THE NEW FACES OF
AMERICAN POVERTY

THE NEW FACES OF AMERICAN POVERTY

A Reference Guide to the Great Recession

VOLUME 2

**Lindsey K. Hanson and
Timothy J. Essenburg, Editors**

 ABC-CLIO

Santa Barbara, California • Denver, Colorado • Oxford, England

Copyright 2014 by ABC-CLIO, LLC

Library of Congress Cataloging-in-Publication Data

The new faces of American poverty : a reference guide to the great recession / Lindsey K. Hanson and Timothy J. Essenburg, editors.

volumes cm

Includes bibliographical references and index.

ISBN 978–1–61069–181–9 (cloth : alk. paper) — ISBN 978–1–61069–182–6 (e-book)

1. Poverty—United States. 2. Poor—United States. 3. Recessions—United States. 4. United States—Economic conditions—2009– 5. United States—Economic policy—2009– I. Hanson, Lindsey K. II. Essenburg, Timothy J.

HC110.P6N393   2014

339.4'60973—dc23   2013020418

ISBN: 978–1–61069–181–9
EISBN: 978–1–61069–182–6

18 17 16 15 14   1 2 3 4 5

This book is also available on the World Wide Web as an eBook.
Visit www.abc-clio.com for details.

ABC-CLIO, LLC
130 Cremona Drive, P.O. Box 1911
Santa Barbara, California 93116-1911

This book is printed on acid-free paper ∞

Manufactured in the United States of America

CONTENTS

Preface   ix

Introduction: Why Care about Poverty?   xiii

VOLUME 1

Section 1: The Great Recession: What Happened?

Introduction to Section 1   3
Global Downturn   7
Great Recession   36
Great Recession vs. Great Depression   73
Housing Crisis   85
Policy, Fiscal (The Federal Government)   99
Policy, Monetary (The Federal Reserve)   116

Section 2: Why Is There Poverty, and How Is Poverty Measured?

Introduction to Section 2   137
Causes and Types of Poverty   140
Economic Insecurity   150
Measurement of Poverty   160
U.S. Poverty Rate in the Great Recession   168

**Section 3: How Did the Great Recession Affect Poverty Rates for
Demographic Groups?**

Introduction to Section 3	179
African Americans	188
Age, 17 or Under (Children)	198
Age, 18–34 (Young Adults)	207
Age, 35–64 (Adults)	217
Age, 65 Plus (Senior Citizens)	223
Asian Americans	232
Disability Status	241
Economic Status, Prior	247
Educational Attainment	256
Hispanic/Latino Americans	265
Immigrants	275
Native Americans	286
Region of the Country	298
Retirees and Potential Retirees	306
Rural Families and Individuals	314
Sex, Female	322
Sex, Male	330
Suburban Families and Individuals	343
United States vs. International Impact	351
Urban Families and Individuals	362
Veterans	371
White Americans	377

**Section 4: How Did the Great Recession Affect Low-Income
Individuals and Families?**

Introduction to Section 4	389
Access to Credit	397
Food Insecurity and Assistance	404
Health Care Assistance	417
Higher Education	424
Hiring Practices	435
Homelessness	444
Housing Assistance Programs and Low-Income Renters	453

VOLUME 2

Impact on Legal System   461
Secondary Effects   470
Social Security   481
Underemployment   493
Unemployment   500
Wages and Income   520
Welfare/Cash Assistance Programs   529

Section 5: How Did Governments Respond to the Great Recession?

Introduction to Section 5   541
Government Response, Local   545
Government Response, State   550
Government Response, Tribal   560
International Government and Nongovernmental Organization Responses 570
Political Parties and Major Legislative Responses   579

Section 6: How Long Will the Effects of the Great Recession Last?

Introduction to Section 6   593
Double Dip Recession Risk   595
A "Normal Economy"—When?   606
Structural Economic Changes   619

Section 7: How Did U.S. Society Respond to Poverty during the Great Recession?

Introduction to Section 7   635
Nonprofit Organizations   639
Political Ideologies   649
Religious Groups   663
Societal View of Poverty   675
Conclusion: What Can Be Done about Poverty in the United States?   685

Primary Documents

Part A. Understanding the Great Recession   713
Part B. The Great Recession and Poverty   785

Recommended Resources   899

About the Editors and Contributors   907

Index   911

PREFACE

We are pleased to present *The New Faces of American Poverty: A Reference Guide to the Great Recession*. This is one of the first works to address the impact of the Great Recession of 2007 to 2009 on poverty in the United States. More than half of people in the United States will experience poverty firsthand before they reach the age of 65, and the Great Recession led to higher rates of poverty than the United States had seen in nearly two decades. During the Recession a housing crisis, rising unemployment and underemployment, and governmental budget crises had dramatic impacts on the poor and poverty rates in the United States. In two volumes *The New Faces of American Poverty* will explore the impact of the worst economic downturn the United States has seen since the Great Depression of the 1930s on the poor in the United States.

This reference work is designed for high school and college researchers, as well as the general reader and scholar who may have little exposure to either economics or poverty issues. We have included a wealth of information in nearly 60 essays and more than 150 graphs, charts, and tables, which provide background information on poverty and economics, along with detailed research on the relationship between the Great Recession and U.S. poverty. Each essay presents information in four sections: "Overview," "The Present," "Outlook," and "Further Reading," which provides references to material discussed in the essay.

CONTENT

The work begins with an introductory essay, "Why Care about Poverty?" which explores religious, nonreligious, ethical, philosophical, historical, and even self-interested reasons to care about poverty alleviation. Following the introduction, the essays are organized alphabetically within seven sections that seek to answer important questions about poverty and the Great Recession. These questions include:

1. **The Great Recession: What happened?** The first section of this work provides necessary background information on the Great Recession, including an overview of both the Great Recession and the global downturn, as well as a comparison of the Great Recession and the Great Depression of the 1930s. In addition, it includes an essay that describes the complicated housing bubble, the bubble burst, and the foreclosure crisis. This section concludes with essays that evaluate the fiscal policy responses of the federal government and monetary policy responses of the Federal Reserve for those with little exposure to the field of economics.

2. **Why is there poverty, and how is poverty measured?** This section investigates the causes and types of poverty in the United States, including temporary, cyclical, chronic, and intergenerational poverty. It also explores the concept and measurement of economic insecurity and methods of poverty measurement utilized in the United States today. Finally, this section provides a general overview of the impact of the Great Recession on poverty rates in the United States to orient the reader for the coming sections that delve more deeply into specific aspects of this topic.

3. **How did the Great Recession affect poverty rates for various demographic groups?** In the third section the impact of the Great Recession on poverty and poverty rates is investigated through a series of essays, each of which covers one demographic group. Demographic groups covered include immigrants, men, women, children, young adults, older adults, retirees and potential retirees, individuals with disabilities, veterans, African Americans, Asian Americans, Hispanic Americans, Non-Hispanic whites, Native Americans, and those living in various regions of the United States as well as in rural, suburban, and urban areas. This section also includes essays that address the impact of the Recession on poverty rates for individuals based on their prior economic status and prior educational attainment.

4. **How did the Great Recession affect low-income individuals and families?** The fourth section of *The New Faces of American Poverty* examines the Recession's effect on low-income individuals and families by exploring topics that are of particular importance to those in poverty. To accomplish this investigative task, essays in this section address access to credit, food insecurity and assistance, health care assistance, access to higher education, hiring practices, homelessness, housing assistance programs and low-income renters, the legal system, Social Security, underemployment, unemployment, wages and income, and welfare/cash assistance programs. In addition, this section includes an essay that discusses some of the more unexpected, or secondary, effects of the Great Recession on low-income individuals and families.

5. **How did governments respond to the Great Recession?** Section 5 presents essays that cover the responses of local, state, federal, and tribal governments in

the United States to poverty during the Great Recession. Essays in this section also address responses of the Republican and Democratic Parties through major legislative efforts, and the response of international governments and nongovernmental organizations to the Recession and U.S. poverty.

6. **How long will the effects of the Great Recession last?** In Section 6 answers to this commonly asked question are explored through essays that investigate the possibility of a double-dip recession and structural changes to the U.S. economy, and by an essay that presents possible answers to the question that many asked during the Recession and its aftermath: "When will the economy be normal?"

7. **How did U.S. society respond to poverty during the Great Recession?** The final section of *The New Faces of American Poverty* considers societal responses to U.S. poverty during the Recession. It includes essays that discuss responses from think tanks and commentators of various political ideologies, nonprofit organizations, religious groups, and public opinion generally.

Each of these seven sections includes an introduction that outlines some of the key points contained in each of its essays. A conclusion essay titled "What Can Be Done about Poverty in the United States?" which follows Section 7, discusses how poverty in the United States might be reduced. It also briefly outlines philosophical, societal, and governmental attitudes toward poverty.

Following the conclusion, a two-part section of 34 selected primary documents helps the reader delve deeper into both the background of the Great Recession and poverty in the United States. These sections provide official documents about the U.S. economy and statistics that describe poverty in the United States from 2008 to 2012. Each document is introduced by a brief commentary and concludes with a source citation. Finally, the "Recommended Resources" section provides a selected bibliography for further reading and research on poverty and the Great Recession. The entire two-volume work also features a comprehensive index.

ACKNOWLEDGMENTS

We would not have been able to publish this series without the work of our editors and more than 20 contributing authors from universities across the country. We would also like to thank Mary Polding, a research and teaching assistant at Bethel University in Saint Paul, Minnesota, who worked for numerous hours capably formatting the figures and tables in this work. For this and her kind encouragement, we express our gratitude.

INTRODUCTION: WHY CARE ABOUT POVERTY?

Lindsey K. Hanson

Before exploring U.S. poverty during the Great Recession, it is vital to understand why domestic poverty is an issue that individuals in the United States should care about. Many people have personal reasons for caring about poverty, perhaps because of their own experience with poverty, or because of the experience of a loved one or friend. Concern for poverty based on personal life experience is important and should not be overlooked, but there are many other reasons to care about poverty. For some, concern for the impoverished is a deeply held religious or philosophical commitment. Others may be concerned about poverty because of its relationship to the American ideal of equal opportunity, or historic injustices in U.S. history that have had long-reaching economic impacts. Still others express concern about poverty for pragmatic economic or political reasons.

RELIGIOUS AND NONRELIGIOUS BELIEF SYSTEMS AND THE IMPORTANCE OF POVERTY ALLEVIATION

The importance of caring for the poor is a tenet of many of the world's major religions including Judaism, Christianity, and Islam. Many nonreligious persons also place moral importance on caring for the poor. Jewish religious teachings mandate certain levels of giving to the poor, and the ancient Jews enforced mandatory giving through a court system (Shapiro 1980). Jewish teachings required that portions of harvests be left for the poor and needy. The first gift of the harvest, *leket*, was the portion of the harvest that was dropped during reaping and left for those who were in need. The second harvest gift, *shich'chah*, was the fruit or sheaves that the owner neglected to harvest, and those too were left for the poor. The *pe'ah*, the third harvest gift, was a portion of a field that was to be deliberately unharvested and left for the poor. It was required that this uncut portion be at least a sixtieth of the total field. Jewish teachings even went so far as to require that the unharvested portion of a field be a less visible area so that the poor would not be subjected to embarrassment as they gathered the crop. Jewish law also provided for a tithe, or a tenth of the harvest, every third and sixth year for the poor (Shapiro 1980). In addition, during the holiday of Purim, Jews were required to give money to at least two people in need (Shapiro 1980). Ancient Jewish instruction also spoke of something called the year of Jubilee. In a Jubilee year, once every 49 or 50 years, all debts were to be forgiven, all land was to return to the original owner, and anyone who had sold themselves into slavery was to be freed (Jacobs 2013). In this way chronic poverty was to be alleviated or prevented. Although modern Jews do not strictly follow these teachings, these historic traditions form the foundation for the modern-day Jewish religious tradition of caring for the poor, the religion's emphasis on the importance of philanthropy, and the practice of tithing 10 percent that is still observed by many modern Jews (Rothner 2013).

Christianity, which has roots in Judaism, also places importance on caring for the poor. "Catholic social teaching," a body of doctrine developed by the Catholic Church, teaches that a basic moral measure of any society or economy is how the poor and vulnerable are treated. The Catholic Church views poverty as not only financial deprivation, but as a denial of full participation in society. The Catholic Church also emphasizes the importance of expanded employment opportunities and just wages for poverty alleviation, and the role of individuals, families, communities, religious institutions, the private sector, and government in combating poverty (U.S. Conference of Catholic Bishops 2013). Many Protestant Christians also place importance on eradicating poverty, but unlike the Catholic tradition, there is no single set of social teaching for Protestants, and beliefs on the topic of poverty vary within the Protestant tradition. Those within the Protestant tradition who place high importance on poverty alleviation and caring for the poor point to Jesus's identification with the poor and the importance he placed on caring for the poor (Birch 1975). The Protestant theology of poverty is informed by more than 290 New Testament verses in which Jesus addressed issues of poverty and justice (DeMoss Group 2013).

Islamic religious instruction likewise addresses issues of poverty in its teachings. *Zakat*, one of the five pillars of Islam, is the giving of one's income as a tax that is to be redistributed to one of eight groups eligible to receive zakat monies. Two of the groups eligible to receive *zakat* funds are the indigent and the needy. *Zakat* is to be paid out of money an individual has had for at least a year, and only those who have a high enough net worth must pay *zakat*. When an individual meets these requirements he or she must pay *zakat* of 2.5 percent. While many Muslim governments no longer require *zakat*, many Muslims still pay it as part of their religious tradition (Khan 2009). In addition to *zakat*, the Islamic religious tradition also encourages voluntary charity, referred to as *sadaqa*, as a means of caring for the needy (Khan 2003).

While the conviction of many people that poverty should be alleviated is based on their religious beliefs and traditions, there are also many nonreligious people who believe that it is important to work toward the alleviation of poverty. Humanists are not theistic (i.e., they do not believe in a deity); rather, they believe that humans have a responsibility to aspire toward the greater good of humanity, which includes the alleviation of poverty. The American Humanist Association (2003), an organization that seeks to educate the public on humanism and advance humanism, publishes the *Humanist Manifesto*. The third and most recent manifesto states that humanists should "seek to minimize the inequities of circumstance and ability" and "support a just distribution of nature's resources and the fruits of human effort so that as many as possible can enjoy a good life" (American Humanist Association 2003).

PHILOSOPHICAL UNDERPINNINGS FOR A BELIEF IN THE IMPORTANCE OF POVERTY ALLEVIATION

In addition to religiously based or humanist beliefs in the importance of poverty alleviation, there are numerous potential philosophical underpinnings for a belief that the alleviation of poverty is an important task. A few commonly held philosophical underpinnings for this belief include arguments from a belief in human rights, an argument from social contract theory, an argument from the virtue ethic of care, and a utilitarian argument.

One can argue that a belief in basic human rights necessitates a belief that poverty alleviation is important or even that freedom from poverty is in itself a basic human right. The idea that basic human rights exist is a familiar one to most people in the United States. Indeed, the idea that there are basic human rights is enshrined in the Declaration of Independence, which declares that "all men are created equal, that they are endowed by their Creator with certain unalienable Rights, that among these are Life, Liberty, and the pursuit of Happiness." One can believe that basic human rights derive from a creator or from national and international law. One could also believe that basic human rights exist due to general consensus across time and culture (e.g., murder is viewed as wrong in all societies) or that basic human rights are those rights for which there are convincing practical or moral reasons to think that they exist in all, or almost all, times and places (Nickel 2012).

However, regardless of the reason one believes in the existence of basic human rights, there is an argument that freedom from poverty is vital to the existence of other human rights and thus is itself a basic right. Henry Shue (1980) argues that minimal economic security is necessary to have, or to exercise, other human rights that are more commonly agreed upon as being human rights. Shue takes minimal economic security to include items such as clean air and water, minimal preventive health care, and adequate shelter, food, and clothing. One more commonly agreed upon human right identified by Shue is the right of physical security (e.g., the right not to be murdered, assaulted, raped). He argues that if someone lacks minimal economic security, they become vulnerable and do not have the ability to exercise other rights often considered more basic human rights, such as the right of physical security. If someone lacks minimal economic security such as food or shelter and cannot live, any right he or she may have to physical security becomes pointless. Shue goes on to argue that if people have a basic right to minimal economic security, it also follows that there is a duty to avoid depriving people of this right, a duty to protect this right, and a duty to help those who have been deprived of this right. This, he points out, is how society treats the right to physical security; for example, there is a duty not to murder someone, and a police force is provided to protect that right (Shue 1980). Thus, there is an argument from a belief in basic human rights that society and individuals have a duty to provide minimal economic security or eradicate, at the very least, deep poverty.

In his "Justice as Fairness: Political Not Metaphysical" the philosopher John Rawls put forward a conception of justice that can also serve as a philosophical framework from which to approach poverty alleviation (Rawls 1985). To make his argument Rawls utilizes a thought experiment in which people are put behind a "veil of ignorance" and must come up with the basic rules (i.e., a social contract) of a society in which they wish to live. From behind the veil of ignorance people do not know what position (e.g., social status, race, ethnicity, gender, belief system) they will have in the society they are choosing the rules for. Rawls argues that from behind the veil of ignorance people would create a society in which everyone would have equal basic freedoms or liberties. Rawls also argues that from behind the veil of ignorance people would create a society in which social and economic inequality would be allowed only to the extent that such inequality served the "least advantaged" and that social and economic inequalities would be attached to "offices and positions" that were open to everyone "under conditions of fair equality and equal opportunity" (Rawls 1985, 227). One can argue that our current society should put into place this same framework because prior to birth humans are essentially behind a veil of ignorance, as they do not know what societal position they will be born into. Creating such a system in our modern society, in which inequality is acceptable only insofar as it benefits the least advantaged (e.g., the poor) and is attached to positions open to all would effectively alleviate poverty.

Another philosophical framework from which to approach the eradication or alleviation of poverty comes from virtue ethics and the virtue of care. A virtue ethic is an approach to ethics that focuses on the development of a certain moral character rather than rules for what does or does not constitute moral behavior, or a consequentialist ethical system that bases the rightness or wrongness of an action on its outcome (Hursthouse 2012). Care, then, is a practice or disposition that one develops toward the world. In the philosophical literature care has been defined in numerous ways. One popular definition is offered by Joan Tronto, who posits that there are four stages of care that one should aim to progress through: "(1) attentiveness, a proclivity to become aware of need; (2) responsibility, a willingness to respond and take care of need; (3) competence, the skill of providing good and successful care; and (4) responsiveness, consideration of the position of others as they see it and recognition of the potential for abuse in care" (quoted in Sander-Staudt 2011). Under this ethical belief system, then, a virtuous person is one who is aware of the needs of others, is willing to respond to and care for those needs, and is able to do so successfully while considering the position of others and retaining an awareness of the potential for abuse. It is not difficult to see how such an ethic could lead one to place importance on the alleviation of poverty. If one believes that being a virtuous person is a worthy project and that a virtuous person is attentive and responsive to the needs of others, a virtuous person would be one who recognizes the need created by poverty and responds competently to that need.

In contrast to a virtue ethic, there is an argument for poverty alleviation from the utilitarian ethic. Utilitarianism is a consequentialist ethic that judges the rightness or wrongness of an action by its outcome. Classical utilitarianism posits that a moral action produces the greatest amount of good for the greatest number of people. Good is defined as pleasure. Thus, roughly speaking, the morally right action is the action that creates the greatest pleasure for the greatest number of people. Peter Singer, a modern utilitarian philosopher, made a utilitarian argument for poverty eradication in his essay *Famine, Affluence, and Morality* (1972). He argues that there is general agreement that lack of shelter, food and medical care are bad, and that if one has the power to prevent something bad from happening without sacrificing something of "comparable moral importance," then one ought, morally, to prevent that bad thing from happening (Singer 1972). For example, he points out that someone walking by a drowning child ought to make the sacrifice of getting her clothes muddy because this mud is insignificant in comparison to a child dying. He argues that the more affluent have the power to prevent lack of food, shelter, and medical care for others without sacrificing anything of comparable moral importance and thus the more affluent ought to do so. By way of example he argues that when a more affluent person buys new clothes simply to be well dressed, that is not an important need, and it would not be a morally significant sacrifice for the more affluent person to continue to wear old clothes and give the money to a cause such as famine relief. Singer argues that this is not simply something the more affluent should do, or which would be good to do, but rather that—it would be wrong not to give the money away (Singer 1972). Although Singer's argument pertains to efforts to eradicate global poverty, this utilitarian argument can also be used to argue for efforts to alleviate domestic poverty.

AMERICAN IDEALS, THE AMERICAN EXPERIENCE, AND A BELIEF IN THE IMPORTANCE OF POVERTY ALLEVIATION

An argument that the alleviation of poverty is an important goal can also come from a belief in the American ideal of equal opportunity. The United States was founded, in part, due to a desire to create a society in which individual effort and hard work were rewarded, and one's economic class at birth was less defining (Isaacs 2008). Indeed, the belief that one can get ahead by hard work and determination in the United States is a central component, if not *the* central component, of the American Dream. The majority of Americans believe that the United States is living up to this ideal, and Americans are more likely to believe that the economic system in their country rewards hard work, and thus provides equal opportunity, than those living in many other countries. In a survey across 27 countries conducted by the International Social Survey Program Americans were the most likely to believe that people are rewarded for "intelligence and skill" and much more likely to believe that "people get rewarded for their effort" (Isaacs 2008). In addition, Americans were much less likely than respondents in other countries to believe that "coming from a wealthy family is essential/very important to getting ahead," that income differentials in their country were too large, and that it is the government's responsibility to reduce income inequality (Isaacs 2008). The belief that the U.S. economic system rewards effort, intelligence, and skill, and that wealth at birth is not a strongly determinative factor in future economic success, serves as justification for the belief that income differentials are not too large and that it is not the government's responsibility to reduce income inequality. American society tends to accept significant gaps between the rich in the poor in large part because of a belief that equal opportunity exists (Isaacs 2008). That is, there is a belief that the rich and poor have chosen their own paths in life by their decisions and work ethic, and anyone who works hard can move up the economic ladder. However, some proponents of this argument for poverty alleviation argue that income inequalities in the United States are not entirely the result of individual skill, effort, and intelligence, but rather are largely determined by one's position at birth. This position provides a stronger argument for intervention, government or private, to reduce income inequality or at least to provide for more equal economic opportunity.

Equal opportunity can be characterized by high economic mobility. In a society with high economic mobility one could expect to see many people "mov[ing] up or down the economic ladder within a lifetime or from one generation to the next"

(Isaacs 2008). If an individual cannot move up or down the economic ladder by virtue of his or her individual life decisions, then equal opportunity does not exist. Proponents of this argument for poverty alleviation go on to argue that while there is certainly some degree of economic mobility in the United States, in reality there is less economic mobility for both the rich and the poor than for those who are born into middle-class families. In addition, while the United States views itself as the land of opportunity, there is actually less economic mobility in this nation than in many other developed countries (Isaacs 2008). Countries such as Norway, Finland, and Canada have high degrees of mobility; Sweden, France, and Germany have middling degrees of mobility; and the United States and the United Kingdom are low-mobility countries (Isaacs 2008). Thus, starting off in a low-income situation is more of a disadvantage in the United States than in these mid- or high-mobility countries (Isaacs 2008).

Forty-two percent of U.S. children born to families with incomes in the bottom fifth remain in the bottom fifth of the income distribution, and 39 percent of children whose parents have incomes in the top fifth remain in the top fifth of the income distribution (Isaacs 2008). A mere 6 percent of children whose families have incomes at the very bottom of the income distribution move to the very top of the income distribution (Isaacs 2008). Children whose parents are in the middle of the income distribution have about an equal chance of moving up or down into an income quintile that is different than that of their parents (Isaacs 2008). These statistics, however, are not the same across race, because economic mobility for black children is not as high as that for white children (Isaacs 2008). Of black children with parents in the lowest quintile, 54 percent stay in the lowest quintile compared to 31 percent of similarly situated white children (Isaacs 2008). In fact, there is more downward and less upward mobility for blacks than for whites (Isaacs 2008). Thus, the economic prospects are, statistically, not as promising for a poor black child as for a poor white child (Isaacs 2008).

The data show that it is by no means impossible for a child born into a low-income family to climb the economic ladder. However, with 65 percent of children born into the lowest income quintile remaining in the lowest two income quintiles (and below the middle income quintile), it is obvious that children born into the lowest income families in the United States are at a disadvantage. Moreover, black children born into the lowest income quintile families are at an even greater disadvantage. With the income of one's parents having such a substantial impact on one's future economic situation and the likelihood that one will be impoverished, poverty alleviation for children is of particular importance because it helps to make the United States the land of equal opportunity it aspires to be.

Still others make an argument for poverty alleviation from the American historic experience. The argument goes something like this: the American historic experience is fraught with examples of injustice that have impoverished some groups while enriching others, so justice demands that society take measures to correct the modern-day impacts of these historic injustices. By way of example, take the experience of African Americans in the United States. Africans were brought to the United States unwillingly and enslaved. Slave owners unjustly derived great economic benefit from the free labor provided by slaves, while the enslaved unjustly were denied the opportunities to which our nation aspired. Once slavery was abolished African Americans continued to experience economic deprivation at the hands of Jim Crow laws. An example of this is segregated schools. Segregated African American schools had fewer resources with which to educate students and were often not able to provide as high a quality of education as schools for whites. The landmark *Brown vs. Board of Education* decision in which the Supreme Court held that state laws segregating schools were unconstitutional was not handed down until 1954, and that only started the process of desegregation. The Civil Rights Act, the federal law that prohibited employment discrimination on the basis of race, was not passed until 1964.

All nations have selective historic memories when it comes to the injustices they have perpetrated. While American culture tends to celebrates its achievements, in this case civil rights legislation, proponents of this argument for poverty alleviation point out that it is important to remember that these changes took place a mere 50 years ago, and that in reality the United States is only a few generations away from slavery. In 2011 more than 13 percent of the U.S. population was 65 years of age or older, meaning that 13 percent of the population was eight years of age or older when the *Brown vs. Board of Education* decision required the desegregation of schools and 18 or older when the Civil Rights Act was enacted (U.S. Census Bureau 2013). The grandparents of today's young adults grew up in a legally segregated United States. Many whites were welcomed into employment, housing, and education opportunities, whereas African Americans and other minority groups entered the employment, housing, and education markets as young adults without the protections of the Civil Rights Act of 1964. Lacking the opportunities and protections provided by today's laws, economic opportunities for all racial minority groups were lessened, and wealth that might otherwise have been accumulated was not. In addition, opportunities to develop social capital, the trusting relationships one has that help one advance in education and employment, that might otherwise have arisen were lost (Loury 1977; Ferguson 1999). Wealth and social capital that was never developed due to the impact of legalized racial injustice was never passed on to the children and grandchildren who are today's young adults. As was covered earlier in this introduction, even today one's economic situation has a substantial impact on the likely economic situation of one's children, so proponents of this argument for poverty alleviation posit that there has not been sufficient opportunity in a mere two or three generations for the impact of the pre-1960s racial injustices to be erased. This is to say nothing about the economic toll of slavery, the toll of the historic trauma of slavery, or even the impacts of contemporary racism. Thus, proponents of this line of reasoning argue that high rates of poverty in the black population of the United States can be directly tied to past legalized racial injustices, and thus the alleviation of black poverty and the creation of an economic system that allows for greater economic equality is a responsibility of government because government policies have greatly contributed to higher rates of black poverty.

In opposition to this stance, an argument may be made that young adults today did not make the historic decisions that created an unjust system and led to the economic deprivation that continues to have a contemporary impact, so they are not responsible for any negative impacts of these historic decisions. In response, those who argue for poverty alleviation on the basis of the American historic experience argue that while it is true that no young adult today, of any race, made the historic decisions that led to these historic economic injustices, it is also true that no one has control over the race or economic situation into which they are born. However, it is true that the ancestors (who may be equally historicly blameless) of many young adults today derived relative benefit simply from the policies and institutions that were unjustly put into place against others and that this benefit has been passed down to some degree due to the effect of family economic status on one's future economic status as discussed previously. Thus, this argument goes, it is the responsibility of American society to alleviate poverty created by its historic injustice.

Similar arguments could be made on the basis of the historic injustices perpetrated against Native Americans whose land was taken in violation of federal treaties and made available to immigrants of European descent. Consider women who have experienced discrimination in employment and pay; Jews who met with anti-Semitism; Catholics who experienced the effects of anti-Catholic sentiment; German, Italian, and Irish immigrants who faced discrimination; Japanese who were interned during World War II (losing the wealth they built up in their homes and business) . . . and the list goes on and on. Thus, it can be argued that historic injustices have had economic impacts that continue today and affect individuals and families across racial, ethnic, and religious boundaries. Across history these injustices have impacted some individuals and families more than others, and the effects have been passed down through some families more than others, in part due to the impact of chance. As a result of these American historic injustices and the impact of one's family's economic status on one's own economic status, and thus the continuing economic impact of these historic injustices, it can be argued that U.S. society has a responsibility to alleviate poverty that it has helped to create.

ARGUMENTS FROM SELF-INTEREST AND A BELIEF IN THE IMPORTANCE OF POVERTY ALLEVIATION

In addition to arguments for the importance of poverty alleviation from religion, philosophy, American ideals, and American history, there are arguments for poverty alleviation that arise from simple self-interest. The argument for poverty alleviation derived from Rawls, discussed earlier, can be viewed as an argument from self-interest because it is based on the simple fact that one does not know what position in society one will be born into, or what level of skill or intelligence one will possess. Thus, it is in one's self-interest to live in a society of equal opportunity where inequalities that are necessary for society to function benefit the least advantaged. However, additional self-interested arguments can be made for poverty alleviation.

First, even in a land of perfect equal opportunity there will always be those who cannot provide for themselves economically due to mental disability, physical disability, or age, and thus there is a strong argument that society should care for these individuals (Haskins 2009). One could argue that society has a moral obligation to care for these individuals, but one could also make the pragmatic argument that it is in the self-interest of individuals to socially contract to provide for these individuals as a sort of insurance policy because at some future date they themselves might have a disability or become unable to economically provide for themselves despite the best future planning.

Second is the argument that a more equal society with less poverty is a more productive and more stable society, which is better for everyone. Children from poor households are at a higher risk for low cognitive development (Brown 2011), which leads to a less productive work force. Children from poor households are also at an increased risk of incarceration (Brown 2011), which is expensive. As of 2010 the United States was spending almost $70 billion a year on the incarceration, probation, and parole of adults and youth (Hawkins 2010). Poverty also increases health risks such as low birthweight and leads to higher rates of hypertension and high cholesterol, and decreased life expectancy (Brown 2011), all of which affect Medicaid and private business expenditures. Poverty weakens the middle class, and a strong middle class serves as a stabilizing factor and safeguard of the democratic system (Brown 2011). Those in poverty also have less access to education and training, which help people become more productive in the workforce and contribute to the economy. As greater percentages of the U.S. population, and particularly children, experience poverty, the United States ultimately becomes less productive and less competitive in the global marketplace because its workers are less skilled, less educated, and less healthy (Brown 2011).

Thus, in addition to personal, religious, humanist, and philosophical reasons, as well reasons based on the American ideal of equal opportunity and the American historic experience, there are self-interested reasons to care about poverty alleviation. Whatever one's reasons for caring about poverty alleviation, considering the impact of the Great Recession on poverty in the United States is important to developing an understanding of contemporary American poverty. Thus, this work will proceed to discuss the Great Recession, the causes and measurements of poverty, and the impact of the Recession on poverty rates for numerous demographic groups in the United States, as well as on individuals, families, governments, the future of the U.S. economy, and American society.

FURTHER READING

American Humanist Association. "Humanist Manifesto III," 2003. Accessed January 15, 2013. http://www.americanhumanist.org/humanism/Humanist_Manifesto_III

Birch, Bruce C. "Hunger, Poverty, and Biblical Religion," June 1975. Accessed January 14, 2013. http://www.religion-online.org/showarticle.asp?title=1855

Brown, Desmond. "10 Reasons Why Cutting Poverty Is Good for Our Nation." Kansas Legal Services, December 2011. Accessed January 16, 2013. http://www.kansaslegalservices.org/node/1257

DeMoss Group. "Poverty and Justice: Bible Facts," 2013. Accessed January 14. http://demossnews.com/americanbible/additional/poverty_and_justice_bible_facts

Ferguson, Ronald F., and William T. Dickens. 1999. "Introduction." In *Urban Problems and Community Development*, ed. Ronald F. Ferguson and William T. Dickens. Washington, D.C.: Brookings Institution Press, 1999, 1–31.

Haskins, Ron, and Isabel Sawhill. *Creating an Equal Opportunity Society*. Washington, D.C.: Brookings Institution Press, 2009.

Hawkins, Steven. "Education vs. Incarceration." *American Prospect*, December 6, 2010. Accessed January 16, 2013. http://prospect.org/article/education-vs-incarceration

Hursthouse, Rosalind. "Virtue Ethics." Stanford Encyclopedia of Philosophy, 2012. Accessed January 15, 2013. http://plato.stanford.edu/entries/ethics-virtue/

Isaacs, Julia B., Isabel V. Sawhill, and Ron Haskins. "Getting Ahead or Losing Ground: Economic Mobility in America," February 2008. Accessed January 14, 2013. http://www.pewtrusts.org/uploadedFiles/wwwpewtrustsorg/Reports/Economic_Mobility/Economic_Mobility_in_America_Full.pdf

Jacobs, Louis. "Sabbatical Year (Shemitah) and Jubilee Year (Yovel)," 2013. Accessed January 14. http://www.myjewishlearning.com/beliefs/Issues/Nature_and_the_Environment/Traditional_Teachings/Sabbatical_and_Jubilee_Years.shtml

Khan, Arshad. *Islam 101: Principles and Practices*. iUniverse, 2003.

Khan, Yusuf. "Islam 101: What Is Zakat?" September 27, 2009. Accessed January 14, 2013. http://www.examiner.com/article/islam-101-what-is-zakat

Loury, Glenn. C. "A Dynamic Theory of Racial Income Differences." In *Women, Minorities and Employment Discrimination*, ed. P. A. Wallace and A. M. Lamonde. Lexington, MA: Lexington Books, 1977, 153–86.

Nickel, James. "Human Rights." Stanford Encyclopedia of Philosophy, 2012. Accessed January 15, 2013. http://plato.stanford.edu/entries/rights-human/

Rawls, John. "Justice as Fairness: Political Not Metaphysical." *Philosophy and Public Affairs* 14, no. 3 (1985): 223–51.

Rawls, John. *A Theory of Justice.* Cambridge, MA: Harvard University Press, 1999.

Rothner, Daniel. "The Jewish Philosophy of Philanthropy," 2013. Accessed January 14, 2013. http://learningtogive.org/faithgroups/voices/tzedakah_jewish_view_of_phil.asp

Sander-Staudt, Maureen. 2011. "Care Ethics." Internet Encyclopedia of Philosophy, March 19, 2011. Accessed January 14, 2013. http://www.iep.utm.edu/care-eth/

Shaprio, Rashi. "Poverty Programs in Jewish Law," December 1980. Accessed January 14, 2013. http://www.bjpa.org/Publications/details.cfm?PublicationID=1580

Shue, Henry. *Basic Rights: Subsistence, Affluence, and U.S. Foreign Policy.* Princeton, NJ: Princeton University Press, 1980.

Singer, Peter. "Famine, Affluence, and Morality," 1972. Accessed January 16, 2013. http://www.utilitarian.net/singer/by/1972——.htm

U.S. Census Bureau. "USA People QuickFacts," 2013. Accessed January 16. http://quickfacts.census.gov/qfd/states/00000.html

U.S. Conference of Catholic Bishops. "Catholic Social Teaching on Poverty, an Option for the Poor, and the Common Good," 2013. Accessed January 14. http://www.usccb.org/about/domestic-social-development/resources/upload/poverty-common-good-CST.pdf

SECTION 4
(CONTINUED)

Impact on Legal System

Lindsey K. Hanson

Here each day the old, the unemployed, the underprivileged, and the largely forgotten people of our Nation may seek help. Perhaps it is an eviction, a marital conflict, repossession of a car, or misunderstanding over a welfare check—each problem may have a legal solution. These are small claims in the Nation's eye, but they loom large in the hearts and lives of poor Americans.

> —*President Nixon's Special Message to Congress May 5, 1971,*
> *proposing the establishment of the Legal Services Corporation*
> *(Legal Services Corporation 2012b).*

OVERVIEW

Individuals in poverty are generally not able to afford a lawyer. Public defender's offices and legal aid programs provide free lawyers for low-income people, but both of these programs have been hit hard by the Recession. The resulting irony is that while more people than ever are eligible for these services, less funding is available to provide them. The judicial system in general has been hard hit by the Recession, but this article will focus on the impact the Recession has had on public defender's offices and legal aid programs because these two programs specifically serve low-income people.

Public defenders prior to Great Recession handled excessive caseloads for comparatively little pay. The Great Recession has only worsened this situation because public defense programs are largely state funded and have thus experienced budget cuts because of state fiscal crises. This has meant fewer public defenders and even higher caseloads. The result has been that some individuals have gone without the effective legal representation they are constitutionally entitled to. Legal aid programs have also experienced reduced funding in light of federal and state budget cuts and reduced interest rates, which result in less funding because many legal aid programs are funded in part by the interest derived from attorney trust accounts.

THE PRESENT

Public Defenders

Public defender's offices provide free court-appointed attorneys to individuals when they have a right to an attorney at government expense. The Sixth Amendment of the U.S. Constitution states: "In all criminal prosecutions, the accused shall enjoy the right to … the Assistance of Counsel for his defense." The Supreme Court, in *Gideon vs. Wainwright* (1963), interpreted this amendment as a requirement that the government provide counsel, at its expense, to anyone charged with a felony who cannot afford an attorney. There is also a right to counsel in interrogations after arrest, in line-ups, and in a number of other situations (National Legal Aid 2012), but further discussion of the right to counsel is outside the scope of this essay.

Around 80 percent of criminal defendants are indigent and need representation through the public defender's office (Hastings 2009). Since the government is constitutionally obligated to pay for attorneys for these indigent individuals funding for public defender's offices cannot be cut completely despite a Recession or budget shortfall. However, even prior to the Great Recession many public defender's offices were underfunded; and before the start of the Recession, taking inflation into account, many states were already reducing spending on public defenders (Constitution Project 2009).

The Recession has only worsened the problem. States are the primary funders of public defender's offices, and the state budget shortfalls that have accompanied the Recession have also meant cuts to public defense programs (Constitution Project 2009). For example, public defense in Maryland lost $400,000 in 2008 when the state needed to cut $432 million from its budget (Constitution Project 2009). The problem faced by the state of Maryland was a common one; during the Recession most states faced budget shortfalls, and in 2012, after the official end of the Recession, all but six states were still projecting a budget shortfall (Combs 2011).

Budget cuts to public defense programs meant growing caseloads for already overworked and undercompensated public defenders (Constitution Project 2009). As these attorneys handle more and more excessive caseloads, the quality of representation suffers (Constitution Project 2009). The practical result can be denial of the constitutional right to effective counsel despite having a court-appointed attorney (Constitution Project 2009). Take, for example, the case of a woman in Mississippi who had been charged with shoplifting $72 worth of merchandise and subsequently spent 14 months in jail because of the public defender crisis. The woman was in jail for 11 months before a lawyer was appointed to her case, and after a lawyer was appointed she spent three more months in jail before pleading guilty (Constitution Project 2009). In South Carolina public defenders were handling an average of 467 cases each during fiscal years (FY) 2009 and 2010 (Kinnard 2011). That represents a 22 percent increase from FY 2007 to 2008 and is well above the national standard, which recommends that defenders with felony cases handle only 125 cases a year (Kinnard 2011).

The crisis in South Carolina and Mississippi was repeated across the country throughout the Recession. Washington State's 2010 report on the status of public defense cited problems with excessive caseloads and poor compensation that had been worsened by the Great Recession. The budget for public defenders in Washington was reduced at both the state and local level—cuts were made in the state's initial 2010 budget and in a special session of the legislature, which made further cuts of 7.6 percent to public defense (Washington State Office of Public Defense 2011). As a result, many Washington counties eliminated attorney and other staff positions, as well as contracts with private attorneys who provided public defense (Washington State Office of Public Defense 2011). The remaining public defenders, who were already handling excessive caseloads, were thus saddled with even more cases (Washington State Office of Public Defense 2011). As in Mississippi, the practical result has been the denial of effective assistance of counsel for some clients. For example, in 2010 a state court in Washington found that a public defender failed to sufficiently consult with his juvenile client before entering a guilty plea to a child molestation charge. The attorney estimated that he spent only around 55 minutes on the case. The court allowed the client to withdraw the guilty plea and a few months later issued rules requiring that prior to the appointment of an attorney the lawyer had to certify that his or her caseload complied with certain standards. However, the implementation of this rule has been delayed pending further clarification of the standards (Washington State Office of Public Defense 2011).

Indigent defendants in New York have also suffered from the public defender crisis. There a woman complained that she waited three weeks in jail after being charged with bringing marijuana into a prison before she was able to meet with a public defender (Meyer 2009). The Defendant said that she met with her court-appointed attorney for only 15 or 20 minutes before her sentencing hearing, and that the attorney simply told her not to fight the charges or the sentence that had been recommended by the prosecutor (Meyer 2009). The New York Civil Liberties Union has filed suit alleging that the public defender's office is failing to provide effective legal assistance to indigent clients because of the excessive caseloads

(Meyer 2009). Lawsuits in at least six other states make similar claims (Meyer 2009).

Already strapped public defenders offices across the nation have been forced to lay off attorneys and other staff. In 2008 Georgia laid off 41 employees in its public defense program. There a defendant charged with murder was in jail for eight months without a public defender because the public defender's office could not afford to provide an attorney. The state of Minnesota cut its public defense budget by $4 million in FY 2009, resulting in layoffs for 23 public defenders. The felony caseload for a public defender in Minnesota at the time was 450 a year and was projected to increase to around 550 a year as a result of the cuts (Constitution Project 2009).

The state of Florida has had similar problems. The Orange-Osceola County public defender's office lost 40 positions and laid off 10 attorneys in 2008 because of budgetary cuts. In Miami-Dade County, the third largest county in the state, the public defender's office experienced a 12 percent budget cut over an 18-month period from late 2007 to June 2009. The average felony caseload for a public defender there was 500, which was an increase of 133 cases over a three-year time period (Hasting 2009). These excessive caseloads negatively impact indigent clients. In one instance, a Miami public defender with 13 cases scheduled for trial in a single day received a plea offer but did not have time to discuss it with her client. The prosecutor rescinded the plea offer of one year, and the client eventually pled guilty and was sentenced to five years (Constitution Project 2009).

Kentucky public defense likewise saw a $2.3 million (6.4 percent) budget reduction in 2008. Consequently, it began to refuse representation in conflict of interest cases, probation and parole violation cases, and certain misdemeanor cases. In 2011 it experienced an additional loss of 1.5 percent of its funding ($500,000). Koppel 2011). In 2008 public defense in Maryland lost $400,000 due to the state's budgetary crisis (Constitution Project 2009). As a result, the public defender's office made the decision to stop paying for private attorneys when the public defender's office could not represent a client because of a conflict of interest (Constitution Project 2009). This cost was passed along to counties, and at least one county claimed it was not able to pay for these conflict of interest public defenders (Constitution Project 2009). The Sacramento County public defender's office in California laid off 34 attorneys in FY 2011, with additional layoffs anticipated. As public defender's offices across the country experience these layoffs and ever increasing caseloads, increasing numbers of indigent defendants will be denied the effective assistance of counsel to which they are constitutionally entitled.

Legal Aid

Legal aid programs are nonprofit legal offices that provide legal advice and representation to low-income individuals. These offices assist individuals with a variety of civil legal cases. Legal aid programs often represent and advise clients in consumer protection, immigration, eviction, tenant's rights, and public benefits cases. Most legal aid offices, and all Legal Services Corporation funded legal aid offices, represent people with household incomes at or below 125 percent of the poverty level (Legal Services Corporation 2012c). Some legal aid offices utilize what is called a judicare model in which private attorneys are paid to handle cases for low-income clients, and the clients pay either reduced legal fees or no fees, depending on their income and the program guidelines (Houseman 2010). Legal aid offices also reach clients through legal clinics where attorneys and other staff assist many clients with a similar legal problem. For example, a legal aid office might hold a clinic on wills and health care directives, and assist numerous clients in one day with these documents. Legal aid offices also publish fact sheets, booklets, and forms that help low-income people represent themselves when an attorney cannot be provided.

Most legal aid programs receive funding from the Legal Services Corporation (LSC), the single largest funder of legal aid programs nationwide (Legal Services Corporation 2012c). In 2010 LSC provided $420 million to legal aid offices across the nation (Legal Services Corporation 2012a). LSC is a nonprofit organization created by Congress and signed into law by President Nixon in 1974 (Legal Services Corporation 2012c). The organization receives federal funding that is then distributed to more than 900 legal aid offices throughout the United States (Legal Services Corporation 2012c). Most LSC-funded offices also receive funding from other sources such as state governments, interest on lawyers' trust accounts, private foundations, and individual donations. Some legal aid offices are funded without the assistance of LSC because LSC funding is limited and brings with it regulations that limit what the legal office can do with its funding, even funding it receives from non-LSC sources. For example, LSC-funded legal aid offices cannot represent undocumented people and cannot lobby or advocate for reform of the welfare system (Houseman 2001).

The Recession has resulted in cuts to most of the sources from which legal aid programs derive funding. The result has been a dramatic reduction in legal aid services despite the increasing poverty rate nationwide. At the federal level LSC experienced budget cuts of less than 2 percent for FY 2004 to 2006 and actually experienced increases for FY 2007 to 2010 (Legal Services Corporation 2012ca). However, LSC experienced funding cuts of around 4 percent for FY 2011 (National Legal Aid 2011), with further funding reductions in FY 2012.

Coupled with reduced LSC funding, funding from private foundations, law firms, and individual donors has also declined because of the Recession (see Section 7, "Nonprofit Organizations," for a discussion of the impact of the Recession on charitable giving). Many legal aid offices also receive funding from the interest on lawyers' trust accounts (IOLTA). Private attorneys often keep retainers and settlement checks in their trust accounts for short periods of time. The interest from these accounts is pooled and referred to as IOLTA. This money is often used to fund legal aid programs. However, the Great Recession has brought with it historically low interest rates, which has led to a drastic decrease in IOLTA revenue to fund legal aid programs. In Minnesota, for example, IOLTA revenue dropped 85 percent between 2007 and 2010, and the IOLTA reserve that helped to fund legal aid for two years was depleted in 2011. Legal aid programs have also been hard hit by the budget shortfalls most states experienced during the Recession. These budgets shortfalls have meant funding cuts for legal aid at the state level in addition to the federal LSC cuts. Eighteen states cut or altogether eliminated funding to legal aid programs in 2011 (Routman 2011).

The combination of cuts from government, donations, and reduced IOLTA funds has meant reduced services, layoffs, and even office closures for many legal aid programs. For example, by 2009 legal aid programs in the District of Columbia reported a budgetary reduction of more than 25 percent and had lost almost 13 percent of their attorneys and 40 percent of other staff. These staff reductions occurred despite cost-saving measures such as freezing pay, furlough days, reduced training budgets, and reductions in salary and benefits. These are measures many other legal aid programs have taken as well.

Montana legal aid had already laid off attorneys and support staff by October 2011 in anticipation of the $500,000 cut it expected due to the reduction in the federal LSC budget (Florio 2011). In 2011 North Carolina legal aid was planning to close three branch offices and reduce services at its other offices because of funding problems (Pacetti 2011). Virginia legal aid estimated that it has experienced a $5 million reduction in its budget over the past few years, and had laid off up to 20 attorneys and 10 support staff as a result (Wilson 2011). From 2008 to 2010 New Jersey legal aid experienced a 35 percent budget reduction, from $72 to $47 million. The result was a 50 percent reduction in attorneys on staff (Leaming 2011). In FY 2011 New Jersey legal aid experienced a $5 million budget cut from the state and anticipated that as a result an additional 100 people would be laid off; three or more offices would be closed; and 10,000 fewer clients would be served in the following year (Delli Santi 2011). Minnesota legal aid was also hard hit by state budget cuts. From 2008 to February of 2011 state funding for legal aid decreased by $1.29 million (Van Berkel 2011). The 2011 budget further reduced state funding for legal aid by $1.6 million (Williams 2011).

Private attorneys have not been able to step in to fill the void left by legal aid. In many states private attorneys who have also been negatively impacted by the Recession have reduced the number of pro bono services they offer. In Nevada, for example, attorneys donated 93,394 hours of free legal services in 2006; 91,917 hours in 2007; and only 73,516 hours in 2008 (Wargo 2009). This is despite an increase of 788 licensed attorneys in the state over that same time period

(Wargo 2009). Attorneys in the state have also reduced the number of hours donated at a reduced rate (Wargo 2009). This pattern can be seen in many other states across the country. With the increased poverty rate that has accompanied the Great Recession and the reduction in services offered by legal aid programs because of reduced funding, many low-income clients with civil legal matters have been left with nowhere to turn for help.

OUTLOOK

The National Right to Counsel Committee recommends that public defenders be adequately funded at the state level with assistance from the federal government so that caseloads can be reduced and indigent clients can receive the effective assistance of counsel to which they are constitutionally entitled (Constitution Project 2009). The Legal Services Corporation and legal aid offices not funded by LSC have highlighted the importance of legal aid in light of the Recession, which has caused an increase in the numbers people eligible for their services (Legal Services Corporation 2009). As private individuals and organizations recover from the Recession, and as interest rates rise (which will provide increased funding for legal aid through IOLTA), legal aid may be able to provide more services to low-income clients. However, until states and the federal government resolve their budgetary shortfalls, a substantial increase in funding for public defenders and legal aid is unlikely. In the meantime, in a nation that aspires to the ideal of "justice for all," many low-income individuals will experience a vastly different justice system than those who are able to afford private attorneys.

FURTHER READING

Combs, David. "State Budget Gaps: How Does Your State Rank?" Pew Charitable Trusts, March 15, 2011. Accessed June 16, 2012.http://www.pewstates.org/projects/stateline/headlines/state-budget-gaps-how-does-your-state-rank-85899375024

Constitution Project: National Right to Counsel Committee. "Justice Denied: America's Continuing Neglect of Our Constitutional Right to Counsel," April 2009. Accessed June 16, 2012. http://www.constitutionproject.org/pdf/139.pdf

Delli Santi, Angela. "N.J. Legal Aid Agency Forced to Cut Caseload." Associated Press, July 28, 2011. Accessed June 16, 2012. http://articles.philly.com/2011-07-28/news/29825097_1_legal-services-domestic-violence-legal-advice

Florio, Gwen. "Budget Cuts Reduce Free Legal Aid for Low-Income Missoula Residents." *Missoulian*, October 24, 2011. Accessed June 16, 2012. http://missoulian.com/news/local/article_046e1934-fdec-11e0-a9fa-001cc4c002e0.html

Gideon vs. Wainwright, 372 U.S. 335 (1963). http://www.uscourts.gov/educational-resources/get-involved/constitution-activities/sixth-amendment/righ-counsel/facts-case-summary-gideon.aspx

Hastings, Deborah. "Nationwide, Public Defender Offices Are in Crisis." Associated Press, June 4, 2009. Accessed June 16, 2012. http://www.michigancampaignforjustice.org/docs/AP 06-04-09.pdf

Holahan, Carol J., and James R. Steiner. "History of Legal Aid in the United States." *Update on Law-Related Education.* 18, no. 3 (1994): 6–13.

Houseman, Alan W., and Linda E. Perle. "Securing Equal Justice for All: A Brief History of Civil Legal Assistance in the United States." Center for Law and Social Policy, January 2007. Accessed June 16, 2012. http://www.clasp.org/admin/site/publications/files/0158.pdf

Houseman, Alan W., and Linda E. Perle. "What Can and Cannot Be Done: Representation of Clients by LSC-Funded Programs." Center for Law and Social Policy, August 9, 2001. Accessed June 16, 2012. http://nhlp.org/node/868

Kinnard, Meg. "S.C.'s Public Defenders Hampered by Recession." Associated Press, April 18, 2011. June 16, 2012. http://www.thesunnews.com/2011/04/18/2107614/scs-public-defenders-hampered.html

Koppel, Nathan. "Public Defenders Stretched Thin by State Cuts." *Wall Street Journal,* April 14, 2011. Accessed June 16, 2012. http://online.wsj.com/article/SB10001424052748704530204576232812464584064.html

Leaming, Jeremy. "Cuts in Legal Services Come at Perilous Times: States, Federal Lawmakers Slashing Funding, Inhibiting Access to Justice." American Constitution Society, August 8, 2011. Accessed June 16, 2012. http://www.acslaw.org/acsblog/cuts-in-legal-services-come-at-perilous-times-states-federal-lawmakers-slashing-funding-inhi

Legal Services Corporation. "Funding History," Accessed June 16, 2012a. http://lsc.gov/congress/lscs-fiscal-year-2012-budget-request-brief/funding-history

Legal Services Corporation. "Legal Services Corporation: History," 2012b. Accessed June 16. http://www.lsc.gov/about/what-is-lsc/history

Legal Services Corporation. "What Is LSC?" 2112c. Accessed June 16. http://www.lsc.gov/about/what-is-lsc

Legal Services Corporation. "LSC Urges Congress to Increase Legal Aid Funding," April 1, 2009. Accessed June 16, 2012. http://www.lsc.gov/media/press-releases/lsc-urges-congress-increase-legal-aid-funding

Meyer, Bill. "Public Defender Offices Are in Crisis Nationwide." *Plain Dealer* (Cleveland, OH), June 3, 2009. Accessed June 16, 2012. http://www.cleveland.com/nation/index.ssf/2009/06/nationwide_public_defender_off.html

National Legal Aid and Defender Association. www.nlada.org/

National Legal Aid and Defender Association. "NLADA Says Budget Deal Comes at Expense of the Poor Who Need Legal Services," April 12, 2011. Accessed June 16, 2012. http://www.nlada.org/News/2011041239514961

National Legal Aid and Defender Association. "History of Right to Counsel," 2012. Accessed June 16. http://www.nlada.org/About/About_HistoryDefender

Pacetti, Andrea. "Three Legal Aid Branches Set to Close due to Budget Cuts." News 14 Carolina, August 15, 2011. Accessed June 16, 2012. http://charlotte.news14.com/content/local_news/sandhills/645355/three-legal-aid-branches-set-to-close-due-to-budget-cuts

Prial, Christopher. "Congress Proposes 13.9% Cut to Legal Services Corporation Budget." New York Law School: Diane Abbey Law Center for Children and Families, November 23, 2011. Accessed June 16, 2012. http://www.justfamilies.org/congress-proposes-13-9-cut-to-legal-services-corporation-budget/

Routman, Brent. "More than Coincidence." *Bench and Bar of Minnesota*, October 12, 2011. Accessed June 16, 2012. http://mnbenchbar.com/2011/10/more-than-coincidence/

Van Berkel, Jessie. "Minnesota's Resources for Legal Aid Are Drying up Fast." *MinnPost*, February 28, 2011. Accessed June 16, 2012. http://www.minnpost.com/stories/2011/02/28/26150/minnesotas_resources_for_legal_aid_are_drying_up_fast

Wargo, Buck. "Hammered by Recession, Nevada Lawyers Cut Pro Bono Work." *Las Vegas Sun*, October 23, 2009. Accessed June 16, 2012. http://www.lasvegassun.com/news/2009/oct/23/hammered-Recession-lawyers-cut-pro-bono-work/

Washington State Office of Public Defense. "2010 Status Report on Public Defense in Washington State," January 2011. http://www.opd.wa.gov/Reports/TrialLevelServices/2010_PublicDefenseStatusReport.pdf

Wice, Paul B. *Public Defenders and the American Justice System*. Westport, CT: Praeger, 2005.

Williams, Brandt. "Uneven Cuts Stressing Minn. Criminal Justice System." Minnesota Public Radio News, November 7, 2011. Accessed June 16, 2012. http://minnesota.public radio.org/display/web/2011/11/07/minnesota-criminal-justice-system-cuts/

Wilson, Patrick. "Virginia Legal Aid Unit Asks for Higher Court Filing Fees." *Virginian-Pilot*, December 31, 2011. Accessed June 16, 2012. http://hamptonroads.com/2011/12/virginia-legal-aid-unit-asks-higher-court-filing-fees

SECONDARY EFFECTS

Bryan Dettrey

OVERVIEW

The effects of the Great Recession were pervasive and damaging, especially for those who entered this economic time period already facing financial constraints. While the other essays in this volume cover in great detail the direct effects of the Great Recession, this essay focuses on the less obvious effects of the Recession on the effects one might expect it to have had which have not been observed. These include the effects of the Recession on household formation, and family size, retirement, health, suicide rates, domestic violence, divorce, crime, and immigration.

THE PRESENT

FAMILY FORMATION AND FAMILY SIZE

Significant life events such as moving out of a parent's residence, marriage, and starting a family were put on pause by many people during the Great Recession. Why would a poor economy affect these life decisions? People often wait until they feel financially secure to get married or start a family. In a poor economy more people are unemployed and thus feel financially insecure; those who are employed may also experience increased uncertainty about the security of their job.

One way to explore the effect the Recession has on these trends is to examine the number of family households in the United States. This is the number of households with related individuals. The Census Bureau has been tracking this number since 1940. More young adults starting their own families and setting up their own households increases the number of households in the United States, the

Many people decided to delay having children during the Recession. (Shutterstock)

inverse decreases the number of households. It is not a surprise that the number of family households has consistently increased over the twentieth century. However, the steady rise in family households was abruptly halted by the Great Recession (U.S. Census Bureau 2013a). In 2009, 2010, and 2011 the number of family households held steady at about 78 million, rather than following the long-run trend of increased households.

The average size of family households is evidence of young people delay moving from their parent's home (U.S. Census Bureau 2013b). Due to the post–World War II baby boom, individuals per household averaged about 3.7 in the late 1950s and 1960s. Since then, there has been a marked decrease in family household size, which was down to 3.13 in 2007. Smaller family units (fewer children) but also robust economic opportunities for young adults to achieve independence caused the average number of individuals in family households to decline. The Great Recession abruptly halted this decline. The average number of people per household was up to 3.18 in 2011 (U.S. Census Bureau 2013b). This is a small but noticeable increase in the average size of family households and reflects the tendency for young adults to remain with their parents for a longer time period of time during severe economic distress.

It is important to point out the reciprocal relationship between these trends. The formation of fewer new households and the increase in household size are caused by the poor economy, but they also affect the economy. The stagnant economy and joblessness causes individuals to delay major life changes, but delaying these changes also contributes to the sluggish economy. For example, new household formation is a significant contributor to the building of homes, which creates many jobs. Starting a family also contributes to the economy because households with new babies need to put money into the economy to pay for items such as cribs, diapers, and visits to health care providers. If economic growth accelerates, some of these trends will revert to their prior trajectory. However, it will also be more difficult for the economy to grow without the formation of many new households. Still, remaining with their parents longer and not forming new households helped many young adults avoid poverty during the Recession. The 2010 poverty rate for 25- to 35-year-olds was 17.4 percent, but the poverty rate for 25- to 35-year-olds living in a multigenerational household was only 9.8 percent (Parker 2012).

DELAYED OR EARLY RETIREMENT

The Great Recession caused many older adults to rethink their retirement plans and in many cases contributed to either early or delayed retirement. For those who retired sooner than anticipated, the Recession led to an increasing number of people applying for early Social Security retirement benefits. The number of applicants peaked in 2009 when 31 percent of those who were eligible applied for benefits (a 4 percentage point increase over the 2007 take-up rate). In 2010 the take-up rate was 28.3 percent, and by 2011 the take-up rate of 26.9 percent was below the 2007 rate (Brandon 2012). The ability to apply for early Social Security benefits provided a much-needed safety net and prevented certain older unemployed individuals from falling into poverty. It also alleviated some pressure on the job market by reducing the number of people looking for scarce job opportunities. However, accepting Social Security benefits before reaching the full retirement age reduces the average monthly payment for the early retiree. For example, a benefit of $1,000 a month at the full retirement age of 66 is reduced to $750 a month for someone who retires at age 62 and $800 a month for someone who retires at age 63 (U.S. Social Security Administration 2012). Foregoing potential wages earned from employment and receiving less money each month may contribute to a lower standard of living than many retirees expected. Reduced financial resources for these retirees also means that they have less money to inject into the economy.

While many retired early during the Great Recession, others delayed retirement. Declining home values, poor returns on retirement investments, and increased financial uncertainty contributed to the decision to delay retirement. The result was an increasing percentage of individuals over the age of 65 in the workforce. The number of those 65 and older in the workforce has been recorded by the Bureau of Labor Statistics since 1948 (see Figure 1). The effects of Social Security

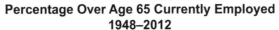

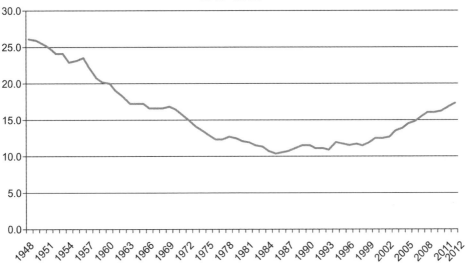

Figure 1

(*Source*: Author's calculations based on Bureau of Labor Statistics Time Series LNU0 2300097Q available at http://data.bls.gov/timeseries/LNU02300097Q?include_graphs =false&output_type=column&years_option=all_years.)

and other retirement plans drove down the percentage of all older workers currently employed from more than 25 percent in 1948 to a low of about 10 percent in the early 1980s. Since that time, the percentage of those older than 65 in the workforce has gradually increased. Improved health care, increased life expectancy, and the transition from blue collar to white collar jobs has enabled individuals to work longer than in previous years. While the increase in older workers was already underway, the Great Recession accelerated it. In the first quarter of 2012, 17.2 percent of those over the age of 65 were employed, which is the same percentage as in 1965. Retaining employment reduces the likelihood of poverty for older Americans. Working for several more years also provides an opportunity for home values or retirement funds to recover their losses and reduces the prospect of depleting retirement funds too quickly in the later years of retirement.

HEALTH

With the stress and hardship created by unemployment, financial stress, and the substantial fallout from the Great Recession it might be expected that the Recession would also bring widespread negative health consequences. However, this does not appear to have happened. For the general U.S. population there is no clear indication that the Recession has negatively impacted overall physical health, and these findings are in line with previous studies on the impact of recessions on health (Burgard 2012). Still, there are signs that the Great Recession may have negatively impacted mental health in the nation. Due to a decrease in health coverage people may have put off dealing with medical care, and this could result in negative health consequences in the future (Burgard 2012). Still, future data may show that those who experienced the most negative consequences of the Recession might also suffer healthwise. Unemployment has been linked to cancer, heart disease, and psychiatric issues (Baker 2012). For example, unemployed men have a 25 percent higher risk of dying of cancer compared to employed men (Baker 2012). Economists who have studied the issue have also found a 50 to 100 percent increase in the death rate for older male workers in the years after the loss of a job (Baker 2012). Still, there may also be some whose health benefits from the downturn. Specifically, male workers who delay retirement may experience better health—research has shown that males who retire early have an increased risk of premature death (Lam 2012).

Suicide Rates

Although widespread health problems as the result of the Recession have not been seen, there are some signs that the Recession contributed to an increased suicide rate. During the early part of the Great Depression of the 1930s the suicide rate increased to around 17 suicides for every 100,000 people (Harris 2011). It is possible that a similar effect was seen during the Great Recession. The suicide rate has been steadily increasing throughout the Great Recession and the slow recovery as shown in Figure 2, but more research is needed to determine whether these increases can be directly tied to the economic downturn. The grey bars in Figure 2 denote the 2001 recession and the Great Recession.

Domestic Violence: Child and Spousal Abuse

Domestic violence, both spousal abuse and child abuse, might also be expected to increase during difficult economic times. The Great Recession does appear to have increased spousal abuse, but the research related to the Recession's impact on child abuse is mixed.

Research has shown that the rate of domestic violence is nearly 7 percentage points higher for couples who feel high levels of financial strain compared to those who feel low levels of financial strain (Renzetti 2009). Other studies have shown that as a female partner's income increases in comparison to the male partner's, the likelihood of the female partner being abused increases (Renzetti 2009). Men who are unemployed are also more likely to be perpetrators of domestic violence.

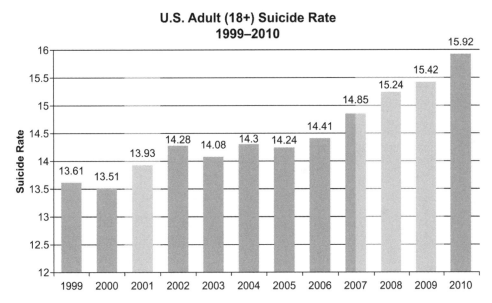

Figure 2

(*Source*: NCHS Vital Statistics System for numbers of deaths. Bureau of Census for population estimates. Can be accessed online at http://webappa.cdc.gov/sasweb/ncipc/mortrate10 _us.html)

Research a few years prior to the Great Recession showed that when the male partner was unemployed the rate of domestic violence increased 2.8 percentage points (Renzetti 2009). The Great Recession has increased the financial strain many households feel and created higher rates of male unemployment than female unemployment. In addition, the Great Recession added to the increasing percentage of working wives making more than their working husbands. (For further discussion of these trends see Section 3, "Sex, Female.") With these trends linked to increasing domestic violence, it is not surprising that early research shows an increase in the rate of domestic violence even though prior to the Recession rates of domestic violence had been falling for 15 years (Cohen 2010). For example, in New York State there was an 18 percent increase in court cases involving assault by family members in 2009, and that same year in Philadelphia there was a 67 percent increase in domestic homicides (Cohen 2010). Additionally, in a 2009 survey of domestic violence shelters 75 percent reported that since September 2008 they had seen an increase in women seeking help due to abuse (Cohen 2010). In surveys of police agencies 40 percent of the agencies said that the bad economy had increased domestic conflict in 2010; for 2011, 56 percent said the same (Johnson 2012).

The impact of the Great Recession on child maltreatment and abuse is less clear. Data from the U.S. Department of Health and Human Services shows decreasing

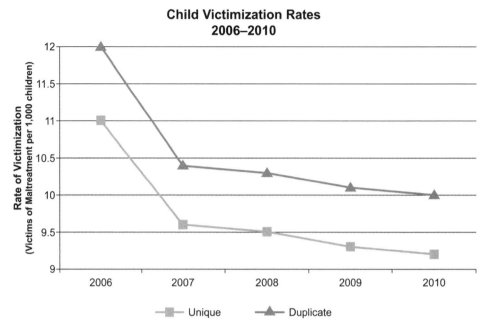

Figure 3
(*Note*: In 2006 and 2007, 51 states and territories reported duplicate counts, and in 2008 to 2010, 52 states and territories reported duplicate counts. In 2006 and 2007, 49 states and territories submitted unique counts; in 2008 and 2009, 50 submitted unique counts; and in 2010, 51 states and territories submitted unique counts. *Source*: U.S. Department of Health and Human Services, Administration on Children, Youth and Families, "Child Maltreatment 2010," 2011, http://www.acf.hhs.gov/programs/cb/resource/child-maltreatment-2010. Tables 3-7 and 3-8.)

rates of child maltreatment, but other prominent studies have linked the Recession with growing rates of child abuse and maltreatment. Figure 3 shows the national rate of victimization for children for the years 2006 to 2010 as reported by the U.S. Department of Health and Human Services. The duplicate count includes a child in the rate of victimization every time she or he is reported to be a victim of maltreatment. The unique count includes a child in the rate of victimization only once, even if the child is reported to be the victim of maltreatment more than once.

Data from 2001 to 2005 are not included in Figure 3 because data for those years are not separated into unique and duplicate counts. However, U.S. Department of Health and Human Services data between 2001 and 2005 show that the rate of victimization dropped by half a percentage point between those years, with the only increase in that time period (of 0.1 percentage point) coming between 2004 and 2005. While data for the years 2001 to 2005 do indicate a slight downward trend, the downward trend from 2006 to 2010 of around two percentage points, for both the unique and duplicate victimization rates, show a greater decrease in victimization than the 2001 to 2005 data do.

Despite these promising reports from the U.S. Department of Health and Human Services, other studies have found that during and after the Recession there was an increase in child abuse. Two studies published in the journal *Pediatrics* reported such increases (Gordon 2012). The first was published in October 2011 and found that between 2004 and 2009 abusive head trauma rates for children increased from 9 out of every 100,000 children to 15 out of every 100,000. The second study published in the same journal in August 2012 found that for children under six years of age the rate of child abuse went up by 0.79 percent from 2000 to 2009 (Gordon 2012). That study also found that the rate of hospital admission for traumatic brain injuries in children under 1 year of age (not including injuries caused by car or other motor vehicle accidents) increased by 3 percent during the same time period (Gordon 2012). The study also reported that during the 2000 to 2009 time period all injuries for children decreased by 0.8 percent per year. A third study presented at an April 2011 meeting of the American Association of Neurological Surgeons found that for children 2 years of age and younger, incidents of abusive head trauma doubled during the Recession (Gordon 2012). While it intuitively seems that the stress and hardship created by the Great Recession would lead to increased child abuse, particularly if it did in fact lead to increased spousal abuse, more research will be needed to determine whether that truly is the case.

OTHER SECONDARY EFFECTS

In addition to the secondary effects discussed earlier in the essay, the media has reported on various other secondary effects of the Recession including crime, immigration and divorce. Crime continued its downward trend throughout the Great Recession (Uggen 2012). Moreover, there is no indication that the long-term trend of decreasing crime is hiding an increase in Recession-related crime, with perhaps the exception of burglary, which has declined less than other crimes since 2007 (Uggen 2012). Immigration, both legal and illegal, has stalled in the wake of the economic downturn, but the migration of temporary workers (which also fell during the Recession) began to increase again in 2009 and 2010 (Massey 2012). (For further discussion of immigration trends, see Section 3, "Immigrants.")

As for divorce, the data is murky. Some economists have found an 18 percent increase in divorce after a husband loses his job and a 1 percent increase when a wife loses her job (Baker 2012). This would suggest that divorce should increase during periods of high unemployment such as the Recession. Some experts theorize that recessions cause stress, which results in more divorce, while other experts suggest that couples avoid or delay divorce during economic downturns because divorces are costly and it is more expensive to live separately than as a couple (Cohn 2012). However, there is no clear data showing the Great Recession has increased divorce rates, and analyzing whether it has decreased or increased divorce rates is greatly complicated by the pre-Recession trend of decreasing divorces (Cohn 2012). Thus, more research will be needed to determine the impact, if any, of the Recession on divorce rates.

OUTLOOK

The effects of the Great Recession are many and varied. This essay identified a few of the less obvious but still important effects of the worst recession in generations. The Recession slowed new household formation, increased the average size of existing family households, led to changes in retirement plans, and stalled immigration to the United States. While the Recession has not impacted crime rates, it may have led to an increase in suicide rates and spousal abuse. Its impact on child abuse, divorce, and health remains less clear.

Additional data will be needed to determine some of the impacts of the Recession, but for the secondary effects for which there are clear trends, one must ask whether these new trends are just temporary adjustments or whether they will continue even years after the Great Recession and subsequent recovery. In the area of immigration there will likely be some growth going forward, but at a slower pace than the nation has seen in recent decades (Singer et al. 2010).

In terms of new household formation, an optimistic scenario suggests that as home prices decline and the job market slowly recovers from the depths of 2008 to 2009, young adults will again venture out on their own and create their own family households. In this case, the pause in household family formation will have been a temporary delay in the long-term trend of household formation growing along with population growth. If family household formation does increase, the average number of people within family households will decrease and return to its historic levels. This would also strengthen the economic recovery because more young adults creating households and purchasing related consumer items will contribute to economic growth.

A more pessimistic scenario suggests the Recession may have more long-term effects on young adults' preferences and choices. If this is the case, the growth in housing may slow relative to the long-term trend. Even as young adults do obtain employment, the wages they can command are likely to be limited, and uncertainty about the future may make for a cautious outlook in many young adults who were affected by the Recession.

The percentage of older workers in the workforce, though accelerated by the Recession, has steady since the early 1980s and will likely continue into the future. Improved health care, longer life expectancies, and slow-to-recover retirement accounts and home values will incentivize older adults to continue working. While this may crowd out some younger workers in an economy with scarce jobs, the overall economic effect of more people working will be increased growth and a healthier economy.

FURTHER READING

Baker, Dean, and Kevin Hassett. "The Human Disaster of Unemployment." *New York Times*, May 12, 2012. Accessed November 4, 2012. http://www.nytimes.com/2012/05/13/ opinion/sunday/the-human-disaster-of-unemployment.html?pagewanted=all&_r=0

Brandon, Emily. "Social Security Claiming Slows," April 17, 2012. Accessed November 4, 2012. http://money.usnews.com/money/blogs/planning-to-retire/2012/04/17/social -security-claiming-slows

Burgard, Sarah. "Health, Mental Health and the Great Recession." Stanford Center on Poverty and Inequality, October 2012. Accessed November 4, 2012. http://www .stanford.edu/group/recessiontrends/cgi-bin/web/sites/all/themes/barron/pdf/Health_fact _sheet.pdf

Cohen, Philip N. "Recession Begets Family Violence," January 2, 2010. Accessed November 3, 2012. http://www.huffingtonpost.com/philip-n-cohen/recession-begets -family-v_b_409502.html

Cohn, D'Vera. "Divorce and the Great Recession," May 2, 2012. Accessed November 3, 2012. http://www.pewsocialtrends.org/2012/05/02/divorce-and-the-great-recession/

Gordon, Serena. "Child Abuse Rises when Economy Sags: Study." *U.S. News and World Report, HealthDay*, July 16, 2012. Accessed November 4, 2012. http://health.usnews .com/health-news/news/articles/2012/07/16/child-abuse-rises-when-economy-sags-study

Harris, Jonathan Daniel. "Suicide Rates up since Recession Began, Debt a 'Way of Life' For 99ers." *Huffington Post*, May 25, 2011. Accessed November 4, 2012. http://www .huffingtonpost.com/2010/07/26/suicide-rates-up-since-re_n_658668.html

Johnson, Kevin. "Domestic Violence Rises in Sluggish Economy, Police Report," April 30, 2012. Accessed November 4, 2012. http://usatoday30.usatoday.com/news/nation/ story/2012-04-29/domestic-violence-police-survey/54633282/1?csp=34news

Lam, Bourree, and Dwyer Gunn. "Early Retirement: Bad for Your Health?" Freakanomics Blog, March 29, 2012. Accessed November 4, 2012. http://www.freakonomics.com/ 2012/03/29/early-retirement-bad-for-your-health/

Massey, Douglas S. "Immigration and the Great Recession." Stanford Center on Poverty and Inequality, October 2012. Accessed November 4, 2012. http://www.stanford.edu/ group/recessiontrends/cgi-bin/web/sites/all/themes/barron/pdf/Immigration_fact_sheet .pdf

Parker, Kim. "The Boomerang Generation." Pew Research Center, March 15, 2012. Accessed June 10, 2012. http://www.pewsocialtrends.org/2012/03/15/the-boomerang -generation/2/

Renzetti, Claire M. "Economic Stress and Domestic Violence," September 2009. Accessed November 3, 2012. http://new.vawnet.org/Assoc_Files_VAWnet/AR_EconomicStress.pdf

Singer, Audrey, and Jill H. Wilson. "The Impact of the Great Recession on Metropolitan Immigration Trends." Brookings Institution, Metropolitan Policy Program, December

2010. Accessed July 8, 2012. http://www.brookings.edu/~/media/research/files/opinions/2011/1/12 migration frey/1216_immigration_singer_wilson.pdf

Uggen, Christopher. "Crime and the Great Recession." Stanford Center on Poverty and Inequality, October 2012. Accessed November 4, 2012. http://www.stanford.edu/group/recessiontrends/cgi-bin/web/sites/all/themes/barron/pdf/Crime_fact_sheet.pdf

U.S. Bureau of Labor Statistics. "Current Population Survey," 2012a. Accessed June 20, 2012. http://www.bls.gov/cps/

U.S. Bureau of Labor Statistics. "Time Series LNU02300097Q," 2012b. Accessed June 30, 2012. Available online at: LNU02300097Q http://data.bls.gov/timeseries/LNU02300097Q?include_graphs=false&output_type=column&years_option=all_years

U.S. Census Bureau. "Families and Living Arrangements," 2012s. Accessed June 20, 2012. http://www.census.gov/hhes/families/data/households.html

U.S. Census Bureau. "Historical Income Tables: Households," 2012b. Accessed June 20, 2012. http://www.census.gov/hhes/www/income/data/historical/household/

U.S. Census Bureau. "Table HH-1: Households, by Type, 1940 to Present," 2013a. Accessed March 11, 2012. http://www.census.gov/hhes/families/data/households.html

U.S. Census Bureau. "Table HH-6: Average Population per Household and Family, 1940 to Present," 2013b. Accessed March 11, 2012. http://www.census.gov/hhes/families/data/households.html

U.S. Department of Health and Human Services, Administration on Children, Youth and Families. "Child Maltreatment 2005," 2007. Accessed November 4, 2012. http://archive.acf.hhs.gov/programs/cb/pubs/cm05/cm05.pdf

U.S. Department of Health and Human Services, Administration on Children, Youth and Families. "Child Maltreatment 2010," 2011. Accessed November 2, 2012. http://www.acf.hhs.gov/programs/cb/resource/child-maltreatment-2010

U.S. Social Security Administration. "When to Start Receiving Retirement Benefits," August 2012. Accessed November 4, 2012. http://www.ssa.gov/pubs/10147.html#a0=1

Social Security

Jack Reardon

OVERVIEW

As capitalism developed during the nineteenth century many believed that some degree of economic security for the vulnerable was needed. In 1889 Otto von Bismarck of the newly formed German nation became the first leader of a major nation to enact a social insurance program for older adults. Within the next 50 years most Western nations followed suit. The United States was one of the last to do so, passing the Social Security Act in 1935 during the midst of the Great Depression. This essay will discuss the debate over the U.S. Social Security program in the midst of the Great Recession, and the role Social Security played in alleviating poverty for the elderly, adults, and children during the Great Recession. First, some background on the historic emergence of the U.S. Social Security program and the Social Security program itself will be necessary.

HISTORIC EMERGENCE OF SOCIAL SECURITY IN THE UNITED STATES

Caring for others is a deeply held human value across cultures and time. Every nation struggles to care for its citizens who are no longer able to provide for themselves, or who are elderly. But the rapid advent of capitalism during the latter part of the nineteenth century made this issue paramount: while capitalism rewards risk-takers and entrepreneurs, others—through no fault of their own—lose their jobs and livelihood, and in some cases fall into poverty. Designing an economic system that maximizes wealth and generates creativity while at the same time caring for the vulnerable, the poor, the infirm, and the aged, is a difficult task.

Perhaps if the Great Depression had never occurred Social Security would never have been implemented, or it would have been different. The Great Depression revolutionized the role of the federal government, which became more active in its economic influence and its role as a provider for the economically vulnerable. With one eye toward the ostensible success of the Soviet Union during the 1930s, and another eye toward the possibility of revolution in the United States, the Social Security Act of 1935 was passed. Criticized by the left for not going far enough (e.g., not providing nationalized health care) and criticized by the right as socialist, the Social Security System provided a collective sense of security for the nation.

One might assume that Social Security specifically earmarks contributions made by each individual for use later in life. If, for example, the government takes $3,000 from an individual's paychecks for Social Security, then that individual is given $3,000 in Social Security payments later in life. However, this is not the case. While such a possibility was considered during the 1930s, the Roosevelt administration, which was worried that future politicians might dismantle all or part of Social Security, explicitly rejected such a system. Instead, Social Security was designed as a pay-as-you-go system. Instead of earmarking specific contributions for use by the same individual later in life, the system funnels each individual's contributions into a trust fund to be used by current recipients of Social Security. The Roosevelt administration felt that a pay-as-you-go system would guarantee institutional survival and reduce the probability of future administrations dismantling all or part of the program by linking future recipients to current contributors. In this respect President Roosevelt's vision for the Social Security program as self-perpetuating has been successful as evidenced by the vociferous objections to any suggestion that the program be changed or eliminated.

Since 1935 the Social Security system has become a vast government program from which 56 million people benefit and that accounts for 20 percent of the federal budget. While most people associate old age pensions (Social Security retirement) with Social Security, it is actually composed of several programs: old age, survivors, disability insurance (OASDI or RSDI for Retirement, Survivors, and Disability Insurance), and the Medicare and Medicaid programs that were established by the 1965 amendments to the Social Security Act. Each of these programs will be explained briefly in the following sections.

An Overview of the U.S. Social Security System: Social Security Retirement or Old Age Pension, and Survivor's Benefits

The most prominent component of the Social Security system is Social Security Retirement, also known as the Old Age Pension. A wage deferred to the future is called a pension. A pension can be provided either by a private company or by the government. Unlike private pensions, which are jointly negotiated between workers and their businesses, nearly all workers must participate in the Old Age Pension provided by the government. As an individual works and pays taxes, she or he accumulates Social Security credits. In 2012 every $1,130 in earnings equaled one credit, and a worker can earn a maximum of four credits per year no matter the income he or she generates. To begin receiving Social Security an individual usually needs 40 credits, or about ten years of employment. The earliest age at which someone can start receiving Social Security Retirement benefits is 62, but benefits are reduced for individuals who receive Social Security before their full retirement age, which is between 65 and 67, depending on an individual's year of birth. Once an individual begins collecting these benefits he or she can continue to do so for life.

The children and spouse of a worker can receive Social Security benefits for their deceased relative if the worker has sufficient credits based on his or her age. The younger the deceased worker, the fewer credits are needed for their survivors to receive benefits. Even if a deceased worker does not have enough credits, his or her children (and spouse who is caring for the children) can receive benefits if the worker has six credits (1.5 years of work) in the three years just prior to death.

To understand how the Old Age Pension works as a program, think of the Social Security Trust Fund, officially known as the Old-Age and Survivors Insurance (OASI) Trust Fund as a giant reservoir, and the level in the reservoir is determined by the relationship between the inflow and the outflow. The inflow to the Social Security Trust Fund is provided by a tax on workers' wages. In 2011 wages comprised approximately 64 percent of personal income earned; profits, interest, and supplemental benefits comprised the remainder, but only wages are taxed for Social Security. The tax on wages is normally 12.4 percent, split between employers and employees. Those who are self-employed pay the entire tax. The tax is applicable to the first $110,000 of wages, which covers about 95 percent of all wages earned in the United States. This wage level increases every year with the rate of inflation. However, the Tax Relief, Unemployment Insurance Reauthorization and Job Creation Act of 2010 reduced the Social Security payroll tax rate by 2 percentage points for workers and the self-employed, and was extended through December 2012.

An Overview of the U.S. Social Security System: Medicare and Medicaid

During the 1930s proposals to adopt universal health care along with Medicare (health insurance for the aged) and Medicaid (health insurance for the indigent) were discussed but ultimately rejected. With the refocus on poverty during the early 1960s these programs once again entered into the national discussion. In 1965 Congress passed an amendment to the 1935 Social Security Act that implemented both Medicare and Medicaid. While often confused, the former is federal program for the aged, while the latter is jointly run between the states and the federal government and is for those with low incomes.

Medicare is divided into five parts. Part A (hospital insurance) is financed primarily by a 1.45 percent tax on employee earnings that is matched by the employer. An individual (or spouse) who is eligible to receive Social Security is also eligible to receive Medicare Part A. Medicare Part B (Medicare medical insurance) is financed by general revenues but also by individual premiums, with individuals earning more than $85,000 paying a higher premium. Anyone eligible for Part A can enroll in Part B. Medicare Part C (Medicare Advantage plans) is offered by private companies, and anyone eligible for Parts A or B is eligible for Part C. Medicare Part D (prescription drug coverage) is optional, and individuals can pay an additional monthly premium for this coverage.

Medicaid programs are funded by states and the federal government but managed by states. Medicaid programs provide health insurance to people with low incomes, but programs and eligibility criterion vary from state to state. This essay will not focus on Medicaid because it is discussed in more detail in other portions of this work (see the essay earlier in this section titled "Health Care Assistance"). The Patient Protection and Affordable Care Act and the State Children's Health Insurance Program also fall under the Social Security Act but are discussed in other portions of this work (see the essay earlier in this section titled "Health Care Assistance").

An Overview of the U.S. Social Security System: Social Security Disability Insurance (SSDI) and Supplemental Security Income (SSI)

Social Security Disability Insurance (SSDI) provides benefits for workers under the age of 65 who become disabled with a condition that will last longer than a year or that will result in death. The SSDI program was created in 1956. To qualify for SSDI an individual must have worked for a requisite number of years depending on their age. For example, an individual must have worked for approximately seven years if she or he becomes disabled before the age of 50; in addition, the individual must have worked very near to the time of injury.

SSDI is not to be confused with Supplementary Security Income (SSI), created in 1974 as a means-tested benefit for individuals with low incomes and is available only for those over 65, blind, or with a disability. Whereas SSDI is funded by the Social Security Trust Fund, SSI is funded by general tax revenues (Berkowitz 2000). The federal Temporary Assistance to Needy Families (TANF) program and the unemployment insurance program also fall under the Social Security Act but are discussed elsewhere in this work (see the essays later in this section titled "Welfare/Cash Assistance Programs" and "Unemployment").

THE PRESENT

The number of people who receive Old Age and Survivors Social Security benefits (OASI), Social Security Disability Insurance (SSDI) benefits, and Medicare has been steadily increasing for decades (see Table 1). By 2011 there were 44.4 million persons receiving OASI benefits, many of whom also received Medicare. It is difficult to say if the Great Recession has significantly affected the number of enrollees in these programs, although there is speculation that disability applications were up during the Recession, and during the height of the Recession there was an increase in individuals choosing to receive Social Security Retirement benefits before the full age of retirement (Brandon 2012; for further discussion see the essay earlier in this section titled "Secondary Effects").

THE VIABILITY OF SOCIAL SECURITY

In the midst of the budget crises and budget debates during the Great Recession, there was a debate about the viability of the Social Security program and the role

Table 1   OASI, SSDI, and Medicare Beneficiaries (in thousands)

Year	OASI	SSDI	Medicare
1945	1,106	—	—
1960	13,740	522	—
1980	30,384	4,734	28,500
2000	38,556	6,606	39,600
2006	40,435	8,428	43,300
2007	40,863	8,739	44,000
2008	41,355	9,065	45,400
2009	42,385	9,475	46,100
2010	43,440	9,958	47,000
2011	44,385	10,428	48,500
2035	78,079	12,894	80,000

Note: The 2035 Medicare figure is for the year 2030.

Sources: OASI and DI from Board of Trustees Federal Old-Age and Survivors Insurance and Federal Disability Insurance Trust Funds. "The 2012 Annual Report of the Board of Trustees of the Federal Old-Age and Survivors Insurance and Federal Disability Insurance Trust Funds," April 25, 2012. Accessed November 4, 2012. http://www.ssa.gov/oact/tr/2012/tr2012.pdf. Table IV.B2: Covered Workers and Beneficiaries 1945–2090. Medicare from Kaiser Family Foundation. "Medicare Spending and Financing," September 2011. Accessed November 4, 2012. http://www.kff.org/medicare/upload/7305-06.pdf.

it should play in providing benefits to those who are economically vulnerable in U.S. society. The Social Security Administration is obligated to make projections into the future concerning the viability of the trust funds. While more money is contributed by current workers than is paid out to beneficiaries on an annual basis, the trust fund's surplus is projected to disappear by the year 2033 if the government does not take action. Thereafter payroll taxes are predicted to cover only 75 percent of projected benefits.

In 2033 a shortfall of $623 billion is projected, with that amount reaching almost $7 trillion in 2086 (Ohlemacher 2012b). Each of these projections is the estimated shortfall for that year only, so the cumulative shortfall by 2086 would be an estimated $134 trillion. To put this into perspective, that cumulative shortfall represents about 11 times the current gross domestic product (GDP), and given current annual returns of 2.9 percent, it would take an investment of $8.6 trillion now (about 15 times the size of Social Security's current budget) to cover it (Ohlemacher 2012b).

The projected deficit is thus substantial for two reasons. First, people are living longer. In 1940 the average life expectancy for males after the age of 65 was 12.7 years, and for females it was 14.7 years. Today the average life expectancy after the age of 65 for males is 17.2 years, and for females it is 19.9 years (U.S. Census Bureau 2013). Second, there are fewer workers for each beneficiary than in prior years due to the aging baby boomer generation and increased life expectancy. In 1960 there were 4.9 workers for each beneficiary, while currently there are 2.8 workers for each beneficiary. This ratio is expected to decrease to 1.9 by 2035 (Ohlemacher 2012b).

The Medicare Part A Trust Fund is facing a similar projected deficit, although its problems are more urgent because it is projected to be depleted in 2024. The reasons for this are similar to those related to the Social Security deficit, with the additional factor of rising health care costs. On the spending side of the federal budget, Social Security accounts for 20 percent, Medicare accounts for 15 percent, and Medicaid 8 percent. In 2011 the combined cost of Social Security and Medicare equaled 8.5 percent of GDP, and this is expected to increase to 12.1 percent in 2035 and 12.8 percent in 2086 (Board of Trustees 2012).

If nothing is done to reduce the shortfall, more government spending will go to Medicare and Social Security, leaving less money available for other programs. Given the projected deficits for both Social Security and Medicare, as well as the millions of people who will be affected by these problems, it is surprising that little corrective action is being undertaken. However, the debate over Social Security and Medicare is entangled with the debate over taxes, spending, and the federal deficit that became even more contentious during the Great Recession and its aftermath (Ohlemacher 2012c).

SOLUTIONS TO THE PROJECTED SOCIAL SECURITY DEFICIT

Though little has actually been done to address the problems related to Social Security's viability, there have been suggested solutions. Some of these solutions are more politically viable than others. Two extreme solutions can be quickly mentioned and dismissed: (1) to do nothing and (2) completely abolish the program. The built-in obligation of current workers to support current beneficiaries and conversely the trust that future beneficiaries have in current workers will ensure that doing nothing remains outside the range of viable options. Abolishing the program is also an extremely unlikely option because of the size of the Social Security program and the vested interest that workers and retirees have in its continuation. Choosing either of these extreme measures will also have dire effects on poverty rates, particularly for older adults.

A third solution, which also has little chance of being enacted, is some type of privatization. For example, instead of sending all of one's Social Security taxes to the federal government, an individual could decide to invest all or part of the money elsewhere, for example, in the stock market. During the stock market boom of the 1990s, it was suggested that individuals could invest perhaps 25 percent of their Social Security taxes in the stock market. While individuals would no doubt benefit during bull markets, they would suffer during bear markets such as during the most recent Recession. Privatization, however, would not address the primary concern: how to increase the flow of revenue into the fund and/or reduce the outflow.

The most practical solutions are to increase the revenue going into the fund and/or decrease the expenditure (i.e., benefits) going out. There are several ways this could be done. The first is to increase taxes. The increase does not have to be substantial if it begins soon and increases cumulatively. For example, if the tax is increased 0.1 percentage point a year until it reaches 14.4 percent in 20 years, this would eliminate 53 percent of the shortfall (Ohlemacher 2012c). However, any tax increase would also have to be reconciled with its potential adverse effect on economic growth. A second practical option is to eliminate the ceiling on taxable wages (i.e., apply the Social Security tax to earnings above $110,000). A third practical option is to extend the Social Security tax to additional forms of income, including rent, interest, and profits.

A fourth option is to stop increasing payment of benefits based on the rate of inflation. In 2008, for example, benefits increased by 2.3 percent to match the increase in the inflation rate. Economists, however, have argued that the official rate of inflation overstates the actual rate because the official rate does not assume that workers will switch away from more expensive to cheaper items. The level of Social Security benefits could instead be linked to a chained consumer price index, which explicitly assumes that individuals reduce their purchases of items that are more expensive while increasing purchases of items that are cheaper. Using the chained index would reduce the annual inflation rate by approximately 0.3 percentage points, which over time could generate significant savings (Ohlemacher 2012c). A fifth practical option would be to increase the age at which individuals become eligible for Social Security Retirement benefits. This could be politically tenable given increased life expectancies and the fact that the full retirement age has been increased numerous times in the past.

Finally, there is the option of reducing monthly benefits by either reducing the absolute sum by a fixed amount or by tinkering with the formula that generates monthly benefit amounts. The formula is currently based on lifetime earnings. Currently, monthly benefits for new recipients average $1,264. Needless to say any decrease in current benefit levels will provoke strong opposition. According to a recent Associated Press–Gfk poll, 53 percent of respondents preferred increasing taxes on current workers to reducing benefits for future generations, with only 36 percent favoring a reduction in benefits (Ohlemacher and Agiesta 2012). Respondents of all political persuasions favored increasing the retirement age over reducing monthly benefits, but not surprisingly a deep political divide exists over increasing taxes—sixty-five percent of Democrats and 53 percent of independents supported increasing taxes, compared to just 38 percent of Republicans (Ohlemacher and Agiesta 2012). Solutions that reduce benefits are more likely to cause an increase in poverty rates than options that address the shortfall by increasing revenues by either increased taxation or other means.

In addition to fixes from within the Social Security system, there are possible solutions to the projected Social Security shortfall that could come from broader changes and policies from outside the Social Security program. Economic expansion that would increase the workforce by increasing the labor force participation rate is one such solution. Given that the main tax base from which Social Security revenues are derived is employee wages, any program that will increase the number of workers would benefit Social Security. During the late 1990s, for example, when economic growth reached 4 percent or higher the labor force participation rate (percentage of person 16 years of age and older that are working or actively looking for work) also reached record numbers, which in turn reduced the projected Social Security deficit. Conversely, slow and negative economic growth will reduce the employment rate and reduce inflow for the Social Security system. Economic expansion would also increase overall revenues for the federal government even if tax rates remain stable, so the government would have more money to invest in Social Security and other programs. Moreover, increased labor force participation could also help to reduce poverty rates, as increased labor force participation means more income for households.

Another way to increase the workforce and thereby decrease the Social Security shortfall would be through increased immigration. This could be accomplished either by allowing more immigration or by granting amnesty to immigrants who are currently in the United States but undocumented. Granting amnesty to the undocumented, while politically controversial, would also reduce poverty rates for this high-poverty demographic because this would give them the ability to work in the United States legally.

While an increase in the labor force participation rate, immigration, and/or work authorization would generate new Social Security revenues, inclusive of funds that support Medicare, and therefore provide additional time before the Trust Funds are depleted, these potential solutions do not address the longer-term financial challenges. The benefits offered by Social Security for retirement will need to be reduced, and Medicare expenditures will also need to be reduced (a combination of lowering benefits and reducing delivery costs). The policy question before Congress is how to do this in a manner that does not result in an increased poverty rate.

Social Security, Medicare, and Poverty during the Great Recession

Social Security significantly prevented poverty for a number of elderly individuals, adults, and children during and after the Great Recession. The program's most drastic impact was on poverty among older adults. Social Security has been chiefly responsible for the sharp decline in the poverty rates of older adults since 1960 (Engelhardt 2004). Since 1960 when federal spending on Social Security dramatically increased, the poverty rate for Americans over the age of 65 fell from 35 to less than 10 percent, where it remains today. This is lower than the poverty rate for any other age demographic.

Table 2 lists the poverty rates since 2006 for all age groups. Notice that since the Recession began in December 2007 the poverty rate for those over the age of 65 have decreased, while the poverty rates for those of all other age groups have increased. This is due in part to the fact that those over the age of 65 are much more likely to be living off of retirement savings and less likely to be working, so they are more insulated from economic downturns. However, the Social Security program also has a dramatic impact on poverty rates among older adults. In 2008, the first full year of the Recession, more than 13.4 million people over the age of 65 were lifted out of poverty by the Social Security program (Van de Water 2010). In 2011, more than two years after the official end of the Great Recession, Social Security was still eliminating poverty for nearly 14.5 million older adults (Van de Water 2012).

Table 2 U.S. Poverty Rate

Year	All Ages	Under 18 Years of Age	18–64 Years of Age	65+ Years of Age
2006	12.3	17.4	10.8	9.4
2007	12.5	18.0	10.9	9.7
2008	13.2	19.0	11.7	9.7
2009	14.3	20.7	12.9	8.9
2010	15.1	22.0	13.8	8.9
2011	15.0	21.9	13.7	8.7

Source: U.S. Bureau of the Census. "Table B-2: Poverty Rates of People by Age, Race and Hispanic Origin, 1959–2011," 2012. Accessed July 17, 2013, www.census.gov/hhes/www/poverty/data/historical/hstpov2.xls.

It is important to keep in mind, though, that Social Security reduces poverty rates for more than just older adults. It also prevents poverty for working age adults and children. Social Security provides income to these individuals because of disability, death of a family member, or simply the fact that these individuals live with a retiree receiving benefits. The loss of a family income due to death or disability is more common than many think. Around 39 percent of males and 31 percent of females will become disabled or die before reaching retirement age. Social Security Disability Insurance or Survivor's benefits will go to these workers or their families (Veghte 2010).

In 2008, the first full year of the Recession, over 1.1 million children avoided poverty because of Social Security, either because they received benefits or because someone in their household did. Social Security also helped nearly 5.3 million adults 64 years of age and younger avoid poverty in 2009. Including those over the age of 65 who avoided poverty because of the program, Social Security resulted in nearly 20 million people being lifted out of poverty or avoiding poverty in 2008 (Van de Water 2010). In 2011 Social Security eliminated poverty for more than 21 million people, including 1.1 million children and 5.8 million adults under the age of 65 (Van de Water 2012). With the older adults who escaped or avoided poverty because of the program in 2011, Social Security eliminated poverty for over 21.4 million people in 2011 (Van de Water 2012).

In addition to reducing poverty for millions of people, Social Security payments may also help to mitigate the effects of a Recession because they provide income to individuals who are often vulnerable and living payment to payment. Thus, the benefits are often spent on consumer goods and services quickly, which injects funds into the economy.

OUTLOOK

The stimulating economic impact of Social Security coupled with the sheer size of the program and its antipoverty effects means that any reforms to the program will have to be weighed carefully to determine the long-term impacts such changes may have on poverty rates and on the overall economy. Based on the projected Social Security shortfall, it is evident that something needs to be done to save the United States' most substantial safety net program, but what these reforms might entail is as yet unclear despite the existence of a variety of feasible solutions. To prevent the surplus from turning into a deficit, it is necessary to undertake corrective measures now. To wait any longer will significantly increase costs. However, based on the current climate in Washington, which appears to have been worsened by the budget battles that accompanied the Great Recession, substantial reform in the near future seems unlikely.

FURTHER READING

Berkowitz, Edward D. "Disability Policy and History." Statement before the Subcommittee on Social Security of the Committee on Ways and Means, July 13, 2000. Accessed November 4, 2012. http://www.ssa.gov/history/edberkdib.html

Board of Trustees, Federal Old-Age and Survivors Insurance and Federal Disability Insurance Trust Funds. "The 2012 Annual Report of the Board of Trustees of the Federal Old-Age and Survivors Insurance and Federal Disability Insurance Trust Funds," April 25, 2012. Accessed November 4, 2012. http://www.ssa.gov/oact/tr/2012/tr2012.pdf

Brandon, Emily. "Social Security Claiming Slows," April 17, 2012. Accessed November 4, 2012. http://money.usnews.com/money/blogs/planning-to-retire/2012/04/17/social-security-claiming-slows

Engelhardt, Gary, and Jonathan Gruber. "Social Security and the Evolution of Elderly Poverty." National Bureau of Economic Research, May 2004. Accessed November 4, 2012. http://www.nber.org/papers/w10466

Kaiser Family Foundation. "Medicare Spending and Financing," September 2011. Accessed November 4, 2012. http://www.kff.org/medicare/upload/7305-06.pdf

Ohlemacher, Stephen. "Is Social Security Still a Good Deal for Workers?" August 5, 2012a. Accessed November 4, 2012. http://news.yahoo.com/social-security-still-good-deal-workers-125016929—finance.html

Ohlemacher, Stephen. "Social Security Surplus Dwarfed by Future Deficit," August 12, 2012b. Accessed November 4, 2012. http://bigstory.ap.org/article/social-security-surplus-dwarfed-future-deficit

Ohlemacher, Stephen. "Analysis: Social Security Is Fixable, but Changes Are Politically Tough," August 20, 2012c. Accessed November 4, 2012. http://www.denverpost.com/nationworld/ci_21350983/analysis-social-security-is-fixable-but-changes-are

Ohlemacher, Stephen, and Jennifer Agiesta. "AP-GfK poll: Raise taxes to save Social Security" August 27, 2012. Accessed November 4, 2012. http://news.yahoo.com/ap-gfk-poll-raise-taxes-save-social-security-142704918.html

U.S. Census Bureau. "Table 105: Life Expectancy by Sex, Age and Race." 2012 Statistical Abstract, 2013. Accessed January 11, 2013. http://www.census.gov/compendia/statab/2012/tables/12s0105.pdf

Van de Water, Paul N., and Arloc Sherman. "Social Security Keeps 20 Million Americans out of Poverty: A State-by-State Analysis," August 11, 2010. Accessed November 4, 2012. http://www.cbpp.org/cms/index.cfm?fa=view&id=3260

Van de Water, Paul N., and Arloc Sherman. "Social Security Keeps 21 Million Americans out of Poverty: A State-by-State Analysis," October 16, 2012. Accessed November 4, 2012. http://www.cbpp.org/cms/index.cfm?fa=view&id=3260

Veghte, Ben, and Virginia P. Reno. "Social Security Is an Anti-Poverty Program," May 24, 2010. Accessed November 4, 2012. http://www.spotlightonpoverty.org/ExclusiveCommentary.aspx?id=8c9cf9cc-c5ba-4f1c-8681-a5fee0a364f9

Underemployment

Jack Reardon

The concept of unemployment is in flux. We knew when the post-war steel-worker was unemployed ... but it is not at all clear how we should apply these categories to today's Internet consultant, temp-worker, or independent sub-contractor ... the future political economy of work will depend very much on the changing world of work and how it is regulated.

—*Baxandall 2004, 3*

OVERVIEW

The Great Recession has undeniably increased the rate of underemployment across demographic boundaries and thus undeniably had a role to play in the increasing poverty rates in the United States during and after the Recession. However, to understand the rising rates of underemployment—particularly among young people, Hispanics, and those with less education—it will first be useful to understand what is meant by the term "underemployment." An individual is underemployed if he or she is employed but working fewer hours than he or she desires; or if he or she is overqualified for the full-time job he or she has. While the government releases official unemployment numbers, there is no official government rate of underemployment, so some background on how rates of under-employment are calculated and how this relates to the unemployment rate will be helpful before delving into the rate of underemployment during the Recession and its impact on poverty.

THE PRESENT

Unemployed, Discouraged, or Underemployed?

The unemployment rate is the most visible and perhaps best known barometer of the labor market. The unemployment rate generally increases during recessions and decreases during expansions. Thus, the longer the expansion, the lower the unemployment rate. The conceptual framework for measuring the labor force was adopted by the thirteenth International Conference of Labor Statisticians in 1982. Whether a person is categorized as unemployed is determined through use of a survey questionnaire that asks the individual about his or her activities during a specific reference point (e.g., a specific week during a previous month).

An individual is considered unemployed if he or she is not working but is actively searching for work. "Actively seeking work" is a matter of the perception of the individual being surveyed. An individual is considered a discouraged worker if he or she wants to work but is not actively seeking work. The U.S. Bureau of Labor Statistics (BLS), which calculates the unemployment rate and other labor market indicators, estimates that in 2006 there were 381,000 discouraged workers but that in 2010, one year after the Recession officially ended, there were 1.2 million discouraged workers. Though the number of discouraged workers had decreased to 989,000 by 2011, this was still more than double the number of discouraged workers as in 2006 (U.S. Department of Labor 2012).

It is important to note that as the number of discouraged workers increases, the unemployment rate decreases, all else equal, because discouraged workers are excluded when calculating the unemployment rate. As economic conditions improve, the number of discouraged workers decreases because people choose to start actively seeking work again, which has the effect of either increasing the unemployment rate or preventing it from decreasing as fast as it otherwise would.

In addition to not accounting for discouraged workers, the official unemployment rate does not account for underemployed workers because an individual is considered employed if he or she worked at least an hour per week in the labor market, regardless of whether he or she wanted to work more hours and whether he or she was fully utilizing his or her talents.

There are two distinct, but not mutually exclusive, categories of underemployment: someone is underemployed if he or she is employed but working less than a desired number of hours, and someone is also considered underemployed if he or she is overqualified for the job he or she is working (Sixteenth International Conference of Labour Statisticians 1998). For example, a young woman is underemployed if she wants to work full-time as a teacher but is able to find only part-time work. However, a man who chooses to work part-time as a teacher because he wants to spend more time with his infant child is not underemployed. A man trained and experienced as an engineer who is working as a janitor would be

To avoid becoming unemployed during the Recession, many Americans worked jobs that offered fewer hours and less pay. (Alice Herden/Dreamstime.com)

underemployed, but an individual with little experience and no formal higher education who is working full-time as janitor is not considered to be underemployed.

While it is relatively easy for an individual to assess whether he or she is working the number of hours he or she wants, it can be much more difficult to determine whether someone is fully utilizing his or her education, experience, and skills (Sixteenth International Conference of Labour Statisticians 1998). For this reason the BLS does not provide official government statistics on the nation's rate of underemployment (U.S. Department of Labor 2012). Because there is no official government measure of underemployment, there is also no official manner in which the underemployment rate is to be calculated. One study utilized a rather simple definition of underemployment, which somewhat captured the first category but ignored the second due to the conceptual difficulties earlier mentioned (Sum 2010). To obtain the rate of underemployment the authors calculated the number of people working part-time who preferred full-time work or preferred to work more hours and divided the number of such part-time workers by the total number of people employed (Sum 2010).

Table 1 utilizes this manner of calculating the underemployment rate. It shows the annual average underemployment rate for every year from 1998 to 2011. In 2000, the last full year of the longest U.S. economic expansion, the rate of underemployment reached a low of 2.4 percent (3.2 million individuals). During the brief recession of 2001, the underemployment rate increased to 2.7 percent and continued increasing until 2002, when it reached a relative peak of 3.9 percent and then decreased to 2.9 percent in 2006. As the Great Recession began in 2007 the underemployment rate increased to 3.0 percent, and by 2009 the underemployment rate had more than doubled. Only in 2011, two years after the official end of the Recession, did the underemployment rate decrease. However, the 2011 underemployment rate of 6.1 percent was much higher than the rate of underemployment prior to the Recession. Despite the growing rate of underemployment during the Recession, the number of Americans who voluntarily chose part-time work has remained relatively constant (at 13.1 percent) since 2001. Thus, the percentage of involuntary part-time workers as a percent of all part-time workers increased from 14.6 percent in 2000 to 31.8 percent in 2011 (U.S. Department of Labor 2012.).

Underemployment significantly increased between 2007 and 2009 for virtually all demographic groups (Sum 2010). However, those most impacted by the

Table 1 Number and Rate of Underemployed in the United States, 1998–2011 (number in thousands; not seasonally adjusted)

Year	Number	Rate[*]
1998	3,665	2.8
1999	3,357	2.5
2000	3,227	2.4
2001	3,715	2.7
2002	4,213	3.9
2003	4,701	3.4
2004	4,567	3.3
2005	4,350	3.1
2006	4,162	2.9
2007	4,401	3.0
2008	5,875	4.0
2009	8,913	6.4
2010	8,874	6.4
2011	8,560	6.1

*Rate = Number of underemployed divided by total employment.

Source: U.S. Department of Labor Bureau of Labor Statistics. 2012. "Access to historical data for the "A" tables of the Employment Situation News Release," Accessed August 5. http://data.bls.gov/pdq/SurveyOutputServlet.

increase in underemployment during the Recession were young people, Hispanics, those with less education, and those in industries heavily affected by underemployment such as private household work and construction (Sum 2010).

For individuals between the ages of 20 and 24 the underemployment rate in late 2009 was estimated at around 10.6 percent, which was a 5.4 percentage point increase from late 2007 (Sum 2010). As the age of workers increased, their underemployment rate decreased, with 25- to 29-year-olds experiencing an underemployment rate of 7.7 percent in late 2009 (a 4.0 percentage point increase from late 2007) and those 70 and older experiencing underemployment of 3.6 percent in late 2009, an increase of 2.0 percentage points from late 2007 (Sum 2010).

The underemployment rate for Hispanics, estimated around 12.0 percent in late 2009, was the highest for all racial/ethnic groups and was also the greatest increase in underemployment in any racial/ethnic group between 2007 and 2009 at 7 percentage points (Sum 2010). Blacks experienced the next highest rate of underemployment during the Recession with an underemployment rate of 7.5 percent in late 2009, which was a 3.7 percentage point increase from the same time the prior year (Sum 2010). The underemployment rate for non-Hispanic whites was 5.2 percent at the end of 2009, which was a 2.7 percentage point increase from the end of 2007 and the smallest increase of all racial/ethnic groups (Sum 2010). For Asians, the underemployment rate was the lowest of all racial/ethnic groups at 4.7 percent in late 2009, a 2.9 percentage point increase from late 2007 (Sum 2010).

Excluding data on current students, both the underemployment rate and the increase in underemployment between late 2007 and late 2009 declined with increasing education (Sum 2010). The rate of underemployment for high school dropouts was the highest at 16.4 percent in late 2009, a 9.0 percentage point increase from late 2007 (Sum 2010). For those with a bachelor's degree the underemployment rate in late 2009 was much lower at 3.5 percent, a 2.0 percentage point increase from late 2007 (Sum 2010).

The industry with the highest underemployment rate in late 2009, at 19.3 percent, was private household work, which was also the industry with the greatest increase (11.3 percentage point) in underemployment (Sum 2010). Construction was the industry with the second highest underemployment rate in late 2009 at 13.6 percent, an increase of 7.7 percentage point from 2007 (Sum 2010). Other industries heavily affected by underemployment during the Recession were retail and food service, as well as other service industries (arts, entertainment, and recreation) and management, administration, and waste services (Sum 2010).

POVERTY AND UNDEREMPLOYMENT

According to the Census Bureau (2012a) in 2010, 46.2 million Americans were officially poor, the largest number since 1959 (when such data was first published).

In 2010 the poverty rate of 15.1 percent, although significantly lower than in 1959, was the highest rate of U.S. poverty since 1993. Given a poverty threshold level of $22,314 in 2010 for a family of four, even households 50 percent above the poverty line were not living comfortably and were often forced to choose between health care, rent, and other basic necessities. The Recession primarily increased poverty by eliminating and reducing household income through unemployment and underemployment.

The impact of underemployment on poverty rates was particularly harsh because underemployment during the Recession was more likely to befall those at the lower end of the income scale. For those in the bottom and second lowest income decile the incidence of underemployment was 20 percent and 17 percent respectively (Sum 2010). However, for those in the middle two deciles the underemployment rate was between 5 and 6 percent, and for the highest two income deciles the incidence of underemployment was 2.5 and 1.6 percent (Sum 2010).

With low-income workers so disproportionately impacted by underemployment during the Recession, many of the underemployed found themselves slipping below the poverty threshold during the Recession. The poverty rate for underemployed workers increased from 12.7 percent in 2007 to 15 percent in 2010. In comparison, the poverty rate for those employed full-time was 2.5 percent in 2007, and 2.6 percent in 2010 (U.S. Census Bureau 2012a). However, these poverty rates may not give the full picture of poverty among the unemployed during the Recession because they do not include the numerous individuals who doubled-up with other households and thus avoided falling below the poverty threshold (Aziz 2011). This is particularly important to note in the context of underemployment because the rate of underemployment among young people, as discussed earlier in this essay, was quite high, as was the rate at which young people doubled-up by moving back in with their parents (around 41 percent of those between the ages of 25 and 29) (Aziz 2011).

OUTLOOK

The Great Recession has increased rates of underemployment for those of every age, race, level of educational attainment, and industry, but as this essay explored, certain demographic groups were more heavily impacted by underemployment during the Recession than others. Unfortunately, the epidemic of underemployment has much more heavily affected lower-income households than middle- or high-income households. The higher rate of underemployment among low-income households will likely continue to contribute to the high U.S. poverty rate that experts predict will remain in the high 14 percent range at least into 2015 (Monea 2011). The increased rate of underemployment among low-income households will also continue to contribute to the growing income inequality between low- and high-income earners (Sum 2010), a rate that had already been increasing since 1979 and that was further exacerbated by the disproportionate impact of the Great Recession on low-income earners (U.S. Census Bureau 2012b).

FURTHER READING

Aziz, Fahima, Tindara Addabbo, and Jack Reardon. "The Effects of the Financial Crisis on the Italian and USA Labour Markets." In *Europe and the Financial Crisis*, ed. Pompeo Della Posta and Leila Simona Talani. Basingstoke, UK: Palgrave, Macmillan, 2011.

Baxandall, Phineas. *Constructing Unemployment: The Politics of Joblessness in East and West*. Burlington, VT: Ashgate, 2004.

Monea, Emily, and Isabel Sawhill. "Simulating the Effect of the 'Great Recession' on Poverty." Brookings Institution, September 17, 2009. Accessed June 14, 2012. http://www.brookings.edu/~/media/research/files/papers/2009/9/10%20poverty%20monea%20sawhill/0910_poverty_monea_sawhill.pdf

Sixteenth International Conference of Labour Statisticians. "Resolution Concerning the Measurement of Underemployment and Inadequate Employment Situations," October 1, 1998. Accessed August 5, 2012. http://www.ilo.org/global/statistics-and-databases/standards-and-guidelines/resolutions-adopted-by-international-conferences-of-labour-statisticians/WCMS_087487/lang—en/index.htm

Sum, Andrew, and Ishwar Khatiwada. "The Nation's underemployed in the 'Great Recession' of 2007–09." *Monthly Labor Review*, November 2010. Accessed August 5, 2012. http://www.bls.gov/opub/mlr/2010/11/art1full.pdf

U.S. Census Bureau. "Table 25: Work Experience and Poverty Status for People 16 Years Old and Over," 2012a. Accessed June 16, 2012. www.census.gov/hhes/www/poverty/data/historical/people.html

U.S. Census Bureau. "Table H-2: Share of Aggregate Income Received by Each Fifth and Top 5 Percent of Households; All Races, 1967 to 2010," 2012b. Accessed June 16, 2012. http://www.census.gov/hhes/www/income/data/historical/household/index.html

U.S. Census Bureau. "Historical Poverty Tables: People," 2012c. Accessed August 5, 2012. http://www.census.gov/hhes/www/poverty/data/historical/people.html

U.S. Department of Labor, Bureau of Labor Statistics. "Access to Historical Data for the 'A' tables of the Employment Situation News Release," 2012. Accessed August 5. http://data.bls.gov/pdq/SurveyOutputServlet

UNEMPLOYMENT

Timothy J. Essenburg

OVERVIEW

It is no secret that the Great Recession has dramatically increased unemployment rates across various demographic groups. However, to understand exactly what this means, and what impact these high unemployment rates have on poverty rates, it is first necessary to understand why employment (and thereby unemployment) is so important to both individuals and the federal government. It is also necessary to understand how the three types of unemployment (cyclical, structural, and frictional) differ from one another, what rates of employment are desirable for the nation, or what the government considers "full employment," and how the government measures employment and unemployment. It is also helpful to understand how education impacts rates of unemployment. This essay will begin by discussing these issues and proceed to discuss the impact that the Great Recession has had on rates of employment and unemployment in the United States. Finally, this essay will address the role of unemployment benefits during the Recession, the impact these benefits, and the extension of these benefits had on poverty rates and what the nation can expect with regards to employment and unemployment in the aftermath of the Great Recession.

THE IMPORTANCE OF EMPLOYMENT

From Enlightenment philosophy—with its emphasis on individual rights, reason, science, and progress—came the idea of consent of the governed. Consent of the governed was institutionalized in the United States by the creation of a democratic government and a market economy (Grenz 1996; Hamson 2010). The market economy, designed through the political processes, was meant to increase the well-being of the individual and society by encouraging people to work and take risks with financial and real assets (Stiglitz 2002). For this reason a market economy and democracy cannot flourish if individuals do not have the opportunity to work. Thus, in the United States employment is considered so important that encouraging it is a central goal of the federal government. The federal government's commitment to high levels of employment can be seen in both the Employment Act of 1946 and the Humphrey-Hawkins Full Employment Act of 1978.

The Employment Act of 1946 stipulates that

> [I]t is the continuing policy and responsibility of the Federal Government to use all practicable means . . . and with the assistance and cooperation of both small and larger businesses, agriculture, labor, and State and local governments, to coordinate and utilize all its plans, functions, and resources for the purpose of creating and maintaining, in a manner calculated to foster and promote free competitive enterprise and the general welfare, conditions which *promote useful employment opportunities*, including self-employment, for those able, willing, and seeking to work, and *promote full employment and production*. . . ..(15 U.S.C. §1021; emphasis added)

In a similar vein, the Humphrey-Hawkins Full Employment Act of 1978 set a target unemployment rate of 4.0 percent for 1983 and all following years and states that

> Unemployment exposes many families to social, psychological, and physiological costs, including disruption of family life, loss of individual dignity and self-respect, and the aggravation of physical and psychological illnesses, alcoholism and drug abuse, crime, and social conflicts.
>
> Increasing job opportunities and full employment would greatly contribute to the elimination of discrimination based upon sex, age, race, color, religion, national origin, handicap, or other improper factors. (15 U.S.C. §3101)

These acts make high employment rates a goal of both fiscal and monetary policy. Fiscal policy includes federal tax, expenditure and regulatory choices enacted by Congress and the president, and monetary policy includes interest rates, liquidity, and financial oversight choices by the Federal Reserve (Federal Reserve Bank of San Francisco 1999). These legislative acts encourage discretionary, or purposeful, changes in fiscal and/or monetary policy to offset undesirable inflation and unemployment rates during a Recession, recovery, or expansion, the three phases of a business cycle. For example, during a Recession the unemployment rate increases. At the discretion of the Federal Reserve it would likely decrease the federal funds interest rate, the key interest rate of monetary policy.

Beyond the fact that high rates of employment are a central goal of the federal government, research confirms that employment significantly contributes to a person's sense of well-being. This sense of well-being arises from consumption and savings generated from income through employment, but it is also the case that employment, even independent of the income it generates, encourages a sense of well-being (Clark 2003; Stiglitz 2002; Blanchflower 2004; Dolan 2008; Tella 2001).

It should also be no surprise that unemployment, which is accompanied by a loss of wages, places people at risk for poverty and all the physical and social ills that so often accompany poverty. This was certainly the case during and after the Great Recession. For example, in 2010 the poverty rate for those unemployed one to 26 weeks was 18.5 percent compared to the 15.1 percent overall poverty rate (Nichols 2011). The poverty rate among those unemployed more than 26 weeks was 30.1 percent (Nichols 2011).

HOW THE GOVERNMENT MEASURES EMPLOYMENT AND UNEMPLOYMENT

Given the importance the federal government places on employment, it collects a great deal of data on unemployment through the Bureau Labor Statistics (BLS). BLS data describes the changes in employment and unemployment during Great Recession, and sheds light on the impact of the Recession on persons with lower incomes.

To track employment and unemployment the BLS uses two monthly surveys to collect data: the Current Population Survey (CPS) (or household survey) and the Current Employment Statistics (CES) survey (more commonly known as the payroll or establishment survey). As their names imply, these surveys take samples from different groups. The CPS targets *households* and gathers data on the activity of persons aged 16 years and older who are neither institutionalized nor on active duty in the military. Persons are then categorized as employed, unemployed, or not in the labor force. The *civilian labor force* is the sum of employed and unemployed persons. A person is *employed* if he or she does any work for pay or profit, works a minimum of 15 unpaid hours in a family business, or is temporarily not working because of illness, inclement weather, vacation, or work dispute. A person is considered *unemployed* only if he or she is jobless and actively looking for work. This means that retirees, stay-at-home parents, and high school students typically are not included in the unemployment rate. Despite being jobless, these people are not actively seeking employment opportunities. In contrast, the CES asks questions of *employers or establishments* to determine the number of *nonfarm payroll jobs* that exist, regardless of the age of the person who holds the job. Finally, it should be noted, that all the data from both of these surveys is *seasonally adjusted*. This means that events such as holidays, weather patterns and school months are taken into consideration. For example, during the holiday season of November and December many jobs are added to meet the increased demands of consumers. This does not result in an increase in employment or payroll jobs reported because is it a seasonal change not reflective of underlying economic changes.

Unemployment data always come from CPS, whereas employment data can come from either CPS or CES Data (U.S. Department of Labor Bureau of Labor Statistics 2012c; U.S. Department of Labor Bureau of Labor Statistics 2012b; U.S Department of Labor Bureau of Labor Statistics 2009). Predictably, these two surveys do not always generate the same data. Take for example the difference in the estimates of the number of jobs lost during the Recession: the CPS estimates that employment declined by 4.14 million persons during the Great Recession, whereas the CES estimates the job loss at 4.97 million (U.S. Department of Labor Bureau of Labor Statistics 2012c).

TYPES OF UNEMPLOYMENT

To understand the impact of the Great Recession on unemployment it is also necessary to understand that there are three different types of unemployment: frictional, structural, and cyclical. *Cyclical* unemployment is unemployment related to the business cycle. Thus, when the economy is in Recession, the number of cyclically unemployed people increases because companies lay-off employees; the reverse is experienced during a robust expansion when people are less likely to be laid off due to economic conditions.

The second type of unemployment is *structural* unemployment. Structural unemployment arises out of a mismatch between a person's human capital (formal education, skills, and life experiences) and the human capital that employers require, and/or a job-seekers geographic location, and the geographic location of employers. Structural unemployment may also arise from technological improvements or international competition. The decline of the manufacturing sector during the 1970s and 1980s, which left many people in this sector unemployed, is one example of this.

The third type of unemployment, *frictional* unemployment, arises from new entrants to the labor force and persons between employment opportunities. Take, for example, the situation of college graduates in early 2007, many of whom experienced frictional unemployment. In 2007 the unemployment rate hovered around 4.5 percent, much lower than the rate during the Recession. However, even with this relatively low rate, many college graduates were still searching for employment after graduation. Economists are least concerned with frictional unemployment because this kind of unemployment arises when persons choose to remain unemployed as they search for a job that more fully utilizes their human capital. Frictional unemployment is considered *voluntary* unemployment, whereas cyclical and structural unemployment are considered *involuntary* unemployment and are of greater concern. Because there are different types of unemployment, different economic policies and conditions are required to reduce them. For example, an increase in aggregate demand will result in a decrease in cyclical unemployment, whereas a reduction in structural unemployment often requires public policy and private choices that lead to changes in human capital and/or geographic location.

While individuals who are underemployed or discouraged are not technically unemployed, and thus do not fall into one of the three categories discussed earlier in this essay, it is important to understand what is meant by these terms. *Underemployment* is when someone is working part-time because full-time employment is not available, or when someone is working a job that does not match their level of human capital (e.g., a college graduate with a degree in social work who earns an income by mowing lawns for $8.50 per hour). The Great Recession has increased the number of underemployed people because of the difficulty of locating work (for further discussion on this topic see the essay earlier in this section titled "Underemployment"). *Discouraged workers* are people who drop out of the labor force because they determine there is no use looking for work. The Great Recession also increased the number of discouraged workers.

WHAT IS FULL EMPLOYMENT?

The notion of *full employment* is conceptually tied, but not exclusively so, to the three unemployment categories: frictional, structural, and cyclical. For starters, because frictional unemployment is considered voluntary, full employment does not mean that 100 percent of the labor force is employed. Cyclical unemployment is involuntary and historically has been considered amenable to discretionary fiscal and monetary policy and the competitive forces that generate longer-term economic growth. This leaves structural unemployment. One way of thinking of full employment is to add the frictional and structural components. For example, assume that 2.5 percent of the labor force is frictionally unemployed and 3 percent is structurally unemployed. In that case, an unemployment rate of 5.5 percent would be considered full employment.

One more way to think about full employment is to ask: "What is the lowest unemployment rate which the nation can sustain without generating unwanted increases in the inflation rate?" This rate is termed the *nonaccelerating inflation rate of unemployment* (NAIRU) and by some estimates was 5.4 percent in 1960, 6.8 percent in 1979, and 4.9 percent in 2000 (Ball 2002). Its rise (1960 to 1979) and subsequent fall (1979 to 2000) is tied to the changes in the structural unemployment rate for a given frictional rate of, for example, 2.5 percent. This means the human capital of the labor force and/or geographic locations better matched the demands of employers in 2000 than they did in 1979. As of 2010 NAIRU estimates range from 6.3 to 7.5 percent, reflecting another increase in structural unemployment (Salas 2010; Estevão 2010; Economist 2010).

THE PRESENT

EMPLOYMENT, UNEMPLOYMENT, AND EDUCATION

It is important to understand the impact levels of educational attainment on unemployment because of the negative implication this has for low-income people. Income can be generated from a number of sources, for example, wages earned as an employee, proprietor's income generated by an entrepreneur, other business income, interest, capital gains, cash transfers (e.g., welfare and social security), pensions, and in-kind income (e.g., employer-paid health care premiums and food stamps). If we divide households into five equal groups of 20 percent each (so there are five quintiles), then wages and proprietor's income combined account for a minimum of 60 percent of all household income, no matter which quintile, with one exception. For the first quintile (the lowest income households), employment income amounts to 53 percent of income. As would be expected, cash-transfers (public benefits) amount to 23 percent (Congressional Budget Office 2008)

Figure 1 shows unemployment rates that are consistently lower for those with higher levels of educational attainment. The unemployment rate for all education levels fell from 1992 to 2000 and then rose due to the recession of 2001. Rates fell again beginning in 2003 until the Great Recession, which began in December 2007. Note the much larger increase in unemployment rates during the Great Recession compared to the recession of 2001. More germane to our focus on education, the unemployment rate for those with a bachelor's degree or higher, for the entire historic period shown, never reaches a value equal to the lowest rate for high school graduates (the years 1997 to 2001) until the end of the Great Recession in 2009. If a 4.6 percent unemployment rate for those with bachelor's degrees feels like a "bad economic disease," it can safely be said that high school graduates and those with less experience fare much worse even when the economy is doing well. The clear implication is that impoverished and lower-income households must contend with a higher unemployment rate than others (Baum 2010). Unfortunately higher levels of educational attainment may be out of reach for many low-income people because of the cost and time involved in obtaining higher levels of education, when that money is needed for basic needs and the time is needed to work to generate income.

People are generally able to establish themselves out of college by age 25, and 64 is traditionally the year prior to retirement, so looking at data for those aged 25 to 64, provides a good picture of the established labor force. Table 1 shows that for those in this age range 40 percent of the labor force has a high school degree or less, and approximately 30 percent have a bachelor's degree or higher.

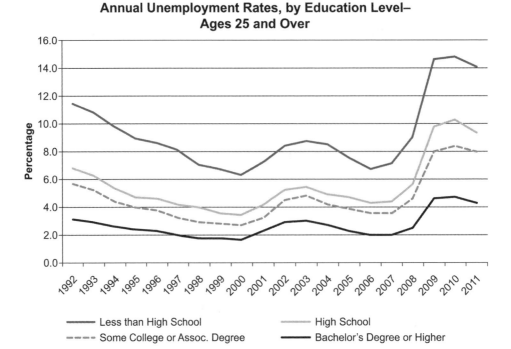

Figure 1
(*Source*: Federal Reserve Bank of St. Louis, Series ID: LNS14027659, LNS14027660, LNS 14027689, and LNS14027662, 2012, http://research.stlouisfed.org/fred2/)

Labor force participation rates show what percent of working-age persons are in the labor force. From the early 1950s until late 1990s the national rate rose from approximately 58 percent to about 67 percent. This aggregate figure masks the differences by sex, age, and education level, among other demographics. Women's participation rose from the low 30s to about 60 percent, with increases across all age levels, most notably among those aged 25 to 54. Men's rates fell from the high 80s to the low 70s, with decreases in all age levels, most notably for the 55-plus age group (Juhn 2006). Participation rates by education level highlight a number of differences, most notably the 30-plus point spread between those with bachelor's degrees and higher, and those with less than a high school diploma; there is approximately a 15-point spread between those with a high school diploma and those with bachelor's degrees and higher.

Looking at this information together, it becomes evident that an economic, and therefore a social experiential, gulf exists between those with a high school diploma and less and those with a bachelor's degree and higher. This has implications for public policy because lower-middle and lower-class groups clearly need greater

Table 1 Percentage Educational Attainment (all persons aged 25–64)

Less than High School	High School Graduate	Some College, No Degree	Associate Degree	Less than Bachelor's Degree	Bachelor's Degree and Higher	Bachelor's Degree	Master's Degree	Professional Degree	Doctoral Degree
10.7	29.4	17.4	10.3	67.8	32.2	21.1	8.2	1.5	1.4

Source: U.S. Census Bureau. "Educational Attainment in the United States, 2011 Detailed Tables," 2012. Accessed June 15, 2012. http://www
.census.gov/hhes/socdemo/education/data/cps/2011/tables.html.

access to education, while local, state, and federal budgets are under great duress. Furthermore, political power, and thus policy decisions that control access to education, are generally held by those in higher classes. Clearly the economic terrain for lower-income persons is more treacherous than for high-income earners in terms of both unemployment rates and labor force participation rates.

Unemployment in the Great Recession

The following figures and tables offer a picture of the Great Recession's impact on employment and unemployment. These data show that labor force participants fared worse during the Great Recession than in all other recessions since the Great Depression. Figures 2 and 3 tell a sobering story about unemployment during the Great Recession. The official unemployment rate rose from a previous low of 4.4 percent in May 2007 to its highest value of 10.0 percent in October 2009. Adjusting this to include discouraged workers, the rate rises to 10.5 percent in October 2009. Subsequently this rate stays virtually the same, while the official rate begins to fall; this indicates a growing number of discouraged workers.

The most comprehensive measure of unemployment includes persons marginally attached and those working part-time because they are unable to find full-time employment. The marginally attached include discouraged workers and others who are not actively seeking employment for reasons that include schooling, family responsibilities, health complications, or transportation difficulties (U.S. Department of Labor April 2009). This rate reaches a maximum of 17.2 percent, also in October 2009. Subsequently, all three rates fell, but by very modest amounts relative to previous Recessions. Figure 3 helps explain why. Prior to the Great Recession the recessions of 1948 (largest decline in employment) and 1981 (large employment loss coupled with a lengthy time to recover lost employment) were the worst since the Great Depression. As Figure 3 shows, 25 months after the 1981 recession began employment was back to pre-recession levels. Not so for the Great Recession; 53 months later employment was still nearly 4 percent below where it was in December 2007 when the Recession started.

Table 2 indicates that the Great Recession, compared to previous recessions listed, saw the largest percentage point increase in the unemployment rate (5.6 percent), the largest percentage increase (127.3 percent), and the highest percent of persons unemployed for 15 weeks or longer (5.9 percent). This is true even when combining the recessions of 1980 and 1981 (as in Table 2, labeled 1980–1982). Median weeks of unemployment (Figure 4) also tell a woeful story. Week "0" represents the beginning of the Great Recession and the 1980 to 1982 recession. Prior to the Great Recession, the recessionary years of 1980 to 1982 were considered the worst labor market since the Great Depression. During the 1980 to 1982 recessionary years the highest median weeks of unemployment reached was 12.3. During

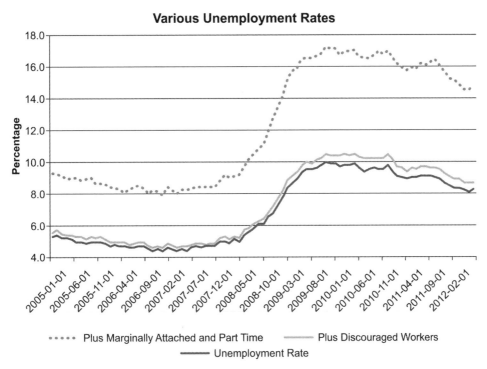

Various Unemployment Rates

Figure 2

(*Source*: Federal Reserve Bank of St. Louis, "UNRATE, U4 and U6," 2012, http://research
.stlouisfed.org/fred2/)

the Great Recession the highest median weeks of unemployment was 25.
Subsequent to the highest median value during the 1980 to 1982 recession noticeable declines were seen; during the Great Recession there was a decrease of five
weeks, from June 2010 to September 2010 (weeks 30 to 33 in Figure 4), but two
years later there was still at a median value of 20 weeks, a 13-week difference.

The data can also be parsed to look at unemployment rates by age, sex, race,
and income quintile. The unemployment rates for all demographic subgroups move
together, but there are still noticeable differences for these groups. There are lower
unemployment rates for those age 25 and older than for teenagers and those in
their early twenties. Historically, male unemployment rates have been lower than
the rates for females (Figure 5). This changed during the 1980s and is a trend that
continues today. There is, however, a noticeable gap—beginning in 2008 and lasting until the end of 2011—that favors women. For this reason, some have called the
Great Recession a "man-cession," although others dispute this (Şahin 2010;
Engemann 2010). It is clear, however, that certain male-dominated industries, such
as construction, were hit hard (for further discussion of the impact of the Recession
based on gender see Section 3, "Sex, Female" and "Sex, Male"). This can be seen in

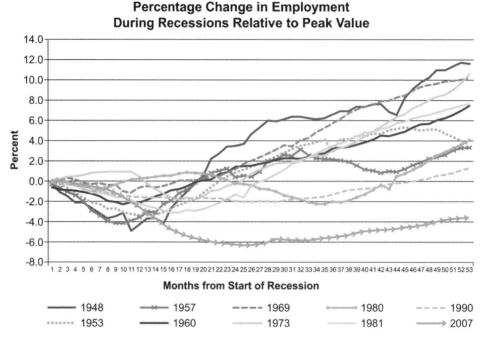

Figure 3

(*Source*: Federal Reserve Bank of Minneapolis, "The Recession and Recovery in Perspective,"
2012, http://www.minneapolisfed.org/publications_papers/studies/recession_perspective/)

Table 3: the percentage loss of construction jobs was 29.4 percent for the Great
Recession, almost double the previous high of a 17.3 percent loss in the recession
of 1973 to 1975.

Table 2   Unemployment Rate Data Associated with Various Recessions

Recession Year(s)	Point Increase	Percentage Increase	Highest Percent Unemployed 15 Weeks or Longer
1969–1970	2.7	79.4	1.5
1973–1975	4.4	95.7	3.1
1980–1982	5.2	92.9	4.2
1990–1991	2.6	50.0	2.9
2001	2.5	65.8	2.5
2008–2009	5.6	127.3	5.9

Source: Federal Reserve Bank of St. Louis. "UNRATE and U1," 2012. Accessed June 15,
2012. http://research.stlouisfed.org/fred2/.

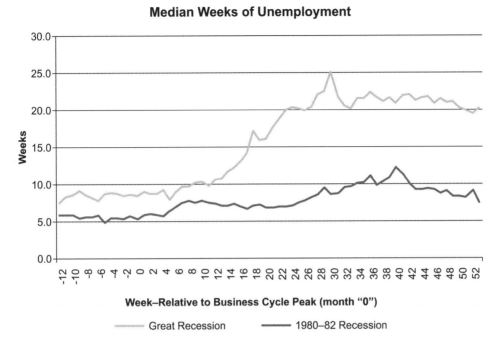

Median Weeks of Unemployment

Figure 4

(*Source*: Federal Reserve Bank of St. Louis, "Median Duration of Unemployment," August 3, 2012, https://research.stlouisfed.org/fred2/series/UEMPMED)

Unemployment rates rose for all racial and ethnic groups as Figure 6 shows. It can be seen that the unemployment rates for blacks and Hispanics are typically 1.5 to 2.0 times higher than that for Asians and whites. The October 2009 white unemployment rate was 9.4 percent, its highest for the Recession. However, going back to 1975, the average black unemployment rate was 12.4 percent, and for Hispanics the average unemployment rate was 9.2 percent. In other words, the harsh labor markets that whites faced for a number of months during the Great Recession is about the norm for Hispanics and actually lower than the norm for blacks. Education is not equally distributed across age and race, and this explains a large portion of the discrepancies in unemployment experienced across demographic groups.

Finally, Table 4 provides data by quintile and for the top 5 percent of earners. Notice that in all cases, excepting the top 5 percent, the percentage of heads of household who are employed fell from 2006 to 2010, and the percentage receiving unemployment compensation increased for all groups (see the subsection "Unemployment Benefits during the Great Recession" later in this essay for more information). When it comes to unemployment rates for the fourth quarter of

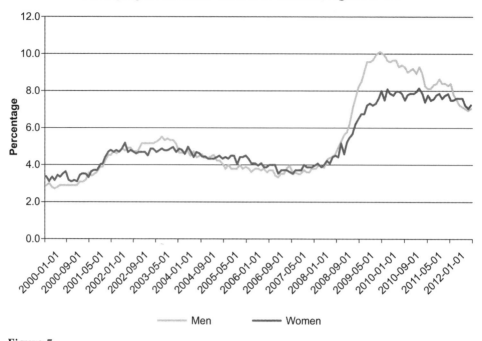

Figure 5
(*Source*: Federal Reserve Bank of St. Louis, Series ID: LNS14000061 and LNS14000062, 2012, http://research.stlouisfed.org/fred2/)

Table 3 Percentage Construction Employment Loss Associated with Recession

Recession Year (s)	Percentage
1948–1949	−2.9
1953–1954	−3.7
1957–1958	−12.8
1960	−7.2
1970	−2.4
1973–1975	−17.3
1980	−6.1
1981–1982	−8.4
1990–1991	−15.7
2001	−3.0
2008–2009	−29.4

Source: Federal Reserve Bank of Minneapolis. "All Employees: Construction," August 3, 2012. Accessed June 15, 2012. http://research.stlouisfed.org/fred2/series/USCONS.

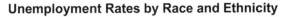

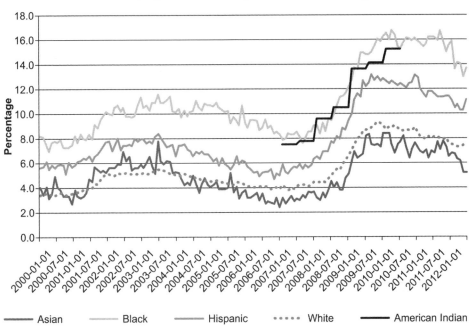

Figure 6

(*Sources*: Federal Reserve Bank of St. Louis, Series ID: LNU04032183 (nonseasonally adjusted), LNS14000006, LNS14000009, and LNS14000003, 2012, http://research .stlouisfed.org/fred2/; Austin, Algernon, "Difference Race, Different Recession: American Indian Unemployment in 2010," Economic Policy Institute, November 18, 2010, http:// www.epi.org/publication/ib289/)

2009, the fourth and fifth quintiles experienced rates below the full-employment rate (or NAIRU), which was estimated to be between 6.3 and 7.5 percent (Salas 2010; Estevão 2010; Economist, 2010). Meanwhile, the lowest quintile suffered a Great Depression rate of unemployment at 25 percent.

Unemployment Benefits during the Great Recession

Beginning with the Social Security Act of 1935 an ever-evolving federal-state system of unemployment insurance has been in place (U.S. Department of Labor 2012a). The program is implemented by each state, with states determining eligibility requirements and weekly cash benefits, and is funded through a combination of state and federal taxes. Each state's unemployment insurance program is not the same. For example, Florida requires a minimum of $2,267 to be earned during one of the five base period quarters, whereas Georgia requires only $756 (U.S. Department of Labor, Employment and Training Administration 2009). When it

Table 4 Work, Unemployment Compensation, Unemployment Rate, Income (by quintile)

| | Percentage of Heads of Household | | | | | |
| | Worked: Full-Time or Part-Time | | Received Unemployment Compensation | | Unemployment Rate | Upper-income Limit |
Quintile	2006	2010	2006	2010	2009(Q4)	2009
Lowest fifth	47.6	44.8	4.0	10.2	25.0	$20,000
Second fifth	63.6	60.0	5.0	12.1	13.7	$38,043
Middle fifth	77.7	73.2	5.8	12.6	8.4	$61,735
Fourth fifth	85.8	82.7	5.3	10.1	5.7	$100,065
Highest fifth	88.4	86.7	3.2	7.5	3.6	NA
Top 5 Percent	86.9	86.8	2.1	5.5	NA	$180,810

Sources: Percentage of Heads of Household: U.S. Census Bureau. "Current Population Survey. FINC—06 Percent Distribution of Families, by Selected Characteristics within Income Quintile and Top 5 Percent in 2006," August 28, 2012. Accessed June 15, 2012. http://www.census.gov/ hhes/www/cpstables/macro/032007/faminc/new06_000.htm. U.S. Census Bureau. "Current Population Survey. FINC—06 Percent Distribution of Families, by Selected Characteristics within Income Quintile and Top 5 Percent in 2010," 2011. Accessed June 15, 2012. http://www.census .gov/hhes/www/cpstables/032011/faminc/new06_000.htm

Unemployment Rates: Author averaged decile rates from Sum, Andrew, and Ishwar Khatiwada. "Labor Underutilization Problems of U.S. Workers across Household Income Groups at the End of the Great Recession: A Truly Great Depression among the Nation's Low Income Workers amidst Full Employment Among the Most Affluent." Center for Labor Market Studies Publications. Paper 26. Northeastern University, 2010. Accessed July 2, 2012. http://iris.lib.neu.edu/cgi/viewcontent.cgi?article=1025&context=clms_pub

Income Limits: U.S. Census Bureau. "Historical Income Tables: Income Inequality, Table H-1," 2012. Accessed June 15. http://www.census.gov/ hhes/www/income/data/historical/inequality/index.html.

comes to average weekly cash benefits, Iowa's is $321, whereas Florida's is $230 (McIntyre 2011).

State unemployment benefits are typically provided for a maximum of 26 weeks. During hard economic times an extended benefits program may provide benefits for an additional 20 weeks. With high unemployment rates over a considerable number of months unemployment benefits played a substantial role in the income of many households during the Great Recession, and various extended benefits programs have been in effect since June 2008 and continued into 2013 (Ludwick 2011). Extended benefits are tiered based on a state's unemployment rate. For example, in May 2012 the unemployment rates in South Dakota, Michigan, and Nevada were 4.3, 8.5, and 11.6 percent respectively. Thus, the maximum number of weeks one could receive unemployment benefits in South Dakota was 60, while in Michigan it was 73, and in Nevada it was 99. These are unprecedented maximums (U.S. Department of Labor Employment and Training Administration 2012). Although some have argued that lengthening the maximum number of weeks for unemployment benefits causes the unemployment rate to remain high because unemployed persons spend more time searching for employment, data suggests otherwise. With so many unemployed during the Great Recession and a comparatively small number of jobs available, work was simply more difficult to come by during the Recession. The national ratio of job seekers to job openings was around 3.5 in April 2012 (Economic Policy Institute 2012). With the Recession so severe, unemployment insurance positively impacted 33 million persons in 2009, reducing the national poverty rate by 1.1 percentage points, from 15.4 to 14.3 percent (Gabe 2011). In 2009 unemployment benefits effectively cut in half (from 21.0 to 10.9 percent) the poverty rate for persons in families that received them.

OUTLOOK

Over the longer term, the U.S. economy has undergone structural transformation from a manufacturing economy to a service sector economy. In both sectors those who will be hired or rehired first mostly likely have the highest human capital (formal education, skills, and life experiences). The implication is that younger persons, those will fewer skills, and people with less formal education will continue to face high unemployment rates and lower participation rates. This means that poverty rates will continue to be high for these groups in particular.

The Federal Reserve Bank of Philadelphia surveys approximately 30 economic forecasters each quarter, gathering information on real gross domestic product (GDP) growth rates, inflation rates, and unemployment rates. Its estimates for the unemployment rate for 2013, 2014, and 2015 are 7.7, 7.2, and 6.6 percent, respectively (Federal Reserve Bank of San Francisco 2012). The Congressional Budget

Office (CBO) forecasts rates of 9.1, 8.7, and 7.4 percent for the same years (2012). The good news is that over the longer term unemployment rates should fall. The bad news is that with a national rate of 7.0 percent (the average of the two forecasts) for 2015, the nation will still be facing an unemployment rate a full 2.5 percentage points above the unemployment rate in mid-2007, just prior to the start of the Great Recession. The NAIRU is also forecast to remain close to a full percentage point above its 2000 value of 5.0 percent, which means that structural unemployment will also likely remain high (Federal Reserve Bank of St. Louis 2012). This will have a particularly adverse effect on those with lower human capital. Thus, it seems that economic difficulties will continue for the foreseeable future, with lower-income households being the most adversely effected, and poverty rates remaining higher than pre-Recession levels even years after the official end of the Great Recession.

FURTHER READING

15 U.S.C. §1021. www.uscode.house.gov/browse/prelim@title15/chapter21&edition=prelim.

15 U.S.C. §3101. www.uscode.house.gov/browse/prelim@title15/chapter58&edition=prelim.

Austin, Algernon. "Difference Race, Different Recession: American Indian Unemployment in 2010." Economic Policy Institute, November 18, 2010. Accessed June 15, 2012. http://www.epi.org/publication/ib289/

Ball, Laurence, and N. Gregory Mankiw. "The NAIRU in Theory and Practice." *Journal of Economic Perspectives*. 16, no. 4 (2002): 115–36.

Baum, Sandy, Jennifer Ma, and Kathleen Payea. "Education Pays 2010." CollegeBoard Advocacy and Policy Center, Trends in Higher Education Series, 2010. Accessed June 22, 2012. http://trends.collegeboard.org/education_pays

Bernard, Tara Siegel. "Extended Unemployment Benefits: F.A.Q." *New York Times*, November 6, 2009. Accessed June 27, 2012. http://bucks.blogs.nytimes.com/2009/11/06/extended-unemployment benefits-faq/

Blanchflower, David G., and Andrew J. Oswald. "Well-Being Over Time in Britain and the USA." *Journal of Public Economics*. 88 (2004): 1359–86.

Clark, Andrew E. "Unemployment as a Social Norm: Psychological Evidence from Panel Data." *Journal of Labor Economics*. 21, no. 2 (2006): 323–51.

Congressional Budget Office. "Historical Effective Tax Rates, 1979 to 2005: Supplement with Additional Data on Sources of Income and High-Income Households," December 2008. Accessed June 22, 2012. http://www.cbo.gov/publication/20374

Congressional Budget Office. "The Budget and Economic Outlook: Fiscal Years 2012 to 2020," January 2012. Accessed June 26, 2012. http://www.cbo.gov/publication/42905

Dolan, Paul, Tessa Peasgood, and Mathew White. "Do We Really Know What Makes Us Happy? A Review of the Economic Literature on Factors Associated with Subjective Well-Being." *Journal of Economic Psychology*. 29 (2008): 94–122.

Economic Policy Institute: The State of Working America. "The Job Shortage," 2012. Accessed June 27, 2012. http://stateofworkingamerica.org/great-recession/the-job-shortage/

Economist. "Is America Facing an Increase in Structural Unemployment?" July 23, 2010. Economics by Invitation. http://www.economist.com/economics/by-invitation/questions/america_facing_increase_structural_unemployment

Engemann, Kristie M., and Howard J. Wall. 2010. "The Effects of Recessions across Demographic Groups." Federal Reserve Bank of St. Louis, January–February 2010. Accessed June 26, 2012. http://research.stlouisfed.org/publications/review/10/01/Engemann.pdf

Estevão, Marcello, and Evridiki Tsounta. "Has the Great Recession Raised U.S. Structural Unemployment?" International Monetary Fun, 2011. Accessed June 22, 2012. http://www.imf.org/external/pubs/ft/wp/2011/wp11105.pdf

Federal Reserve Bank of St. Louis. "Natural Rate of Unemployment (Long-Term) (NROU)," 2012. Accessed August 6, 2012. http://research.stlouisfed.org/fred2/series/NROU

Federal Reserve Bank of Minneapolis. "All Employees: Construction," August 3, 2012. Accessed June 15, 2012. http://research.stlouisfed.org/fed2/series USCONS

Federal Reserve Bank of Minneapolis. "The Recession and Recovery in Perspective," 2012. Accessed June 15. http://www.minneapolisfed.org/publications_papers/studies/recession_perspective/

Federal Reserve Bank of San Francisco. "The Goals of U.S. Monetary Policy," January 29, 1999. Accessed June 22, 2012. http://www.frbsf.org/econrsrch/wklyltr/wklyltr99/el99-04.html

Federal Reserve Bank of San Francisco. "Survey of Professional Forecasters," May 11, 2012. Accessed June 26, 2012. http://www.phil.frb.org/research-and-data/real-time-center/survey-of-professional-forecasters/

Federal Reserve Bank of St. Louis. "Series ID: LNS14027659, LNS14027660, LNS14027689, LNS14027662," 2012a. Accessed June 15. http://research.stlouisfed.org/fred2/

Federal Reserve Bank of St. Louis. "Series ID—LNS11327659, LNS11327660, LNS11327689, LNS11327662,"2012b. Accessed June 15.http://research.stlouisfed.org/fred2/

Federal Reserve Bank of St. Louis. "Series ID: LNS14000012, LNS14000036, LNS14000089, LNS14000091, LNS14000093, LNS14024230," 2012c. Accessed June 15. http://research.stlouisfed.org/fred2/

Federal Reserve Bank of St. Louis. "Series ID: LNS14000061, LNS14000062," 2012d. Accessed June 15, 2012d. http://research.stlouisfed.org/fred2/

Federal Reserve Bank of St. Louis. "Series ID: LNU04032183 (non-seasonally adjusted), LNS14000006, LNS14000009, LNS14000003," Accessed June 15, 2012e. http://research.stlouisfed.org/fred2/

Federal Reserve Bank of St. Louis. "Median Duration of Unemployment," August 3, 2012f. Accessed June 15, 2012. https://research.stlouisfed.org/fred2/series/UEMPMED

Federal Reserve Bank of St. Louis. "UNRATE, U4 and U6," 2012g. Accessed June 15. http://research.stlouisfed.org/fred2/

Federal Reserve Bank of St. Louis. "UNRATE and U1," 2012h. Accessed June 15. http://research.stlouisfed.org/fred2/

Gabe, Thomas, and Julie M. Whittaker. "Antipoverty Effects of Unemployment Insurance." Congressional Research Service, Report for Congress: R41777, 2011. Accessed

July 2, 2012. http://greenbook.waysandmeans.house.gov/sites/greenbook.waysand
means.house.gov/files/images/R41777_gb.pdf

Grenz, Stanley J. *A Primer on Postmodernism*. Grand Rapids, MI: William B. Eerdmans,
1996.

Hamson, Darryl. 2010. "Thomas Jefferson and the Consent of the Governed," September 10.
American History. Accessed June 21, 2012. http://suite101.com/article/thomas-jefferson
-and-the-consent-of-the-governed-a284561

Juhn, Chinhui,and Simon Potter. "Changes in Labor Force Participation in the United
States." *Journal of Economic Perspectives* 20, no. 3 (2006): 27–46.

Ludwick, Mark S., and Benjamin A. Mandel. "Analyzing Federal Programs Using BEA
Statistics: A Look at Unemployment Insurance Benefits Payments." *Survey of Current
Business. Bureau of Economic Analysis* 91, no. 9 (2011): 14–17. Accessed June 27,
2012. http://www.bea.gov/scb/pdf/2011/09%20September/0911_unemploy.pdf

McIntyre, Douglas. "The 10 Best States for Unemployment Benefits, and the 10 Worst."
Daily Finance, May 12, 2011. Accessed July 2, 2012. http://www.dailyfinance.com/
2011/05/12/unemployment-benefits-best-worst-states/.

Nichols, Austin. "Poverty in the United States." Urban Institute, September 13, 2011.
Accessed June 30, 2012. http://www.urban.org/uploadedpdf/412399-Poverty-in-the
-United-States.pdf

Şahin, Ayşegül, Joseph Song, and Bart Hobjin. "The Unemployment Gender Gap during the
2007 Recession." *Current Issues in Economics and Finance*. 16, no. 2 (2010): 1–7.
Accessed June 26, 2012. http://www.newyorkfed.org/research/current_issues/ci16-2.pdf

Salas, Caroline. "In Search of the Ideal Jobless Rate," *BusinessWeek*, June 7–13, 2010,
12–13.

Stiglitz, Joseph. 2002. "Employment, Social Justice and Societal Well-Being." *International
Labour Review*.141, no. 1–2 (2002): 9–29.

Sum, Andrew, and Ishwar Khatiwada. 2010. "Labor Underutilization Problems of U.S.
Workers Across Household Income Groups the End of the Great Recession: A Truly
Great Depression among the Nation's Low Income Workers amidst Full Employment
among the Most Affluent." Center for Labor Market Studies Publications: Paper 26;
Northeastern University, 2010. Accessed July 2, 2012. http://iris.lib.neu.edu/cgi/view
content.cgi?article=1025&context=clms_pub

Di Tella, Rafael, Robert J. MacCulloch, and Andrew J. Oswald. 2001. "Preferences over
Inflation and Unemployment: Evidence from Surveys of Happiness." *American
Economic Review*. 90, no.1 (2001): 335–41.

U.S. Census Bureau. "Educational Attainment in the United States, 2011: Detailed Tables,"
2012. Accessed June 15, 2012. http://www.census.gov/hhes/socdemo/education/data/
cps/2011/tables.html

U.S. census Bureau. "Historical Income Tables: Income Inequality, Table H-1." Accessed
June 15, 2012. http://www.census.gov/hhes/www/income/data/historical/inequality/
index.html

U.S. Department of Labor, Bureau of Labor Statistics. "Highlights of Women's Earnings in
2000," August 2001. Accessed June 22, 2012. http://www.bls.gov/cps/cpswom2000.pdf

U.S. Department of Labor, Bureau of Labor Statistics. "Highlights of Women's Earnings in 2005," September 2006. Accessed June 22, 2012. http://www.bls.gov/cps/cpswom 2005.pdf

U.S Department of Labor Bureau of Labor Statistics. "How the Government Measures Unemployment," February 2009a. Accessed June 21, 2012. http://www.bls.gov/cps/ cps_htgm.pdf

U.S. Department of Labor, Bureau of Labor Statistics. "Ranks of Discouraged Workers and Others Marginally Attached to the Labor Force Rise during Recession," April 2009b. Issues in Labor Statistics. Accessed July 2, 2012. http://www.bls.gov/opub/ils/pdf/ opbils74.pdf

U.S. Department of Labor, Bureau of Labor Statistics. "Highlights of Women's Earnings in 2010," July 2011. Accessed June 22, 2012. http://www.bls.gov/cps/cpswom2010.pdf

U.S. Department of Labor, Bureau of Labor Statistics. "Chronology of Federal Unemployment Compensation Laws," April 11, 2012a. Accessed June 27, 2012. http:// www.oui.doleta.gov/unemploy/pdf/chronfedlaws.pdf

U.S. Department of Labor, Bureau of Labor Statistics. "Employment from the BLS Household and Payroll Surveys: Summary of Recent Trends," June 1, 2012b. Accessed June 21, 2012. http://www.bls.gov/web/empsit/ces_cps_trends.pdf

U.S. Department of Labor, Bureau of Labor Statistics. "The Employment Situation: July 2012," August 3, 2012c. Accessed June 21, 2012. http://www.bls.gov/news .release/pdf/empsit.pdf.

U.S. Department of Labor Employment and Training Administration. "Comparison of State Unemployment Laws," 2009. Accessed July 2, 2012. https://www.ows.doleta.gov/ unemploy/uilawcompar/2009/comparison2009.asp

U.S. Department of Labor Employment and Training Administration. "Maximum Potential Weeks of UI Benefits for New Claimants," 2012. Accessed June 27, 2012. http://ows .doleta.gov/unemploy/docs/potentialWeeksMap-6-17-2012.pdf

WAGES AND INCOME

Behroz Baraghoshi

OVERVIEW

A market economy such as the U.S. economy experiences ups and downs in economic activity over time. This kind of volatility cannot be avoided, and these ups (expansions) and downs (recessions) are known among economists as business cycles. Wages and salaries—the main source, if not the only source, of income for most individuals and families—are negatively impacted by recessions. Due to a lack of assets, a good portion of all workers in the United States are vulnerable to lows in the business cycle. Particularly vulnerable are low-wage and low-salary earners. A low-wage job pays two-thirds of the national median hourly wage, and almost 25 percent (38 million people) of all U.S. workers are in low-wage jobs (Schmitt 2011). When low-wage jobs are a career path toward higher paying jobs, it is not a serious social problem. However, when low-wage jobs offer no path to higher future earnings, they contribute to growing income inequality (Schmitt 2011). The latter seems to be the case in the United States today, and those with lower levels of educational achievement are particularly likely to suffer as a result. Workers with low levels of formal education are more likely to be working in low-wage jobs, and low-wage workers are more likely to experience unemployment and underemployment. They also generally lack the assets necessary to weather the loss of wages that result. Thus, these low-wage workers are much more likely to experience poverty than those with higher levels of education and higher earnings, who are more likely to be employed full-time, year-round even in periods of economic downturn such as the Great Recession.

THE PRESENT

INTERRELATIONSHIP BETWEEN WAGES, UNEMPLOYMENT, AND EDUCATION

Those with lower levels of education are more likely to work in low-wage jobs and are more likely to experience wage loss due to unemployment. The unemployment rate for persons with less than a high school diploma (14.1 percent) is almost three times the rate for persons with a bachelor's degree (4.9 percent). In addition to enduring much higher unemployment rates, persons with less than a high school diploma earn less than half the weekly income of those with a bachelor's degree ($451 versus $1,053) (U.S. Department of Labor 2012). Figure 1 and Table 1 provide a picture of the stark economic reality for those with lower levels of education.

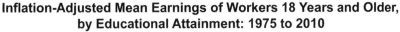

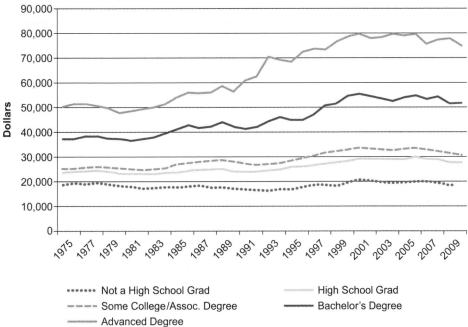

Figure 1

(*Note*: Nominal values adjusted by use of the December values for the Personal Consumption Expenditure: Chain-type Price Index. *Sources*: U.S. Census Bureau, Table A-3: "Selected Measures of Household Income Dispersion: 1967 to 2010," 2012, http://www.census.gov/hhes/www/income/data/historical/inequality/IE-1.pdf; Federal Reserve Bank of St. Louis, "Personal Consumption Expenditures: Chain-type Price Index (PCEPI)," July 31, 2012, http://research.stlouisfed.org/fred2/series/PCEPI)

Table 1   Percentage Change in Inflation-Adjusted Mean Earnings of Workers 18 Years and Older (by education)

Years	Not a High School Graduate	High School Graduate	Some College/ Associate's Degree	Bachelor's Degree	Advanced Degree
1975–2000	4.8	19.9	30.7	47.2	55.8
2000–2006	3.0	5.9	1.3	0.2	1.2
2006–2010	−7.3	−7.6	−8.2	−6.1	−5.7
2000–2010	−4.5	−2.2	−7.0	−5.8	−4.6
1975–2010	0.1	17.3	21.6	38.6	48.7

Note: Nominal values adjusted by use of the December values for the Personal Consumption Expenditure: Chain-type Price Index.
Sources: U.S. Census Bureau. "Educational Attainment, CPS Historical Time Series Table," 2012. Accessed June 15. http://www.census.gov/hhes/socdemo/education/data/cps/historical/index.html; Federal Reserve Bank of St. Louis. "Personal Consumption Expenditures: Chain-Type Price Index (PCEPI)," July 31, 2012. Accessed June 15, 2012. http://research.stlouisfed.org/fred2/series/PCEPI.

Higher levels of education have always been associated with higher earnings, but around 1990 the earnings gap grew between those with bachelor's degrees and higher and those with lower levels of education.

The information in Figure 1 is provided with greater precision in Table 1. From 1975 to 2000 the inflation-adjusted mean earnings for those with a bachelor's degree increased more than twice the earnings for high school graduates: 47.2 versus 19.9 percent. Between 2000 and 2006 (the last year with year-over-year gains) all education levels saw gains in earnings, with those with a high school education and less gaining on the other groups. However, as the 2006 to 2010 data show, the Recession brought earnings losses for all educational levels. Finally, over the entire period shown in Table 1 (1975 to 2010) the gains in earnings for those with a bachelor's degree outpaced the gains in earnings for those with a high school education twofold (38.6 versus 17.3 percent). Additionally, employees with a bachelor's degree or higher compared to high school graduates have much higher probabilities of securing both employer-provided retirement plans (68 versus 50 percent) and health care (70 versus 55 percent) (Baum 2010). These data make it clear that formal education brings with it financial gain.

However, it is also worth noting that students entering the labor force during a recession experience long-term wage loss even if they are able to obtain full-time employment. A study published by the National Bureau of Economic Research found that students who graduate during a recession (when the unemployment rate is 5 points higher than its previous low) earn approximately 10 percent less than those who graduate during an economic expansion. This income shortfall declines slowly but takes eight years to disappear (Nesvisky 2006).

LOSS OF WAGES AND POVERTY DUE TO UNEMPLOYMENT

While the previously discussed data show that wages fell for those of all educational levels during the Great Recession, the greatest impact on wages during the Recession was for those who lost their jobs and thereby altogether lost their wages. The Great Recession resulted in more long-term unemployment (unemployment that lasts for more than 12 months) than had been seen in the United States since the government began keeping such records in 1948 (Seefeldt 2012). The unemployed not only face a complete temporary loss of their wages, they will also likely experience a reduction in their long-term wages for two reasons. First, firm-specific knowledge does not transfer well with someone who secures employment at a new organization. Second, general knowledge accumulation will slow, and even come to a halt, for those who are unemployed for longer periods of time (Kumar 2011). Workers who lose their jobs during a recession, on average, experience an 11.6 percent decrease in their wages every year after reemployment for more than 20 years (Barnette 2012). A study by Henry S. Farber found that workers who lost their jobs during the Recession and found new jobs made on average 17.5 percent less than they did in their previous employment (Pear 2011). The temporary loss of wages and long-term reduction in wages puts the unemployed at a greater risk of poverty. Figure 2 indicates that historically, and during the Great Recession, the unemployment rate and poverty rate move together. (For further discussion of unemployment's impact on poverty see the essay earlier in this section titled "Unemployment.")

REDUCED WAGES AND POVERTY DUE TO UNDEREMPLOYMENT

In addition to high unemployment, the Great Recession led to growing underemployment and thereby reduced wages for workers. Underemployed workers are employed workers who want to work full-time but are unable to find full-time jobs or workers whose level of skill and education do not match the job in which they are working. According to a report in November 2010, the number of underemployed workers who wanted to work full-time but were able to find only part-time employment grew from 4.2 million in November 2007 (just prior to the official start of the Great Recession in December 2007) to 8.9 million in December 2009 (right after the official end of the Recession in June 2009), which is an increase of more than 100 percent (Sum 2010). The underemployed experience reduced income because they are working fewer hours and lower wages because they are working

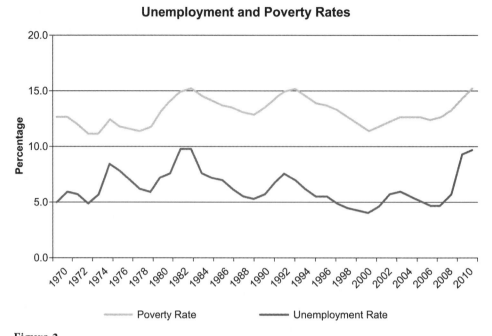

Figure 2

(*Note*: Average unemployment rates based on Timothy J. Essenburg calculations. *Sources*: U.S. Census Bureau, Historical Poverty Tables—People, 2012, http://www.census.gov/hhes/www/poverty/data/historical/people.html; Federal Reserve Bank of St. Louis, "Civilian Unemployment Rate (UNRATE)," August 3, 2012, http://research.stlouisfed.org/fred2/series/UNRATE)

at jobs that require fewer skills and less education than they possess and therefore pay less than what their human capital would command during a strong economy.

Underemployment is more prevalent among those with less than a high school diploma—approximately 20 percent compared to around 7 percent for those with bachelor's degrees (Sum 2010). However, the long-term loss of income due to temporary underemployment is greater for employees with bachelor's degrees. Estimates of long-term wage loss for this group range from 10 to 15 percent after six years of full-time employment (Kumar 2011). Decreased wages for the underemployed lead some to be impoverished. In fact, the poverty rate for underemployed workers increased from 12.7 percent in 2007 to 15 percent in 2010. In comparison, the poverty rate for those employed full-time was 2.5 percent in 2007 and 2.6 percent in 2010 (U.S. Census Bureau 2012). (For further discussion on underemployment during the Recession see the essay earlier in this section titled "Underemployment.")

More than 2.7 million full-time year-round workers and just over 7.3 million part-time workers were poor in 2008, the middle of the Great Recession. By 2010 the numbers were 2.6 million and 8.0 million, respectively (U.S. Census Bureau 2012). Tables 2 and 3 provide a clearer picture of work status and poverty. In both tables the years 2000 and 2007 have a double-lined border, representing the year before Recessions started; the grey-shaded years of 2008 and 2009 indicate that during these years the country was in the Great Recession. In 2007 (see Table 2) the total number of employees was 158.47 million, which fell by more than 5 million jobs by 2010. During this same time period the percentage of full-time employees dropped from 68.5 to 64.8 percent, and the percentage of part-time workers increased from 31.5 to 35.2 percent. This decrease in full-time employment and increase in part-time employment led to a decrease in wages and income, which are predictive of an increase in poverty. This is precisely what happened, as Table 3 shows. For full-time, year-round workers the poverty rate remained relatively steady in the 2.5 to 2.7 percent range. However, for those employed part-time the poverty rate increased from 12.7 to 15.0 percent. For those who did not work the poverty rate increased from 21.5 to 23.9 percent.

Table 2   Work Status for Persons 16 Years of Age and Older

Year	Percentage of All Employees			Absolute Number of All Employees (in millions)
	Full-Time, Year-Round	Part-Time, Year-Round	Did Not Work	
2000	66.8	33.2	41.9	151.63
2001	66.4	33.6	44.0	151.04
2002	66.4	33.6	45.9	151.55
2003	66.4	33.6	47.4	151.55
2004	67.0	33.0	47.7	153.05
2005	67.6	32.4	47.5	155.13
2006	68.5	31.5	47.3	157.35
2007	68.5	31.5	47.6	158.47
2008	65.7	34.3	49.1	158.32
2009	64.2	35.8	53.8	154.77
2010	64.8	35.2	56.7	153.14

Source: U.S. Census Bureau. "Table 25: Work Experience and Poverty Status for People 16 Years Old and Over," 2012. Accessed June 16, 2012. www.census.gov/hhes/www/poverty/data/historical/people.html.

Table 3 Poverty Rate by Work Status

Year	All Workers	Full-Time, Year-Round	Part-Time, Year-Round	Did Not Work
2000	5.6	2.4	12.1	19.8
2001	5.6	2.6	11.8	20.6
2002	5.9	2.6	12.4	21.0
2003	5.8	2.6	12.2	21.5
2004	6.1	2.8	12.8	21.7
2005	6.0	2.8	12.8	21.8
2006	5.8	2.7	12.6	21.1
2007	5.7	2.5	12.7	21.5
2008	6.4	2.6	13.5	22.0
2009	6.9	2.7	14.5	22.7
2010	7.0	2.6	15.0	23.9

Source: U.S. Census Bureau. "Table 25: Work Experience and Poverty Status for People 16 Years Old and Over," 2012. Accessed June 16. www.census.gov/hhes/www/poverty/data/historical/people.html.

OUTLOOK

Economic business cycles are an inevitable component of a market economy, but macroeconomic policies can affect the impact these business cycles have on society. The Great Depression of 1930s was a negative period in U.S. history. However, because of protective measures put in place as a result of the Great Depression, such as unemployment insurance and Social Security retirement income, the hardship experienced during the recent Great Recession was somewhat mitigated, and what the nation has learned as a result of the Great Recession may result in further protections that will benefit those who sustain large income losses in future recessions. For example, The Fair Employment Opportunity Act of 2011 would make it illegal for potential employers to discriminate against the unemployed in the hiring process. This act did not pass during the Congressional Session in which it was introduced, but it may be re-introduced at some future time. Policies such as this could help to mitigate the income loss experienced by unemployed workers in future recessions.

The data discussed in this essay make it clear that future worker earnings depend on economic growth and educational attainment. It is apparent that increased access to education for low-income earners is necessary to increase income and reduce poverty rates for this group. The Great Recession reminded the nation of the volatility of market economies and has hopefully taught it something about wage and income losses due to unemployment and underemployment that will call forth private and public sector changes to alleviate some of the pain of future recessions.

FURTHER READING

Barnette, Justin, and Amanda Michaud. "Wage Scars from Job Loss." University of Minnesota, February 22, 2012. Accessed June 15, 2012. http://www.econ.umn.edu/~micha292/rg/Barnette_Michaud_WageScarsJobLoss.pdf

Baum, Sandy, Jennifer Ma, and Kathleen Payea. "Education Pays: The Benefits of Higher Education for Individuals and Society." Trends in Higher Education Series, 2010. Accessed August 1, 2012. http://trends.collegeboard.org/downloads/Education_Pays_2010.pdf

Fair Employment Opportunity Act of 2011, HR 2501. 112th Congress. Accessed June 9, 2012. http://www.opencongress.org/bill/112-h2501/text

Federal Reserve Bank of St. Louis. "Civilian Unemployment Rate (UNRATE)," August 3, 2012a. Accessed June 14, 2012. http://research.stlouisfed.org/fred2/series/UNRATE

Federal Reserve Bank of St. Louis. "Personal Consumption Expenditures: Chain-type Price Index (PCEPI)," July 31, 2012b. Accessed June 15, 2012. http://research.stlouisfed.org/fred2/series/PCEPI

Kumar, Anil, and Michael Weiss. "Underemployment Poses Long-Term Financial Risk to More Workers." Federal Reserve Bank of Dallas, 2011. Accessed July 11, 2012. http://www.dallasfed.org/assets/documents/research/swe/2011/swe1103g.pdf

Nesvisky, Matt. "The Career Effects of Graduating in a Recession." National Bureau of Economic Research, July 16, 2012. Accessed July 16, 2012. http://www.nber.org/digest/nov06/w12159.html

Pear, Robert. "Recession Officially Over, U.S. Incomes Kept Falling." *New York Times*, October 9, 2011. Accessed July 7, 2012. http://www.nytimes.com/2011/10/10/us/recession-officially-over-us-incomes-kept-falling.html?_r=1

Schmitt, John. "Low-Wage Lessons." Center for Economic and Policy Research, January 2012. Accessed August 5, 2012. http://www.cepr.net/documents/publications/low-wage-2012-01.pdf

Seefeldt, Kristin, Gordon Abner, Joe A. Bolinger, Lanlan Xu, and John D. Graham. "At Risk: America's Poor during and after the Great Recession." School of Public and Environmental Affairs Indiana University Bloomington, January 2012. Accessed August 5, 2012. http://www.tavistalks.com/remakingamerica/wp-content/uploads/2011/12/Indiana-University_White-Paper_EMBARGOED-UNTIL-WED_JAN.-11-AT-8AM1.pdf

Sum, Andrew, and Ishwar Khatiwada. "The Nation's Underemployed in the 'Great Recession' of 2007–2009." *Monthly Labor Review* 133 (November 2010): 3–15. Accessed July 11, 2012. http://bls.gov/opub/mlr/2010/11/art1full.pdf

U.S. Census Bureau. "Educational Attainment, CPS Historical Time Series Table," 2012. Accessed June 15, 2012. http://www.census.gov/hhes/socdemo/education/data/cps/historical/index.html

U.S. Census Bureau. "Historical Poverty Tables: People," 2012. Accessed June 14, 2012. http://www.census.gov/hhes/www/poverty/data/historical/people.html

U.S. Census Bureau. "Table A-3: Selected Measures of Household Income Dispersion, 1967 to 2010," 2012. Accessed June 14, 2012. http://www.census.gov/hhes/www/income/data/historical/inequality/IE-1.pdf

U.S. Census Bureau. "Table 25: Work Experience and Poverty Status for People 16 Years Old and Over," 2012. Accessed June 16, 2012. www.census.gov/hhes/www/poverty/data/historical/people.html

U.S. Department of Labor, Bureau of Labor Statistics. "Education Pays," March 23, 2012. Accessed June 15, 2012. http://www.bls.gov/emp/ep_chart_001.htm

WELFARE/CASH ASSISTANCE PROGRAMS

Stephen Pimpare

OVERVIEW

This essay examines the responsiveness of Temporary Assistance for Needy Families (TANF), federal and state Earned Income Tax Credit (EITC) programs, and state-level General Assistance (GA) benefits to the needs of families and individuals during the Great Recession. Each of these government programs offers cash payments to individuals and families who meet income and other guidelines. As this essay will explore, the reach and generosity of TANF and GA programs had been eroding for many years prior to the Great Recession, while the EITC had been expanding during the same time period. Despite the severity of the economic crisis, however, that pattern changed little during the Great Recession. The EITC has responded to the new needs created by the Great Recession, while TANF and GA have, for the most part, not risen to meet the increased need brought on by the Recession. The EITC has become an effective program of poverty reduction in the United States, both during periods of recession and in "normal" times, while GA and TANF have, at best, marginal effects on the overall poverty rate in the United States in both good times and bad.

THE PRESENT

TEMPORARY ASSISTANCE FOR NEEDY FAMILIES

To understand TANF, EITCs, and GA during the Recession, an understanding of the origins and operations of these programs prior to the Recession will be helpful. Temporary Assistance for Needy Families (TANF) is the program often referred to as "welfare." TANF is funded by the federal government but is run at the state level—states are given an annual lump-sum block grant to run the TANF program in the state. TANF programs often go by different names in different states. For example, the TANF program in Minnesota is called the Minnesota Family Investment Program (MFIP), and the TANF program in North Carolina is called Work First.

TANF is particularly important to an analysis of the role of government cash assistance in responding to poverty during the Great Recession because of the prominent role it plays in American social policy debates. An analysis of TANF's responsiveness to the Great Recession also provides an opportunity to evaluate the accuracy of the warnings of critics who claimed that the 1996 restructuring of the welfare program would make it particularly vulnerable in periods of economic crisis.

TANF is the successor to Aid to Families with Dependent Children (AFDC), a legacy of the Great Depression and the Social Security Act of 1935. TANF was created in 1996 by the Personal Responsibility and Work Opportunity Reconciliation Act (PRWORA). TANF, as with AFDC, offers modest cash payments that go primarily to poor single mothers. However, under TANF states have significantly more discretion than they did under AFDC to set the rules for, and manage, their programs. Benefit levels continued to vary significantly, as they did under AFDC. For example, during the same time period in 2007 a family of three in Virginia would receive $1,383 per month while a family of three in Arkansas would receive $204 a month (Rowe 2008). With some exceptions, TANF recipients must engage in work or job search activities after receiving two years of benefits (although in practice such requirements apply much earlier in most locales), and—with some exceptions—an individual can receive benefits for no more than a total of five years over the course of their adult lives.

AFDC rolls were already declining when the PRWORA was enacted in 1996, but the decline accelerated afterward. By 2007 the welfare rolls had fallen to just under 4 million recipients from the peak of over 14 million in 1994 (U.S. Department of Health and Human Services 2012). Compared to 1979, when 82 percent of all poor families received benefits, by the PRWORA's tenth anniversary in 2006, only some 30 percent received welfare benefits. That same year the median maximum monthly cash benefit for a family of three hovered around 29 percent of the poverty line, while it had reached 35 percent of the poverty line in 1996 and 52 percent in 1981 (U.S. House of Representatives 2008). By 2006 the average monthly TANF benefit was only 65 percent of what it was at the peak in the late 1970s (U.S. Department of Health and Human Services 2012). In 1996, right before the PRWORA reforms, AFDC lifted 1 percent of poor people above the poverty line (Pavetti 2011). By way of comparison, the figures were 5 percent for the Supplemental Nutrition Assistance Program (SNAP, or food stamps), and 10 percent for the EITC (Pavetti 2011). By 2006, with an average monthly benefit of

$372 per family (in nominal dollars, that is, dollars not adjusted for inflation) and 1.8 million families on the rolls, TANF reduced the national official poverty rate by only 0.6 percentage points (Pavetti 2011). The comparable figures in 2006 for other programs were 2 to 3 percentage points for SNAP, and 5 percentage points for the EITC and Child Tax Credit (Meyer 2009; Gabe 2008). So, even prior to the Great Recession, cash welfare benefits had only a marginal effect on the poverty rate in the United States.

Never in the history of the AFDC or TANF programs were the benefits these programs provided generous enough in any state, even when combined with food stamps, to bring a family above the poverty level on their own. However, in previous periods of high unemployment, AFDC rolls tended to rise as unemployment rates rose, providing a temporary offset to drops in household income (Pavetti 2011). During the Great Recession, unlike Unemployment Insurance and SNAP, TANF was minimally responsive to the rising need the Recession and its aftermath brought. During the official Recession, December 2007 to June 2009, TANF caseloads actually continued to fall in six states, while they rose less than 10 percent in another 16 states (Pavetti 2011). Overall, TANF rolls rose by only 13 percent nationwide during the Recession (Pavetti 2011). By way of comparison, SNAP rolls

A woman prepares a food basket for donation at the Latin American Community Center in Wilmington, Delaware, on November 16, 2006. A single mother of five children, she relies on welfare. (AP Photo/Ron Soliman)

increased 45 percent over the Recession, and state spending on Unemployment Insurance more than doubled (Pavetti 2011). This is even more striking when one considers that TANF enrollment was already historically low just prior to the Great Recession.

In four states, already low TANF benefit levels declined even further during the Recession. For example, in South Carolina TANF benefits dropped to $214 per month for a family of three, which is about 14 percent of the poverty line (Pavetti 2011). Additionally, during the Recession some states also reduced the number of months families and individuals could receive assistance (Pavetti 2011). By 2009, the year the Great Recession officially ended, fewer than 28 percent of poor families were receiving TANF, and in some states as few as 10 percent of poor families were receiving TANF assistance (Executive Office of the 2012). This is in comparison to the 75 percent of poor families nationwide that were receiving assistance in 1995 (Executive Office of the President 2012). Federal TANF expenditures of $18.1 billion in 2010 delivered benefits or services to some 4.4 million people. Federal EITC expenditures in 2010, by contrast, were $59.5 billion and benefited 26.8 million people (Executive Office of the President 2012). Even after the official end of the Great Recession, with most states facing budget deficits, manyenacted even deeper cuts to TANF programs.

Structural changes to the TANF program may help to explain why the program was relatively unresponsive to the impact of the Great Recession. The 1996 PRWORA reforms ended AFDC's limited entitlement status, which ensured that everyone who qualified would receive benefits no matter how many people qualified or how much costs increased. This was accomplished under AFDC because the federal government and the states shared the costs of the program based on a set formula. However, under TANF, states receive a block grant, a single annual lump sum to be used for the state's TANF program. Should a state spend the entire block grant, its options are to cut back access to the state's TANF program, reduce benefit levels, or find the funding elsewhere in the state budget. Worse because the block grant level has not increased over time, it has lost almost 30 percent of its original value due to the impact of inflation (Pavetti 2011). The result is that even before taking inflation into account, TANF funding was lower in 2012 than in 1996, despite the higher rates of poverty, child poverty, and unemployment brought on by the Great Recession (Pavetti 2011). One of the consequences is that between 17 and 26 percent of all low-income single mothers became "disconnected," meaning that they did not have income from either work or from TANF. Eighty-two percent of these disconnected single mothers live in poverty. The poverty rate for single mothers who are not disconnected is 54 percent. These disconnected single mothers and their children are more likely to face hunger, health problems, a loss of electricity and other utilities in their homes, are more likely to have to move in with family or friends to survive (Loprest 2011).

A modest exception to the general pattern of decline in TANF assistance was the TANF emergency fund. The emergency fund was enacted in 2009 as part of the American Recovery and Reinvestment Act (the so-called stimulus bill). It set aside $5 billion in additional funds for states to access under certain broad conditions. About $1.3 billion of this supplemental funding was used to create or expand subsidized employment programs, efforts ultimately undertaken by 39 states. It supported some 260,000 private sector jobs for low-income women and summer jobs for youth (Executive Office of the President 2012). However, the emergency fund expired in late 2010, while the after effects of the Great Recession continued, and general TANF funding remained relatively unresponsive to the impact of the Recession.

EARNED INCOME TAX CREDIT: FEDERAL AND STATE

Established in 1975, the Earned Income Tax Credit (EITC) is a refundable tax credit available to families with children, and some individuals, who have earned income and yet remain poor or low-income. The EITC program is limited to those with annual incomes below $36,000 to $49,000, depending on family size. By 1996, the year the PRWORA was enacted, EITC spending surpassed that of combined federal and state spending on AFDC (Urban Institute and Brookings Institution 2012).

The EITC program is widely identified by scholars and policy analysts as among the most effective poverty-reduction programs in the United States. EITC is particularly effective at reducing poverty among children. Research suggests that the EITC also functions as a work incentive because the way its payout scheme is structured means that those who work more generally receive a greater tax credit. Additionally, the lump-sum tax-time payment is often used by recipients to fund education expenses or capital expenditures (e.g., a better car) and other investments that can secure a family's current status and increase future earnings potential. The EITC program may even have positive effects on children's performance in school and on household health outcomes (National Community Tax Coalition 2012). Research indicates that states with their own EITC programs have higher infant birthweights and less maternal smoking; it also suggests that increasing a family's income by only $1,000 through programs such as EITC, resulted in a 2.1 increase in children's math scores and a 3.6 percent increase in reading scores (Dahl 2005).

In addition to the federal EITC program, 23 states and the District of Columbia have their own EITC programs, although in three states the credit is nonrefundable, which means that the refund cannot exceed the actual amount of taxes paid. Three local jurisdictions also have their own EITCs: New York City, San Francisco, and Montgomery Country, Maryland (Center on Budget and Policy Priorities 2011). Even prior to the Great Recession, use of the EITC was widespread. One study found that between 1989 and 2006 nearly half of all American families with children used the program at least once: the majority for one or two years, and one-fifth for five years or more (Dutta-Gupta 2011). By 2006 total federal EITC spending had grown to $45 billion. Total federal spending on the EITC rose to $49 billion in 2007 (Russell Sage Foundation 2011), the first year of the Great Recession, and rose again to $51 billion in 2008, reaching 25 million families. The federal credit cost over $57 billion by 2009, when 27 million American families benefitted, collecting an average of $2,700 each (although the average benefit was only $259 for single adults without children). In 2010, 26 million claimed the credit, receiving an average of $2,220 for a total cost of more than $58 billion (Executive Office of the President and the Council of Economic Advisers 2012). State-level EITCs added another $2 billion to those total expenditures in 2008. For 2011, the maximum federal credit for someone with 3 or more children was $5,751, a large amount indeed for a low-income household (Center on Budget and Policy Priorities December 13, 2011).

By 2010 the EITC was lifting almost 6 million Americans above the poverty line annually, half of them children (Berube 2007). The expansion of the program through the 2009 American Recovery and Reinvestment Act, which included provisions that raised benefit levels for families with three or more children, lifted some 500,000 people above the official poverty line alone. In addition to its effects on poverty reduction, work participation, health, education, and long-term investments by poor households, many economists conclude that the EITC can have positive effects upon the overall economy thanks to its "multiplier effect" (Berube 2007). The multiplier effect may create as much as $1.50 in economic activity for each $1.00 spent on the EITC (Berube 2007). Because of the manner in which poverty is concentrated, this multiplier effect may particularly benefit poorer urban areas (Berube 2007). During times of economic downturn the EITC helps to reduce poverty, especially among children, while also helping create the demand that can spur general economic recovery (Berube 2007).

General Assistance

General Assistance (GA) refers to state, county, or local programs that provide cash assistance to low-income people who are not eligible for federal assistance. General Assistance programs are usually the public benefit of last resort (Kost 1996). In most states that still offer General Assistance, applicants must demonstrate that they are unable to work and ineligible for aid from all other state and federal sources before they can receive benefits under the program. These cash assistance programs go by different names in different states and cities (e.g., general assistance, cash assistance, home relief, general relief, poor relief, interim assistance). Most of these programs have their genesis in the late nineteenth century or the Great Depression.

GA programs are typically, although not exclusively, used by working-age men for brief periods of time; about six to seven months, on average. Many of these men are ineligible for federal Unemployment Insurance due to inconsistent work histories. Some research suggests that General Assistance programs are also more likely to be used by men with criminal records, perhaps due to the difficulties these men face finding employment even in good economic times. GA programs are also more likely to be utilized by those with a physical disability or mental illness (Washington State Institute for Public Policy 2009). Many individuals who receive GA are awaiting a determination of their eligibility for Supplemental Security Income, a federal program that provides cash for basic needs for the low-income older adults, blind people, and individuals with disabilities (Washington State Institute for Public Policy 2009).

General Assistance benefits are typically very low; and although the benefits provided under GA have always been low, the benefit amount has been declining for decades. When Wisconsin eliminated its GA program in 1995, for example, its average benefits were $205 per month, about one-third the value of a minimum wage job (Kost 1996). GA recipients are often eligible for Medicaid, and some can qualify for food stamps, although other regulations tend to limit most to a maximum of three months of benefits. Even so, combined GA and food stamp (SNAP) benefits generally bring recipients to about half the value of a minimum wage job.

Always limited in their reach and generosity, these programs were cut back or entirely abolished in most states in the 1980s and 1990s. By 1997 just 11 states contained 93 percent of the national GA caseload (Ucello 1997). There were, as a result, fewer programs still in existence that could have responded to the Great Recession. As with TANF, instead of expanding, many of these programs continued to contract, since the Recession hit state budgets particularly hard, and most were looking to make budget cuts. GA programs were, in this regard, low-hanging fruit, given the weakness of the client base and the few interests that would be likely to object. And indeed, by 2011, only 30 states operated GA programs at all. Two states, Illinois and Kansas, abolished GA programs that year, and another five reduced the services and benefits available through their programs (Schott 2011). In 2011 in all but one of the states with a remaining General Assistance program the maximum benefits were below 50 percent of the official poverty line. Benefits were below 25 percent in most states (Schott 2011). The Great Recession, then, saw the continuation of the trend toward reducing or eliminating GA programs.

OUTLOOK

As many states continue to face budget shortfalls and search for ways to cut spending, TANF and GA programs will remain vulnerable. Even in those states that do not further reduce or eliminate benefits, it seems unlikely that any expansion of these programs is on the horizon, despite continued high rates of poverty, child poverty, unemployment, and long-term unemployment. The EITC, by contrast, is likely to continue to be effective and responsive to economic conditions. This may be in part because of the EITC's relative "invisibility" (because it is administered through the tax code) and because it is available only to working adults, generally identified by many as the more "worthy" of the poor. In contrast, General Assistance programs tend to support those who are often thought of as the least "deserving": working-age men with histories of incarceration and addiction. GA programs are, in this way, more vulnerable. However, state-level EITC programs may be in jeopardy as well—governors in at least seven states undertook efforts in 2012 to eliminate or reduce their state's income taxes, which could end the refundable income tax credits that accompany them (Tax Credits for Working Families 2012).

FURTHER READING

Berube, Alan. "The Importance of the EITC to Urban Economies." Brookings Institution, July 13, 2007. Accessed June 9, 2012. http://www.brookings.edu/~/media/research/files/speeches/2007/7/13childrenfamilies berube/20070713_berube.pdf

Center on Budget and Policy Priorities. "Policy Basics: State Earned Income Tax Credits," January 13, 2011. Accessed June 10, 2012. http://www.cbpp.org/cms/index.cfm?fa=view&id=2506

Center on Budget and Policy Priorities. "Earned Income Credit Benefits for Tax Year 2011 at Various Income Levels," December 13, 2011. Accessed June 10, 2012. http://eitcoutreach.org/wp-content/uploads/2008/03/Final_Benefits1-12-13-11.pdf

Dahl, Gordon B., and Lance Lochner. "The Impact of Family Income on Child Achievement." National Bureau of Economic Research, April 2005. Accessed June 9, 2012. http://www.nber.org/papers/w11279.pdf

Dutta-Gupta, Indivar. "New Research Highlights Importance of EITC for Working Families." Center on Budget and Policy Priorities, October 19, 2011. Accessed June 9, 2012. http://www.offthechartsblog.org/new-research-highlights-importance-of-eitc-for-working-families/

Executive Office of the President and the Council of Economic Advisers. "Economic Report of the President, 2012," February 17, 2012. Accessed June 9, 2012. http://www.fdlp.gov/component/content/article/1191-erp-2012

Gabe, Thomas. "Trends in Welfare, Work, and the Economic Well-Being of Female-Headed Families with Children, 1987–2006." Congressional Research Service, January 29, 2008. Accessed June 10, 2012. http://wlstorage.net/file/crs/RL30797.pdf

Kost, Kathleen A. " 'A man without a job is a dead man': The Meaning of Work and Welfare in the Lives of Young Men" Institute for Research on Poverty, October 1996. Accessed June 9, 2012. http://www.irp.wisc.edu/publications/dps/pdfs/dp111296.pdf

Loprest, Pamela J. "Disconnected Families and TANF." Urban Institute, November 2011. Accessed June 9, 2012. http://www.acf.hhs.gov/programs/opre/other_resrch/tanf_ccdf/reports/disconnected.pdf

Meyer, Bruce D. "The Effects of the EITC and Recent Reforms." Harris School of Public Policy Studies University of Chicago, December 2009. Accessed June 10, 2012. http://harrisschool.uchicago.edu/about/publications/working-papers/pdf/wp_09_10.pdf

National Community Tax Coalition. "The Earned Income Tax Credit: Good for Our Families, Communities and Economy," January 2012. Accessed June 9, 2012. http://www.taxcreditsforworkingfamilies.org/wp-content/uploads/2012/01/NCTC-EITC-paper_Jan2012.pdf

Pavetti, LaDonna, and Liz Schott. "TANF's Inadequate Response to Recession Highlights Weakness of Block-Grant Structure." Center on Budget and Policy Priorities, June 14 2011. Accessed June 9, 2012. http://www.cbpp.org/cms/?fa=view&id=3534

Rowe, Gretchen, Mary Murphy, and James Kaminski. "Welfare Rules Databook: State TANF Policies as of July 2007." Urban Institute, December 2008. Accessed June 9, 2012. http://www.urban.org/uploadedpdf/412261-Welfare-Rules-Databook-2007.pdf

Russell Sage Foundation. 2011. "Social and Economic Effects of the Great Recession: Tables, Figures, and Analyses," 2011. Accessed June 9, 2012. http://www.russellsage.org/research/chartbook/great-recession

Schott, Liz, and Clare Cho. "General Assistance Programs: Safety Net Weakening Despite Increased Need." Center on Budget and Policy Priorities, 2011. Accessed June 9, 2012. http://www.cbpp.org/cms/?fa=view&id=3603

Tax Credits for Working Families. "Efforts to Reduce or Eliminate State Income Taxes Threaten Family Tax Credits," February 19, 2012. Accessed June 9, 2012. http://www.taxcreditsforworkingfamilies.org/2012/02/efforts-reduce-eliminate-state-income-taxes-threaten-family-tax-credits/

Ucello, Cori E., and L. Jerome Gallagher. "General Assistance Programs: The State-Based Part of the Safety Net." Urban Institute, 1997. Accessed June 10, 2012. http://www.urban.org/publications/307036.html

Urban Institute and Brookings Institution. "Spending on the EITC, Child Tax Credit, and AFDC/TANF, 1975–2009," 2012. Accessed June 10, 2012. http://www.taxpolicycenter.org/taxfacts/displayafact.cfm?Docid=266

U.S. Department of Health and Human Services, Administration for Children and Families. "TANF: Data and Reports," 2012. Accessed June 10, 2012. http://www.acf.hhs.gov/programs/ofa/data-reports/index.htm

U.S. House of Representatives Ways and Means Committee. "Green Book," May 5 2008. Accessed June 10, 2012. http://democrats.waysandmeans.house.gov/media/pdf/110/tanf.pdf.

Washington State Institute for Public Policy. "General Assistance Programs for Unemployable Adults," December 2009. Accessed June 9, 2012. http://www.wsipp.wa.gov/rptfiles/09-12-4101.pdf

SECTION 5

HOW DID GOVERNMENTS RESPOND TO THE GREAT RECESSION?

INTRODUCTION TO SECTION 5

Lindsey K. Hanson

The essays in this section explore the response of governments (local, state, tribal, international and national) as well as the response of nongovernmental organizations (NGOs) to the Great Recession and in particular to Recession-era increases in poverty. Understanding these responses to the Recession helps paint a picture of just how deep the economic downturn was. The following summaries present some of the key findings of these essays.

GOVERNMENT RESPONSE, LOCAL

- The term "local government" encompasses the governments of counties, municipalities (i.e., incorporated towns and cities), townships, and special-purpose local governments such as school districts.
- The effect of the Great Recession on local governments was more delayed than the impact on the federal government and states.
- In the aftermath of the Recession state aid to local governments and property tax revenues declined at the same time for the first time since the 1980s.
- Aid from states to local governments, which on average accounts for around a third of local government revenue, fell by 2.6 percent in fiscal year (FY) 2010, with states reporting further cuts in FY 2011 and 2012.
- Property taxes constitute nearly 74 percent of local government revenue. In 2010 revenue from property taxes declined 2.5 percent from the prior year. This was the first yearly decline in property tax revenues since the mid-1990s, as well as the largest decline in 30 years. Property tax revenues again decreased in 2011, this time by 3.1 percent, with further declines expected in 2012 and 2013.

- In response to the budget crises created by reduced state aid and reduced property tax revenues, some local governments raised taxes and fees, but most addressed budget concerns by cutting spending.
- Local government spending cuts included layoffs, staff reduction through attrition and furlough, hiring and pay freezes, benefit reductions, and reduced services that included, in some areas, reduced social services for low-income individuals.

GOVERNMENT RESPONSE, STATE

- The Recession resulted in historically unprecedented losses of state government tax revenue.
- The vast majority of states experienced budget shortfalls during the Recession and its aftermath.
- States dealt with Recession-era budget shortfalls in a number of ways, including utilizing federal stimulus funds (e.g., American Recovery and Reinvestment Act of 2009), borrowing money, shifting funds, delaying spending, selling assets, raising taxes, and cutting spending.
- In FY 2009 states cut services by 4.2 percent, and in FY 2010 states cut services by 6.8 percent.
- Thirty-one or more states cut services, which resulted in a reduction of health care access or health insurance eligibility for low-income children or families.
- Many state services that assist those in poverty across the nation were eliminated or reduced during the Recession.

GOVERNMENT RESPONSE, TRIBAL

- A tribal government is the government of a Native American tribe that is recognized by the federal government. Tribal governments and the U.S. federal government carry on government-to-government relations.
- Tribes operating manufacturing facilities, particularly those with government defense contracts, have weathered the Recession well because there were not been major cuts in defense spending during the Recession.
- Timber is also a source of revenue for many tribes. Due to the decline in the housing market the timber industry suffered during the Recession, and tribes saw declining revenue from the timber industry.
- Alaska Natives often receive funds from Alaska Native corporations that lease land for oil and other resource extraction and that generate income from a wide variety of investments the corporations have made. Regional corporations have experienced diverse results during and since the Recession. About half saw profits decline in 2008, while the others saw little change or even improvement.
- Social services on reservations are primarily funded by the federal government. During and since the Recession a number of special programs have been implemented to help individuals and families who are unable to receive the assistance

they need from other organizations. For example, the Bureau of Indian Affairs' Financial Assistance and Social Services program provides funds for clothing, food, utilities, and shelter. This program is available to American Indians and Native Alaskans who live on or near an "approved service area."

- In 2009, 50 percent of tribal casinos saw revenue decrease, although about half said revenues were down 10 percent or less.

INTERNATIONAL GOVERNMENT AND NGO RESPONSES

- Some of the world's increasingly powerful economic nations, such as China and Brazil, gained new prominence in helping manage the world response through multilateral organizations such as the International Monetary Fund (IMF) and the G-20. Other international organizations (e.g., the International Labor Organization and United Nations) sought to coordinate global plans to combat poverty.
- International governments increasingly responded to the Recession in the United States by turning to emerging markets to pick up the slack left by the U.S downturn.
- During the Recession Mexican immigrants increasingly chose to return to Mexico, faced growing numbers of deportation proceedings in the United States, or simply chose to stay in Mexico and not immigrate to the United States. Mexican president Felipe Calderón's administration created the Humanitarian Repatriation Program in 2008 to minimize the time returning migrants spent in ports of entry.
- Greece's political leaders, desperate for rescue credit from the IMF, the European Central Bank, and the European Union, imposed austerity measures that, despite the resistance of both unions and employers, included lowering the minimum wage.
- Some international NGOs addressed U.S. poverty directly by providing development assistance and other international aid to support the poor in the United States.
- U.S. poverty, particularly as it related to housing deprivation and a lack of economic opportunities for immigrants, came under fire from a number of governments and international NGOs in 2010 and 2011.
- Emerging economic powers made some progress in gaining on the United States and European powers in the decades prior to the Recession, but the economic influence of the North was not fundamentally altered.

POLITICAL PARTIES AND MAJOR LEGISLATIVE RESPONSES

- The bipartisan Economic Stimulus Act was signed into law by President Bush in February of 2008. It provided tax rebates for low- and middle-income taxpayers, tax incentives to businesses, and increased maximum limits for mortgages that could be purchased by Fannie Mae and Freddie Mac.
- The bipartisan Emergency Stabilization Act of 2008, often referred to as the "bailout" for the U.S. financial system, created the Troubled Asset Relief Program (TARP) and authorized the U.S. secretary of the treasury to buy mortgage-backed

securities in order to provide cash to banks and other financial institutions. It also included other initiatives meant to mitigate the foreclosure crisis.

- The Democratic American Recovery and Reinvestment Act of 2009 (ARRA) provided around $800 billion in funding meant to increase jobs and address the widespread impacts of the Recession. It included numerous initiatives that directly impacted low-income families.
- The bipartisan Tax Relief, Unemployment Insurance Reauthorization, and Job Creation Act of 2010 extended Bush-era income tax cuts and various investment incentives that were enacted in 2001 and 2003, and also provided for a one-year payroll tax reduction.
- When the new Congress took office in January 2011 Republicans controlled the House and Democrats controlled the Senate and the presidency. The result was partisan gridlock and an ongoing debate over the federal deficit, debt, and debt ceiling.

GOVERNMENT RESPONSE, LOCAL

Lindsey K. Hanson

OVERVIEW

During the Great Recession, and particularly in its aftermath, local governments experienced reduced tax revenues and reduced aid from states. While some local governments responded by raising taxes, most responded by cutting costs through reductions in staff, benefits, and services. Some of these service and staff reductions were in the area of social services and thus directly negatively impacted a growing number of low-income individuals during the Recession era. This essay discusses these Recession-era phenomena in more depth, but to understand these phenomena some background on local government is first necessary.

This essay utilizes the Census Bureau definition of "local government" that includes the governments of counties, municipalities (i.e., incorporated towns and cities), townships, and special-purpose local governments such as school districts. The structure of local governments varies from state to state and even within states. For example, Rhode Island and Connecticut do not have counties, and across the nation not all geographic counties also have a county government (U.S. Census Bureau 2013). It is also important to know that local governments derive income from a variety of sources, including the federal government, state governments, and property and sales taxes. Local governments also derive income from some of the services they provide, including school lunches, parks, utilities, garbage disposal services, and hospitals. Local governments often provide police and fire protection, and they care for public facilities such as roads and local airports. Many also administer and/or fund certain social service and income maintenance programs (U.S. Census Bureau 2012).

THE PRESENT

THE GREAT RECESSION'S IMPACT ON LOCAL GOVERNMENT REVENUE

The effect of the Great Recession on local governments was more delayed than the impact on the federal government and states. Along with the federal government and states, local governments experienced revenue declines from decreasing income tax due to high unemployment and decreasing sales tax due to lowered consumption during the Recession. However, the greatest impacts on local government revenues occurred after the official end of the Recession because local governments rely heavily upon aid from states and from property taxes, and both of these revenue sources experienced significant declines in the aftermath of the Great Recession (Urahn 2012). This was the first time since the 1980s that both state aid and property taxes had declined at the same time (Urahn 2012).

While funds from the federal government were provided to stabilize state and local governments through the American Recovery and Reinvestment Act of 2009 (ARRA), this was early in the Recession before the full effect of the decline in property tax revenues was felt (Dadayan 2012). Despite federal stimulus funding, aid from states to local governments—which on average accounts for around a third of local government revenue—fell by 2.6 percent ($12.6 billion) in FY 2010, with

On March 2, 2011, parents pick up children from Farmers Branch Elementary School. They walk by a sign calling for education funding. Teacher layoffs across Texas hurt some local economies by cutting 100,000 jobs in Texas. (AP Photo/LM Otero)

states reporting further cuts in FY 2011 and 2012 (Urahn 2012). Reductions in aid from states were particularly drastic in New Mexico, California, Arizona, Nevada, Minnesota, Texas, Virginia, and Wyoming (Urahn 2012).

In addition to aid from states, property taxes are an important source of revenue for local governments, constituting nearly 74 percent of local government revenue (Dadayan 2012). The housing crisis that accompanied the Great Recession (see Section 1, "Housing Crisis") reduced home values, and when home values decline there is less to tax and therefore property tax revenues decrease. However, the effect of declining home values takes time to impact property taxes because property taxes are based on home value assessments that are generally not done every year. Research suggests that it takes three or more years for a decline in home values to impact property taxes (Dadayan 2012), and the impact of the Great Recession on property tax revenues seems to bear this out. In 2010 revenue from property taxes declined 2.5 percent from the prior year (Urahn 2012). This was the first yearly decline in property tax revenues since the mid-1990s, as well as the largest decline in 30 years (Urahn 2012). Property tax revenues again decreased in 2011, this time by 3.1 percent, with further declines expected in 2012 and 2013 (Urahn 2012). These declines in property tax revenues coupled with declines in other taxes such as sales and income taxes meant that by late 2009 local tax revenue was down 13 percent from its pre-Recession level (Urahn 2012).

LOCAL GOVERNMENTS RESPOND TO THE GREAT RECESSION

With aid from states and tax revenues declining, local governments (like the federal government and the vast majority of state governments) were facing budget crises (see Section 1, "Policy, Fiscal" and an essay later in this section titled "Government Response, State"). Some local governments raised taxes and fees in response, but most addressed budgetary concerns by cutting spending (Urahn 2012). Local governments cut spending by reducing services, instituting pay freezes, laying off employees, and reducing benefits (Urahn 2012). For example, Cleveland, Ohio, cut $36 million from its FY 2012 budget in part by laying off more than 300 employees, including many police officers and firefighters; leaving 145 open positions vacant; and cutting six trash crews (Urahn 2012). Cleveland was not alone. Across the nation from September 2008 to December 2011, 3.4 percent of local government jobs were lost through layoffs, furloughs, hiring freezes, and attrition. Many of the lost jobs were in the area of education (Urahn 2012).

While reductions in government services and personnel across the nation impacted everyone living in the affected localities, including low-income residents, certain local government cuts hit low-income individuals in particular. Counties (and sometimes cities) administer and may provide some funding for welfare, food assistance, workforce development, and health care and housing for low-income individuals. With rising poverty rates during the Great Recession (see Section 2, "U.S. Poverty in the Great Recession") the demand for these services increased, which put additional strain on local governments. For example, Hartford County in Maryland reported that county residents seeking SNAP benefits (food stamps) doubled during the Recession, and Racine County in Wisconsin reported increased participation in rent and energy assistance programs, food and child care support programs, and Medicaid (Urahn 2012).

At the same time additional strain was being put on local governments due to increased eligibility and demand, local governments were laying off social services personnel. In 2010, 52 percent of counties and 26 percent of cities reported personnel cuts in the social services area (United States Conference of Mayors 2010). The effect was reduced, delayed, and less effective services. For example, in Ohio, Alabama, and California child protection social workers were handling protection cases involving vulnerable adults, and in New York City the Public Housing Authority had such a substantial backlog of repairs (280,000) that a special task force was created to address the issue (Urahn 2012). New York City also cut $4 million in funding for programming to help poor people and older adults get health insurance and health services (United States Conference of Mayors 2012). In Mecklenburg County, North Carolina, 74 percent of county funding for nonprofit organizations was lost, as was a program for elderly homebound veterans (United States Conference of Mayors 2010).

Cuts, however, were not the only way that local governments addressed Recession-era budget crises. Some local governments chose to increase property taxes to deal with declining property tax revenue (Urahn 2012). The city of Sarasota, Florida, is one such example. Sarasota had lost $3.5 billion in revenue since 2009 and responded by raising property taxes in September 2011 (Urahn 2012). However, it should be noted that most local governments do not have completely free reign to increase tax revenue. All but four states, including Florida, have at least some restrictions on how local governments can raise taxes (Urahn 2012). In addition to cuts and tax increases many local governments chose to dip into emergency funds to cope with Recession-era revenue losses. In 2011, 40 percent of local governments reported using emergency or "rainy day" funds, and an even higher percentage reported delaying purchases or repairs to address declining revenue (Urahn 2012).

Despite the challenges faced by local governments during the Recession era, through a variety of cost reducing and revenue raising measures, most local governments avoided bankruptcy and default. While some local governments, such as the city of Central Falls, Rhode Island, did declare bankruptcy during the Recession era, the rate of local government bankruptcies did not increase during the Recession era (Urahn 2012).

OUTLOOK

With federal and state budget crises continuing, neither the federal government nor state governments are likely to provide substantial aid to local governments in the near future. Local governments are likely to continue to suffer from a decline in property tax revenues as a result of the decline in housing values experienced during the Recession (Dadayan 2012). Just as the negative impact of the decline in the housing market took time to trickle into local government revenues, so too will the slow recovery in the housing market take time to positively affect local government revenues. While local governments wait for revenues to increase they will continue to struggle with increased demand for social services while the poverty rate remains elevated for years to come and the nation slowly recovers from the Great Recession.

FURTHER READING

Dadayan, Lucy. "Impact of the Great Recession on Local Property Taxes." Nelson A. Rockefeller Institute of Government, July 2012. Accessed February 23, 2013. http://www.rockinst.org/pdf/government_finance/2012-07-16-Recession_Local_%20Property_Tax.pdf

United States Conference of Mayors. "Local Governments Cutting Jobs and Services: Job Losses Projected to Approach 500,000," July 2010. Accessed February 23, 2013. http://usmayors.org/pressreleases/uploads/LJAreport.pdf

Urahn, Susan K. "The Local Squeeze: Falling Revenues and Growing Demand for Services Challenge Cities, Counties, and School Districts." Pew Charitable Trusts, June 2012. Accessed February 23, 2013. http://www.pewstates.org/uploadedFiles/PCS_Assets/2012/Pew_Cities_Local%20Squeeze_report.pdf

U.S. Census Bureau. "Population of Interest: Criteria for Classifying Governments," 2013. Accessed February 23. http://www.census.gov/govs/go/population_of_interest.html

U.S. Census Bureau. "Table 1: State and Local Government Finances by Level of Government and by State, 2009–10," September 21, 2012. Accessed February 23, 2013. http://www2.census.gov/govs/estimate/10slsstab1a.xls

GOVERNMENT RESPONSE, STATE

Lindsey K. Hanson

OVERVIEW

The Great Recession resulted in historically unprecedented losses of revenue for state governments due mostly to a loss of tax revenue (Oliff 2012). As a result, the vast majority of states experienced budget shortfalls during the Recession and its aftermath. This was also true for the federal government. However, unlike the federal government, which borrows to cover revenue shortfalls and thereby accumulates debt, states do not engage in this practice because constitutional or statutory requirements mandate balanced budgets (sometimes over a two-year period) and/or preclude carrying debt forward to the next fiscal year (National Conference of State Legislatures 2010). The only exception is Vermont (Oliff 2012). The debate over how to respond to these shortfalls raged on throughout, and after, the Great Recession with some favoring increased taxes, particularly on the wealthy, and others favoring budget cuts, particularly to entitlement programs (see the essay later in this section titled "Political Parties and Major Legislative Responses"). The ways in which state governments responded to the Great Recession, and particularly to increased poverty as a result of the Recession, were undoubtedly influenced by the budget shortfalls faced by states at the same time.

To understand how states responded to the Great Recession and the increased poverty created by the Recession this essay will first provide a more in-depth explanation of why the Recession resulted in budget shortfalls for states and what those budget shortfalls looked like. The second half of this essay will then explore the impact of state budgets on state services, particularly on programs that assist low-income individuals and families, as well as the impact of state budget shortfalls on the economy more generally. The essay will conclude by discussing the outlook for state government budgets and state programs that assist low-income people as the nation moves out of the Great Recession.

THE PRESENT

WHY DID THE GREAT RECESSION RESULT IN BUDGET SHORTFALLS FOR STATES?

A state has a budget shortfall when its revenue falls short of its spending. State budget shortfalls during the Great Recession were caused primarily by decreased tax revenue (Oliff 2012). States do not uniformly gain tax revenues from the same sources. For example, Florida has no personal income tax and raises almost 70 percent of its funds through various sales taxes. In contrast, California raises approximately 45 percent of revnue from personal income tax and 35 percent of revenue from various sales taxes (Index Mundi 2012). This only adds to the diversity of observed budget shortfalls during and after the Great Recession. Government budget shortfalls can occur even when the overall economy is doing well, but budget shortfalls tend to accompany economic downturns such as the Great Recession for a number of reasons, which will be discussed in this section.

First, increased unemployment, which accompanies recessions, results in decreased tax revenues. This is because the unemployed no longer have the same amount of taxable income. The unemployed also lack new income to spend, thus tending to be careful with savings and spending less. Because unemployed workers spend less, state governments receive less revenue in sales taxes (Moffatt 2012). The Great Recession resulted in high unemployment rates, many discouraged or underemployed workers, and substantial long-term unemployment, all of which combined to a decrease state tax revenues (see Section 4, "Unemployment" and "Underemployment").

High unemployment also contributes to state budget problems in other ways. When unemployment is high many people who are employed fear unemployment and feel less confident about the overall economy. As a result, people tend to spend less, save more, and pay down debt, all of which decrease sales tax revenues for states. All three of these phenomena occurred during the Great Recession and its aftermath (see Section 4, "Access to Credit"). In addition, if unemployment reaches high enough levels, unemployment taxation on employers will not generate enough revenue to cover benefits paid out to the unemployed, and state budgets will suffer (Scherer 2011). This also occurred during the Great Recession; as a result, 30 states had to borrow money from the federal government to make unemployment insurance payments (Scherer 2011). The housing crisis that was part of the Great Recession (see Section 1, "Housing Crisis") also contributed to decreased sales tax revenues for states because it resulted in less home construction and thus fewer purchases of construction materials and fewer home purchases, which meant reduced consumption in terms of new home furnishings and appliances (Oliff 2012). Moreover, with housing prices declining during the Recession, property tax revenues (which help fund local governments and schools) declined. As local governments struggled they tended to turn to states to help them maintain services (Oliff 2012). In addition, as consumers spend less and the general economy declines corporate profits go down (Moffatt 2012). Reduced corporate profits means less corporate income for states to collect tax revenue off of, and thus state revenues continue to decline (Moffatt 2012). Reductions in corporate profits also lead to more layoffs, which in turn decreases state revenue (as discussed earlier in this essay).

Finally, during recessions government spending tends to increase (Moffatt 2012). These increases can be due to increased eligibility for programs due to more poverty or unemployment, or they can be due to programs meant to stimulate the economy and lead the country out of recession. Both occurred during the Great Recession, although increased state stimulus spending was primarily funded by the federal government through legislation such as the American Recovery and Reinvestment Act, commonly known as the federal stimulus. Still, in addition to increased eligibility for unemployment benefits, states experienced increased eligibility for other programs, which put a strain on state budgets. Take, for example, Medicaid, a health care program for eligible low-income people that is funded by both the federal government and states. From 2008 to 2012 the number of individuals eligible for Medicaid increased an estimated 4.8 million due to job loss and employers who stopped offering health insurance benefits (Oliff 2012). While additional federal funds were provided to states to deal with increased Medicaid eligibility during and after the Recession, this enhanced federal funding ended in the summer of 2011 while many states were still grappling with budget shortfalls (Oliff 2012). In the end, the depth of state budget shortfalls meant reductions in Medicaid services in many states despite federal assistance. These service reductions and cuts will be discussed in greater depth later in this essay. Due to all of these factors, during the Great Recession state government revenues decreased, spending increased, and budget shortfalls resulted. The following sections explore what these state budget shortfalls looked like during the Great Recession and the years that followed.

State Budget Shortfalls during and after the Great Recession

Unlike the federal government every state (except Vermont) is required to balance its budget every fiscal year (Oliff 2012) and thus cannot carry budget shortfalls from one fiscal year to another. This requires states to make difficult decisions about how to close budget gaps. All but a few states were faced with this dilemma during the Great Recession. Between fiscal year (FY) 2009 (which began for most states on July 1, 2008) and FY 2012 (which ended for most states on June 30, 2012) the combined budget shortfall for states was more than $540 billion (Oliff 2012). Only Montana and North Dakota did not experience a budget shortfall at any point during this time period (Oliff 2012).

In FY 2009 California, Arizona, and Rhode Island faced the most substantial budget shortfalls as a percentage of the state's general fund. In 2010 Arizona, California, and Nevada faced the most substantial shortfalls, and in 2011 Nevada, Illinois, and Arizona experienced the largest shortfalls. In 2012 New Jersey, Nevada, and California were struggling with the largest shortfalls (Oliff 2012). As a percentage of the state's general fund, the largest shortfall during the Recession and its aftermath was in Arizona during FY 2010 when the state's shortfall as a percentage of its general fund was 65.0 percent, or $5.1 billion (Oliff 2012). In absolute dollar value the largest budget shortfall was in California, which had a shortfall of $45.5 billion in FY 2010 (Oliff 2012). As Figure 1 shows, overall state budget shortfalls peaked in FY 2010 and have since been on a general decline. However, as this figure also shows, budget deficits remained a problem as of at least fiscal year 2013.

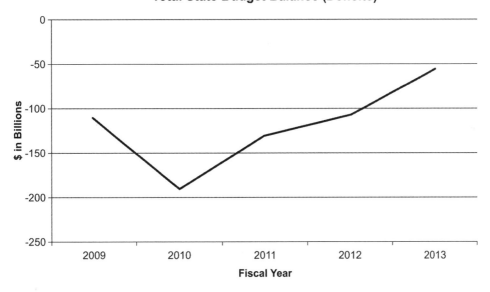

Figure 1
(*Note*: The fiscal year for most states begins July 1 and ends June 30 (Oliff 2012). For example, the 2013 fiscal year for most states began July 1, 2012, and ended June 30, 2013. *Source*: Oliff, Phil, Chris Mai, and Vincent Palacios, "States Continue to Feel Recession's Impact," Center on Budget and Policy Priorities, June 27, 2012, http://www.cbpp.org/cms/index.cfm?fa=view&id=711)

On July 16, 2009, Governor Arnold Schwarzenegger talks to reporters outside his Capitol office in Sacramento, California, during ongoing budget negotiations. (AP Photo/Rich Pedroncelli)

States dealt with Great Recession–era budget shortfalls in a number of ways, including utilizing federal stimulus funds, borrowing money, shifting funds, delaying spending, selling assets, raising taxes, and cutting spending (Gordon 2011). Tax increases were smaller during the Great Recession than in previous recessions (Gordon 2011). Still, California and New York did temporarily increase income taxes on high-income earners, although those measures have since expired (Gordon 2011). Overall, at least 30 states increased taxes (Oliff 2012).

Federal stimulus funding provided through the American Recovery and Reinvestment Act (ARRA) helped states weather shortfalls in FY 2009 to FY 2011 (Oliff 2012). During these years the federal stimulus provided $135 to $140 billion (approximately 30 to 40 percent of projected shortfalls) to states to withstand the Recession (Oliff 2012). This stimulus money prevented many state service reductions, and reductions in Medicaid in particular, as a large portion of the stimulus funding was for Medicaid. However, federal funding did not completely prevent Medicaid cuts, and when federal stimulus funding to states ended in June 2011 the majority of states were still facing budget shortfalls despite the fact that the

Recession had officially ended two years earlier. As a result, many states reduced services and cut budgets even more after the Recession than during its height (Oliff 2012).

Impact of State Budget Shortfalls

While the demand for many state services went up during the Great Recession, significantly due to increasing poverty rates, services available actually decreased (Johnson 2011). From FY 2008 through at least FY 2013 many states were continuing to experience budget shortfalls and continuing to cut services (Oliff 2012). In FY 2009 states cut services by 4.2 percent, and in FY 2010 states cut services by 6.8 percent (Johnson 2011). From 2008 to early 2011, 46 states and Washington, D.C., cut funding for at least one major state service (Johnson 2011). Thirty-one states cut health care spending; 29 states and Washington, D.C., cut services for people with disabilities and older adults; 43 state cut higher education spending; and 34 states and Washington, D.C., cut funding for K-12 education (Johnson 2011). These service reductions would have been even greater if it were not for federal stimulus funding (Johnson 2011). For example, federal money helped to save child care services in Arizona and Alabama, and tuition assistance and prescription drug help for seniors in the state of New York (Johnson 2011).

Federal money also helped states meet some of the increased demand for Medicaid during the Recession (Johnson 2011). However, not all Medicaid cuts were prevented. In Arizona more than 1 million low-income people lost access to certain services previously provided by Medicaid (Johnson 2011), including some vital services such as emergency dentistry, insulin pumps, prosthetics, and dentures (Johnson 2011). In Connecticut more than 220,000 people lost coverage for most nonprescription medications, and in Massachusetts 700,000 low-income people saw their Medicaid dental benefits reduced (Johnson 2011). Numerous other states also made cuts to their Medicaid programs despite the federal assistance provided in this area (Johnson 2011).

Thirty-one or more states cut services that resulted in a reduction of health care access or health insurance eligibility for low-income children or families (Johnson 2011). Massachusetts did away with a health insurance program for low-income legal immigrants, and Michigan ended a health insurance program for adults with children who had transitioned from welfare to work but could not afford employer health insurance premiums and were no longer eligible for a 12-month transitional medical assistance program (Johnson 2011). New Jersey ended Children's Health Insurance Program (CHIP) eligibility for legal immigrant parents who had been in the United States for less than five years. Combined with other cuts to health insurance programs 50,700 low-income adults lost health care coverage in New Jersey in FY 2011 (Johnson 2011).

Many other state services that assist those in poverty across the nation were also eliminated or reduced during the Great Recession. For example, Arizona reduced the time limit for temporary cash assistance by 24 months, which resulted in 8,200 families losing cash assistance (Johnson 2011). In Minnesota cash bonus payments for those effectively moving from welfare to work were reduced by half to $25 (Johnson 2011). Rhode Island reduced funding for affordable housing programs and made welfare for children more difficult to access (Johnson 2011). California completely cut funding for domestic violence shelters (Johnson 2011), which is particularly important for those whose abusers may have complete control of finances and those who come from low-income households. California also ended cost of living adjustments to its cash assistance programs for low-income families and reduced child care subsidies (Johnson 2011). Financial support for homeless services in the District of Columbia was reduced by $12 million (20 percent). Washington, D.C., also reduced cash assistance for low-income families and services that are meant to assist low-income families stay in their homes (Johnson 2011). In Georgia layoffs reduced the number of workers available to help low-income people access services and public benefits, and in Idaho the closure of health and welfare offices made it more difficult for low-income people to access services (Johnson 2011). Texas, Massachusetts, and Ohio made reductions in child care assistance programs (Johnson 2011).

At least 29 states and the District of Columbia made cuts to services for low-income seniors and/or people with disabilities (Johnson 2011). In Idaho cash assistance for 1,250 low-income seniors and/or individuals with disabilities ended completely or decreased (Johnson 2011). Cash assistance for low-income individuals with disabilities in New Mexico who could not work and were not eligible for Temporary Assistance for Needy Families (TANF, or welfare) benefits eligible went down by a third, and Pennsylvania reduced its state Supplemental Security Income (SSI) payments by $5 a month for each individual (Johnson 2011). In the state of Washington monthly benefits for individuals with disabilities who cannot work were reduced by an average of $81 per person (Johnson 2011).

Cuts to K-12 and higher education that had particularly dire impacts for low-income individuals were also made during the Recession. Illinois ended a grant program that was meant to assist at-risk kindergarten to sixth grade students (Johnson 2011). There was a 21 percent funding cut to a North Carolina program that helped provide nurses and social workers for small schools in low-income areas, and Head Start funding in Rhode Island was reduced (Johnson 2011). Higher education also suffered during the Recession. In Minnesota 19 percent of students receiving financial aid grants saw their grants reduced, while 9,400 students actually lost state financial aid grants completely (Johnson 2011). Missouri eliminated 60 percent of its funding for the only need-based financial aid program in the state. Despite the offsetting impact of other scholarship funds, the end result was a 24 percent decrease in need-based aid in Missouri (Johnson 2011). Need-based scholarships in New Mexico also suffered when 80 percent of funding for the State's College Affordability Endowment fund was eliminated (Johnson 2011).

State budget problems also impacted the overall economy and poverty rates because they led to layoffs, hiring freezes, and salary and benefit reductions for state employees. A minimum of 44 states and the District of Columbia utilized some form of cuts that impacted state employees to control costs, including job elimination, holding off on filling open positions, and requiring furlough (unpaid leave) for employees (Johnson 2011). For example, Utah, Oregon, and Wisconsin, in addition to numerous other states, cut state employee pay or required furloughs (Johnson 2011).

From August 2008 to 2011 the number of people employed by state or local governments went down by more than 400,000 (Johnson 2011). Nearly 200 state employees were laid off in Iowa, 115 employees in Arizona were laid off when 11 Department of Motor Vehicle offices were closed, and 124 Department of Human Services employees in Mississippi were laid off (Johnson 2011). At the mid-point of FY 2010 Missouri had to lay off 700 employees in order to deal with its budget shortfall (Johnson 2011). Two thousand positions were eliminated in Tennessee through layoffs and buyouts in which employees retired early (Johnson 2011). In addition, many states utilized hiring freezes, including Kansas, Louisiana, and New Hampshire (Johnson 2011). As state employees are laid off, or their pay or benefits are reduced, they may become impoverished and thereby increase the poverty rate. In addition, state government layoffs contributed to the overall high rate of unemployment during the Recession and to widespread economic decline.

State budget cuts also impact poverty in more unexpected ways because they effectively slow recovery (Oliff 2012). When states cut spending during a Recession they decrease overall demand and can deepen a recession or slow are-covery, thereby indirectly prolong relatively high poverty rates (Oliff 2012). This is so because in addition to state spending cuts that result in layoffs (i.e., more unemployment), cuts can also mean less money flowing to businesses and nonprofits through government contracts (Oliff 2012). As a result, there is less money flowing into the state's overall economy (Oliff 2012). If states choose to increase taxes to address budget shortfalls during recessions, it can harm the economy because people have less money to spend to stimulate the economy (Oliff 2012). It should be noted, however, that if taxes are increased on those with higher incomes, the impact is not as drastic because those with higher incomes tend to save more of their money (Oliff 2012). During severe recessions this savings is not immediately borrowed for productive investment in items such a manufacturing plant, equipment, inventory, and software. Undoubtedly the combination of tax increases, service reductions, layoffs, and other measures states were forced to utilize during the

Recession to address massive budget shortfalls has contributed to the slow rate of recovery in the aftermath of the Recession.

OUTLOOK

Recovery of state budgets generally occurs after recovery of the overall economy (Oliff 2012). Due to the depth of the state budget crisis brought on by the Great Recession, state revenues are unlikely to recover from the Recession in the near future, and cuts to state services are likely to continue for a few years. In FY 2013, 31 states are estimated to have a total budget shortfall of $55 billion (Oliff 2012). While this is a decline from previous Great Recession years, it is still high in comparison to prior recessions and historic norms (Oliff 2012). State revenues in the form of taxes have increased but not enough to deal with the remaining shortfalls. In FY 2011 states brought in 8.3 percent more in taxes compared to the prior fiscal year (Oliff 2012). However, even in the unlikely event that tax revenues grow this much in the upcoming years, it would be seven years until state budgets fully recovered (Oliff 2012). Unemployment remains high, which means less income and sales tax revenue for states, and state revenues were still 5.5 percent lower than prior to the Recession as of the first quarter of 2012 (Oliff 2012).

In addition, federal stimulus funds are being replaced by federal budget cuts that will further harm state budgets (Oliff 2012). A third of the federal government's discretionary spending (defense spending excluded) goes through state governments and local governments for services such as law enforcement, education, health care, and human services (Oliff 2012). If the federal government makes substantial cuts, states and local governments will have less money to spend on these types of services and will likely have to make additional cuts to state services in order to balance their budgets (Oliff 2012). States will also face additional difficulties as they attempt to address current and future budget deficits because they have already taken drastic measures to address billions of dollars of shortfalls throughout the Recession (Oliff 2012). Due to this combination of factors, states are unlikely to have the income necessary to restore programs and services that were made during the Recession and its aftermath for many years, and, in fact, are likely to continue to make cuts to services in the coming years (Oliff 2012). Still, when the overall economy's unemployment rate drops to the 5.50 to 5.75 percent range and remains there for the foreseeable future, the financial position of most state governments will improve (Oliff 2012).

FURTHER READING

Gordon, Tracy. "State Budgets in Recession and Recovery," October 27, 2011. Accessed December 18, 2012. http://www.brookings.edu/research/reports/2011/10/27-state-budgets -gordon

Index Mundi. "United States Tax Revenue: All Tax Types, Q3 2011," 2012. Accessed December 27, 2012. http://www.indexmundi.com/facts/united-states/state-taxes/all -states/all-tax-types/tax-revenue#map

Johnson, Nicholas, Phil Oliff, and Erica Williams. "An Update on State Budget Cuts." Center on Budget and Policy Priorities, February 9, 2011. Accessed December 18, 2012. http://www.cbpp.org/cms/index.cfm?fa=view&id=1214

Moffatt, Mike. "Why Do Government Budget Shortfalls Grow During Recessions?" 2012. Accessed December 18, 2012. http://economics.about.com/od/Recessions/a/budget _shortfalls.htm

National Conference of State Legislatures. "NCSL Fiscal Brief: State Balanced Budget Provisions," 2010. Accessed December 27, 2012. http://www.ncsl.org/documents/ fiscal/StateBalancedBudgetProvisions2010.pdf

Oliff, Phil, Chris Mai, and Vincent Palacios. "States Continue to Feel Recession's Impact." Center on Budget and Policy Priorities, June 27, 2012. Accessed December 18, 2012. http://www.cbpp.org/cms/index.cfm?fa=view&id=711

Scherer, Ron. "Unemployment 101: Who Pays for Jobless Benefits, Anyway?" *Christian Science Monitor*, February 9, 2011. Accessed December 18, 2012. http://www .csmonitor.com/USA/Politics/2011/0209/Unemployment-101-Who-pays-for-jobless -benefits-anyway

GOVERNMENT RESPONSE, TRIBAL

Wayne Edwards

OVERVIEW

Many people in the general population are not familiar with the role of tribal governments and may not even know that such governments exist in the United States. However, for many Native Americans, particularly those living on reservations, tribal governments have the potential to provide assistance and relief during times of economic downturn such as the Great Recession. Yet, tribal benefits to families and individuals are sometimes difficult to acquire because of complicated legal issues, the truncated authority of tribal governments, and the limited resources of many tribal governments. The response of tribal authorities and organizations to the Great Recession, in some ways, can be seen as a continuation of their ongoing efforts to improve the lives and well-being of their tribal members. Having faced high unemployment and poverty for decades, the recent downturn and slow recovery has worsened already poor prospects for gains. To make matters worse, looming budget cuts at the federal level threaten to reduce financial flows through the Bureau of Indian Affairs (BIA) and other organizations that provide support to tribes and individuals. Tribal governments continue to seek new sources of revenue and additional ways to serve their members.

This essay will cover these topics, beginning with defining terms and providing a background understanding of tribal governments. It will proceed by discussing the demographic makeup of the population served by tribal governments, federal budget allocations made for Indian Affairs Programs (which are often administered through tribal governments), and other tribal revenue sources. It will then explore Recession-era developments for Alaska Native corporations, tribal economic bonds, lobbying efforts by tribal governments, social services, and the outlook for tribal governments in the aftermath of the Great Recession.

TERMINOLOGY

The Census Bureau considers "a person having origins in any of the original peoples of North and South America (including Central America) who maintains tribal affiliation or community attachment" to belong to the American Indian and Native Alaskan (AINA) demographic category (Norris 2012). Throughout this essay the term "American Indian" will refer to native peoples in the contiguous United States. The term "Native American" will refer to American Indians and Alaska Natives. Native Hawaiians will not be discussed in this essay because Native Hawaiians are not recognized by the U.S. government as a tribal entity. As such, there is no tribal government or organization of Native Hawaiians with any statutory authority to make decisions about income or commodity distributions to members. Individuals who are Native Hawaiians are, of course, eligible as U.S. citizens to receive any federal or state assistance they qualify for on another basis besides race, such as low-income status or unemployment (see Section 3, "Native Americans").

WHAT IS A TRIBAL GOVERNMENT?

To understand the role of tribal governments during the Recession, it is important to have at least some background understanding of tribal governments. A tribal government is the government of a Native American tribe that is recognized by the federal government. Tribal governments and the U.S. federal government thus carry on government-to-government relations. While usually relatively small, tribal governments are not like a county government or other local government entity because they are the government of a sovereign nation. Still, tribes are considered "domestic dependent nations" and are not entirely separate governments from the federal government, as they are allowed to pursue self-determination only within stated boundaries. While the ability of a tribal organization to respond to the needs of its constituents is more often limited by available funds than by legal restrictions on its authorized activities, legal restrictions have also limited economic development in Indian Country.

Tribal governments often consist of a tribal council that functions as a legislative body and is headed by a chairperson, president, or chief. Many tribal governments also have a tribal court system. The authority and jurisdiction of tribal governments varies from state to state. Some tribal courts have both civil and criminal jurisdiction, while others have only certain types of civil jurisdiction. Tribal governments often maintain their own human services programs that administer many of the public assistance programs meant to aid those in poverty, for example, public housing. Tribes may also administer their own Temporary Assistance to Needy Families (TANF, commonly known as welfare) programs and energy assistance programs. Tribal governments vary greatly, and not all tribes administer these programs. Tribal members may also receive such assistance from the county if the tribe in not administering these programs.

THE PRESENT

DEMOGRAPHICS

The role of tribal governments in responding to the Great Recession, and the impact of the Great Recession on tribal governments, cannot be fully understood without some understanding of the demographics of the population tribal governments serve. Native Americans are a diverse group of people comprised of individuals belonging to 565 federally recognized tribes. In all, data are collected for 617 American Indian legal and statistical areas. According to the 2010 Census the U.S. population was 308.7 million, of which 5.2 million (1.7 percent) identified as belonging to the AINA category alone or in combination with one or more races. Those who identified themselves as AINA alone totaled 2.9 million (0.9 percent). In the 2010 Census, the AINA population was shown to have grown faster than the total population, both in the AINA alone category and in the AINA in combination with one or more other races category. The largest proportion of AINA people lived in the West, with the greatest shares residing in California and Oklahoma. The area with the largest proportion of AINA was Anchorage, Alaska. In 2010 the overwhelming majority of the AINA population, about 78 percent, lived outside of American Indian and Alaska Native areas. In 2010 the Navajo Nation had the largest AINA population of all reservations (169,000), and the Cherokee tribal grouping had the largest American Indian population (819,000). In Alaska the Yup'ik tribal grouping had the largest population (34,000), while Knik had the largest AINA population in a native village statistical area (Norris 2012).

In terms of demographic characteristics, the AINA population faces a number of challenges. In 2010, 54 percent of AINA householders owned their own homes, compared to 65 percent in the total population. In the total population, 86 percent had a high school diploma and 28 percent had a bachelor's degree or higher, while in the AINA population the numbers are 77 and 13 percent, respectively. Median household income among the AINA population was $35,062, while in the total population median income was $50,046. In 2010 the poverty rate for AINA persons was 28.4 percent, almost double the total population rate of 15.3 percent. Health insurance coverage rates were similarly disparate with 29.2 percent of the AINA population lacking health insurance coverage, compared to 15.5 percent of the population overall (U.S. Census Bureau 2011).

The AINA population has made many advances over the past decade. While income has increased and unemployment has fallen, income among white Americans is still 50 percent higher and unemployment is 50 percent lower, on average, than among AINA groups. Many of the negative outcomes and socioeconomic indicators that are common among other racial minorities are also evidenced by AINA experiences. Native Americans have been impacted more severely by recessions in the past, taking longer to return to pre-recession levels of income and unemployment than other groups. The Great Recession, with its markedly slow recovery, is likely to be particularly trying for Native Americans (Muhammad 2009). The following subsections discuss some of the issues that will have the biggest effect on Native Americans in the coming years, including federal funding, tribal governance, and self-determination.

FEDERAL BUDGET ALLOCATIONS FOR INDIAN AFFAIRS PROGRAMS

Indian Affairs programs through the Department of the Interior include education systems, social services and economic development programs, programs designed to improve housing, natural resources management, law enforcement and detention, and the administration of tribal courts (U.S. Department of the Interior 2013). About 63 percent of appropriations through Indian Affairs programs are provided directly to tribes and tribal organizations through grants, contracts, and compacts for tribes to administer such programs (U.S. Department of the Interior 2012).

The total fiscal year (FY) 2013 budget request was $2.6 billion, down from the 2012 enacted budget of $2.7 billion and the actual 2011 budget of $2.8 billion (U.S. Department of the Interior 2012). Much of the reduction from the 2012 request, which is relatively small in any case, reflects a stable budget with adjustments for funding related to the settlement of legal claims that was no longer necessary. Funds were also made available through other sources, allowing the Indian Affairs budget to redirect money to needed programs. For example, the American Recovery and Reinvestment Act (Recovery Act) of 2009 resulted in a Department of Justice grant of $225 million for detention centers and a separate Indian Affairs grant of $285 million for schools (U.S. Department of the Interior 2012).

In addition to the Indian Affairs budget request, the Indian Health Service (IHS) 2013 request was $5.5 billion, up slightly from the 2012 budget request. IHS is a division of the Department of Health and Human Services. While the budget might seem large, there are 2,080,934 people in IHS's service population. Services are delivered directly by the IHS and through tribes via contracts. In the IHS system there are 45 hospitals, 320 health centers, and 287 health stations, school centers, and Alaska village clinics. In some cases funds are expended outside the system when facilities are not available locally for individuals. Roughly 54 percent of the budget is administered by tribes under the Indian Self-Determination and Education Assistance Act of 1975. IHS takes the position, in line with federal policy, that Native Americans should administer allocations as much as possible because they are more aware of, and have a better understanding of, issues and problems their members face (U.S. Department of Health and Human Services 2012). IHS has used Recovery Act funds to further its mission through construction and facility improvements. Specific projects include a new 138,000-square-foot, 10-bed Cheyenne River Health Center in Eagle Butte, South Dakota, that opened on January 16, 2012, and a Nome, Alaska, hospital that opened in November 2012 (U.S. Department of Health and Human Services 2012).

To the extent that funds continue to flow from the federal government to aid in the recovery, poverty will be reduced, or at least remain steady, compared to poverty increases that could have occurred if the budget allocation had been substantially reduced. There is reason to be concerned, however, because all spending is potentially subject to looming budget cuts as Congress and the White House debate tax reform and spending in an effort to reduce the trillion-dollar budget deficits that accompanied the Great Recession. If the resolution of the budget compromise results in less spending on existing programs that result in employment opportunities on reservations, unemployment would rise and poverty would increase as a consequence.

TRIBAL REVENUE SOURCES

In addition to the transfers tribes receive from the federal government, they also have land holdings totaling about 56 million acres, not counting Alaska (Getches 2005). The land is not evenly distributed across tribes. Some of the land has valuable resources on it such as oil, natural gas, and minerals. Much of the revenue the land generates comes from leases administered by the Bureau of Land Management of the Department of the Interior. Mineral rights are typically administered by the Minerals Management Service (Getches 2005). Increasingly, tribes are beginning to take over the administration of their own leases. In line with the self-determination mission of the federal government, this shift is welcomed by legislators. It is also preferred by more and more tribal entities, which believe that making day-to-day decisions regarding the disposition of subsurface wealth is a positive step. Timber is also a source of revenue for many tribes. Unfortunately, due to the decline in the housing market the timber industry suffered during the Recession (Muhammad 2009).

Some tribes operate casinos. There is no denying that revenues from casino operations provide much-needed funds, but casinos remain controversial. Some say the operations generate negative externalities such as crime in areas surrounding casinos, and many tribes have deliberately stayed out of the gaming business on moral grounds. Like most other businesses in the economy, casinos have been impacted by the Great Recession. Revenues for casinos were down in 2009. Some casinos even laid off employees for the first time since they opened (Falmouth Institute 2010). In 2009, 50 percent of tribal casinos said that revenue had decreased, although about half said revenues were down 10 percent or less (Falmouth Institute 2010). Casinos, however, are not the only Native-owned businesses. Many tribes own a wide variety of businesses, from cement plants to electronics manufacturing facilities. Like businesses owned by any other group of people, some are more successful than others (Getches 2005). Tribes operating manufacturing facilities, particularly ones with government defense contracts, have weathered the Recession well because there were not been major cuts in defense spending during the Recession. In addition, many tribes are moving toward diversification of businesses to insulate themselves from economic shocks. Acquiring contracts from state and local governments, rather than exclusively from the federal government, is increasingly common (Kennard 2011). Finally, tribes have the right to levy taxes in Indian country and, to an extremely limited extent, outside of it (Pevar 2004). For the most part opportunities to tax are therefore limited to non-Indians operating businesses in Indian Country and tribal members. As a result, tax revenue does not supply a large stream of income for tribal governments.

Alaska Native Corporations

Alaska Natives often receive funds from Alaska Native corporations that receive revenue from leasing land for oil and other resource extraction, along with a wide variety of investments the corporations have made. The corporations were created through the Alaska Native Claims Settlement Act (1971), which was intended to settle all disputes with Natives in Alaska. There are 13 regional corporations and more than 200 village corporations. Not every Alaska Native corporation controls land equally rich in potential revenue sources. The difference is partially offset by mandatory profit sharing between the corporations, but the dividends paid are still substantially different from one institution to the next, and this disparity affects poverty rates and the economic well-being of members. The arrangements are different in Alaska than in the contiguous states, and tribal governance, as such, occurs primarily at the village level, while the bulk of economic distributions to members come from the corporations, each of which spans many villages (Edwards 2008). Some village corporations do generate large revenues, but they are the small minority. Regional corporations have experienced diverse results during and since the Great Recession. About half saw profits decline in 2008, while others saw little change or even improvement. Many regional corporations have made efforts to keep dividend distributions at steady or increasing levels even during years when their revenue and profit declined substantially. This sort of moderating behavior helps protect members from economic shocks and reduces poverty (LaFleur 2010).

TRIBAL ECONOMIC DEVELOPMENT BONDS

Section 1402 of the 2009 Recovery Act amends the Indian Tribal Governmental Tax Status Act of 1982 to permit, for the first time, Tribal Economic Development Bonds. Previously, tribal governments were not allowed to issue bonds for commercial purposes and could raise funds through bond issues only for schools and other essential functions of government. Still, there are restrictions on the bonds, primarily that bonds cannot exceed $2 billion or be used for buildings housing or for class II or III gaming, and the development project being funded must on a reservation. These new regulations make tribal governments more like state governments and therefore further the federal policy of building nation-to-nation relationships with tribal entities. While bond proceeds are not a revenue source, they do provide needed funds at a relatively low cost to tribal governments (National Indian Justice Center 2012).

TRIBAL LOBBYING

Like any constituency in the United States, AINA groups have discovered that to create policy change, representatives are needed to argue their case to politicians. In the context of the slow recovery following the Great Recession, tribal governments were particularly concerned about the Budget Control Act of 2011, which mandated a cap on discretionary funds, because experts projected that the act might mean as much as $841 billion in discretionary fund cuts in the next 10 years, and some of the funding from Indian Affairs and the IHS is discretionary. Lobbyists for AINA governments and other organizations called for cuts to the BIA budget to be as small as possible. In addition, lobbying efforts were made to influence a number of pieces of legislation. Some of these initiatives included relaxing restrictions on energy production on tribal lands, allowing tribes to run their own banks, and increasing tribal sovereignty, to give tribes the ability to levy taxes on nonmembers. Relaxing restrictions on energy production and increasing the tax authority of tribal governments both would allow direct increases in revenue streams for AINA groups. Allowing tribes to run their own banks would increase financial flexibility and allow expenditures on financial services to remain with AINA organizations (Armstrong 2011).

SOCIAL SERVICES

Social services on reservations are primarily funded by the federal government. During and since the Recession, special programs have been implemented to help individuals and families who are unable to receive the assistance they need from other organizations. For example, the BIA Financial Assistance and Social Services program provides funds for clothing, food, utilities, and shelter. This program is available to American Indians and Native Alaskans who live on or near an "approved service area" (Benefits.gov 2012). As long as budget appropriations are not cut significantly, these programs will help lessen the impact of income poverty over the coming years. AINA peoples on and off reservations who meet eligibility requirements can also receive services through the same programs that other U.S. citizens and eligible noncitizens can receive, including health care assistance, housing assistance, unemployment insurance benefits, and welfare (see corresponding essays in Section 4).

OUTLOOK

In the coming years further economic development will be led by the tribes themselves rather than being directed by outside organizations of the federal government. The projects will provide jobs and, if profitable, will also generate distributable earnings for tribal members. There is some evidence of a trend in this direction as tribes diversify in their entrepreneurial activity. New regulations allowing tribal governments expanded authority to issue economic development bonds should provide more flexibility in economic development projects and improve the overall outlook for the future. As development brings more employment opportunities for AINA on reservations, the high poverty rates that have been the historical norm should decline at least slightly, although they are also likely to remain higher than the overall poverty rate for the nation. As the overall economy recovers and the gaming and timber industries improve, the economic situation for tribal governments dependent upon these industries should improve along with them.

If federal and state funding that is allocated to state and local governments were also allocated to tribal governments, tribes could use more resources to aid their recovery from the Great Recession. Several attempts have been made in the past by legislators and political figures, both at the tribal and federal level to do just this. Lobbying efforts continue, but so far have yielded little success. There is some reason to believe that continued efforts will eventually be rewarded by desired reform, but there is no way to know how soon significant changes will occur. More importantly, it is not known if any such changes will manifest into substantial improvements in the lives of Native Americans, particularly when it comes to policy changes meant to increase employment opportunities on reservations and thereby reduce high poverty rates.

FURTHER READING

Armstrong, Joshua. "Arizona Tribal Leaders Lobby in Washington on Budget Cuts, Regulations." Cronkite News, October 11, 2011. Accessed July 14, 2012. http://cronkite newsonline.com/2011/10/arizona-tribal-leaders-lobby-in-washington-on-budget -cuts-regulations/

Benefits.gov. "Bureau of Indian Affairs (BIA) Financial Assistance and Social Services," 2012. Accessed December 17. http://www.benefits.gov/benefits/benefit-details/801

Edwards, Wayne, and Tara Natarajan. "ANCSA and ANILCA: Capabilities Failure?" *Native Studies Review* 17, no. 2 (2008): 69–97.

Falmouth Institute. "Recession Not Over for Tribal Casino," September 27, 2010. Accessed July 14, 2012. http://www.americanindianreport.com/wordpress/2010/09/Recession -not-over-for-tribal-casinos/

Getches, David H., Charles F. Wilkinson, and Robert A. Williams Jr. *Cases and Materials on Federal Indian Law*. St. Paul, MN: Thomson West, 2005.

Kennard, Matt. "Native American Economies Feel Sharp Impact of Recession." *Financial Times*, May 22, 2011. Accessed December 12, 2012. http://www.ft.com/intl/cms/s/0/ 66d39808-84af-11e0-afcb-00144feabdc0.html

LaFleur, Jennifer, and Michael Grabell. "Alaska Native Corporations Annual Reports," December 15, 2010. Accessed December 18, 2012. http://projects.propublica.org/ tables/alaska-native-corporations-annual-reports

Muhammad, Dedrick. *Challenges to Native American Advancement: The Recession and Native America*. Washington, D.C.: Institute for Policy Studies, 2009.

National Indian Justice Center. "Tribal Economic Development Bonds: An Executive Summary for Tribal Leaders," 2012. Accessed July 14, 2012. http://www.nijc.org/pdfs/ TTAP/Tribal Economic Development Bonds.pdf

Norris, Tina, Paula L. Vines, and Elizabeth M. Hoeffel. "The American Indian and Alaska Native Population: 2012." U.S. Census Bureau, January 2012. Accessed July 14, 2012. http://www.census.gov/prod/cen2010/briefs/c2010br-10.pdf

Pevar, Stephen L. *The Rights of Indians and Tribes*. New York: New York University Press, 2004.

U.S. Census Bureau. "American Indian and Alaska Native Heritage Month: November 2011," November 1, 2011. Accessed July 14, 2012. http://www.census.gov/ newsroom/releases/archives/facts_for_features_special_editions/cb11-ff22.html

U.S. Department of Health and Human Services. "Fiscal Year 2013 Budget in Brief," 2012. Accessed July 14, 2012. http://www.hhs.gov/budget/budget-brief-fy2013.pdf

U.S. Department of the Interior. "Budget Justifications and Performance Information Fiscal Year 2013," 2012. Accessed July 14, 2012. http://www.bia.gov/cs/groups/public/documents/text/idc016442.pdf

U.S. Department of the Interior. "What We Do," 2013. Accessed January 13, 2013. http://www.bia.gov/WhatWeDo/index.htm

INTERNATIONAL GOVERNMENT AND NONGOVERNMENTAL ORGANIZATION RESPONSES

Eric Larson

OVERVIEW

As fears of national decline and threats of economic apocalypse crackled through the news media in the year leading up to the 2012 U.S. presidential elections, one Argentine commentator offered an equally damning forecast for the future of the United States and Europe: the historically rich global North, he asserted, was lurching toward its own "Lost Decade," a decade akin to the 10 years of debt default, violently polarized politics, and austerity that afflicted much of Latin America in the 1980s. Though predicting the eminent collapse of the United States is practically a pastime for the nation's public figures and politicians, the first decade of the twenty-first century did indeed present rich Euro-American nation-states with a global economic landscape significantly different than the landscape of even 20 years earlier. This essay explores how the ascending power of the BRICS (Brazil, Russia, Indian, China, and South Africa) and other emerging economies shaped, and helps to explain, how foreign governments, multilateral economic organizations, and the international nongovernmental organization (NGO) sector reacted to the Great Recession and poverty in the United States.

Foreign governments and international NGOs responded to the rapidly declining economy of the United States during and after the Great Recession in a variety of ways. Some of the world's increasingly powerful economic nations, such as China and Brazil, gained new prominence in helping manage the world response through multilateral organizations like the International Monetary Fund (IMF) and the Group of 20 (G-20). Other international organizations, like the International Labor Organization and United Nations, sought to coordinate global plans to combat poverty. Some international development NGOs even turned their attention to the United States as poverty there increased during the Recession. NGOs also responded to the direct economic repercussions of poverty in the United States, including the sudden outflow of U.S.-based investment dollars to emerging markets. As in any matter of prospective international coordination, the proposals and initiatives of governments and NGOs were also shaped by national and international political rivalries and alliances.

THE PRESENT

As in other economic crises, the financial crisis that spurred the Great Recession both reflected and reinforced deeper economic problems. The United States was by far the world's biggest national economy when the Great Recession started, so sudden changes in U.S. demand, production, and wealth inevitably rippled through the world economy. The bursting of the U.S. housing bubble and the collapse of the country's biggest financial institutions quickly spread to other countries, both through financial markets and international trade. In the two decades prior to the Great Recession the United States had also increasingly become the world's "consumer of last resort," particularly after the Asian economic crisis of the late 1990s. Debt-fueled spending helped make the United States responsible for around one-third of the world's consumption in the first decade of the twenty-first century, as U.S. consumer debt helped counter declines in global demand caused by decades of wage stagnation (Guttmann 2010). With the world economy so intimately connected to the U.S. economy prior to the Recession it should be no surprise that the economic downturn in the United States brought numerous international responses.

INTERNATIONAL GOVERNMENTS RESPOND TO THE U.S. RECESSION

International governments increasingly responded to the Recession in the United States by turning to emerging markets to pick up the slack left by the U.S downturn. The Great Recession's effect on the U.S. economy helped many of that country's pundits and political leaders argue during the 2012 election cycle that the rest of the world did not need the United States as much as it once did. While the Recession did deflate emerging markets outside of Europe, many of these markets recovered relatively quickly. The quick recovery was in part due to commercial ties to other up-and-coming economies, rather than to ties to the United States or the North Atlantic. For example, China's continued growth fed Brazil's airplane and agriculture export industries, and both countries' thirst for raw materials helped create substantial economic growth in sub-Saharan Africa. Turkey, despite a quick downturn due to a drop in export sales, emerged as what some have identified as one of the "winners" of the Great Recession. This was due in part due to its growing trade relations with North Africa and the Middle East (Keating 2012; Goldstone 2011). In addition, despite their mutual animosity, India and Pakistan relied on recently forged trade relations to withstand the worst of the downturn, and most of Asia and the Arab states avoided recessions. Much of Latin America recovered from the relatively muted impact in the region quickly, though the country most closely tied to the U.S. economy, Mexico, fared worse than most in the years after 2007 (Fair 2012; Cho 2011).

Meanwhile, the financial crisis hit European and other rich countries, particularly those tightly interwoven through financial markets, much harder. The burst housing bubble in the United States helped lead to the collapse of housing and bond markets in Ireland, Spain, Portugal, and Greece, all of which continued to struggle with debt and joblessness years after the official end of the Great Recession in the United States. Greece's political leaders, desperate for rescue credit from the IMF, the European Central Bank, and the European Union, imposed austerity measures that included lowering the minimum wage despite the resistance of both unions and employers (Athens News 2012). Creditors targeted Greece and other southern European countries only after they had intervened in the European Union's eastern extremities. Baltic states, some of which faced double digit drops in gross domestic product (GDP), were hit particularly hard by the financial crisis and Recession. The IMF had not transferred emergency funds to a rich northern country since the 1970s, but after the crisis it made such transfers to Iceland and several others.

Despite the ability of emerging markets to compensate for the U.S. downturn in many ways, governments around the world were forced to respond to the domestic effects of dramatic drops in U.S. demand for goods and labor. The export zones in places such as the Caribbean, China, and Southeast Asia, for instance, were highly sensitive to swings in world demand, and they competed against each to offer the cheapest prices to retailers and their middlemen. The price of labor often determined profit and loss in such industries, and their workers faced some of the most difficult adjustments during the Great Recession. In China around 20 million rural migrant workers had lost their jobs in the country's export factories by 2009, and the fast-growing region often known as the "world's factory" suddenly became its most stagnant. Fretting that a growth rate less than 8 percent could lead to more discontent and social protests, the Chinese government created programs to help move laborers back to their rural homes and retrain them, though corruption and lack of arable land presented persistent obstacles to the successful implementation of these policies (Wing Chan 2010; Economist 2009).

The U.S. decline in demand for low-waged labor also led governments, Mexico's in particular, to respond to the sudden decline in emigration. During the Recession Mexican immigrants increasingly chose to return to Mexico, faced growing numbers of deportation proceedings in the United States, or simply chose to stay in Mexico in the first place. Mexican president Felipe Calderón's administration created the Humanitarian Repatriation Program in 2008 to minimize the time returning migrants spent in ports of entry. His government expanded the program during the Great Recession as well. In some cases, according to one international NGO working in the area, agri-businesses were taking advantage of the new flows of poor migrants in northern Mexico to demand particularly difficult working conditions for the migrants, many of whom were indigenous. Elsewhere, in the border area, governments collaborated with international organizations such as the International Organization of Migration (IOM) to burnish federal programs or assist others (Rodríguez Santos 2008; París Pombo 2010; IOM 2011). The advisory boards of the Institute of Mexicans in the Exterior (CC-IME) responded to economic conditions in the U.S. by advising consulates to sponsor "Labor Rights Weeks," and consulates in places like Saint Paul, Minnesota, and Raleigh, North Carolina, opened "Labor Windows" in consular offices, based on CC-IME recommendations. The CC-IME also created a coalition to contest anti-immigrant fervor in the wake of the Recession (Bayes 2010; Letras Libres 2009).

During the Great Recession investment money and migrants flowed out of the United States and into other countries; national governments responded in turn. For example, although John Deere made its fortune in the U.S. agricultural "heartland," it unveiled plans to build all of its seven new factories in BRICS countries. Like other multinational agricultural companies, it hoped to expand its already substantial investment in countries like Brazil in search of stronger domestic consumer markets and investment conditions (Schneider 2012; Gruley 2012). The aggressive stimulus policies of the U.S. government and the U.S. Federal Reserve helped to expand the investment money flowing away from the United States and toward emerging economies. It also forced national governments in places like Brazil and South Korea to equally aggressively monitor their currencies after 2007, as sharp increases against a lower dollar would have endangered their export industries (Economist 2010). Spain, for its part, responded to the crisis in its own country by looking not to the United States, but to other nations for the recapitalization of its businesses and real estate markets. Only a decade after Spain initiated its own wave of speculation in Latin America, the country increasingly turned to the southern reaches of the Western hemisphere in search of investors. In addition, it offered immediate residency permits to anyone willing to buy residential real estate worth at least 160,000 Euros (about $200,000), and that offer was directed primarily at Russian and Chinese investors. A similar initiative in the United States helped inspire Spain's plan (Ceberio Belaza 2012). The Chinese and Indian governments, for their part, actively sought to recruit return migrants (U.S. residents of Chinese or Indian heritage, particularly), who were seeking better opportunities in their countries of origins or in other emerging economies (Jain 2010).

INTERNATIONAL NGOS AND MULTILATERAL ORGANIZATIONS

In response to the Great Recession and the rise in poverty, foreign governments and NGOs from outside the United States sought out methods to mitigate the negative impact of the Great Recession. Some of these international NGOs addressed U.S. poverty directly by providing development assistance and other international aid to support the poor in the United States. For example, the Bangladesh-based Grameen Bank, known for its microlending to the poverty-stricken of the developing world, opened offices in the United States to offer $1,500 loans at below-market rates to small businesses in poor communities (Shevory 2010). Other groups with a U.S. base but with histories in international development, like Kiva.org, began microlending in the United States as well. All of their U.S.-based "field partners" listed in 2012 initiated their relationship with the microloan process in 2008 or the following years (Kiva.org 2012). Though neither microlending nor foreign aid were new to the United States, strategic politicking and the poverty exacerbated by the Great Recession helped many to recognize the importance of continuing these antipoverty efforts. For example, after the U.S.-based subsidiary of Venezuela's state-run oil company discontinued its low-price oil shipments to poor U.S. communities in 2009, Venezuela's president Hugo Chavez "intervened directly" to continue the program through the U.S.-based nonprofit Citizens Energy (James 2009).

U.S. poverty, particularly as related to housing deprivation and a lack of economic opportunities for immigrants, came under fire from a number of governments and international NGOs in 2010 and 2011. In November 2010 the United States presented its first country report to the UN Human Rights Council and the Universal Periodic Review process. Participating governments and NGOs consistently cited the growing poverty in the United States as contradictory to its government's frequent demands for human rights compliance from other nations. The United States received 228 recommendations in the 2011 review process, and though the U.S. delegation suggested that certain social and economic rights (e.g., housing) would be important areas of focus in the future, delegations from countries such as Morocco and Bolivia lamented the response as incomplete and vague (International Service for Human Rights 2010; UN Office of the High Commissioner for Human Rights 2011). As the Obama administration deported record numbers of immigrants during the Recession, NGOs and governments used the opportunity to criticize the country's treatment of detained immigrants and its failure to view economic rights as human rights by ratifying the International Covenant on Economic, Social, and Cultural Rights (ICESCR) (Centre for Housing Rights and Evictions 2010; Columbia Law School Human Rights Institute 2011).

OUTLOOK

After the recession ended, the UN Economic and Social Council headlined the summary of a meeting with the following: "South-South Cooperation Softening Impact of Crisis, but No Substitute for Traditional North-South Cooperation." If emerging economic powers "dented the privileges" of the North Atlantic world in the two decades prior to the Great Recession, they had yet to fundamentally alter its economic influence (Prashad and Chandra 2012). However, unlike the aforementioned headline, contestation, not cooperation, defined much of the international government and NGO response to the U.S. Great Recession and its reverberations abroad.

The revised frameworks of international coordination that emerged during the Great Recession are still in flux. Emerging economies continue to exert increasing pressure to be included in meetings to manage the international reaction to the Recession. The G-20, rather than the G-7, became the executive committee for the world's response to the Recession. Despite a degree of unity in 2009 and multinational efforts to inject funds into the world economy and prevent a depression, national interests and divisions between the North and the South, particularly in response to the Eurozone crisis, shaped policy discussions and responses. For example, according to the Council on Foreign Relations, the quantitative easing of the U.S. Federal Reserve and China's currency policies "undermined the G20's cooperative agenda" after 2009 (Council on Foreign Relations 2012). The G-20 did agree to empower the IMF with new capital and a reaffirmed mandate, but newly powerful countries like China struggled with the United States and other rich nations over how its increased financial obligations to the fund should relate to decision-making power (Woods 2010; Mattoo 2008; Aljazeera 2011; Council of Foreign Relations 2012). Despite calls from European leaders (e.g., Nicholas Sarkozy of France) and international NGOs (e.g., the Third World Network) for large-scale regulatory reforms, political conflict in Europe led leaders to temper their hope for global coordination, and powerful countries disagreed on how to implement regulatory reforms meant to stabilize and coordinate the banking system globally (Bennhold 2011; Third World Network 2012; Council of Foreign Relations 2012).

By the end of 2012 the effects of the U.S. downturn continued to ripple through the world economy, and the Eurozone crisis continued as well. Dropping U.S. demand for machinery led even Europe's bulwark, Germany, into recession. The BRICS' growth rates also slowed considerably, as did growth rates in Turkey and other emerging economies. Changes in the global economy and deepening inequality in much of the world helped spur a wave of popular movements that often overshadowed NGOs and even toppled governments. Youth unemployment in particular was a fundamental issue to the protestors and their occasional international NGO allies from the Arab Spring to the Occupy Movement to the *Indignados* in Spain (Agencia AFP 2011). Thus, the Great Recession and U.S. poverty helped spur a number of political and economic changes, and governments and international NGOs responded by using the opportunity to better situate themselves in a shifting, increasingly multipolar world system.

FURTHER READING

Agencia France-Presse (AFP). "De Madrid a Nueva York, ira contra las desigualdades." *El Heraldo*, December 30, 2011. Accessed November 30, 2012. http://www.elheraldo.hn/Secciones-Principales/Mundo/De-Madrid-a-Nueva-York-ira-contra-las-desigualdades

Aljazeera. "G20 Seeks Stronger IMF to Fight Debt Crisis," November 5, 2011. Accessed December 11, 2012. http://www.aljazeera.com/news/europe/2011/11/201111464940325870.html

Athens News. "Unions Mull Wage Cut Options," December 10, 2012. Accessed December 14, 2012. http://www.athensnews.gr/portal/1/52151

Bayes, Jane H., and Laura Gonzalez. "Globalization, Transnationalism and Intersecting Geographies of Power: The Case of the Consejo Consultivo del Instituto de los Mexicanso en el Exterior (CC-IME): A Preliminary Study of Progress." Paper prepared for the Canadian Political Science Association Meeting, June 1–3, 2010.

Bennhold, Katrin. "French Leader Scales Back Ambitions for New Monetary System," January 27, 2011. Accessed November 19, 2012. http://dealbook.nytimes.com/2011/01/27/french-leader-scales-back-ambitions-for-new-monetary-system/?ref=brettonwoodssystem

Ceberio Belaza, Mónica. "El Gobierno planea otorgar la residencia a quienes compren pisos de 160.000 euros." *El País* (Madrid), November 19, 2012. Accessed November 20, 2012. http://politica.elpais.com/politica/2012/11/19/actualidad/1353320638_988833.html

Centre for Housing Rights and Evictions. "United States Must Not Betray Its Commitment to Freedom from Want, Human Rights Groups Say," 2010. Accessed November 14, 2012. http://www.cohre.org/news/press-releases/united-states-must-not-betray-its-commitment-to-freedom-from-want-human-rights-g

Cho, Yoonyoung, and David Newhouse. "How Did the Great Recession Affect Different Types of Workers? Evidence from 17 Middle-Income Countries." Institute for the Study of Labor (IZA) Discussion Paper No. 5681, April 2011. Accessed November 23, 2012. http://ftp.iza.org/dp5681.pdf

Columbia Law School Human Rights Institute. "Implementing Recommendations from the Universal Periodic Review: A Toolkit for State and Local Human Rights and Human Relations Commissions," 2011. Accessed November 19, 2012. http://www.law.columbia.edu/ipimages/Human_Rights_Institute/UPR%20Toolkit.pdf

Council on Foreign Relations. "The Global Finance Regime: Issue Brief," July 10, 2012. Accessed November 28, 2012. http://www.cfr.org/us-strategy-and-politics/global-finance-regime/p20177

Department of Public Information, U.N. Economic and Social Council. 2010. "Economic and Social Council Examines U.N. Response to Economic Crisis." July 7, 2010. Accessed Jan. 14, 2013. http://www.un.org/News/Press/docs/2010/ecosoc6437.doc.htm

Economist. "Beyond Bretton Woods 2: Is There a Better Way to Organize the World's Currencies?" November 4, 2010. Accessed November 21, 2012. http://www.economist .com/node/17414511

Economist. "A Great Migration into the Unknown: Global Recession Is Hitting China's Workers Hard," January 29, 2009. Accessed November 10, 2012. http://www .economist.com/node/13012736

Fair, C. Christine. "Pakistan in 2011: Ten Years of the 'War on Terror.'" *Asian Survey* 52, no. 1 (2012).

Goldstone, Jack A. "Rise of the TIMBIs." *Foreign Policy*, December 2, 2011. Accessed November 28, 2012. http://www.foreignpolicy.com/articles/2011/12/02/rise_of_the_timbis ?page=0,2

Gruley, Bryan, and Shruti Date Singh. "Deere's Big Green Profit Machine." *Bloomberg Businessweek*, July 5, 2012. Accessed November 12, 2012. http://www.businessweek .com/articles/2012-07-05/deeres-big-green-profit-machine#p5

Guttmann, Robert, and Dominique Plihon. "Consumer Debt and Financial Fragility." *International Review of Applied Economics* 24, no. 3 (2010).

International Organization for Migration (IOM). "Ciudad Juárez Municipality and IOM Sign Agreement for Migrant Assistance Program," 2011. Accessed November 28, 2012. http://www.iom.int/cms/en/sites/iom/home/news-and-views/press-briefing-notes/pbn-2011/ pbn-listing/ciudad-juarez-municipality-and-iom-sign.html

International Service for Human Rights. "UPR of the United States: No New Commitments," 2010. Accessed November 1, 2012. http://www.ishr.ch/upr/942-upr-of-the-united-states -no-new-commitments

Jain, Sonali. "For Love and Money: Second-Generation Indian Americans 'Return' to India," October 2010. Accessed October 29, 2012. http://www.migrationinformation.org/ Feature/display.cfm?ID=804

James, Ian. "Venezuela to Keep Sending Free Fuel to US Poor." Council on Hemispheric Affairs, January 8, 2009. Accessed November 4, 2012. http://www.coha.org/venezuela -to-keep-sending-free-fuel-to-us-poor/

Keating, Joshua E. "Who Won the Great Recession? These 7 Countries." *Foreign Policy*, November 10, 2012. Accessed November 20, 2012. http://www.foreignpolicy.com/ articles/2012/10/08/these_7_countries

Kiva.org. "Our Field Partners." Accessed November 25, 2012. http://www.kiva.org/partners

Letras Libres. "A diez anos del Instituto de los Mexicanos en el Exterior," January 9, 2013. Accessed January 11, 2013. http://www.letraslibres.com/blogs/frontera-adentro/diez -anos-del-instituto-de-los-mexicanos-en-el-exterior

Mattoo, Aaditya, and Arvind Subramanian. "India and Bretton Woods II." *Economic and Political Weekly*, November 8, 2008. Accessed November 21, 2012. http://www.epw .in/special-articles/india-and-bretton-woods-ii.html

París Pombo, María Dolores. "Procesos de repatriación. Experiencias de las personas devuel- tas a México por las autoridades estadounidenses." Working paper, El Colegio de la

Frontera Norte and the Woodrow Wilson International Center for Scholars, Mexico Institute, 2010. Accessed December 2, 2012. http://www.wilsoncenter.org/sites/default/files/PARIS%20POMBO%20PAPER.pdf

Prashad, Vijay, and Pratyush Chandra. "'Arab Spring Is Part of the General Strike of the South': An Interview with Vijay Prashad," May 15, 2012. Accessed November 29, 2012. http://radicalnotes.com/2012/05/15/arab-spring-is-part-of-the-general-strike-of-the-south-an-interview-with-vijay-prashad/

Rodríguez Santos, Bertha. "La comunicación indígena en un mundo globalizado: Las estrategias del FIOB en sus luchas en México y EEUU." Programa de las Américas, December 30, 2008. Accessed November 28, 2012. http://www.cipamericas.org/es/archives/1733

Schneider, Howard. "In Sign of Growing Clout, Brazil's Corn Helps Hold up U.S. Market." *Washington Post*, November 8, 2012. Accessed November 30, 2012. http://articles.washingtonpost.com/2012-11-18/business/35504609_1_cotton-growers-cotton-farmers-cotton-programs

Shevory, Kristina. "With Squeeze on Credit, Microlending Blossoms." *New York Times*, July 28, 2010. Accessed October 30, 2012. http://www.nytimes.com/2010/07/29/business/smallbusiness/29sbiz.html

Third World Network. "Towards a Lasting Solution to Sovereign Debt Problems," 2012. Accessed December 15, 2012. http://www.item.org.uy/node/59

UN Office of the High Commissioner for Human Rights. "Council Adopts Outcome of Universal Periodic Review on the United States, Holds General Debate on the Universal Periodic Review," March 18, 2011. Accessed November 29, 2012. http://www.ohchr.org/en/NewsEvents/Pages/DisplayNews.aspx?NewsID=10867&LangID=E

Wing Chan, Kam. "The Global Financial Crisis and Migrant Workers in China: 'There Is No Future as a Labourer; Returning to the Village Has No Meaning.'" *International Journal of Urban and Regional Research* 34, no. 3 (2010): 659–77.

Woods, Ngaire. "The G20 Leaders and Global Governance." Global Economic Governance Programme Working Paper, Oxford University, October 2010. Accessed January 14, 2012. http://www.globaleconomicgovernance.org/wp-content/uploads/Woods-2010-The-G20-and-Global-Governance.doc.pdf

Political Parties and Major Legislative Responses

Lindsey K. Hanson

OVERVIEW

The Great Recession and its aftermath became increasingly characterized by partisan politics. The chasm between the two major political parties, Democrats and Republicans, was perhaps nowhere as apparent as in the debates over the federal deficit, debt, and fiscal cliff. Still, many of the major federal legislative responses to the Great Recession were, in the end at least, largely bipartisan. This essay will explore the responses of the Republican and Democratic Parties to the Great Recession by discussing some of the major legislation of the Great Recession, the party politics behind this legislation, and the Recession-era mid-term 2010 elections and the 2012 presidential election.

THE PRESENT

PRESIDENT BUSH AND THE BIPARTISAN ECONOMIC STIMULUS AND EMERGENCY STABILIZATION ACTS

The Recession began in December 2007 when President George W. Bush was in office, and the Senate and House were controlled by Democrats. While it was apparent that the nation was entering an economic downturn, the beginning of the Recession was not officially identified by the National Bureau of Economic Research (NBER) until December 2008, one month after Barack Obama became president-elect and shortly before Obama took office in January of 2009 (National Bureau of Economic Research 2008). In response to the downturn, the Economic Stimulus Act and Emergency Stabilization Act were enacted prior to Obama's first inauguration and prior to the NBER's announcement that a recession was underway.

The Economic Stimulus Act was signed into law by President Bush in February 2008. The act had both Republican and Democratic co-sponsors and passed with the support of both parties (Govtrack.us 2008a). In the House 215 Democrats and 165 Republicans voted for the act, and six Democrats and 28 Republicans voted against it (Govtrack.us 2008a). In the Senate 47 Democrats and 32 Republicans voted for passage, with no Democrats and 16 Republicans voting against it (Govtrack.us 2008a). The act provided tax rebates for low- and middle-income taxpayers of up to $600, with an additional $300 for each child of an eligible taxpayer (Govtrack.us 2008a). It also provided tax incentives to businesses, including increasing deductible expenses allowed for depreciable business assets (Govtrack.us 2013). Finally, the act increased the maximum limit for mortgages that could be purchased by Fannie Mae and Freddie Mac (Govtrack.us 2008a).

The Emergency Stabilization Act, often referred to as the "bailout" for the U.S. financial system, was introduced with numerous Republican and Democrat co-sponsors. It also passed with the support of both parties. In the Senate 40 Democrats and 33 Republicans voted in favor of the bill, and 9 Democrats and 15 Republicans voted against it (Govtrack.us 2008b). In the House 172

A newspaper headline is taped to a booth on the New York Stock Exchange floor. The Emergency Economic Stabilization Act of 2008 was signed into law on October 3, 2008. (AP Photo/Richard Drew)

Democrats and 91 Republicans voted "Yes," and 63 Democrats and 108 Republicans voted "No" (Govtrack.us 2008b). Bush signed the act into law on October 3, 2008 (Govtrack.us 2008b). The act created the Troubled Asset Relief Program (TARP) and authorized billions of dollars for the U.S. secretary of the treasury to buy distressed assets, and in particular mortgage-backed securities, in order to provide cash to banks and other financial institutions (Govtrack.us 2008b). When mortgages or mortgage-backed securities were purchased through TARP, the Economic Stabilization Act of 2008 provided that the secretary of the treasury had to create a plan to encourage mortgage servicers to modify loans and take other measures to avoid foreclosures (Govtrack.us 2008b). The act also required other federal entities such as the Federal Housing Finance Agency (FHFA), the Federal Deposit Insurance Corporation (FDIC), and the Federal Reserve to create plans to mitigate foreclosures (Govtrack.us 2008b). In addition it regulated compensation for executives who sold troubled assets to the federal government and raised the debt ceiling (Govtrack.us 2008b). The Economic Stimulus Act and the Emergency Stabilization Act were the most expansive Bush administration responses to the Great Recession, but even more expansive legislative responses were in store as the Recession continued into the Obama administration.

President Obama and the Democratic American Recovery and Reinvestment Act of 2009 (ARRA)

In the November 2008 elections the Democrats won the presidency and expanded their control in both the House and the Senate, where they retained majorities. Early in Obama's first term the American Recovery and Reinvestment Act of 2009 (ARRA) was enacted in response to the downturn. Unlike the Economic Stimulus Act and Economic Stabilization Acts of 2008, the ARRA was partisan legislation that passed both chambers almost completely on the basis of Democratic votes. In the House 246 Democrats and 0 Republicans voted for the bill, while six Democrats and 177 Republicans voted against it (Govtrack.us 2009). In the Senate 56 Democrats and 2 Republicans voted in favor, and 0 Democrats and 38 Republicans voted "No" (Govtrack.us 2009).

The ARRA, which provided around $800 billion in funding, was intended to create, or save, an estimated 3.5 million jobs (Brass 2009). It was also estimated that it would cause a deficit increase of $787.2 billion over 11 years due to reduced revenue and increased spending (Brass 2009). The ARRA included many measures too numerous to outline in this essay. However, it included many provisions that impacted low-income individuals, and some of those provisions are discussed here. The ARRA temporarily increased the Earned Income Tax Credit (EITC), a tax credit for working low-income people with children. It also provided tax incentives for businesses to hire unemployed veterans and 16- to 24-year-olds, bonds for job training education, and investment in locations with high unemployment, including tribal economic development bonds (see the essay earlier in this section titled "Government Response, Tribal"). The ARRA provided funding for homelessness prevention (see Section 4, "Homelessness") and low-income housing (see Section 4, "Housing Assistance Programs and Low-Income Renters"), as well as for Medicare and Medicaid (see Section 4, "Health Care Assistance"). In addition, the ARRA provided funding for Supplemental Nutrition Assistance Programs (SNAP, or food stamps) (see Section 4, "Food Insecurity and Assistance") and Temporary Assistance for Needy Families (TANF, or welfare) (see Section 4, "Welfare/Cash Assistance Programs"). The ARRA also provided one-time payments to Social Security beneficiaries, including those receiving Supplemental Security Income (SSI), and to Veterans Affairs and Railroad Retirement Board Beneficiaries (Recovery.gov 2013). The Executive Office of the President reports, among other positive impacts, that as of the second quarter of 2011 the ARRA had resulted in 2.2 million to 4.2 million more jobs than would have otherwise existed, and had raised the gross domestic product (GDP) 2.0 to 2.9 percent higher than it would have been without the ARRA (2011).

While the Recession officially ended in June 2009 (which the NBER announced in September of 2010), the slow recovery felt like a continued Recession to many (National Bureau of Economic Research 2010). In addition, concerns over the federal deficit were growing, and the Tea Party movement was coming to the forefront, neither of which would bode well for the Democratic Party in the 2010 mid-term elections.

RISE OF THE TEA PARTY AND THE MID-TERM 2010 ELECTIONS

The Tea Party movement began in 2008 in response to the Economic Stimulus Act and financial bailout (New York Times 2012). It took its name from the pre–Revolutionary War Boston Tea Party in which a group of protestors destroyed tea by throwing it into the Boston Harbor in protest of British taxation policies. The Tea Party was not a movement with a clearly defined agenda, rather, it was a more conservative offshoot of the Republican party with libertarian leanings; the movement was largely concerned with reducing the deficit, taxes, government spending (particularly on entitlements), and the size of the federal government (New York Times 2012; Hunt 2010).

The Tea Party began its rise to prominence in early 2009, around the time Obama took office and the ARRA was enacted. By the 2010 mid-term elections four out of 10 voters were expressing support for the Tea Party (New York Times 2012), and the growth in popular support for the movement had caused even non–Tea Party Republicans to shift toward the right (Hunt 2010). The Tea Party helped the

Republican Party regain control of the House and make gains in the Senate in the November 2010 mid-term elections. The elections were largely viewed as a Republican victory.

One month before the new Congress took office in January of 2011, the Tax Relief, Unemployment Insurance Reauthorization, and Job Creation Act was enacted. That act was co-sponsored by Democrat and Republican members of Congress, and it passed the House with 139 Democrats and 138 Republicans voting in favor (112 Democrats and 36 Republicans were opposed) (Govtrack.us 2010). In the Senate 43 Democrats and 37 Republicans voted "Yes," and 13 Democrats and five Republicans voted "No" (Govtrack.us 2010). The Tax Relief, Unemployment Insurance Reauthorization, and Job Creation Act of 2010 extended Bush-era income tax cuts and various investment incentives that were enacted in 2001 and 2003, and it provided for a one-year payroll tax reduction (Govtrack.us 2010). The act also extended the expansion of the Earned Income Tax Credit (EITC) under the ARRA for an additional two years (Govtrack.us 2010) and reduced the marriage penalty; these two measures combined meant an average of $600 for families with three or more children (IRS 2013). It also extended the Child Tax Credit provisions of the ARRA (and prior Bush-era legislation) that allowed families with lower incomes to receive this credit (Govtrack.us 2010; IRS 2013). In addition, it provided for a 13-month extension of unemployment benefits for the eligible unemployed and extended the American Opportunity Tax Credit for college students and their families (Govtrack.us 2010).

Partisan Gridlock, the Federal Deficit, and Debt Ceiling Debates

When the new Congress took office in January 2011 Republicans controlled the House, and Democrats controlled the Senate. The result was partisan gridlock. The debt ceiling, which had been raised numerous times before, was suddenly a point of massive contention in the face of growing deficits and the burgeoning influence of Tea Party Republicans. Tea Party supporters and Republicans who were not backed by the Tea Party were refusing to raise the debt ceiling without substantial reductions in spending (National Priorities Project 2013). The debate over the deficit and debt ceiling that would mark the coming years began in earnest.

In 2011 Paul Ryan, chair of the House Budget Committee who later ran as Mitt Romney's vice presidential candidate in the 2012 elections, put forward a budget plan to address the deficit. His budget plan garnered a great deal of attention. According to the Bipartisan Policy Center, the Ryan budget would have raised the debt ceiling while reducing the debt-to-GDP ratio to 62 percent by 2022, a lower ratio than Obama's proposal, which called for a debt-to-GDP ratio of 76 percent (Adler 2012). The Ryan budget would also have repealed the expansion of

Medicaid and the Children's Health Insurance Program (CHIP) that were included in the Affordable Care Act (Adler 2012). The expansions in the Affordable Care Act extended coverage to most low-income children and low-income adults who were not elderly and thereby eligible for Medicare (Adler 2012). In addition to not expanding Medicare and CHIP coverage, the Ryan budget would have reduced funding for these programs by around $160 billion by 2022 (Adler 2012). The Ryan budget also included provisions that would gradually increase the Medicare eligibility age to 67 by 2034, up from the current age of 65 (Adler 2012).

In addition, Ryan's budget would lower the corporate tax rate from 35 to 25 percent and reduce individual income tax rates to two brackets (10 and 25 percent). While this would reduce revenue, Ryan maintained this he intended to offset these losses and losses from the repeal of certain tax provisions in the Affordable Care Act (losses of an estimated $4.6 trillion over the course of a decade) by eliminating certain deductions, credits, and exemptions in the current income tax code (Adler 2012). The Ryan budget would also have changed the funding structure for the Supplemental Nutrition Assistance Program (SNAP, commonly called food stamps) and create SNAP time limits and work requirements (Adler 2012). Had these changes to the SNAP program been enacted it would have meant a loss of SNAP benefits for 8 to 10 million people (Merrick 2012). The Ryan budget would also have limited the expansion of Pell grants, a program that provides funds to low-income students for undergraduate degrees, and would have made cuts to job training programs (Adler 2012). It also called for increased antifraud efforts for Medicare, Medicaid, Supplemental Security Income, and Disability Insurance (Adler 2012). The Center on Budget and Policy Priorities found that a minimum of 62 percent of the $5.3 trillion in nondefense cuts in Ryan's budget would come from programs for low-income people (Merrick 2012). A budget plan based on the Ryan budget did pass the House in April of 2011 with all Democrats voting against it and all but four Republicans voting for in favor (New York Times 2013). However, the measure never went to the Senate for a vote.

With no budget and the United States approaching its debt ceiling which is the highest level of debt the government can legally hold (National Priorities Project 2013), House Republicans introduced the Cut, Cap, and Balance Act. The act, which was introduced in July 2011, raised the debt ceiling contingent on the passage of a constitutional amendment that required a balanced budget, capped spending at a percentage of GDP, and required all future tax increases to be approved by two-thirds of the House and Senate (Library of Congress 2011). While the bill had Republican, and particularly Tea Party, support, there was no hope of it being approved by the Democratic-controlled Senate and President Obama had promised to veto it. In combination with the fact that raising the debt ceiling under the act would have required the passage of a constitutional amendment, it was largely viewed as a symbolic gesture. Still, the House passed the Cut,

Cap, and Balance Act with only five Democrats voting "Yes" and only nine Republicans voting "No" (Library of Congress 2011).

With no resolution to the debt ceiling debate and the U.S. government at its debt ceiling in August 2011, Congress needed to raise the ceiling so that the federal government could keep paying on its debts and avoid default (National Priorities Project 2013). Faced with partisan gridlock, negotiation efforts continued. In order to temporarily put an end to the debate and raise the debt ceiling, and thereby avoid default, the largely bipartisan Budget Control Act of 2011 was enacted in August 2011 (National Priorities Project 2013). In the House 174 Republicans and 95 Democrats voted in favor, and 66 Republicans and 95 Democrats were opposed (Govtrack.us 2011). In the Senate 45 Democrats and 28 Republicans voted in favor of the Budget Control Act of 2011, and six Democrats and 19 Republicans opposed it (Govtrack.us 2011). The act raised the debt ceiling by a minimum of $2.1 trillion and a maximum of $2.4 trillion under certain conditions (Heniff 2011). It required a 12-member "super-committee" of members of both parties to come up with a plan to reduce the deficit by at least $1.2 trillion in the next 10 years, or automatic cuts (known as sequestration) of $917 billion to discretionary funding over a decade would go into effect in early January 2013 (National Priorities Project 2013). Unable to overcome the partisan politics that had resulted in the need for the Budget Control Act of 2011, and facing a presidential election year that both parties hoped would change the political tides, the super-committee failed to create this plan (National Priorities Project 2013).

THE 2012 ELECTIONS, THE AMERICAN TAXPAYER RELIEF ACT OF 2012, AND THE NO BUDGET NO PAY ACT OF 2013

However, the turning political tides that both parties hoped for did not materialize. In the November 2012 elections Obama defeated Republican candidate Mitt Romney to win re-election, Democrats maintained control of the Senate, and Republicans retained control of the House. With the balance of political power remaining at the status quo, in early January the American Taxpayer Relief Act of 2012 was implemented. In the Senate the Bill passed with 47 Democrats and 40 Republicans in favor, and three Democrats and 5 Republicans opposed (Govtrack.us 2012). In the House 85 Republicans and 172 Democrats voted in favor of the act, and 151 Republicans and 16 Democrats voted "No" (Govtrack.us 2012). The act extended the deadline for congressional action on the budget required by the Budget Control Act of 2011 to March of 2013 (Govtrack.us 2012). It also extended Bush-era tax cuts for individuals whose taxable income is at or below $400,000 annually (or $450,000 for a joint return of a married couple). The income threshold level for these tax cuts was set to increase with inflation (Govtrack.us 2012). For individuals with incomes higher than this threshold the

Bush-era tax cuts expired as of January 1, 2013, and were not extended. Effectively this meant a top marginal tax rate increase of 4.6 percentage points (Govtrack.us 2012). The act also caps tax credits and deductions for filers with upper-level incomes (Govtrack.us 2012). The payroll tax cut provision of the ARRA was not extended through the American Taxpayer Relief Act, but the act did make the Child Tax Credit (discussed earlier in this essay) permanent and extended the expansion of the Earned Income Tax Child Tax Credit and American Opportunity Tax Credit through 2017 (Govtrack.us 2012). Additionally, it extended federal unemployment benefits and froze pay for members of Congress (Govtrack.us 2012).

With another temporary stopgap in place the debt ceiling still loomed and negotiations between the parties continued. On February 4, 2013, President Obama signed H.R. 325, commonly referred to as the No Budget, No Pay Act of 2013. The act temporarily eliminated restrictions on federal government spending, thus raising the debt ceiling, until May 19, 2013. It also required a fiscal year (FY) 2014 budget resolution from the House and the Senate by April 15, 2013, or congressional representatives' salaries would be placed in escrow until their chamber passed a budget or the end of the 113th Congress (Govtrack.us 2013).

While the No Budget, No Pay Act of 2013 raised the debt ceiling it did not prevent sequestration (the automatic cuts to discretionary spending mandated by the Budget Control Act of 2011). Sequestration went into effect March 1, 2013, after the super-committee and Congress failed to create a deficit reduction plan even after the American Taxpayer Relief Act of 2012 delayed sequestration and gave Congress until March 2013 to act (Govtrack.us 2012; National Women's Law Center 2013). While sequestration did go into effect, Congress avoided a government shutdown by passing an appropriations bills in late March 2013 that funded the federal government through the end of FY 2013 (National Women's Law Center 2013).

While the House and Senate both met the April 15, 2013, deadline for a budget resolution imposed by the No Budget, No Pay Act of 2013, no budget had been agreed upon as of mid-2013 (National Women's Law Center 2013). Moreover, the United States hit its debt ceiling on May 19, 2013, with the U.S. Treasury employing what it called "extraordinary measures" to continue spending without going over the legal debt limit; the Treasury estimated that it will be able to continue spending without breaching the debt limit into the autumn of 2013 if necessary (Boccia 2013).

OUTLOOK

While the debate and partisan politics surrounding the federal debt continued well into 2013, the Tea Party, which arguably started that debate in earnest, had seen its influence fall dramatically since the 2010 mid-term elections. This led commentators to question whether the movement had ended, with one expert stating that "the Tea Party was of a moment and that moment was the recession" (NPR 2012). The Tea Party is unlikely to regain the prominence it had during the 2010 mid-term elections, but it did start a national conversation about the size of government and the government deficitthat will continue for some time.

The Tea Party also helped to create debate about, and within, the Republican Party about the Party's principles and place in the future of the United States. In the wake of its loss in the 2012 presidential election the Republican Party was re-evaluating itself in light of the changing demographics of U.S. society. The Party was particularly concerned about attracting young people and minorities in light of the changing social views of young people, particularly on the issue of gay marriage, and the growing minority population in the United States. In January 2013 GOP Louisiana governor Bobby Jindahl gave a highly publicized speech in which he argued that the Republican Party was too focused on Washington and that it had failed to pursue votes from the entire populace, particularly minority voters (Cillizza 2013). The Republican Party will continue to evaluate itself in preparation for the 2016 presidential election in an attempt to appeal to young voters with more liberal social views and to minority voters.

While the Republican Party looks inward, the partisan politics playing out between Republicans and Democrats are likely to continue at least until the mid-term elections of 2014 when voters will once again decide whether the power balance in Washington will remain status quo or shift toward the right or left. In the meantime, while the heated discussion over the debt, deficit, and debt ceiling persists, programs and benefits for low-income individuals and families will also continue to be hotly debated and will remain particularly vulnerable to funding cuts.

FURTHER READING

Adler, Loren, and Shai Akabas. "Paul Ryan's Fiscal Year 2013 Budget: 2013," March 21, 2012. Accessed February 1, 2013. http://bipartisanpolicy.org/blog/2012/03/paul-ryan%E2%80%99s-fiscal-year-2013-budget-details

Boccia, Romina. "Treasury Employs Extraordinary Measures to Spend Beyond Debt Limit," J une 6, 2013. Accessed June 13, 2013. http://blog.heritage.org/2013/06/06/treasury-employs-extraordinary-measures-to-spend-beyond-debt-limit/

Brass, Clinton T., Carol Hardy Vincent, Pamela J. Jackson, Jennifer E. Lake, Karen Spar, and Robert Keith. "American Recovery and Reinvestment Act of 2009 (P.L. 111-5): Brief Summary," April 20, 2009. Accessed January 29, 2013. http://waxman.house.gov/sites/waxman.house.gov/files/documents/UploadedFiles/ARRA.pdf

Cillizza, Chris, and Aaron Blake. "Bobby Jindal Speaking Truth to GOP Power." *Washington Post*, January 24, 2013. Accessed February 1, 2013. http://www.washingtonpost.com/blogs/the-fix/wp/2013/01/24/bobby-jindal-speaking-truth-to-gop-power/

Executive Office of the President of the United States. "The Economic Impact of the American Recovery and Reinvestment Act of 2009: Eighth Quarterly Report," December 9, 2011. Accessed February 1, 2013. http://www.whitehouse.gov/sites/default/files/cea_8th_arra_report_final_draft.pdf

Govtrack.us. "H.R. 5140 (110th): Economic Stimulus Act of 2008," January 28, 2008a. Accessed February 1, 2013. http://www.govtrack.us/congress/bills/110/hr5140

Govtrack.us. "H.R. 1424 (110th): Emergency Economic Stabilization Act of 2008," October 3, 2008b. Accessed February 1, 2013. http://www.govtrack.us/congress/bills/110/hr1424

Govtrack.us. "H.R. 1 (111th): American Recovery and Reinvestment Act of 2009," February 17, 2009. Accessed February 1, 2013. http://www.govtrack.us/congress/bills/111/hr1

Govtrack.us. "H.R. 4853 (111th): Tax Relief, Unemployment Insurance Reauthorization, and Job Creation Act of 2010," December 17, 2010. Accessed February 1, 2013. http://www.govtrack.us/congress/bills/111/hr4853

Govtrack.us. "S. 365 Budget Control Act of 2011," August 2, 2011. Accessed February 1, 2013. http://www.govtrack.us/congress/bills/112/s365

Govtrack.us. "H.R. 8 (112th): American Taxpayer Relief Act of 2012," January 2, 2012. Accessed February 1, 2013. http://www.govtrack.us/congress/bills/112/hr8

Govtrack.us. "H.R. 325: To Ensure the Complete and Timely Payment of Obligations of the United States Government until May …," January 31, 2013. Accessed February 3, 2013. http://www.govtrack.us/congress/bills/113/hr325

Heniff, Bill Jr., Elizabeth Rybicki, and Shannon M. Mahan. "The Budget Control Act of 2011: Summary." Congressional Research Service, August 19, 2011. Accessed January 28, 2013. http://www.fas.org/sgp/crs/misc/R41965.pdf

Hunt, Albert R. "Tea Party Doesn't Need Votes to Win U.S. Elections," September 26, 2010. Accessed February 1, 2013. http://www.nytimes.com/2010/09/27/us/27iht-letter.html

Internal Revenue Service (IRS). "Tax Relief, Unemployment Insurance Reauthorization, and Job Creation Act of 2010: Information Center," January 7, 2013. Accessed June 13, 2013. http://www.irs.gov/uac/Tax-Relief,-Unemployment-Insurance-Reauthorization,-and-Job-Creation-Act-of-2010:-Information-Center

Library of Congress. "H.R. 2560," July 22, 2011. Accessed February 1, 2013. http://thomas.loc.gov/cgi-bin/bdquery/z?d112:H.R.2560:

Merrick, Kelsey, and Jim Horney. "Chairman Ryan Gets 62 Percent of His Huge Budget Cuts from Programs for Lower-Income Americans," March 23, 2012. Accessed February 1, 2013. http://www.cbpp.org/cms/index.cfm?fa=view&id=3723

National Bureau of Economic Research. "Determination of the December 2007 Peak in Economic Activity," December 1, 2008. Accessed January 28, 2013. http://wwwdev.nber.org/dec2008.html

National Bureau of Economic Research. "Business Cycle Dating Committee, National Bureau of Economic Research," September 20, 2010. Accessed January 28, 2013. http://www.nber.org/cycles/sept2010.html

National Public Radio. "End of the Tea Party as We Know It?" April 22, 2012. Accessed February 1, 2013. http://www.npr.org/2012/04/22/151146854/end-of-the-tea-party-as-we-know-it

National Priorities Project. "Federal Budget Timeline: Beyond the Fiscal Cliff 2013," January 9, 2013. Accessed February 1, 2013. http://nationalpriorities.org/analysis/2013/federal-budget-timeline-beyond-fiscal-cliff-2013/

National Women's Law Center. "A Roadmap to the 2013 Federal Budget Debates," May 17, 2013. Accessed June 13, 2013. http://www.nwlc.org/resource/roadmap-2013-federal-budget-debates

New York Times. "House Vote 277, Passes Ryan Budget Bill," April 15, 2013. Accessed February 1, 2013. http://politics.nytimes.com/congress/votes/112/house/1/277

New York Times. "Tea Party Movement," December 26, 2012. Accessed February 1, 2013. http://topics.nytimes.com/top/reference/timestopics/subjects/t/tea_party_movement/index.html

Recovery.gov. "Breakdown of Funding by Category," 2013. Accessed January 28. http://www.recovery.gov/Transparency/fundingoverview/Pages/fundingbreakdown.aspx

SECTION 6

HOW LONG WILL THE EFFECTS OF THE GREAT RECESSION LAST?

INTRODUCTION TO SECTION 6

Timothy J. Essenburg

Typically the economic effects of a recession linger for a few years after the official end of the recession. With the Great Recession, however, fully 3.5 years after its official end (in June 2009) unemployment and poverty rates remained high. This has led many to wonder how long the Recession's aftermath will linger. To explore answers to the question "How Long Will the Effects Last?" this section discusses fears of a double dip Recession, addresses questions about when the economy will again be "normal," and examines the possibility of structural changes to the economy wrought by the Recession.

DOUBLE DIP RECESSION RISK

- A double dip recession occurs when a second recession starts 12 or fewer months after the end of a previous recession. There have been three such occurrences in the past 100 years: 1913, 1920, and 1981.
- Data from 2006 to 2012 demonstrates that there was no double dip recession accompanying the Great Recession. The Great Recession ended in June 2009 with no second recession, although it was followed by a weak recovery that felt like a recession to many.
- Despite the fact that there was no double dip, concerns remained even at the start of 2013. These concerns included (1) the European Union's relapse into a second recession in 2012, (2) remaining uncertainties regarding the Arab Spring, (3) China's potential real estate bubble, and (4) the fact that the United States has yet to formalize a longer-term plan for reducing deficits.

A NORMAL ECONOMY—WHEN?

- The economy is a socially alive ever-evolving system. In some sense there is no "normal," but there are desirable and nondesirable economic conditions.
- Variables to consider when determining what a normal, or desirable, economy looks like include: the growth rate of gross domestic product (GDP), the unemployment rate, the inflation rate, income distribution, the poverty rate, and deficit and debt as a percentage of total output.
- By all of the previously mentioned measures, with the exception of the poverty rate, the decade of the 1960s is the U.S. standard for desirable conditions. During the 1960s the GDP growth rate averaged 3.5 percent. The unemployment rate from 1965 to 1969 averaged 3.8 percent. In comparison, from 1970 on the unemployment rate reached 3.8 percent or lower for only a single month (April 2000). Inflation was also low in the 1960s—below 3.0 percent from 1960 to 1966. In addition, deficits were less than 1.5 percent of GDP for much of the 1960s, and debt as a percentage of GDP was less than 40 percent. Income inequality, as measured by the Gini coefficient, was also lowest in the 1960s.
- Poverty rates in the 1960s were relatively high but declining. They reached lows in the mid-1970s. This was the case because civil rights legislation and programs associated with the War on Poverty, both implemented in the 1960s, took time to take their full effect.
- In the aftermath of the Recession and slow recovery near-term GDP growth rates will not be strong, and concerns about federal deficits and debt will continue. As a result: (1) near-term economic growth, on its own, will not reduce the unemployment rate to below 6.0 percent or the poverty rate to below 12.0 percent, and (2) no substantial federal antipoverty measures are likely to be implemented in the near future. Thus, the effects of the Great Recession are likely to continue to linger for some time.

STRUCTURAL ECONOMIC CHANGES

- The Great Recession brought longer-lasting changes to the economy than are associated with most recessions.
- The Great Recession most likely brought about a decline in potential GDP and caused an increase in structural unemployment.
- The middle class, due to unemployment and plummeting housing values, lost substantial income and wealth.
- In the aftermath of the Recession credit was more difficult to obtain, and households continued to reduce debt to cope with economic uncertainty.
- Concerns over the federal debt and deficit are likely to linger for some time along with concerns arising from the future solvency of Social Security and Medicare.
- It is unlikely that the coming years will bring substantial economic growth that will lead to greater employment of those with lower skills and to increasing wages. In addition, low-income individuals are likely to be impacted by federal budget cuts in the near future. As a result it will be many years before the poverty rate falls below 11.5 percent.

DOUBLE DIP RECESSION RISK

Timothy J. Essenburg

OVERVIEW

There were concerns during the Great Recession and the years that followed that the economy would enter a second recession, or double dip recession. This essay will discuss these concerns and will begin by further defining and explaining what a double dip recession is, and why a double dip recession did not occur as part of the Great Recession.

A business cycle corresponds to the time period from peak economic activity through a trough (the low point of economic activity) and to the next peak. A business cycle has three phases: recession, recovery, and expansion. The standard definition of a recession is a six-month downturn in inflation-adjusted gross domestic product (GDP). Although all recessions in the past 100 years meet this criterion, the Dating Committee of the National Bureau of Economic Research (NBER), the group that "officially" declares when U.S. recessions begin and end, uses the following definition of a recession: "a significant decline in economic activity spread across the economy, lasting more than a few months, normally visible in real GDP, real income, employment, industrial production, and wholesale-retail sales" (National Bureau of Economic Research 2013). When an economy enters the recovery phase, policymakers, businesspersons, and economists wonder if the recovery will eventually transition into sustained economic expansion, or if it will falter and possibly result in another recession. When a recession closely follows the end of a previous recession, it is said to be a "double dip" recession. A double dip recession can be thought of as inflation-adjusted GDP tracing out a "W" (each downward line representing a recession) in a relatively short time period.

A teenager reenacts a scene of a boy selling apples during the Great Depression in front of the New York Stock Exchange on September 30, 2008, following the market's plunge. (AP Photo/Mark Lennihan)

A double dip recession can be said to be a time period when a second recession starts 12 or fewer months after the end of a previous recession. There have been three such occurrences in the past 100 years (National Bureau of Economic Research 2013). The second recession of each of these double dip recession began at the following times: January 1913, January 1920, and July 1981. Figure 1 depicts the most recent double dip recession. Note how the value of inflation-adjusted GDP traces out the gray-colored "W." The relative strength of the economy is reflected in unemployment rates. As the economy expands and more persons are hired, the unemployment rate falls; the reverse is true for a recessionary economy. The result is that the unemployment rate moves in the opposite direction of inflation-adjusted GDP, and traces out an "M" during a double dip period (see Figure 2). Without a strong recovery and expansion, the poverty rate also increases through this time period.

The Federal Reserve (Fed) began operations in 1914, but the Open Market Committee (the policy branch of the Fed) came later, with the Banking Act of 1935 (History of the Federal Reserve 2013; See also Section 1, "Policy, Monetary"). Thus, the first two examples of double dip recessions took place prior to today's economic system in which the full policy options available to the Fed can be employed. As a result, it makes sense to focus on the 1981 double dip recession for comparative purposes. In the case of that double dip recession, in late 1979 the Fed began a concerted effort to bring down the inflation rate by increasing interest rates (Goodfriend 2005). The idea was that if the cost of borrowing were increased, less lending would take place, thereby decreasing expenditures, and it worked. The inflation rate fell from a high of 12.0 percent in March of 1980 to a low of 3.5 by April 1983 (Federal Reserve Bank of St. Louis 2013). Thankfully, inflation was not of concern for the Fed during the Great Recession. To understand this

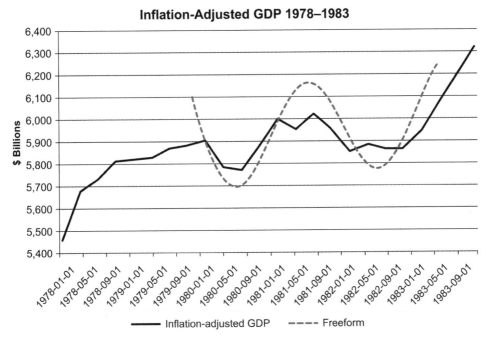

Figure 1
(*Source*: FRED Data, Federal Reserve Bank of St. Louis, GDCC1, http://research
.stlouisfed.org/fred2/series/GDPC1)

and the ongoing concerns with a second recession, this article presents data from
2006 to 2012 and concludes with an economic outlook for the coming years.

THE PRESENT

The idea of a double dip recession was an ongoing concern from the official end
of the Great Recession in June 2009 through mid-2012 (Halo 2011; Norris 2011;
Rickards 2012; Roubini 2009, 2010, 2011). These concerns were for good reason.
Not only was the recovery weak by historic standards, as measured by GDP growth
rates (see Figure 3 and note the rate almost fell below 0.00 percent in 2011), but the
Economic Cycle Research Institute's U.S. Weekly Leading Index (a predictor of the
strength of economic growth) in both 2010 and 2011 offered data forecasting a possible recession. Craig Elwell, a macroeconomist for the Congressional Research
Service, wrote four reports for Congress between 2010 and 2012 voicing concerns
over a double dip recession. Not until the end of 2012 was he confident enough
to write a report that focused on sustaining growth (Elwell 2010, 2011a, 2011b,
2012a, 2012b).
   Data from 2006 to 2012 demonstrate that no double dip, or second, recessionary
period occurred. This is because the Great Recession ended in June 2009, and

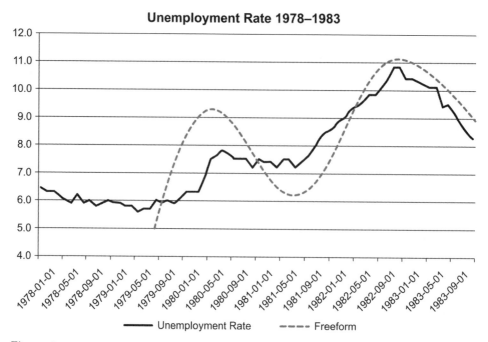

Figure 2

(*Source*: FRED Data, Federal Reserve Bank of St. Louis: UNRATE, http://research
.stlouisfed.org/fred2/series/UNRATE)

there was no intervening recession. GDP growth rates (Figure 3) and the output
ratios (Figure 4) both indicate weak economic performance following the
Recession. The downward trend of growth rates from a high of 4.03 percent in
2009 Quarter 3 to a low of 0.08 percent in 2011 Quarter 1, followed by another
downward trend from 2011 Quarter 3 to 2012 Quarter 2 more or less traces out a
"W." Fortunately, the economy never slipped into recession number two.
Reflective of this weak growth is a continued low value for the output ratio, the ratio
of actual GDP to its potential value if resources were fully utilized. A desirable
value is at or above 1.00. At the close of the Recession the value stood at 0.925
and has increased minimally since then.

Anemic GDP growth can be seen in unemployment statistics (Figure 5). Reaching
a high of 10.0 percent in October 2009, the unemployment rate falls to 7.8 percent in
September 2012. There is no "M" traced out (see Figure 2). However, the labor market remained weak. Corresponding to this slow and minimal decline in the unemployment rate are the values for the median number of weeks unemployed and the
percentage of the unemployed who experienced unemployment for 27 weeks or more
(long-term unemployment). Both of these values remained high in July 2012 at
39 weeks and 18.8 percent, respectively, and were essentially unchanged from the

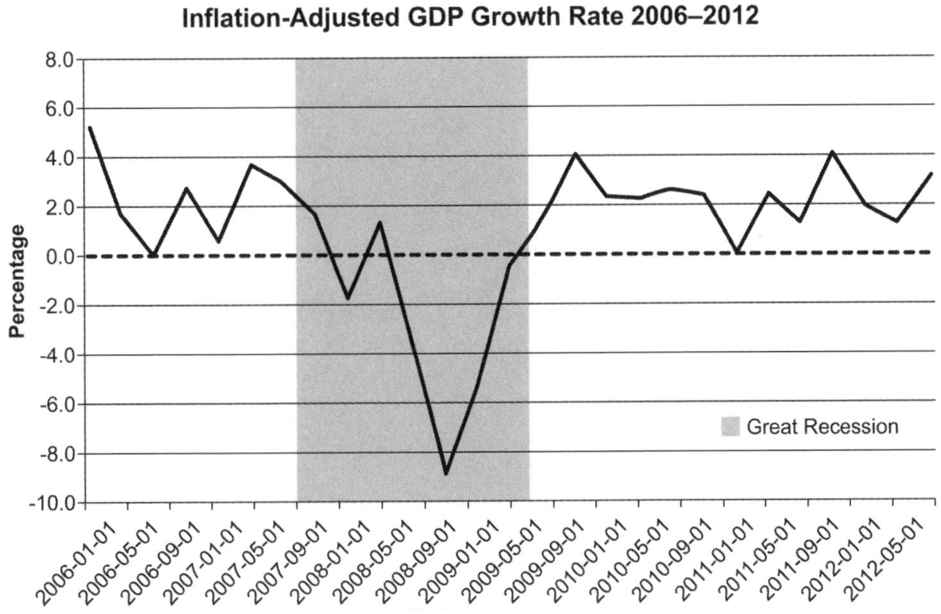

Inflation-Adjusted GDP Growth Rate 2006–2012

Figure 3
(*Source:* Calculations based on FRED Data, Federal Reserve Bank of St. Louis, GDCC1, http://research.stlouisfed.org/fred2/series/GDPC1)

late 2009 values. Weak economic growth and high unemployment coupled with lengthy spells of unemployment also contributed to high poverty rates.

Unlike the high inflation rates of the late 1970s and early 1980s that resulted in contractionary monetary policy and a double dip recession as shown in Figure 1, the inflation rate during, and subsequent to, the Great Recession remained in check. If there was a concern, it was over deflation. Concerns over deflation surface when the inflation rate runs into the negatives as it did October 2008 through May 2009. Deflation is a concern for two reasons. First, if prices on consumer goods and services are falling, then consumers have an incentive to postpone purchasing consumer durables such as cars and home appliances while they wait for prices to fall further. In turn, this can lead to further price discounts as retailers try to move merchandise. Second, as wages fall it makes it more difficult for households to make monthly payments on debts (e.g., mortgages). Both of these results adversely affect economic growth (Bordo 2005; Fuhrer 2003–2004; Krugman 2010). Despite falling prices from October 2008 to May 2009, consumers did not foresee a full-fledged deflationary period. Consumer expectations for the inflation rate remained in the 2.0 to 4.0 percent range.

During and after the Great Recession the Federal Reserve engaged in aggressive monetary policy (see Section 1, "Policy, Monetary"). The Fed put more than a trillion dollars of new money into the economy. One might expect that this would

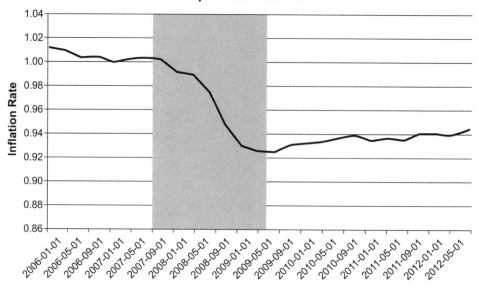

Figure 4

(*Note*: Shaded area indicates the Great Recession. *Source*: Calculations based on FRED Data, Federal Reserve Bank of St. Louis, GDCC1 and GDPPOT, http://research.stlouisfed .org/fred2/series/GDPC1 and http://research.stlouisfed.org/fred2/series/GDPPOT)

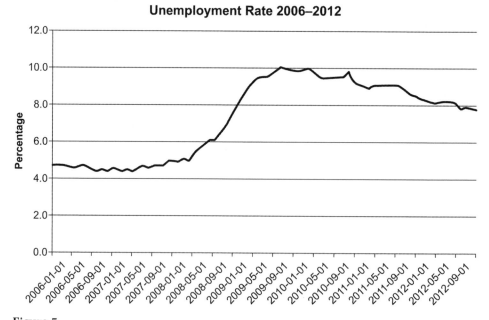

Figure 5

(*Source*: FRED Data, Federal Reserve Bank of St. Louis, UNRATE, http://research.stlouisfed .org/fred2/series/UNRATE)

cause both increasing inflation and inflation expectation rates. However, this did not occur because banks decided to keep these funds out of circulation. (For a further explanation of why this was the case see Section 1, "Policy, Monetary.") With inflation and inflation expectations in check, the Fed did not contemplate raising interest rates as it did in the early 1980s.

OUTLOOK

As this essay has discussed, there was no double dip recession associated with the Great Recession. Instead, there was weak economic growth leading to continued relatively high unemployment and poverty rates (i.e., a slow recovery). Table 1 offers forecasts for 2013 and 2014 with respect to GDP growth rates, unemployment rates, and inflation rates, from four forecasting organizations. Note first that only the Congressional Budget Office (CBO) forecasts a recession for 2013 (GDP has negative growth, –0.5). The CBO forecast assumes that Congress and the president would not agree to changes to avoid the 2012 "fiscal cliff," which would have resulted in automatic increases in federal tax rates and decreases in federal expenditures in January 2013. Fortunately, however, Congress and President Obama came to an agreement in late December 2012, and Congress passed the American Taxpayer Relief Act, avoiding the fiscal cliff (Henchman 2013). Provisions of the act include retaining current tax rates for all except those with incomes over $400,000; extending emergency unemployment compensation and benefits for 2013; and ending the 2 percent payroll tax cut. However, no action was taken on the debt ceiling (Henchman 2013). Barring unforeseen circumstances, the act and subsequent agreements will forestall any fiscal cliff–induced recession. The last columns of the table represent average values, excluding the CBO estimates. Accordingly, the average forecast inflation rates of 1.9 and 2.0 percent look good, and the unemployment rates remain fairly high at 7.8 and 7.4 percent. This latter outcome is a reflection of continued tepid economic growth of 2.1 and 2.8 percent for 2013 and 2014 respectively. One result of this slow growth will be poverty rates remaining relatively high.

Averting the fiscal cliff enables the economy to move forward without a recession. However, concerns remain. First, the European Union has relapsed into a second recession and continues to have financial difficulties with respect to the Euro currency (Chan 2012; Charlemagne 2012; Eurostat 2013; Associated Press 2012; Mead 2012; Steen 2013). A weakened European Union reduces U.S. exports to this region, and Euro currency difficulties continue to cause uncertainty in financial markets. Second, the Arab Spring, which has encompassed protests, political changes, and civil war in the Middle East and North African regions, is ongoing and has increased political instability in the Middle East (and particularly in Syria and Iran) and Egypt (Tripline 2013; National Staff 2011). Turmoil in this region

Table 1 Forecast for 2013 and 2014

Variable	The Livingston Survey		Survey of Professional Forecasters		Federal Reserve*		Congressional Budget Office		Average Values[T]	
	2013	2014	2013	2014	2013	2014	2013	2014	2013	2014
GDP growth rate	1.9	2.5	2.0	2.7	2.5	3.3	-0.5	4.4	2.1	2.8
Unemployment rate	7.8	7.4	7.8	7.5	7.8	7.4	9.1	8.4	7.8	7.4
Personal Consumption Expenditures (PCE) inflation rate	NA	NA	2.0	2.2	1.8	1.8	1.4	1.7	1.9	2.0
Consumer Price Index (CPI) inflation rate	2.1	2.1	NA	NA	NA	NA	NA	NA	2.1	2.1

*Values are the average of the central tendency range given.

[T]Average values exclude the Congressional Budget Office values and utilize only other values given.

NA Data not available.

Sources: Congressional Budget Office. "An Update to the Budget and Economic Outlook, Fiscal Years 2012–2022." Congressional Budget Office, August, 2012. Accessed ay 14, 2013. http://www.cbo.gov/sites/default/files/cbofiles/attachments/08-22-2012-Update_to_Outlook.pdf.

Federal Reserve Bank of Philadelphia. "Survey of Professional Forecasters." November 9, 2012. Accessed June 4, 2013. http://www.phil.frb.org/research-and-data/real-time-center/survey-of-professional-forecasters/2012/spfq412.pdf.

Federal Reserve Bank of Philadelphia. "The Livingston Survey." December 12, 2012. Accessed May 14, 2013. http://www.philadelphiafed.org/research-and-data/real-time-center/livingston-survey/2012/livdec12.pdf.

has relevance to the United States because of its commitment to Israel and its dependence on foreign oil. Third, with the ascendency of China as a world economic power there is concern over its potential real estate bubble and its need to transition from a very high savings rate economy to more of a consumer economy (Cowen 2012; Tian 2012; Yang 2012). A real estate bubble burst in China would negatively affect financial markets, and its high savings rate will forestall greater exports to China. Finally, as of mid-2013 there is no long-term plan for decreasing federal deficits and significantly slowing the growth of the U.S. debt. If any one, or more, of the four concerns mentioned in this paragraph materializes into a major problem, U.S. economic growth, unemployment, and poverty will be negatively affected, and the possibility of the economy slipping into a recession increases.

FURTHER READING

Associated Press. "Eurozone Back in Recession," November 15, 2012. Accessed January 11, 2013. http://www.cbsnews.com/8301-505123_162-57550157/eurozone-back-in-Recession/

Aversa, Jeannine. "A 'Double-Dip Recession Defined." *Huffington Post*, July 1, 2010. Accessed January 9, 2013. http://www.huffingtonpost.com/2010/07/01/a-doubledip-Recession-def_n_633004.html

Bordo, Michael, and Andrew Filardo. "Deflation in Historical Perspectives." Bank for International Settlements, Working Papers No. 186, November 2005. Accessed January 11, 2013. http://www.bis.org/publ/work186.htm

Chan, Tsu Ping. "Eurozone in Double-Dip Recession: As It Happened." *Telegraph*, November 15, 2012. Accessed January 11, 2013. http://www.telegraph.co.uk/finance/debt-crisis-live/9679140/Eurozone-in-double-dip-recession-as-it-happened.html

Charlemagne. "The Lingering Limbo." *Economist*, October 8, 2012. Accessed January 10, 2013. http://www.economist.com/blogs/charlemagne/2012/10/euro-crisis/print

Cowen, Tyler. "Two Prisms for Looking at China's Problems." *New York Times*, August 11, 2012. Accessed January 10, 2013. http://www.nytimes.com/2012/08/12/business/two-ways-to-see-chinas-problems-economic-view.html?_r=0

Economic Cycle Research Institute. "Indexes," 2013. Accessed January 9, 2013. http://www.businesscycle.com/ecri-reports-indexes/all-indexes#

Elwell, Craig K. "Double-Dip Recession: Previous Experience and Current Prospect," December 3, 2010. Congressional Research Service Report for Congress. Accessed January 9, 2013. http://www.hsdl.org/?view&did=12006

Elwell, Craig K. "Double-Dip Recession: Previous Experience and Current Prospect," August 31, 2011a. Congressional Research Service Report for Congress. Accessed January 9, 2013. www.hsdl.org/?view&did=718935

Elwell, Craig K. "Double-Dip Recession: Previous Experience and Current Prospect," December 9, 2011b. Congressional Research Service Report for Congress. Accessed January 9, 2013. http://www.hsdl.org/?view&did=718384

Elwell, Craig K. "Double-Dip Recession: Previous Experience and Current Prospect," June 19, 2012a. Congressional Research Service Report for Congress. Accessed January 9, 2013. http://www.hsdl.org/?view&did=713663

Elwell, Craig K. "Economic Recovery: Sustaining U.S. Economic Growth in a Post-Crisis Economy." Congressional Research Service Report for Congress, November 29, 2012b. Accessed January 9, 2013. http://www.hsdl.org/?view&did=726877

Eurostat. "Most Popular Databases (Real GDP Growth Rate, Unemployment Rate)," 2013. Accessed January 11. http://epp.eurostat.ec.europa.eu/portal/page/portal/eurostat/home/

Federal Reserve Bank of St. Louis. "FRED Economic Data. Series: PCEPI, MICH," 2013. Accessed January 11. http://research.stlouisfed.org/fred2/

Federal Reserve Education. "History of the Federal Reserve," 2013. Accessed January 9. http://www.federalreserveeducation.org/about-the-fed/history/

Financial Times. "Double-Dip Recession," 2013. Accessed January 9, 2013. http://lexicon.ft.com/Term?term=double_dip-recession

Fuleky, Peter. "Details of the Fiscal Cliff Deal." Economic Research Organization at the University of Hawai'I, January 3, 2013. Accessed January 10, 2013. http://www.uhero.hawaii.edu/news/view/205

Fuhrer, Jeffrey, and Geofffrey Tootell. "What Is the Cost of Deflation?" Federal Reserve Bank of Boston, 2003–2004. Accessed January 10, 2013. http://www.bos.frb.org/economic/nerr/rr2004/q1/index.htm

Goodfriend, Marvin, and Robert G. King. "The Incredible Volcker Disinflation." *Journal of Monetary Economics* 52, no. 5 (2005): 981–1015.

Halo, Li. "US Double Dip Recession 2012: ECRI, Roubini Say It's Coming." *International Business Times*, March 15, 2011. Accessed January 9, 2013. http://www.ibtimes.com/us-double-dip-recession-2012-ecri-roubini-say-it%E2%80%99s-coming-425660

Henchman, Joseph. "Details of the Fiscal Cliff Tax Deal." Tax Foundation, January 1, 2013. Accessed January 10, 2013. http://taxfoundation.org/blog/details-fiscal-cliff-tax-deal

Krugman, Paul. "Why Is Deflation Bad?" *New York Times*, August 2, 2010. Accessed January 11, 2013. http://krugman.blogs.nytimes.com/2010/08/02/why-is-deflation-bad/

Leonhardt, David. "Rising Fears of Recession." *New York Times*, September 2011. Accessed January 9, 2013. http://www.nytimes.com/2011/09/08/business/economy/american-economy-on-the-verge-of-a-double-dip-recession.html?_r=0

Mead, Nick, and Garry Blight. "Eurozone Crisis: A Timeline of Key Events." *Guardian*, November 2, 2012. Accessed January 10, 2013. http://www.guardian.co.uk/business/interactive/2012/oct/17/eurozone-crisis-interactive-timeline-three-years

National Bureau of Economic Research. "US Business Cycle Expansions and Contractions," 2013. Accessed January 9. http://www.nber.org/cycles.html

National Staff. "The Arab Spring Country by Country." *National*, June 17, 2011. Accessed January 10, 2013. http://www.thenational.ae/news/world/middle-east/the-arab-spring-country-by-country

Norris, Floyd. "Time to Say It: Double Dip Recession May Be Happening." *New York Times*, August 4, 2011. Accessed January 9, 2013. http://www.nytimes.com/2011/08/05/business/economy/double-dip-Recession-may-be-returning.html

Rickards, James. "Why We Should Still Be Worried about a Double-Dip Recession." *US News*, February 27, 2012. Accessed January 9, 2013. http://www.usnews.com/opinion/blogs/economic-intelligence/2012/02/27/why-we-should-still-be-worried-about-a-double-dip-Recession

Roubini, Nouriel. "The Risk of a DoubleDip Recession Is Rising." *Financial Times*, August 23, 2009. Accessed January 9, 2013. http://www.ft.com/cms/s/0/90227fdc-900d-11de-bc59-00144feabdc0.html#axzz2HUihbBmT

Roubini, Nouriel. "Double-Dip Days." Project Syndicate, July 16, 2010. Accessed January 9, 2013. http://www.project-syndicate.org/commentary/double-dip-days

Roubini, Nouriel. "That Stalling Feeling." *Slate*, June 22, 2011. Accessed January 9, 2013. http://www.slate.com/articles/business/project_syndicate/2011/06/that_stalling_feeling.html

Steen, Michael. "ECB Hails Financial Market 'Normalisation.'" *Financial Times*, January 10, 2013. Accessed January 10, 2013. http://www.ft.com/intl/cms/s/0/02fcff3a-5b14-11e2-8d06-00144feab49a.html#axzz2Hbya4bFr

Tian, Wei. "Housing Prices at 16-Month Low." *China Daily*, June 2, 2012. Accessed January 10, 2013. http://europe.chinadaily.com.cn/business/2012-06-02/content_15454712.htm

Tripline. "Map of the Arab Spring Protests," 2013. Accessed January 10, 2013. http://tripline.net/trip/Map_of_the_Arab_Spring_Protests-2173004375451003A9ECA90105EA623D?text=1

Tseng, Nin-Hai. "What's a Double Dip? No One Really Knows." CNNMoney, July 8, 2010. Accessed January 9, 2013. http://money.cnn.com/2010/07/08/news/economy/double_dip_Recession.fortune/index.htm#

Yang, Jia Lynn. "As China's Economy Slows, Real Estate Bubble Looms." *Washington Post*, October 2, 2012. Accessed January 10, 2013. http://articles.washingtonpost.com/2012-10-02/business/35500560_1_home-prices-real-estate-chinese-home-buyers

A "NORMAL ECONOMY"— WHEN?

Timothy J. Essenburg

OVERVIEW

"When will the economy be normal?" implies that there actually is some concrete definition of normality. However, the economy is a socially alive ever-evolving system. In some sense there is no normal, but there are desirable and nondesirable economic conditions. The U.S. economy has experienced a great deal of fluctuation even in modern times. Prior to the Great Recession the time period characterized as the most "abnormal" would be Great Depression, the decade of the 1930s. After that, the first half of the 1940s was substantially influenced by World War II, and the remainder of the 1940s was spent adjusting to millions of GIs returning home and transitioning from a war-supporting economy to a civilian-oriented economy. The 1950s offered a clear break from World War II and the transition afterward.

This essay will discuss the time period from the 1960s to the present in more depth in order to further explore the question: "When will the economy be normal?" After examining data on various economic measures from these decades (where data is available) and the years surrounding the Great Recession, it will become apparent that despite the difficulty of defining normality, one might define normal/desirable as national unemployment rates below 5.0 percent, poverty rates below 11.5 percent, and strong wage growth for the lower 40 percent of households that results in declining income inequality. It will also become clear that the time period of the 1960s represented a desirable normal to which the nation could hope to aspire. Using this definition of normal, this essay will explore the outlook for the

A help wanted sign hangs in a cafe window. As the economy turned around, investors became more confident and more jobs became available despite the fact that unemployment rates remained stubbornly high. (Lauri Wiberg/iStockPhoto.com)

U.S. economy in the years after the Great Recession and conclude that a normal/desirable economic state is not in the foreseeable future.

THE PRESENT: DEFINING TODAY'S NORMAL BY LOOKING TO THE PAST

There are three key variables by which the U.S. economy is assessed: (1) inflation-adjusted gross domestic product (GDP) growth rate, (2) unemployment rate, and (3) inflation rate. In addition to these variables, broadly described, this section also provides data on poverty, distribution of income, federal deficits and debt, and health insurance. These variables will offer a data-driven picture of the performance of the U.S. economy over time. From this data emerges an understanding of the historical time periods during which economic conditions were favorable and some definition of normality, or at least desirable economic outcomes.

THE BIG THREE: GDP, UNEMPLOYMENT, AND INFLATION

There are three ways of looking at GDP data. Figure 1 presents data on actual and estimated potential growth rates. The potential growth rate is an estimate

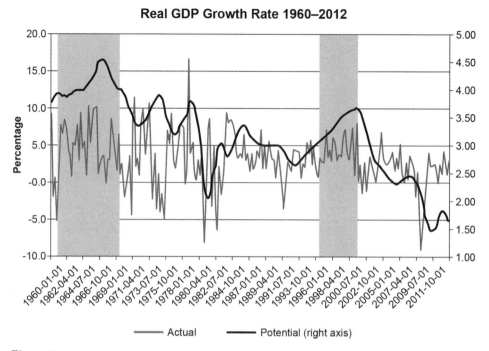

Figure 1

(*Note:* Gray shaded areas represent time periods of three or more consecutive years for which the potential growth rate exceeded 3.0 percent and actual average growth rate was at or above 3.5 percent. *Source:* Calculations based on FRED Data, Federal Reserve Bank of St. Louis, GDCC1 and GDPPOT, http://research.stlouisfed.org/fred2/series/GDPC1 and http://research.stlouisfed.org/fred2/series/GDPPOT)

of GDP if resources are fully employed. During the time periods marked by the gray shaded areas in Figure 1 there were three or more consecutive years of both potential growth rates in excess of 3.0 percent and average actual growth rates at or above 3.5 percent. Comparing the two gray shaded areas the 1960s shows the best growth rates for the longest period of time.

An output ratio (actual GDP divided by potential GDP) of 1.00 implies that the economy is at its potential. Time periods with an output ratio of 1.01 or more for at least 2.5 years have happened just twice in the past 50 years, most recently in the late 1990s. As with Figure 1, Figure 2 shows that the 1960s had the best output ratio for the longest time.

Unemployment data corroborates the fact that the economy was strong during the 1960s. Figure 3 combines two variables, the actual employment rate and the employment rate economists estimate will exist when the GDP is equal to its potential. The "line" in Figure 3 that acts as a floor for the rising portions of the chart (the "stalagmite" years) and as a ceiling for the dropping portion (the "stalactite" years) is a representation of this unemployment measure created by economists. It ranges

Output Ratio 1960–2012

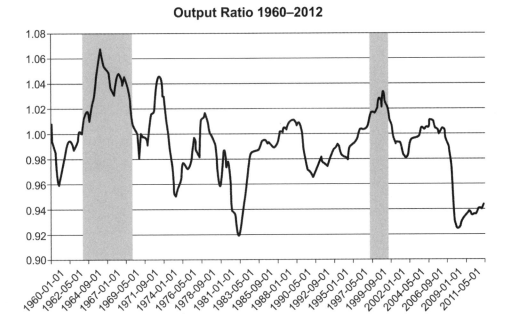

Figure 2

(*Note:* Gray shaded areas represent time periods of at least 2.5 years when the output ratio equaled 1.01 or higher. *Source:* Calculations based on FRED Data, Federal Reserve Bank of St. Louis, GDCC1 and GDPPOT, http://research.stlouisfed.org/fred2/series/GDPC1 and http://research.stlouisfed.org/fred2/series/GDPPOT)

from 5.0 to 6.27 percent. In the past 50 years the 1960s, particularly the late 1960s, stands out. From 1965 to 1969 the monthly unemployment rate rose above 5.0 percent only once, and the average for the entire five years was 3.8 percent. From 1970 through 2012 there was only a single month (April 2000) with an unemployment rate as low as 3.8 percent.

Figure 4 provides more evidence that the 1960s is the kind of economic normal that the vast majority of persons desire. The latter months of the 1960s (the only months for which data are available) saw the shortest periods of unemployment (around five weeks) and the lowest percentage of the unemployed who experienced unemployment for 27 weeks or more (around 5 percent). Going forward these values only worsen (the thin lines represent the trends), with the worst performance associated with the Great Recession.

The last of the "big three" is inflation. Until January 2012 the Fed had never set an inflation rate target value or range. Historical monetary policy changes taken by the Fed would indicate that the it acted as if a range between 1.0 and 3.0 percent were the targeted range. This changed in January 2012 when the Fed announced a target value of 2.0 percent (Board of Governors 2012). Because the actual inflation rate in any shorter time period will differ from the target, the 1.0 to 3.0 percent range

Unemployment Rate 1960–2012

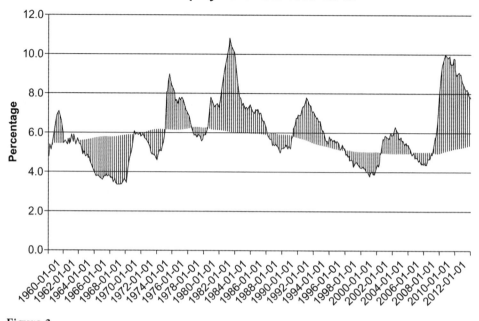

Figure 3

(*Source*: FRED Data, Federal Reserve Bank of St. Louis, UNRATE and NROU, http://research
.stlouisfed.org/fred2/series/UNRATE and http://research.stlouisfed.org/fred2/series/NROU)

Unemployment Data, 1967–2012

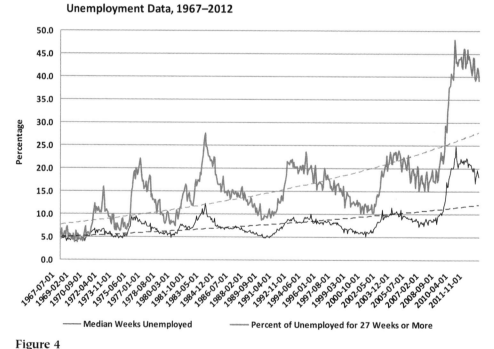

Median Weeks Unemployed   Percent of Unemployed for 27 Weeks or More

Figure 4

(*Note:* The dashed lines are trend lines for each of the unemployment measures. *Source*: FRED
Data, Federal Reserve Bank of St. Louis, UMPMED, http://research.stlouisfed.org/fred2/series/
UEMPMED and /LNU03025703-http://research.stlouisfed.org/fred2/series/LNU03025703)

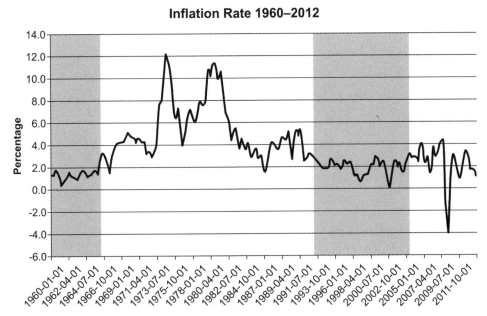

Figure 5

(*Note:* Gray shaded areas indicate an inflation rate below 3.0 percent for more than 3 years. *Source:* FRED Data, Federal Reserve Bank of St. Louis, PCECTPI, http://research .stlouisfed.org/fred2/series/PCECTPI?cid=9. *Note:* Calculations for annualized inflation rates based on quarterly data and using six-month intervals.)

is used here as a desirable range. Looking at Figure 5 there are two periods where the inflation rate remained below 3.0 percent for more than 3 years: 1960 to 1966 and 1992 to 2003. Desirable GDP growth rates during the 1963 to 1966 and 1995 to 1999 time periods, and the unemployment rates experienced during the 1964 to 1966 and 1997 to 2001 time periods overlapped with some of the preferable inflation rate years.

FEDERAL DEFICITS AND DEBT

During the aftermath of the Great Recession it was clear that politicians and the public felt that federal deficits and debt had reached undesirable levels, and both groups expressed a desire to see federal deficits and debt at a more desirable, or normal, level. However, what is normal or desirable in terms of the federal deficit and debt? Deficits were less than 1.5 percent of GDP for much of the 1960s and the latter part of the 1990s through 2002. These time periods are highlighted in Figure 6 and can be considered times during which the federal deficit was at desirable levels. In fact, the situation was so good during the second Clinton administration that small surpluses were generated. Looking at the federal debt as a percentage of GDP, the country was at 32 percent when Reagan took office in

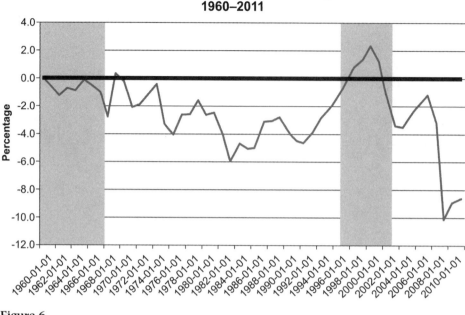

Figure 6

(*Note:* Gray shaded areas represent time periods when the federal budget balance is at desirable levels. *Source:* FRED Data, Federal Reserve Bank of St. Louis, FYFSGDA188S, http://research.stlouisfed.org/fred2/series/FYFSGDA188S)

1981. Large increases came during the Reagan and George H. W. Bush years (1980 to 1992; during the earlier part of Reagan's first term there was a severe recession). At the beginning of the Great Recession, in December 2007, the federal debt was 65 percent of GDP. Over the last year of the George W. Bush's second term through Obama's first term the percentage rose to 99 percent. Significantly, the relatively low and declining values of the federal debt as a percentage of GDP during the latter 1960s were associated with the buildup for the Vietnam War. The years of war with Iraq and Afghanistan, starting in 2003 and going to the beginning of the Great Recession, were not associated with similar declines.

Summarizing the big three (GDP, unemployment, and inflation) and federal deficits and debt, the clear "winning" years occurred during the 1960s. The second best economic time period was the late 1990s. However, this ranking is reversed when poverty rates are considered.

POVERTY

If the 1960s saw the best economic performance over the past 50 years, why is this not true for poverty rates? The answer is twofold. First, poverty was not a public policy concern, per se, until the mid-1960s when the Johnson administration waged its War on Poverty beginning in 1964. Second, civil rights legislation prohibiting discrimination based on race and sex was enacted during the 1960s. This allowed women and persons of color to secure better education and employment, and thus improve their economic situation and reduce poverty. Ten years after these public policy changes took effect brings the nation up to 1975, so looking at the time period from 1975 to 2011 provides a set of poverty rates that is less reflective of the initial impact of the War on Poverty and civil rights policy shifts. As Figure 7 shows, excepting for the latter part of the 1970s the only other time of relatively low poverty rates was in the latter part of the 1990s.

Turning to the demographics of poverty (age, sex, race, and socioeconomic class), rates for children and females have actually increased since 1975, with the exception of the late 1990s. This is tied to the rise in female-headed households. Over this same time period poverty rates by race indicate stagnation at best. Finally, there has been no reduction in the percentage of persons with incomes at various ratios (0.75, 1.25, and 1.75) of the poverty threshold. (An income to poverty ratio is calculated by dividing a household's income by the poverty threshold for the household size.) Together these figures indicate that across age, sex, race, and class, no substantial or more permanent decline in poverty has occurred during the 1975 to 2011 time period. Thus, there really is no desirable set of years regarding the poverty rate from which to set a desirable normal. The United States has not done well over the past 35 years in terms of poverty reduction.

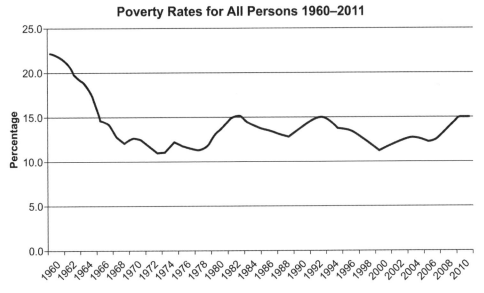

Figure 7
(*Source*: U.S. Census, Historical Poverty Tables-People, Table 2: "Poverty Status of People by Family Relationship, Race, and Hispanic Origin: 1959 to 2011," http://www.census.gov/hhes/www/poverty/data/historical/people.html)

DISTRIBUTION OF INCOME

Although the 1960s and mid-1990s to 2000 were strong economic growth years with low unemployment rates, these data do not describe the distribution of income generated during these times. The Gini coefficient is a measure of income inequality across households (Figure 8). It ranges from a low of 0.00 to a high of 1.00, where higher values represent greater income inequality. Of interest here is the fact that the strong economy of the 1960s (Figures 1 to 6) and the decade in which poverty rates also fell substantially (Figure 7) also came with the lowest Gini coefficient values of the past 50 years. Current international data indicate that the lowest country value is 0.23 (Sweden) and the highest value is 0.71 (Namibia) (CIA 2013). Out of 138 countries for which data is available, the United States ranks ninety-fifth (CIA 2013). If the United States had maintained its 0.348 value from 1968, today it would rank fiftieth.

This inequality is borne out by the data presented in Table 1. Inflation-adjusted average incomes for each fifth (or quintile) of the total families are given, where the middle three quintiles can be thought of as the middle class. For example, in 2005 the average family income in the lower-income group was $16,492 and for the upper-income set of families it was $196,891. While all quintiles saw income gains from 1966 to 2005, clearly the greatest gains were experienced by the top two quintiles. Over a 40-year period the lowest quintile saw gains of 19.5 percent, compared

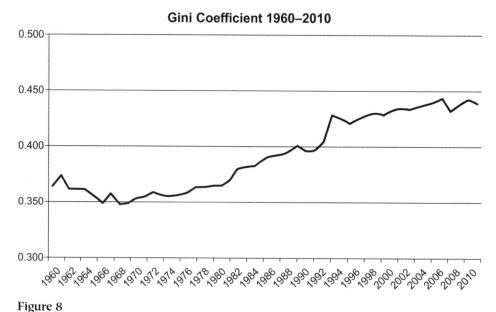

Figure 8

(*Source*: U.S Census, Historical Income Tables-Income Inequality, Table F-4, "Gini Ratios for Families, by Race and Hispanic Origin of Householder: 1947 to 2010," http://www.census .gov/hhes/www/income/data/historical/inequality/)

Table 1   Distribution of Income by Quintile and Top 5 Percent (2010 dollars)

Year	Lowest Fifth	Second Fifth	Third Fifth	Fourth Fifth	Highest Fifth	Top 5 Percent
1966	13,803	30,643	43,845	58,695	100,174	153,820
1975	16,091	34,017	50,580	69,254	116,705	171,198
1985	15,206	34,893	53,874	77,223	137,238	205,088
1995	16,003	36,871	57,728	84,464	169,693	291,025
2005	16,492	39,243	62,797	93,921	196,891	344,699
Percentage Increase, 1966 to 2005	19.5	28.1	43.2	60.0	96.5	124.1

Source: U.S Census Bureau. "Historical Income." *Tables*: Income Inequality, Table F-3. Mean Income Received by Each Fifth and Top 5 Percent of Families, All Races: 1966 to 2010." http://www.census.gov/hhes/www/income/data/historical/inequality/.

to 96.5 percent and 124.1 percent income increases for the top fifth and top 5 percent, respectively. A significant body of research indicates that large and growing income inequalities are associated with lower social well-being (e.g., Senik 2009; Centre for Confidence and Well Being 2013; Equality Trust 2013). In this sense, the 1960s again represents desirable outcomes, or a desirable normal.

HEALTH INSURANCE

While the United States is the only high-income country that does not provide health insurance to all residents, it did complement private insurance (employment-based and direct purchase) with Medicare for retired persons and Medicaid for lower-income persons starting in the 1960s. Available data, starting in 1987, show that the percentage of persons with health insurance coverage has declined slightly, from 87.1 percent in 1987 to 84.3 percent in 2011 (Figure 9). However, what is hidden by these data is the source of health insurance. Health insurance can be private (employee-based or direct purchase) or government-based (Medicare, Medicaid, and military). The percentage of persons with private care has fallen, while the percentage of those with government-based insurance has risen. This is due in part to the fact that the U.S. population is aging (as a larger percentage moves into retirement age, a greater percentage use Medicare) and in part to economic reasons (a growing percentage of persons are eligible for, and are accessing, Medicaid as poverty increases). In terms of a desirable outcome, or desirable normal, it would be encouraging to see a greater percentage of the population with health insurance.

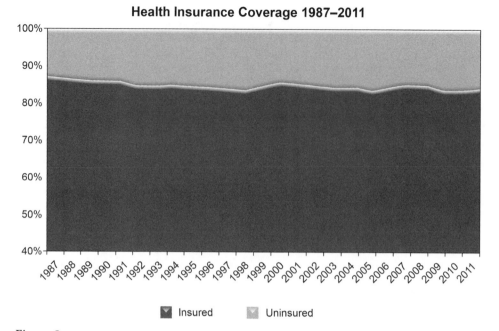

Figure 9

(*Source*: U.S. Census, Historical Health Insurance Tables, Table HI-1: "Health Insurance Coverage Status and Type of Coverage by Sex, Race and Hispanic Origin: 1987 to 2005," http://www.census.gov/hhes/www/hlthins/data/historical/orghihistt1.html; Health Insurance Historical Tables, HIB Series, Table HIB-1: "Health Insurance Coverage Status and Type of Coverage by Sex, Race and Hispanic Origin," http://www.census.gov/hhes/www/hlthins/data/historical/HIB_tables.html. *Note:* Data for 1987-2005 used Table HI-1 data, where the two entries for 1999 were averaged. Data for 2006–2011 use Table HIB-1 data.)

Summary

As this essay has discussed, answering the question "When will the economy be normal?" depends on how one defines normal. This essay has, in essence, defined normal as desirable. Thus, this essay addresses the underlying question "When will the economy be as good as it used to be?" Looking at data from the past 50 years the, big three economic variables (GDP, unemployment, and inflation) identify the 1960s and the late 1990s as time periods when economic conditions were desirable. These time periods represent a normal to which many would like to return. In terms of deficits and debt, again it is the 1960s that stand out as a desirable economic time. Income distribution in terms of poverty rates, Gini coefficients, and quintiles tell a similar story. Income inequality has increased over the past 35 years, and the various poverty rates have remained within the same numerical ranges, with the exception of increasing childhood and female poverty. Health insurance coverage also has not improved in the past 25 years. Thus, it is the 1960s that set the economic bar to which the nation would like to return.

OUTLOOK

Prior to the Great Recession the largest previous financial crash was associated with the Great Depression. By all accounts the Great Depression was worse than the Great Recession, due in large part to the fact that monetary policy during the Great Depression was inferior to that employed during the Great Recession (see Section 1, "Policy, Monetary"). One way to think about the outlook for the United States in the aftermath of the Recession is to gauge the future based on the past. As this essay has discussed, the economic state of the 1960s provides a normal to which the nation can aspire. That economically desirable time period began 30 years after the start of the Great Depression. Only the latter part of the 1990s has come close to the desirable normal of the 1960s. It might be that less desirable economic outcomes will persist going forward because the nation's economic system is ever-changing.

The U.S. economy pulled out of the Great Recession at the end of 2009. The GDP growth and inflation rates for all of 2009 were –0.08 percent and 1.37 percent, respectively, while the poverty rate was 14.3 percent. Excepting the inflation rate, these are abysmal values. Near-term forecasts for real GDP growth rates range from 2.0 to 2.6 for 2013 (see "Forecasts" in the following "Further Reading" section). However, these growth rates will not be strong enough to bring back the "good old days" of 3.0 to 4.0 percent GDP growth rates, unemployment rates of 5.0 percent or lower, and commendable increases in the incomes of the lowest-income households. This means that the poverty rate will also remain relatively high for the foreseeable future, barring a change in public policy resulting in higher incomes for the lowest quintile of households. The likelihood of this is slim as politicians grapple with the financial difficulties presented by deficits and debt in the Recession's aftermath. It appears that instead a "new normal" of higher unemployment and poverty rates will be here for some time.

FURTHER READING

Board of Governors of the Federal Reserve System. "Press Release," January 25, 2012. Accessed January 9, 2013. http://www.federalreserve.gov/newsevents/press/monetary/20120125c.htm

Central Intelligence Agency (CIA). "The World Fact Book," 2013. Accessed January 8, 2013. https://www.cia.gov/library/publications/the-world-factbook/rankorder/2172rank.html

Centre for Confidence and Well Being. "Society," 2013. Accessed January 8, 2013. http://www.centreforconfidence.co.uk/flourishing-lives.php?pid=171

Equality Trust. "The Equality Trust, Home," 2013. Accessed January 8, 2013. http://www.equalitytrust.org.uk/

European Central Bank. "Map of Euro Area 1999–2011," 2013. Accessed January 8, 2013. http://www.ecb.int/euro/intro/html/map.en.html

FORECASTS

Board of Governors of the Federal Reserve System. "Monetary Report to the Congress," July 17, 2012. Accessed October 8, 2012.http://www.federalreserve.gov/monetary policy/files/20120717_mprfullreport.pdf

Congressional Budget Office. "The Budget and Economic Outlook: Fiscal Years 2012 through 2022," January 2012. Accessed October 8, 2012. http://www.cbo.gov/sites/default/files/cbofiles/attachments/01-31-2012_Outlook.pdf

Economist. "The Economists Pool of Forecasters, July Averages," 2012. Accessed October 8, 2012. http://www.economist.com/node/21558296

Federal Reserve Bank of Philadelphia. "Livingston Survey," June 2012. Accessed October 8, 2012. http://www.phil.frb.org/research-and-data/real-time-center/livingston-survey/

Federal Reserve Bank of Philadelphia. "Third Quarter 2012 Survey of Professional Forecasters," August 2012. Accessed October 8, 2012. http://www.philadelphiafed.org/research-and-data/real-time-center/survey-of-professional-forecasters/2012/survq312.cfm

International Monetary Fund. "An Update of the Key WEO Projections," July 16, 2012. Accessed October 8, 2012. http://www.imf.org/external/pubs/ft/weo/2012/update/02/pdf/0712.pdf

Organization for Economic Co-Operation and Development. "United States: Economic Forecast Summary," May 2012. Accessed October 8, 2012. http://www.oecd.org/eco/economicoutlookanalysisandforecasts/unitedstates-economicforecastsummarymay2012.htm

Senik, Claudia. "Income Distribution and Subjective Happiness." OECD Social, Employment and Migration Working Paper 96, 2009. Accessed January 8, 2013. http://dx.doi.org/10.1787/218860720683

STRUCTURAL ECONOMIC CHANGES

Timothy J. Essenburg

OVERVIEW

A structural economic change occurs when there is a long-term, or permanent, change in how an economy operates. A cyclical change, unlike a structural change, is a change that occurs in response to the business cycle (the ups and downs of the economy) but that reverses within a few years. For example, an unemployment rate that remains elevated for two years during a recession would be a cyclical change, but an unemployment rate that remains elevated for much longer would be a structural change.

One way to understand the difference between these types of economic changes is to think of the sea and sea floor as the U.S. economy. Underneath the sea is a mountain with an active volcano; in this case the active volcano is the U.S. housing market. As the mountain grew from 2002 to 2006 it provided food and shelter for the surrounding sea creatures, and they flourished as a result. Then one day in mid-2006 the volcano erupted. The surrounding sea creatures that had once benefited from the food and shelter provided from the mountain began to suffer, and as the volcano erupted large waves spread throughout the sea. How long after the volcano goes dormant does the sea settle down and return to how it used to be? Does the sea ever return to how it was, or did the volcano cause long-term, or even permanent, change? Long-term, or permanent, changes would be structural changes, but if the changes are more temporary in nature they would be considered cyclical changes (Swanson 2012).

Recessions brought on by financial crises, such as the Great Recession, have more potential to bring about structural economic changes (Papell 2012). This is

A computer screen displays a stock market analysis. Structural changes are long-term changes in the economy that transcend a single business cycle. (Pgiam/iStockPhoto.com)

because financial crises like the Great Recession tend to bring deeper recessions and prolonged recoveries (Papell 2012; Reinhart 2009). By one account the average number of years elapsing before GDP comes back to its pre–financial crisis trend is nine, compared to only 1.5 years for non–financial crisis recessions (Papell 2012). This essay explores some of the structural economic changes arising from the Great Recession, including changes to potential gross domestic product (GDP), structural unemployment, the financial sector, middle-class income and wealth, the federal debt, and ultimately poverty. Whether the Great Recession has, or will, result in structural changes in each of these areas is not uniformly agreed upon by economists. Nonetheless, there is data that clearly indicates that, at a minimum, the changes wrought by the Great Recession will be long-lived even if they are not permanent.

THE PRESENT

CHANGE AS AN INEVITABLE PART OF A MARKET ECONOMY

While it is important to consider how an economy changes over time, it is also important to recognize that, to some degree, change itself is part of the very nature of a market economy. In 1942 an economist by name of Joseph A. Schumpeter published *Capitalism, Socialism and Democracy*. In that work Schumpeter argued that capitalism is an always changing economic system rooted in the idea of creative destruction. He put it this way:

> The essential point to grasp is that in dealing with capitalism we are dealing with an evolutionary process ... [which] is by nature a form or method of economic change and not only never is but never can be stationary. ... The fundamental impulse that sets and keeps the capitalist engine in motion comes from the new consumers' goods, the new methods of production or transportation, new markets, the new forms of industrial organization that capitalist enterprise creates. ... [This] industrial mutation ... incessantly revolutionizes the economic structure *from within*, incessantly destroying the old one, incessantly creating a new one. This process of Creative Destruction is the essential fact about capitalism. (Schumpeter 1976, 82–83)

There are three important points to take from Schumpeter's observations: (1) creative destruction comes "from within" the economic system, (2) what is changed by creative destruction is the "economic structure," and (3) the ongoing revolutions Schumpeter refers to are the inherent ups and downs (business cycles) of a market economy (Schumpeter 1976, 83 footnote 2). The Great Recession (December 2007 to June 2009) certainly fits within Schumpeter's description. The Great Recession was brought about from within. Within the United States there were new kinds of mortgages (e.g., subprime and adjustable rate), and new kinds of securities (e.g., collateralized debt obligations and credit default swaps) (see Section 1, "Housing Crisis"). These new mortgages and securities, combined with additional factors, restructured the labor market by increasing the size of the construction industry and restructuring the banking industry by increasing the role of shadow banking, or banking carried out by financial intermediaries (e.g., hedge funds) that are not subject to the same regulatory oversight that commercial banks are. These were some of the factors that brought about the creative destruction (i.e., Great Recession) of the U.S. economy from within. This creative destruction led to changes in the economic structure of the U.S. economy as well as a downturn in the economy. These structural changes will be discussed in the following sections, beginning with potential GDP.

STRUCTURAL CHANGES: POTENTIAL GROSS DOMESTIC PRODUCT (GDP)

One way to look at the relative strength of the economy is to compare the inflation-adjusted actual and potential GDP (subsequently "inflation-adjusted" is implied) (Figure 1). Note the relatively smooth dashed line for potential GDP. This line is the estimate of GDP assuming resources, most importantly labor, are

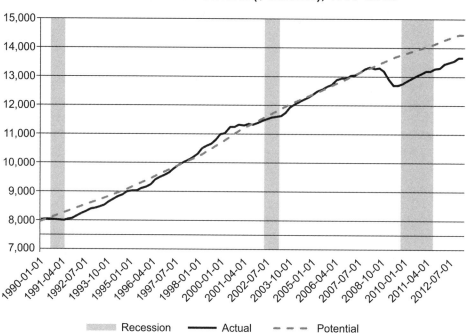

Figure 1

(*Source:* FRED Economic Data, GDPC1 and GDPPOT)

fully utilized. The smoothness of the line is reflective of the steady improvements in technology and employees' skills, and the steady growth of the labor force. These three factors are not subject to the same ups and downs of the business cycle (solid line). The solid line reflects the actual GDP and highlights the severity of the Great Recession in comparison to the recessions of 1991 and 2001.

To determine whether the Great Recession resulted in a structural change to potential GDP, one must first ask whether the Great Recession influenced the path of potential GDP. According to Federal Reserve data it has and the fact that it has can be seen in Figure 2. The solid line represents potential GDP from 2000 to 2016. The slight decrease in the slope of the line beginning with the Great Recession is almost imperceptible. However, the dashed line represents potential GDP assuming the potential GDP would have continued to grow at the average rate it did from 2004 to 2007 (i.e., if the Great Recession had not occurred). The gap between the two lines is thus indicative of a structural change. While there is debate over whether the changes to potential GDP will be permanent, the changes will certainly be long term in light of the slow recovery and thus can be considered structural.

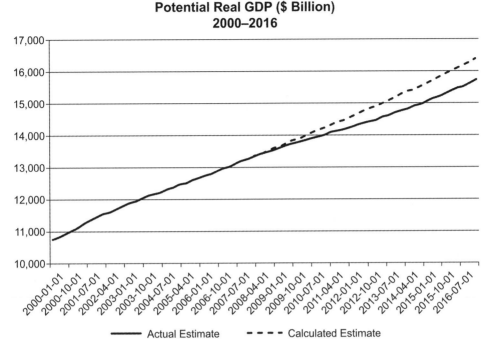

Figure 2

(*Source:* FRED Economic Data, GDPPOT. Calculations for "Calculated Estimate" based on the average annualized quarterly growth rate for 2004-2007.)

STRUCTURAL CHANGES: UNEMPLOYMENT

Likewise, there is debate over whether changes to the unemployment rate will be permanent. The full unemployment rate, or the natural unemployment rate, is the lowest rate of unemployment an economy can sustain over the long term. The gray line in Figure 3 depicts the full, or natural, unemployment rate. Notice the values range from a high of approximately 6.25 percent in 1979 to a low of 5.0 percent from 2001 through 2006. As Figure 3 shows, the actual unemployment goes up and down with the ebbs and flows of business cycles while the full, or natural, unemployment rate is less volatile. From 1957 to 1980 the natural rate rose approximately 1 percentage point. From the 1980 recession until the Great Recession the natural rate fell 1.25 points. The trend toward a declining natural rate was abruptly reversed with the onset of the Great Recession, when the natural unemployment rate rose 0.5 percentage points, or approximately 800,000 workers.

Another way to detect a change in the natural unemployment rate is to analyze the Beveridge curve. This curve matches the vacancy rate (job openings) with the unemployment rate for each quarter over a specified time period. Figure 4 shows this for 2002 to 2012, breaking it up into three periods: growth after the

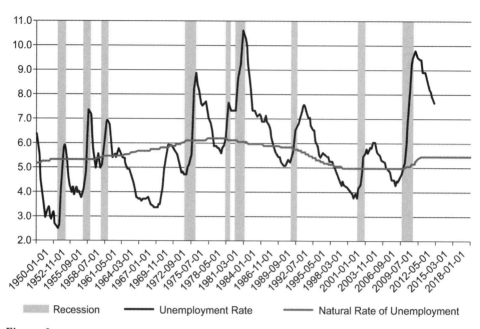

Figure 3

(*Source:* FRED Economic Data, UNRATE and NROU)

recession of 2001, the Great Recession, and recovery and expansion. In addition to these periods are trend lines for each of the three periods represented by the solid straight lines. The years of growth following the recession of 2001 exhibit a fairly uniform relationship between the unemployment rate and vacancy rate, where a 1-point change in the unemployment rate is correlated with a 0.5-point change in the vacancy rate. The Great Recession more or less follows this pattern for its nine months and then demonstrates large increases in the unemployment rate for relatively smaller decreases in the vacancy rates, something to be expected in the Great Recession. This means the trend line for the Great Recession is flatter than the trend line for the growth following the 2001 recession. The third portion of the curve starts right after the end of the Great Recession (June 2009) and runs through the end of 2012. Of importance here is that as vacancy rates once again increased, and the unemployment rates did not decrease in a pattern associated with either the Great Recession or prior growth. If there were not structural changes, one would expect the increases in the vacancy rate to be matched with decreases in unemployment, which are very close to the previous values. Instead, what occurs is a kind of shift in the curve, which is indicated by its trend line. Data have the vacancy rate around 2.7 and the unemployment rate around 7.8 percent. Compared to previous vacancy rates of 2.7, the curve predicts an unemployment

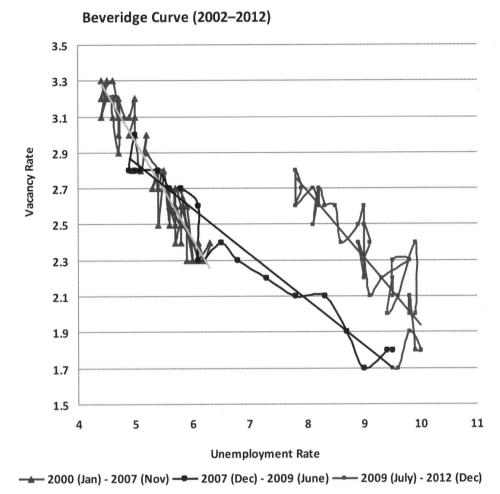

Beveridge Curve (2002–2012)

Figure 4
(*Source:* Vacancy Rate, Bureau of Labor Statistics, Job Openings and Labor Turnover Survey, JTS00000000JOR, Unemployment Rate, FRED Economic Data, UNRATE)

rate around 6.0 percent. This difference of 1.8 percentage points may represent structural change in the unemployment rate. Disaggregating the data, one can see that the shift is due primarily to three demographic groups: those unemployed for longer than 27 weeks and two sectors, government and construction, that were hard hit by the Recession (author's calculations).

STRUCTURAL CHANGES: MIDDLE CLASS INCOME AND WEALTH

The unprecedented length of unemployment spells during the Great Recession leads to concerns regarding accompanying declines in income and wealth. The unemployed are hit particularly hard with loss of income and frequently draw down available savings (wealth) during their unemployment spell. In addition, following unemployment spells associated with recessions re-employed workers, compared to those who retained employment, earn annual incomes 9 to 20 percent less, depending on the length of the unemployment spell and the degree to which an individual's job skills have deteriorated (Davis 2011; Greenstone 2011; Jacobson 2011; Oreopoulos 2008; Stevens 1997). Declining income and wealth for those who lose jobs during a Recession may also affect the educational performance of their children and the long-term income levels of their children (Stevens 2009; Stevens 2013).

The Great Recession also brought on an additional loss of wealth that affected the unemployed and employed alike: the loss in housing values. The burst housing bubble, financial crisis, and high unemployment rates all led to a substantial loss of income and wealth for middle-class families. Table 1 shows that Recession-era median family income and median family wealth percentage losses were greater for middle-class families (those in the 20 to 79.9 percent ranges in Table 1) than losses for either lower-class or upper-class families. Furthermore, median leverage ratios (the ratio of debt to assets) for the middle class increased significantly. This is because as housing values declined, homeowners lost equity (assets) while their debt (mortgage owed) remained the same. These losses decreased economic security for much of the middle class. For example, in a 2012 Pew Research survey 85 percent of middle-class respondents said it was more difficult than 10 years ago to maintain a middle-class lifestyle, and 43 percent said it would take them five or more years to recover from the Great Recession (Pew Research Center 2012). These changes have led to growing concerns about the middle class and constitute a structural change because while the loss of income and wealth for the middle class may not be permanent, it is certainly a long-term concern.

STRUCTURAL ECONOMIC CHANGES: FINANCE (DEBT AND CREDIT)

Due in large part to the loss of income and wealth experienced by many during the Recession, the Recession also led to structural changes in the area of finance, namely, restricted access to credit and declining household debt. Housing prices have remained fairly stable since the middle of 2009, but at the end of 2012 they were still only 70 percent of their 2006 high (Federal Reserve Bank of St. Louis 2013b). Mindful of this loss of wealth, and other wealth and income losses experienced during the Recession, households reduced their debt payments from 14.0 percent of disposable income in 2007 to 10.6 percent at the end of 2012. While there was a substantial credit crunch (see Section 4, "Access to Credit") during the Recession, credit conditions, as measured by the National Financial Condition Index of the Chicago Federal Reserve, began to improve six months after the official June 2009 end of the Recession. Still, households did not take

Table 1 Changes in U.S. Family Finances, by Percentile of Income (2001–2010; 2010 dollars)

What Is Measured	Year			Percentage Change	
	2004	2007	2010	2004 to 2010	2007 to 2010
Median before-Tax Family Income ($1,000s)					
0–19.9%	12.8	12.9	13.4	4.7	3.9
20–39.9%	29.5	30.1	28.1	−4.7	−6.6
40–59.9%	49.8	49.6	45.8	−8.0	−7.7
60–79.9%	78.5	78.7	71.7	−8.7	−8.9
80–89.9%	120.5	119.5	112.8	−6.4	−5.6
90–100%	212.7	216.8	205.3	−3.5	−5.3
Median Family Net Worth ($1,000s)					
0–19.9%	8.6	8.5	6.2	−27.9	−27.1
20–39.9%	38.8	39.6	25.6	−34.0	−35.4
40–59.9%	82.8	92.3	65.9	−20.4	−28.6
60–79.9%	184.0	215.7	128.6	−30.1	−40.4
80–89.9%	360.9	373.2	286.6	−20.6	−23.2
90–100%	1,069.7	1,172.3	1,194.3	11.6	1.9
Leverage Ratio (debt to assets)					
0–19.9%	15.1	13.5	18.3	21.2	35.6
20–39.9%	19.4	18.6	21.4	10.3	15.1
40–59.9%	23.2	24.3	26.5	14.2	9.1
60–79.9%	21.6	25.3	27.7	28.2	9.5
80–89.9%	22.7	23.3	23.0	1.3	−1.3
90–100%	9.1	8.3	9.8	7.7	18.1

Source: Bricker, Jesse, Arthur B. Kennickell, Kevin B. Moore, and John Sabelhaus. "Changes in U.S. Family Finances from 2007 to 2010: Evidence from the Survey of Consumer Finances." Federal Reserve Bulletin, Board of Governors of the Federal Reserve System, 2012. Accessed February 20, 2013. http://www.federalreserve.gov/pubs/bulletin/2012/PDF/scf12.pdf.

advantage of improving credit conditions by taking out more debt. The tendency for households to reduce debt rather than incur more debt is another structural change wrought by the Great Recession.

Reduced access to credit is another structural change brought on by the Great Recession. While credit conditions have improved since the end of the Recession (as discussed earlier in this essay), they still remained tighter than prior to the Recession, particularly in the area of mortgages. For example, in 2007 a prospective home buyer could get a 30-year, fixed-rate, prime loan for 100 percent of the home's sale price with a credit score as low as 630, and she could spend almost 38 percent of herincome on housing (Professional Risk Mangers 2012; Wessel 2011). Four years later a prime loan required up to 20 percent down (and therefore a maximum of 80 percent borrowed), a minimum credit score of 680, and a maximum of 33 percent of income spent on housing. These new credit conditions represent a structural change in the housing market. They are likely to continue and dampen the recovery of the housing industry (Professional Risk Mangers 2012; Wessel 2011). Although a much smaller market, credit conditions in the area of auto finance companies also remained restricted in the aftermath of the Recession. Before the Recession lenders were willing to make loans worth 95 to 100 percent of the car's value, but by 2011 many lenders were willing to make loans for only 80 percent of the car's value (FRED Economic Data 2013).

STRUCTURAL ECONOMIC CHANGES: FINANCE (THE DODD-FRANK ACT)

Structural changes in the area of finance were also brought about by the Financial Oversight and Consumer Protection Act of 2010 (Dodd-Frank Act). Dodd-Frank has significantly changed the regulatory framework for the financial system in response to the Great Recession. The act creates additional oversight and consumer protections in three areas of the financial services sector: (1) systemic risk and supervision, (2) oversight and control of depository and financial institutions, and (3) consumer protection (Table 2). Collectively the 398 rules of the Dodd-Frank Act are meant to increase the safety and trustworthiness of the financial system. Its provisions range from lowering debit card fees and increasing capital requirements to providing greater derivative oversight and more disclosure requirements for mortgages and credit cards (Klein 2010). Of particular note, the Dodd-Frank Act establishes four new federal organizations: (1) the Financial Stability and Oversight Council, (2) the Office of Financial Research, (3) the Federal Insurance Office, and (4) the Consumer Financial Protection Bureau. Although the act passed in 2010, of the 398 new rules to be written and implemented, only 148 were finalized as of early 2013. Of the 250 remaining rules, 129 had yet to be even proposed (Davis Polk 2013). Thus, the full structural effect of the Dodd-Frank Act remains to be seen. However, the tighter regulatory framework it creates around financial institutions and the various financial products they sell will decrease the availability of credit in comparison to the 2002 to 2006 credit boom.

Table 2 Wall Street Reform and Consumer Protection Act of 2010 (Dodd-Frank Act)

Systemic Risk and Supervision

    Financial Stability Oversight Council

    Office of Financial Research

    Authority to Act on Distressed Financial Companies

Oversight and Control of Depository and Financial Institutions

    Federal Insurance Office

    Abolished the Office of Thrift Supervision

    Capital Adequacy and Lending Standards

    Volcker Rule

    FDIC Insurance

    Derivatives, including Swaps and Asset Backed Securities

    Credit Rating Agencies

    Investment Advising

    Investor Protections

    Compensation of Executives

Consumer Protections

    Consumer Financial Protection Bureau

    Debit Card Fee

    Residential Mortgage Lending Controls

Source: Klein, Carter H., and Lee E. Dionne. "An Executive Summary of the Dodd-Frank Financial Reform Act." Jenner & Block LLP, August 2010. Accessed February 20, 2013. http://jenner.com/system/assets/publications/273/original/Dodd_Frank_Financial_Reform _Act_8.2.2010.pdf?1319809629.

STRUCTURAL ECONOMIC CHANGES: FEDERAL DEBT AND DEFICIT

The Clinton years resulted in a decline in the debt-to-GDP ratio, and the last 4 years of the Clinton Administration only (1998–2001) added $500 billion to the federal debt (see Figure 5). The declining debt-to-GDP ratio was a consequence of strong economic growth and an increase in income taxes on top income earners. However, this stellar financial picture changed beginning in 2001. In 2000 the accumulated federal debt, from over the past 225 years, was $5.7 trillion. Annual deficits beginning 2001 and ending in 2011 resulted in an additional $9.0 trillion of debt. Of this $9.0 trillion, $5.7 trillion came from the Great Recession and subsequent years, the majority of which was due to lost tax

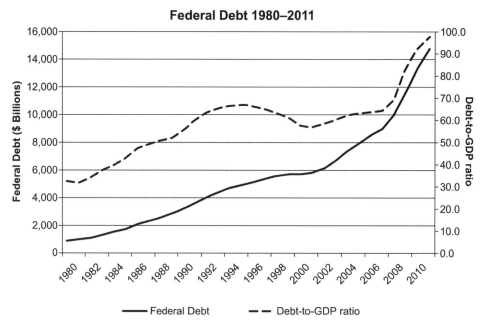

Figure 5

(*Source:* FRED Economic Data, GFDEBTN and GFDEGDQ188S)

revenues, not fiscal policy initiatives taken by the Bush and Obama administrations. During the Recession era the federal debt and deficit became a growing concern, and congressional discussions over dealing with the problem have been mired in partisan debate (see Section 5, "Political Parties and Major Legislative Responses"). The debate over the federal debt and deficit is likely to continue for some time, and thus the growing concern over this issue represents a structural shift. In addition, the decisions the federal government makes or fails to make affect the confidence of investors and the overall economy.

OUTLOOK

The Great Recession brought longer-lasting changes to the economy than are associated with most recessions, largely because it was precipitated by a financial crisis. Although economists do not uniformly agree on what constitutes a structural economic change or on what structural economic changes have occurred as a result of the Great Recession, the Recession most likely brought about structural changes in terms of a decline in potential GDP and an increase in structural unemployment. In addition, the middle class, due to unemployment and plummeting housing values, lost a great deal of income and wealth. As a result, discussions surrounding the well-being of the middle class will likely dominate political debate for some time.

In the aftermath of the Recession, households faced stricter credit conditions, which will persist for the foreseeable future. Households also reduced their debt as a way of coping with lost wealth and economic uncertainty. In the midst of these financial changes Congress passed the Financial Oversight and Consumer Protection Act of 2010 (Dodd-Frank Act) in an effort to increase the health and wellness of the financial system. This act brought further structural change to the financial system, and its full extent remains to be seen. Finally, Congress continues to grapple with the federal debt, both the additional $5.7 trillion in debt accumulated in the past four years, and future debts arising from commitments to Social Security and Medicare.

Where do all of these structural changes leave low-income families and individuals? Unfortunately, these changes leave the low-income in a difficult position. In 2000 the poverty rate was 11.3 percent, the lowest level since 1974. The poverty rate was low in 2000 largely because strong economic growth brought more employment opportunities and higher wages for those with lower levels of skill and/or educational attainment. In the aftermath of the Recession neither strong economic growth nor substantially increased employment opportunities are likely. In addition, programs and benefits for low-income persons will likely be negatively impacted by coming federal budget cuts. As a result, the poverty rate will remain elevated for years to come, and thus an elevated poverty rate is also a structural change wrought by the Great Recession.

FURTHER READING

Bricker, Jesse, Arthur B. Kennickell, Kevin B. Moore, and John Sabelhaus. "Changes in U.S. Family Finances from 2007 to 2010: Evidence from the Survey of Consumer Finances." Federal Reserve Bulletin, Board of Governors of the Federal Reserve System, 2012. Accessed February 20, 2013. http://www.federalreserve.gov/pubs/bulletin/2012/PDF/scf12.pdf

Davis Polk. "Dodd-Frank Progress Report," 2013. Accessed February 22, 2013. http://www.davispolk.com/Dodd-Frank-Rulemaking-Progress-Report/

Davis, Steven J., and Till von Wachter. "Recessions and the Cost of Job Loss." Brookings Papers on Economic Activity, 2011. Accessed February 21, 2013. http://www.brookings.edu/~/media/projects/bpea/fall%202011/2011b_bpea_davis.pdf

Federal Reserve Bank of St. Louis. "FRED Economic Data," 2013a. Accessed February 20. http://research.stlouisfed.org/fred2/

Federal Reserve Bank of St. Louis. "FRED Economic Data: SPCS20RSA, TDSP," 2013b. Accessed January 12. http://research.stlouisfed.org/

Greenstone, Michael, and Adam Looney. "Unemployment and Earnings Losses: The Long-Term Impacts of the Great Recession on American Workers." Hamilton Project,

2011. Accessed February 21, 2013. http://www.hamiltonproject.org/files/downloads
_and_links/110411_jobs_greenstone_looney.pdf

Jacobson, Louis S., Robert J. LaLonde, and Daniel G. Sullivan. "Policies to Reduce
High-Tenured Displaced Workers' Earnings Losses Through Retraining," 2011.
Accessed February 19, 2013. http://www.hamiltonproject.org/files/downloads_and
_links/11_displaced_JLS_paper.pdf

Klein, Carter H., and Lee E. Dionne. "An Executive Summary of the Dodd-Frank Financial
Reform Act." Jenner & Block LLP, August 2010. Accessed February 20, 2013. http://
jenner.com/system/assets/publications/273/original/Dodd_Frank_Financial_Reform_Act
_8.2.2010.pdf?1319809629

Oreopoulos, Philip, Marianne Page, and Ann Huff Stevens. "The Intergenerational Effects of
Worker Displacement." *Journal of Labor Economics* 26, no. 3 (2008): 455–83.

Papell, David H., and Ruyxandra Prodan. "The Statistical Behavior of GDP after Financial
Crises and Sever Recessions." *B.E. Journal of Macroeconomics* 12, no. 3 (2012): 1–31.

Pew Research Center. "Fewer, Poorer, Gloomier: The Lost Decade of the Middle Class." Pew
Research Center, August 22, 2012. Accessed February 19, 2013. http://www.pew
socialtrends.org/2012/08/22/the-lost-decade-of-the-middle-class/

Professional Risk Mangers' International Association. "US Consumer Credit Risk:
Trends and Expectations," 2012. Accessed February 22, 2013. http://www.fico.com/
en/Company/News/Pages/FICO-Surveys.aspx

Reinhart, Carmen M., and Kenneth S. Rogoff. *This Time Is Different: Eight Centuries of
Financial Folly.* Princeton, NJ: Princeton University Press, 2009.

Schumpeter, Joseph A. *Capitalism, Socialism and Democracy.* New York: Harper Torchbooks,
1976.

Stevens, Ann Huff. "Persistent Effects of Job Displacement: The Importance of Multiple Job
Losses." *Journal of Labor Economics* 15, no. 1 (1997): 165–88.

Stevens, Ann Huff. "Effects of Job Loss on Individuals and Families." Center for Poverty
Research at University of California–Davis, 2013. Accessed February 19, 2013. http://
uccs.ucdavis.edu/assets/event-assets/event-presentations/a-stevens-presentation

Stevens, Ann Huff, and Jessamyn Schaller. "Short-Run Effects of Parental Job Loss on
Children's Academic Achievement," November 2009. Accessed May 14, 2013. http://
www.nber.org/papers/w15480

Swanson, Eric. "Structural and Cyclical Economic Factors." *Economic Letter.* Federal
Reserve Bank of San Francisco. 2012. Accessed February 19, 2013.

U.S. Bureau of Labor Statistics. "Job Openings and Labor Turnover Survey," 2013. Accessed
February 22, 2013. http://data.bls.gov/timeseries/JTS00000000JOR

Wessel, David. "Prime-Mortgage Standards Tighter Than Pre-Boom Levels." *Wall Street
Journal,* November 17, 2011. Accessed February 22, 2013. http://blogs.wsj.com/
economics/2011/11/17/prime-mortgage-standards-tighter-than-pre-boom-levels/

SECTION 7

HOW DID U.S. SOCIETY RESPOND TO POVERTY DURING THE GREAT RECESSION?

INTRODUCTION TO SECTION 7

Lindsey K. Hanson

This section addresses societal responses to poverty during the Great Recession. The following essays explore societal responses from nonprofit organizations, as well as from diverse political ideologies, religious groups, and the general public. Some of the key findings from these essays follow.

NONPROFIT ORGANIZATIONS

- There was decreased funding from government, corporations, individuals, foundations, and endowments to nonprofit organizations.
- As governments at the federal, state, and local levels experienced budget deficits, many eliminated or reduced funding provided to nonprofit organizations. A 2009 study reported that 56 percent of nonprofit organizations received reduced revenue from state government, 49 percent received reduced funding from local governments, and 31 percent experienced a decrease in funding from the federal government.
- As the stock market declined and interest rates fell nonprofit endowments, like other investments, suffered.
- Private foundation grants to nonprofit organizations fell. In one survey, 53 percent of nonprofits that reported decreased funding in 2010 stated that the decreased funding was due to a decrease in grants from private foundations.
- Corporate cash donations to nonprofits dropped from the start of the Recession in 2007 to the official end of the Recession in 2009 and rebounded somewhat in 2010.
- Individual giving to nonprofits decreased. Data from the Internal Revenue Service (IRS) showed that individual donations to charities were down 10.6 percent in 2008 and 14.0 percent in 2009.

- The number of nonprofits reporting a significant increase in demand for services increased. By 2010, 41 percent of nonprofits reported a significant increase in the demand for services.
- Rising costs and decreasing funds resulted in budget deficits at many nonprofits. In 2008, 32 percent of nonprofits reported a budget deficit. This percentage increased to 39 percent in 2009.
- Nonprofit organizations responded to the decreased funding and increased demand for services in a variety of ways. Some closed their doors, while others weathered the Recession through staff layoffs, salary freezes, reduced employee benefits, and/or cutbacks on the services offered to clients.
- Nonprofit leaders, for the most part, remain optimistic about the future of their organizations and their organization's ability to continue to meet the increased demand created by the Recession, which they expect will last for some time.

POLITICAL IDEOLOGIES

- Conservatives criticized the federal government's main response, stimulus spending. Conservatives, for the most part, believed that the government's main response should have been tax cuts for businesses.
- Many liberals argued that government spending was a useful counterimpact to the decline in private sector activity. Many liberals believed that the stimulus funding that was provided was too small and favored transferring federal funds to stabilize state and local governments so that those governments did not have to cut jobs.
- Liberals tended to favor additional government programs to address poverty and related problems, while conservatives did not.
- Liberals tended to favor tax increases, particularly for the highest income earners, while conservatives favored tax cuts.
- Conservatives were more likely than liberals to believe that someone in the United States who works hard can get ahead.

RELIGIOUS GROUPS

- Religious Americans were concerned about poverty during the Great Recession. A 2010 Pew survey found that 63 percent of Americans favored additional government assistance to the poor, including 54 percent of white evangelicals, 57 percent of white mainline Protestants, 64 percent of Catholics, and 81 percent of black Protestants.
- There was relative agreement among religious groups about appropriate public policy responses. In 2011 most religious groups reacted with strong opposition as federal and state governments began proposing massive budget cuts to poverty reduction programs.
- The U.S. Conference of Catholic Bishops (USCCB) was active in calling for changes in public policy. In 2010 it called upon Congress to extend unemployment

insurance benefits, the child tax credit, and earned income tax credits. It also urged Congress to provide $1 billion for low-income housing through the National Housing Trust Fund.

- The National Council of Churches, an umbrella group for mainline Protestants, expressed concern about the deterioration of the safety net in the previous 10 to 15 years, as well as state cuts to health insurance programs for children and the poor. The organization predicted that the financial crisis would cause conditions to worsen for the poor in America.

- The National Association of Evangelicals (NAE) asserted that deficit reduction should not involve abandoning commitments to the poor. The NAE took the view that churches have an obligation to help the poor but also argued that government shares in the responsibility to meet the basic needs of the poor.

- The Jewish Council for Public Affairs (JCPA) lobbied in favor of the stimulus package because of its support for Medicaid, food stamps, unemployment insurance, investments in the green economy, and support for other programs that meet human needs. The JCPA opposed the House Republican budget plan because of its proposed cuts to programs affecting needy people and its deprioritizing of programs for the most vulnerable.

- In 2008 an interfaith initiative of Catholics, Protestants, Jews, and Muslims called on political leaders to develop plans to combat poverty and expressed concern about job losses, foreclosures, and the health crisis.

- In 2009 almost three dozen Christian, Muslim, Hindu, and Jewish organizations came together to pressure political leaders to invest in green jobs for the poor that would provide livable wages and benefits.

- A dissenting position came from a group of conservative Christian leaders who formed a group called Christians for a Sustainable Economy (CASE). The group was not composed of religious denominations, but instead represented individuals and some conservative advocacy organizations. CASE criticized a letter from over 60 religious leaders and organizations for legitimizing big government and defending ineffective and counterproductive federal welfare programs. CASE emphasized the need to rely on economic freedom and growth to encourage productivity and generosity but resolutely opposed wealth redistribution. The group encouraged charity toward the poor that also addressed the spiritual needs of the poor.

SOCIETAL VIEW OF POVERTY

- Theories as to why poverty exists can be roughly divided into structuralist and non-structuralist explanations. Those who hold to more structuralist theories of poverty believe that poverty exists because of the very structure of society (e.g., the political or economic system). In contrast, those who posit nonstructuralist explanations for poverty believe that poverty exists because of lack of effort, or some other fault, on the part of those who are impoverished.

- The Great Recession led to an increasing sense of conflict between the rich and the poor in the United States. Researchers found that 66 percent of those surveyed in 2011 felt that there was "strong" or "very strong" conflict between the rich and the poor. This was a substantial increase from the 47 percent who believed the same in 2009.
- The Great Recession led to a slight increase in the percentage of people who offer more structuralist explanations for poverty.
- In a survey of Americans, living standards of the poor ranked eighth on a list of 10 economic problems facing the nation. Thus, while U.S. constituents believed that it was important to address the living standards of the poor, there were many other issues, including the federal deficit and U.S. debt, that were of greater importance to the bulk of the population.

Nonprofit Organizations

Lindsey K. Hanson

OVERVIEW

Many nonprofit organizations serve low-income individuals and families. These nonprofits help people access public benefits, navigate the legal system, find housing and jobs, and provide child care, education, mental health treatment, crisis intervention, and addiction prevention and treatment, among other services. For example, legal aid offices advise and represent low-income clients with legal issues, and organizations such as Habitat for Humanity help low-income people buy a home of their own. Nonprofits like Catholic Charities and Volunteers of America, as well as many others, help low-income people find housing and provide a variety of other services to low-income people to help them escape poverty.

On a more systemic level, many nonprofit organizations are committed to public policy research, lobbying, and economic development that is advantageous to low-income families and individuals. Organizations such as the Sargent Shriver National Center on Poverty Law, the Southern Poverty Law Center, the National Law Center on Homelessness and Poverty, and the National Center for Children in Poverty engage in this type of work.

Like the clients they serve, the Great Recession has brought with it a variety of obstacles for nonprofit organizations. The Recession has resulted in decreased funding for nonprofit organizations from government, corporations, individuals, foundations, and endowments. At the same time the Great Recession increased the poverty rate and thereby increased the demand for the services many nonprofit organizations provide. Nonprofit organizations have responded to the dilemma created by the Recession in a variety of ways. Some have simply had to close their doors, while others have weathered the Recession through staff layoffs, salary freezes, reduced employee benefits, and/or cutbacks to the services offered to clients. Still, despite these difficulties, many nonprofits report increasing client services in response to the needs created by the Recession. Nonprofit leaders, for the most part, remain optimistic about the future of their organizations, and their organization's ability to continue to meet the increased demand created by the Recession, which will likely last for some time.

THE PRESENT: DECREASED FUNDING, INCREASED COSTS, AND DEMAND FOR SERVICES

As the federal government, as well as state and local governments, faced budgetary deficits during the Recession, government funding to nonprofits decreased. Along with reductions in government funding, nonprofits faced reduced endowment revenue as nonprofit investments suffered along with other investments during the market downturn and as interest rates dropped. Coupled with these funding reductions, nonprofits were also faced with decreased funding from private foundations (which were also facing reductions in their own funding from endowments) and decreased corporate and individual giving as corporations and individuals tightened their purse strings to weather the economic downturn. The resulting budget deficits forced nonprofits to find a variety of creative ways to reduce expenditures, including reducing staff hours, instituting salary freezes, and collaborating with other organizations. The timing for this reduction in funding could not have been worse—because as the nation faced its worst economic decline since the Great Depression, the demand for the services offered by many nonprofits drastically increased.

Decreased and Uncertain Government Funding

Government funding through grants and contracts often plays an important role in a nonprofit organization's budget and its ability to further its mission and provide client services. For example, a nonprofit organization may have a contract with the county to help individuals access public benefits such as Supplemental Nutrition Assistance Program (SNAP, formerly known as food stamps) benefits, or it may have a grant from the federal government to provide legal services to individuals facing domestic violence. Almost 33,000 nonprofit organizations classified as human service nonprofits, a type of nonprofit that often serves low-income people, received government funding in 2009 (Boris 2010). The Urban Institute found that in 2009 there were almost 200,000 contracts between nonprofits and government at all levels; these contracts totaled approximately $100 billion (Boris 2010). For

Volunteers pick up food at the Emergency Food Bank in Stockton, California, on May 7, 2008. The food will be distributed to people in need. (AP Photo/Marcio Jose Sanchez)

the majority of nonprofits surveyed, government funding was their main revenue source (Boris 2010).

As governments at the federal, state, and local levels experienced budget deficits during the Great Recession, many eliminated or reduced funding provided to nonprofit organizations. A 2009 study reported that 56 percent of nonprofit organizations received reduced revenue from state government, 49 percent received reduced funding from local governments, and 31 percent experienced a decrease in funding from the federal government (Boris 2010). In a 2010 study 32 percent of nonprofit organizations surveyed by the Nonprofit Resources Collaborative reported that a decrease in government funding negatively impacted the organization's budget (Nonprofit Research Collaborative 2010). In a second 2010 study 45 percent of nonprofits surveyed reported receiving some government funding, and of that 45 percent, 38 percent reported a decrease in government funding that year. While more nonprofits than not saw their government funding reduced, not all nonprofits faced the same fate; 32 percent reported stable government funding, and 31 percent actually reported an increase in government funding for 2010 (Nonprofit Research Collaborative 2011).

However, even among those organizations that experienced stable or increased government funding, the organization's financial concerns were further complicated by the budgetary battles being waged in the U.S. Congress and in state legislatures across the nation. As politicians battled over budgets, payments to nonprofit organizations were often delayed, and nonprofits faced uncertain future funding (Salamon 2009). In 2009, 57 percent of nonprofits that received funding from government contracts were faced with the cancellation of contracts, reductions in payments, or delayed payments. The percentage of organizations reporting late government payments was 41 percent (Boris 2010). The credit crunch that accompanied the Recession made it difficult for some cash-strapped nonprofits to access the credit needed to help the organization wait out the late payments. Some organizations had to seek emergency funding from private donors, or place staff on furlough while government payments remained delayed or uncertain (Strom 2009).

DECREASED FUNDING FROM ENDOWMENTS

Government funding was not the only concern for many nonprofits. Endowment income also fell during the Recession. An endowment is a set of funds in which a nonprofit invests to create a steady stream of income for the organization and ensure its existence long into the future. Many nonprofits, particularly larger nonprofits, have endowments. The success of endowment investments depends on the overall economic and financial performance of the economy and where the money is invested. With the declining stock market and falling interest rates during the Recession, nonprofit endowments—like other investments—suffered.

Of those endowed nonprofits surveyed by Johns Hopkins University, 80 percent lost endowment revenue between September 2008 and March 2009 because of the negative impact the Recession had on investments. Two of three nonprofits with endowments reported decreases of 20 percent or more. Interestingly, the Johns Hopkins survey actually found that nonprofit organizations experienced increased revenues in 2008 from all sources but endowments (Salamon 2009). This shows that endowment revenue was perhaps the first major impact of the Recession on nonprofits. Endowment income continued its decline in 2009, when other sources of income also began to decline. The Urban Institute found that in 2009 72 percent of nonprofit organizations saw reductions in revenue from savings and investments that year (Boris 2010).

DECREASED FOUNDATION FUNDING

Decreased endowment funding brings with it decreased funding from private foundations because private foundations are themselves nonprofit organizations that rely on funding from their own endowments to provide grants to other nonprofit organizations. Some of the nation's largest foundations include the Bill and Melinda Gates Foundation, the Ford Foundation, the Robert Wood Johnson

Foundation, and the Pew Charitable Trusts. The assets of private foundations took a major hit when the stock market crashed in 2008. Accounting for inflation, the 10 largest foundations lost around $25 billion between 2007 and 2011. Private foundation grants to nonprofit organizations fell dramatically as a result. In one survey 53 percent of nonprofits that reported decreased funding in 2010 reported that the decreased funding was due to a decrease in grants from private foundations (Nonprofit Research Collaborative 2010).

Giving from private foundations recovered slightly in 2009 and 2010, but with the largest private foundations seeing a 3.5 percent decrease from 2010 to 2011 (on average), most foundations did not increase their giving in 2011 (Nonprofit Research Collaborative 2010; Barton 2012). Overall inflation-adjusted foundation giving declined slightly in 2011, with early estimates showing that foundation giving did increase slightly in 2012 (Lawrence 2012).

DECREASED CORPORATE GIVING

There is a great deal of overlap between corporate giving and foundation giving because many large corporations have a corporate foundation that makes grants to charitable organizations (e.g., the Walmart Foundation, the Wells Fargo Foundation, and the Verizon Foundation). As corporations experienced reduced profits and market uncertainty during the Recession, they responded by reducing philanthropic efforts. Nonprofits have felt the crunch from reduced corporate giving. Fifty-five percent of organizations that experienced decreased funding from 2009 to 2010 stated that decreases in the organization's budget were primarily due to decreased corporate funding (Nonprofit Research Collaborative 2010). Detailed data on corporate giving throughout the Recession is somewhat conflicting. However, some overall trends can be seen in the data.

Corporate cash donations dropped from the start of the Recession in 2007 to the official end of the Recession in 2009 and rebounded somewhat in 2010. A survey of major corporations found that corporate giving dropped from $4.57 billion in 2007 to $4.21 billion by 2009. Most corporations (67 percent) reported reduced cash donations in 2009. The trend reversed in 2010, with 61 percent reporting increased cash donations that year, although the data showed that this increase was largely focused on disaster response efforts in Haiti (Philanthropy Journal 2011) and thus did not positively affect nonprofits focused on domestic clients. One data set showed that corporate giving was down 7.5 percent in 2009 but rose an estimated 13 percent in 2010; and when in-kind donations were accounted for the increase was 20 percent (Frazier 2011).

Corporate giving was expected to remain relatively stable throughout 2011 and 2012, and while most experts believe that corporate giving is around pre-Recession levels, or is expected to reach pre-Recession levels in the near future, the Recession has changed the face of corporate giving. Throughout the Recession corporations focused more philanthropic efforts on in-kind donations of goods and volunteer services rather than cash donations, and that trend continued after the official end of the Recession. Overall in-kind donations from major corporations increased from $5.9 billion in 2008 to $8.27 billion by 2010 (Philanthropy Journal 2011). Pharmaceutical companies in particular were responsible for a great deal of the increase in in-kind donations through their patient assistance programs that provide prescription drugs to low-income individuals (Philanthropy Journal 2011). However, the trend toward in-kind donations as opposed to cash donations gives nonprofit organizations less flexibility in meeting the needs they see as most pressing. Additionally, because a high percentage of the in-kind donations were made by pharmaceuticals directly to individual patients, nonprofit organizations never saw many of these in-kind donations.

In addition to corporations being more likely to provide in-kind than cash donations, the Recession also saw corporations more likely to focus their donations in one or two areas rather than on a variety of needs. From 2009 to 2010, 33 percent of corporations spent more than half of their donation funds on one or two issues, which was up from 24 percent prior to 2009 (Philanthropy Journal 2011). This translates to reduced budgets for many nonprofit organizations and fewer nonprofit organizations benefiting from corporate philanthropy. Corporate donors also reported that the Recession led to different types of requests. During the Recession era many nonprofits were asking corporations for assistance with items such as utility bills and rent, rather than for money to fund endowments or major long-term projects (Philanthropy Journal 2011).

DECREASED INDIVIDUAL DONATIONS

Donations from individuals play an important role in the budgets of most nonprofit organizations. Unsurprisingly, the downturn in the economy also had a negative impact on individual donations as people struggled to make ends meet and chose not to maintain pre-Recession giving patterns. Data from the Internal Revenue Service (IRS) show that individual donations to charities were down approximately 10.6 percent in 2008 and 14 percent in 2009 (McCambridge 2011). Giving USA estimates that individual donations increased by about 3.8 percent (or 2.1 percent when inflation is accounted for) from 2009 to 2010. However, an increase of 2.1 percent would still represent an 11 percent decline from pre-Recession giving levels (McCambridge 2011).

The Nonprofit Research Collaborative found that in 2010 organizations in the Midwest were slightly more likely to report increased contributions, and organizations in the West were slightly more likely to report decreased contributions. Larger organizations were more likely to report an increase, while smaller organizations were more likely to report that contributions remained stable (Salamon 2009). For nonprofits that reported decreased funding in 2010 compared to 2009, the organizations most commonly reported fewer individual donations and smaller donations as the cause of the decrease (Salamon 2009). In fact, 53 percent of organizations reported decreased funding from individual donors between 2009 and 2010 (Salamon 2009).

INCREASED DEMAND FOR SERVICES

While the Recession brought with it decreased funding for nonprofits organizations from all sources, it also brought an increased demand for services. In 2008, 31 percent of nonprofits surveyed by the Nonprofit Finance Fund reported a significant increase in demand for services, and 42 percent reported a slight increase in demand for services (Nonprofit Finance Fund 2011). In 2009 even more nonprofits, 35 percent, were reporting a significant increase in demand for services, while 36 percent were reporting a slight increase in demand for services (Nonprofit Finance Fund 2011). The number of nonprofits reporting a significant increase in demand for services again increased in 2010, this time to 41 percent, with 36 percent reporting a slight increase in demand for services (Nonprofit Finance Fund 2011).

Unsurprisingly, as nonprofits reported an increased demand for services from 2008 to 2010, nonprofits also increasingly reported an inability to meet the demand for these services. Nonprofits reporting an inability to meet the demand for services increased from 44 percent, to 49 percent, to 54 percent between 2008 and 2010 respectively (Nonprofit Finance Fund 2011). The greatest increase in demand for services was for human services nonprofits, with 78 percent of nonprofits in this sector reporting an increase. Conversely, arts organizations were the most likely to have reported a decreased demand for services (Nonprofit Research Collaborative 2011). The data clearly imply that the increased demand for services was related to the increasing poverty rate as people sought help from human services providers.

BUDGET DEFICITS

Rising costs and decreasing funds meant budget deficits at many nonprofit organizations during the Recession. In 2008, 32 percent of nonprofits reported a budget deficit. That percentage increased to 39 percent in 2009 and then decreased after the official end of the Recession in 2010, to 34 percent. Still, 26 percent of nonprofits surveyed in 2010 expected to run a deficit in 2011 (Nonprofit Research Collaborative 2011). While many organizations expected 2011 to bring increased budgets, 7 percent were concerned that their organization would have to close in

2011 due to financial problems (Nonprofit Research Collaborative 2011). Eighty-three percent of nonprofit organizations surveyed by Johns Hopkins University reported "fiscal stress" between September 2008 and March 2009. Forty percent reported that this fiscal stress was "severe" or "very severe" in nature. Mid-sized organizations were the most likely to have experienced fiscal stress (Salamon 2009).

Organizations dealt with budget deficits in a variety of ways. In 2011, 36 percent of nonprofits surveyed by the Nonprofit Finance Fund reported relying more on volunteers (Nonprofit Finance Fund 2011). For the first nine months of 2010, 22 percent of nonprofits reported utilizing volunteers to do work that was previously performed by paid staff, representing a 15 percent increase over 2009 (Nonprofit Research Collaborative 2011). Thirty-four percent reported freezing or reducing employee salaries, and 27 percent said the organization had reduced staffing levels. Nineteen percent reduced employee benefits, and 17 percent reduced staff hours. Still, many nonprofits (44 percent) made new hires, gave staff raises (39 percent), and improved staff benefits (11 percent) (Nonprofit Finance Fund 2011).

Despite budget concerns, when surveyed by the Nonprofit Finance Fund, the majority of nonprofits reported adding or expanding services (55 percent). Many organizations (47 percent) collaborated with other organizations to accomplish this. Only 26 percent reported a reduction in services provided to clients, and 49 percent reported serving more clients in 2011 than in 2010 (Nonprofit Finance Fund 2011).

A Johns Hopkins study found that almost 75 percent of nonprofits reported that between September 2008 and March 2009 the organization maintained or increased services. Conversely, only 27 percent reported service reductions. For organizations serving the economically disadvantaged, an amazing 92 percent reported maintaining or increasing services (Salamon 2009). This percentage was so high for a number of reasons. First, organizations serving the economically disadvantaged were more likely to belong to categories of service providers less likely to report financial stress because organizations most likely to report financial stress were theaters and orchestras (Salamon 2009). Theaters and orchestras also experienced greater stress from decreased donations because these types of organizations rely more heavily on donations (Salamon 2009). Still, 42 percent of human services organizations (which are likely to serve the economically disadvantaged) had a budget deficit in 2009 (Boris 2009). The ability of these nonprofits to maintain or increase services is likely due to their creative efforts to weather the Recession in order to serve their clients by instituting the staffing, volunteer, and organizational changes discussed earlier in this essay.

OUTLOOK

The resiliency that many nonprofits showed throughout the Recession is reflected in the optimistic outlook many nonprofit leaders have for the years to come. Many experts, however, express continued concerns about the nonprofit sector as the country slowly recovers from the Great Recession.

Overall fund-raising was up 3.4 percent in the first 11 months of 2011 as compared to 2010. Still, when inflation is accounted for, this is not a return to pre-Recession levels (Blackbaud 2012). While many state budgets had recovered by 2012, the ongoing debate over the federal deficit means that overall government funding is unlikely to increase for nonprofit organizations in the near future. Experts also warn that foundation grant-making will likely not rebound until 2015 (Barton 2012). Initial 2012 data showed that corporate giving increased somewhat (Lawrence 2012). Individual giving is expected to rebound somewhat faster, but the slow recovery will also mean a slow rebound for individual giving. Overall charitable giving is not expected to reach pre-Recession levels until sometime between 2015 and 2017 (Center on Philanthropy 2011).

Still, nonprofit organizations themselves remain largely hopeful for the future. Looking forward, nonprofit organizations anticipate increased demand for services to continue, and they are increasingly optimistic that revenues will go up and that they will be able to hire in order to meet the increased demand for services (Blackbaud 2011).

FURTHER READING

Barton, Noelle, and Maria di Mento. "Big Grant Makers Don't Expect to Increase Giving in 2012." *Chronicle of Philanthropy*, March 18, 2012. Accessed June 16, 2012. http://philanthropy.com/article/Grant-Makers-Won-t-Increase/131193/

Blackbaud. "2011 State of the Nonprofit Industry Survey: Executive Overview," October 2011. Accessed June 16, 2012. https://www.blackbaud.com/files/resources/downloads/Research_SONI_2011_ExecutiveOverview.pdf

Blackbaud. "Blackbaud Index," 2012. Accessed June 16, 2012. https://www.blackbaud.com/nonprofit-resources/blackbaud-index.aspx

Boris, Elizabeth T., Erwin de Leon, Katie L. Roeger, and Milena Nikolova. "National Study of Nonprofit-Government Contracting State Profiles." Urban Institute, October 7, 2010. Accessed June 16, 2012. http://www.urban.org/UploadedPDF/412227-National-Study -of-Nonprofit-Government.pdf

Center on Philanthropy at Indiana University. "U.S. Charitable Giving Shows Modest Uptick in 2010 Following Two Years of Declines," June 20, 2011. Accessed June 16, 2012. http://www.philanthropy.iupui.edu/news/2011/06/pr-GUSA.aspx

Frazier, Eric, and Marisa López-Rivera. "Corporate Giving Slow to Recover as Economy Remains Shaky." *Chronicle of Philanthropy*, July 24, 2011. Accessed June 16, 2012. http://philanthropy.com/article/Big-Businesses-Won-t/128327/

Giving USA Foundation. "Giving USA 2010: The Annual Report on Philanthropy for the Year 2009," 2010. Accessed May 28, 2012. http://www.cfbroward.org/cfbroward/media/Documents/Sidebar Documents/GivingUSA_2010_ExecSummary_Print.pdf

Lawrence, Steven. "Foundation Growth and Giving Estimates." *Foundation Center,* June 2012. Accessed May 17, 2013. http://foundationcenter.org/gainknowledge/research/pdf/fgge12.pdf

McCambridge, Ruth, and Rick Cohen. "The Other America's Philanthropy: What Giving USA Numbers Reveal in 2011." *Nonprofit Quarterly,* June 20, 2011. Accessed June 16, 2012. http://www.nonprofitquarterly.org/index.php?option=com_content&view=article&id=13306:the-other-americas-philanthropy-what-giving-usa-numbers-reveal-in-2011&catid=153:features&Itemid=336

Nonprofit Finance Fund. "2011 State of the Sector Survey," 2011. Accessed June 16, 2012. http://nonprofitfinancefund.org/files/docs/2011/2011survey_brochure.pdf

Nonprofit Research Collaborative. "Nonprofit Research Collaborative 2011," November 2010. Accessed June 16, 2012. http://www2.guidestar.org/ViewCmsFile.aspx?ContentID=3117

Nonprofit Research Collaborative. "The 2010 Nonprofit Fundraising Survey: Funds Raise in 2010 Compared with 2009." March 2011. Accessed June 16, 2012. http://foundationcenter.org/gainknowledge/research/pdf/nrc_survey2011.pdf

Philanthropy Journal. "Recession's Effects on Corporate Giving Vary," December 13, 2011. Accessed June 16, 2012. 'http://www.philanthropyjournal.org/news/top-stories/recession's-effects-corporate-giving-vary

Salamon, Lester M., Stephanie M. Geller, and Kasey L. Spence. "Impact of the 2007–09 Economic Recession on Nonprofit Organizations." Listening Post Project, Johns Hopkins University Center for Civil Society Studies, 2009. Accessed June 16, 2012. http://www.educational-access.org/Documents/Impactof2007_09EconomicRecessiononNonprofitOrganizations.pdf

Strom, Stephanie. "Credit Crisis Is Leaving Charities Low on Cash." *New York Times,* January 23, 2009. Accessed June 16, 2012. http://www.nytimes.com/2009/01/24/us/24liquidity.html?_r=1&scp=5&sq=Credit Crisis&st=cse

POLITICAL IDEOLOGIES

Fred Van Geest

OVERVIEW

All societies have a wide range of political viewpoints on different issues, and this is also true when it comes to the issue of poverty. However, in the United States these different viewpoints coalesce around two main perspectives: conservative and liberal ideologies, with moderates in between. Ideologies can be defined as a set of interrelated ideas that embody individual, social, and cultural aspirations of people. They entail different values and assumptions about the role of government, society, the nature of human beings, and justice. These differing assumptions in turn affect how people view poverty and the solutions proposed for dealing with it during the Great Recession.

While individual Americans broadly hold to these ideological views on poverty, institutions work hard to define and shape specific viewpoints and policy proposals within these ideologies. Think tanks are one set of these institutions. Think tanks are important reflections of individual political viewpoints on poverty, but they also help individuals develop their own perspectives on ideologies. The first part of this essay will present data illustrating the different ideological perspectives individual Americans have on poverty. The second half of this essay will present and discuss a representative sample of viewpoints from several think tanks that have tackled the issue of poverty during the Great Recession.

THE PRESENT

CONSERVATIVE AND LIBERAL VIEWS HELD BY AMERICANS ON POVERTY IN THE GREAT RECESSION

To illustrate commonly held conservative and liberal viewpoints that many Americans hold about how poverty should be dealt with in light of the Great Recession it is helpful to explore how leading conservative and liberal economists approach the issue in the media. The viewpoints of Stephen Moore, a senior economics writer with the conservative publication the *Wall Street Journal* is a good example of the perspective of conservative Americans. Moore, like many conservatives, is critical of the government's main response to the Recession: the stimulus legislation. Moore suggests that the stimulus legislation was political payback to Democratic interest groups. He criticized the "hundreds of billions of dollars for welfare programs" and claimed the legislation would not have much effect in creating jobs. Moore, like many conservatives, believed the legislation might even have a dampening effect on job creation. He also criticized investments in mass transit and other provisions in the bill to create "green jobs" in the renewable energy sector, saying that they supported "hopelessly inefficient technologies." For Moore and many conservatives, the fact that the private sector is not investing in certain technologies is evidence that they are not worthwhile. Although some conservatives, like House Speaker John Boehner, favored certain infrastructure spending in the stimulus bills, most conservatives hold the belief that the government's main response to the Recession should have been tax cuts for businesses to stimulate the economy (National Public Radio 2009a; National Public Radio 2009b).

A contrasting liberal view on the stimulus can be found in James Galbraith, a professor of economics from the University of Texas. Galbraith, like many liberals, argues that government spending is a useful counterimpact to a decline in private sector activity during a recession. In contrast to Moore, Galbraith claimed that the $1 trillion spending package was too small. In addition to government spending, Galbraith also favored transferring federal funds to stabilize state and local governments so that those governments did not have to cut jobs. In contrast to conservatives, Galbraith believes that tax cuts for businesses are not a practical response to a recession because in recessionary times, many businesses are not making enough profit to tax in the first place (National Public Radio 2009b).

These contrasting views on the stimulus package, and government responses to the Recession more generally, are held by many Americans. A report from the Pew Research Center in 2011 categorized Americans into nine different political typologies along the ideological spectrum (Pew Research Center 2011). To simplify, one can look at the two groups at each end of the political spectrum that match the views of Moore and Galbraith. At one end are "staunch conservatives" and at the other are "solid liberals." Table 1 shows the relative size of these groups, which

Table 1 General Characteristics of Polar Political Viewpoints in the United States

	Staunch Conservatives	Solid Liberals	Total Public
% of general public	9	14	100
% Republican	84	0	24
% Democrat	0	75	33
% Independent	16	24	43
% claiming a personal liberal ideology	3	60	21
% claiming a personal conservative ideology	88	9	39
% claiming to have a moderate ideology	3	31	36
% saying recession had no major impact on their personal finances	32	35	34
% not satisfied with their personal financial situation	43	41	51

Source: Pew Research Center. "Beyond Red vs. Blue Political Typology," May 4, 2011. Accessed January 5, 2012. http://www.people-press.org/files/legacy-pdf/Beyond-Red-vs-Blue-The-Political-Typology.pdf.

make up a relatively small proportion of the population and represent more strongly held views than those of the average American. Yet, they serve as a helpful approximation of the main ideological perspectives that are more broadly held in the population.

Table 2 shows the different views that conservatives and liberals have on poverty and other issues related to the Recession. For example, even though the financial services and banking industries had a role in contributing to the Recession, most conservatives believe that corporations make fair and reasonable profits. More conservatives than not believe that Wall Street helps more than hurts the U.S. economy. In contrast, very few liberals believe that corporations make fair profits, and a strong majority believe that Wall Street does more harm to the U.S. economy than good. Table 2 also shows that conservatives do not favor additional government programs for poverty and related problems. Eighty-seven percent of conservatives believe that government cannot afford to do much more to help the needy, while 74 percent of liberals take the opposite view.

Clearly, what is "affordable" is a highly subjective matter. However, liberals argue that as an empirical reality, the affordability argument made by conservatives does not add up when one examines historic and comparative data. Federal spending as a percentage of gross domestic product (GDP), they point out, has

Table 2   Political Viewpoints on Poverty and Related Issues in the Great Recession

	Staunch Conservatives	Solid Liberals	Total Public
% believing government is wasteful and inefficient	90	22	55
% believing most corporations make a fair and reasonable profit	78	17	39
% believing Wall Street hurts American economy more than it helps	39	59	47
% believing Wall Street helps American economy more than it hurts	48	32	38
% believing government today can't afford to do much more to help the needy	87	21	51
% believing government should do more to help needy Americans, even if it means going deeper into debt	9	74	41
% believing best way to reduce deficit is by cutting major programs	59	2	20
% favoring tax increases to reduce deficit	0	23	6
% favoring both program cuts and tax increases to reduce deficit	34	70	64
% believing new health care law will have a mostly bad effect on U.S. health care	80	1	27
% believing new health care law will have mostly good effect on health care	0	43	17
% saying most can get ahead if they work hard	79	45	62

Source: Pew Research Center. "Beyond Red vs. Blue Political Typology," May 4, 2011. Accessed January 5, 2012. http://www.people-press.org/files/legacy-pdf/Beyond-Red-vs -Blue-The-Political-Typology.pdf.

not increased dramatically. Federal spending as a percentage of GDP during the Recession (when one might expect more spending) between 2007 and 2010 averaged 22.27 percent of GDP, a rate similar to that in previous decades. Moreover, overall government spending at all levels in the United States in 2008 was 38.77 percent of GDP, significantly below the average of 41.37 percent of GDP for the 33 other advanced industrial economies in the Organization for Economic Cooperation and Development (OECD). However, many conservatives believe that government spending in relation to GDP should be kept as low as possible, and that even prior to the Recession government spending was too high (Google Public Data Explorer 2012).

On the taxation side, between 2007 and 2010 federal tax revenue averaged 16.45 percent of GDP, a rate that has not been so low since the 1950s (Office of Management and Budget 2012). During this same period the top tax rates for high-income people fell. The top marginal tax rate fell from highs of more than 70 percent for several decades in the middle of the twentieth century to lows of 35 percent at the end of the first decade of the twenty-first century. With the exception of three years in the early 1990s, rates have not been as low since just before the Great Depression (Tax Policy Center 2012). Many liberals argue that current taxation rates, particularly those on high-income earners, are too low. With increased taxation revenue, they argue, the government could do more to combat poverty and boost the economy. On the other hand, many conservatives argue that taxes are too high and that reducing taxes will stimulate the economy, which would reduce poverty.

The viewpoints liberals and conservatives hold about the ability of the poor to escape poverty also vary and may contribute to the different approaches liberals and conservatives take in addressing poverty. Seventy-nine percent of conservatives believe it is possible in the United States to get ahead if you work hard, but only 45 percent of liberals take this view (Pew Research Center 2011).

This highlights how decisions about government taxation and spending are more dependent on political viewpoints than on what is objectively possible. Of course, political viewpoints on spending decisions that affect the needy might also be contingent on the size of the federal deficit, which grew massively during the Recession. Yet, there are three ways of resolving a deficit: raising taxes, cutting spending, or a combination of both. While all options are definitely possible, the different perspectives are stark. As shown in Table 2, 59 percent of conservatives favor only cutting government programs to reduce the deficit, but only 2 percent of liberals take this view. On the other hand, 70 percent of liberals favor a combination of tax increases and programs cuts, while only 34 percent of conservatives do so. Overall, the conservative view has become more influential in the past decade. Though there are more needy people during a recession, a higher percentage of Americans believed that helping the poor and the needy was a top priority for the president and Congress before the Recession (59 percent) than believed so during the Recession (52 percent) (Pew Research Center 2011).

CONSERVATIVE, LIBERAL, AND MODERATE VIEWS IN MORE
DEPTH: THINK TANK PERSPECTIVES

Individuals have a limited ability to articulate their views in the political process, and the degree to which an individual's political viewpoints are well informed varies greatly. This is why think tanks play an important role in shaping and

Table 3   Selected U.S. Think Tanks Categorized by Political Viewpoint

Conservative	Liberal	Moderate
American Enterprise Institute	Economic Policy Institute	Urban Institute
Hoover Institution	Joint Center for Political and Economic Studies	Brookings Institution
Manhattan Institute	Center on Budget and Policy Priorities	National Bureau of Economic Research
Hudson Institute	Institute for Policy Studies	Carnegie Endowment
Cato Institute		Progressive Policy Institute
Heritage Foundation		Institute for International Economics
		Economic Strategy Institute

Source: Categorization based on ideological classification by Rich, Andrew. *Think Tanks, Public Policy, and the Politics of Expertise*. Cambridge: Cambridge University Press, 2004.

representing individual views in the larger political process. Think tanks are independent nonprofit organizations that employ experts on various subjects to conduct research and analysis in order to influence the policymaking process. A think tank often has considerable financial and intellectual resources that allow it to articulate its views through the media and lobbying efforts. As such, think tanks are good sources for understanding, in greater depth, the ideas and positions that are associated with the ideological perspectives described earlier in this essay.

Think tanks are often thought of as neutral and objective, basing their work on sound social science research. While this is true, many think tank experts effectively function as advocates of certain ideological viewpoints, rather than as neutral analyzers of information and data. Table 3 presents a list of think tanks categorized by their ideological perspective.

The remaining portion of this essay will examine the perspective of three of these think tanks: the conservative American Enterprise Institute, the liberal Economic Policy Institute, and the moderate Urban Institute, as they relate to poverty and the Great Recession. These three think tanks are among the largest, most well funded, and most influential of all think tanks (Groseclose 2005; Rich 2004).

American Enterprise Institute (Conservative)

Established in 1943, the American Enterprise Institute (AEI) describes itself as "a community of scholars and supporters committed to expanding liberty, increasing individual opportunity and strengthening free enterprise" (American Enterprise

Institute 2012). AEI is financed by investment earnings, as well as contributions from corporations, foundations, and individuals. AEI conducts research and promotes its ideas through a variety of media outlets.

One conservative tendency of AEI is to highlight perceived gains in economic conditions and to minimize hardships. In keeping with this tendency, one AEI study during the Recession reported considerable improvements in well-being for the poor and middle class over the past three decades (Meyer 2011). This AEI report challenges prevailing views that things have gotten worse for the poor and the middle class, arguing that common poverty definitions (which rely only on income) are insufficient because they ignore the benefits that have gone to the poor in recent years: food stamps, lower tax rates, expanded tax credits, and ownership of durables (i.e., consumer goods that do not have to be purchased frequently, such as appliances, furniture, and automobiles).

A second AEI report downplays the growing awareness of income inequality in recent years and instead argues that while wage growth has not been very strong (and probably understated), gains in employment benefits have been greater, thereby reducing the seriousness of poverty (Barone 2011). This same AEI article makes the case that poverty is not as bad as some make it out to be because of other gains in general well-being that come from the greater availability of consumer electronics at lower prices, greater selection of food in supermarkets, and lower prices for clothing.

In keeping with the controversy over how poverty is measured, another report from AEI applauds the new Supplemental Poverty Measure (SPM) released by the Census Bureau because the inclusion of cost of living differences, receipt of public benefits, and tax benefits in the SPM provides a more accurate depiction of poverty (Conover 2011). While conservatives often argue that poverty is being overestimated, it is interesting to see support for the SPM from AEI, even though the measure shows that poverty has increased.

Another AEI study claims that the existing array of tax credits for needy people is too complicated and ineffective (Roden 2010). Tax credits are cash refunds that go to people upon the filing of their tax returns. According to this AEI study, the Making Work Pay credit introduced as part of the stimulus package during the Recession unnecessarily adds to the complexity of the tax system. AEI contends that the complexity of the system results in the failure of many to apply for the credit, requires people to pay for tax professionals, creates confusion over eligibility, and results in persons who do not have need claiming tax credits. The study recommends consolidating credits, streamlining eligibility requirements, and reducing the disincentive to work associated with increasing marginal tax rates at some income levels when applying tax credits. Another AEI author also criticizes the work disincentives associated with the seven different tax credits for low-income earners (Hassett 2009). The article expresses concern at the rising cost of these credits and questions their effectiveness in reducing poverty.

Conservatives often have a preference for voluntary charitable giving to address poverty rather than the use of government programs. The president of AEI, Arthur Brooks, has taken this conservative position on charitable giving (Brooks 2009). Brooks argues that AEI research shows that conservatives not only have higher charitable giving rates than liberals, but that in times of recession, conservatives are less likely to cut back on their giving than liberals.

One prominent writer for AEI, Norman Ornstein, has a concern over one effect of the Recession that is unusual among AEI writers and conservatives generally. Ornstein claims that hunger was worse during the Recession because of high food costs, and he has expressed concern about possible cutbacks to government programs aimed at reducing hunger. He noted that the food stamp program is not particularly generous, and he has worried about possible cutbacks to the Emergency Food Assistance Program, which gives food to food banks. While Ornstein expresses concern about the weakness of these government programs, his primary emphasis is consistent with conservative ideology: he stresses the need for individuals to give more to charity and the need to increase tax credits for business to encourage businesses to donate more food to nonprofits (Ornstein 2011).

Economic Policy Institute (Liberal)

Established in 1986, the Economic Policy Institute (EPI) aims to "broaden discussions about economic policy to include the needs of low- and middle-income workers" (Economic Policy Institute 2012). EPI believes every working person deserves a good job with fair pay, affordable health care, and retirement security. Like AEI, EPI conducts research and analysis and attempts to influence public policy through the media and other outlets. Also like AEI, EPI employs scholars with advanced graduate degrees and emphasizes their rigorous research (Economic Policy Institute 2012).

However, the emphasis of EPI studies is much different than those of AEI. For instance, EPI writers tend to show how recession statistics underestimate the extent of the problems low- and middle-income earners face. For example, one EPI report on falling unemployment in 2011 explained that this statistic masked a more serious problem: workers dropping out of the labor force altogether and therefore not being counted in the unemployment figures (Mishel 2011).

EPI writers are also very critical of Republican policies affecting public employment. For instance, one article criticizes Republican efforts to finance a "jobs bill" to extend a payroll tax cut by forcing 280,000 job cuts in government employment (Fieldhouse 2011b). While conservatives generally favor cuts to government jobs, liberals are much more likely to support public sector employment, especially in times of recession.

The liberal support for government programs is also illustrated by EPI writers who praise the Census Bureau's new Supplemental Poverty Measure (SPM) because it shows the positive effects of government programs in reducing poverty (Cooper and Gould 2011). However, liberals are quick to point out that while government programs have helped, they do not go nearly far enough because the poverty rate is still unacceptably high. EPI writers also express concern over data from the 2010 American Community Survey that show the effects of the Great Recession on the poor. These effects include reduced median incomes, rising inequality, fewer people with health insurance, higher than average poverty in certain regions, and increased reliance on cash assistance (Cooper and Sabadish 2011).

The liberal perspective on taxes, poverty, and inequality is evident in EPI's response to a speech President Obama gave in which he criticized the conservative preference for cutting regulations and taxes for the wealthy. An EPI writer endorses Obama's view that the Bush tax cuts did not contribute to job growth in the first decade of the twenty-first century (Fieldhouse 2011c).

This same EPI writer sympathized with the concern about inequality expressed by the Occupy Wall Street movement, which grew out of the Great Recession (Fieldhouse 2011a). This concern with inequality is also seen in criticism of House Majority Leader Eric Cantor's efforts to keep high tax deduction rates for wealthy Americans. Cantor was opposed to an Obama proposal that would have reduced these deductions for the wealthy because he claimed it would indirectly hurt the poor and the needy, as wealthier people would be less motivated to give to charitable causes. The EPI writer also criticized proposals by Republicans in the House to cut food stamps and health insurance for the poor and needy by half over a 20-year time period (Fieldhouse 2011a).

Urban Institute (Moderate)

Much like AEI and EPI, the Urban Institute (UI) conducts research and analysis of public policy and seeks to educate while disseminating its findings. It is usually classified as a moderate or centrist think tank without a clear ideological perspective. UI has spent considerable resources focusing on the effects of the Great Recession on Americans. To that end, in 2010 it produced a six-part series called *Recession and Recovery*.

These reports provide a great deal of factual information on the Recession that illuminates the effects of the Recession on average Americans. UI's reports document that lower-income households have seen greater declines in income than other households and that it takes these households longer to recover. UI studies also explain that many of the unemployed do not receive unemployment insurance because they choose not to, or are ineligible, and that this was a growing problem

A protester plays a guitar at the Occupy Wall Street camp in Zuccotti Park in New York City. The Occupy Wall Street movement was concerned with corruption in the financial services industry and economic inequality. The movement began in New York in September of 2011 and spread across the United States. (Mira Agron/Dreamstime.com)

during the Recession: the percentage of the unemployed receiving benefits in the 1970s was as high as 60 percent but has been at 40 percent in recent decades and was only 36.3 percent in 2007. UI studies also note other problems with unemployment insurance, specifically that unemployment insurance benefits do not replace health insurance and retirement contributions that often come with employment, and are an increasingly important part of an employee's total compensation package. Additionally, not all the unemployed qualify for Medicaid, and many newly unemployed become uninsured. The UI urges increased federal transfers to states to limit cutbacks to programs that exist to help some people in these circumstances. UI points out that in previous recessions, because of pressure on state budgets, programs like these for needy people have been cut (Dorn 2008).

Despite these problems with unemployment insurance, UI contends that the federal government's extension of unemployment benefits was a great help to many during the Recession. UI also praises the Unemployment Insurance Modernization Act of 2008. That Act incentivizes states to establish alternative base periods that allow more people to qualify for unemployment insurance (Simms 2008). It also provides compensation for those who are otherwise eligible but are looking for part-time work, for those who are participating in certain training programs, and for those who left jobs because of disability, personal or family illness, or domestic violence. Still, another writer for the UI says that extensions of unemployment insurance do not go far enough and that "labor market policies that will provide long-term income support and speed reemployment" are needed (Vroman 2010).

According to UI experts, unemployment insurance was particularly important during the Great Recession because of the scaling back of the social safety net in recent decades. These experts note that in previous recessions welfare assistance rose along with increased unemployment, but that legislative changes in 1996 designed to motivate people to move from welfare to work resulted in a decline in welfare caseloads during the 2001 recession and at the beginning of the 2008 Recession. These events have led UI to recommend that Congress revisit the work requirements and assistance time limits imposed by the 1996 welfare reform law and consider increasing block grants to states to fund welfare programs (Zedlewski 2008).

UI writers have outlined a number of policies to respond to the problems of the Recession: extension of unemployment benefits, more generous funding for food stamps, support for states to maintain benefits under Medicaid, and funding to help people maintain health coverage after job loss, as well as "general purpose" aid to state governments. UI authors have expressed concern that elements of the stimulus package would expire before the Recession was over and urged longer-term investments in child care and education. Additionally, they recommend tax credits for companies that hire unemployed workers (Edelman 2010; Finegold 2008).

UI is a strong advocate of the Earned Income Tax Credit (EITC), a cash benefit that goes to the working poor upon the filing of their tax return. UI claims that although it is one of the most helpful provisions for the poor, it is not enough for low-income families during a Recession with unemployment rates on the rise because it is obtained only after a tax return has been filed, which is too late for many. An advance distribution (of about $35 per week in 2009) is available, but only 2 percent of eligible workers choose this option (Williams 2008).

The UI is conscious of the expense associated with many of its recommendations and the reality of large budget deficits. Instead of targeting programs for the poor and needy, UI suggests working to restrain health care costs, reforming Social Security, and looking at reducing fast growing expenditures in defense and homeland security (Edelman 2011). It also states that deficit reduction in the long term will require increased revenues and that we "... should not sacrifice sensible cost-effective investments in poverty reduction over the longer term that will contribute to GDP growth and ultimately to fiscal balance as well ... [because] failure to make these improvements leads to reduced earnings capacity, higher crime rates, and poor health among the poor, which in turn generate enormous economic costs on the United States" (Edelman 2011, 8). In keeping with the centrist viewpoint, UI favors both a reduction in expenditures and an increase in revenues, and highlights the long-term national economic impact of poverty (Edelman 2011).

OUTLOOK

Given the ideological divide among Americans it is likely that there will continue to be differences of opinion on what caused the Recession, the real extent of poverty, the capacity of government programs to respond to poverty, and on how government should deal with budget deficits. The ascendency of more conservative views, though, suggests an overall waning of political commitment to the government's role as a protector for the well-being of the poor. Still, most people across the ideological spectrum acknowledge the overall severity of poverty and growing human need during the Recession, and see at least some limited role for government in responding to it. Moreover, as shown in Table 2, large numbers of Americans in the middle are willing to consider both tax increases and spending cuts to manage deficits and sustain important programs that serve the poor. For people from a variety of ideological perspectives, many of these programs, flawed as they may be, are viewed as important for the poor in the United States.

FURTHER READING

American Enterprise Institute. "AEI's Organization and Purposes," 2012. Accessed August 5, 2012. http://www.aei.org/

Barone, Michael. "Personal Well-Being Overshadows Income Inequality." American Enterprise Institute, January 2, 2011. Accessed January 5, 2012. www.aei.org/article/society-and-culture/poverty/personal-well-being-overshadows-income-inequality/

Brooks, Arthur. "Conservatives Have Answered Obama's Call." American Enterprise Institute, January 22, 2009. Accessed January 5, 2012. http://www.aei.org/article/society-and-culture/poverty/conservatives-have-answered-obamas-call/

Conover, Christopher. "In Sickness or in Wealth," American Enterprise Institute, November 30, 2011. Accessed January 5, 2012. http://www.aei.org/search/In+sickness+or+in+wealth

Cooper, David, and Elise Gould. "New Poverty Measure Highlights Positive Effect of Government Assistance." Economic Policy Institute, November 17, 2011. Accessed January 5, 2012. http://www.epi.org/publication/poverty-measure-highlights-dire-circumstances/

Cooper, David, and Natalie Sabadish. "American Community Survey Paints a Bleak Landscape." Economic Policy Institute, September 22, 2011. Accessed January 5, 2012. http://www.epi.org/blog/american-community-survey-poverty/

Dorn, Stan. "Health Coverage in a Recession." Urban Institute, December 2008. Accessed January 5, 2012. http://www.urban.org/UploadedPDF/411812_health_coverage_in _a_recession.pdf

Economic Policy Institute. "About," 2012. Accessed August 5, 2012. http://www.epi.org/ about

Edelman, Peter B., Olivia A. Golden, and Harry J. Holzer. "Reducing Poverty and Economic Distress after ARRA: Next Steps for Short-Term Recovery and Long-Term Economic Security." Urban Institute, July 2010. Accessed January 5, 2012. http://www.urban .org/UploadedPDF/412150-next-steps-ARRA.pdf

Fieldhouse, Andrew. "Ryan's Budget Proposals Belie Concerns about Inequality." Economic Policy Institute, November 29, 2011a. Accessed January 5, 2012. http://www.epi.org/ blog/paul-ryan-budget-proposals-inequality-concerns/

Fieldhouse, Andrew. "Paying for a Jobs Bill by Cutting Federal Jobs?" Economic Policy Institute, December 2, 2011b. Accessed January 5, 2012. http://www.epi.org/ publication/paying-jobs-bill-cutting-federal-jobs/

Fieldhouse, Andrew. "Supply-Side's Abject Failure." Economic Policy Institute, December 7, 2011c. Accessed January 5, 2012. http://www.epi.org/blog/supply-side-abject-failure/

Finegold, Kenneth. "SNAP and the Recession." Urban Institute, December 2008. Accessed January 5, 2012. http://www.urban.org/UploadedPDF/411810_SNAP_and_the_Recession .pdf

Google Public Data Explorer. "Central Government Expenditures," 2012. Accessed January 5. http://www.google.com/publicdata/explore?ds=ltjib1m1uf3pf_&ctype=l &strail=false&bcs=d&nselm=h&met_y=govdefct_t3&scale_y=lin&ind_y=false&rdim =country_group&idim=country_group:oecd:non-oecd&idim=country:USA&ifdim=country _group&tstart=-600631200000&tend=2555128800000

Groseclose, T., and J. Milyo. "A Measure of Media Bias." *Quarterly Journal of Economics* 120 (2005): 1191–1238.

Hassett, Kevin A., and Aparna Mathur. "Simplifying Tax Credits for Low-Income People: Reforming an Inefficient System." American Enterprise Institute, October 5, 2009. Accessed January 5, 2012. http://www.aei.org/search/Simplifying+Tax+Credits+for +Low-Income+People

Meyer, Bruce D., and James X. Sullivan. "The Material Well-Being of the Poor and Middle Class since 1980." American Enterprise Institute, October 25, 2011. Accessed January 5, 2012. http://www.aei.org/files/2011/10/25/Material-Well-Being-Poor-Middle -Class.pdf

Mishel, Lawrence. "Why Falling Unemployment May Not Make Voters Happy." Economic Policy Institute, December 2, 2011. Accessed January 5, 2012. http://www.epi.org/ blog/unemployment-impact-on-voters/

National Public Radio. "Conservative View on Stimulus: Stephen Moore," February 4, 2009a. Accessed January 5, 2012. http://www.npr.org/templates/transcript/transcript. php?storyId=100241769

National Public Radio. "Liberal View on Stimulus: James Galbraith," February 5, 2009b. Accessed January 5, 2012. http://www.npr.org/templates/story/story.php?storyId=10 0241766

Office of Management and Budget. "Historical Tables, Summary of Receipts, Outlays, and Surpluses or Deficits as Percentages of GDP, 1930–2016," 2012. Accessed January 5, 2012. http://www.whitehouse.gov/omb/budget/Historicals/

Ornstein, Norman J. "Perfect Storm Puts Hunger Back on the Agenda." American Enterprise Institute, September 21, 2011. Accessed January 5, 2012. http://www.aei.org/search/Perfect+Storm+Puts+Hunger+Back+on+the+Agenda

Pew Research Center. "Beyond Red vs. Blue Political Typology," May 4, 2011. Accessed January 5, 2012. http://www.people-press.org/files/legacy-pdf/Beyond-Red-vs-Blue-The-Political-Typology.pdf

Rich, Andrew. Think Tanks, Public Policy, and the Politics of Expertise. Cambridge: Cambridge University Press, 2004.

Roden, Amy. "No Way to Help the Poor." American Enterprise Institute, January 5, 2010. Accessed January 5, 2012. http://www.aei.org/search/No+Way+to+Help+the+Poor

Simms, Margaret C., and Daniel Kuehn. "Unemployment Insurance during a Recession." Urban Institute, December 2008. Accessed January 5, 2012. http://www.urban.org/UploadedPDF/411808_unemployment_insurance.pdf

Tax Policy Center. "Historical Top Tax Rate," April 13, 2012. Accessed June 14, 2012. http://www.taxpolicycenter.org/taxfacts/displayafact.cfm?Docid=213

Vroman, Wayne. "The Great Recession, Unemployment Insurance, and Poverty: Summary," July 15, 2010. Accessed January 5, 2012. http://www.urban.org/publications/412147.html

Williams, Roberton, and Elaine Maag. "The Recession and the Earned Income Tax Credit." Urban Institute, December 2008. Accessed January 5, 2012. http://www.urban.org/UploadedPDF/411811_recession_and_EITC.pdf

Zedlewski, Sheila. "The Role of Welfare during a Recession." Urban Institute, December 2008. Accessed January 5, 2012. http://www.urban.org/UploadedPDF/411809_role_of_welfare.pdf

RELIGIOUS GROUPS

Fred Van Geest

OVERVIEW

Many Americans, including many religious Americans, believe that the government should do more to help the needy. A 2007 Pew survey found that 62 percent of Americans believed that government should do more to help the needy even if it meant going deeper into debt (Pew Forum on Religion and Public Life 2008). Many religious Americans also agreed with this sentiment, including 57 percent of evangelical Christians, 58 percent of mainline Protestants, 63 percent of Catholics, 68 percent of Jews, 73 percent of Muslims, and 79 percent of black Protestants (Pew Forum on Religion and Public Life 2008, 102).

Some studies indicate that this level of support continued almost unchanged after the official end of the Great Recession in June 2009. A 2010 Pew survey found that 63 percent of Americans favored additional government assistance to the poor, including 54 percent of white evangelicals, 57 percent of white mainline Protestants, 64 percent of Catholics, and 81 percent of black Protestants (Pew Research Center 2010). In 2011 two different surveys from the Pew Forum addressed the question of government spending, but in slightly different ways. In one study, conducted in February 2011, respondents wanted to see spending maintained or increased in 15 of 18 areas (Pew Research Center 2011a). Of those areas, 83 percent indicated a preference for maintaining or increasing spending on Medicare, 76 percent for aid to the needy in the United States, 74 percent on Social Security, and 71 percent on health care spending (Pew Research Center 2011a). However, a second Pew survey, conducted a few weeks prior, found that only 41 percent of respondents believed that the government should do more to help needy Americans, even if it meant going deeper into debt (Pew Research Center 2011b). Regardless, it is clear that many Americans, and many religious Americans, are concerned about poverty in the United States and the government's role in combating that poverty. Therefore, it should be no surprise that the uptick in poverty rates during the Great Recession drew a great deal of attention from various religious groups.

What was striking about the responses of religious groups was the relative agreement among them about appropriate public policy responses to the Recession. This relative agreement continued into 2011, when most religious groups reacted with strong opposition as federal and state governments, in the midst of huge budget deficits, began proposing massive budget cuts to poverty reduction programs. Many religious groups expressed deep opposition to proposed program cuts that would, in their view, harm the poor and the needy in the United States. This essay will discuss the responses of these various religious groups to poverty in the midst of the Great Recession.

THE PRESENT

CHRISTIAN DENOMINATIONAL RESPONSES

Roman Catholic

The U.S. Conference of Catholic Bishops (USCCB) is the main leadership body in the United States for Roman Catholics. In making public pronouncements, the USCCB usually refers to longstanding principles of Catholic Social Teaching (CST) and reminds people of the connection between these principles and poverty. For instance, CST holds that poverty and unemployment undermine human dignity, freedom, and creativity and can also cause psychological and spiritual suffering. The Catholic principle of subsidiarity is central to CST and is based on the idea that higher-level institutions (e.g., the federal government) should not do what lower-level institutions (e.g., families, communities, and local governments) can do. Also central to CST is the idea that one of the most important basic moral tests of a society is how well it treats its most vulnerable members.

CST articulates a clear view of the different responsibilities of government and nongovernmental institutions when it comes to dealing with issues such as poverty. A statement by the USCCB called "A Catholic Framework for Economic Life" lays out principles for economic life that explain the roles of government and nongovernmental organizations (1996). The bishops explain that, in their view, free markets have both strengths and weaknesses, as do voluntary groups. They argue that neither of these institutions is sufficient on its own and that government action may be necessary to ensure the meeting of basic human needs. In CST, the market needs to be appropriately controlled by the state and society to ensure that basic human needs are met. CST also emphasizes the importance of work to human dignity, arguing that long-term reliance on public or private assistance can cause suffering on spiritual and psychological levels.

The USCCB was active in calling for changes in public policy during the Recession. For instance, in 2010 it lamented the fact that despite the stimulus package, unemployment, poverty, and foreclosures remained high. An action alert called on the 111th Congress to extend Unemployment Insurance (UI) benefits, the Child Tax Credit, and Earned Income Tax Credit (EITC) and provide $1 billion for low-income housing through the National Housing Trust Fund (U.S. Conference of Catholic Bishops 2010b).

The USCCB also expressed great concern about the foreclosure crisis during the Recession and urged a number of policy responses. It condemned predatory lending as a cause of the foreclosure crisis and noted the inconsistency of such practices with Catholic teaching. It expressed support for the Obama administration's Home Affordable Modification Program (HAMP) because of its view that the initiative helped many homeowners. However, the bishops also argued that it did not go nearly far enough to meet the needs of homeowners. USCCB has also urged Americans to lobby for other increases in federal funding to address the housing crisis. For example, one action alert issued in 2010 urged people to contact their representatives to pass the American Jobs and Closing Tax Loopholes Act of 2010, which would have provided funding for the National Housing Trust Fund (U.S. Conference of Catholic Bishops 2010a).

Additionally, the USCCB has urged people to contact their representatives to lobby for more funding for home counseling and other foreclosure programs. This funding is particularly important to Catholic agencies that have been directly involved in responding to the foreclosure crisis but have been unable to meet demand. The USCCB also has a ministry to families at risk of foreclosure through its Campaign for Human Development, a general antipoverty program.

The USCCB expressed grave concern for those who experienced greater hunger during the Recession. It urged voters to contact their elected officials to lobby for restoring cuts and increasing funding for all programs that ensure adequate nutrition and reduce hunger, for example, Women, Infants, and Children (WIC); the food stamp program; and summer feeding programs. The USCCB also called on people to educate the needy about eligibility for government benefits, and to work with local agencies, food banks, churches, and others that serve immigrants and low-income families (U.S. Conference of Catholic Bishops 2011).

Catholics have addressed the problems of the Recession in many direct ways as well, most prominently through Catholic Charities (CC), one of the largest networks of charitable organizations in the United States. Its motto is "Working to reduce

A volunteer with Catholic Charities organizes bread that will be delivered to community members at the Bishop Cosgrove Center in Cleveland, Ohio. Catholic Charities is one of the largest charitable organizations in the United States. (AP Photo/Tony Dejak)

poverty in America," and it has extensive programs that labor to do so. These programs directly serve millions of Americans in need every year. Not surprisingly, the work CC undertakes has been profoundly affected by the Recession. A 2009 survey of agencies in its network found that most were experiencing significant drops in funding from their usual revenue sources: state and local government, investment income, and corporate donations. While it was experiencing this decline in revenue, the demand for services rose. This higher demand came from the working poor, the homeless, and middle-class families. Increases in domestic violence were reported, along with an increased need for child protective services, Medicaid, children's health insurance, and food stamps. Additionally, these charities saw greater demands for assistance with clothing, counseling and other mental health services, food, foreclosure prevention, job training and replacement, permanent housing, prescription assistance, temporary housing, utilities assistance, and emergency financial assistance. Given the mismatch between demand and resources, the report expressed doubt about the ability of CC to continue to offer adequate services to the needy (Catholic Charities 2009).

Mainline Protestant

One of the most historically influential Protestant groups in the United States has been the National Council of Churches (NCC). The NCC is an umbrella group for mainline Protestant denominations that tend to be more theologically liberal. The group includes some of the largest denominations in the United States and claims to represent more than 45 million Americans. The NCC has had a long history of activism on poverty and related issues, and it has remained active throughout the Great Recession.

For example, in 2008 the NCC wrote a letter to presidential candidates John McCain and Barack Obama calling on them to prioritize the concerns of the poor and the needy in the United States and around the world, noting that both candidates had more often spoken of the needs of the middle class than the poor (National Council of Churches 2008b). The letter expressed concern about the deterioration of the safety net in the previous 10 to 15 years and state cuts to health insurance programs for children and the poor. They also predicted that the financial crisis would cause conditions to worsen for the poor in America.

Many of the NCC's efforts on poverty are undertaken through coordinated campaigns with other religious groups. Frequently, the NCC is the main organization leading these efforts. In the past several years the NCC has joined together with other religious, civic, and community organizations to work toward cutting poverty in half over 10 years. This effort, called Fighting Poverty with Faith, started at the beginning of the Great Recession and was co-sponsored by Catholic Charities USA and the Jewish Council for Public Affairs. It calls attention to the causes of poverty, highlights strategies to reduce it, and works toward new economic opportunities for the needy. It has pursued a wide range of strategies, and over 50 national faith based organizations have signed on to its mobilization statement. Various efforts have included extensive education, action to influence public policy, a food stamp challenge in which people are encouraged to see what it is like to live on food stamps, a "hunger banquet," writing op-eds, candidate forums, poverty simulations, prayer, and various other local events throughout the country (National Council of Churches 2010b).

Evangelical Protestant

Evangelical Protestant Christians are one of the largest religious groups in the United States. However, they are much more decentralized and therefore do not act as often in a coordinated way like Catholics or mainline Protestants. However, many evangelical denominations are represented by the National Association of Evangelicals (NAE). The NAE claims to represent tens of millions of Christians in more than 40 different denominations and 45,000 local churches.

The NAE has made important statements on poverty, particularly global poverty. For instance, in one of their "take action" items the NAE recommends getting to know poor people, supporting poverty relief through church organizations and ministries, volunteering in ministries that help the poor, joining Teach for America, and joining the Micah Challenge, a global effort to cut poverty in half by 2015 (National Association of Evangelicals 2009).

On the domestic front, in their "Lowering the Debt, Raising the Poor" statement, the NAE said that when attempting to combat government deficits, both revenues and spending should be reviewed. Unlike Catholics and mainline Protestants, the NAE does not often comment on specific policies. However, in this statement, the NAE asserts that deficit reduction should not involve abandoning commitments to the poor. Like other religious traditions, the NAE takes the view that churches have an obligation to help the poor but also that government shares in the responsibility to meet the basic needs of the poor. Like the emphasis in Catholic Social Teaching, the NAE also believes that it is important to help poor people become productive and contributing members of society (National Association of Evangelicals 2011).

Jewish

American Jews have been active in many of the interfaith efforts described in the following section, but they have also been active on their own, sharing many of the perspectives of the groups mentioned earlier in this essay. The Jewish Council for Public Affairs (JCPA) represents many American Jewish individuals and organizations in public affairs. It has lobbied in favor of the stimulus package debated in Congress because of its support for Medicaid, food stamps, Unemployment Insurance, investments in the green economy, and support for other programs meeting human needs. The JCPA opposed the House Republican budget plan because of its proposed cuts to programs affecting needy people and its deprioritizing of programs for the most vulnerable. Additionally, it maintains a Confronting Poverty program in which it encourages support for interfaith initiatives to combat poverty and focuses on health care, housing, and hunger issues. The JCPA also sponsored an "e-postcard" campaign expressing concern over the increase in poverty during the Great Recession and urging the president to commit to cutting poverty in half in 10 years. In 2012 the JCPA urged Congress to extend unemployment insurance benefits for people still struggling to recover from the Recession (Jewish Council on Public Affairs 2012).

Interfaith

In recent years it has become quite common for people from different religious traditions to work together in addressing poverty. One example comes from a broad coalition established in 2006 representing 100 million Christians in a wide range of denominations, called Christian Churches Together in the USA (CCT). CCT issued public statements and met with President Obama shortly after his inauguration to urge him to include provisions for the poor in the stimulus package. Calling poverty a scandal, CCT emphasized the need for more personal responsibility and to strengthen families; it also called for greater societal responsibility and public investments by government. CCT emphasizes concrete action by churches, neighborhood communities, faith-based organizations, government, individuals, families, and the market to reduce child poverty by half in 10 years.

CCT also echoed a popular refrain during the Recession expressing concern that more attention was being given to Wall Street than to the neediest people in society. It specifically called for adequate funding for the EITC and adequate schooling for children. The group has developed a domestic poverty initiative and shares resources and the antipoverty efforts of member denominations (Christian Churches Together 2012).

A second interfaith initiative took place in 2008 when religious leaders from Catholic, Protestant, Jewish, and Muslim traditions called on political leaders to develop plans to combat poverty and give attention to it at the national political party conventions. A related statement expressed concern about job losses, foreclosures, and the health crisis. The group said that even though their religious groups work hard to meet the needs of the poor and vulnerable, this was not enough to meet the national need, and called for additional efforts from political leaders (National Council of Churches 2008a).

In a third example from 2009, almost three dozen Christian, Muslim, Hindu, and Jewish organizations came together to pressure political leaders to invest in green jobs for the poor, jobs that would provide livable wages and benefits. This request was part of a week-long effort by the group called Fighting Poverty with Faith. The activities included programs on job training in the green economy, home retrofitting, and tours of green job facilities. In addition, the group encouraged government at all levels to enact policies that would help low-income families with their energy and housing costs (National Council of Churches 2009).

A fourth effort in 2010 came from the Interreligious Working Group on Domestic Human Needs. This group focused on urging Congress to develop a budget with continuing and new investments that reflect a priority for child welfare programs, housing assistance, and job training. Specifically, the group called for increased funding for the National Housing Trust Fund and a permanent extension of the increases to the Child Tax Credit and the EITC (National Council of Churches 2010a). Like other groups, this group claims that the needs of vulnerable people will not be met through congregations running soup kitchens and homeless shelters alone.

A fifth example of an interfaith effort took place in 2011. An interfaith religious coalition launched an 18-month campaign warning public officials that churches and congregations could not shoulder the burden of budget cuts affecting the poor and vulnerable. The group urged public officials to maintain commitments to both domestic and international poverty reduction programs. This campaign included meetings with public officials and daily prayer vigils (National Council of Churches 2011b).

Final examples of interfaith efforts include a 2011 fasting campaign launched to protest budget cuts that would have affected the poor and vulnerable (Falsani

2011), and a 2010 effort called Faith Advocates for Jobs, which provides toolkits for congregations and encourages them to develop "worker support committees" to help working families by providing social and economic support (Faith Advocates for Jobs 2012).

Budget cutting in the 112th Congress

One of the most extraordinary combined efforts of religious groups came in the middle of 2011. The specific catalyst that mobilized these religious groups was a concurrent budget resolution introduced in May in the House of Representatives by Republican Paul Ryan. House Concurrent Resolution 234 was the official Republican attempt to establish budget levels for 2012 and following years. After their significant gains in the elections in the fall of 2010, the Republican Party felt emboldened and hoped to reverse some of the direction taken in the stimulus legislation. It planned to introduce large cuts to important programs affecting the weaker and more vulnerable members of society, such as Social Security, Medicare, Medicaid, food stamps, and education. The resolution ultimately failed in the Senate and did not become law, perhaps in part because of the aggressive opposition of religious groups.

Both traditionally conservative and liberal religious groups in many different denominations expressed strong opposition to the attempts to cut taxes for wealthier Americans and enact program cuts that would harm the poor and the needy. These efforts came together in a document called the Circle of Protection, which was signed by leaders of more than 60 religious denominations and other organizations. In criticizing the general philosophy behind House Concurrent Resolution 234, the Circle of Protection statement sought to defend programs that protect the life and dignity of poor and vulnerable people by opposing budget cuts. Further, the statement asked for improvements in poverty assistance programs. To tackle the deficit, these religious leaders proposed an examination of tax revenues, military spending, and entitlements.

Individual denominations also worked hard in 2011 to oppose these proposed budget cuts. One typical letter from church leaders opposing cuts to domestic anti-poverty programs expressed criticism of increased military spending and tax cuts for the rich as causes of the deficit, and argued that discretionary programs that serve the poor and vulnerable are a small portion of the budget (National Council of Churches 2011a). Proposed cuts, they argued, would be devastating to those living in poverty, possibly costing jobs and even hurting, rather than helping, the overall fiscal situation whileseverely diminishing the government's ability to meet the needs of those most affected by the Recession (National Council of Churches 2011a).

The NAE reported that Circle of Protection leaders from across the spectrum met with President Obama and made the case that any deficit control agreements should exempt cuts to programs serving poor and hungry people (National Council of Churches 2011a). The NAE reiterated its position that it embraces the church's call to care for the poor, but the group also emphasized the government's responsibility. The statement also took a position against cutting aid programs for the poor in other countries (National Council of Churches 2011a).

A DISSENTING VIEW ON BUDGET CUTTING AND ANTIPOVERTY PROGRAMS

The religious groups backing the Circle of Protection clearly represent the overwhelming majority of religious interests in the United States. They represent most of the official and organized religious groups to which Americans belong. However, there are some dissenting voices. One notable voice of dissent comes from Richard Land, who heads the Ethics and Religious Liberty Commission, an arm of the Southern Baptist Convention (SBC). The SBC is one of the larger denominations in the United States. Land chose not to sign on to the Circle of Protection statement, taking a more conservative approach and urging Americans in 2011 to support the Cut, Cap, and Balance Bill that would have cut spending by $111 billion in the following fiscal year and capped future spending as a percentage of gross domestic product (GDP). The recommendation from Land did not come with any call to protect poverty reduction programs (Land 2011). Additionally, in a debate with Jim Wallis of Sojourners, Land was critical of antipoverty programs, arguing that they were unsustainable and that they were key contributors to the deficit. Land also asserted that absent fathers and single parenthood were the main causes of poverty, and he recommended eliminating no-fault divorce laws as a solution (Jones 2011).

Another more organized dissenting position came from a group of conservative Christian leaders who formed a group called Christians for a Sustainable Economy (CASE). Unlike the Circle of Protection group, the members of CASE do not include any religious denominations, but instead represent individuals and some conservative advocacy organizations (e.g., the Institute on Religion and Democracy, Concerned Women for America, the Acton Institute, Ethics and Public Policy Center, and the Family Research Council).

CASE wrote a letter to President Obama, Majority Leader Harry Reid, and Speaker John Boehner stating that the authors of the Circle of Protection did not speak for all Christians. They criticized the Circle of Protection statement for legitimizing the idea of big government and defending ineffective and counterproductive federal welfare programs. To CASE these government programs harm the poor by creating long-term dependency and are unwise, uncompassionate, and unjust. For solutions, CASE emphasized the need to rely on economic freedom and growth to encourage productivity and generosity but resolutely opposed wealth redistribution. The group encouraged charity toward the poor, but a type of charity that also addresses spiritual needs.

Despite this criticism of government programs, CASE does still believe that government-provided safety nets are useful for those in need. However, it is strongly opposed to any additional taxes, preferring program cuts instead and believing that the deficit is not due to tax cuts and declining revenue, but rather stems from excessive spending. Although the group does not specify where program cuts are to come from, it did say that poverty reduction programs were not "sacrosanct" (Christians for a Sustainable Economy 2012).

CASE is a relatively lone voice among religious advocacy groups. Far more typical is the view expressed in a 2011 advertisement entitled "Listen to Your Pastors." It was sponsored by the Christian group Sojourners and another group established in 2006 by 40 religious leaders from different backgrounds called Faith in Public Life. The ad highlighted the positive aspects of government programs such as food stamps, WIC, Medicaid, and Head Start (Faith in Public Life 2011).

OUTLOOK

Given the relative consensus and widespread agreement among religious groups with regards to the appropriate response of government to poverty in the Great Recession, it is possible that religious interests in the United States will have some significant impact. Religious organizations can have an impact both through sophisticated programs run by groups such as Catholic Charities and awareness-raising programs and direct assistance orchestrated through local churches. However, religious interests may also have some influence in the political arena, given their aggressive, repeated, and coordinated lobbying efforts to protect poverty reduction programs and prevent budget cuts to these programs during the Recession.

FURTHER READING

The American Jobs and Closing Tax Loopholes Act of 2010, HR 4213, 111th Congress. www.waysandmeans.house.gov/media/pdf/111/hwc_711_xml.pdf

Catholic Charities USA. "The Impact of the Recession and How We Are Responding," Fall 2009. Accessed January 5, 2012. http://www.catholiccharitiesusa.org/NetCommunity/Document.Doc?id=1887

Christian Churches Together in the USA. "Domestic Poverty Initiative," 2012. Accessed January 5. http://www.christianchurchestogether.org/initiative/

Christians for a Sustainable Economy. 2012. Accessed August 5, 2012. http://www.case 4america.org/

A Circle of Protection. "A Circle of Protection: A Statement on Why We Need to Protect Programs for the Poor," 2012. Accessed August 5. http://www.circleofprotection.us/

Concurrent Resolution, H. Con. Res. 234, 110th Congress, 1st Session.

Faith Advocates for Jobs. 2012. Accessed August 5, 2012. http://faithadvocatesforjobs .wordpress.com/

Faith in Public Life. 2011. Accessed June 9, 2012. http://www.faithinpubliclife.org/

Falsani, Cathleen. "Fasting and Prayer as Protest," April 2, 2011. Accessed August 5, 2012. http://www.washingtonpost.com/todays_paper/Metro/2011-04-02/B/2/18.0.20764936 99_epaper.html

Fighting Poverty with Faith. "Endorsing Organizations," 2012. Accessed August 5, 2012. http://fightingpovertywithfaith.com/f2/about/endorsing-organizations/

Interreligious Working Group on Domestic Human Needs. 2012. Accessed August 5, 2012. http://www.domestichumanneeds.org/

Jewish Council on Public Affairs. 2012. Accessed August 5, 2012. http://engage.jewish publicaffairs.org/p/salsa/web/common/public/content?content_item_KEY=2205

Jones, Whitney. "Budget Debt Discussion Reveals Surprising Agreement," July 14, 2011. Accessed January 5, 2012. http://www.baptiststandard.com/index.php?option=com _content&task=view&id=12743&Itemid=53

Land, Richard. "The Ethics and Religious Liberty Commission of the Southern Baptist Convention," July 21, 2011. Accessed January 5, 2012. http://erlc.com/article/urge -senate-to-support-house-passed-cut-cap-and-balance-bill/

National Association of Evangelicals. "Aid to the World's Poorest People," Fall 2009.

National Association of Evangelicals. "Lowering the Debt, Raising the Poor 2011," 2011. Accessed January 5, 2012. http://www.nae.net/government-relations/policy-resolutions/ 541-lowering-the-debt-raising-the-poor-2011

National Council of Churches. "Interfaith Leaders Call on Candidates to Make Major Statements on Poverty," August 4, 2008a. Accessed January 5, 2012. http://www .ncccusa.org/news/080804povertystatement.html

National Council of Churches. "Religious Leaders Urge the Presidential Candidates to Use Their Voices for Persons Living in Poverty," October 13, 2008b. Accessed January 5, 2012. http://www.ncccusa.org/news/081013lettertocandidates.html

National Council of Churches. "Christians, Jews, Muslims, Hindus Advocate for Green Job Creation for Those in Poverty," October 13, 2009. Accessed January 5, 2012. http:// www.ncccusa.org/news/091013greenjobs.html

National Council of Churches. "National Council Joins Religious Coalition Calling for a Moral Budget and Jobs Bill," February 5, 2010a. Accessed January 5, 2012. http:// www.ncccusa.org/news/100205dhnbudget2.html

National Council of Churches. "People of Faith Aim to Cut U.S. Poverty in Half by the End of the Next Decade," October 5, 2010b. Accessed January 5, 2012. http://www.ncccusa .org/news/101005povertymobilization.html

National Council of Churches. "Church Leaders Tell Congress They Oppose Deep Cuts in Domestic Spending and Poverty-Focused Foreign Aid," March 1, 2011a. Accessed January 5, 2012. http://www.ncccusa.org/news/110301budget.html

National Council of Churches. "Prominent Christians, Jews, Muslims Unite to Protect Funding for Poverty Assistance," July 14, 2011b. Accessed January 5, 2012. http://www.ncccusa.org/news/110714budgetcoalition.html

Pew Forum on Religion and Public Life. "U.S. Religious Landscape Survey," June 2008. Accessed January 5, 2012. http://religions.pewforum.org/pdf/report2-religious-landscape-study-full.pdf

Pew Research Center. "Few Say Religion Shapes Immigration, Environment Views: Results from the 2010 Annual Religion and Public Life Survey," September 17, 2010. Accessed January 5, 2012. http://www.people-press.org/files/legacy-pdf/655.pdf

Pew Research Center. "Changing Views of Federal Spending: Fewer Want Spending to Grow, But Most Cuts Remain Unpopular," February 10, 2011a. Accessed January 30, 2012. http://www.people-press.org/files/2011/02/702.pdf

Pew Research Center. "Beyond Red vs. Blue Political Typology," May 4, 2011b. Accessed January 5, 2012. http://www.people-press.org/files/legacy-pdf/Beyond-Red-vs-Blue-The-Political-Typology.pdf

U.S. Conference of Catholic Bishops. "A Catholic Framework for Economic Life: A Statement of the U.S. Catholic Bishops," November 1996. Accessed January 5, 2012. http://www.usccb.org/issues-and-action/human-life-and-dignity/economic-justice-economy/upload/catholic-framework-economic-life.pdf

U.S. Conference of Catholic Bishops. "Help Families Impacted by the Economic Recession!" May 24, 2010a. Accessed January 5, 2012. http://old.usccb.org/sdwp/national/2010-05-21-aa-help-families-in-economic-recession.pdf

U.S. Conference of Catholic Bishops. "Action Alert!: Tell Congress to Help Poor and Unemployed Families," November 12, 2010b. Accessed January 5, 2012. http://www.usccb.org/upload/action-alert-jobs-111-Congress.pdf

U.S. Conference of Catholic Bishops. "Food and Nutrition Programs," February 2011. Accessed January 5, 2012. http://www.usccb.org/about/domestic-social-development/resources/upload/food-nutrition-backgrounder-2011.pdf

Societal View of Poverty

Samuel Zalanga

OVERVIEW

Theories as to why poverty exists can be roughly divided into structuralist and nonstructuralist explanations. Those who hold to more structuralist theories of poverty believe that poverty exists because of the very structure of society (e.g., the political system or economic system). In contrast, those who posit nonstructuralist explanations for poverty believe that poverty exists because of lack of effort or some other fault of those who are impoverished. While the views of individuals often fall somewhere in between a wholly structuralist or wholly nonstructuralist explanation for the existence of poverty, categorizing views based on whether they are more structuralist or more nonstructuralist in nature provides a way to understand shifts in U.S. society's explanations for poverty over time.

To better understand societal views of poverty in the United States it is helpful to understand some of the historic and philosophical foundations that underlie Americans' beliefs about poverty. With this information as background, the impact of the Great Recession on U.S. society's understanding of poverty can be explored. The Great Recession has led to an increasing sense of conflict between the rich and the poor in the United States, but it has also led to an increase in the percentage of people who offer more structuralist explanations for poverty. However, increasingly structuralist explanations for poverty do not necessarily translate into the political will to alleviate poverty, particularly in times of economic strain like the Great Recession.

Philosophical Foundation for Societal View of Poverty in the United States

To understand explanations Americans offer for why poverty exists, it is important to understand the significance that U.S. society places on the concept of "radical individualism." The concept of radical individualism undergirds Social Darwinist explanations for poverty and the culture of poverty theory. These theories stand in contrast to structuralist explanations for poverty, which are not based in the concept of radical individualism.

Radical individualism is historically rooted in the early settlement of the United States by the Puritans and European immigrants who moved westward from the east coast. It was also influenced by Protestant theology, which underscores personal responsibility in one's religious struggle for salvation (Gossett 1970). The concept of radical individualism provides philosophical and moral justification for the rights of individuals, laissez faire economics, freedom of speech and religion, market competition, and the presumed existence of equal opportunity (Marger 2008). The concept of radical individualism can also form the basis for viewpoints of poverty that blame the poor for their poverty and thus deny that society has any duty or obligation to help alleviate poverty. Still, radical individualism in the American tradition often makes concessions for the elderly, children, and those affected by natural disasters. These three social groups are often categorized as the "deserving poor."

Radical individualism is one of the philosophical foundations for Social Darwinism; Social Darwinism could be viewed as radical individualism and nonstructuralism taken to the extreme. Social Darwinists believe that the concept of "survival of the fittest" applies to human society and that social conflicts between groups should be allowed to play out so that superior peoples outcompete those who are inferior and society can progress. Thus, Social Darwinists believe that public policies should not seek to aid the disadvantaged, including the poor, because this would impede the survival of the fittest and thus impede progress. Social Darwinists see poverty as a function of the moral failure and deficient character of the poor, evidenced by laziness, mismanagement of finances, and lack of self-restraint and perseverance. This view of poverty can be traced back to American scholar William Graham Sumner and British sociologist Herbert Spencer. Spencer introduced the application of the concept of survival of the fittest to human society as a justification for a society where the best and smartest succeed and the incompetent fall by the wayside (Spencer 1864). Both men believed that the poor were morally deficient and that there were biological explanations for that deficiency (Hawkins 1997). Thus, Sumner and Spencer were opposed to any attempt to develop comprehensive public policy aimed at alleviating poverty.

In the last quarter of the twentieth century two influential books, *Losing Ground* by Charles Murray, and *The Bell Curve* by Murray and Richard Herrnstein, elaborated upon and affirmed the "validity" of Spencer's arguments. Murray and Herrnstein were strongly opposed to welfare because they believed it encouraged laziness and a lack of personal responsibility. *The Bell Curve* maintained that people were impoverished for genetic reasons, and more specifically believed that poverty was directly connected to low IQ scores. Thus, they also believed that little could be done to change the condition of the poor. Murray and Herrnstein's research project generated serious scholarly challenge. Scholars who disputed *The Bell Curve* thesis asserted that poverty resulted in lower IQ scores, not that people were poor because they had lower IQ scores (Russell 1995).

A second view of poverty, which is also rooted in the concept of radical individualism, is the culture of poverty thesis: poor people perpetuate poverty by internalizing and maintaining a culture of poverty (Gossett 1970). The origin of this theory can be found in the works of social anthropologist Oscar Lewis (Lewis 1959). Lewis's primary argument was that some children raised in poverty internalize poverty to the point that it becomes an integral part of their personality and way of life. Lewis theorized that a culture of poverty exists at the personal, family, and community levels. For instance, Lewis argued that the poor were less apt to participate in normative social institutions in society (e.g., schools, marriage, and employment) and were more likely to interact with welfare system institutions and the criminal justice system. Lewis also believed that poor children experienced shortened childhoods and earlier sexual experiences. Furthermore, Lewis believed that in poor communities mothers often abandoned their children, that the institution of marriage was weakened, and that households tended to be female headed and female centered. At the personal level he theorized that the poor feel helpless, dependent, marginal, inferior in relation to others, and that they lack self-confidence, are fatalistic in their thinking, tend to act impulsively, and are less willing to defer gratification than others.

The third view of poverty, the structuralist view, is not rooted in the concept of radical individualism and stands in contrast to the two preceding theories which are nonstructuralist in their approach (Kerbo 2003). In the structuralist view, poverty is believed to be the result of unequal economic and political power due to the structure of the political and economic system. Urban sociologist William Julius Wilson is a proponent of the structuralist view (Wilson 1996, 1987). Wilson does not deny the empirical observations of Oscar Lewis's culture of poverty theory. However, Wilson challenges Lewis's causal reasoning. Wilson observes that the culture of poverty theory gives the impression that the poor are impoverished because of their unique social characteristics, and argues instead that structural conditions produce poverty and the culture of poverty that Lewis observed. From the structuralist viewpoint, the poor face a limited set of choices and options because of structural constraints in society, and only within these constraints do the social values, behaviors, and choices observed by Lewis make sense.

From the structuralist viewpoint one way that economic institutions create poverty is by not providing a sufficient number of jobs that pay wages adequate to keep people out of poverty. Thus, the structuralists argue, people are poor because they lack education and skill sets that are highly valued in the marketplace, and therefore have great difficulty in earning an above-poverty income. The relative lack of education and skills are considered the outcome of lower-quality education systems. Since the 1970s the labor market in the United States has undergone a restructuring, due to outsourcing of jobs overseas, labor-saving technologies, and competition from international businesses. As a result, fewer jobs for unskilled workers are available in the United States, and wages for the unskilled are depressed because of increased global competition for these jobs. If the educational institutions of society do not provide the poor with access to the training and education necessary to secure these jobs, the poor are unlikely to escape poverty. However, increased educational access is largely dependent upon the political process, and the poor also have relatively little political power and access. Political power is all too often derived from economic power, which the poor, by nature of being impoverished, lack. As a result, the poor are represented by fewer interest groups than their middle and upper class counterparts, and tend to be ignored by the political system. The end result, structuralists point out, is that the poor remain poor not because they are lazy or deficient in some way, but because the economic and political systems in place prevent them from escaping poverty.

While the structuralist versus nonstructuralist dichotomy provides a simple way to understand changing viewpoints on poverty over time, it is important to note that the viewpoints of individuals are often more complicated and cannot be fully explained by these two categories alone. Still, research has shown that certain demographical groups are more likely to hold to nonstructuralist views of poverty (i.e., are more likely to believe that poverty is the result of a lack of effort by the poor). These groups include Hispanics, Republicans, and those with a high school education or less. It may be surprising that Hispanics are more likely to hold to a nonstructuralist view of poverty because this demographic group experiences higher rates of poverty than the norm, but this is likely explained by the fact that a significant percentage of Hispanics are Catholic and Catholic religious affiliation is also correlated with nonstructuralist views of poverty (Hunt 2002). In contrast, those most likely to hold to structuralist views of poverty (i.e., that poverty is the result of circumstances beyond the control of the poor) are individuals with postgraduate education, Democrats, and Liberals (Belden Russonello and Stewart 2007).

THE PRESENT

With an understanding of some of the explanations for poverty that are offered in the United States the impact of the Great Recession on U.S. society's views on poverty can be explored. The Great Recession has led to an increased sense of class conflict, but it has also led more people to offer structuralist explanations for poverty. Nevertheless, this does not appear to have translated into an increased political will to alleviate poverty.

According to the Pew Research Center, in the aftermath of the Great Recession an increasing number of Americans believe that strong conflict exists between the rich and the poor (Morin 2012). Researchers found that 66 percent of those surveyed in 2011 felt that there was "strong" or "very strong" conflict between the rich and the poor in the United States (Morin 2012). This was a substantial increase from the 47 percent who believed a "strong" or "very strong" conflict existed between the rich and poor in 2009 (Morin 2012). In 2009 the sense of the rich-poor conflict reported was lower than that for the conflict between the native and foreign born; but between 2009 and 2011 the sense of the rich-poor conflict escalated to the top of the list above conflict between the native born and foreign born, the young and the old, and racial conflict between blacks and whites (Morin 2012).

In both the 2009 and 2011 surveys blacks and Hispanics were more likely to report "strong" or "very strong" conflict between the rich and poor than whites (Morin 2012). However, the percentage of whites reporting "strong" or "very strong" conflict increased 22 percentage points between 2009 and 2011, while there was only a 6 percentage point increase for Hispanics and an 8 percentage point increase for blacks (Morin 2012). Democrats and Independents were more likely to report that "strong" or "very strong" conflict exists between the rich and poor in both 2009 and 2011, as were those between the ages of 18 and 34 (Morin 2012). People over the age of 65 were less likely to report class conflict in both 2009 and 2011 (Morin 2012). Women were more likely than men to report class conflict, and those with some college education were more likely to report class conflict than college graduates or those with a high school education or less; those with a high school education or less were least likely to report class conflict (Morin 2012).

An increased percentage of people from all economic classes reported rich-poor conflict between 2009 and 2011. The increase in reported class conflict was relatively equal across income levels between 2009 and 2011, with slightly greater increases among those with incomes between $40,000 and $75,000 (Morin 2012). The economic group reporting the greatest sense of rich-poor conflict in 2009 (49 percent) earned an income of $75,000 or more a year, with the group earning between $20,000 and $40,000 reporting the least amount conflict (46 percent) (Morin 2012). In 2011 those making between $40,000 and $75,000 reported the most class conflict (71 percent), and those making less than $20,000 reported the least conflict (64 percent) (Morin 2012).

While Pew Researchers found an increasing sense of class conflict, they found no significant change in the nation's perception of the wealthiest Americans (Morin 2012). In 2011 around 43 percent of those surveyed believed that the wealthy became wealthy due to their "own hard work, ambition or education," a 1 percentage point increase from 2008 (Morin 2012). Virtually equal percentages of people with the highest incomes (over $100,000) and lowest incomes (less than $20,000) believed that being born in the right family or knowing the right people explains most wealth (47 percent and 46 percent respectively) (Morin 2012). Republicans are much more likely to attribute wealth to hard work rather than luck or connections (58 percent), than are Independents (45 percent) or Democrats (32 percent). Women and younger people are also more likely to believe that wealth comes from luck or connections (Morin 2012).

While the Great Recession has led to a greater sense of class conflict, it also seems to have resulted in increasingly structuralist explanations for poverty. Figure 1 shows data from 1964 through April 2012 (for years data is available) on the explanations survey respondents gave for why people are in poverty. The "lack of effort" response is a nonstructuralist explanation for poverty, and the "circumstances beyond their control" response can be roughly equated to a structuralist explanation for poverty. Research suggests that structuralist explanations for poverty are more prevalent during difficult economic or social times (Roller 2009). One way of measuring difficult economic times is by looking at the performance of the economy as measured by the unemployment rate. When the unemployment rate decreases (good economic times) there is an increase in the percentage of respondents who believe that poverty is generally the result of "lack of effort" (e.g., 1964 to 1967). When the unemployment rate increases (difficult economic times) there is an increase in respondents who believe that poverty is due to "circumstances beyond the control" of the poor (e.g., 1989 to 1992). The years 2007 to 2010, inclusive of the Great Recession, saw increasing unemployment rates and Figure 1 shows an increasing percentage of respondents identifying circumstance beyond the control of the poor as an explanation for poverty.

While the preceding data show that the Great Recession may have led to overall slightly more favorable views of the poor, more favorable views of those in poverty does not necessarily correlate with a political will to alleviate poverty. This may be particularly true in times of recession when resources are more limited than normal. In fact, research at the University of California–Berkeley has shown that the Great Recession made people less altruistic (i.e., less willing to redistribute their income to those with less to increase equality) in laboratory games. Subjects participating in the laboratory games before the Recession were more altruistic than those who participated in the same game after the Recession began; and subjects who

"In your opinion, which is generally more often to blame if a person is poor? Lack of effort on his or her own part, or circumstances beyond his or her control?"

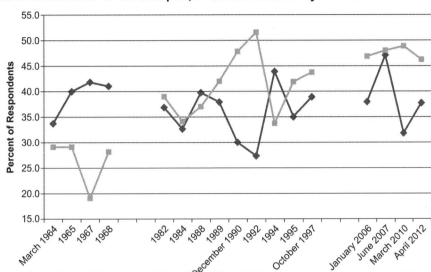

—◆— Lack of Effort–Individualist   —■— Circumstances Beyond Their Control–Structuralist

Figure 1

(*Note*: Percentages do not add to 100 percent due to rounding and additional choices ("Both" and "Don't Know/Refuse") responses offered on some of the surveys. *Source*: Survey by the Pew Research Center from http://www.people-press.org/files/legacy-questionnaires/Values%20topline%20for%20release.pdf; 1968 data are from Washington Post/Kaiser/Harvard Survey Project, American Values: 1998 National Survey of Americans on Values. Washington Post/Kaiser/Harvard Survey Project, American Values: 1998 National Survey of Americans on Values; January 26, 2006 data are from Survey by NBC News, Wall Street Journal conducted by Hart and McInturff Research at http://www.ropercenter.uconn.edu/cgi-bin/hsrun.exe/roperweb/pom/pom.htx;start=ipollsearch?TopID=327; June 2007 data are from Survey by The Opportunity Agenda conducted by Belden Russonello & Stewart at http://www.ropercenter.uconn.edu/cgi-bin/hsrun.exe/roperweb/pom/pom.htx;start=ipollsearch?TopID=327)

participated in laboratory games designed to imitate the impact of the Recession were also less altruistic (Fisman 2012).

It makes intuitive sense that people would be less willing to share resources in times of economic hardship, and research such as this can help to explain, in a new light, the vehement political debates that surrounded public benefits programs throughout the Great Recession. Still, despite the intense debate over public benefits, a Gallup survey in May 2012 revealed that 69 percent of respondents believed that "living standards for the poorest Americans" was an "extremely important" or "very important" economic issue facing the country (Saad 2012). However, the living standards of the poor ranked eighth on a list of 10 economic problems facing the nation. Thus, while U.S. constituents may believe that it is important to address the living standards of the poor, there are many other issues, including the federal deficit and U.S. debt (which ranked third), that are of greater importance to the bulk of the population.

In addition, many Americans believe that the poor have become too dependent on government assistance. A 2007 survey found that 71 percent of Americans were concerned that poor people in the United States were too dependent on government assistance (Belden Russonello and Stewart 2007). A 2011 survey found that 87 percent of respondents believed that the poor had become too dependent on government assistance (Public Religion Research Institute 2011). The heightened sense of limited resources during the Great Recession coupled with the decreased altruism found by researchers at Berkeley and the relatively low importance individuals place on poverty reduction in comparison to other economic issues, can help to explain why so many government programs aimed at the alleviation of poverty were the center of political debate during and after the Recession despite signs that the Recession may actually have slightly increased structuralist views even in the midst of a growing sense of class conflict.

OUTLOOK

Given the tough economic realities brought on by the Great Recession, characterized by significant loss of household wealth and income, unemployment rates which remain high, a large federal debt, and stagnant tax revenues, it will be all too easy for the concerns of the poor to remain a low priority issue. Despite the increasingly structuralist explanations for poverty offered by survey respondent's during the Great Recession, it does not appear that the United States possesses the political will to make substantial progress towards the alleviation of poverty.

Structuralist explanations for poverty are likely to wane somewhat as the economy recovers and the structural economic conditions that perpetuate poverty are no longer as obvious. In fact, data for April 2012 show that this is already happening. Between March 2010 and April 2012 there was a 6 percentage point increase in those who believed poverty was mostly the result of a lack of effort, and a 3 percentage point decrease in those who believed that poverty was mostly the result of circumstances beyond the control of the poor. Still, the split in opinion over structuralist and nonstructuralist explanations for poverty will remain, as will the uneasy tension between structuralist explanations for poverty and the United States' conception of itself as a nation of radical individualism and equal opportunity.

FURTHER READING

Belden Russonello and Stewart for The Opportunity Agenda. "Human Rights in the U.S.: Opinion Research with Advocates, Journalists, and the General Public," August 2007. Accessed August 5, 2012 http://opportunityagenda.org/pdfs/HUMAN%20RIGHTS%20REPORT.PDF

Fisman, Raymond, Pamela Jakiela, and Shachar Karivy. "How Did the Great Recession Impact Social Preferences?" University of California–Berkeley, May 31, 2012. Accessed August 5, 2012. http://emlab.berkeley.edu/~kariv/FJK_I.pdf

Fraser, Steven. *The Bell Curve Wars: Race, Intelligence and the Future of America*. New York: Basic Books, 1995.

Gans, Herbert J. "The Uses of Poverty: The Poor Pay All." *Social Policy* July/August 1971: 20–24. Accessed August 5, 2012. http://www.sociology.org.uk/as4p3.pdf

Gossett, Thomas F. *Race: The History of an Idea in America*. New York: Schocken, 1970.

Hawkins, Mike. *Social Darwinism in European and American Thought, 1860–1945: Nature as a Model and Nature as a Threat*. New York: Cambridge University Press, 1997.

Hunt, Matthew O. "Religion, Race/Ethnicity, and Beliefs About Poverty." *Social Science Quarterly* 83, no. 2 (September 2002). Accessed May 17, 2013. http://nuweb.neu.edu/mhunt/articles/SSQ%2002.pdf

Jacoby, Russell, and Naomi Glauberman. *The Bell Curve Debate*. New York: Three Rivers, 1995.

Kerbo, Harold R. *Social Stratification and Inequality: Class Conflict in Historical, Comparative, and Global Perspective*. 5th ed. Boston: McGraw Hill, 2003.

Lewis, Oscar. *Five Families: Mexican Case Studies in the Culture of Poverty*. New York: Basic Books, 1959.

Marger, Martin N. *Social Inequality: Patterns and Processes*. 4th ed. Boston: McGraw Hill, 2008.

Morin, Rich. "Rising Share of Americans See Conflict between Rich and Poor." Pew Research Center, January 11, 2012. Accessed July 21, 2012. http://www.pewsocialtrends.org/2012/01/11/rising-share-of-americans-see-conflict-between-rich-and-poor/

Public Religion Research Institute. "PRRI/RNS Religion News Survey, November 10–14, 2011," November 16, 2011. Accessed August 5, 2012. http://publicreligion.org/site/wp-content/uploads/2011/11/November-PRRI-RNS-2011-Topline.pdf

Roller, John Edwin. "Support for Social Programs: Effects of Class, Race, Political Ideology, and Poverty Beliefs." College of Graduate Studies of Georgia Southern University, May 2009. Accessed August 5, 2012. http://www.georgiasouthern.edu/etd/archive/spring2009/john_e_roller/roller_john_e_200901_mass.pdf

Saad, Lydia. "Obama, Romney Each Has Economic Strengths with Americans." Gallup, May 12, 2012. Accessed August 5, 2012. Http://Www.Gallup.Com/Poll/154727/Obama-Romney-Economic-Strengths-Americans.Aspx

Spencer, Herbert. *The Principles of Biology*. London: Williams and Norgate, 1864.

Wilson, William Julius. *The Truly Disadvantaged: The Inner City, the Underclass, and Public Policy*. Chicago: University of Chicago Press, 1987.

Wilson, William Julius. *When Work Disappears: The World of the New Urban Poor*. New York: Knopf, 1996.

Conclusion: What Can Be Done About Poverty in the United States?

Timothy J. Essenburg

OVERVIEW

This work began by discussing why many people care about reducing poverty in the United States (see the introduction), and the essays presented in this text have explored the face of poverty in the United States in the context of the Great Recession and its immediate aftermath. Understanding why one might care about poverty and what poverty in the United States looks like is important, but this discussion may leave one wondering what can be done about poverty in the United States today. Scholars, economists, politicians, and lay people have suggested numerous public and private solutions for the poverty problem in the United States. This conclusion delves deeply into at least one possible solution that has been put forth by prominent poverty researchers. This conclusion is divided into two parts. Part I explores institutional constraints on poverty alleviation in the United States, and Part II explores some suggestions for poverty alleviation from within these institutional constraints, as well as the likelihood that these proposals will be implemented in the coming years.

Part I explains what is meant by the term "institutional constraints" by exploring the concepts of worldview, institutions, and path dependency. With a basic understanding of these important terms one can see how the enlightenment worldview, the prevailing worldview at the time the United States was founded, still influences U.S. society today and how this impacts poverty alleviation efforts. With this background, Part I outlines institutional reform efforts that affected poverty alleviation in the turbulent decades of the 1930s and 1960s, as well as the backlash response (i.e., conservative revolution) to these reform efforts, which was aimed at returning

U.S. institutions to their pre-reform state, more in line with the enlightenment worldview. Finally, Part I presents public opinion polling data from the United States and other countries to show how the enlightenment worldview plays out in modern U.S. institutions and how this influences poverty alleviation efforts in the United States today.

With the understanding of institutional constraints on poverty alleviation in the United States covered in Part I, Part II presents a suggestion for public poverty alleviation in the United States that attempts to work within these U.S. institutional constraints. This suggestion comes from prominent poverty scholars Isabel Sawhill and Ron Haskins and is based on the idea that the United States should strive to become an opportunity society, in essence a society that is characterized by equal opportunity and a high degree of economic mobility such that those born into poverty have a very real chance of escaping it. Sawhill and Haskins theorize that this opportunity society can be created by implementing policies that encourage individuals to live their lives in a "success sequence" in which they first attain education, then employment, then a family. After discussing specific policy reforms suggested by Sawhill and Haskins to encourage this success sequence, Part II then discusses the likelihood that these policy reforms will be made in the coming years.

THE PRESENT

PART I: INSTITUTIONAL CONSTRAINTS ON POVERTY ALLEVIATION IN THE UNITED STATES

Worldview

A worldview can be thought of as an all-inclusive structure composed of one's fundamental views about life (Wolters 1985). A worldview is the filter through which one understands his or her world and his or her role in it. It answers important questions such as How did the universe come into being? What is my purpose in life? What values should govern human interaction? What type of political economy should a nation implement? More pertinent to the topic at hand, it also provides answers to the question: Should society be concerned about poverty, and if so, how should it display this concern? Worldviews are shaped by many elements, but most importantly they are shaped by life experiences (American Scientific Affiliation 2013). Worldviews are not only personal, they are also displayed in the structure of societies and are thus linked to power because the group, or groups, with power embed their worldview into societal institutions (North 1991, 1994).

Institutions

To understand what it means to embed one's worldview into institutions it is first important to understand what an institution is. Institutions are comprised of four parts: (1) people doing something (i.e., human action and interaction); (2) rules for what people are doing, including both formal rules (e.g., constitutions, antitrust law, law regarding property rights) and informal rules (e.g., customs and traditions); (3) enforcement mechanisms that uphold the rules (again, both formal and informal in nature); and (4) stories people tell that answer the "why questions" (i.e., why people act and interact as they do, and why the rules of a society exist), in so doing, these stories justify actions, interactions, and rules in society (Hodgson 2006; Neale 1987; North 1991, 1994). Because institutions are upheld by the worldviews of those who have power, changing institutions requires those in power to see things differently and/or those without power to somehow gain power.

Path Dependency

Institutions constrain human behavior and give it predictability, thus making problem solving path dependent (Neale 1987; North 1991, 1994). "Path dependence" is a term used in the field of economics and social science to explain that the array of current options is constrained by past circumstance and decisions. Path dependency, in its most general sense, conveys the idea that history matters in terms of understanding current realities and making current decisions. Thus, institutions are carriers of history and constrain current decisions, but they do not fully determine current decisions.

By way of example take the QWERTY keyboard, the U.S. Constitution, and the distribution of assets. The QWERTY keyboard constrains computer makers' choice of ordering letters on a keyboard because the QWERTY system is all that most current U.S. users know. The Declaration of Independence and Constitution constrain policy options. For example, a presidential declaration could not raise income taxes because the Constitution does not give the executive branch the authority to do this. The Constitution reserves this power for Congress. Finally, the distribution of privately owned assets today is a function of history and thus constrains the market-generated incomes of tomorrow (David 1994; Page 2006).

Because path dependency carries on the worldview of those who create a society's institutions, it is important to understand the historic worldview that is being carried on in a modern society's institutions. Institutions in the United States are the product of an Enlightenment worldview because the United States was founded, and its most important institutions created (including its representative democracy and market economy), during the Enlightenment era. The Enlightenment worldview is thus ingrained into U.S. institutions, and even though the Enlightenment era is over, its ideals have been carried on in the United States through U.S. institutions due to path dependency. For this reason, to understand the United States today it is important to have a sense of the Enlightenment worldview.

The Enlightenment Worldview and the Founding of the United States

Broadly conceived, Enlightenment philosophy, which began in western Europe in the mid-1600s, can be thought of as focusing on what is true, good, and beautiful. In the Enlightenment worldview truth is believed to come through skeptical human reasoning, and in particular science and the scientific method. The good, in the political sense, is understood as being derived from the consent of the governed, which is undergirded by the notions of freedom, equality, and individual rights. The Enlightenment conception of the beautiful focuses on human pleasure and what is discoverable by reason, science, and the laws of nature. In contrast to earlier eras, the Enlightenment worldview turns away from the political and social hierarchies of monarchies and the church, and with them the unscientific grounding of tradition, myth, and miracles (Bristow 2011). These ideas are foundational to the Western worldview and are expressed today in a constitutional and limited government, individual freedoms, and beliefs in the importance of freedom from religious tyranny, private property rights, a free-market economy, and the belief that nature is understood through reason (Hanson 2009).

The Enlightenment worldview can perhaps best be understood through its most prominent thinkers. Three Enlightenment thinkers stand out, each of whom played a key role in the founding and development of the United States: John Locke, Adam Smith, and Thomas Jefferson. John Locke (1632–1704) believed that human rights precede governments and are therefore natural rights. These natural rights, according to Locke, are the right to life, liberty, property, and health (Uzgalis 2012). Locke reasoned that the first property one owns is oneself. For example, when one puts one's own labor into placing fences on land and tilling soil, the fences and the fruit of the land are then one's private property. He also reasoned that consent of the governed was a requirement of all legitimate governments because then the basis of such a government would be individual rights.

Adam Smith (1723–1790) penned *An Inquiry into the Nature and Causes of the Wealth of Nations* (1776). In that work he made the case for doing away with mercantilism and instituting what today is called a market economy. Smith, like many other Enlightenment thinkers, believed in a deistic god, a God that created and then abandoned the universe, leaving it to run on natural law free from supernatural intervention. Thus, Smith believed that there were natural laws that governed social interaction. These laws, he reasoned, would lead to harmonious social outcomes in the economic sphere of life (Jensen 1976). For example, if people adhere to their own self-interest in a competitive environment, a kind of harmonious order arises from the chaos of individual decision making, with the outcome being that governments increase their tax revenues and citizens experience an increasing standard of living.

Finally, Thomas Jefferson (1743–1826), another Enlightenment thinker and deist, defended inalienable individual rights such as consent of the governed and freedom from religious tyranny. Jefferson was the lead author of the Declaration of Independence, and these beliefs can clearly be seen in this document, which—in one of its most oft-quoted segments—reads:

> We hold these truths to be self-evident, that all men are created equal, that they are endowed by their Creator with certain unalienable Rights, that among these are Life, Liberty and the pursuit of Happiness.—That to secure these rights, Governments are instituted among Men, deriving their just powers from the consent of the governed, — That whenever any Form of Government becomes destructive of these ends, it is the Right of the People to alter or to abolish it, and to institute new Government, laying its foundation on such principles and organizing its powers in such form, as to them shall seem most likely to effect their Safety and Happiness.

The political economic system which was "most likely to effect ... [the] Safety and Happiness" was, in the view of the nation's founders, a representative democracy and a market economy, both of which were congruent with Enlightenment beliefs as discussed earlier in this essay. It is important to note that nothing in a representative democracy requires specific attention to poverty or distribution of income, except insofar as it creates and upholds the laws of private property, individual rights, and a competitive market economy. It does not require public laws that seek to benefit the impoverished. In the Enlightenment view, then, Americans were to make it on their own in a market economy, as equals before the laws of the land. The role of government was to set up formal rules that would enable persons who act responsibly and live out the values of life, liberty, and the pursuit of happiness to remain above some culturally determined baseline of material well-being and human dignity (Messmore 2012). The bulk of the responsibility for social justice fell to civil society, that is, private philanthropic and religious organizations and the efforts of good neighbors (Messmore 2012). Americans, by and large, approve of this kind of a political economy.

As with all worldviews and institutions, the Enlightenment worldview and its institutions contain both strengths and weaknesses. One of the weaknesses arose when the creators and enforcers of the formal rules of society (e.g., the federal government, courts, and state governments) intentionally or unintentionally denied certain groups of persons life, liberty, and/or the pursuit of happiness. This becomes an even greater problem when the informal rules and enforcement mechanisms in society also deny access to certain groups. Historically when this occurs poverty ensues. The only recourse persons have is to "alter or abolish" the formal rules and mechanisms. There are four groups of persons who were historically denied such access by the spirit of the Declaration of Independence and/or the rights guaranteed by the Constitution. These include women, Native Americans, African Americans,

Mexican Americans, and Asian Americans. In facts the Declaration of Independence *de facto* (in practice) and the Constitution *de jure* (in law) made available to white males rights not available to white women and all persons of color. However, because white women were associated with white men through family (i.e., wives, daughters, female cousins, aunts, and grandmothers), their material well-being was not compromised to the same extent as that of minorities.

While the Enlightenment worldview, with both its strengths and weaknesses, remains deeply ingrained in U.S. institutions and is perpetuated by path dependency, U.S. institutions have not been unaltered since the founding of the nation. Efforts have been made by some to address what they see as weaknesses in U.S. institutions. These changes are often easier to make in times of national turmoil when society as a whole tends to question institutions more deeply. Thus, it is useful to discuss some of the institutional changes that took place in two turbulent decades in U.S. history: the 1930s and the 1960s.

Institutional Reform in the 1930s

The Great Depression occurred in the 1930s; during that decade economic conditions were desperate for many people. According to the Federal Reserve Bank of St. Louis, the economy experienced deflation in three consecutive years (1930 to 1932), inflation-adjusted gross domestic product (GDP) fell for four consecutive years (1930 to 1933), and the annual unemployment rate for the entire decade (excepting 1930) exceeded the highest unemployment rate for all subsequent years through 2012. In fact, the unemployment rate for the decade averaged approximately 18 percent, with a high of 25 percent in 1933. In the face of this national turmoil Adam Smith's notion of harmonious economic outcomes was called into question.

Two noteworthy changes arose from this questioning: first, the Social Security Act (SSA) of 1935 and the Fair Labor Standards Act (FLSA) of 1938 were signed into law. SSA provided income support to older adults and to survivors (spouse and children), and instituted the first welfare program, Aid to Families with Dependent Children (AFDC). AFDC provided income supplements to single parents with children. These programs marked a significant change from the Enlightenment view that called only for "negative" freedoms (e.g., freedom from the tyranny of monarchy and religion) rather than the "positive" freedom of freedom from want. Old age and survivor benefits, and AFDC (provided by the Social Security Act) thus reflected a change in political thinking. FLSA specified a minimum wage, a definite violation of the noninterventionist government vis-à-vis the market economy envisioned by the founders and Adam Smith.

Second, the discipline of economics itself underwent significant change. Prior to the Great Depression there were other recessions and financial panics. Still, economic theory predicted that market competition would soon restore the economy to full employment and held that persons who were unemployed voluntarily chose to be unemployed. This changed when John Maynard Keynes published *The General Theory of Employment, Interest, and Money* (1936). Among other arguments, Keynes posited that unemployment may be involuntary and that an economy could remain below full employment for a number of years. From this, while still maintaining a commitment to the benefits of a market economy, Keynes demonstrated the need for active monetary and fiscal policy (see Section 1 of this work). In other words, he provided a theoretical argument for the federal government playing an active role in guiding the economy to full employment. Both the new federal programs and Keynes's version of macroeconomics broke with the dominant thinking prior to the Depression. Path dependency made these breaks difficult, but they were by no means unmanageable, particularly in a time of national turmoil like the Great Depression. Path dependency certainly prevented the United States from turning to a communist system because this would have almost entirely violated the Enlightenment worldview imbedded in U.S. institutions. However, path dependence did leave room for less dramatic reforms.

Institutional Reform in the 1960s

The 1960s was another tumultuous decade in U.S. history. It brought the civil rights movement, protests against the Vietnam War, and changing sexual mores. Poverty rates in communities of color were particularly high at this time. In addition to the passage of the Civil Rights Act of 1964, the federal government sought to develop programs targeting persons in poverty, thus emphasizing positive freedoms. In this context President Johnson declared a War on Poverty and persuaded Congress to enact legislation to reduce poverty through various programs such as Head Start, Job Corps, Community Action Programs (CAP), the Office of Economic Opportunity, Volunteers in Service to America (VISTA), TRIO (an educational program, not an acronym), and Legal Services (Germany 2013). The focus of the War on Poverty was on education and employment. There was also debate during this time that the government should guarantee some minimum level of income, but this was opposed by President Johnson over concerns that the measure did not encourage people to work (Mason 2013). This concern is evidence that Enlightenment thinking, through path dependency, continued to play a role in policy decisions even in this time of national questioning.

The Impact of the Institutional Reforms of the 1930s and 1960s on Poverty

The Social Security Act of 1935 (old age and survivors benefits, AFDC), the minimum wage guaranteed by the Fair Labor Standards Act of 1938, the civil rights legislation of the 1960s, and the War on Poverty that began in the mid-1960s reduced poverty rates (see Figures 1 and 2). All three age groups shown (Figure 1) experienced declines in poverty rates. Those 65 and older in particular experienced declining poverty rates, which highlights the impact of the Social Security Act of 1935. Figure 2 presents poverty rates by race. Note in particular the decline of 25 percentage points in the African American poverty rate. It is possible to conclude that civil rights legislation and targeted benefit programs combined with a strong economy to reduce poverty this substantially.

Not only did Society Security provisions (Old Age and Survivors benefits Medicare) reduce the poverty rate among older adults when it was enacted, but even today it prevents the poverty rate for this age group from being higher than it otherwise would be. For example, the Center on Budget and Policy Priorities estimated that the 2011 poverty rate among those 65 and older would have been

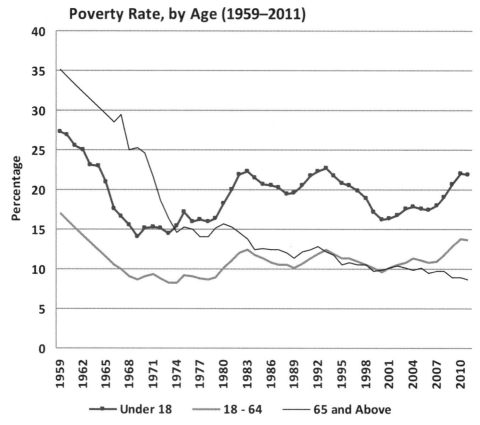

Figure 1
(*Note*: Lines for 18-64 and 65 and Above connect 1959 with 1966 because of missing data. Source: U.S. Census, Historical Poverty Tables—People, Table 3: "Poverty Status of People, by Age, Race, and Hispanic Origin: 1959 to 2011," http://www.census.gov/hhes/www/poverty/data/historical/people.html)

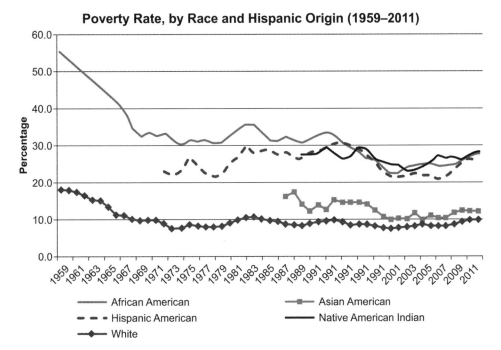

Figure 2

(*Note*: African American: Black (1959-2001; 1959 connected to 1966 due to missing data) Black Alone (2002-2011). Asian American: Asian and Pacific Islander (1987-2001) Asian Alone (2002-2011). Hispanic American: Hispanic (1972-2011). Native American Indian: American Indian and Alaska Native (1989-2001) American Indian and Alaska Native Alone (2002-2011). White: White (1959-1972, White Non-Hispanic (1973-2001), White Alone, Non-Hispanic (2002-2011). *Source:* African American, Asian American, White from U.S. Census. Historical Poverty Tables—People. Table 2. Poverty Status of People by Family Relationship, Race, and Hispanic Origin: 1959 to 2011. http://www.census.gov/ hhes/www/poverty/data/historical/people.html. Native American from U.S. Census. Historical Poverty Tables—People. Table 24. Number in Poverty and Poverty Rate by Race and Hispanic Origin Using 3-Year Averages: 1987 to 2011. http://www.census.gov/ hhes/www/poverty/data/historical/people.html.)

43.6 percent, rather than the actual poverty rate of 8.7 percent, without Social Security (Van de Water 2012).

   With the record that Social Security has in reducing poverty among older adults, one might ask why the government does not institute similar programs for persons aged 64 and younger. One could argue that Social Security recipients are simply getting back what they put in during their working lives. However, the Social Security system has always been a pay as you go system. This means that the current labor force is taxed and those funds are transferred to today's older adults, rather than today's older adults actually receiving funds they put in during their working years. Thus, it is a transfer program, just as unemployment compensation and cash assistance welfare are. If U.S. society is at least relatively comfortable being taxed so that funds can be transferred to older adults, why is it seemingly less inclined to tax so that funds can be transferred to the poor 64 years of age and younger in order to further reduce poverty? The simple answer is that society finds it acceptable for persons 65 and older not to work and thus believes that generous welfare (Old Age and Survivors benefits, Medicare) for this group is acceptable. In contrast, U.S. society is significantly less comfortable providing such benefits to those aged 18 to 64, primarily because they are considered working age and thus should generate their own income for themselves and their children. Regardless of whether one agrees with this sentiment, it is further evidence that the Enlightenment-era beliefs in property and a free market continue in U.S. institutions today. Because of these beliefs a conservative movement developed to respond to those in the United States concerned that the institutional reforms of the 1930s and 1960s pushed the country too far from the important Enlightenment-era concepts of free markets, a noninterventionist government, and private property.

The Conservative Revolution in Three Phases

In response to the Great Depression the role of the federal government expanded considerably. From the extensive reforms of the Social Security Act to the creation of various administrative agencies (e.g., Federal Housing Administration, Civil Aeronautics Board, National Labor Relations Board, Federal Communications Commission), many conservatives became concerned with the expanding reach of the federal government. Thus began what some have called a conservative revolution. Phase one in this revolution was the Republican Party's endorsement of Barry Goldwater as its presidential nominee for the 1964 election. However, Democratic nominee Lyndon Johnson won in a landslide (61.1 percent of the popular vote and 90.3 percent of the electoral vote) (Gayner 1995; American Presidency Project 2013). Thus, the Johnson administration continued its Great Society with the War on Poverty, Medicare and Medicaid, and civil rights legislation that included Affirmative Action programs. Despite their lack of political power at the time, conservatives continued the movement to redefine the federal government's role in society.

Phase two of the conservative revolution came in 1980 with the election of President Ronald Reagan and the Reagan Revolution (Gayner 1995). Reagan addressed the political and economic agenda of conservatives by pursuing four goals: (1) cutting the growth of federal spending, (2) reducing personal and corporate income tax rates, (3) continuing the deregulation started by the Carter administration, and (4) reducing the inflation rate (Niskanen 1993). Reagan succeeded in all four of his aims. The Reagan Revolution was followed by the presidencies of George H. W. Bush and Bill Clinton.

In Clinton's first term he pushed for health care reform characterized by managed competition and universal coverage, which conservatives strongly opposed (Pfiffner 2013). In response Republicans galvanized themselves and won back a majority in the House of Representatives during the mid-term elections of 1994. In that election Republicans made a promise to the American people outlined in their "Contract with America." This contract constitutes phase three of the conservative revolution. It identified 10 reforms "aimed at restoring the faith and trust of the American people in their government" (National Center for Public Policy Research 1994). The proposed reforms can be placed into three categories: (1) family, (2) economy, and (3) politics. Conservatives promised to reduce taxes, make government smaller, and focus on the importance of family. As part of these efforts the Personal Responsibility and Work Opportunity and Reconciliation Act (PRWORA) was signed into law in 1996. The act begins with a section on findings:

> The Congress makes the following findings: (1) Marriage is the foundation of a successful society. (2) Marriage is an essential institution of a successful society which promotes the interest of children. (3) Promotion of responsible fatherhood and motherhood is integral to successful child rearing and the well-being of children. (4) In 1992, only 54 percent of single-parent families with children had a child support order established and, of that 54 percent, only about one-half received the full amount due ... (5) The number of individuals receiving ... AFDC ... has more than tripled since 1965. More than two-thirds of these recipients are children ... [Over the same time period] the total number of children in the United States aged 0 to 18 has declined by 5.5 percent. (H.R. 3734 1996).

The upshot of the act was to turn AFDC into Temporary Assistance for Needy Families (TANF) and to make TANF a block grant program that gave each state the flexibility to design its own delivery system. The federal financial commitment to TANF was capped. The legislation also limited adult lifetime use to five years and put in place work requirements. The findings contained in PRWORA imply that its reform efforts were aimed at encouraging marriage and work to reduce poverty rather than reducing poverty through government benefits. This represents a return to conceptions of the government's role in poverty reduction that are closer to Enlightenment-era beliefs.

While governmental commitment to lower-income persons waned during the 1980s and 1990s, there was one exception: the Earned Income Tax Credit (EITC). EITC was part of the Tax Reduction Act of 1975 and is now considered one of the main poverty reduction programs for working families. In 2011 it raised 6.1 million people, including 3.1 million children, out of poverty (Forman 2013; Center on Budget and Policy Priorities 2013). That year it provided a maximum credit of

$5,028 to two-child families with an income of $16,420 and phases out to $0 when income reaches $40,295 (Tax Policy Center 2013). The EITC became permanent in 1978 and was expanded in 1984, 1986, 1990, 1993, and 2001, always receiving bipartisan support (Forman 2013). The program is popular because it incentivizes people to work and reduces the incidence of poverty. There is even some evidence that it results in improved school performance of children (Charite 2012; Hotz 2003). Its main limitation is that recipients must be employed, a condition that was much more difficult to meet during the Great Recession and its aftermath. It must also be observed that EITC guarantees working families neither economic security nor a basic needs level of income (see Section 2, "Economic Insecurity"). Still, the EITC has been able to elicit continual bipartisan support in part because its work requirements comport with American conceptions of personal responsibility and work that align with the Enlightenment worldview that is embedded in modern U.S. institutions.

Enlightenment Worldview in Modern U.S. Society

The dominant worldview in the United States today, in line with Enlightenment thinking, emphasizes personal responsibility, individualism, and the freedom to pursue one's goals (i.e., life, liberty, and the pursuit of happiness) in the context of a representative democracy and market economy. In contrast to beliefs in many other countries, the majority of Americans believe that this freedom to pursue personal goals is more important than having a society in which everyone is free from need. This can be seen in the data provided in Table 1. Britain, the country the United States fought to gain independence from, and France and Spain, allies in the pursuit of that independence, all clearly value freedom from material need for all more than the freedom to pursue life's goals. Among these three countries an average of 62 percent ranked "nobody in need" over "freedom to pursue life's goals." In contrast, only 25 percent of Americans ranked having no one in need as more important than freedom to pursue life's goals.

This is not simply evidence that Americans fail to see poverty as a problem or do not care about poverty; rather, it is evidence of the American path-dependent relationship with freedom and individualism. In fact, in polling prior to the Recession a majority of Americans reported believing that poverty in the United States was a big problem (Table 2). Respondents from lower-income households were more likely to believe that poverty was a big problem, but even among respondents above 200 percent of the poverty level a slight majority agreed (Table 2).

Thus, most Americans believe poverty is a problem but think that freedom to pursue one's life goals is more important than everyone being from free from need. American beliefs about individualism can help tie these two poll results together. Not only is individualism valued in and of itself (i.e., it is seen as a virtue),

Table 1 Nobody in Need vs. Individual Freedom

Which Is More Important?		
Social Value		
Country	Nobody in Need	Freedom to Pursue Life's Goals
Britain	55%	38%
Germany	62%	36%
France	64%	36%
Spain	67%	30%
United States	25%	58%

Source: Stokes, Bruce. "Public Attitudes toward the Next Social Contract." New American Foundation, 2013. Accessed February 8, 2013. http://www.pewglobal.org/2013/01/15/public-attitudes-toward-the-next-social-contract/.

but it is also thought to play the dominant role in success in life (Table 3). While 36 percent of Americans think success in life is determined by forces outside of individual control, Europeans—and most particularly Germans (72 percent)—view success as significantly more dependent on forces outside of individual control.

The tension between American beliefs in freedom and individualism and concern about poverty can be seen in Table 4. The data presented in Table 4 indicate that the majority of people (60 percent) believe that it is difficult to escape poverty and that poverty is trap (59 percent). However, 49 percent think a good work ethic is all that is needed to escape poverty, and 55 percent think that eliminating poverty is not even possible.

The importance Americans place on individualism and personal effort also comes through when Americans are asked about what plays the biggest role in

Table 2 Is Poverty a Big Problem?

Poverty Is a Big Problem, by Income (2001)	
Income Level Relative to the Poverty Threshold	Percentage
Less than 100%	67
100–200%	63
More than 200%	52

Source: "Poverty In America." NPR/Kaiser/Kennedy School Poll, May 2001. Accessed May 15, 2013. http://www.npr.org/programs/specials/poll/poverty/summary.html.

Table 3   Views on Individualism

| | Success in Life Is Determined by Forces outside Our Control? | | |
| | Percentage Response | | |
Country	Agree	Disagree	Don't Know
Germany	72	27	1
France	57	43	0
Spain	50	47	3
Britain	41	55	4
United States	36	62	3

Source: Stokes, Bruce. "Public Attitudes toward the Next Social Contract." New American Foundation, 2013. Accessed February 8, 2013. http://www.pewglobal.org/files/2013/01/Stokes_Bruce_NAF_Public_Attitudes_1_2013.pdf.

getting more opportunity and getting ahead: education, the state of the economy, race/ethnicity, skills, or income level. In polling, very few Americans think that race or income level plays the biggest role in getting ahead (Mizell 2012). Instead, polling shows Americans believe that the most important factors in getting ahead are a person's educational background and skills (Mizell 2012). Race/ethnicity, income level, and even the state of the overall economy are seen as being less important (Mizell 2012). This highlights the importance Americans place on factors that are believed to be within an individual's own control in success in life.

Table 4   Perceptions of Poverty, 2012

Statement	Percentage Response in Agreement
Once you become poor, it is really hard to find a way out of poverty.	60
If we gave poor people more assistance, they would take advantage of it.	47
A good work ethic is all you need to escape poverty.	49
Poverty is a trap some Americans just can't escape, no matter how hard they try.	59
It's not possible to eliminate poverty in our society.	55

Source: Salvation Army. "Perception of Poverty: The Salvation Army's Report to America," 2012. Accessed May 15, 2013. http://www.salvationarmy.com/usn/2012povertyreport.pdf.

The American commitment to individual freedom and the sense of being in control of one's destiny are a kind of path dependency in the United States that constrains public poverty alleviation efforts to those that, for the most part, do not violate these important American beliefs. Thus, when considering what types of public efforts toward poverty alleviation will be at least politically viable in the United States, these constraints are important to understand. The second section of this conclusion will discuss policy reform suggestions from poverty scholars who attempt to work within these constraints toward public efforts to alleviate poverty in the United States.

PART II: PUBLIC EFFORTS FOR POVERTY ALLEVIATION FROM WITHIN THE U.S. INSTITUTIONAL FRAMEWORK

In the unique context of American beliefs about freedom and personal responsibility, which stem from the Enlightenment worldview imbedded in modern U.S. institutions, there are certain types of public efforts toward poverty alleviation that are simply not politically viable in the United States despite the fact that they may be viable in other countries. One politically unviable option is large-scale government tax transfers to the poor, while one more politically viable option is based on policy reform efforts to create an opportunity society, or a society characterized by equal opportunity and a high degree of economic mobility. These two approaches will be discussed in the coming section along with the likelihood of either of these approaches being adopted in the coming years.

Politically Unviable Poverty Alleviation: Large-Scale Cash Transfers

Conservative scholar Michael Tanner published an article in 2012 entitled "The American Welfare State: How We Spend Nearly $1 Trillion a Year Fighting Poverty: And Fail." He totaled all government spending (federal, state, and local) on welfare programs and found that it amounted to an average of $59,233 for a poor family of three. His conclusion was that welfare programs have failed the poor and taxpayers because if a family of three had simply been given $59,233, they would no longer be poor. First, it must be noted that poverty thresholds are based on cash incomes on a before-tax basis (U.S. Census Bureau 2013). Thus, poverty rates do not factor the "income" from EITC, Medicaid, Supplemental Nutrition Assistance Program (SNAP/food stamps), Section 8 housing vouchers, subsidized school lunch programs, and the like. Still, if U.S. governments at all levels are really spending this much money on poverty alleviation, one might ask why governments do not simply transfer these funds to households in order to bring the poverty rate to 0.0 percent. The fundamental reason is that this goes against the national commitment to individual responsibility that was discussed earlier in this essay

(Gilens 1999). This commitment to individual responsibility results in a general opposition to welfare because welfare recipients are viewed as not fulfilling their personal responsibilities. Though Americans want others to do well, this charitableness conflicts with the value of commitment to personal responsibility. Therefore, cash transfers sufficient to bring every family to 200 percent of the poverty threshold, even if financially feasible, are extremely unlikely to be enacted.

Politically Viable Poverty Alleviation: Creation of an Opportunity Society

If the United States is not likely to simply transfer funds to the poor in order to reduce poverty, a more politically viable option that works within American beliefs about freedom and personal responsibility, must be generated. One option is to work from American beliefs about the importance of equal opportunity. Americans overwhelmingly favor equal opportunity. Public opinion polling over the past 25 years has shown 86 to 94 percent (90.3 percent on average) support for the concept of equal opportunity (Mizell 2012). However, there is no agreement on whether the United States is actually a society with equal opportunity or if more should be done to ensure equal opportunity. An average of 43.3 percent of those polled over the past 25 years thought that society had gone too far in trying to provide equal rights, while 53.6 percent thought society has not gone far enough in providing equal rights (Mizell 2012). Thus, Americans strongly favor equal opportunity but are split as to whether they believe more should be done to ensure equal opportunity. Still, with data showing that 42 percent of U.S. children born to families with incomes in the bottom fifth remain in the bottom fifth of the income distribution, and 39 percent of children whose parents have incomes in the top fifth remain in the top fifth of the income distribution (Isaacs 2008), there is reason to believe that the United States is not yet a society characterized by truly equal opportunity.

Thus, poverty scholars Ron Haskins (a developmental psychologist and Republican) and Isabel Sawhill (an economist and Democrat) have put forth a comprehensive suggestion for alleviating poverty in the United States by creating an *opportunity society*, or a society in which there is equal opportunity and thus a high degree of economic mobility so that children born into poverty have a real chance of escaping it. According to Haskins and Sawhill, the creation of an opportunity society requires the formation of institutions (rules, enforcement mechanisms, and stories that justify the rule and enforcement mechanisms) that nurture certain values and behavior. The values and behaviors that should be nurtured to this end are those that lend themselves to a "success sequence" that will increase the probability that individuals and households will gain economic security by their own efforts. Following the success sequence entails attaining education, then employment, and finally a family. If this success sequence is followed, the United

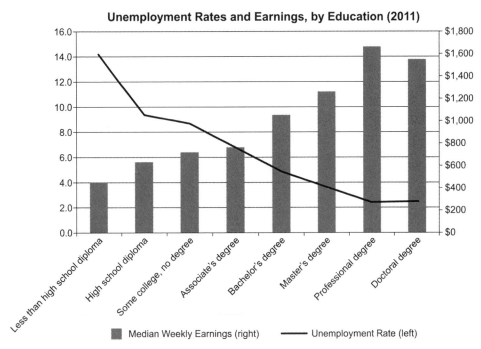

Figure 3

(*Source:* Bureau of Labor Statistics, Current Population Survey, http://www.bls.gov/emp/ ep_chart_001.htm. *Note:* Data are for persons age 25 and over. Earnings are for full-time wage and salary workers.)

States will—through private and government efforts—become an opportunity society (Haskins 2009).

The first step in the success sequence is education. Educational outcomes are thought to depend on genes, environment, and effort, all of which interact with each other. As a result, some children will need more help than others in attaining an education due to genes and environment. Thus, access to quality preschool and K-12 schools, particularly for low-income children, is a crucial component of creating an opportunity society.

The second step in the success sequence is attaining employment. This step comes after education because those with higher levels of educational attainment generally have higher earnings and suffer less from unemployment (Figure 3). Not only does median weekly income increase as education levels increase, but unemployment rates also drop (Haskins 2009). For example, when a high school graduates' median weekly income was $638, the median weekly income was $1,053 for those with a bachelor's degree. This amounts to an $865,000 income difference over a 40-year work life. In addition there is almost a 50 percent reduction in the probability of being unemployed for those with a bachelor's degree compared to high school graduates (from 9.4 percent for high school graduates to 4.9 percent for those with bachelor's degrees).

Finally, the third step in the success sequence is family formation: marriage and then children. The data show that marriage is good for reducing poverty, and conservatives often champion marriage as the key to reducing poverty (Rector 2010; Murray 2008; Kass 2012). There is, in fact, a link between marriage and poverty: data from 2006 to 2008 show that during that time period married households had a poverty rate nearly 30 percentage points lower than the poverty rate for single-parent families headed by a female (Rector 2010). Some may think that most nonmarital births are to teenage mothers. However, 77 percent of nonmarital births are to women 20 years of age and older (Rector 2010). Thus, reducing nonmarital births to teens will not substantially reduce childhood poverty. Instead, increasing both marriage rates and educational attainment are important to reducing poverty—the poverty rate for single-parent families drops 15.3 percentage points when the parent is a high school graduate, and there is an additional 22.8 percentage point drop for single parents with a college degree (Rector 2010). Thus, while marriage is an important component of poverty reduction, so too is education because of the improved employment outcomes achieved with greater educational attainment.

If the success sequence is followed, how much will poverty be reduced? Figure 4 compares the role of each of the three elements of the success sequence in reducing poverty. It also compares the impact on poverty reduction of reducing family sizes and doubling cash welfare. As Figure 4 shows, the most important factor in reducing poverty is working more hours, followed by increasing marriage, and then increasing educational attainment. However, these factors are interdependent because the likelihood of being employed and working more hours depends on the level of education obtained, and the income generated from work depends on education (see Figure 3). This reality can also be seen in Table 5. Although poor families do have, on average, more children (0.35 children) than families who are not poor, the bigger differences between poor and nonpoor families are related to marital status, education levels, and working full-time versus part-time or versus being unemployed. These factors combine to bring about large income differentials. They also tell the same story as Figure 4. Marriage, education, and income combine to reduce childhood poverty and increase educational outcomes for children, who then have greater earning power in adulthood.

Policy Proposals for the Creation of an Opportunity Society

Having shown that their success sequence serves to increase opportunity and reduce poverty, Haskins and Sawhill (Haskins 2009) also provide policy proposals for how societal institutions might encourage individuals to follow the success sequence. Educational proposals include:

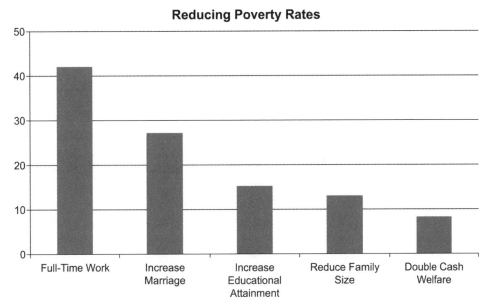

Figure 4

(*Source*: Sawhill, Isabel. "Solutions to Poverty." Before the Ways and Means Committee, Income Security and Family Support Subcommittee. U.S. House of Representatives, April 26, 2007.)

- Targeting preschool education for children below 150 percent of the poverty threshold
- Establishing national standards for K-12 education
- Establishing and funding more schools that provide more instructional time, a culture that highlights academic success, and more comprehensive monitoring of student learning
- Attracting and retaining the best teaching talent, in part by reviewing tenure programs and by recruiting non–education degree majors

Table 5   Differences between Nonpoor and Poor Families, 2001

Characteristic (averages)	Nonpoor	Poor
Number of children	1.78	2.13
Married (%)	81.0	39.5
Education	Some college	Less than high school graduate
Hours worked (annually)	2,151	1,017
Family income (annual)	$75,288	$9,465

Timothy J. Essenburg. *Source*: Haskins, Ron and Isabel Sawhill. "Work and Marriage: The Way to End Poverty and Welfare," September 2003. The Brookings Institution. Accessed February 11, 2013. http://www.brookings.edu/~/media/research/files/papers/2003/9/children families%20haskins/pb28.pdf.

- Increasing application assistance, funding, and degree-completion support for college and trade schools, for lower-income students and students of color in paraticular

Policy proposals for the second step of the success sequence, employment, include:

- Increasing the EITC and expanding it to include workers with no children
- Allowing education to meet work requirements for TANF recipients
- Increasing the quality of, and funding for, preschool options for families moving off of welfare and those earning modest incomes
- Breaking the link between TANF eligibility and Medicare (something the Affordable Care Act addresses; see Section 4, "Health Care Assistance")
- Expanding income eligibility and the level of benefits available for food stamps
- Increasing child support enforcement and suspending payments in arrears for parents with modest incomes, providing that they make payments going forward

Policy proposals for the third step of the success sequence, marriage and then family, pose greater difficulties. The Personal Responsibility and Work Opportunity and Reconciliation Act (PRWORA), initiated by Republicans and endorsed by a sufficient numbers of Democrats to become law in 1996, was one attempt to encourage the formation of two-parent families. A second noteworthy attempt was made by President George W. Bush, who publically championed marriage and allocated $100 million in competitive grants to fund programs for strengthening marriage among lower-income households (Haskins 2009). Thus far, however, neither initiative has had the desired effect of increasing marriage. Despite the difficulty of encouraging marriage through public policy, increasing marital births is readily seen as a crucial step toward reducing poverty and has bipartisan support (Haskins 2009).

There are theoretically three ways to increase marital births: (1) decrease the number of nonmarital births, (2) increase marriage rates, or (3) a combination of the two. Research indicates that 50 percent of nonmarital births are not planned. President Obama's hotly debated proposal to require employer health insurance coverage to include free birth control could thus contribute to a reduction in nonmarital births (Haskins 2009). Another way to reduce nonmarital births is by expanding Medicaid family planning services for women whose family income is below 200 percent of the poverty threshold. Not only would there be an increase in contraceptive use, but the Congressional Budget Office estimates that the reduction in costs due to the decrease in unplanned pregnancies would pay for the program and even generate savings (Congressional Budget Office 2008). Promoting marriage is more difficult because cultural norms supporting marriage are waning. Thus, the primary proposal presented by Haskins and Sawhill to encourage marriage is a national marketing campaign that would tout the benefits of marriage and having children after marriage (Haskins 2009).

OUTLOOK: THE LIKELIHOOD OF MAJOR POVERTY ALLEVIATION EFFORTS IN THE NEAR FUTURE

FUNDING FOR POVERTY ALLEVIATION EFFORTS

Haskins and Sawhill estimate that to carry out the policy proposals needed to encourage the success sequence and thereby create an opportunity society and alleviate poverty, $21 billion in funding would be needed (Haskins 2009). This represents 0.8 percent of the 2006 pre-Recession budget (Office of Management and Budget 2010). Funding could also come from state budgets and private philanthropy. If 0.8 percent of state budgets ($668 billion exclusive of federal transfer payments) and 0.8 percent of private philanthropy funds ($298.42 billion in 2011) were set aside for this programming, it would amount to an additional $7.7 billion in funding (National Governors Association and the National Association of State Budget Officers 2012; Center on Philanthropy 2012).

However, it is not likely that such funding will be available in the near future. The federal government and states continue to face smaller budgets and budget deficits. Neither is in a position to increase funding for an opportunity society by implementing the policies proposed by Haskins and Sawhill. Instead, programming for low-income individuals and families is at risk in the midst of the debate regarding the federal debt and deficit (see Section 5, "Political Parties and Major Legislative Responses"). When surveyed a slight majority (53 percent) of Republican respondents approved of cutting funding to low-income households to reduce the federal deficit and debt, and 24 percent of Democrats approved (Table 6). The lack of political will to address poverty was evident in 2011 and 2012 during the presidential campaign and election season, during in which the issue of poverty was avoided almost entirely. Despite the fact that the poverty rate was at its highest level since 1993, neither Barack Obama nor Mitt Romney championed new initiatives for the poor. Similarly, with the exception of statements from the expected interest groups (e.g., Catholic Charities USA, Sojourners, the Economic Policy Institute, and the Children's Defense Fund), there was little heard on the topic. Thus, additional funding for programming to help low-income individuals and families is unlikely, and in fact funding cuts to programs for low-income families are a more likely alternative.

What of the $298.42 billion in private giving to nonprofits? Might there be $21 billion available for the opportunity society characterized by the success sequence? While the proposed budget of $21 billion amounts to 7 percent of total giving in 2011, there is not sufficient giving to programs focused on education, work and income, and family formation to support the implementation of Haskins's and

Table 6 Reduce the National Deficit and Debt by Cutting Funding to Help Low-Income Households

Answer	Percentage Response			Difference between Republicans and Democrats
	Republicans	Democrats	Independents	
Approve	53	24	39	+29 for R's
Disapprove	43	73	57	−30 for R's

Source: Stokes, Bruce. "Public Attitudes toward the Next Social Contract." New American Foundation, 2013. Accessed February 8, 2013. http://www.pewglobal.org/2013/01/15/public-attitudes-toward-the-next-social-contract/.

Sawhill's policy proposals for an opportunity society (Center on Philanthropy 2012). Instead, most private giving goes to programming aimed at the middle class (Center on Philanthropy 2012).

In summary, data indicate that no new large-scale public or private sector initiatives will be forthcoming. Furthermore, with concerns over the federal deficit and debt, state budgets, divided perceptions on the seriousness of poverty, and even concerns over whether poverty can be eliminated, there is unlikely to be a groundswell of support for large-scale public or private programs to address poverty. Instead, the focus will turn to the struggles of the middle class in the aftermath of the Great Recession. The implication is that lower-income households that lost employment, income, and housing will find it increasingly difficult to stabilize their financial situation. It appears that the United States has not seized the opportunity afforded by the Great Recession to rethink its stories about poverty, and without such a rethinking no institutional changes will be forthcoming. The United States will remain a charitable country committed to equal opportunity but not structurally committed to the creation of an opportunity society for lower-income households. However, the seriousness of the poverty problem in the aftermath of the Great Recession is no reason to refrain from acting. Instead, the seriousness of the problem is a reason to take action, no matter how seemingly small, because only with such action can the political and private will be created to alleviate poverty in the United States.

FURTHER READING

American Presidency Project. "Election of 1964," 2013. Accessed February 6, 2013. http://www.presidency.ucsb.edu/showelection.php?year=1964

American Scientific Affiliation. "What Is a Worldview? Definitions and Introduction," 2013. Accessed January 18. http://www.asa3.org/ASA/education/views/index.html

Bristow, William. 2011. "Enlightenment." In *Stanford Encyclopedia of Philosophy* (summer ed.), ed. Edward N. Zalta. Accessed January 18, 2013. http://plato.stanford.edu/archives/sum2011/entries/enlightenment/

Center on Budget and Policy Priorities. "The Earned Income Tax Credit," February 1, 2013. Accessed February 7, 2013. http://www.cbpp.org/files/policybasics-eitc.pdf

Center on Philanthropy. "Giving USA 2012: The Annual Report on Philanthropy for the Year 2011." Giving USA, 2012. Accessed February 12, 2013. http://store.givingusareports.org/2012-Giving-USA-The-Annual-Report-on-Philanthropy-for-the-Year-2011-Executive-Summary-P43.aspx

Charite, Jimmy, Indivar Dutta-Gupta, and Chuck Marr. "Studies Show Earned Income Tax Credit Encourages Work and Success in School and Reduces Poverty." Center on Budget and Policy Priorities, June 26, 2012. Accessed February 7, 2013. http://www.cbpp.org/files/6-26-12tax.pdf

Congressional Budget Office. "Budget Options: Vol 1. Health Care," 2008. Accessed February 11, 2013. http://www.cbo.gov/sites/default/files/cbofiles/ftpdocs/99xx/doc9925/12-18-healthoptions.pdf

David, Paul A. "Why Are Institutions the 'Carriers of History'?: Path Dependence and the Evolution of Conventions, Organizations and Institutions." *Structural Change and Economic Dynamics* 5, no. 2 (1994): 205–20.

Federal Reserve Bank of St. Louis. "The Great Depression, 1929–1939: A Curriculum for High School Students," 2007. Accessed January 25, 2013. http://www.stlouisfed.org/greatdepression/curriculum.html

Forman, Jonathan Barry. "Earned Income Tax Credit." Tax Policy Center, 2013. Accessed February 7. http://www.taxpolicycenter.org/UploadedPDF/1000524.pdf

Gayner, Jeffrey B. "The Contract with America: Implementing New Ideas in the U.S." Heritage Foundation, 1995. Accessed February 5, 2013. http://s3.amazonaws.com/thf_media/1995/pdf/hl549.pdf

Germany, Kent B. "War on Poverty." University of Virginia, 2013. Accessed January 25, 2013. http://www.faculty.virginia.edu/sixties/readings/War%20on%20Poverty%20entry%20Poverty%20Encyclopedia.pdf

Gilens, Martin. *Why Americans Hate Welfare: Race, Media, and the Politics of Antipoverty Policy.* Chicago: University of Chicago Press, 1999.

Govtrack.us. "H.R. 3734 Personal Responsibility and Work Opportunity Reconciliation Act of 1996," August 22, 1996. Accessed February 6, 2013. http://www.govtrack.us/congress/bills/104/hr3734

Hanson, Victor Davis. "The Future of Western War," 2009. Accessed January 23, 2013. http://www.hillsdale.edu/news/imprimis/archive/issue.asp?year=2009&month=11

Haskins, Ron, and Isabel Sawhill. "Work and Marriage: The Way to End Poverty and Welfare." Brookings Institution, September 2003. Accessed February 11, 2013. http://www.brookings.edu/~/media/research/files/papers/2003/9/childrenfamilies%20haskins/pb28.pdf

Haskins, Ron, and Isabel Sawhill. *Creating an Opportunity Society.* Washington, D.C.: Brookings Institution Press, 2009.

Hodgson, Geoffrey M. "What Are Institutions?" *Journal of Economic Issues* 40, no. 1 (2006): 125.

Hotz, Joseph V., and John Karl Scholz. "The Earned Income Tax Credit." National Bureau of Economic Research, 2003. Accessed February 7, 2013. http://www.nber.org/chapters/c10256.pdf

Huston, Aletha C., Cynthia Miller, Lashawn Richburg-Hayes, Greg J. Duncan, Carolyn A. Eldred, Julia B. Isaacs, Isabel V. Sawhill, and Ron Haskins. "Getting Ahead or Losing Ground: Economic Mobility in America," February 2008. Accessed January 14, 2013. http://www.pewtrusts.org/uploadedFiles/wwwpewtrustsorg/Reports/Economic_Mobility/Economic_Mobility_in_America_Full.pdf

Jensen, Hans E. "Sources and Contours of Adam Smith's Conceptualized Reality in the *Wealth of Nations*." *Review of Political Economy* 34, no. 3 (1976): 259–74.

Kass, Leon R. "The Other War on Poverty: Finding Meaning in America." Irving Kristol Lecture, American Enterprise Institute, May 2, 2012. Accessed February 11, 2013. http://www.aei.org/speech/society-and-culture/free-enterprise/the-other-war-on-poverty-finding-meaning-in-america/

Liebowitz, Stan J., and Stephen E. Margolis. "Path Dependence." Encyclopedia of Law and Economics, 2013. Accessed February 16, 2013. http://encyclo.findlaw.com/0770book.pdf

Mankiw, Greg. "Does the EITC Reduce the Poverty Rate?" September 4, 2006. Accessed February 7, 2013. http://gregmankiw.blogspot.com/2006/09/does-eitc-reduce-poverty-rate.html

Mason, Kikora. "A Brief History of the EITC." National Community Tax Coalition, January 24, 2013. Accessed January 25, 2013. http://taxcoalition.wordpress.com/2012/01/24/a-brief-history-of-the-eitc/

Messmore, Ryan. "Justice, Equality, and the Poor." National Affairs, 2012. Accessed February 16, 2013. http://www.nationalaffairs.com/publications/detail/justice-inequality-and-the-poor

Mizell, Jill. "Public Opinion Research: An Overview of Research on Attitudes toward Expanding Opportunity." Opportunity Agenda, November 2012. Accessed February 9, 2013. http://opportunityagenda.org/attitudes_expanding_opportunity

Moynihan, Daniel Patrick. "The Negro Family: The Case for National Action." Office of Policy Planning and Research. U.S. Department of Labor, March 1965. Accessed February 11, 2013. http://www.stanford.edu/~mrosenfe/Moynihan%27s%20The%20Negro%20Family.pdf

Murray, Charles. "Poverty and Marriage, Income Inequality and Brains." Society and Culture, American Enterprise Institute, January 1, 2008. Accessed February 11, 2013. http://www.aei.org/article/society-and-culture/poverty-and-marriage-income-inequality-and-brains/

National Center for Public Policy Research. "Contract with America," 1994. Accessed February 6, 2013. http://www.nationalcenter.org/ContractwithAmerica.html

National Governors Association and the National Association of State Budget Officers. "The Fiscal Survey of States," 2012. Accessed February 12, 2013. http://www.nasbo.org/sites/default/files/Spring%202012%20Fiscal%20Survey%20of%20States.pdf

Neale, Walter C. "Institutions." *Journal of Economic Issues* 21, no. 3 (1987): 1177–1206.

Niskanen, William A. "Reganomics." Concise Encyclopedia of Economics, Library of Economics and Liberty, 1993. Accessed February 5, 2013. http://www.econlib.org/library/Enc1/Reaganomics.html

North, Douglass C. "Institutions." *Journal of Economic Perspectives* 1, no. 1(1991): 97–122.

North, Douglass C. "Economic Performance through Time." *American Economic Review* 84, no. 3 (1994): 359–68.

North, Douglass C. "Five Propositions about Institutions Change," 2013. Accessed January 3, 2013. http://128.118.178.162/eps/eh/papers/9309/9309001.pdf

Office of Management and Budget. "Historical Tables: Fiscal Year 2012 Budget of the U.S. Government." Executive Office of the President of the United States, 2010. Accessed February 12, 2013. http://www.whitehouse.gov/sites/default/files/omb/budget/fy2012/assets/hist.pdf

Page, Scott E. "Path Dependence." *Quarterly Journal of Political Science* 1, no. 1 (2006): 87–115.

Pfiffner, James P. "President Clinton's Health Care Reform Proposals of 1994," 2013. Accessed February 6, 2013. http://www.thepresidency.org/storage/documents/President_Clintons_Health_Care_Reform_Proposals.pdf

Rector, Robert. "Marriage: America's Greatest Weapon against Child Poverty." Heritage Foundation, September 16, 2010. Accessed February 11, 2013. http://www.heritage.org/research/reports/2010/09/marriage-america-s-greatest-weapon-against-child-poverty

Sawhill, Isabel. "Solutions to Poverty." Before the Ways and Means Committee, Income Security and Family Support Subcommittee. U.S. House of Representatives, April 26, 2007. Accessed February 11, 2013. http://www.brookings.edu/~/media/research/files/testimony/2007/4/26poverty%20sawhill/20070426.pdf

Sawhill, Isabel. "Are We Headed toward a Permanently Divided Society?" Center on Children and Families, Brookings Institution, March 2012a. Accessed February 11, 2013. http://www.brookings.edu/research/papers/2012/03/30-divided-society-sawhill

Sawhill, Isabel. "20 Years Later, It Turns out Dan Quayle Was Right about Murphy Brown and Unmarried Moms." *Washington Post*, May 25, 2012b. Accessed February 11, 2013. http://articles.washingtonpost.com/2012-05-25/opinions/35457123_1_father-moves-marriage-biological-parents

Sawhill, Isabel, and Adam Thomas. "A Hand Up from the Bottom Third: Toward a New Agenda for Low-Income Working Families." Brookings Institution, 2001. Accessed February 11, 2013. http://www.brookings.edu/~/media/research/files/papers/2001/5/useconomics%20sawhill/20010522

Tanner, Michael. "The American Welfare State: How We Spend Nearly $1 Trillion a Year Fighting Poverty: And Fail." CATO Institute, 2012. Accessed February 7, 2013. http://www.cato.org/publications/policy-analysis/american-welfare-state-how-we-spend-nearly-$1-trillion-year-fighting-poverty-fail

Tax Policy Center. "Historical EITC Parameter," January 28, 2013. Accessed February 7, 2013. http://www.taxpolicycenter.org/taxfacts/displayafact.cfm?DocID=36&Topic2id=40&Topic3id=42

U.S. Census Bureau. 2013. "How the Census Bureau Measures Poverty," Accessed February 7. http://www.census.gov/hhes/www/poverty/about/overview/measure.html

Uzgalis, William. "John Locke." Stanford Encyclopedia of Philosophy, 2012. Accessed January 23, 2013. http://plato.stanford.edu/archives/fall2012/entries/locke/

Van de Water, Paul N., and Arloc Sherman. "Social Security Keeps 21 Million Americans out of Poverty: A State-by-State Analysis." Center on Budget and Policy Priorities, October 16, 2012. Accessed January 25, 2013. http://www.cbpp.org/files/10-16-12ss.pdf

Wolters, Albert M. *Creation Regained: Biblical Basis for a Reformational Worldview.* Grand Rapids, MI: William B. Eerdmans, 1985.

PRIMARY DOCUMENTS

Lindsey K. Hanson

PART A: UNDERSTANDING THE GREAT RECESSION

To understand the impact the Great Recession has had on poverty in the United States, some background understanding of the recession is necessary. Following are primary documents to aid in this understanding. They are provided in chronological order, from early 2008 through 2012. Part A of the primary documents focus on the Great Recession. Part B will present documents illustrating the impact of the recession on poverty. Each document begins with an explanatory introduction and ends with the source of the document.

A-1. ECONOMIC STIMULUS ACT OF 2008

Even before the U.S. Great Recession became official it was apparent that the country was entering an economic downturn, and government began taking action. On February 13, 2008, the Economic Stimulus Act of 2008 was enacted by then President George W. Bush in response to the beginnings of the economic downturn. The Congressional Research summary of that Bill is reproduced here.

Bill Summary & Status
110th Congress (2007–2008)
H.R.5140
CRS Summary

H.R.5140
Latest Title: Economic Stimulus Act of 2008
Sponsor: Rep Pelosi, Nancy [CA-8] (introduced 1/28/2008) Cosponsors (15)
Related Bills: H.R.5107, S.2539
Latest Major Action: Became Public Law No: 110-185

SUMMARY AS OF:
2/13/2008—Public Law. (There are 3 other summaries)

(This measure has not been amended since it was passed by the Senate on February 7, 2008. The summary of that version is repeated here.)

Economic Stimulus Act of 2008—**Title I: Recovery Rebates and Incentives for Business Investment**—(Sec. 101) Amends the Internal Revenue Code to grant tax rebates of the lesser of net income tax liability or $600 to individual taxpayers ($1,200 for married taxpayers filing joint returns). Allows additional rebates of $300 for each child of an eligible taxpayer.

Provides for a minimum tax rebate of $300 ($600 for married taxpayers filing joint returns) for taxpayers with earned income of at least $3,000. Includes social security retirement benefits and compensation and pension benefits paid to disabled veterans for purposes of determining income eligibility for rebates.

Reduces the amount of such rebates by 5% of the amount that exceeds an adjusted gross income of $75,000 ($150,000 for married taxpayers filing joint returns).

Directs the Secretary of the Treasury to pay tax rebates as rapidly as possible. Prohibits: (1) payment of rebates after December 31, 2008; and (2) payment of a rebate to a taxpayer without a valid identification number (i.e., social security number).

Provides for payment of comparable tax rebates to residents of the Commonwealths of Puerto Rico and the Northern Mariana Islands.

Provides that the payment of a tax rebate shall not be considered income for purposes of determining eligibility for federal and federally-assisted state benefit programs.

Makes appropriations for FY2008 to implement payment of the tax rebates. Directs the Secretary to submit a plan and quarterly reports to the Senate and House Committees on Appropriations on actual and expected expenditures of appropriated funds.

(Sec. 102) Increases in 2008: (1) the expensing allowance for depreciable business assets to $250,000; and (2) the maximum investment phase-out threshold for such expensing allowance to $800,000.

(Sec. 103) Increases to 50% (from 30%) the amount of the adjusted basis of certain depreciable property (e.g., equipment and computer software) that may be claimed as a deductible expense in 2008.

Title II: Housing GSE and FHA Loan Limits—(Sec. 201) Raises the statutory ceiling on the maximum original principal obligation of a mortgage originated between July 1, 2007, and December 31, 2008, that may be purchased by either the Federal National Mortgage Association (Fannie Mae) or the Federal Home Loan Mortgage Corporation (Freddie Mac). Disregards mortgages purchased with the increased ceiling amount for purposes of meeting certain housing goals established under the Housing and Community Development Act of 1992.

Expresses the sense of Congress that Fannie Mae and Freddie Mac should securitize mortgages acquired pursuant to the increased conforming loan limits of this Act if the manner of securitization does not: (1) impose additional costs for mortgages originated, purchased, or securitized under existing limits; or (2) interfere with the goal of adding liquidity to the market.

(Sec. 202) Establishes a temporary loan limit increase for FHA-insured mortgages in specified high-cost areas for which a borrower received credit approval by December 31, 2008.

Grants the Secretary of Housing and Urban Development (HUD) discretionary authority to increase loan limits in 2008 based upon the size and location of residences in particular areas.

Directs the Secretary to publish the median house prices and mortgage principal obligation limits as revised by this Act not later than 30 days after its enactment.

Title III: Emergency Designation—Designates all provisions of this Act as emergency requirements and necessary to meet emergency needs for certain budgetary purposes

Source: Library of Congress. "Bill Summary and Status 110th Congress (2007–2008) H.R. 5140 CRS Summary," February 13, 2008. Accessed January 28, 2013. http://thomas.loc.gov/cgi-bin/bdquery/z?d110:HR05140:@@@D&summ2=m&

A-2. THE EMERGENCY STABILIZATION ACT (THE FINANCIAL SYSTEM BAILOUT) AND THE TROUBLED ASSET RELIEF PROGRAM (TARP)

The Emergency Stabilization Act is commonly referred to as the financial system bailout. It was passed with bipartisan support in October 2008 and signed into law by President George W. Bush on October 3, 2008.

It created the Troubled Asset Relief Program (TARP) and authorized the U.S. secretary of the treasury to buy distressed assets, particularly mortgage-backed securities, in order to provide cash to banks and other financial institutions. The Congressional Research Services' summary of the Paul Wellstone Mental Health and Addiction Equity Act of 2007 is reproduced below, Division A of this act is the Emergency Stabilization Act. Senate leaders added the Emergency Stabilization Act as a rider to the Paul Wellstone Mental Health and Addiction Equity Act of 2007 in order to get around the Constitutional requirement that all bills raising revenues originate in the House of Representatives.

Bill Summary & Status
110th Congress (2007–2008)
H.R.1424
CRS Summary

H.R.1424

Latest Title: Paul Wellstone Mental Health and Addiction Equity Act of 2007

Sponsor: Rep Kennedy, Patrick J. [RI-1] (introduced 3/9/2007) Cosponsors (274)

Related Bills: H.RES.1014, H.RES.1525, H.R.493, H.R.1367, H.R.6983, H.R. 7202, H.R.7207, S.358, S.558

Latest Major Action: Became Public Law No: 110-343

House Reports: 110-374 Part 1, 110-374 Part 2, 110-374 Part 3

Note: Emergency Economic Stabilization Act of 2008. H.R.1424 is the vehicle for the economic rescue legislation. Division A is the Emergency Economic Stabilization Act of 2008; Division B is the Energy Improvement and Extension Act of 2008; and Division C is the Tax Extenders and Alternative Minimum Tax Relief Act of 2008.

SUMMARY AS OF:

10/3/2008—Public Law. (There are 6 other summaries)

(This measure has not been amended since it was passed by the Senate on October 1, 2008. The summary of that version is repeated here.)

Division A: Emergency Economic Stabilization—Emergency Economic Stabilization Act of 2008—**Title I: Troubled Assets Relief Program**—(Sec. 101) Authorizes the Secretary of the Treasury (Secretary) to establish the Troubled Asset Relief Program (TARP) to purchase troubled assets from any financial institution, in accordance with terms, conditions, policies, and procedures the Secretary develops.

Directs the Secretary to establish within the Office of Domestic Finance of the Department of the Treasury an Office of Financial Stability, through which TARP shall be implemented.

Authorizes the Secretary to: (1) designate financial institutions as financial agents of the federal government; and (2) establish vehicles to purchase, hold, and sell troubled assets and issue obligations.

Directs the Secretary to prevent unjust enrichment of participating financial institutions, including any sale of a troubled asset (with certain exceptions) to the Secretary at a price higher than what the seller paid to purchase the asset. Exempts from this requirement any troubled assets acquired in a merger or acquisition, or a purchase of assets from a financial institution that is either under conservatorship or receivership, or that has initiated bankruptcy proceedings.

(Sec. 102) Requires the Secretary, if TARP is established, to establish also a program to guarantee troubled assets originated or issued before March 14, 2008, including mortgage-backed securities.

Establishes the Troubled Assets Insurance Financing Fund for deposit of premiums collected from participating financial institutions in order to fund such guarantee program.

(Sec. 104) Establishes the Financial Stability Oversight Board to review and report to Congress on the authorities created under this Act and their effect in assisting American families in preserving home ownership, stabilizing financial markets, and protecting taxpayers.

(Sec. 105) Requires the Secretary to report periodically to Congress regarding: (1) transactions (tranche reports); (2) purchases; (3) liabilities; and (4) the status of regulatory oversight over financial markets.

(Sec. 106) Authorizes the Secretary to enter into financial transactions regarding any troubled asset purchased under this Act. Requires deposit into the Treasury of all revenues and proceeds from the sale of troubled assets.

(Sec. 107) Authorizes the Secretary to waive specific provisions of the Federal Acquisition Regulation if urgent and compelling circumstances make compliance with them contrary to the public interest. Requires submission of such a waiver, and its justification, to certain congressional oversight committees.

Requires the Secretary, in any solicitation or contract containing such a waiver, to develop and implement standards and procedures to ensure the inclusion and utilization of minorities and women, and minority- and women-owned businesses, in that solicitation or contract, including contracts to asset managers, servicers, property managers, and other service providers or expert consultants.

Makes the Federal Deposit Insurance Corporation (FDIC) eligible for, and requires its consideration in, the selection of asset managers for residential mortgage loans and residential mortgage-backed securities. Requires the Secretary to reimburse the FDIC for any services rendered.

(Sec. 108) Directs the Secretary to prescribe regulations or guidelines to address and manage or to prohibit conflicts-of-interest that may arise in connection with the administration and execution of the authorities under this Act.

(Sec. 109) Directs the Secretary, to the extent that he or she acquires mortgages, mortgage-backed securities, and other assets secured by residential real estate, and the Federal Housing Finance Agency, as conservator of the Federal National Mortgage Association (Fannie Mae) and the Federal Home Loan Mortgage Corporation (Freddie Mac), to implement a plan to maximize assistance for home owners and encourage the servicers of the underlying mortgages to take advantage of the HOPE for Homeowners Program under the National Housing Act or other available programs to minimize foreclosures. Authorizes the Secretary to use loan guarantees and credit enhancements to facilitate loan modifications to prevent avoidable foreclosures.

(Sec. 110) Directs federal property managers (the Federal Housing Finance Agency, as conservator of Fannie Mae and Freddie Mac, the FDIC, and the Board of Governors of the Federal Reserve System), to the extent that they hold, own, or control mortgages, mortgage-backed securities, and other assets secured by residential real estate, including multifamily housing, to implement a plan that seeks to maximize assistance for homeowners and use its authority to encourage the servicers of the underlying mortgages to take advantage of the HOPE for Homeowners Program or other available programs to minimize foreclosures.

(Sec. 111) Subjects any financial institution that sells troubled assets to the Secretary to specified executive compensation requirements.

Directs the Secretary to require a financial institution to meet appropriate standards for executive compensation and corporate governance whenever:

(1) the purposes of this Act are best met through direct purchases of troubled assets from an individual financial institution where no bidding process or market prices are available; and (2) the Secretary receives a meaningful equity or debt position in the financial institution as a result of the transaction.

Requires such standards to include: (1) limits on compensation that exclude incentives for senior executive officers to take unnecessary and excessive risks that threaten the financial institution's value during the period the Secretary holds an equity or debt position in it; (2) a provision for the recovery by the financial institution of any bonus or incentive compensation paid to a senior executive officer based on statements of earnings, gains, or other criteria that are later proven to be materially inaccurate; and (3) a prohibition on the institution's making any golden parachute payment to its senior executive officer during the period that the Secretary holds an equity or debt position in the financial institution.

Requires the Secretary, upon a determination that specified auction purchases of troubled assets best meet the purposes of this Act, to prohibit, for certain financial institutions, any new employment contract with a senior executive officer that provides a golden parachute in the event of an involuntary termination, bankruptcy filing, insolvency, or receivership.

(Sec. 112) Instructs the Secretary to coordinate with foreign financial authorities and central banks to work toward the establishment of similar programs by such authorities and central banks.

States that, to the extent the foreign entities hold troubled assets as a result of extending financing to financial institutions that have failed or defaulted on such financing, such troubled assets qualify for purchase under this title.

(Sec. 113) Prescribes requirements for purchase and sale of assets by the Secretary, using market mechanisms, in a manner that will minimize any potential long-term negative impact on the taxpayer and maximize the return on investment for the federal government, including by making such purchases at the lowest price determined to be consistent with this Act. Authorizes the Secretary, if the Secretary determines that use of a market mechanism is not feasible or appropriate, and the purposes of the Act are best met through direct purchases from an individual financial institution, to pursue additional measures to ensure that prices paid are reasonable and reflect the asset's underlying value. Provides requirements for warrants and senior debt instruments.

(Sec. 114) Requires the Secretary to: (1) make available to the public a description, amounts, and pricing of assets acquired under this Act within two business days of purchase, trade, or other disposition; and (2) determine whether the disclosure required of financial institutions that sell troubled assets to the Secretary with respect to off-balance sheet transactions, derivatives instruments, contingent liabilities, and similar sources of potential exposure adequately provides sufficient information to the public regarding the true financial position of the institutions (market transparency).

Requires the Secretary to recommend additional disclosure requirements to the relevant regulators if disclosure pursuant to this market transparency requirement is not adequate for that purpose.

(Sec. 115) Limits the Secretary's authority to purchase troubled assets under this Act to: (1) $250 billion outstanding at any one time; (2) $350 billion outstanding at any one time if, at any time, the President certifies to Congress that the Secretary needs to exercise authority for up to such an amount; and (3) $700 billion outstanding at any one time if, at any time after such a certification, the President reports to Congress a plan of the Secretary to exercise the authority ... for up to such an amount, unless Congress enacts a joint resolution of disapproval within 15 calendar days of transmission of the plan.

Requires a joint resolution of disapproval to receive fast track consideration in the House and the Senate.

(Sec. 116) Directs the Comptroller General to: (1) perform ongoing oversight of TARP activities and performance and its agents and representatives, including vehicles established by the Secretary under this Act; and (2) study and report to Congress on the extent to which leverage and sudden deleveraging of financial institutions was a factor behind the current financial crisis.

(Sec. 118) Authorizes the Secretary to use proceeds from the sale of government bonds to pay the costs of administering authorities under this Act.

Declares that funds expended or obligated by the Secretary for actions authorized by this Act, including the payment of administrative expenses, shall be deemed appropriated at the time of expenditure or obligation.

(Sec. 119) Subjects the actions of the Secretary under this Act to judicial review, with specified limitations.

(Sec. 120) Terminates the authorities under sections 101 and 102, with a certain exception, on December 31, 2009. Authorizes a two-year extension of such authorities if the Secretary submits a specified certification to Congress.

(Sec. 121) Establishes the Office of the Special Inspector General for TARP to conduct oversight of the purchase, management, and sale of assets by the Secretary, including the management of any program established under this Act.

(Sec. 122) Increases the statutory limit on the public debt to $11.315 trillion.

(Sec. 124) Amends the National Housing Act, with respect to extinguishment of subordinate liens for refinanced mortgages, to authorize the Secretary to make payments, which shall be accepted as payment in full of all indebtedness to any holder of an existing subordinate mortgage in lieu of certain future appreciation payments.

(Sec. 125) Establishes the Congressional Oversight Panel to review and report to Congress on the status of the financial markets and regulatory system.

(Sec. 126) Amends the Federal Deposit Insurance Act to prohibit false advertising, misuse of Federal Deposit Insurance Corporation (FDIC) names, and misrepresentation of insured status.

(Sec. 127) Requires the federal financial regulatory agencies to cooperate with the Federal Bureau of Investigation (FBI) and other law enforcement agencies investigating fraud, misrepresentation, and malfeasance regarding development, advertising, and sale of financial products.

(Sec. 128) Amends the Financial Services Regulatory Relief Act of 2006 to accelerate from October 1, 2011, to October 1, 2008, the effective date for the Board of Governors of the Federal Reserve (Board) to: (1) pay interest on balances maintained at a Federal Reserve bank; and (2) employ increased flexibility to set reserve requirements for member banks.

(Sec. 129) Instructs the Board to submit periodic updates to certain congressional committees regarding its exercise of loan authority.

(Sec. 131) Directs the Secretary to reimburse the Exchange Stabilization Fund for any funds that are used for the Treasury Money Market Funds Guaranty Program for the U.S. money market mutual fund industry.

Prohibits the Secretary from using the Exchange Stabilization Fund to establish any future guaranty programs for the U.S. money market mutual fund industry.

(Sec. 132) Authorizes the Securities and Exchange Commission (SEC) to suspend application of Statement Number 157 (about mark-to-market accounting) of the Financial Accounting Standards Board.

Instructs the SEC to study and report to Congress on the applicability of such standard to financial and depository institutions.

(Sec. 133) Directs the SEC to study and report to Congress on Statement Number 157.

(Sec. 134) Instructs the Director of the Office of Management and Budget (OMB) to report to Congress, after five years, on the net amount within TARP.

Instructs the President, in case of a shortfall within TARP, to submit to Congress a legislative proposal that recoups from the financial industry an amount equal to such shortfall in order to ensure that TARP does not add to the deficit or national debt.

(Sec. 136) Increases from $100,000 to $250,000, until December 31, 2009, the amount of deposit and share insurance coverage offered under the Federal Deposit Insurance Act and the Federal Credit Union Act.

Title II: Budget-Related Provisions—(Sec. 201) Requires all information used by the Secretary in connection with activities authorized under this Act (including the records to which the Comptroller General is entitled) to be made available, upon request, to the Congressional Budget Office (CBO) and the Joint Committee on Taxation to assist congressional committees with conducting oversight, monitoring, and analysis of such authorized activities.

(Sec. 202) Requires OMB to report to the President and Congress semiannually: (1) an estimate of the cost of troubled assets and their guarantees; (2) the information used to derive such estimate; and (3) a detailed analysis of how the estimate has changed from the previous report.

Requires the second and each ensuing report to explain the differences between CBO's required estimate and prior OMB estimates.

Requires CBO to assess and report to Congress on OMB's report, including: (1) the cost of the troubled assets and their guarantees; (2) the information and valuation methods used to calculate such cost; and (3) the impact on the deficit and the debt.

Authorizes appropriations.

(Sec. 203) Requires the President's annual budget request to Congress to include as supplementary materials a separate analysis of the budgetary effects for all prior fiscal years, the current fiscal year, the fiscal year for which the budget is submitted, and ensuing fiscal years of the Secretary's actions taken or to be taken using any authority provided in this Act.

(Sec. 204) Designates all provisions of this Act as an emergency requirement necessary to meet emergency needs. Prohibits rescissions of any amounts provided in it from being counted for budget enforcement purposes.

Title III: Tax Provisions—(Sec. 301) Provides for ordinary income or loss treatment of gain or loss from the sale or exchange of any applicable preferred stock by any applicable financial institution. Defines "applicable preferred stock" as preferred stock in Fannie Mae or Freddie Mac that was held on September 6, 2008, or that was sold or exchanged on or after January 1, 2008, and before September 7, 2008. Defines "applicable financial institution" as a banking, financial, or investment institution or a depository institution holding company. Allows the Secretary of the Treasury to apply ordinary gain or loss treatment to certain sales of preferred stock not held on September 6, 2008. Authorizes the Secretary to prescribe regulations to carry out this section.

(Sec. 302) Denies certain employers whose assets have been purchased under the Troubled Asset Relief Program (TARP) a tax deduction for the payment of compensation or other benefits in excess of $500,000 to their executives or other highly compensated employees. Makes tax penalties for excess parachute payments applicable to employers who participate in TARP and their executives.

(Sec. 303) Extends through 2012 the exclusion from gross income of income attributable to a discharge of indebtedness on a principal residence.

Division B: Energy Improvement and Extension Act of 2008—Energy Improvement and Extension Act of 2008—**Title I: Energy Production Incentives—Subtitle A: Renewable Energy Incentives**—(Sec. 101) Extends through 2009 the tax credit for producing electricity from wind and refined coal facilities. Extends through 2010 such tax credit for other facilities, including closed and open-loop biomass, solar energy, small irrigation power, landfill gas, trash combustion, and hydropower. Modifies rules for and definitions of refined coal, trash and biomass facilities, and hydropower production.

(Sec. 102) Includes marine and hydrokinetic renewable energy as a renewable resource for purposes of the tax credit for producing electricity from renewable resources.

(Sec. 103) Extends through 2016 the energy tax credit for solar energy, fuel cell, and microturbine property. Allows a new energy tax credit for combined heat and power system property. Increases to $1,500 the credit limitation for fuel cell property. Modifies energy tax credit rules to allow: (1) offsets of tax credit amounts against alternative minimum tax (AMT) liabilities; and (2) public utility property to qualify for such credit.

(Sec. 104) Allows a new energy tax credit for 30% of expenditures for wind turbines used to generate electricity in a residence and for geothermal heat pump systems.

(Sec. 106) Extends through 2016 the tax credit for residential energy efficient property. Eliminates the limitation on the tax credit for solar electric property. Allows a residential energy tax credit for 30% of small wind energy and geothermal heat pump property expenditures.

(Sec. 107) Allows a new tax credit for investment in new clean renewable energy bonds for capital investment in renewable energy facilities.

Extends through 2009 the authority to issue clean renewable energy bonds.

(Sec. 108) Includes steel industry fuel as a renewable resource for purposes of the tax credit for producing electricity from renewable resources. Defines "steel industry fuel" as fuel that: (1) is produced by liquefying coal waste sludge and distributing it on coal; and (2) is used as a feedstock for the manufacture of coke.

(Sec. 109) Extends through 2009 the deferral of tax on the gain on sales of transmission property by vertically-integrated electric utilities to independent transmission companies approved by the Federal Energy Regulatory Commission (FERC).

Subtitle B: Carbon Mitigation and Coal Provisions—(Sec. 111) Allows a 30% investment tax credit rate for advanced coal-based generation technology projects and increases the maximum credit amounts allocable for such projects to $2.55 billion.

Authorizes additional carbon energy projects, including projects for the capture and and sequestration of carbon dioxide.

(Sec. 112) Increases to 30% the investment tax credit rate for coal gasification projects and the aggregate credit amount for such projects.

(Sec. 113) Extends the excise tax on coal until the earlier of January 1, 2019, or the day after the first December 31 after December 31, 2007, on which there is no balance of repayable advances made to the Black Lung Disability Trust Fund and no unpaid interest on such advances. Makes a one-time appropriation to the Trust Fund to pay the difference between the market value of outstanding repayable advances (plus accrued interest) and the proceeds from the obligations issued by such Trust Fund to the Secretary of the Treasury.

(Sec. 114) Sets forth special rules for refund claims of the coal excise tax by certain coal producers and exporters.

(Sec. 115) Allows a new tax credit for carbon dioxide sequestration.

(Sec. 116) Provides for the treatment of certain income and gains from industrial source carbon dioxide as qualifying income for publicly traded partnerships.

(Sec. 117) Directs the Secretary of the Treasury to contract with the National Academy of Sciences for a comprehensive review of Internal Revenue Code provisions that have the largest effects on carbon and other greenhouse gas emissions and an estimate of the magnitude of such effects. Requires the Academy to report to Congress on the results of such study within two years after the enactment of this Act. Authorizes appropriations.

Title II: Transportation and Domestic Fuel Security Provisions—(Sec. 201) Includes cellulosic biofuel within the definition of biomass ethanol plant property for purposes of the bonus depreciation allowance.

(Sec. 202) Increases and extends through 2009 income and excise tax credits for biodiesel and renewable diesel used as fuel.

(Sec. 203) Disqualifies foreign-produced fuel that is used or sold for use outside the United States from the income and excise tax credits for alcohol, biodiesel, and alternative fuel production.

(Sec. 204) Extends through 2009 the excise tax credit for alternative fuel and fuel mixtures. Requires such fuels to include compressed or liquefied biomass gas and to meet certain carbon capture requirements.

(Sec. 205) Allows a new tax credit for new qualified plug-in electric drive motor vehicles. Limits the amount of such credit based upon the gross vehicle weight rating of such vehicles. Terminates such credit after 2014.

(Sec. 206) Allows an exclusion from the heavy truck excise tax for idling reduction devices and advanced insulation used in certain heavy trucks and trailers.

(Sec. 207) Extends through 2010 the tax credit for alternative fuel vehicle refueling property expenditures. Includes electricity as a clean burning fuel for purposes of such credit.

(Sec. 208) Provides for the treatment of certain income and gains from alcohol, biodiesel, and alternative fuels and mixtures as qualifying income for publicly traded partnerships.

(Sec. 209) Extends through 2013 the taxpayer election to expense costs of certain refinery property.

(Sec. 210) Extends the suspension of the taxable income limit on percentage depletion for oil and natural gas produced from marginal properties.

(Sec. 211) Allows employees to exclude reimbursements for bicycle commuting expenses from gross income.

Title III: Energy Conservation And Efficiency Provisions—(Sec. 301) Allows a new tax credit for investment in qualified energy conservation bonds for capital expenditures to reduce energy consumption in public buildings, implement green community programs, develop alternative and renewable energy sources, and promote mass commuting facilities.

(Sec. 302) Extends through 2009 the tax credit for nonbusiness energy property expenditures. Includes energy-efficient biomass fuel stoves as property eligible for such tax credit. Modifies tax credit standards for water heaters, geothermal heat pumps, and energy efficiency improvements.

(Sec. 303) Extends through 2013 the tax deduction for energy efficient commercial buildings.

(Sec. 304) Extends through 2009 the tax credit for residential energy efficiency improvements.

(Sec. 305) Modifies tax credit amounts and standards for energy efficient household appliances produced after 2007.

(Sec. 306) Allows an accelerated 10-year recovery period for the depreciation of qualified smart electric meters and smart electric grid systems.

(Sec. 307) Extends through FY2012 the authority to issue tax-exempt bonds for qualified green building and sustainable design projects.

(Sec. 308) Allows a 50% depreciation allowance for reuse and recycling property used to collect, distribute, or recycle certain materials, including scrap, fibers, and metals.

Title IV: Revenue Provisions—(Sec. 401) Reduces by 3% the tax deduction for income attributable to domestic production activities for taxpayers with income derived from activities related to oil, gas, or any primary products thereof.

(Sec. 402) Revises the tax treatment of foreign oil and gas extraction income and foreign oil related income for purposes of the foreign tax credit.

(Sec. 403) Includes within the reporting requirements of investment brokers the adjusted basis of any publicly traded security owned by customers of such brokers.

(Sec. 404) Extends through 2009 the 0.2% Federal Unemployment Tax Act (FUTA) surtax.

(Sec. 405) Increases the Oil Spill Liability Trust Fund financing rate and extends such rate through 2017.

Division C: Tax Extenders and Alternative Minimum Tax Relief—Tax Extenders and Alternative Minimum Tax Relief Act of 2008—**Title I: Alternative Minimum Tax Relief**—(Sec. 101) Amends the Internal Revenue Code to extend through 2008 for individual taxpayers: (1) the offset of nonrefundable personal tax credits against regular and alternative minimum tax (AMT) liability; and (2) the increased AMT exemption amounts.

Increases the AMT refundable credit amount for individuals who have long-term unused minimum tax credits from prior taxable years. Abates any underpayment of tax attributable to the application of special AMT rules for the treatment of incentive stock options.

Title II: Extension of Individual Tax Provisions—(Sec. 201) Extends through 2009: (1) the tax deduction for state and local sales taxes in lieu of state and local income taxes; (2) the tax deduction for qualified tuition and related expenses; (3) the tax deduction for certain expenses of elementary and secondary school teachers; (4) the additional standard tax deduction from gross income for real property taxes; (5) tax-free distributions from individual retirement plans for charitable purposes; (6) the exemption from withholding of tax of interest-related and short-term capital gain dividends received from a regulated investment company (RIC) and the special rule for RIC stock held in the estate of a nonresident non-citizen; and (7) the inclusion of an RIC within the definition of "qualified investment entity" for income tax purposes.

Title III: Extension of Business Tax Provisions—(Sec. 301) Extends through 2009: (1) the tax credit for increasing research activities; (2) the new markets tax credit; (3) the subpart F income exemption for active financing income; (4) special rules for related controlled foreign corporations and for the tax treatment of certain payments to tax-exempt organizations by a controlled subsidiary; (5) accelerated depreciation for qualified leasehold and restaurant improvements and for certain improvements to retail space; (6) the special rule for reductions in the basis of S corporation stock for charitable contributions of property; (7) the increase in alcohol excise taxes payable to Puerto Rico and the Virgin Islands; (8) the economic development credit for American Samoa; (9) tax incentives for mine rescue team training and advanced mine safety equipment; (10) the tax deduction for income attributable to domestic production activities in Puerto Rico; (11) issuance authority for qualified zone academy bonds; (12) the Indian employment tax credit; (13) accelerated depreciation of business property on Indian reservations and of motorsports racing track facilities; (14) the tax credit for railroad track maintenance; (15) expensing allowances for film and television production costs and for environmental remediation costs; (16) work opportunity tax credit eligibility for Hurricane Katrina employees (through August 28, 2009); (17) the increased rehabilitation tax credit for property in the Gulf Opportunity (GO) Zone; (18) the tax deduction for corporate contributions of computer technology and equipment for educational purposes; (19) tax incentives for investment in the District of Columbia; and (20) the expanded tax deductions for charitable contributions of food and book inventories by noncorporate taxpayers.

(Sec. 325) Extends through 2014: (1) the suspension of tariff duties on certain wool products; and (2) the Wool Research, Promotion, and Development Trust Fund.

Title IV: Extension of Tax Administration Provisions—(Sec. 401) Makes permanent the authority of the Internal Revenue Service (IRS) to: (1) conduct undercover operations; and (2) disclose tax return information related to terrorist activities.

Title V: Additional Tax Relief and Other Tax Provisions—Subtitle A: General Provisions—(Sec. 501) Lowers in 2008 (from $10,000 to $8,500) the earned income threshold amount for determining the refundable portion of the child tax credit.

(Sec. 502) Amends Internal Revenue Code provisions relating to the tax deduction for domestic film and television productions to: (1) include within the income base for such deduction compensation for services performed in the United States by actors, production personnel, directors, and producers and any copyrights, trademarks, or other intangibles with respect to a film production; and (2) allow a deduction for partners or S corporation shareholders who own at least a 20% interest in a film project.

(Sec. 503) Exempts from the excise tax on bows and arrows certain shafts consisting of all natural wood that, after assembly, measure 5/16 of an inch or less in diameter and that are not suitable for use with bows that would otherwise be subject to such tax (having a peak draw weight of 30 pounds or more).

(Sec. 504) Allows taxpayers who are plaintiffs in the civil action *In re Exxon Valdez*, No. 89-095-CV (HRH) (Consolidated) (D. Alaska), or their heirs or dependents, to: (1) elect to average, for income tax purposes, income received in settlement of such civil action; and (2) make a limited contribution of such settlement income to certain tax-exempt retirement plans in the year such income is received.

(Sec. 505) Allows accelerated depreciation (i.e., five-year recovery period) for certain farming business machinery or equipment placed in service before January 1, 2010.

(Sec. 506) Modifies the standards for imposing penalties on tax return preparers for understatements of tax to require: (1) substantial authority for a position with respect to an item on a tax return if such position was not disclosed with the return; and (2) a reasonable basis for a position that was disclosed with the return.

Requires tax return preparers to have a reasonable belief that a position with respect to a tax shelter or a reportable transaction (a transaction having a potential for tax avoidance or evasion) will more likely than not be sustained on its merits.

Subtitle B: Paul Wellstone and Pete Domenici Mental Health Parity and Addiction Equity Act of 2008—(Sec. 511) Paul Wellstone and Pete Domenici Mental Health Parity and Addiction Equity Act of 2008—Amends the Employee Retirement Income Security Act of 1974 (ERISA), the Public Health Service Act, and the Internal Revenue Code to require a group health plan that provides both medical and surgical benefits and mental health or substance use disorder benefits to ensure that: (1) the financial requirements, such as deductibles and copayments, applicable to such mental health or substance use disorder benefits are no more restrictive than the predominant financial requirements applied to substantially all medical and surgical benefits covered by the plan; (2) there are no separate cost sharing requirements that are applicable only with respect to mental health or substance use disorder benefits; (3) the treatment limitations applicable to such mental health or substance use disorder benefits are no more restrictive than the predominant treatment limitations applied to substantially all medical and surgical benefits covered by the plan; and (4) there are no separate treatment limitations that are applicable only with respect to mental health or substance use disorder benefits.

Requires the criteria for medical necessity determinations and the reason for any denial of reimbursement or payment for services made under the plan with respect to mental health or substance use disorder benefits to be made available by the plan administrator.

Requires the plan to provide out-of network coverage for mental health or substance use disorder benefits if the plan provides coverage for medical or surgical benefits provided by out-of network providers.

Exempts from the requirements of this Act a group health plan if the application of this Act results in an increase for the plan year of the actual total costs of coverage with respect to medical and surgical benefits and mental health and substance use disorder benefits by an amount that exceeds 2% for the first plan year and 1% for each subsequent plan year. Requires determinations as to increases in actual costs under a plan to be made and certified by a qualified and licensed actuary.

Requires determinations for such an exemption to be made after such plan has complied with this Act for the first six months of the plan year.

Sets forth requirements for notifications of exemptions under this Act, including notification of the Secretary of Health and Human Services, the appropriate state agencies, and participants and beneficiaries in the plan.

Authorizes the Secretary and the appropriate state agency to audit the books and records of a group health plan relating to an exemption.

Directs the Secretary to: (1) report to the appropriate congressional committees on compliance of group health plans with the requirements of this Act; and (2) publish guidance and information concerning the requirements of this Act and provide assistance concerning such requirements and the continued operation of applicable state law.

Requires the Comptroller General to report to Congress on the specific rates, patterns, and trends in coverage and exclusion of specific mental health and substance use disorder diagnoses by health plans and health insurance.

Title VI: Other Provisions—(Sec. 601) Revises the provisions of the Secure Rural Schools and Community Self-Determination Act of 2000.

Provides for: (1) calculating payments to eligible states, counties, and territories for FY2008-FY2011 and; (2) the making of transition payments for FY2008-FY2010 to California, Louisiana, Oregon, Pennsylvania, South Carolina, South Dakota, Texas, and Washington. Sets forth distribution, election, and expenditure rules.

Permits eligible electing counties to expend a portion of funds received for the protection, restoration, and enhancement of fish and wildlife habitat, and other consistent resource objectives upon project approval.

Sets forth requirements for a merchantable timber contracting pilot program.

Revises provisions concerning resource advisory committees and the use and availability of project funds for projects submitted by such committees. Terminates authority to initiate projects on September 30, 2011.

Revises provisions for the use of county funds for certain projects. Requires certification by participating counties that county funds have been expended only for authorized uses. Terminates authority to initiate such projects on September 30, 2011.

Authorizes appropriations for FY2008-FY2011 to carry out the Secure Rural Schools and Community Self-Determination Act of 2000.

Amends the Act of May 23, 1908, and the Weeks Law to prescribe that an amount equal to the annual average of 25% of all amounts received for the applicable fiscal year and each of the preceding six fiscal years from each national forest (under current law, 25% of all moneys received during any fiscal year) be paid at the end of such year to eligible states and counties for the benefit of public schools and public roads in which such forests are situated.

Amends federal law regarding payment in lieu of taxes to provide, for FY2008-FY2012, for each county or other eligible unit of local government to be entitled to payment for entitlement land (certain land owned by the U.S. government).

(Sec. 602) Amends the Surface Mining Control and Reclamation Act of 1977 to require the transfer of $9 million on October 1, 2010, to the United Mine Workers of America Combined Benefit Fund to provide for refunds of certain health benefit premiums, death benefit premiums, and unassigned beneficiaries premiums.

Title VII: Disaster Relief—Subtitle A: Heartland and Hurricane Ike Disaster Relief—Heartland Disaster Tax Relief Act of 2008—(Sec. 702) Makes certain provisions of the Internal Revenue Code providing tax benefits to residents of the Gulf Opportunity (GO) Zone and the Hurricane Katrina disaster areas, including provisions for tax-exempt bond financing, the low-income housing tax credit, an increased rehabilitation tax credit, education and housing tax benefits, employee retention tax credits, and tax-exempt bond financing, applicable to residents of the Midwestern disaster area on a similar basis. Defines "Midwestern disaster area" as an area in which a major disaster has been declared by the President on or after May 20, 2008, and before August 1, 2008, under the Robert T. Stafford Disaster Relief and Emergency Assistance Act by reason of severe storms, tornados, or flooding occurring in any of the states of Arkansas, Illinois, Indiana, Iowa, Kansas, Michigan, Minnesota, Missouri, Nebraska, and Wisconsin.

(Sec. 703) Includes within the reporting requirements of tax-exempt public charities information about disaster relief activities and contributions received for those purposes.

(Sec. 704) Extends through 2010 tax-exempt bond financing and low-income housing tax credit benefits to the Hurricane Ike disaster area. Defines the "Hurricane Ike disaster area" as an area in Texas or Louisiana that was declared a major disaster area by the President by reason of Hurricane Ike and that was determined by the President to warrant federal assistance.

Subtitle B: National Disaster Relief—(Sec. 706) Waives the 10% adjusted gross income limitation on personal casualty losses for losses sustained from a federally declared disaster occurring before January 1, 2010. Defines "federally declared disaster" as any disaster determined by the President to warrant federal assistance under the Robert T. Stafford Relief and Emergency Assistance Act.

Increases the standard tax deduction by a taxpayer's net disaster loss (i.e., personal casualty losses in a disaster area over personal casualty gains).

Increases until December 31, 2009, the threshold for deductible casualty losses (from $100 to $500).

(Sec. 707) Allows the expensing of business-related costs incurred due to a federally declared disaster for: (1) the abatement or control of hazardous substances; (2) removal of debris or demolition of damaged structures; or (3) repair of damaged property.

(Sec. 708) Provides for a five-year carryback period for net operating losses attributable to a federally declared disaster. Allows such losses as a deduction in computing alternative minimum taxable income.

(Sec. 709) Modifies certain mortgage revenue bond requirements for principal residences damaged or destroyed in a federally declared disaster occurring before January 1, 2010.

(Sec. 710) Allows accelerated depreciation and increases the expensing allowance for qualified disaster assistance property. Defines "qualified disaster assistance property" to include nonresidential real or residential rental property in a federally declared disaster area.

Title VIII: Spending Reductions and Appropriate Revenue Raisers for New Tax Relief Policy—(Sec. 801) Requires the inclusion in gross income for income tax purposes of employee compensation deferred under a nonqualified deferred compensation plan of a nonqualified entity when there is no substantial risk of forfeiture of the rights to such compensation. Defines "nonqualified entity" as any foreign corporation unless substantially all of its income is: (1) effectively connected with a trade or business in the United States; or (2) subject to a comprehensive foreign income tax. Includes certain partnerships within such definition.

Source: Library of Congress. "Bill Summary and Status 100th Congress (2007–2008) H.R. 1424 CRS Summary," October 3, 2008. Accessed January 31, 2013. http://thomas.loc.gov/cgi-bin/bdquery/z?d110:HR01424:@@@D&summ2=m&

A-3. THE OFFICIAL START AND END OF THE GREAT RECESSION

The U.S. government does not officially announce start and end dates for reces-sions. The National Bureau of Economic Research (NBER), a private nonprofit research organization, is generally considered the authority on start and end dates for U.S. recessions. It usually takes the NBER six to 18 months after the start or end of a recession to announce an official start or end date. This is because it takes time for eco-nomic data to become available and for economic trends to become apparent. When the NBER considers whether the U.S. economy has entered or ended a recession, it considers a variety of economic indicators.

On December 1, 2008, the NBER announced that the U.S. economy had entered a recession in December 2007 based on the December 2007 peak (and thus the decline that follows a peak) in personal incomes and the number of jobs in the economy, as well as on the peak in real manufacturing and wholesale retail trade in June 2008, and the peak in industrial production in January 2008. The following press release below is the official NBER announcement that the U.S. economy had entered a recession.

Determination of the December 2007 Peak in Economic Activity

The Business Cycle Dating Committee of the National Bureau of Economic Research met by conference call on Friday, November 28. The committee maintains a chronol-ogy of the beginning and ending dates (months and quarters) of U.S. recessions. The committee determined that a peak in economic activity occurred in the U.S. economy in December 2007. The peak marks the end of the expansion that began in November 2001 and the beginning of a recession. The expansion lasted 73 months; the previous expansion of the 1990s lasted 120 months.

A recession is a significant decline in economic activity spread across the economy, lasting more than a few months, normally visible in production, employment, real income, and other indicators. A recession begins when the economy reaches a peak of activity and ends when the economy reaches its trough. Between trough and peak, the economy is in an expansion.

Because a recession is a broad contraction of the economy, not confined to one sec-tor, the committee emphasizes economy-wide measures of economic activity. The committee believes that domestic production and employment are the primary conceptual measures of economic activity.

The committee views the payroll employment measure, which is based on a large survey of employers, as the most reliable comprehensive estimate of employment.

This series reached a peak in December 2007 and has declined every month since then.

The committee believes that the two most reliable comprehensive estimates of aggregate domestic production are normally the quarterly estimate of real Gross Domestic Product and the quarterly estimate of real Gross Domestic Income, both produced by the Bureau of Economic Analysis. In concept, the two should be the same, because sales of products generate income for producers and workers equal to the value of the sales. However, because the measurement on the product and income sides proceeds somewhat independently, the two actual measures differ by a statistical discrepancy. The product-side estimates fell slightly in 2007Q4, rose slightly in 2008Q1, rose again in 2008Q2, and fell slightly in 2008Q3. The income-side estimates reached their peak in 2007Q3, fell slightly in 2007Q4 and 2008Q1, rose slightly in 2008Q2 to a level below its peak in 2007Q3, and fell again in 2008Q3. Thus, the currently available estimates of quarterly aggregate real domestic production do not speak clearly about the date of a peak in activity.

Other series considered by the committee including real personal income less transfer payments, real manufacturing and wholesale-retail trade sales, industrial production, and employment estimates based on the household survey all reached peaks between November 2007 and June 2008.

The committee determined that the decline in economic activity in 2008 met the standard for a recession, as set forth in the second paragraph of this document. All evidence other than the ambiguous movements of the quarterly product-side measure of domestic production confirmed that conclusion. Many of these indicators, including monthly data on the largest component of GDP, consumption, have declined sharply in recent months.

The committee's primary role is to maintain a monthly chronology of the business cycle. For this purpose, the committee mainly relies on monthly indicators. It also considers quarterly indicators and maintains a quarterly chronology. In its deliberations, the committee relied on a number of monthly and quarterly economic indicators published by government agencies. The Appendix to this announcement lists these indicators and their sources. The Appendix also describes the calculations required to reproduce the series that the NBER committee examined in its deliberations.

THE MONTH OF THE PEAK

The committee identified December 2007 as the peak month, after determining that the subsequent decline in economic activity was large enough to qualify as a recession.

Payroll employment, the number of filled jobs in the economy based on the Bureau of Labor Statistics large survey of employers, reached a peak in December 2007 and has declined in every month since then. An alternative measure of employment, measured by the BLS's household survey, reached a peak in November 2007, declined early in 2008, expanded temporarily in April to a level below its November 2007 peak, and has declined in every month since April 2008. For a discussion of the difference between payroll and household survey employment measures, see Mary Bowler and Teresa L. Morisi, Understanding the Employment Measures from the CPS and CES Surveys, *Monthly Labor Review*, February 2006, pp. 23–38.

The committee uses real personal income less transfer payments from the Bureau of Economic Analysis as a monthly measure of output. The deduction of transfer payments places the data closer to the desired measure, real gross domestic income. To adjust personal income less transfer payments from nominal to real terms (that is, to remove the effects of price changes), the committee uses the deflator for gross domestic product. Because this deflator is only available quarterly, the committee interpolates the published series to approximate a monthly price index for GDP. The resulting monthly measure of real personal income less transfers is an imperfect measure of monthly real output because of definitional differences between personal income less transfers and gross national income and because we use the interpolated price index. Our measure of real personal income less transfers peaked in December 2007, displayed a zig-zag pattern from then until June 2008 at levels slightly below the December 2007 peak, and has generally declined since June.

Real manufacturing and wholesale-retail trade sales from the Census Department is another monthly indicator of output. It is an imperfect measure of the production of goods and services for at least three reasons. First, it covers only goods and not services. Second, it does not deduct the sales of imported goods. Because the real value of imports declined substantially over the relevant period, the measure understates the growth of output. Third, the government does not publish a price index corresponding to the coverage of the measure. The committee uses the same interpolated GDP deflator as discussed above. Real manufacturing and wholesale-retail trade sales reached a well-defined peak in June 2008.

The last monthly measure of production is the Federal Reserve Board's index of industrial production. This measure has quite restricted coverage it includes manufacturing, mining, and utilities but excludes all services and government. Industrial production peaked in January 2008, fell through May 2008, rose slightly in June and July, and then fell substantially from July to September. It rose somewhat in

October with the resumption of oil production disturbed by hurricanes in the previous month. The October value of the industrial production index remained a substantial 4.7 percent below its value in January 2008.

The committee noted that the behavior of the quarterly estimates of aggregate production was not inconsistent with a peak in late 2007. The income-side estimate of output reached its peak in the third quarter of 2007. The product-side estimate reached a temporary peak in the same quarter, but rose to a higher level in the second quarter of 2008.

THE QUARTER OF THE PEAK

The committee determined that the peak quarter of economic activity was the fourth quarter of 2007. When the monthly peak occurs in the last month of a quarter, the NBERs long-standing procedures dates the quarterly peak either in the quarter containing the monthly peak or in the subsequent quarter. Thus, the committee could have dated the quarterly peak in 2008Q1 if it had determined that economic activity was higher in that quarter than in 2007Q4. However, the committee determined that this was not the case. Most notably, both payroll employment and the income-side estimate of domestic production were lower in 2008Q1 than in 2007Q4, and the product-side estimate of domestic production was only slightly higher. The committee found that the peak quarter was the one containing the peak month, 2007Q4.

FURTHER COMMENTS

Although the indicators described above are the most important measures considered by the NBER in developing its business cycle chronology, there is no fixed rule about which other measures may contribute information to the process in any particular episode.

Committee members participating in the decision were: Robert Hall, Stanford University (chair); Martin Feldstein, Harvard University and NBER President Emeritus; Jeffrey Frankel, Harvard University; Robert Gordon, Northwestern University; James Poterba, MIT and NBER President; David Romer, University of California, Berkeley; and Victor Zarnowitz, the Conference Board. Christina Romer of the University of California, Berkeley, resigned from the committee on November 25, 2008, and did not participate in its deliberations of November 28.

For more information, see the FAQs below and also see http://www.nber.org/cycles .html.

FAQs

Q: The financial press often states the definition of a recession as two consecutive quarters of decline in real GDP. How does that relate to the NBERs recession dating procedure?

A: Most of the recessions identified by our procedures do consist of two or more quarters of declining real GDP, but not all of them. As an example, the last recession, in 2001, did not include two consecutive quarters of decline. As of the date of the committee's meeting, the economy had not yet experienced two consecutive quarters of decline.

Q: Why doesn't the committee accept the two-quarter definition?

A: The committee's procedure for identifying turning points differs from the two-quarter rule in a number of ways. First, we do not identify economic activity solely with real GDP, but use a range of indicators. Second, we place considerable emphasis on monthly indicators in arriving at a monthly chronology. Third, we consider the depth of the decline in economic activity. Recall that our definition includes the phrase, a significant decline in activity. Fourth, in examining the behavior of domestic production, we consider not only the conventional product-side GDP estimates, but also the conceptually equivalent income-side GDI estimates. The differences between these two sets of estimates were particularly evident in 2007 and 2008.

Q: Isn't a recession a period of diminished economic activity?

A: It's more accurate to say that a recession the way we use the word is a period of *diminishing* activity rather than *diminished* activity. We identify a month when the economy reached a peak of activity and a later month when the economy reached a trough. The time in between is a recession, a period when economic activity is contracting. The following period is an expansion.

Q: How do the movements of unemployment claims inform the Bureau's thinking?

A: A bulge in jobless claims would appear to forecast declining employment and rising unemployment, but we do not use the initial claims numbers in our discussions, partly because there is a lot of week-to-week noise in the series.

Q: What about the unemployment rate?

A: Unemployment is generally a lagging indicator, particularly after the trough in economic activity determined by the NBER. For instance, the unemployment rate peaked 15 months after the NBER trough month in the 1990–91 recession and 19 months after the NBER trough month in the 2001 recession. The unemployment rate (which the committee does not use) tends to lag behind employment (which the committee *does* use) on account of variations in labor-force participation.

Q: Is the expansion of real GDP (as measured using the product-side estimates) in the first quarter of 2008 consistent with the identification of a recession starting in December 2007?

A: The committee considers a range of indicators of economic activity, and many of them suggest declining activity in the first quarter of the current calendar year. These include payroll employment and the income-side estimates of domestic production.

Q: In December 2007, was there a clear peak in economic activity or was there a flat period around that time?

A: The committee found that economic activity measured by production was close to flat from roughly September 2007 to roughly June 2008, while activity measured by employment reached a clear peak in December 2007. The committee judged that the weight of the evidence suggested that the peak occurred in December 2007.

Q: Are there estimates of monthly real GDP?

A: Yes. Macroeconomic Advisers, a consulting firm, prepares estimates of monthly real GDP. Many of the ingredients of the quarterly GDP figures are published at a monthly frequency by the Bureau of Economic Analysis. Macroeconomic Advisers aggregates them, and then uses a statistical procedure to adjust the monthly estimates for each quarter to make them consistent with the Commerce Department's official quarterly figure. The monthly GDP numbers are fairly noisy and are subject to considerable revision. Estimated monthly real GDP reached one peak in January 2008 and another, higher peak in June 2008.

Q: Has the committee ever changed a cycle date?

A: In the past, the NBER has made some small changes to cycle dates, most recently in 1975. No changes have occurred since 1978 when the Business Cycle Dating Committee was formed. The committee would change the date of a recent peak or trough if it concluded that the date it had chosen was incorrect.

Q: Typically, how long after the beginning of a recession does the BCDC declare that a recession has started? After the end of the recession?

A: Anywhere from 6 to 18 months. The committee waits long enough so that the existence of a recession is not at all in doubt. It waits until it can assign an accurate date.

Q: When the BCDC says that the recession began in December, is there a specific date in December?

A: The committee identifies the month when the peak occurred, without taking a stand on the date in the month. Thus, December 2007 is both the month when the recession began and the month when the expansion ended.

Q: Does the NBER identify depressions as well as recessions in its chronology?

A: The NBER does not separately identify depressions. The NBER business cycle chronology identifies the dates of peaks and troughs in economic activity. We refer to the period between a peak and a trough as a contraction or a recession, and the period between the trough and the peak as an expansion. The term depression is often used to refer to a particularly severe period of economic weakness. Some economists use it to refer only to the portion of these periods when economic activity is declining. The more common use, however, also encompasses the time until economic activity has returned to close to normal levels. The most recent episode in the United States that is generally regarded as a depression occurred in the 1930s. The NBER determined that the peak in economic activity occurred in August 1929, and the trough in March 1933. The NBER identified a second peak in May 1937 and a trough in June 1938. Both the contraction starting in 1929 and that starting in 1937 were very severe; the one starting in 1929 is widely acknowledged to have been the worst in U.S. history. According to the Bureau of Economic Analysis, real GDP declined 27 percent between 1929 and 1933, roughly ten times as much as in the worst postwar recession. If the term Great Depression is used to mean the period of exceptional decline in economic activity, it refers to the period from August 1929 to March 1933. If it is used to also include the period until economic activity had returned to approximately normal levels, most economists would judge that it ended sometime in 1940 or 1941. However, just as the NBER does not define the term depression or identify depressions, there is no formal NBER definition or dating of the Great Depression.

Q: When did the NBER first establish its business cycle dates?

A: The NBER was founded in 1920, and published its first business cycle dates in 1929.

Q: When was your committee first formed?

A: When Martin Feldstein became president of the NBER in 1978. Robert Hall has chaired the committee since its inception.

Q: How is the committee's membership determined?

A: The President of the NBER appoints the members, who include directors of the macro-related programs of the NBER plus other members with specialties in business-cycle research.

Q: How long does the committee expect the recession to last?

A: The committee does not forecast.

WEBSITES:

Federal Reserve Board industrial production index: http://www.federalreserve.gov/releases/g17/iphist/iphist_sa.txt

Bureau of Economic Analysis, U.S. Department of Commerce: http://www.bea.gov/national/nipaweb/SelectTable.asp?Selected=N

BLS payroll survey: http://data.bls.gov/cgi-bin/surveymost?ce

BLS household survey: http://data.bls.gov/cgi-bin/surveymost?ln

Table A-3   Data Sources and Calculations

Indicator	Source and method
Industrial production	FRB index B50001
Quarterly real GDP	BEA Table 1.1.6, line 1
Quarterly real gross domestic income, GDI	BEA Table 1.10, line 1, divided by BEA Table 1.1.9, line 1
Monthly real personal income less transfers	BEA Table 2.6, line 1 less line 14, both deflated by a monthly interpolation (see below) of BEA Table 1.1.9, line 1
Monthly payroll employment	BLS Series CES0000000001
Monthly household employment	BLS Series LNS12000000
Monthly real manufacturing and trade sales	Census series tbtsla, adjusted, total business, deflated by monthly interpolation of BEA Table 1.1.9, line 1

Census data on manufacturing and trade sales: http://www.census.gov/mtis/www/data/text/mtis-sales.txt

Interpolation of GDP deflator:

The value of the index in the first month of the quarter is one third of the past quarter's value plus two-thirds of the current quarter's value. In the second month, it is the quarter's value. In the third month, it is two-thirds of the quarter's value plus one third of the next quarter's value.

Source: National Bureau of Economic Research. 2008. "Determination of the December 2007 Peak in Economic Activity," December 1. Accessed January 28, 2013. http://wwwdev.nber.org/dec2008.html. Used by permission.

A-4. PRESIDENT BARACK OBAMA'S ADDRESS ON THE HOME MORTGAGE CRISIS

The depths of the housing crisis and its impact on the U.S. economy as a whole are highlighted in the following address from President Obama. These remarks were made to high school students in Arizona, one of the states hardest hit by the downturn in the housing market.

For Immediate Release February 18, 2009

REMARKS BY THE PRESIDENT
ON THE HOME MORTGAGE CRISIS
Dobson High School
Mesa, Arizona
10:25 A.M. MST

THE PRESIDENT: Thank you very much. (Applause.) Please, everybody have a seat. Thank you. Well, it is good to be back in Arizona. (Applause.) Thank you. Are you excited? (Applause.) Thank you, thank you. And thank you for arranging for such a beautiful day. I want to stick around, but I got to go back to work. But it is wonderful to be here. And to all of you, I know that attending these kinds of events, oftentimes you have to wait in line and there's all kinds of stuff going on. But I appreciate you being here very much. And to all the officials here at the school, the principal and the student body, everybody who helped make this possible, thank you so much to all of you. (Applause.)

I'm here today to talk about a crisis unlike we've ever known—but one that you know very well here in Mesa, and throughout the Valley. In Phoenix and its surrounding suburbs, the American Dream is being tested by a home mortgage crisis that not only threatens the stability of our economy, but also the stability of families and neighborhoods. It's a crisis that strikes at the heart of the middle class: the homes in which we invest our savings and build our lives, raise our families and plant roots in our communities.

So many Americans have shared with me their personal experiences of this crisis. Many have written letters or emails or shared their stories with me at rallies and along rope lines. Their hardship and heartbreak are a reminder that while this crisis is vast, it begins just one house—and one family—at a time.

It begins with a young family—maybe in Mesa, or Glendale, or Tempe—or just as likely in a suburban area of Las Vegas, or Cleveland, or Miami. They save up. They search. They choose a home that feels like the perfect place to start a life. They secure a fixed-rate mortgage at a reasonable rate, and they make a down payment, and they make their mortgage payments each month. They are as responsible as anyone could ask them to be.

But then they learn that acting responsibly often isn'' enough to escape this crisis. Perhaps somebody loses a job in the latest round of layoffs, one of more than 3.5 million jobs lost since this recession began—or maybe a child gets sick, or a spouse has his or her hours cut.

In the past, if you found yourself in a situation like this, you could have sold your home and bought a smaller one with more affordable payments, or you could have refinanced your home at a lower rate. But today, home values have fallen so sharply that even if you make a large down payment, the current value of your mortgage may still be higher than the current value of your house. So no bank will return your calls, and no sale will return your investment.

You can't afford to leave, you can't afford to stay. So you start cutting back on luxuries. Then you start cutting back on necessities. You spend down your savings to keep up with your payments. Then you open the retirement fund. Then you use the credit cards. And when you've gone through everything you have, and done everything you can, you have no choice but to default on your loan. And so your home joins the nearly 6 million others in foreclosure or at risk of foreclosure across the country, including roughly 150,000 right here in Arizona.

But the foreclosures which are uprooting families and upending lives across America are only part of the housing crisis. For while there are millions of families who face foreclosure, there are millions more who are in no danger of losing their homes, but who have still seen their dreams endangered. They're the families who see the "For Sale" signs lining the streets; who see neighbors leave, and homes standing vacant, and lawns slowly turning brown. They see their own homes—their single largest asset—plummeting in value. One study in Chicago found that a foreclosed home reduces the price of nearby homes by as much as 9 percent. Home prices in cities across the country have fallen by more than 25 percent since 2006. And in Phoenix, they've fallen by 43 percent.

Even if your neighborhood hasn't been hit by foreclosures, you're likely feeling the effects of this crisis in other ways. Companies in your community that depend on the housing market—construction companies and home furnishing stores and painters and landscapers—they're all cutting back and laying people off. The number of residential construction jobs has fallen by more than a quarter million since mid-2006. As businesses lose revenue and people lose income, the tax base shrinks, which means less money for schools and police and fire departments. And on top of this, the costs to local government associated with a single foreclosure can be as high as $20,000.

So the effects of this crisis have also reverberated across the financial markets. When the housing market collapsed, so did the availability of credit on which our economy depends. And as that credit has dried up, it's been harder for families to find affordable loans to purchase a car or pay tuition, and harder for businesses to secure the capital they need to expand and create jobs.

In the end, all of us are paying a price for this home mortgage crisis. And all of us will pay an even steeper price if we allow this crisis to continue to deepen—a crisis which is unraveling home ownership, the middle class, and the American Dream itself. But if we act boldly and swiftly to arrest this downward spiral, then every American will benefit. And that's what I want to talk about today.

The plan I'm announcing focuses on rescuing families who've played by the rules and acted responsibly, by refinancing loans for millions of families in traditional mortgages who are underwater or close to it, by modifying loans for families stuck in sub-prime mortgages they can't afford as a result of skyrocketing interest rates or personal misfortune, and by taking broader steps to keep mortgage rates low so that families can secure loans with affordable monthly payments.

At the same time, this plan must be viewed in a larger context. A lost home often begins with a lost job. Many businesses have laid off workers for a lack of revenue and available capital. Credit has become scarce as markets have been overwhelmed by the collapse of security backed—securities backed by failing mortgages. In the end, the home mortgage crisis, the financial crisis, and this broader economic crisis are all interconnected, and we can't successfully address any one of them without addressing them all.

So yesterday, in Denver, I signed into law the American Recovery and Reinvestment Act, which will create or save—(applause.) The act will create or save 3.5 million jobs over the next two years—including 70,000 right here in Arizona, right here—(applause)—doing the work America needs done. And we're also going to work to stabilize, repair and reform our financial system to get credit flowing again to families and businesses.

And we will pursue the housing plan I'm outlining today. And through this plan, we will help between 7 and 9 million families restructure or refinance their mortgages so they can afford—avoid foreclosure. And we're not just helping homeowners at risk of falling over the edge; we're preventing their neighbors from being pulled over that edge, too—as defaults and foreclosures contribute to sinking home values, and failing local businesses, and lost jobs.

But I want to be very clear about what this plan will not do: It will not rescue the unscrupulous or irresponsible by throwing good taxpayer money after bad loans. It will not help speculators—(applause)—it will not help speculators who took risky bets on a rising market and bought homes not to live in but to sell. (Applause.) It will not help dishonest lenders who acted irresponsibly, distorting the facts— (applause)—distorting the facts and dismissing the fine print at the expense of buyers who didn't know better. And it will not reward folks who bought homes they knew from the beginning they would never be able to afford. (Applause.) So I just want to make this clear: This plan will not save every home.

But it will give millions of families resigned to financial ruin a chance to rebuild. It will prevent the worst consequences of this crisis from wreaking even greater havoc on the economy. And by bringing down the foreclosure rate, it will help to shore up housing prices for everybody. According to estimates by the Treasury Department, this plan could stop the slide in home prices due to neighboring foreclosures by up to $6,000 per home.

So here's how my plan works: First, we will make it possible for an estimated 4 to 5 million currently ineligible homeowners who receive their mortgages through Fannie Mae or Freddie Mac to refinance their mortgages at a lower rate. (Applause.)

Today, as a result of declining home values, millions of families are what's called "underwater," which simply means that they owe more on their mortgages than their homes are currently worth. These families are unable to sell their homes, but they're also unable to refinance them. So in the event of a job loss or another emergency, their options are limited.

Also right now, Fannie Mae and Freddie Mac—the institutions that guarantee home loans for millions of middle-class families—are generally not permitted to guarantee refinancing for mortgages valued at more than 80 percent of the home's worth. So families who are underwater or close to being underwater can't turn to these lending institutions for help.

My plan changes that by removing this restriction on Fannie and Freddie so that they can refinance mortgages they already own or guarantee. (Applause.)

And what this will do is it will allow millions of families stuck with loans at a higher rate to refinance. And the estimated cost to taxpayers would be roughly zero. While Fannie and Freddie would receive less money in payments, this would be balanced out by a reduction in defaults and foreclosures. (Applause.)

I also want to point out that millions of other households could benefit from historically low interest rates if they refinance, though many don't know that this opportunity is available to them—meaning some of you—an opportunity that could save your families hundreds of dollars each month. And the efforts we are taking to stabilize mortgage markets will help you, borrowers, secure more affordable terms, too.

A second thing we're going to do under this plan is we will create new incentives so that lenders work with borrowers to modify the terms of sub-prime loans at risk of default and foreclosure.

Sub-prime loans—loans with high rates and complex terms that often conceal their costs—make up only 12 percent of all mortgages, but account for roughly half of all foreclosures. Right now, when families with these mortgages seek to modify a loan to avoid this fate, they often find themselves navigating a maze of rules and regulations, but they're rarely finding answers. Some sub-prime lenders are willing to renegotiate; but many aren't. And your ability to restructure your loan depends on where you live, the company that owns or manages your loan, or even the agent who happens to answer the phone on the day that you call.

So here's what my plan does: establishes clear guidelines for the entire mortgage industry that will encourage lenders to modify mortgages on primary residences. Any institution that wishes to receive financial assistance from the government, from taxpayers, and to modify home mortgages, will have to do so according to these guidelines—which will be in place two weeks from today. (Applause.)

Here's what this means: If lenders and home buyers work together, and the lender agrees to offer rates that the borrower can afford, then we'll make up part of the gap between what the old payments were and what the new payments will be. Under this plan, lenders who participate will be required to reduce those payments to no more than 31 percent of a borrower's income. And this will enable as many as 3 to 4 million homeowners to modify the terms of their mortgages to avoid foreclosure.

So this part of the plan will require both buyers and lenders to step up and do their part, to take on some responsibility. Lenders will need to lower interest rates and share in the costs of reducing monthly payments in order to prevent another wave of foreclosures. Borrowers will be required to make payments on time in return for this opportunity to reduce those payments.

And I also want to be clear that there will be a cost associated with this plan. But by making these investments in foreclosure prevention today, we will save ourselves the costs of foreclosure tomorrow—costs that are borne not just by families with troubled loans, but by their neighbors and communities and by our economy as a whole. Given the magnitude of these crises, it is a price well worth paying. (Applause.)

There's a third part of the plan: We will take major steps to keep mortgage rates low for millions of middle-class families looking to secure new mortgages.

Today, most new home loans are backed by Fannie Mae and Freddie Mac, which guarantee loans and set standards to keep mortgage rates low and to keep mortgage financing available and predictable for middle-class families. Now, this function is profoundly important, especially now as we grapple with a crisis that would only worsen if we were to allow further disruptions in our mortgage markets.

Therefore, using the funds already approved by Congress for this purpose, the Treasury Department and the Federal Reserve will continue to purchase Fannie Mae and Freddie Mac mortgage-backed securities so that there is stability and liquidity in the marketplace. Through its existing authority, Treasury will provide up to $200 billion in capital to ensure that Fannie Mae and Freddie Mac can continue to stabilize markets and hold mortgage rates down.

And we're also going to work with Fannie and Freddie on other strategies to bolster the mortgage markets, like working with state housing finance agencies to increase their liquidity. And as we seek to ensure that these institutions continue to perform what is a vital function on behalf of middle-class families, we also need to maintain transparency and strong oversight so that they do so in responsible and effective ways.

Fourth, we will pursue a wide range of reforms designed to help families stay in their homes and avoid foreclosures.

And my administration will continue to support reforming our bankruptcy rules so that we allow judges to reduce home mortgages on primary residences to their fair market value—as long as borrowers pay their debts under court-ordered plans. (Applause.) I just want everybody to understand, that's the rule for investors who own two, three, and four homes. So it should be the rule for folks who just own one home—(applause)—as an alternative to foreclosure.

In addition, as part of the recovery plan I signed into law yesterday, we are going to award $2 billion in competitive grants to communities that are bringing together stakeholders and testing new and innovative ways to limit the effects of foreclosures. Communities have shown a lot of initiative, taking responsibility for this crisis when many others have not. And supporting these neighborhood efforts is exactly what we should be doing.

So taken together, the provisions of this plan will help us end this crisis and preserve for millions of families their stake in the American Dream. But we also have to acknowledge the limits of this plan.

Our housing crisis was born of eroding home values, but it was also an erosion of our common values, and in some case, common sense. It was brought about by big banks that traded in risky mortgages in return for profits that were literally too good to be true; by lenders who knowingly took advantage of homebuyers; by homebuyers who knowingly borrowed too much from lenders; by speculators who gambled on ever-rising prices; and by leaders in our nation's capital who failed to act amidst a deepening crisis. (Applause.)

So solving this crisis will require more than resources; it will require all of us to step back and take responsibility. Government has to take responsibility for setting rules of the road that are fair and fairly enforced. Banks and lenders must be held accountable for ending the practices that got us into this crisis in the first place. And each of us, as individuals, have to take responsibility for their own actions. That means all of us have to learn to live within our means again and not assume that—(applause)—and not assume that housing prices are going to go up 20, 30, 40 percent every year.

Those core values of common sense and responsibility, those are the values that have defined this nation. Those are the values that have given substance to our faith in the American Dream. Those are the values we have to restore now at this defining moment.

It will not be easy. But if we move forward with purpose and resolve—with a deepened appreciation of how fundamental the American Dream is and how fragile it can be when we fail to live up to our collective responsibilities, if we go back to our roots, our core values, I am absolutely confident we will overcome this crisis and once again secure that dream not just for ourselves but for generations to come.

Thank you. God bless you. God bless the United States of America. (Applause.)

Source: White House Office of the Press Secretary. "Remarks by the President on the Home Mortgage Crisis," February 18, 2009. Accessed January 29, 2013. http://www.whitehouse.gov/the-press-office/remarks-president-mortgage-crisis

A-5. THE STIMULUS PACKAGE ACT (THE AMERICAN RECOVERY AND REINVESTMENT ACT) OF 2009

The federal government responded to the crisis created by the Great Recession with a series of tax cuts, tax credits, and government spending in the American Recovery and Reinvestment Act of 2009 (ARRA), which became known as the stimulus package based on the government's intent to stimulate the economy with these measures.

The largest allocations in the ARRA were for tax credits for low- and middle-income individuals and families. However, many programs that specifically target low-income individuals and families also benefited middle-income persons. As can be seen in the following document, the ARRA provided funding for food stamps, rental assistance programs, homelessness prevention, housing assistance, and funds to states for Medicaid. The following document provides a summary of the ARRA from the Congressional Research Service.

American Recovery and Reinvestment Act of 2009 (P.L. 111-5): Brief Summary

Summary

President Barack Obama signed H.R. 1, the American Recovery and Reinvestment Act (ARRA) of 2009, into law on February 17, 2009, as P.L. 111-5 (123 Stat. 115-521). The act is seen as one of the most significant legislative responses made thus far to the current economic turmoil. This report provides a summary and legislative history of ARRA and identifies other resources that provide additional information regarding its content and implementation.

ARRA is a relatively lengthy and complex act, amounting to just over 400 pages (in slip law form) and melding together hundreds of billions of dollars in discretionary spending, mandatory spending, and revenue provisions encompassing the jurisdiction of several House and Senate committees. The act consists of two major divisions. Division A (Appropriations Provisions) includes supplemental appropriations for FY2009 (and later fiscal years) covering by separate titles all 12 of the regular appropriations acts, as well as four additional titles dealing with health information technology, a state fiscal stabilization fund, accountability and transparency, and general provisions. Division B (Tax, Unemployment, Health, State Fiscal Relief, and Other Provisions) consists of seven separate titles. Division A includes the discretionary spending provisions, but some significant substantive provisions as well; Division B includes the mandatory spending and revenue provisions, with some exceptions.

ARRA provides almost $800 billion through extensive discretionary spending, mandatory spending, and revenue provisions that the Administration estimates will save or create some 3.5 million jobs. Funding is provided for existing and some new programs in the 15 Cabinet-level departments and 11 independent agencies. Some of the funds are distributed to states, localities, other entities, and individuals through a combination of formula and competitive grants and direct assistance. In addition to new spending and tax provisions, new policies are created regarding unemployment compensation, health insurance, health information technology, broadband communications, and energy, among others.

Numerous oversight, accountability, and transparency provisions are contained in the act. They include various reporting requirements and funding for offices of inspector general, the Government Accountability Office, and a newly established Recovery Accountability and Transparency Board.

With regard to its specific impact on the budget, the act is estimated by the Congressional Budget Office to increase the deficit by $787.2 billion over the 11-year period covering FY2009-FY2019. The estimated deficit impact reflects spending increases of $575.3 billion (in outlays) and revenue reductions of $211.8 billion. The total spending increases consist of $311.2 billion in discretionary new budget authority (yielding $308.3 billion in outlays) and $269.5 billion in mandatory new budget authority (yielding $267.0 billion in outlays).

About 21% of total outlays ($120.1 billion) under ARRA are estimated to occur by the end of FY2009. By the end of FY2010, 59% of total outlays ($339.4 billion) are expected to occur, and by the end of FY2011, 81% of total outlays ($465.6 billion) are expected to occur. Revenue reductions occur more quickly, with reductions of $64.8 billion in FY2009 and $180.1 billion in FY2010, offset somewhat in later years by modest revenue increases.

This report will not be updated.

Source: Brass, Clinton T., Carol Hardy Vincent, Pamela J. Jackson, Jennifer E. Lake, Karen Spar, and Robert Keith. "American Recovery and Reinvestment Act of 2009 (P.L. 111-5): Brief Summary," April 20, 2009. Accessed January 29, 2013. http://waxman.house.gov/sites/waxman.house.gov/files/documents/UploadedFiles/ARRA.pdf

A-6. RECOVERY.GOV: A WEBSITE FOR ACCOUNTABILITY AND TRANSPARENCY FOR THE AMERICAN RECOVERY AND REINVESTMENT ACT

The following document is from the website Recovery.gov. The American Recovery and Reinvestment Act of 2009 (ARRA) required that the Recovery.gov website be created to provide accountability and transparency during the implementation of the ARRA. (For more background on the ARRA see A-5 earlier in this section.)

BREAKDOWN OF FUNDING BY CATEGORY

Total Funds Allocated:

$840 BILLION
Estimated American Recovery and Reinvestment Act tax, entitlement, and contract, grant, and loan expenditures have been increased from $787B to $840B to be consistent with the President's 2012 budget and with scoring changes made by the Congressional Budget Office since the enactment of the Recovery Act in February 2009.

BREAKDOWN OF FUNDS PAID OUT BY CATEGORY

For a complete list of all programs in a category, click the category name.

Individual Tax Credits

$131.8B
First-Time Homebuyers. Transportation Subsidy. Education benefits. Earned Income Tax Credits.

Making Work Pay
$104.4B
$400 tax credit for working individuals; $800 for working married couples

Tax Incentives For Businesses
$32.6B
The Work Opportunity Tax Credit added unemployed veterans and 16-to-24 year olds to the list of new hires that businesses could claim. The Net Operating Loss Carryback allows small businesses to offset losses by receiving refunds on taxes paid up to five years ago.

Energy Incentives
$10.9B
Tax credits for energy efficient improvements to residences. Tax credits for alternative energy equipment. Electric Vehicles Tax Credit

Manufacturing & Economic Recovery, Infrastructure Refinancing, Other
$7.3B
Tax-exempt bonds to expand industrial development. Bonds for investment in Infrastructure, job training, and education in high unemployment areas. Increased available New Market credits

COBRA

$3.7B

Assistance with Continuation of Health Coverage

Education

$91.7B

State Fiscal Stabilization Fund. Student Aid. Training and Employment Services. Aid for the Disadvantaged. Special Education and Rehabilitative Services

Transportation

$36.9B

Highway Infrastructure. High-Speed Rail Corridors. Grants for Railroads and Airports

Infrastructure

$31.0B

Broadband. Federal Building Fund. Highway Construction. Rural Water and Waste Disposal Account

Energy / Environment

$28.4B

Energy Efficient and Renewable Energy Program. Defense Environmental Clean-up. Electricity Delivery and Energy Reliability Program. Water and Related Resources Superfund Program

Research & Development / Science

$14.4B

Fossil Energy R&D. National Science Foundation. National Institutes of Health

Housing

$13.8B

Public and Indian Housing. Rental Assistance Programs. Homelessness Prevention Programs. Homeowners Assistance Fund

Health

$11.5B

Centers for Disease Control & Prevention. Indian Health Service. Food & Nutrition Service. National Institutes of Health

Other Programs
$5.8B
Some administrative and Operation Costs for Recovery Programs. Offices of the Inspectors General Recovery Administration Costs

Public Safety
$5.4B
Wild land Fire Management. FEMA Firefighter Assistance Grants and Emergency Food and Shelter. Violence Against Women Programs. Customs and Border Protection

Family
$5.0B
Health Resources and Services. Veterans Health Administration. Centers for Disease Control and Prevention. Indian Health Services. Food and Nutrition Services. Supplemental Nutrition Program for Women, Infants, and Children

Job Training / Unemployment
$4.7B
Community Service Employment for Older Americans. Training and Employment Services. Special Education and Rehabilitative Services. Trade Adjustment Assistance for Farmers.

Medicaid/Medicare
$96.9B
Medicaid Grants to States; Medicare HITECH Incentive Payments; Program Management

Unemployment Insurance Programs
$61.2B

Family Services
$45.2B
Foster Care and Adoption Assistance; Child Support; Food Stamp Program; Assistance for Needy Families

Energy
$17.8B
Grants for Specified Energy Property in Lieu of Tax Credits; Bonneville Power Administration Fund; Western Area Power Administration, Borrowing Authority

Economic Recovery Payments

$13.8B

One-time $250 payments to Social Security beneficiaries; Railroad Board payments; Veterans payments

Housing

$5.6B

Grants to States for Low-Income Housing in Lieu of Low-Income Tax Credits

Agriculture

$1.0B

Assistance for Farm and Aquaculture Revenue Losses Due to Natural Disasters. Trade Adjustment Assistance for Farmers

- Most of the tax credits authorized under the Recovery Act have expired. The Office of Tax Analysis submitted final data as of June 2012.

Source: Recovery.gov. "Breakdown of Funding by Category," 2013. Accessed January 28, 2013. http://www.recovery.gov/Transparency/fundingoverview/Pages/fundingbreakdown.aspx

A-7. REMARKS BY THE PRESIDENT ON THE EMERGENCY RESTRUCTURING OF GM, 2009

The U.S. auto industry suffered so deeply during the Great Recession that the federal government had to intervene to prevent its collapse from deepening the economic crisis in the country. In the summer of 2009 President Obama announced restructuring plans for GM and additional government investments of $30 billion in the company. The scale of the federal government's intervention and the president's remarks (which follow) highlight the depths of the crisis the United States was facing.

THE WHITE HOUSE
Office of the Press Secretary
For Immediate Release June 1, 2009
REMARKS BY THE PRESIDENT
ON GENERAL MOTORS RESTRUCTURING
Grand Foyer

11:51 A.M. EDT

THE PRESIDENT: Good morning, everybody. Just over two months ago, I spoke with you in this same spot about the challenges facing our auto industry, and I laid out what needed to be done to save two of America's most storied automakers— General Motors and Chrysler. These companies were facing a crisis decades in the making, and having relied on loans from the previous administration, were asking for more.

From the beginning, I made it clear that I would not put any more tax dollars on the line if it meant perpetuating the bad business decisions that had led these companies to seek help in the first place. I refused to let these companies become permanent wards of the state, kept afloat on an endless supply of taxpayer money. In other words, I refused to kick the can down the road.

But I also recognized the importance of a viable auto industry to the well-being of families and communities across our industrial Midwest and across the United States. In the midst of a deep recession and financial crisis, the collapse of these companies would have been devastating for countless Americans, and done enormous damage to our economy—beyond the auto industry. It was also clear that if GM and Chrysler remade and retooled themselves for the 21st century, it would be good for American workers, good for American manufacturing, and good for America's economy.

I decided, then, that if GM and Chrysler and their stakeholders were willing to sacrifice for their companies' survival and success; if they were willing to take the difficult, but necessary steps to restructure, and make themselves stronger, leaner, and more competitive, then the United States government would stand behind them.

The original restructuring plans submitted by GM and Chrysler earlier this year did not call for the sweeping changes these companies needed to survive—and I couldn't in good conscience proceed on that basis. So we gave them a chance to develop a stronger plan that would put them on a path toward long-term viability. The 60 days GM had to submit its revised plans have now elapsed, and I want to say a few words about where we are and what steps will be taken going forward. But before I do, I want to give you an update on where things stand with Chrysler.

When my administration took office and began going over Chrysler's books, the future of this great American car company was uncertain. In fact, it was not clear whether it had any future at all. But after consulting with my Auto Task Force, industry experts, and financial advisors, and after asking many tough questions, I became convinced that if Chrysler were willing to undergo a restructuring, and if it were able to form a partnership with a viable global car company, then Chrysler could get a new lease on life.

Well, that more promising scenario has now come to pass. Today, after taking a number of painful steps, and moving through a quick, efficient, and fair bankruptcy process, a new, stronger Chrysler is poised to complete its alliance with Fiat. Just 31 days after Chrysler's Chapter 11 bankruptcy filing, a court has approved the Chrysler-Fiat alliance, paving the way for a new Chrysler to emerge from bankruptcy in the next few days.

What happens next is in the hands of their executives, managers, and workers—as it is for any private company. But what the completion of this alliance means is that tens of thousands of jobs that would have been lost if Chrysler had liquidated will now be saved, and that consumers have no reason at all to worry about a restructuring—even one as painful as what Chrysler underwent.

And keep in mind—many experts said that a quick, surgical bankruptcy was impossible. They were wrong. Others predicted that Chrysler's decision to enter bankruptcy would lead to an immediate collapse in consumer confidence that would send car sales over a cliff. They were wrong, as well. In fact, Chrysler sold more cars in May than it did in April, in part because consumers were comforted by our extraordinary commitment to stand behind a quick bankruptcy process. All in all, it's a dramatic—an outcome dramatically better than what appeared likely when this process began.

Now the situation we found at General Motors was very different from what we found at Chrysler—largely because GM is a different kind of company. It is much larger and much more complex, with operations all over the globe. In this context, GM's management team—including its new CEO, Fritz Henderson, its interim chairman, Kent Kresa, and all of their colleagues—have worked—has worked tirelessly to produce a plan that meets the strict standards I laid out at the beginning: to streamline GM's brands, clean up GM's balance sheet, and make it possible for GM to compete and succeed.

Working with my Auto Task Force, GM and its stakeholders have produced a viable, achievable plan that will give this iconic American company a chance to rise again. It's a plan tailored to the realities of today's auto market; a plan that positions GM to move toward profitability, even if it takes longer than expected for our economy to fully recover; and it's a plan that builds on GM's recent progress in making better cars. As this plan takes effect, GM will start building a larger share of its cars here at home, including fuel-efficient cars. In fact, if all goes according to plan, the share of GM cars sold in the United States that are made here will actually grow for the first time in three decades.

Now, any time a business as large as General Motors goes through a restructuring, it is extremely difficult to find common ground among all of the company's stakeholders. But while the deal that has been worked out is tough, it is also fair.

It will require the United Auto Workers to make further cuts in compensation and retiree health care benefits—painful sacrifices on top of all that they have already done.

It will require GM shareholders to give up the remaining value of their shares—just as they would have had to do in any private restructuring of this kind.

And it will also provide unsecured bondholders with an equitable outcome—an outcome that will let them recover more than the current value of their claims, and substantially more than they would have recovered if the government had not intervened and GM had liquidated. That's why a majority of GM's bondholders already support this deal.

Throughout this process, I wanted to ensure that none of GM's stakeholders receives special treatment because of our government's involvement. That's why I instructed my Auto Task Force to treat all of GM's stakeholders fairly and to ensure that this restructuring was carried out in a way that was consistent with past precedent—and it was.

What we have, then, is a credible plan that is full of promise. But GM can't put this plan into effect on its own. Executing this plan will require a substantial amount of money that only a government can provide. Considering GM's extensive operations within their borders, the governments of Canada and Ontario have agreed to do their part with an investment in GM's future, and I want to thank them for doing so. I also want to thank the government of Germany for working diligently to reach a Memorandum of Understanding on the sale of a major stake in GM's European Division and for providing interim funding that will make it possible for that transaction to be finalized.

But of course GM is an American company with tens of thousands of employees in this country, and responsibility for its future ultimately rests with us. That's why our government will be making a significant additional investment of about $30 billion in GM—an investment that will entitle American taxpayers to ownership of about 60 percent of the new GM.

Now, let me talk about this. I recognize that this may give some Americans pause. So let me explain as clearly as possible why we are making this investment. We inherited a financial crisis unlike any that we've seen in our time. This crisis crippled private capital markets and forced us to take steps in our financial system—and with our auto companies—that we would not have otherwise even considered. These steps have put our government in the unwelcome position of owning large stakes in private companies for the simple and compelling reason that their survival and the success of our overall economy depend on it.

Understand we're making these investments not because I want to spend the American people's tax dollars, but because I want to protect them. Instead of taking so much stock in GM, we could have simply offered the company more loans. But for years, GM has been buried under an unsustainable mountain of debt. And piling an irresponsibly large debt on top of the new GM would mean simply repeating the mistakes of the past. So we are acting as reluctant shareholders— because that is the only way to help GM succeed.

What we are not doing—what I have no interest in doing—is running GM. GM will be run by a private board of directors and management team with a track record in American manufacturing that reflects a commitment to innovation and quality. They—and not the government—will call the shots and make the decisions about how to turn this company around. The federal government will refrain from exercising its rights as a shareholder in all but the most fundamental corporate decisions. When a difficult decision has to be made on matters like where to open a new plant or what type of new car to make, the new GM, not the United States government, will make that decision.

In short, our goal is to get GM back on its feet, take a hands-off approach, and get out quickly.

Exiting a restructuring of this scale, however, requires not only new investment. It also requires giving GM a chance to start anew by clearing away the massive past debts that are weighing the company down. And that's why earlier today, GM did what Chrysler has successfully done and filed for Chapter 11 bankruptcy with the support of its key stakeholders and the United States government.

In all likelihood, this process will take more time for GM than it did for Chrysler because GM is a bigger, more complex company. But Chrysler's extraordinary success reaffirms my confidence that GM will emerge from its bankruptcy process quickly, and as a stronger and more competitive company. And I want to remind everyone that if you are considering buying a GM car during this period of restructuring, your warrantees will be safe and government-backed.

So I'm confident that the steps I'm announcing today will mark the end of an old GM, and the beginning of a new GM; a new GM that can produce the high-quality, safe, and fuel-efficient cars of tomorrow; that can lead America towards an energy independent future; and that is once more a symbol of America's success.

But I want to be honest with you. Building a leaner GM will come at a cost. It will take a painful toll on many Americans who have relied on General Motors throughout the generations. So I want to say a word directly to all the men and women watching today, wondering what all of this will mean as far as their own lives are concerned.

I know you've already seen more than your fair share of hard times. We saw 400,000 jobs lost in the auto industry in the year before this restructuring even began. I will not pretend the hard times are over. Difficult days lie ahead. More jobs will be lost. More plants will close. More dealerships will shut their doors, and so will many parts suppliers.

But I want you to know that what you're doing is making a sacrifice for the next generation—a sacrifice you may not have chose to make, but a sacrifice you were nevertheless called to make so that your children and all of our children can grow up in an America that still makes things; that still builds cars; that still strives for a better future.

As our autoworkers and auto communities pass through these difficult times, we, as a nation, must do our part. That's why, in March, I appointed Ed Montgomery Director of Recovery for Auto Communities and Workers. That's why two weeks ago Ed announced a green jobs training program for autoworkers in hard-hit communities. And that's why last week Ed and Karen Mills, my Small Business Administration chief, traveled to Indiana to announce a new plan to provide loans to auto, RV, and boat dealers to help finance floor plans. That's why we are accelerating the purchase of a federal fleet of cars to jumpstart demand and give the industry a boost at a time when it needs one. And that's why I'm calling on Congress to pass fleet modernization legislation that can provide a credit to consumers who turn in old cars and purchase cleaner, more fuel-efficient cars. These are important steps on the long road to overcoming a problem that didn't happen overnight and will not be solved overnight.

I recognize that today's news carries a particular importance because it's not just any company we're talking about—it's GM. It's a company that's not only been a source of income, but a source of pride for generations of autoworkers and generations of Americans. But while the GM of the future will be different from the GM of the past, I am absolutely confident that if well managed, a new GM will emerge that can provide a new generation of Americans with a chance to live out their dreams, that can out-compete automakers around the world, and that can once again be an integral part of America's economic future. And when that happens, we can truly say that what is good for General Motors and all who work there is good for the United States of America.

Thank you, everybody.

Source: White House Office of the Press Secretary. "Remarks by the President on General Motors Restructuring," June 1, 2009. Accessed January 29, 2013. http://www.whitehouse.gov/the-press-office/remarks-president-general-motors-restructuring

A-8. BUSINESS CYCLE DATING

The U.S. government does not officially announce start and end dates for recessions. The National Bureau of Economic Research (NBER), a private nonprofit research organization, is generally considered the authority on start and end dates for U.S. recessions. On September 20, 2010, the NBER announced the official end of what had become the longest recession since World War II. The NBER's announcement was based on the fact that gross domestic product (GDP) and gross domestic income (GDI) were 3.1 percent above the low, which was experienced in the second quarter of 2009. The NBER dated the official end of the recession as June 2009 but indicated that GDP and GDI were still 1.3 percent below the peak in the fourth quarter of 2007. Simply put, the official end of the recession did not mean that the economy was "normal" or "good," but that economic indicators showed that any new economic decline would be a second recession, not a continuation of the previous recession.

Business Cycle Dating Committee, National Bureau of Economic Research

CAMBRIDGE September 20, 2010—The Business Cycle Dating Committee of the National Bureau of Economic Research met yesterday by conference call. At its meeting, the committee determined that a trough in business activity occurred in the U.S. economy in June 2009. The trough marks the end of the recession that began in December 2007 and the beginning of an expansion. The recession lasted 18 months, which makes it the longest of any recession since World War II. Previously the longest postwar recessions were those of 1973–75 and 1981–82, both of which lasted 16 months.

In determining that a trough occurred in June 2009, the committee did not conclude that economic conditions since that month have been favorable or that the economy has returned to operating at normal capacity. Rather, the committee determined only that the recession ended and a recovery began in that month. A recession is a period of falling economic activity spread across the economy, lasting more than a few months, normally visible in real GDP, real income, employment, industrial production, and wholesale-retail sales. The trough marks the end of the declining phase and the start of the rising phase of the business cycle. Economic activity is typically below normal in the early stages of an expansion, and it sometimes remains so well into the expansion.

The committee decided that any future downturn of the economy would be a new recession and not a continuation of the recession that began in December 2007. The basis for this decision was the length and strength of the recovery to date.

The committee waited to make its decision until revisions in the National Income and Product Accounts, released on July 30 and August 27, 2010, clarified the 2009 time path of the two broadest measures of economic activity, real Gross Domestic Product (real GDP) and real Gross Domestic Income (real GDI). The committee noted that in the most recent data, for the second quarter of 2010, the average of real GDP and real GDI was 3.1 percent above its low in the second quarter of 2009 but remained 1.3 percent below the previous peak which was reached in the fourth quarter of 2007.

Identifying the date of the trough involved weighing the behavior of various indicators of economic activity. The estimates of real GDP and GDI issued by the Bureau of Economic Analysis of the U.S. Department of Commerce are only available quarterly. Further, macroeconomic indicators are subject to substantial revisions and measurement error. For these reasons, the committee refers to a variety of monthly indicators to choose the months of peaks and troughs. It places particular emphasis on measures that refer to the total economy rather than to particular sectors. These include a measure of monthly GDP that has been developed by the private forecasting firm Macroeconomic Advisers, measures of monthly GDP and GDI that have been developed by two members of the committee in independent research (James Stock and Mark Watson, (http://www.princeton.edu/~mwatson/ mgdp_gdi.html), real personal income excluding transfers, the payroll and household measures of total employment, and aggregate hours of work in the total economy. The committee places less emphasis on monthly data series for industrial production and manufacturing-trade sales, because these refer to particular sectors of the economy. Movements in these series can provide useful

additional information when the broader measures are ambiguous about the date of the monthly peak or trough. There is no fixed rule about what weights the committee assigns to the various indicators, or about what other measures contribute information to the process.

The committee concluded that the behavior of the quarterly series for real GDP and GDI indicates that the trough occurred in mid-2009. Real GDP reached its low point in the second quarter of 2009, while the value of real GDI was essentially identical in the second and third quarters of 2009. The average of real GDP and real GDI reached its low point in the second quarter of 2009. The committee concluded that strong growth in both real GDP and real GDI in the fourth quarter of 2009 ruled out the possibility that the trough occurred later than the third quarter.

The committee designated June as the month of the trough based on several monthly indicators. The trough dates for these indicators are:

    Macroeconomic Advisers' monthly GDP (June)
    The Stock-Watson index of monthly GDP (June)
    Their index of monthly GDI (July)
    An average of their two indexes of monthly GDP and GDI (June)
    Real manufacturing and trade sales (June)
    Index of Industrial Production (June)
    Real personal income less transfers (October)
    Aggregate hours of work in the total economy (October)
    Payroll survey employment (December)
    Household survey employment (December)

The committee concluded that the choice of June 2009 as the trough month for economic activity was consistent with the later trough months in the labor-market indicators–aggregate hours and employment–for two reasons. First, the strong growth of quarterly real GDP and real GDI in the fourth quarter was inconsistent with designating any month in the fourth quarter as the trough month. The committee believes that these quarterly measures of the real volume of output across the entire economy are the most reliable measures of economic activity. Second, in previous business cycles, aggregate hours and employment have frequently reached their troughs later than the NBER's trough date. In particular, in 2001–03, the trough in payroll employment occurred 21 months after the NBER trough date. In 2009, the NBER trough date is 6 months before the trough in payroll employment. In both the 2001–03 and 2009 cycles, household employment also reached its trough later than the NBER trough date.

The committee noted the contrast between the June trough date for the majority of the monthly indicators and the October trough date for real personal income less transfers. There were two reasons for selecting the earlier date. The first was described above—the fact that quarterly real GDP and GDI rose strongly in the fourth quarter. The second was that real GDI is a more comprehensive measure of income than real personal income less transfers, as it includes additional sources of income such as undistributed corporate profits. The committee's use of income-side measures, notably real GDI, is based on the accounting principle that the value of output equals the sum of the incomes that arise from producing the output. Apart from a random statistical discrepancy, real GDI satisfies that equality while real personal income does not.

The committee also maintains a quarterly chronology of business cycle peak and trough dates. The committee determined that the trough occurred in the second quarter of 2009, when the average of quarterly real GDP and GDI reached its low point.

For more information, see the FAQs and the more detailed description of the NBER's business cycle dating procedure at http://www.nber.org/cycles/recessions.html. An Excel spreadsheet containing the data and the figures for the indicators of economic activity considered by the committee is available at that page as well.

The current members of the Business Cycle Dating Committee are: Robert Hall, Stanford University (chair); Martin Feldstein, Harvard University; Jeffrey Frankel, Harvard University; Robert Gordon, Northwestern University; James Poterba, MIT and NBER President; James Stock, Harvard University; and Mark Watson, Princeton University. David Romer, University of California, Berkeley, is on leave from the committee and did not participate in its deliberations

Source: National Bureau of Economic Research. "Business Cycle Dating Committee, National Bureau of Economic Research," September 20, 2010. Accessed January 28, 2013. http://www.nber.org/cycles/sept2010.html

A-9. TAX RELIEF, UNEMPLOYMENT INSURANCE REAUTHORIZATION, AND JOB CREATION ACT OF 2010

The bipartisan Tax Relief, Unemployment Insurance Reauthorization, and Job Creation Act of 2010 extended Bush-era income tax cuts. It provided for a one-year payroll tax reduction, extended the expansion of the Earned Income Tax Credit under the ARRA for an additional two years, and extended the Child Tax Credit provisions of the ARRA. In addition, it provided for a 13-month extension of unemployment benefits for the eligible unemployed and extended a tax credit to college students and their families. The Congressional Research Services' summary of this act follows.

Bill Summary & Status
111th Congress (2009–2010)
H.R.4853
CRS Summary

H.R.4853

Latest Title: Tax Relief, Unemployment Insurance Reauthorization, and Job Creation Act of 2010

Sponsor: Rep Oberstar, James L. [MN-8] (introduced 3/16/2010) Cosponsors (5)

Related Bills: H.RES.1745, H.RES.1766, H.R.1512, H.R.3607, H.R.4217, H.R. 4915, H.R.4957, H.R.5147,

H.R.5611, H.R.5900, H.R.6190, H.R.6467, H.R.6473, S.3187

Latest Major Action: Became Public Law No: 111-312

SUMMARY AS OF:

12/17/2010—Public Law. (There are 4 other summaries)

Tax Relief, Unemployment Insurance Reauthorization, and Job Creation Act of 2010—**Title I: Temporary Extension of Tax Relief**—Extends through December 31, 2012: (1) the Economic Growth and Tax Relief Reconciliation Act of 2001 (EGTRRA), Public Law 107-16; (2) provisions of the Jobs and Growth Tax Relief Reconciliation Act of 2003, Public Law 108-27, reducing income tax rates on dividend and capital gain income; (3) increases in the Hope Scholarship tax credit, the child tax credit, and the earned income tax credit; and (4) increases in the tax credit for adoption expenses and the tax exclusion for employer-provided adoption assistance.

Title II: Temporary Extension of Individual AMT Relief—(Sec. 201) Extends through 2011 the increased exemption from the alternative minimum tax (AMT)

for married and single taxpayers. Repeals the terminating date in EGTRRA (i.e., December 31, 2010) applicable to increases in the AMT exemption amounts. (Sec. 202) Extends through 2011 the offset against regular and AMT tax liability of certain nonrefundable income tax credits.

Title III: Temporary Estate Tax Relief—(Sec. 301) Reinstates the estate, gift, and generation-skipping transfer tax, subject to modifications to such tax made by this Act. Allows estates of decedents dying after December 31, 2009, and before January 1, 2011, an election to apply current estate tax provisions of EGTRRA.

Extends for nine months after the enactment of this Act filing deadlines for estate tax returns of decedents who die after December 31, 2009, and for generation-skipping transfers made after such date.

(Sec. 302) Amends the Internal Revenue Code to: (1) allow an estate tax exclusion of $5 million, adjusted for inflation for estates of decedents who die in a calendar year after 2011; and (2) establish a maximum estate tax rate of 35%.

(Sec. 303) Increases the estate tax exclusion amount of a surviving spouse by the unused portion of a deceased spouse's exclusion amount.

(Sec. 304) Terminates the estate, gift, and generation-skipping transfer provisions of EGTRRA and the provisions of this title after December 31, 2012.

Title IV: Temporary Extension of Investment Incentives—(Sec. 401) Extends through 2012: (1) the additional depreciation allowance for business and investment property; (2) the 100% expensing allowance for business and investment property; and (3) the election to accelerate the AMT and research tax credits in lieu of bonus depreciation.

(Sec. 402) Extends through 2012 the increased expensing allowance (i.e., $125,000) for depreciable business and investment property and the adjusted gross income threshold (i.e., $500,000) for calculating reductions in such allowance. Allows an inflation adjustment to such increased amounts beginning in 2012. Extends through 2012 the designation of certain computer software as depreciable property for purposes of such allowance.

Title V: Temporary Extension of Unemployment Insurance and Related Matters—(Sec. 501) Amends the Supplemental Appropriations Act, 2008 with respect to the state-established individual emergency unemployment compensation account. Extends the final date for entering a federal-state agreement under the Emergency Unemployment Compensation (EUC) program through January 3, 2012. Postpones the termination of the program until June 9, 2012.

Amends the Assistance for Unemployed Workers and Struggling Families Act to extend until January 4, 2012, requirements that federal payments to states cover 100% of EUC.

Amends the Unemployment Compensation Extension Act of 2008 to exempt weeks of unemployment between enactment of this Act and June 10, 2012, from the prohibition in the Federal-State Extended Unemployment Compensation Act of 1970 against federal matching payments to a state for the first week in an individual's eligibility period for which extended compensation or sharable regular compensation is paid if the state law provides for payment of regular compensation to an individual for his or her first week of otherwise compensable unemployment (thus allowing temporary federal matching for the first week of extended benefits for states with no waiting period).

(Sec. 502) Amends the Federal-State Extended Unemployment Compensation Act of 1970 to authorize a state to apply certain requirements of the Act, with specified substitutions, for determining an extended unemployment compensation period. Requires the state's "on" and "off" indicators to be based on its rate of insured unemployment and rate of total unemployment for the period beginning on the date of enactment of this Act (or, if later, the date established pursuant to state law) and ending on or before December 31, 2011.

(Sec. 503) Amends the Internal Revenue Code, as amended by the Claims Resolutions Act of 2010, to make a technical correction to the definition of a "covered unemployment compensation debt" relating to the amount that states may receive from a reduction of an overpayment otherwise payable to a person who owes such debt.

(Sec. 504) Amends the Claims Resolution Act of 2010 to make a technical correction regarding the limitation on distributions relating to repeal of a continued dumping and subsidy offset. Requires that no payments be distributed under certain provisions of the Tariff Act of 1930 with respect to entries of any goods that are: (1) unliquidated; (2) not in litigation; and (currently, or) (3) under an order of liquidation from the Department of Commerce.

(Sec. 505) Amends the Railroad Unemployment Insurance Act to extend through December 31, 2011, the temporary increase in extended unemployment benefits for employees with 10 or more years of service and for those with less than 10. Makes pre-existing appropriated funds under such Act available to cover the cost of such extended unemployment benefits as well as the costs of current benefits.

Title VI: Temporary Employee Payroll Tax Cut—Reduces by 2% in calendar year 2011 (the payroll tax holiday period) employment and self-employment tax rates. Requires a transfer of amounts from the Treasury to the Federal Old Age and Survivors Trust Fund, the Federal Disability Insurance Trust Fund, and the Social Security Equivalent Benefit Account to compensate for revenue lost as a result of such reduction in the employment and self-employment tax rates.

Title VII: Temporary Extension of Certain Expiring Provisions—Subtitle A: Energy—(Sec. 701)—Extends through 2011 expiring tax provisions related to energy production and conservation, including: (1) income and excise tax credits (and outlay payments) for biodiesel and renewable diesel used as fuel; (2) the tax credit for investment in refined coal facilities; and (3) the new energy efficient home tax credit.

(Sec. 704) Extends through 2011 the excise tax credits and outlay payments for alternative fuel and alternative fuel mixtures. Denies such credit for any fuel (including lignin, wood residues, or spent pulping liquors) derived from the production of paper or pulp.

(Sec. 705) Extends through 2011 the deferral of gain, for income tax purposes, on sales of electric transmission property by vertically integrated electric utilities to independent transmission companies approved by the Federal Energy Regulatory Commission (FERC).

(Sec. 706) Extends through 2011 the suspension of the taxable income limitation for purposes of percentage depletion of oil and gas from marginal properties.

(Sec. 707) Amends the American Recovery and Reinvestment Act of 2009 to extend through 2011 the programs of grants for renewable and alternative energy property in lieu of tax credits for such property.

(Sec. 708) Extends through 2011 the income and excise tax credits for alcohol used as fuel and payments for alcohol fuel mixtures. Amends the Harmonized Tariff Schedule of the United States to extend through 2011 the additional tariff on ethyl alcohol blends (ethanol) used as fuel.

(Sec. 709) Extends through 2011 the tax credit for energy efficient appliances (i.e., clothes washers, dishwashers, and refrigerators). Modifies the energy efficiency standards for such appliances.

(Sec. 710) Extends through 2011 the tax credit for nonbusiness energy property. Revises the limitations and standards for such credit.

(Sec. 711) Extends through 2011 the tax credit for alternative fuel vehicle refueling property expenditures.

Subtitle B: Individual Tax Relief—(Sec. 721) Extends through 2011: (1) the tax deduction for certain expenses of elementary and secondary school teachers; (2) the deduction of state and local sales taxes in lieu of state and local income taxes; (3) the deduction for contributions of capital gain real property made for conservation purposes; (4) the deduction (from gross income) for qualified tuition and related expenses; and (5) the tax exemption for distributions from individual retirement accounts (IRAs) for charitable purposes.

(Sec. 726) Extends through 2011 the tax rule for stock of regulated investment companies (RICs) held in the estate of nonresidents of the United States.

(Sec. 727) Extends through 2011 the equalization of the tax exclusion for employer-provided mass transit and parking benefits.

(Sec. 728) Requires a disregard of any tax refund or advance payment with respect to a refundable tax credit in determining eligibility for benefits or assistance under any federal program or under any federally-assisted state or local program.

Subtitle C: Business Tax Relief—(Sec. 731) Extends through 2011: (1) the tax credit for increasing research activities; (2) the Indian employment tax credit; (3) the new markets tax credit; (4) the railroad track maintenance tax credit; (5) the mine rescue team training tax credit; (6) the tax credit for differential payments to employees who are active duty members of the uniformed services; (7) accelerated depreciation (15-year recovery period) of qualified leasehold improvements, qualified restaurant buildings and improvements, and qualified retail improvements; (8) accelerated depreciation (7-year recovery period) for motorsports entertainment complexes; (9) accelerated depreciation for business property on an Indian reservation; (10) the expansion of the tax deductions for charitable contributions of food and book inventories and for charitable deductions for contributions by corporations of computer technology and equipment for educational purposes; (11) the election to expense mine safety equipment; (12) expensing of certain film and television production costs; (13) expensing of environmental remediation costs; and (14) the tax deduction with respect to income attributable to domestic production activities in Puerto Rico; and (15) the exclusion from gross income of 100% of the gain from the sale of qualified small business stock held for more than five years.

(Sec. 747) Extends through 2011 the tax rule for the treatment of payments of rents, royalties, annuities, or interest income by a controlled organization to a controlling tax-exempt organization as unrelated business taxable income.

(Sec. 748) Extends through 2011 the tax rule exempting from withholding the interest-related dividends and short term capital gain dividends received from an RIC.

(Sec. 749) Extends through 2011 the inclusion of RICs within the definition of qualified investment entity for income tax purposes.

(Sec. 750) Extends through 2011 the exemption of subpart F income from foreign personal holding company income for active financing income (e.g., income from insurance, banking, financing, or similar businesses) earned on business operations overseas.

(Sec. 751) Extends through 2011 tax rules relating to payments between related controlled foreign corporations.

(Sec. 752) Extends through 2011 the basis adjustment to stock of S corporations making charitable contributions of property.

(Sec. 753) Extends through 2011 the period for designation of empowerment zones for purposes of allowing certain tax incentives for investment in such zones, including wage credits, accelerated depreciation of business equipment, tax-exempt bond financing, and deferral of capital gains on the sale of business and investment property.

(Sec. 754) Extends through 2011 tax incentives for investment in the District of Columbia, including tax-exempt bond financing, zero-percent capital gains tax rate, and the first-time homebuyer tax credit.

(Sec. 755) Extends through 2011: (1) the increase in the limit on the amount of distilled spirits covered (paid over) into the treasuries of the Commonwealth of Puerto Rico and the U.S. Virgin Islands; and (2) the American Samoa economic development tax credit.

(Sec. 757) Extends through December 31, 2011, the work opportunity tax credit.

(Sec. 758) Extends through 2011 the authority for issuing qualified zone academy bonds and increases the limit on such bonds to $400 million in 2011.

(Sec. 759) Extends through 2011 the tax deduction for mortgage insurance premiums.

Subtitle D: Temporary Disaster Relief Provisions—Subpart A: New York Liberty Zone—(Sec. 761) Extends through 2011 tax-exempt bond financing for investment in the New York Liberty Zone.

Subpart B: GO Zone—(Sec. 762) Extends through 2011: (1) the increase in the rehabilitation tax credit in the Gulf Opportunity (GO) Zone; (2) the placed-in-service deadline for buildings in the GO Zone for purposes of the low-income housing tax credit; (3) tax-exempt financing for GO Zone investments; and (4) bonus depreciation allowances for qualified GO Zone property.

Title VIII: Budgetary Provisions—(Sec. 801) Provides for compliance of the budgetary effects of this Act with the Statutory Pay-As-You-Go Act of 2010.

(Sec. 802) Designates this Act as an emergency requirement pursuant to provisions of: (1) the Statutory Pay-As-You-Go Act of 2010, subject to the current policy adjustments under such Act; and (2) the concurrent resolution on the budget for fiscal year 2010.

Source: Library of Congress. "Bill Summary and Status 111th Congress (2009–2010) H.R. 4853 CRS Summary," December 17, 2010. Accessed January 31, 2013. http://thomas.loc.gov/cgi-bin/bdquery/z?d111:HR04853:@@@D&summ2=m&

A-10. THE BUDGET CONTROL ACT OF 2011: RAISING THE DEBT CEILING

The Great Recession and its aftermath were marked by intense debates over how the government should respond to the economic downturn in light of the federal deficit. While many Republicans argued for spending cuts, many Democrats argued that spending cuts would harm the economy and perhaps even cause the country to enter a second recession. With the federal government about to hit its debt ceiling, the ceiling needed to be raised to avoid a default, but the fiery debate in Congress over the federal deficit raged on for months before a bill raising the debt ceiling was finally signed by the president on August 2, 2011. The following document provides a summary of the Budget Control Act of 2011, the bill that eventually resulted after much debate.

The Budget Control Act of 2011

Summary

The Budget Control Act (BCA) is the result of negotiations between the President and Congress held in response to the federal government having nearly reached its borrowing capacity. The BCA authorized increases in the debt limit of at least $2.1 trillion dollars (and up to $2.4 trillion under certain conditions), subject to a disapproval process that would likely require securing the support of two-thirds of each chamber to prevent a debt limit increase. It established caps on the amount of money that could be spent through the annual appropriations process for the next 10 years, which the Congressional Budget Office (CBO) estimates will reduce federal spending by $917 billion. The BCA also created a Joint Select Committee on Deficit Reduction that is instructed to develop a bill to reduce the federal deficit by at least another $1.5 trillion over the 10 year period ending in FY2021.

The legislation resulting from the joint committee recommendations can be considered under special procedures that prevent amendment and limit debate in both chambers. These procedures could have a significant impact in the Senate because they allow the bill to advance with simple majority support; under regular Senate procedures it can be necessary to obtain agreement among at least three-fifths of the Senate (normally 60 Senators) to advance consideration of legislation.

If a joint committee proposal cutting the deficit by at least $1.2 trillion is not enacted by January 15, 2012, then the BCA established an automatic spending reduction process that includes sequestration (the cancellation of budgetary resources). The process presumably is intended to encourage agreement on deficit reduction, either by enacting the joint committee legislation by early 2012, or possibly by enacting other legislation (presumably through existing congressional procedures) by the beginning of 2013, when the automatic process would make reductions. If the enacted bill cuts the deficit by more than $1.2 trillion, an additional increase in the debt limit becomes available in the amount of the excess, up to $0.3 trillion.

The Budget Control Act has two additional elements. First, it directs that the House and Senate must each vote on a proposal to amend the Constitution to require that the budget of the federal government be balanced. The BCA does not alter the procedures for taking up such a measure in the Senate, and therefore the Senate might not be able to vote on passage of a constitutional amendment unless the support of 60 Senators can be secured to begin consideration. The only procedural consequence of not voting specified in the BCA is that, if Congress does not approve a constitutional amendment, the second of two conditions under which the act would permit an additional increase of $0.3 trillion in the debt ceiling, will not be available.

Second, the BCA also makes changes to the William D. Ford Federal Direct Loan (DL) program and the Federal Pell Grant program, two federal student aid programs authorized under Title IV of the Higher Education Act of 1965, as amended (HEA; P.L. 89-329). Effective July 1, 2012, the BCA eliminates the availability of Subsidized Stafford Loans to graduate and professional students and eliminates all but one type of repayment incentives on future DL program loans. CBO estimates these changes would reduce direct spending by $21.6 billion over the FY2012-FY2021 period. Approximately $17 billion of the $21.6 billion in estimated savings from the changes in the DL program would be directed to the Pell Grant program for future general use in FY2012 and FY2013.

Source: Heniff, Bill Jr., Elizabeth Rybicki, and Shannon M. Mahan. "The Budget Control Act of 2011: Summary." Congressional Research Service, August 19, 2011. Accessed January 28, 2013. http://www.fas.org/sgp/crs/misc/R41965.pdf

A-11. AMERICAN TAXPAYER RELIEF ACT OF 2012

The American Taxpayer Relief Act of 2012 extended the deadline for congressional action on the budget required by the Budget Control Act of 2011 from early January 2013 to March 2013. It also extended Bush-era tax cuts for individuals with incomes below a certain threshold ($400,000 or below for an individual). For individuals with incomes higher than this threshold the Bush-era tax cuts expired as of January 1, 2013, and were not extended. The act also capped tax credits and deductions for filers with upper-level incomes. It made the Child Tax Credit (discussed previously) permanent and extended the expansion of the Earned Income Tax Child Tax Credit and American Opportunity Tax Credit through 2017. It also extended federal unemployment benefits and froze pay for members of Congress.

Bill Summary & Status
112th Congress (2011–2012)
H.R.8
CRS Summary

H.R.8
Latest Title: American Taxpayer Relief Act of 2012
Sponsor: Rep Camp, Dave [MI-4] (introduced 7/24/2012) Cosponsors (28)

Related Bills: H.RES.747, H.RES.844, H.R.1173, H.R.6169, H.R.6688, S.720, S.3401, S.3413, S.3417, S.3521
Latest Major Action: Became Public Law No: 112-240
Note: Enactment of the "fiscal cliff bill" averted scheduled income tax rate increases and the spending reductions required by the sequestration process.

SUMMARY AS OF:

1/2/2013—Public Law. (There are 3 other summaries)

(This measure has not been amended since it was passed by the Senate on January 1, 2013. The summary has been expanded for this version.)

American Taxpayer Relief Act of 2012—**Title I: General Extensions**—(Sec. 101) Makes permanent the Economic Growth and Tax Relief Reconciliation Act of 2001 for individual taxpayers whose taxable income is at or below a $400,000 threshold amount ($450,000 for married couples filing a joint return).

Amends the Internal Revenue Code to: (1) revise income tax rates for individual taxpayers whose taxable income is at or below the $400,000 threshold amount ($450,000 for married couples filing a joint return) and increase the rate to 39.6% for taxpayers whose taxable income exceeds the threshold, (2) set the threshold for the phaseout of personal tax exemptions and itemized deductions at $250,000 for individual taxpayers ($300,000 for married couples filing a joint return), and (3) increase the top marginal estate tax rate from 35% to 40%.

(Sec. 102) Makes permanent for individual taxpayers whose taxable income is at or below a $400,000 threshold ($450,000 for married couples filing a joint return) provisions of the Jobs and Growth Tax Relief Reconciliation Act of 2003 that reduce tax rates for capital gain and dividend income.

Increases the capital gains tax rate from 15% to 20% for taxpayers whose taxable income exceeds the $400,000 threshold amount.

(Sec. 103) Extends through 2017: (1) the American Opportunity tax credit, (2) the child tax credit, and (3) the increased earned income tax credit.

Makes permanent the disregard of tax refunds for determining eligibility for benefits or assistance under any federal program or state or local program financed in whole or in part with federal funds.

(Sec. 104) Establishes a permanent $78,750 exemption from the alternative minimum tax (AMT) for married taxpayers filing a joint tax return ($50,600 for individual taxpayers). Provides for an annual inflation adjustment to such exemption amounts for calendar years after 2012.

Title II: Individual Tax Extenders—(Sec. 201) Extends through 2013 expiring tax provisions relating to individual taxpayers, including:

- the tax deduction for certain expenses of elementary and secondary school teachers;
- the exclusion from gross income of amounts attributable to the discharge of qualified principal residence indebtedness;
- the equalization of the exclusion from gross income of employer-provided commuter transit and parking benefits;
- the tax deduction for mortgage insurance premiums;
- the election to deduct state and local general sales taxes in lieu of state and local income taxes;
- the tax deduction for contributions of capital gain real property made for conservation purposes;
- the tax deduction for qualified tuition and related expenses; and
- the exemption from tax of distributions from individual retirement accounts (IRAs) made for charitable purposes.

(Sec. 209) Makes permanent the authority of the Secretary of the Treasury to disclose tax returns and other information to federal and state prison officials for inmates who may have filed or facilitated the filing of false or fraudulent tax returns. Allows disclosures of such information to contractors responsible for the operation of a federal or state prison and to the legal representatives of the Federal Bureau of Prisons, a state agency, a contractor charged with the responsibility for administration of prisons, or the incarcerated individual accused of filing the false or fraudulent return.

Title III: Business Tax Extenders—(Sec. 301) Extends through 2013 expiring tax provisions relating to business taxpayers, including:

- the tax credit for increasing research activities;
- the 9% low-income housing tax credit rate for newly constructed non-federally subsidized buildings;
- the exemption of the basic military housing allowance from the income test for programs financed by tax-exempt housing bonds;
- the Indian employment tax credit;
- the new markets tax credit;

- the tax credit for qualified railroad track maintenance expenditures;
- the tax credit for mine rescue team training expenses;
- the tax credit for differential wage payments to employees who are active duty members of the Uniformed Services;
- the work opportunity tax credit;
- the authority for issuing qualified zone academy bonds;
- accelerated depreciation for qualified leasehold, restaurant, and retail improvements, for motorsports entertainment complexes, and for business property on Indian reservations;
- the deduction for contributions of food inventory by taxpayers other than C corporations;
- increased expensing allowances for depreciable business property;
- the election to expense advanced mine safety equipment and expensing of film and television production expenses;
- the deduction for income attributable to domestic production activities in Puerto Rico;
- tax rules relating to payments between related foreign corporations;
- rules for the tax treatment of certain dividends of regulated investment companies (RICs);
- the subpart F income exemption for income derived in the active conduct of a banking, finance, or insurance business;
- the 100% exclusion from gross income of gain from the sale or exchange of certain small business stock;
- the rule for adjusting stock of an S corporation making charitable contributions of property;
- the reduction of the recognition period for the built-in gains of S corporations;
- tax incentives for investment in empowerment zones;
- the authority for issuing New York Liberty Zone bonds;
- the increased limitation for payments of excise taxes on distilled spirits into the treasuries of Puerto Rico and the Virgin Islands;
- the tax credit for investment in American Samoan economic development activities; and
- the additional depreciation allowance (bonus depreciation) for business assets and the election to accelerate the AMT in lieu of bonus depreciation.

Title IV: Energy Tax Extenders—(Sec. 401) Extends through 2013 expiring energy-related tax provisions, including:

- the tax credit for residential energy efficiency improvements;
- the tax credit for alternative fuel vehicle refueling property expenditures;
- the tax credit for two- or three-wheeled plug-in electric vehicles;
- the income tax credit for biodiesel and renewable diesel used as fuel;
- the tax credit for producing electricity from Indian coal production facilities;

- the tax credit for energy efficient new homes;
- the tax credit for energy efficient appliances;
- tax rules relating to sales required to implement federal and state restructuring policy for qualified electric facilities; and
- the excise tax credit for alternative fuels.

(Sec. 404) Extends through 2013 the cellulosic biofuel producer tax credit. Modifies the definition of "cellulosic biofuel" for purposes of such credit to mean any liquid fuel which is derived by, or from, qualified feedstocks. Defines "qualified feedstocks" as any lignocellulosic or hemicellulosic matter that is available on a renewable or recurring basis and any cultivated algae, cyanobacteria, or lemna.

(Sec. 407) Extends through 2013 placed-in-service dates for renewable energy facilities eligible for the tax credit for producing electricity from renewable resources, including wind, biomass, landfill gas, trash, hydropower, and marine and hydrokinetic renewable energy facilities.

(Sec. 410) Extends through 2013 the special depreciation allowance (bonus depreciation) for cellulosic biofuel plant property. Modifies the definition of "cellulosic biofuel" for purposes of bonus depreciation to mean any liquid fuel which is derived by, or from, qualified feedstocks.

Title V: Unemployment—(Sec. 501) Amends the Supplemental Appropriations Act, 2008 to extend emergency unemployment compensation (EUC) payments for eligible individuals to weeks of employment ending on or before January 1, 2014.

(Sec. 502) Amends the Assistance for Unemployed Workers and Struggling Families Act to extend until December 31, 2013, requirements that federal payments to states cover 100% of EUC.

Amends the Unemployment Compensation Extension Act of 2008 to exempt weeks of unemployment between enactment of this Act and June 30, 2014, from the prohibition in the Federal-State Extended Unemployment Compensation Act of 1970 (FSEUCA of 1970) against federal matching payments to a state for the first week in an individual's eligibility period for which extended compensation or sharable regular compensation is paid if the state law provides for payment of regular compensation to an individual for his or her first week of otherwise compensable unemployment. (Thus allows temporary federal matching for the first week of extended benefits for states with no waiting period.)

Amends the FSEUCA of 1970 to postpone similarly from December 31, 2012, to December 31, 2013, termination of the period during which a state may determine its "on" and "off" indicators according to specified temporary substitutions in its formula.

(Sec. 503) Amends the Supplemental Appropriations Act, 2008 to appropriate funds out of the employment security administration account through FY2014 to assist states in providing reemployment and eligibility assessment activities.
(Sec. 504) Amends the Railroad Unemployment Insurance Act to extend through December 31, 2013, the temporary increase in extended unemployment benefits.

Title VI: Medicare and Other Health Extensions—Subtitle A: Medicare Extensions—(Sec. 601) Amends title XVIII (Medicare) of the Social Security Act (SSA) to extend for one year the Medicare physician payment rates without change.

Authorizes eligible professionals to receive incentive payments under Medicare for reporting on quality measures by participating in a qualified clinical data registry.

Requires the Comptroller General (GAO) to study the potential of clinical data registries to improve the quality and efficiency of care in the Medicare program.

(Sec. 602) Extends through 2013 the floor at 1.0 on the work geographic index in the formula for determining relative values for physicians' services for the Medicare physician payment.

(Sec. 603) Revises requirements for Medicare payments for outpatient therapy services, including to extend through December 31, 2013, the period of incurred expenses for which an enrollee may request an exception to the ceiling on such expenses.

(Sec. 604) Extends: (1) the temporary increase in payment for ground ambulance services, (2) the increase in payment for certain urban air ambulance services, and (3) the increase in the assistance for rural providers furnishing (super rural ambulance) services in low-population density areas. Requires the Secretary of Health and Human Services (HHS) to study issues related to ambulance services.

(Sec. 605) Extends through 2013 the additional Medicare payment for inpatient services for low-volume hospitals.

(Sec. 606) Extends through FY2013 the current methodology for payment to subsection (d) hospitals for inpatient hospital services furnished to individuals under the Medicare-dependent, small rural hospital (MDH) program. (Generally, a subsection [d] hospital is an acute hospital, particularly one that receives payments under Medicare's inpatient prospective payment system [IPPS] when providing covered inpatient services to eligible beneficiaries.)

(Sec. 607) Extends through December 31, 2014, Medicare Advantage plans that exclusively serve special needs individuals.

(Sec. 608) Extends Medicare authorization for reasonable cost contracts through December 31, 2013.

(Sec. 609) Reauthorizes through FY2013 the requirements that the HHS Secretary contract with a consensus-based entity to develop health care performance measurements. Requires the Secretary to develop a strategy to provide data for performance improvement in a timely manner to applicable providers under the Medicare program. Requires the Comptroller General to study private sector and Medicare information sharing activities.

(Sec. 610) Amends the Medicare Improvements for Patients and Providers Act of 2008 to extend grants for outreach to Medicare beneficiaries.

Subtitle B: Other Health Extensions—(Sec. 621) Amends SSA title XIX (Medicaid) to extend for one year the Qualifying Individual (QI) Program through which the QI program pays the Medicare Part B premiums of Medicare beneficiaries with incomes between 120% and 135% of the official poverty line.

(Sec. 622) Extends the program to provide continued short-term eligibility for Medicaid beneficiaries who become ineligible due to increased hours of, or increased income from, employment (transitional medical assistance program).

(Sec. 623) Extends through September 30, 2014, the authority of states to base eligibility determinations for Medicaid or the Children's Health Insurance Program (CHIP) on findings by an Express Lane agency.

(Sec. 624) Amends SSA title V (Maternal and Child Health Services Block Grant) to extend the program for the development and support of family-to-family health information centers for children with disabilities or special health care needs.

(Sec. 625) Amends the Public Health Service Act to reauthorize for FY2014: (1) a research program for the prevention and cure of Type I diabetes, and (2) a program to provide services through Indian health facilities for the prevention and treatment of diabetes.

Subtitle C: Other Health Provisions—(Sec. 631) Directs the HHS Secretary to apply certain prospective documentation and coding adjustments (made in response to the implementation of the Medicare Severity Diagnosis Related Group [MS-DRG] system under the Medicare IPPS) for discharges occurring during FY2008, FY2009, and FY2010. Directs the Secretary to make an additional adjustment

-

to the standardized amounts for inpatient hospital services based upon the Secretary's estimates for discharges occurring only during FY2014-FY2017 to offset $11 billion (which represents the amount of the increase in aggregate payments from FY2008-FY2013 for which an adjustment was not previously applied).

(Sec. 632) Requires the Secretary to make reductions in Medicare payments for renal dialysis services.

Directs GAO to update its report to Congress on the impact on Medicare beneficiary access to high-quality dialysis services of including specified oral drugs furnished for the treatment of end stage renal disease in the related bundled prospective payment system.

(Sec. 633) Makes reductions to Medicare payments for multiple therapy services provided to the same patient on the same day.

(Sec. 634) Reduces payments for certain hospital outpatient department services (stereotactic radiosurgery).

(Sec. 635) Revises utilization rates for purposes of Medicare payment for the use of expensive diagnostic imaging equipment.

(Sec. 636) Makes Medicare reimbursement for diabetic supplies that are non-mail order equal to the single payment amounts established under the national mail order competition for diabetic supplies.

(Sec. 637) Reduces Medicare payment by 10% for ambulance services consisting of non-emergency basic life support services involving transport of an individual with end-stage renal disease (ESRD) for renal dialysis services furnished other than on an emergency basis by a provider of services or a renal dialysis facility.

(Sec. 638) Extends from three years to five years the length of time the Secretary has to collect Medicare overpayments.

(Sec. 639) Revises the coding adjustment factor for health status under Medicare Advantage plans.

(Sec. 640) Eliminates funding for the Medicare Improvement Fund starting in FY2014.

(Sec. 641) Revises state disproportionate share hospital (DSH) allotments under Medicaid.

(Sec. 642) Repeals the Community Living Assistance Services and Supports Act or the CLASS Act, as added to the Public Health Service Act by the Patient Protection and Affordable Care Act, which establishes a national, voluntary insurance program for purchasing community living assistance services and supports in order to provide individuals with functional limitations with tools that will allow them to maintain their personal and financial independence and live in the community.

Amends the Deficit Reduction Act of 2005 to repeal appropriations through FY2015 for the National Clearinghouse for Long-Term Care Information.

(Sec. 643) Establishes the Commission on Long-Term Care to develop a plan for a system to ensure the availability of long-term services and supports for individuals in need of such services.

(Sec. 644) Requires the Secretary to establish a fund to be used to provide assistance and oversight to qualified nonprofit health insurance issuers that have been awarded loans or grants under the Consumer Operated and Oriented Plan (CO-OP) program to offer qualified health plans in the individual and small group markets. Transfers to this new fund 10% of the appropriations to the CO-OP program. Rescinds all other unobligated funds appropriated to the CO-OP program.

Title VII: Extension of Agricultural Programs—(Sec. 701) Extends programs under the Food, Conservation, and Energy Act of 2008 through September 30, 2013, with specified exceptions including Pigford claim discrimination determinations.

Extends: (1) the dairy product price support program through December 31, 2013, and (2) the milk income loss contract program.

Extends specified commodity programs to crop year 2013, including programs for sugar cane, sugar beets, and peanuts.

Suspends price support authorities for: (1) covered commodities, peanuts, sugar-cane, and sugar through the 2013 crop or production year; and (2) milk through December 31, 2013.

Amends the Food Security Act of 1985 to extend the conservation reserve program through FY2013.

Authorizes appropriations through FY2013 for the voluntary public access and habitat incentive program.
Amends the Food and Nutrition Act of 2008 to reduce FY2013 funding for the supplemental nutrition assistance program (SNAP, formerly the food stamp program) employment and training.

Revises FY2012 through FY2015 funding for the nutrition education and obesity prevention grant program.

Amends the Food, Agriculture, Conservation, and Trade Act of 1990 to authorize FY2013 appropriations for: (1) the organic agriculture research and extension initiative, and (2) the specialty crop research initiative.

Amends the Farm Security and Rural Investment Act of 2002 to authorize FY2013 appropriations for: (1) the beginning farmer and rancher development program, (2) the biobased markets program, (3) biorefinery assistance, (4) repowering assistance, (5) the bioenergy program for advanced biofuels, (6) the biodiesel fuel education program, (7) the rural energy for America program, (8) biomass research and development, (9) the rural energy self-sufficiency initiative, (10) the biomass crop assistance program, (11) the forest biomass for energy program, and (12) the community wood energy program.

Authorizes the feedstock flexibility program for energy producers through FY2013.

Amends the Farmer-to-Consumer Direct Marketing Act of 1976 to authorize FY2013 appropriations for the farmers market promotion program.

Amends the Food, Conservation, and Energy Act of 2008 to authorize FY2013 appropriations for the national clean plant network.

Amends the Farm Security and Rural Investment Act of 2002 regarding the national organic certification cost-share program to: (1) make specified Commodity Credit Corporation (CCC) funds available for FY2008 through FY2012, and (2) authorize FY2013 appropriations.

Authorizes FY2013 appropriations for organic production and market data initiatives.

Amends the Food, Agriculture, Conservation, and Trade Act of 1990 to authorize FY2013 appropriations for outreach and technical assistance for socially disadvantaged farmers or ranchers.

(Sec. 702) Amends the Federal Crop Insurance Act to authorize FY2012-FY2013 appropriations for payments to eligible producers for: (1) livestock death losses in excess of the normal mortality due to adverse weather, including losses from hurricanes, floods, blizzards, disease, wildfires, and extreme heat or cold; (2) grazing losses for covered livestock due to drought or fire; (3) emergency relief to eligible producers of livestock, honey bees, and farm-raised fish for losses due to disease, adverse weather, or other conditions such as blizzards and wildfires; and (4) orchardists and nursery tree growers for commercial losses caused by natural disasters.

Title VIII: Miscellaneous Provisions—(Sec. 801) Amends the National Defense Authorization Act for Fiscal Year 2013 to modify requirements concerning presidential notification of any reduction of strategic delivery systems to state that the President shall certify whether the Russian Federation is in compliance (currently, "that" it is in compliance) with its strategic arms control obligations (currently, "arms control obligations") with the United States and is not violating or acting inconsistently with such obligations.

(Sec. 802) Prohibits any cost-of-living adjustment to the rate of pay for Members of Congress during FY2013.

Title IX: Budget Provisions—Subtitle A: Modifications of Sequestration—(Sec. 901) Amends the Balanced Budget and Emergency Deficit Control Act of 1985 to reduce the required amount of deficit reduction calculated for FY2013 by $24 billion.

Implements the FY2013 spending reductions required by the Balanced Budget and Emergency Deficit Control Act of 1985 on March 27, 2013 (current law requires a sequestration to eliminate a budget-year breach within 15 calendar days after Congress adjourns).

Postpones from January 2, 2013, until March 1, 2013, the sequestration required under the Budget Control Act of 2011 if a joint committee bill achieving a deficit reduction greater than $1.2 trillion was not enacted by January 15, 2012.

Reduces FY2013 discretionary spending limits to those applicable for FY2012. Reduces FY2014 limits from $1.066 trillion to $1.058 trillion.

(Sec. 902) Amends the Internal Revenue Code to permit an applicable tax-deferred retirement plan that includes a qualified Roth contribution (a program under which an employee may elect to make designated Roth contributions in lieu of all or a portion of elective deferrals the employee is otherwise eligible to make under the plan) to allow an individual to elect to have the plan transfer any amount not otherwise distributable to a designated Roth account maintained for the individual's benefit. Treats such a transfer as a taxable rollover distribution to the account. (Roth account contributions are made with after-tax funds.) Exempts such a plan, including the federal Thrift Savings Plan, from certain normally applicable restrictions because of such a transfer.

Subtitle B: Budgetary Effects—(Sec. 911) Exempts the budgetary effects of this Act from the PAYGO scorecard requirements of the Statutory Pay-As-You-Go Act of 2010 and S.Con.Res. 21, 110th Congress (setting forth the congressional budget for the government for FY2008).

Source: Library of Congress. "Bill Summary and Status 112th Congress (2011–2012) H.R. 8 CRS Summary," January 2, 2012. Accessed January 31, 2013. http://thomas.loc.gov/cgi-bin/bdquery/z?d112:HR00008:@@@D&summ2=m&

PART B: THE GREAT RECESSION AND POVERTY

With a background understanding of the Great Recession in place, Part B of the documents section explores in greater detail the impact of the recession on poverty in the United States. The U.S. Office of Management and Budget (OMB) establishes official poverty thresholds every year. The official poverty thresholds set the amount of income someone needs, according to their family size, to be considered poor or not poor by the government. This measure is used to determine eligibility for government assistance and for statistical calculations by government agencies. The following 23 documents, most of them tables, illuminate how the U.S. government tracks and measures poverty.

B-1. HOW THE CENSUS BUREAU MEASURES POVERTY

The following article, from the U.S. Census Bureau, explains more about how this official poverty measure works and how income and family size are calculated.

Following the Office of Management and Budget's (OMB) Statistical Policy Directive 14, the Census Bureau uses a set of money income thresholds that vary by family size and composition to determine who is in poverty. If a family's total income is less than the family's threshold, then that family and every individual in it is considered in poverty. The official poverty thresholds do not vary geographically, but they are updated for inflation using Consumer Price Index (CPI-U). The official poverty definition uses money income before taxes and does not include capital gains or noncash benefits (such as public housing, Medicaid, and food stamps).

INCOME USED TO COMPUTE POVERTY STATUS (MONEY INCOME)

- Includes earnings, unemployment compensation, workers' compensation, Social Security, Supplemental Security Income, public assistance, veterans' payments, survivor benefits, pension or retirement income, interest, dividends, rents, royalties, income from estates, trusts, educational assistance, alimony, child support, assistance from outside the household, and other miscellaneous sources.
- Noncash benefits (such as food stamps and housing subsidies) **do not** count.
- Before taxes
- Excludes capital gains or losses.
- If a person lives with a family, add up the income of all family members. (Non-relatives, such as housemates, do not count.)

MEASURE OF NEED (POVERTY THRESHOLDS)

Poverty thresholds are the dollar amounts used to determine poverty status. Each person or family is assigned one out of 48 possible poverty thresholds Thresholds vary according to:

- Size of the family
- Ages of the members

The same thresholds are used throughout the United States (do not vary geographically).
Updated annually for inflation using the Consumer Price Index for All Urban Consumers (CPI-U).
Although the thresholds in some sense reflect families needs,

- They are intended for use as a statistical yardstick, not as a complete description of what people and families need to live.
- Many government aid programs use a different poverty measure, the Department of Health and Human Services (HHS) poverty guidelines, or multiples thereof.

Poverty thresholds were originally derived in 1963–1964, using:

- U.S. Department of Agriculture food budgets designed for families under economic stress.
- Data about what portion of their income families spent on food.

COMPUTATION

If total family income is less than the threshold appropriate for that family,

- The family is in poverty.
- All family members have the same poverty status.

- For individuals who do not live with family members, their own income is compared with the appropriate threshold.

If total family income equals or is greater than the threshold, the family (or unrelated individual) is not in poverty.

EXAMPLE

Family A has five members: two children, their mother, father, and great-aunt. Their threshold was $27,517 in 2011. (See poverty thresholds for 2011). Suppose the members' incomes in 2011 were:

Table B-1

Mother	$10,000
Father	8,000
Great-aunt	10,000
First Child	0
Second Child	0
Total Family Income	**$28,000**

Compare total family income with their family's threshold:

$$\text{Income} / \text{Threshold} = \$28,000 / \$27,517 = 1.02$$

Since their income was greater than their threshold, Family A is not "in poverty" according to the official definition.

The income divided by the threshold is called the **Ratio of Income to Poverty**.
– Family A's ratio of income to poverty was 1.02.

The difference in dollars between family income and the family's poverty threshold is called the **Income Deficit** (for families in poverty) or **Income Surplus** (for families above poverty)
– Family A's income surplus was $483 (or $28,000—$27,517).

PEOPLE WHOSE POVERTY STATUS CANNOT BE DETERMINED

Unrelated individuals under age 15 (such as foster children):

- Income questions are asked of people age 15 and older.
- If someone is under age 15 and not living with a family member, we do not know their income.
- Since we cannot determine their poverty status, they are excluded from the "poverty universe" (table totals).

People in:

- Institutional group quarters (such as prisons or nursing homes)
- College dormitories
- Military barracks
- Living situations without conventional housing (and who are not in shelters)

AUTHORITY BEHIND OFFICIAL POVERTY MEASURE

The official measure of poverty was established by the Office of Management and Budget (OMB) in Statistical Policy Directive 14.

To be used by federal agencies in their statistical work.

Government aid programs do not have to use the official poverty measure as eligibility criteria.

- Many government aid programs use a different poverty measure, the Department of Health and Human Services (HHS) poverty guidelines, or variants thereof.
- Each aid program may define eligibility differently.

Official poverty data come from the Current Population Survey (CPS) Annual Social and Economic Supplement (ASEC), formerly called the Annual Demographic Supplement or simply the "March Supplement."

Source: U.S. Census Bureau. "How the Census Bureau Measures Poverty," 2012. Accessed July 1. http://www.census.gov/hhes/www/poverty/about/overview/measure .html

POVERTY THRESHOLDS, 2006–2011

The following documents (B-2 to B-7) show the official poverty thresholds for the years 2006 to 2011. These poverty thresholds are important to be aware of because they form the basis for understanding official government data on who was in poverty during and after the recession. For example, as shown in B-2, the poverty threshold for a single person under the age of 65 in 2006 was $10,488. In other words, any single person in the United States under the age of 65 whose income was less than $10,488 that year was considered poor by government standards.

B-2. POVERTY THRESHOLDS, 2006

Table B-2 Poverty Thresholds for 2006 by Size of Family and Number of Related Children Under 18 Years

Size of Family Unit	Weighted Average Thresholds	Related Children under 18 Years								
		None	One	Two	Three	Four	Five	Six	Seven	Eight or More
One person (unrelated individual)	10,294									
Under 65 years	10,488	10,488								
65 years and over	9,669	9,669								
Two people	13,167									
Householder under 65 years	13,569	13,500	13,896							
Householder 65 years and over	12,201	12,186	13,843							
Three people	16,079	15,769	16,227	16,242						
Four people	20,614	20,794	21,134	20,444	20,516					
Five people	24,382	25,076	25,441	24,662	24,059	23,691				
Six people	27,560	28,842	28,957	28,360	27,788	26,938	26,434			
Seven people	31,205	33,187	33,394	32,680	32,182	31,254	30,172	28,985		
Eight people	34,774	37,117	37,444	36,770	36,180	35,342	34,278	33,171	32,890	
Nine people or more	41,499	44,649	44,865	44,269	43,768	42,945	41,813	40,790	40,536	38,975

Source: U.S. Census Bureau. "Poverty Thresholds 2006," 2012. Accessed July 1, 2012. http://www.census.gov/hhes/www/poverty/data/threshld/thresh06.html

B-3. Poverty Thresholds, 2007

Table B-3

Size of Family Unit	Weighted Average Thresholds	Related Children under 18 Years								
		None	One	Two	Three	Four	Five	Six	Seven	Eight or More
One person (unrelated individual)	10,590									
Under 65 years	10,787	10,787								
65 years and over	9,944	9,944								
Two people	13,540									
Householder under 65 years	13,954	13,884	14,291							
Householder 65 years and over	12,550	12,533	14,237							
Three people	16,530	16,218	16,689	16,705						
Four people	21,203	21,386	21,736	21,027	21,100					
Five people	25,080	25,791	26,166	25,364	24,744	24,366				
Six people	28,323	29,664	29,782	29,168	28,579	27,705	27,187			
Seven people	32,233	34,132	34,345	33,610	33,098	32,144	31,031	29,810		
Eight people	35,816	38,174	38,511	37,818	37,210	36,348	35,255	34,116	33,827	
Nine people or more	42,739	45,921	46,143	45,529	45,014	44,168	43,004	41,952	41,691	40,085

Source: U.S. Census Bureau. "Poverty Thresholds 2007," 2012. Accessed July 1, 2012. http://www.census.gov/hhes/www/poverty/data/threshld/thresh07.html

B-4. POVERTY THRESHOLDS, 2008

Table B-4

Size of Family Unit	Weighted Average Thresholds	Related Children under 18 Years							
		None	One	Two	Three	Four	Five	Six	Seven	Eight or More
One person (unrelated individual)	10,991									
Under 65 years	11,201	11,201								
65 years and over	10,326	10,326								
Two people	14,051									
Householder under 65 years	14,489	14,417	14,840							
Householder 65 years and over	13,030	13,014	14,784							
Three people	17,163	16,841	17,330	17,346						
Four people	22,025	22,207	22,570	21,834	21,910					
Five people	26,049	26,781	27,170	26,338	25,694	25,301				
Six people	29,456	30,803	30,925	30,288	29,677	28,769	28,230			
Seven people	33,529	35,442	35,664	34,901	34,369	33,379	32,223	30,955		
Eight people	37,220	39,640	39,990	39,270	38,639	37,744	36,608	35,426	35,125	
Nine people or more	44,346	47,684	47,915	47,278	46,743	45,864	44,656	43,563	43,292	41,624

Source: U.S. Census Bureau. "Poverty Thresholds 2008," 2012. Accessed July 1, 2012. http://www.census.gov/hhes/www/poverty/data/threshld/thresh08.html

B-5. POVERTY THRESHOLDS, 2009

Table B-5 Poverty Thresholds for 2009 by Size of Family and Number of Related Children Under 18 Years

Size of Family Unit	Weighted Average Thresholds	Related Children under 18 Years								
		None	One	Two	Three	Four	Five	Six	Seven	Eight or More
One person (unrelated individual)	10,956									
Under 65 years	11,161	11,161								
65 years and over	10,289	10,289								
Two people	13,991									
Householder under 65 years	14,439	14,366	14,787							
Householder 65 years and over	12,982	12,968	14,731							
Three people	17,098	16,781	17,268	17,285						
Four people	21,954	22,128	22,490	21,756	21,832					
Five people	25,991	26,686	27,074	26,245	25,603	25,211				
Six people	29,405	30,693	30,815	30,180	29,571	28,666	28,130			
Seven people	33,372	35,316	35,537	34,777	34,247	33,260	32,108	30,845		
Eight people	37,252	39,498	39,847	39,130	38,501	37,610	36,478	35,300	35,000	
Nine people or more	44,366	47,514	47,744	47,109	46,576	45,701	44,497	43,408	43,138	41,476

Note: The poverty thresholds are updated each year using the change in the average annual Consumer Price Index for All Urban Consumers (CPI-U). Since the average annual CPI-U for 2009 was lower than the average annual CPI-U for 2008, poverty thresholds for 2009 are slightly lower than the corresponding thresholds for 2008.

Source: U.S. Census Bureau. "Poverty Thresholds 2009," 2012. Accessed July 1, 2012. http://www.census.gov/hhes/www/poverty/data/threshld/thresh09.html

B-6. POVERTY THRESHOLDS, 2010

Table B-6 Poverty Thresholds for 2010 by Size of Family and Number of Related Children Under 18 Years

Size of Family Unit	Weighted Average Thresholds	Related Children under 18 Years								
		None	One	Two	Three	Four	Five	Six	Seven	Eight or More
One person (unrelated individual)	11,139									
Under 65 years	11,344	11,344								
65 years and over	10,458	10,458								
Two people	14,218									
Householder under 65 years	14,676	14,602	15,030							
Householder 65 years and over	13,194	13,180	14,973							
Three people	17,374	17,057	17,552	17,568						
Four people	22,314	22,491	22,859	22,113	22,190					
Five people	26,439	27,123	27,518	26,675	26,023	25,625				
Six people	29,897	31,197	31,320	30,675	30,056	29,137	28,591			
Seven people	34,009	35,896	36,120	35,347	34,809	33,805	32,635	31,351		
Eight people	37,934	40,146	40,501	39,772	39,133	38,227	37,076	35,879	35,575	
Nine people or more	45,220	48,293	48,527	47,882	47,340	46,451	45,227	44,120	43,845	42,156

Source: U.S. Census Bureau. "Poverty Thresholds 2010," 2012. Accessed July 1, 2012. http://www.census.gov/hhes/www/poverty/data/threshld/thresh10.xls

B-7. POVERTY THRESHOLDS, 2011

Table B-7 Poverty Thresholds for 2011 by Size of Family and Number of Related Children Under 18 Years

Size of Family Unit	Weighted Average Thresholds	Related Children under 18 Years								
		None	One	Two	Three	Four	Five	Six	Seven	Eight or More
One person (unrelated individual)	11,484									
Under 65 years	11,702	11,702								
65 years and over	10,788	10,788								
Two people	14,657									
Householder under 65 years	15,139	15,063	15,504							
Householder 65 years and over	13,609	13,596	15,446							
Three people	17,916	17,595	18,106	18,123						
Four people.	23,021	23,201	23,581	22,811	22,891					
Five people	27,251	27,979	28,386	27,517	26,844	26,434				
Six people	30,847	32,181	32,309	31,643	31,005	30,056	29,494			
Seven people	35,085	37,029	37,260	36,463	35,907	34,872	33,665	32,340		
Eight people	39,064	41,414	41,779	41,027	40,368	39,433	38,247	37,011	36,697	
Nine people or more	46,572	49,818	50,059	49,393	48,835	47,917	46,654	45,512	45,229	43,487

Source: U.S. Census Bureau. "Poverty Thresholds 2011," 2012. Accessed July 1, 2012. http://www.census.gov/hhes/www/poverty/data/threshld/thresh11.xls

Using the poverty thresholds shown earlier (B-2 to B-7), the U.S. Census Bureau compiles statistics on poverty in the United States based on data from the Current Population Survey (CPS) Annual Social and Economic Supplement (ASEC), which the Census Bureau conducts as a joint effort with the U.S. Bureau of Labor Statistics. This data, seen in B-8 to B-10, is the official U.S. government data on poverty.

B-8 provides information on who was poor in the United States from 1959 to 2011 by age, race, and Hispanic origin. This data can help to provide historical background in which to situate an understanding of poverty in the United States during and after the Great Recession.

Table B-8

Year and Characteristic	Under 18 Years						18 to 64 Years			65 Years and Over		
	All People			Related Children in Families								
	Total	Below Poverty Level		Total	Below Poverty Level		Total	Below Poverty Level		Total	Below Poverty Level	
		Number	Percent		Number	Percent		Number	Percent		Number	Percent
All Races												
2011	73,737	16,134	21.9	72,568	15,539	21.4	193,213	26,492	13.7	41,507	3,620	8.7
2010 17/	73,873	16,286	22.0	72,581	15,598	21.5	192,481	26,499	13.8	39,777	3,558	8.9
2009	74,579	15,451	20.7	73,410	14,774	20.1	190,627	24,684	12.9	38,613	3,433	8.9
2008	74,068	14,068	19.0	72,980	13,507	18.5	189,185	22,105	11.7	37,788	3,656	9.7

(continued)

Table B-8 (Continued)

Year and Characteristic	Under 18 Years — All People Total	Below Poverty Level Number	Percent	Related Children in Families Total	Below Poverty Level Number	Percent	18 to 64 Years Total	Below Poverty Level Number	Percent	65 Years and Over Total	Below Poverty Level Number	Percent
2007	73,996	13,324	18.0	72,792	12,802	17.6	187,913	20,396	10.9	36,790	3,556	9.7
2006	73,727	12,827	17.4	72,609	12,299	16.9	186,688	20,239	10.8	36,035	3,394	9.4
2005	73,285	12,896	17.6	72,095	12,335	17.1	184,345	20,450	11.1	35,505	3,603	10.1
2004 14/	73,241	13,041	17.8	72,133	12,473	17.3	182,166	20,545	11.3	35,209	3,453	9.8
2003	72,999	12,866	17.6	71,907	12,340	17.2	180,041	19,443	10.8	34,659	3,552	10.2
2002	72,696	12,133	16.7	71,619	11,646	16.3	178,388	18,861	10.6	34,234	3,576	10.4
2001	72,021	11,733	16.3	70,950	11,175	15.8	175,685	17,760	10.1	33,769	3,414	10.1
2000 12/	71,741	11,587	16.2	70,538	11,005	15.6	173,638	16,671	9.6	33,566	3,323	9.9
1999 11/	71,685	12,280	17.1	70,424	11,678	16.6	171,146	17,289	10.1	33,377	3,222	9.7
1998	71,338	13,467	18.9	70,253	12,845	18.3	167,327	17,623	10.5	32,394	3,386	10.5
1997	71,069	14,113	19.9	69,844	13,422	19.2	165,329	18,085	10.9	32,082	3,376	10.5
1996	70,650	14,463	20.5	69,411	13,764	19.8	163,691	18,638	11.4	31,877	3,428	10.8
1995	70,566	14,665	20.8	69,425	13,999	20.2	161,508	18,442	11.4	31,658	3,318	10.5
1994	70,020	15,289	21.8	68,819	14,610	21.2	160,329	19,107	11.9	31,267	3,663	11.7
1993 10/	69,292	15,727	22.7	68,040	14,961	22.0	159,208	19,781	12.4	30,779	3,755	12.2

Year												
1992 9/	68,440	15,294	22.3	67,256	14,521	21.6	157,680	18,793	11.9	30,430	3,928	12.9
1991 8/	65,918	14,341	21.8	64,800	13,658	21.1	154,684	17,586	11.4	30,590	3,781	12.4
1990	65,049	13,431	20.6	63,908	12,715	19.9	153,502	16,496	10.7	30,093	3,658	12.2
1989	64,144	12,590	19.6	63,225	12,001	19.0	152,282	15,575	10.2	29,566	3,363	11.4
1988	63,747	12,455	19.5	62,906	11,935	19.0	150,761	15,809	10.5	29,022	3,481	12.0
1987 7/	63,294	12,843	20.3	62,423	12,275	19.7	149,201	15,815	10.6	28,487	3,563	12.5
1986	62,948	12,876	20.5	62,009	12,257	19.8	147,631	16,017	10.8	27,975	3,477	12.4
1985	62,876	13,010	20.7	62,019	12,483	20.1	146,396	16,598	11.3	27,322	3,456	12.6
1984	62,447	13,420	21.5	61,681	12,929	21.0	144,551	16,952	11.7	26,818	3,330	12.4
1983 6/	62,334	13,911	22.3	61,578	13,427	21.8	143,052	17,767	12.4	26,313	3,625	13.8
1982	62,345	13,647	21.9	61,565	13,139	21.3	141,328	17,000	12.0	25,738	3,751	14.6
1981 5/	62,449	12,505	20.0	61,756	12,068	19.5	139,477	15,464	11.1	25,231	3,853	15.3
1980	62,914	11,543	18.3	62,168	11,114	17.9	137,428	13,858	10.1	24,686	3,871	15.7
1979 4/	63,375	10,377	16.4	62,646	9,993	16.0	135,333	12,014	8.9	24,194	3,682	15.2
1978	62,311	9,931	15.9	61,987	9,722	15.7	130,169	11,332	8.7	23,175	3,233	14.0
1977	63,137	10,288	16.2	62,823	10,028	16.0	128,262	11,316	8.8	22,468	3,177	14.1
1976	64,028	10,273	16.0	63,729	10,081	15.8	126,175	11,389	9.0	22,100	3,313	15.0
1975	65,079	11,104	17.1	64,750	10,882	16.8	124,122	11,456	9.2	21,662	3,317	15.3
1974 3/	66,134	10,156	15.4	65,802	9,967	15.1	122,101	10,132	8.3	21,127	3,085	14.6
1973	66,959	9,642	14.4	66,626	9,453	14.2	120,060	9,977	8.3	20,602	3,354	16.3
1972	67,930	10,284	15.1	67,592	10,082	14.9	117,957	10,438	8.8	20,117	3,738	18.6

(continued)

Table B-8 (Continued)

Year and Characteristic	Under 18 Years						18 to 64 Years			65 Years and Over		
	All People			Related Children in Families								
		Below Poverty Level			Below Poverty Level			Below Poverty Level			Below Poverty Level	
	Total	Number	Percent	Total	Number	Percent	Total	Number	Percent	Total	Number	Percent
1971 2/	68,816	10,551	15.3	68,474	10,344	15.1	115,911	10,735	9.3	19,827	4,273	21.6
1970	69,159	10,440	15.1	68,815	10,235	14.9	113,554	10,187	9.0	19,470	4,793	24.6
1969	69,090	9,691	14.0	68,746	9,501	13.8	111,528	9,669	8.7	18,899	4,787	25.3
1968	70,385	10,954	15.6	70,035	10,739	15.3	108,684	9,803	9.0	18,559	4,632	25.0
1967 1/	70,408	11,656	16.6	70,058	11,427	16.3	107,024	10,725	10.0	18,240	5,388	29.5
1966	70,218	12,389	17.6	69,869	12,146	17.4	105,241	11,007	10.5	17,929	5,114	28.5
1965	69,986	14,676	21.0	69,638	14,388	20.7	(NA)	(NA)	(NA)	(NA)	(NA)	(NA)
1964	69,711	16,051	23.0	69,364	15,736	22.7	(NA)	(NA)	(NA)	(NA)	(NA)	(NA)
1963	69,181	16,005	23.1	68,837	15,691	22.8	(NA)	(NA)	(NA)	(NA)	(NA)	(NA)
1962	67,722	16,963	25.0	67,385	16,630	24.7	(NA)	(NA)	(NA)	(NA)	(NA)	(NA)
1961	66,121	16,909	25.6	65,792	16,577	25.2	(NA)	(NA)	(NA)	(NA)	(NA)	(NA)
1960	65,601	17,634	26.9	65,275	17,288	26.5	(NA)	(NA)	(NA)	(NA)	(NA)	(NA)
1959	64,315	17,552	27.3	63,995	17,208	26.9	96,685	16,457	17.0	15,557	5,481	35.2
White Alone												
2011	54,186	10,103	18.6	53,268	9,643	18.1	151,416	18,007	11.9	35,732	2,739	7.7

Year												
2010 17/	54,490	10,092	18.5	53,573	9,590	17.9	151,218	18,353	12.1	34,274	2,638	7.7
2009	56,266	9,938	17.7	55,397	9,440	17.0	152,367	17,391	11.4	33,414	2,501	7.5
2008	56,153	8,863	15.8	55,339	8,441	15.3	151,681	15,356	10.1	32,714	2,771	8.5
2007	56,419	8,395	14.9	55,483	8,002	14.4	150,875	14,135	9.4	31,839	2,590	8.1
2006	56,205	7,908	14.1	55,330	7,522	13.6	150,143	14,035	9.3	31,270	2,473	7.9
2005	56,075	8,085	14.4	55,152	7,652	13.9	148,450	14,086	9.5	30,905	2,700	8.7
2004 14/	56,053	8,308	14.8	55,212	7,876	14.3	146,974	14,486	9.9	30,714	2,534	8.3
2003	55,779	7,985	14.3	54,989	7,624	13.9	145,783	13,622	9.3	30,303	2,666	8.8
2002	55,703	7,549	13.6	54,900	7,203	13.1	144,694	13,178	9.1	29,980	2,739	9.1
White												
2001	56,089	7,527	13.4	55,238	7,086	12.8	143,796	12,555	8.7	29,790	2,656	8.9
2000 12/	55,980	7,307	13.1	55,021	6,834	12.4	142,164	11,754	8.3	29,703	2,584	8.7
1999 11/	55,833	7,639	13.7	54,873	7,194	13.1	139,974	12,085	8.6	29,553	2,446	8.3
1998	56,016	8,443	15.1	55,126	7,935	14.4	138,061	12,456	9.0	28,759	2,555	8.9
1997	55,863	8,990	16.1	54,870	8,441	15.4	136,784	12,838	9.4	28,553	2,569	9.0
1996	55,606	9,044	16.3	54,599	8,488	15.5	135,586	12,940	9.5	28,464	2,667	9.4
1995	55,444	8,981	16.2	54,532	8,474	15.5	134,149	12,869	9.6	28,436	2,572	9.0
1994	55,186	9,346	16.9	54,221	8,826	16.3	133,289	13,187	9.9	27,985	2,846	10.2
1993 10/	54,639	9,752	17.8	53,614	9,123	17.0	132,680	13,535	10.2	27,580	2,939	10.7
1992 9/	54,110	9,399	17.4	53,110	8,752	16.5	131,694	12,871	9.8	27,256	2,989	11.0
1991 8/	52,523	8,848	16.8	51,627	8,316	16.1	130,312	12,097	9.3	27,297	2,802	10.3

(continued)

Table B-8 (Continued)

Year and Characteristic	Under 18 Years — All People			Under 18 Years — Related Children in Families			18 to 64 Years			65 Years and Over		
	Total	Below Poverty Level Number	Percent	Total	Below Poverty Level Number	Percent	Total	Below Poverty Level Number	Percent	Total	Below Poverty Level Number	Percent
1990	51,929	8,232	15.9	51,028	7,696	15.1	129,784	11,387	8.8	26,898	2,707	10.1
1989	51,400	7,599	14.8	50,704	7,164	14.1	128,974	10,647	8.3	26,479	2,539	9.6
1988	51,203	7,435	14.5	50,590	7,095	14.0	128,031	10,687	8.3	26,001	2,593	10.0
1987 7/	51,012	7,788	15.3	50,360	7,398	14.7	126,991	10,703	8.4	25,602	2,704	10.6
1986	51,111	8,209	16.1	50,356	7,714	15.3	125,998	11,285	9.0	25,173	2,689	10.7
1985	51,031	8,253	16.2	50,358	7,838	15.6	125,258	11,909	9.5	24,629	2,698	11.0
1984	50,814	8,472	16.7	50,192	8,086	16.1	123,922	11,904	9.6	24,206	2,579	10.7
1983 6/	50,726	8,862	17.5	50,183	8,534	17.0	123,014	12,347	10.0	23,754	2,776	11.7
1982	50,920	8,678	17.0	50,305	8,282	16.5	121,766	11,971	9.8	23,234	2,870	12.4
1981 5/	51,140	7,785	15.2	50,553	7,429	14.7	120,574	10,790	8.9	22,791	2,978	13.1
1980	51,653	7,181	13.9	51,002	6,817	13.4	118,935	9,478	8.0	22,325	3,042	13.6
1979 4/	52,262	6,193	11.8	51,687	5,909	11.4	117,583	8,110	6.9	21,898	2,911	13.3
1978	51,669	5,831	11.3	51,409	5,674	11.0	113,832	7,897	6.9	20,950	2,530	12.1
1977	52,563	6,097	11.6	52,299	5,943	11.4	112,374	7,893	7.0	20,316	2,426	11.9
1976	53,428	6,189	11.6	53,167	6,034	11.3	110,717	7,890	7.1	20,020	2,633	13.2

Year												
1975	54,405	6,927	12.7	54,126	6,748	12.5	109,105	8,210	7.5	19,654	2,634	13.4
1974 3/	55,590	6,223	11.2	55,320	6,079	11.0	107,579	7,053	6.6	19,206	2,460	12.8
1973	(NA)	(NA)	(NA)	56,211	5,462	9.7	(NA)	(NA)	(NA)	(NA)	2,698	14.4
1972	(NA)	(NA)	(NA)	57,181	5,784	10.1	(NA)	(NA)	(NA)	(NA)	3,072	16.8
1971 2/	(NA)	(NA)	(NA)	58,119	6,341	10.9	(NA)	(NA)	(NA)	(NA)	3,605	19.9
1970	(NA)	(NA)	(NA)	58,472	6,138	10.5	(NA)	(NA)	(NA)	(NA)	4,011	22.6
1969	(NA)	(NA)	(NA)	58,578	5,667	9.7	(NA)	(NA)	(NA)	(NA)	4,052	23.3
1968	(NA)	(NA)	(NA)	(NA)	6,373	10.7	(NA)	(NA)	(NA)	17,062	3,939	23.1
1967 1/	(NA)	(NA)	(NA)	(NA)	6,729	11.3	(NA)	(NA)	(NA)	16,791	4,646	27.7
1966	(NA)	(NA)	(NA)	(NA)	7,204	12.1	(NA)	(NA)	(NA)	16,514	4,357	26.4
1965	(NA)	(NA)	(NA)	(NA)	8,595	14.4	(NA)	(NA)	(NA)	(NA)	(NA)	(NA)
1964	(NA)	(NA)	(NA)	(NA)	(NA)	(NA)	(NA)	(NA)	(NA)	(NA)	(NA)	(NA)
1963	(NA)	(NA)	(NA)	(NA)	(NA)	(NA)	(NA)	(NA)	(NA)	(NA)	(NA)	(NA)
1962	(NA)	(NA)	(NA)	(NA)	(NA)	(NA)	(NA)	(NA)	(NA)	(NA)	(NA)	(NA)
1961	(NA)	(NA)	(NA)	(NA)	(NA)	(NA)	(NA)	(NA)	(NA)	(NA)	(NA)	(NA)
1960	(NA)	(NA)	(NA)	(NA)	11,229	20.0	(NA)	(NA)	(NA)	(NA)	(NA)	(NA)
1959	(NA)	(NA)	(NA)	(NA)	11,386	20.6	(NA)	(NA)	(NA)	(NA)	4,744	33.1

White Alone, not Hispanic

Year												
2011	38,955	4,850	12.5	38,322	4,554	11.9	123,101	12,112	9.8	32,904	2,210	6.7
2010 17/	39,437	4,866	12.3	38,823	4,544	11.7	123,731	12,230	9.9	31,616	2,155	6.8
2009	40,917	4,850	11.9	40,319	4,518	11.2	125,511	11,658	9.3	30,736	2,022	6.6

(continued)

Table B-8 (Continued)

Year and Characteristic	Under 18 Years						18 to 64 Years			65 Years and Over		
	All People			Related Children in Families								
	Total	Below Poverty Level		Total	Below Poverty Level		Total	Below Poverty Level		Total	Below Poverty Level	
		Number	Percent		Number	Percent		Number	Percent		Number	Percent
2008	41,309	4,364	10.6	40,707	4,059	10.0	125,482	10,380	8.3	30,149	2,280	7.6
2007	41,979	4,255	10.1	41,304	3,996	9.7	125,161	9,598	7.7	29,442	2,179	7.4
2006	42,212	4,208	10.0	41,563	3,930	9.5	124,847	9,761	7.8	28,990	2,044	7.0
2005	42,523	4,254	10.0	41,867	3,973	9.5	124,326	9,708	7.8	28,704	2,264	7.9
2004 14/	42,978	4,519	10.5	42,363	4,190	9.9	123,481	10,236	8.3	28,639	2,153	7.5
2003	43,150	4,233	9.8	42,547	3,957	9.3	123,110	9,391	7.6	28,335	2,277	8.0
2002	43,614	4,090	9.4	43,017	3,848	8.9	122,511	9,157	7.5	28,018	2,321	8.3
White, not Hispanic												
2001	44,095	4,194	9.5	43,459	3,887	8.9	122,470	8,811	7.2	27,973	2,266	8.1
2000 12/	44,244	4,018	9.1	43,554	3,715	8.5	121,499	8,130	6.7	27,948	2,218	7.9
1999 11/	44,272	4,155	9.4	43,570	3,832	8.8	120,341	8,462	7.0	27,952	2,118	7.6
1998	45,355	4,822	10.6	44,670	4,458	10.0	120,282	8,760	7.3	27,118	2,217	8.2
1997	45,491	5,204	11.4	44,665	4,759	10.7	119,373	9,088	7.6	26,995	2,200	8.1
1996	45,605	5,072	11.1	44,844	4,656	10.4	118,822	9,074	7.6	27,033	2,316	8.6
1995	45,689	5,115	11.2	44,973	4,745	10.6	118,228	8,908	7.5	27,034	2,243	8.3

Year											
1994	46,668	5,823	12.5	45,874	5,404	11.8	119,192	9,732	8.2	26,684	2,556	9.6
1993 10/	46,096	6,255	13.6	45,322	5,819	12.8	118,475	9,964	8.4	26,272	2,663	10.1
1992 9/	45,590	6,017	13.2	44,833	5,558	12.4	117,386	9,461	8.1	26,025	2,724	10.5
1991 8/	45,236	5,918	13.1	44,506	5,497	12.4	117,672	9,244	7.9	26,208	2,580	9.8
1990	44,797	5,532	12.3	44,045	5,106	11.6	117,477	8,619	7.3	25,854	2,471	9.6
1989	44,492	5,110	11.5	43,938	4,779	10.9	116,983	8,154	7.0	25,504	2,335	9.2
1988	44,438	4,888	11.0	43,910	4,594	10.5	116,479	8,293	7.1	25,044	2,384	9.5
1987 7/	44,461	5,230	11.8	43,907	4,902	11.2	115,721	8,327	7.2	24,754	2,472	10.0
1986	44,664	5,789	13.0	44,041	5,388	12.2	115,157	8,963	7.8	24,298	2,492	10.3
1985	44,752	5,745	12.8	44,199	5,421	12.3	114,969	9,608	8.4	23,734	2,486	10.5
1984	44,886	6,156	13.7	44,349	5,828	13.1	114,180	9,734	8.5	23,402	2,410	10.3
1983 6/	44,830	6,649	14.8	44,374	6,381	14.4	113,570	10,279	9.1	22,992	2,610	11.4
1982	45,531	6,566	14.4	45,001	6,229	13.8	113,717	10,082	8.9	22,655	2,714	12.0
1981 5/	45,950	5,946	12.9	45,440	5,639	12.4	112,722	9,207	8.2	22,237	2,834	12.7
1980	46,578	5,510	11.8	45,989	5,174	11.3	111,460	7,990	7.2	21,760	2,865	13.2
1979 4/	46,967	4,730	10.1	46,448	4,476	9.6	110,509	6,930	6.3	21,339	2,759	12.9
1978	46,819	4,506	9.6	46,606	4,383	9.4	107,481	6,837	6.4	20,431	2,412	11.8
1977	47,689	4,714	9.9	47,459	4,582	9.7	106,063	6,772	6.4	19,812	2,316	11.7
1976	48,824	4,799	9.8	48,601	4,664	9.6	104,846	6,720	6.4	19,565	2,506	12.8
1975	49,670	5,342	10.8	49,421	5,185	10.5	103,496	7,039	6.8	19,251	2,503	13.0
1974 3/	50,759	4,820	9.5	50,520	4,697	9.3	101,894	6,051	5.9	18,810	2,346	12.5

(continued)

Table B-8 (Continued)

Year and Characteristic	Under 18 Years All People Total	Below Poverty Level Number	Percent	Related Children in Families Total	Below Poverty Level Number	Percent	18 to 64 Years Total	Below Poverty Level Number	Percent	65 Years and Over Total	Below Poverty Level Number	Percent
Black Alone or in Combination												
2011	12,968	4,849	37.4	12,815	4,762	37.2	25,962	6,241	24.0	3,718	640	17.2
2010 17/	13,015	4,923	37.8	12,759	4,814	37.7	25,815	6,031	23.4	3,555	643	18.1
2009	12,655	4,480	35.4	12,445	4,349	34.9	24,815	5,441	21.9	3,405	655	19.2
2008	12,388	4,202	33.9	12,201	4,104	33.6	24,404	5,017	20.6	3,305	663	20.0
2007	12,380	4,178	33.7	12,227	4,106	33.6	23,968	4,742	19.8	3,215	748	23.3
2006	12,375	4,086	33.0	12,206	3,977	32.6	23,510	4,652	19.8	3,128	710	22.7
2005	12,159	4,074	33.5	11,975	3,972	33.2	23,338	4,735	20.3	3,053	708	23.2
2004 14/	12,190	4,059	33.3	12,012	3,962	33.0	22,842	4,638	20.3	3,005	714	23.8
2003	12,215	4,108	33.6	11,989	3,977	33.2	22,355	4,313	19.3	2,933	688	23.5
2002	12,114	3,817	31.5	11,931	3,733	31.3	22,170	4,376	19.7	2,922	691	23.6
Black Alone												
2011	11,138	4,320	38.8	11,005	4,247	38.6	24,831	5,980	24.1	3,640	630	17.3
2010 17/	11,173	4,355	39.0	10,953	4,271	39.0	24,667	5,775	23.4	3,443	617	17.9
2009	11,282	4,033	35.7	11,102	3,919	35.3	23,953	5,264	22.0	3,320	647	19.5

Year											
2008	11,172	3,878	34.7	10,998	3,781	34.4	23,565	4,855	20.6	3,229	646	20.0
2007	11,302	3,904	34.5	11,174	3,838	34.3	23,213	4,602	19.8	3,150	731	23.2
2006	11,315	3,777	33.4	11,168	3,690	33.0	22,907	4,570	19.9	3,085	701	22.7
2005	11,136	3,841	34.5	10,962	3,743	34.2	22,659	4,627	20.4	3,007	701	23.3
2004 14/	11,244	3,788	33.7	11,080	3,702	33.4	22,226	4,521	20.3	2,956	705	23.8
2003	11,367	3,877	34.1	11,162	3,750	33.6	21,746	4,224	19.4	2,876	680	23.7
2002	11,275	3,645	32.3	11,111	3,570	32.1	21,547	4,277	19.9	2,856	680	23.8
Black												
2001	11,556	3,492	30.2	11,419	3,423	30.0	21,462	4,018	18.7	2,853	626	21.9
2000 12/	11,480	3,581	31.2	11,296	3,495	30.9	21,160	3,794	17.9	2,785	607	21.8
1999 11/	11,488	3,813	33.2	11,260	3,698	32.8	21,518	4,000	18.6	2,750	628	22.8
1998	11,317	4,151	36.7	11,176	4,073	36.4	20,837	4,222	20.3	2,723	718	26.4
1997	11,367	4,225	37.2	11,193	4,116	36.8	20,400	4,191	20.5	2,691	700	26.0
1996	11,338	4,519	39.9	11,155	4,411	39.5	20,155	4,515	22.4	2,616	661	25.3
1995	11,369	4,761	41.9	11,198	4,644	41.5	19,892	4,483	22.5	2,478	629	25.4
1994	11,211	4,906	43.8	11,044	4,787	43.3	19,585	4,590	23.4	2,557	700	27.4
1993 10/	11,127	5,125	46.1	10,969	5,030	45.9	19,272	5,049	26.2	2,510	702	28.0
1992 9/	10,956	5,106	46.6	10,823	5,015	46.3	18,952	4,884	25.8	2,504	838	33.5
1991 8/	10,350	4,755	45.9	10,178	4,637	45.6	18,355	4,607	25.1	2,606	880	33.8
1990	10,162	4,550	44.8	9,980	4,412	44.2	18,097	4,427	24.5	2,547	860	33.8
1989	10,012	4,375	43.7	9,847	4,257	43.2	17,833	4,164	23.3	2,487	763	30.7

(continued)

Table B-8   (Continued)

Year and Characteristic	Under 18 Years						18 to 64 Years			65 Years and Over		
	All People			Related Children in Families								
		Below Poverty Level			Below Poverty Level			Below Poverty Level			Below Poverty Level	
	Total	Number	Percent	Total	Number	Percent	Total	Number	Percent	Total	Number	Percent
1988	9,865	4,296	43.5	9,681	4,148	42.8	17,548	4,275	24.4	2,436	785	32.2
1987 7/	9,730	4,385	45.1	9,546	4,234	44.4	17,245	4,361	25.3	2,387	774	32.4
1986	9,629	4,148	43.1	9,467	4,037	42.7	16,911	4,113	24.3	2,331	722	31.0
1985	9,545	4,157	43.6	9,405	4,057	43.1	16,667	4,052	24.3	2,273	717	31.5
1984	9,480	4,413	46.6	9,356	4,320	46.2	16,369	4,368	26.7	2,238	710	31.7
1983 6/	9,417	4,398	46.7	9,245	4,273	46.2	16,065	4,694	29.2	2,197	791	36.0
1982	9,400	4,472	47.6	9,269	4,388	47.3	15,692	4,415	28.1	2,124	811	38.2
1981 5/	9,374	4,237	45.2	9,291	4,170	44.9	15,358	4,117	26.8	2,102	820	39.0
1980	9,368	3,961	42.3	9,287	3,906	42.1	14,987	3,835	25.6	2,054	783	38.1
1979 4/	9,307	3,833	41.2	9,172	3,745	40.8	14,596	3,478	23.8	2,040	740	36.2
1978	9,229	3,830	41.5	9,168	3,781	41.2	13,774	3,133	22.7	1,954	662	33.9
1977	9,296	3,888	41.8	9,253	3,850	41.6	13,483	3,137	23.3	1,930	701	36.3
1976	9,322	3,787	40.6	9,291	3,758	40.4	13,224	3,163	23.9	1,852	644	34.8
1975	9,421	3,925	41.7	9,374	3,884	41.4	12,872	2,968	23.1	1,795	652	36.3
1974 3/	9,439	3,755	39.8	9,384	3,713	39.6	12,539	2,836	22.6	1,721	591	34.3

Year												
1973	(NA)	(NA)	(NA)	9,405	3,822	40.6	(NA)	(NA)	(NA)	1,672	620	37.1
1972	(NA)	(NA)	(NA)	9,426	4,025	42.7	(NA)	(NA)	(NA)	1,603	640	39.9
1971 2/	(NA)	(NA)	(NA)	9,414	3,836	40.4	(NA)	(NA)	(NA)	1,584	623	39.3
1970	(NA)	(NA)	(NA)	9,448	3,922	41.5	(NA)	(NA)	(NA)	1,422	683	48.0
1969	(NA)	(NA)	(NA)	9,290	3,677	39.6	(NA)	(NA)	(NA)	1,373	689	50.2
1968	(NA)	(NA)	(NA)	(NA)	4,188	43.1	(NA)	(NA)	(NA)	1,374	655	47.7
1967 1/	(NA)	(NA)	(NA)	(NA)	4,558	47.4	(NA)	(NA)	(NA)	1,341	715	53.3
1966	(NA)	(NA)	(NA)	(NA)	4,774	50.6	(NA)	(NA)	(NA)	1,311	722	55.1
1965	(NA)	(NA)	(NA)	(NA)	5,022	65.6	(NA)	(NA)	(NA)	(NA)	711	62.5
Asian Alone or in Combination												
2011	4,572	607	13.3	4,495	566	12.6	11,660	1,397	12.0	1,581	185	11.7
2010 17/	4,308	586	13.6	4,256	560	13.2	11,414	1,265	11.1	1,515	214	14.1
2009	3,996	531	13.3	3,946	507	12.9	9,898	1,154	11.7	1,378	216	15.7
2008	3,717	494	13.3	3,678	476	12.9	9,507	1,031	10.8	1,319	162	12.3
2007	3,606	431	11.9	3,558	402	11.3	9,531	892	9.4	1,293	144	11.2
2006	3,573	408	11.4	3,530	398	11.3	9,553	897	9.4	1,205	142	11.8
2005	3,472	359	10.3	3,435	352	10.2	9,115	999	11.0	1,144	144	12.6
2004 14/	3,406	329	9.7	3,367	311	9.2	8,780	819	9.3	1,104	147	13.3
2003	3,316	420	12.7	3,279	406	12.4	8,510	956	11.2	1,065	152	14.2
2002	3,199	353	11.0	3,159	338	10.7	8,292	804	9.7	995	86	8.7

(continued)

Table B-8 (Continued)

Year and Characteristic	Under 18 Years						18 to 64 Years			65 Years and Over		
	All People			Related Children in Families								
		Below Poverty Level			Below Poverty Level			Below Poverty Level			Below Poverty Level	
	Total	Number	Percent	Total	Number	Percent	Total	Number	Percent	Total	Number	Percent
Asian Alone												
2011	3,657	494	13.5	3,600	466	13.0	10,873	1,297	11.9	1,555	182	11.7
2010 17/	3,431	494	14.4	3,399	477	14.0	10,696	1,191	11.1	1,484	214	14.4
2009	3,311	463	14.0	3,271	444	13.6	9,344	1,069	11.4	1,350	213	15.8
2008	3,052	446	14.6	3,016	430	14.2	8,961	974	10.9	1,296	157	12.1
2007	2,980	374	12.5	2,932	345	11.8	9,012	832	9.2	1,265	143	11.3
2006	2,956	360	12.2	2,915	351	12.0	9,039	851	9.4	1,182	142	12.0
2005	2,871	317	11.1	2,842	312	11.0	8,591	941	11.0	1,118	143	12.8
2004 14/	2,854	281	9.9	2,823	265	9.4	8,294	774	9.3	1,083	146	13.5
2003	2,759	344	12.5	2,726	331	12.1	8,044	907	11.3	1,052	151	14.3
2002	2,683	315	11.7	2,648	302	11.4	7,881	764	9.7	977	82	8.4
Asian and Pacific Islander												
2001	3,215	369	11.5	3,169	353	11.1	8,352	814	9.7	899	92	10.2
2000 12/	3,294	420	12.7	3,256	407	12.5	8,500	756	8.9	878	82	9.3
1999 11/	3,212	381	11.9	3,178	367	11.5	7,879	807	10.2	864	96	11.1

Year												
1998	3,137	564	18.0	3,099	542	17.5	6,951	698	10.0	785	97	12.4
1997	3,096	628	20.3	3,061	608	19.9	6,680	753	11.3	705	87	12.3
1996	2,924	571	19.5	2,899	553	19.1	6,484	821	12.7	647	63	9.7
1995	2,900	564	19.5	2,858	532	18.6	6,123	757	12.4	622	89	14.3
1994	1,739	318	18.3	1,719	308	17.9	4,401	589	13.4	513	67	13.0
1993 10/	2,061	375	18.2	2,029	358	17.6	4,871	680	14.0	503	79	15.6
1992 9/	2,218	363	16.4	2,199	352	16.0	5,067	568	11.2	494	53	10.8
1991 8/	2,056	360	17.5	2,036	348	17.1	4,582	565	12.3	555	70	12.7
1990	2,126	374	17.6	2,098	356	17.0	4,375	422	9.6	514	62	12.1
1989	1,983	392	19.8	1,945	368	18.9	4,225	512	12.1	465	34	7.4
1988	1,970	474	24.1	1,949	458	23.5	4,035	583	14.4	442	60	13.5
1987 7/	1,937	455	23.5	1,908	432	22.7	4,010	510	12.7	375	56	15.0
Hispanic (of any race)												
2011	17,600	6,008	34.1	17,276	5,820	33.7	31,643	6,667	21.1	3,036	569	18.7
2010 17/	17,371	6,059	34.9	16,964	5,815	34.3	30,740	6,948	22.6	2,860	516	18.0
2009	16,965	5,610	33.1	16,655	5,419	32.5	29,031	6,224	21.4	2,815	516	18.3
2008	16,370	5,010	30.6	16,138	4,888	30.3	28,311	5,452	19.3	2,717	525	19.3
2007	15,647	4,482	28.6	15,375	4,348	28.3	27,731	4,970	17.9	2,555	438	17.1
2006	15,147	4,072	26.9	14,907	3,959	26.6	27,209	4,698	17.3	2,428	472	19.4
2005	14,654	4,143	28.3	14,361	3,977	27.7	26,051	4,765	18.3	2,315	460	19.9
2004 14/	14,173	4,098	28.9	13,929	3,985	28.6	25,324	4,620	18.2	2,194	403	18.4

(continued)

Table B-8 (Continued)

Year and Characteristic	Under 18 Years						18 to 64 Years			65 Years and Over		
	All People			Related Children in Families								
		Below Poverty Level			Below Poverty Level			Below Poverty Level			Below Poverty Level	
	Total	Number	Percent	Total	Number	Percent	Total	Number	Percent	Total	Number	Percent
2003	13,730	4,077	29.7	13,519	3,982	29.5	24,490	4,568	18.7	2,080	406	19.5
2002	13,210	3,782	28.6	12,971	3,653	28.2	23,952	4,334	18.1	2,053	439	21.4
2001	12,763	3,570	28.0	12,539	3,433	27.4	22,653	4,014	17.7	1,896	413	21.8
2000 12/	12,399	3,522	28.4	12,115	3,342	27.6	21,734	3,844	17.7	1,822	381	20.9
1999 11/	12,188	3,693	30.3	11,912	3,561	29.9	20,782	3,843	18.5	1,661	340	20.5
1998	11,152	3,837	34.4	10,921	3,670	33.6	18,668	3,877	20.8	1,696	356	21.0
1997	10,802	3,972	36.8	10,625	3,865	36.4	18,217	3,951	21.7	1,617	384	23.8
1996	10,511	4,237	40.3	10,255	4,090	39.9	17,587	4,089	23.3	1,516	370	24.4
1995	10,213	4,080	40.0	10,011	3,938	39.3	16,673	4,153	24.9	1,458	342	23.5
1994	9,822	4,075	41.5	9,621	3,956	41.1	16,192	4,018	24.8	1,428	323	22.6
1993 10/	9,462	3,873	40.9	9,188	3,666	39.9	15,708	3,956	25.2	1,390	297	21.4
1992 9/	9,081	3,637	40.0	8,829	3,440	39.0	15,268	3,668	24.0	1,298	287	22.1
1991 8/	7,648	3,094	40.4	7,473	2,977	39.8	13,279	3,008	22.7	1,143	237	20.8
1990	7,457	2,865	38.4	7,300	2,750	37.7	12,857	2,896	22.5	1,091	245	22.5
1989	7,186	2,603	36.2	7,040	2,496	35.5	12,536	2,616	20.9	1,024	211	20.6

Year											
1988	7,003	2,631	37.6	6,908	2,576	37.3	12,056	2,501	20.7	1,005	225	22.4
1987 7/	6,792	2,670	39.3	6,692	2,606	38.9	11,718	2,509	21.4	885	243	27.5
1986	6,646	2,507	37.7	6,511	2,413	37.1	11,206	2,406	21.5	906	204	22.5
1985	6,475	2,606	40.3	6,346	2,512	39.6	10,685	2,411	22.6	915	219	23.9
1984	6,068	2,376	39.2	5,982	2,317	38.7	10,029	2,254	22.5	819	176	21.5
1983 6/	6,066	2,312	38.1	5,977	2,251	37.7	9,697	2,148	22.5	782	173	22.1
1982	5,527	2,181	39.5	5,436	2,117	38.9	8,262	1,963	23.8	596	159	26.6
1981 5/	5,369	1,925	35.9	5,291	1,874	35.4	8,084	1,642	20.3	568	146	25.7
1980	5,276	1,749	33.2	5,211	1,718	33.0	7,740	1,563	20.2	582	179	30.8
1979 4/	5,483	1,535	28.0	5,426	1,505	27.7	7,314	1,232	16.8	574	154	26.8
1978	5,012	1,384	27.6	4,972	1,354	27.2	6,527	1,098	16.8	539	125	23.2
1977	5,028	1,422	28.3	5,000	1,402	28.0	6,500	1,164	17.9	518	113	21.9
1976	4,771	1,443	30.2	4,736	1,424	30.1	6,034	1,212	20.1	464	128	27.7
1975	(NA)	(NA)	(NA)	4,896	1,619	33.1	(NA)	(NA)	(NA)	(NA)	137	32.6
1974 3/	(NA)	(NA)	(NA)	4,939	1,414	28.6	(NA)	(NA)	(NA)	(NA)	117	28.9
1973	(NA)	(NA)	(NA)	4,910	1,364	27.8	(NA)	(NA)	(NA)	(NA)	95	24.9

Note: Numbers in thousands. People as of March of the following year.

Source: U.S. Bureau of the Census, Current Population Survey, Annual Social and Economic Supplements.

For information on confidentiality protection, sampling error, nonsampling error, and definitions, see http://www.census.gov/apsd/techdoc/cps/cpsmar12.pdf

Footnotes are available at http://www.census.gov/hhes/www/poverty/histpov/footnotes.html.

Historical Poverty Tables—Footnotes

NA—Not available.

1. Implementation of a new March CPS processing system.

2. Implementation of 1970 census population controls.

3. Implementation of a new March CPS processing system. Questionnaire expanded to ask eleven income questions.

4. Implementation of 1980 census population controls. Questionnaire expanded to show 27 possible values from 51 possible sources of income.

5. Implemented three technical changes to the poverty definition. See Characteristics of the Population Below the Poverty Level: 1980; Series P-60, No. 133.

6. Implementation of Hispanic population weighting controls.

7. Implementation of a new March CPS processing system.

8. CPS file for March 1992 (1991 data) was corrected after the release of the 1991 Income and Poverty reports. Weights for nine person records were omitted on the original file. (See P60-184 for further details.)

9. Implementation of 1990 census population controls.

10. Data collection method changed from paper and pencil to computer-assisted interviewing. In addition, the March 1994 income supplement was revised to allow for the coding of different income amounts on selected questionnaire items. Limits either increased or decreased in the following categories: earnings increased to $999,999; Social Security increased to $49,999; Supplemental Security Income and Public Assistance increased to $24,999; Veterans' Benefits increased to $99,999; Child Support and Alimony decreased to $49,999.

11. Implementation of Census 2000 based population controls.

12. Implementation of Census 2000 based population controls and sample expanded by 28,000 households.

13. Beginning in 2003, CPS ASEC offered respondents the option of choosing more than one race. The 2002 and 2001 CPS ASEC recorded only one race for each respondent. The 3-year averages for 2002 are based on combining the 2003 CPS ASEC race categories shown in the stub with the relevant single race categories of White, Black, American Indian or Alaska Native, or Asian and Pacific Islander recorded in the 2002 and 2001 CPS ASEC.

14. The 2004 data have been revised to reflect a correction to the weights in the 2005 ASEC.

15. The "Outside metropolitan statistical areas" category includes both micropolitan statistical areas and territory outside of metropolitan and micropolitan statistical areas. For more information, see "About Metropolitan and Micropolitan Statistical Areas" at www.census.gov/popest/about/index.html

16. Work experience: Refers to the longest job held in the previous calendar year. The work experience categories are based on the number of weeks worked, and the number of hours worked per week. Full-time year-round: Worked at least 35 hours per week, for at least 50 weeks last year (including paid sick leave and vacations). Not full-time year-round: Worked for at least 1 week last year, but for less than 50 weeks, or less than 35 hours per week, or both.

17. Implementation of Census 2010-based population controls.

A. People of Hispanic origin may be of any race. Data for Hispanic origin not available prior to 1972.

B. Beginning in January 1978, the Bureau of Labor Statistics introduced a new price index for all urban consumers (CPI-U) that forms a continuous series with the earlier index for urban wage earners and for clerical workers as of December 1997.

C. Prior to 1979 unrelated subfamilies were included in all families. Beginning in 1979 unrelated subfamilies are excluded from all families.

Note: The 2003 Current Population Survey asked respondents to choose one or more races. White alone refers to people who reported White and did not report any other race category. The use of this single-race population does not imply that it is the preferred methods of presenting or analyzing data. The Census Bureau use variety of approaches. Information on people who reported more than one race, such as "White and American Indian and Alaska Native" or "Asian and Black or African American," is available from Census 2000 through American FactFinder. About 2.6 percent of people reported more than one race in 2000. Black alone refers to people who reported Black and did not report any other race category. Asian alone refers to people who reported Asian and did not report any other race category. Asian and/or Native Hawaiian and Other Pacific Islander refers to people who reported either or both of these categories, but did not report any other category.

Source: U.S. Census Bureau. "Table 3: Poverty Status of People, by Age, Race, and Hispanic Origi;:: 1959 to 2011," 2013. Accessed January 28, 2013. http://www.census.gov/hhes/www/poverty/data/historical/hstpov3.xls

B-9. U.S. GOVERNMENT POVERTY DATA, 1959–2011

The following table provides official U.S. government poverty data for the years 1959 to 2011. This data describes the number and percentage of people at the poverty line and just above the poverty line and thus at risk of poverty.

Table B-9   People Below 125 Percent of Poverty Level and the Near Poor: 1959 to 2011

Year	Total	Below 1.25		Between 1.00–1.25	
		Number	Percent	Number	Percent
2011	308,456	60,949	19.8	14,702	4.8
2010 17/	306,130	60,669	19.8	14,326	4.7
2009	303,820	56,840	18.7	13,271	4.4
2008	301,041	53,805	17.9	13,977	4.6
2007	298,699	50,876	17.0	13,601	4.6
2006	296,450	49,688	16.8	13,229	4.5
2005	293,135	49,327	16.8	12,377	4.2
2004 14/	290,617	49,693	17.1	12,653	4.4
2003	287,699	48,687	16.9	12,826	4.5
2002	285,317	47,084	16.5	12,514	4.4
2001	281,475	45,320	16.1	12,413	4.4
2000 12/	278,944	43,612	15.6	12,030	4.3
1999 11/	276,208	45,030	16.3	12,239	4.4
1998	271,059	46,036	17.0	11,560	4.3
1997	268,480	47,853	17.8	12,280	4.6
1996	266,218	49,310	18.5	12,781	4.8
1995	263,733	48,761	18.5	12,336	4.7
1994	261,616	50,401	19.3	12,342	4.7
1993 10/	259,278	51,801	20.0	12,536	4.8
1992 9/	256,549	50,592	19.7	12,578	4.9
1991 8/	251,192	47,527	18.9	11,819	4.7
1990	248,644	44,837	18.0	11,252	4.5
1989	245,992	42,653	17.3	11,125	4.5
1988	243,530	42,551	17.5	10,806	4.4
1987 7/	240,982	43,032	17.9	10,811	4.5

Table B-9 (Continued)

Year	Total	Below 1.25		Between 1.00–1.25	
		Number	Percent	Number	Percent
1986	238,554	43,486	18.2	11,116	4.7
1985	236,594	44,166	18.7	11,102	4.7
1984	233,816	45,288	19.4	11,588	5.0
1983 6/	231,700	47,150	20.3	11,847	5.1
1982	229,412	46,520	20.3	12,122	5.3
1981 5/	227,157	43,748	19.3	11,926	5.3
1980	225,027	40,658	18.1	11,386	5.1
1979 4/	222,903	36,616	16.4	10,544	4.7
1978	215,656	34,155	15.8	9,658	4.5
1977	213,867	35,659	16.7	10,939	5.1
1976	212,303	35,509	16.7	10,534	5.0
1975	210,864	37,182	17.6	11,305	5.4
1974 3/	209,362	33,666	16.1	10,296	4.9
1973	207,621	32,828	15.8	9,855	4.7
1972	206,004	34,653	16.8	10,193	4.9
1971 2/	204,554	36,501	17.8	10,942	5.3
1970	202,183	35,624	17.6	10,204	5.0
1969	199,517	34,665	17.4	10,518	5.3
1968	197,628	35,905	18.2	10,516	5.3
1967 1/	195,672	39,206	20.0	11,437	5.8
1966	193,388	41,267	21.3	12,757	6.6
1965	191,413	46,163	24.1	12,978	6.8
1964	189,710	49,819	26.3	13,764	7.3
1963	187,258	50,778	27.1	14,342	7.7
1962	184,276	53,119	28.8	14,494	7.9
1961	181,277	54,280	30.0	14,652	8.1
1960	179,503	54,560	30.4	14,709	8.2
1959	176,557	54,942	31.1	15,452	8.7

Note: numbers in thousands
Source: U.S. Bureau of the Census, Current Population Survey, Annual Social and Economic Supplements. For information on confidentiality protection, sampling error, nonsampling error, and definitions, see http://www.census.gov/apsd/techdoc/cps/cpsmar12.pdf

Footnotes are available at http://www.census.gov/hhes/www/poverty/histpov/footnotes.html.

Footnotes:

NA—Not available.

1. Implementation of a new March CPS processing system.
2. Implementation of 1970 census population controls.
3. Implementation of a new March CPS processing system. Questionnaire expanded to ask eleven income questions.
4. Implementation of 1980 census population controls. Questionnaire expanded to show 27 possible values from 51 possible sources of income.
5. Implemented three technical changes to the poverty definition. See Characteristics of the Population Below the Poverty Level: 1980; Series P-60, No. 133.
6. Implementation of Hispanic population weighting controls.
7. Implementation of a new March CPS processing system.
8. CPS file for March 1992 (1991 data) was corrected after the release of the 1991 Income and Poverty reports. Weights for nine person records were omitted on the original file. (See P60-184 for further details.)
9. Implementation of 1990 census population controls.
10. Data collection method changed from paper and pencil to computer- assisted interviewing. In addition, the March 1994 income supplement was revised to allow for the coding of different income amounts on selected questionnaire items. Limits either increased or decreased in the following categories: earnings increased to $999,999; Social Security increased to $49,999; Supplemental Security Income and Public Assistance increased to $24,999; Veterans' Benefits increased to $99,999; Child Support and Alimony decreased to $49,999.
11. Implementation of Census 2000 based population controls.
12. Implementation of Census 2000 based population controls and sample expanded by 28,000 households.
13. Beginning in 2003, CPS ASEC offered respondents the option of choosing more than one race. The 2002 and 2001 CPS ASEC recorded only one race for each respondent. The 3-year averages for 2002 are based on combining the 2003 CPS ASEC race categories shown in the stub with the relevant single race categories of White, Black, American Indian or Alaska Native, or Asian and Pacific Islander recorded in the 2002 and 2001 CPS ASEC.
14. The 2004 data have been revised to reflect a correction to the weights in the 2005 ASEC.
15. The "Outside metropolitan statistical areas" category includes both micropolitan statistical areas and territory outside of metropolitan and micropolitan statistical areas. For more information, see "About Metropolitan and Micropolitan Statistical Areas" at www.census.gov/popest/about/index.html
16. Work experience: Refers to the longest job held in the previous calendar year. The work experience categories are based on the number of weeks worked, and the number of hours worked per week. Full-time year-round: Worked at least 35 hours per week, for at least 50 weeks last year (including paid sick leave and vacations).

Not full-time year-round: Worked for at least 1 week last year, but for less than 50 weeks, or less than 35 hours per week, or both.

17. Implementation of Census 2010-based population controls.

A. People of Hispanic origin may be of any race. Data for Hispanic origin not available prior to 1972.

B. Beginning in January 1978, the Bureau of Labor Statistics introduced a new price index for all urban consumers (CPI-U) that forms a continuous series with the earlier index for urban wage earners and for clerical workers as of December 1997.

C. Prior to 1979 unrelated subfamilies were included in all families. Beginning in 1979 unrelated subfamilies are excluded from all families.

Note: The 2003 Current Population Survey asked respondents to choose one or more races. White alone refers to people who reported White and did not report any other race category. The use of this single-race population does not imply that it is the preferred methods of presenting or analyzing data. The Census Bureau use variety of approaches. Information on people who reported more than one race, such as "White and American Indian and Alaska Native" or "Asian and Black or African American," is available from Census 2000 through American FactFinder. About 2.6 percent of people reported more than one race in 2000. Black alone refers to people who reported Black and did not report any other race category. Asian alone refers to people who reported Asian and did not report any other race category. Asian and/or Native Hawaiian and Other Pacific Islander refers to people who reported either or both of these categories, but did not report any other category.

Source: U.S. Census Bureau. "Table 6: People Below 125 Percent of Poverty Level and the Near Poor: 1959 to 2011," 2013. Accessed January 28. http://www.census.gov/hhes/www/poverty/data/historical/hstpov6.xls

B-10. POVERTY IN THE UNITED STATES, STATE BY STATE, 1980–2011

The following table provides official U.S. government data on the number and percentage of people who were poor in each state and the District of Columbia for each year from 1980 to 2011.

Table B-10 Number of Poor and Poverty Rate, by State: 1980 to 2011

State	Total	Number	Standard Error	Percent	Standard Error
2011					
Alabama	4,765	732	74	15.4	1.53
Alaska	712	83	9	11.7	1.33
Arizona	6,547	1,128	107	17.2	1.66
Arkansas	2,909	545	46	18.7	1.58

(continued)

Table B-10   (Continued)

State	Total	Number	Standard Error	Percent	Standard Error
California	37,592	6,352	202	16.9	0.55
Colorado	5,016	661	54	13.2	1.07
Connecticut	3,514	356	33	10.1	0.93
Delaware	902	123	9	13.7	0.97
D.C.	619	123	9	19.9	1.44
Florida	18,986	2,822	136	14.9	0.72
Georgia	9,681	1,783	122	18.4	1.25
Hawaii	1,337	162	18	12.1	1.35
Idaho	1,574	248	26	15.7	1.73
Illinois	12,697	1,807	109	14.2	0.87
Indiana	6,344	989	83	15.6	1.31
Iowa	3,027	315	24	10.4	0.80
Kansas	2,807	402	32	14.3	1.17
Kentucky	4,302	689	60	16.0	1.38
Louisiana	4,494	947	75	21.1	1.63
Maine	1,328	178	14	13.4	1.06
Maryland	5,806	537	43	9.3	0.76
Massachusetts	6,514	688	55	10.6	0.85
Michigan	9,689	1,449	100	15.0	1.03
Minnesota	5,276	528	46	10.0	0.88
Mississippi	2,932	510	40	17.4	1.39
Missouri	5,892	910	98	15.4	1.65
Montana	986	163	16	16.5	1.64
Nebraska	1,823	187	22	10.2	1.25
Nevada	2,682	414	34	15.5	1.26
New Hampshire	1,300	99	12	7.6	0.89
New Jersey	8,642	988	76	11.4	0.88
New Mexico	2,037	451	36	22.2	1.78
New York	19,329	3,085	144	16.0	0.74
North Carolina	9,504	1,459	130	15.4	1.39
North Dakota	675	67	10	9.9	1.42

State	Total	Number	Standard Error	Percent	Standard Error
Ohio	11,309	1,708	129	15.1	1.16
Oklahoma	3,763	522	47	13.9	1.24
Oregon	3,850	553	51	14.4	1.33
Pennsylvania	12,697	1,604	106	12.6	0.84
Rhode Island	1,038	139	10	13.4	1.02
South Carolina	4,605	874	64	19.0	1.39
South Dakota	808	117	20	14.5	2.45
Tennessee	6,324	1,030	104	16.3	1.66
Texas	25,554	4,458	196	17.4	0.77
Utah	2,812	309	29	11.0	1.02
Vermont	615	71	6	11.6	0.99
Virginia	7,971	907	70	11.4	0.87
Washington	6,812	854	74	12.5	1.09
West Virginia	1,820	318	34	17.5	1.77
Wisconsin	5,676	743	60	13.1	1.08
Wyoming	562	60	8	10.7	1.43
2010 17/					
Alabama	4,717	812	83	17.2	1.79
Alaska	695	87	10	12.5	1.45
Arizona	6,426	1,208	108	18.8	1.69
Arkansas	2,879	440	45	15.3	1.58
California	37,240	6,073	212	16.3	0.57
Colorado	4,995	615	54	12.3	1.08
Connecticut	3,541	303	27	8.6	0.76
Delaware	890	109	10	12.2	1.07
D.C.	604	118	8	19.5	1.29
Florida	18,759	3,006	127	16.0	0.68
Georgia	9,650	1,814	104	18.8	1.10
Hawaii	1,311	162	15	12.4	1.18
Idaho	1,543	213	23	13.8	1.53
Illinois	12,784	1,798	101	14.1	0.79

(*continued*)

Table B-10 (Continued)

State	Total	Number	Standard Error	Percent	Standard Error
Indiana	6,390	1,041	95	16.3	1.49
Iowa	2,977	307	30	10.3	1.00
Kansas	2,766	400	39	14.5	1.44
Kentucky	4,270	754	65	17.7	1.56
Louisiana	4,418	949	69	21.5	1.62
Maine	1,298	164	15	12.6	1.16
Maryland	5,786	628	50	10.9	0.86
Massachusetts	6,532	711	68	10.9	1.06
Michigan	9,751	1,530	110	15.7	1.12
Minnesota	5,217	563	43	10.8	0.83
Mississippi	2,920	658	44	22.5	1.48
Missouri	5,929	890	79	15.0	1.36
Montana	979	142	17	14.5	1.80
Nebraska	1,804	184	20	10.2	1.15
Nevada	2,696	446	35	16.6	1.31
New Hampshire	1,294	84	8	6.5	0.65
New Jersey	8,733	966	89	11.1	1.01
New Mexico	2,033	372	30	18.3	1.52
New York	19,116	3,062	147	16.0	0.77
North Carolina	9,359	1,633	90	17.4	0.96
North Dakota	653	82	6	12.6	0.87
Ohio	11,341	1,746	118	15.4	1.06
Oklahoma	3,697	603	62	16.3	1.68
Oregon	3,752	537	44	14.3	1.17
Pennsylvania	12,530	1,535	84	12.2	0.68
Rhode Island	1,042	146	11	14.0	1.04
South Carolina	4,563	773	53	16.9	1.16
South Dakota	799	109	9	13.6	1.14
Tennessee	6,315	1,052	85	16.7	1.34
Texas	25,200	4,633	196	18.4	0.79
Utah	2,768	278	30	10.0	1.11

Table B-10   (Continued)

State	Total	Number	Standard Error	Percent	Standard Error
Vermont	624	67	7	10.8	1.10
Virginia	7,837	835	73	10.7	0.94
Washington	6,713	779	73	11.6	1.08
West Virginia	1,816	306	23	16.8	1.32
Wisconsin	5,626	567	52	10.1	0.92
Wyoming	550	53	5	9.6	0.85
2009					
Alabama	4,655	770	60	16.6	1.28
Alaska	688	81	8	11.7	1.20
Arizona	6,508	1,381	84	21.2	1.29
Arkansas	2,846	538	40	18.9	1.39
California	36,742	5,638	177	15.3	0.48
Colorado	4,969	613	58	12.3	1.17
Connecticut	3,472	292	35	8.4	1.01
Delaware	883	109	11	12.3	1.19
D.C.	595	107	9	17.9	1.53
Florida	18,385	2,676	116	14.6	0.63
Georgia	9,657	1,775	91	18.4	0.94
Hawaii	1,250	156	14	12.5	1.16
Idaho	1,524	209	19	13.7	1.22
Illinois	12,759	1,690	94	13.2	0.73
Indiana	6,342	1,023	70	16.1	1.10
Iowa	2,987	319	34	10.7	1.14
Kansas	2,737	374	35	13.7	1.29
Kentucky	4,276	727	58	17.0	1.35
Louisiana	4,450	636	55	14.3	1.24
Maine	1,297	148	16	11.4	1.27
Maryland	5,662	543	54	9.6	0.96
Massachusetts	6,623	717	60	10.8	0.90
Michigan	9,797	1,376	83	14.0	0.84
Minnesota	5,200	576	54	11.1	1.03

(continued)

Table B-10 (Continued)

State	Total	Number	Standard Error	Percent	Standard Error
Mississippi	2,847	658	44	23.1	1.53
Missouri	5,963	926	68	15.5	1.14
Montana	971	131	12	13.5	1.23
Nebraska	1,778	176	20	9.9	1.10
Nevada	2,629	343	32	13.0	1.24
New Hampshire	1,313	103	13	7.8	0.99
New Jersey	8,660	806	66	9.3	0.76
New Mexico	1,971	381	31	19.3	1.56
New York	19,158	3,018	125	15.8	0.65
North Carolina	9,336	1,576	88	16.9	0.94
North Dakota	632	69	7	10.9	1.14
Ohio	11,441	1,526	87	13.3	0.76
Oklahoma	3,632	468	44	12.9	1.22
Oregon	3,821	510	49	13.4	1.27
Pennsylvania	12,401	1,376	84	11.1	0.68
Rhode Island	1,030	134	14	13.0	1.32
South Carolina	4,501	618	55	13.7	1.21
South Dakota	799	113	9	14.1	1.17
Tennessee	6,240	1,031	70	16.5	1.12
Texas	24,632	4,262	154	17.3	0.63
Utah	2,794	270	26	9.7	0.94
Vermont	617	58	7	9.4	1.14
Virginia	7,767	831	65	10.7	0.84
Washington	6,697	781	65	11.7	0.97
West Virginia	1,801	285	22	15.8	1.23
Wisconsin	5,545	599	56	10.8	1.00
Wyoming	540	50	6	9.2	1.11
2008					
Alabama	4,716	675	57	14.3	1.20
Alaska	672	55	7	8.2	1.03
Arizona	6,529	1,172	79	18.0	1.21

Table B-10 (Continued)

State	Total	Number	Standard Error	Percent	Standard Error
Arkansas	2,822	431	36	15.3	1.28
California	36,637	5,344	174	14.6	0.47
Colorado	4,908	541	55	11.0	1.13
Connecticut	3,433	276	34	8.1	1.00
Delaware	861	82	9	9.6	1.08
D.C.	590	98	9	16.5	1.49
Florida	18,022	2,370	110	13.1	0.61
Georgia	9,541	1,477	84	15.5	0.88
Hawaii	1,255	125	13	9.9	1.05
Idaho	1,515	185	18	12.2	1.16
Illinois	12,687	1,564	90	12.3	0.71
Indiana	6,288	901	66	14.3	1.06
Iowa	2,986	285	32	9.5	1.08
Kansas	2,716	346	34	12.7	1.26
Kentucky	4,246	724	58	17.1	1.36
Louisiana	4,326	788	60	18.2	1.38
Maine	1,317	158	17	12.0	1.28
Maryland	5,528	481	51	8.7	0.93
Massachusetts	6,420	727	60	11.3	0.94
Michigan	9,806	1,273	80	13.0	0.81
Minnesota	5,120	506	51	9.9	0.99
Mississippi	2,900	525	40	18.1	1.39
Missouri	5,861	780	63	13.3	1.07
Montana	973	125	12	12.9	1.21
Nebraska	1,774	188	20	10.6	1.14
Nevada	2,581	278	30	10.8	1.15
New Hampshire	1,300	91	12	7.0	0.95
New Jersey	8,515	787	65	9.2	0.76
New Mexico	1,977	381	31	19.3	1.55
New York	19,309	2,734	120	14.2	0.62
North Carolina	9,234	1,285	80	13.9	0.87

(*continued*)

Table B-10 (Continued)

State	Total	Number	Standard Error	Percent	Standard Error
North Dakota	625	74	7	11.8	1.19
Ohio	11,386	1,557	88	13.7	0.77
Oklahoma	3,550	484	45	13.6	1.26
Oregon	3,806	403	44	10.6	1.15
Pennsylvania	12,178	1,335	83	11.0	0.68
Rhode Island	1,042	132	14	12.7	1.30
South Carolina	4,462	624	55	14.0	1.23
South Dakota	794	104	9	13.1	1.13
Tennessee	6,163	924	67	15.0	1.09
Texas	24,174	3,834	148	15.9	0.61
Utah	2,754	209	23	7.6	0.85
Vermont	610	55	7	9.0	1.13
Virginia	7,735	799	64	10.3	0.83
Washington	6,526	680	61	10.4	0.93
West Virginia	1,796	260	21	14.5	1.19
Wisconsin	5,548	544	53	9.8	0.96
Wyoming	529	54	6	10.1	1.17
2007					
Alabama	4,566	662	56	14.5	1.23
Alaska	675	51	7	7.6	1.00
Arizona	6,365	912	71	14.3	1.12
Arkansas	2,803	387	35	13.8	1.23
California	36,247	4,589	163	12.7	0.45
Colorado	4,872	478	52	9.8	1.07
Connecticut	3,471	309	36	8.9	1.04
Delaware	861	80	9	9.3	1.07
D.C.	580	104	9	18.0	1.55
Florida	18,044	2,250	108	12.5	0.60
Georgia	9,486	1,294	80	13.6	0.84
Hawaii	1,264	94	12	7.5	0.91
Idaho	1,501	149	16	9.9	1.07

Table B-10 (Continued)

State	Total	Number	Standard Error	Percent	Standard Error
Illinois	12,680	1,262	82	10.0	0.65
Indiana	6,258	740	61	11.8	0.98
Iowa	2,965	264	31	8.9	1.05
Kansas	2,720	319	33	11.7	1.21
Kentucky	4,202	653	55	15.5	1.32
Louisiana	4,186	673	56	16.1	1.34
Maine	1,312	142	16	10.9	1.23
Maryland	5,560	491	52	8.8	0.93
Massachusetts	6,336	707	59	11.2	0.94
Michigan	9,919	1,076	74	10.8	0.75
Minnesota	5,188	482	50	9.3	0.96
Mississippi	2,895	655	44	22.6	1.51
Missouri	5,783	742	62	12.8	1.06
Montana	938	122	12	13.0	1.23
Nebraska	1,751	174	20	9.9	1.11
Nevada	2,566	250	28	9.7	1.10
New Hampshire	1,312	76	11	5.8	0.87
New Jersey	8,548	742	63	8.7	0.74
New Mexico	1,941	271	27	14.0	1.38
New York	19,021	2,757	121	14.5	0.63
North Carolina	9,170	1,423	84	15.5	0.92
North Dakota	614	57	7	9.3	1.08
Ohio	11,280	1,446	85	12.8	0.76
Oklahoma	3,551	476	44	13.4	1.25
Oregon	3,761	481	47	12.8	1.26
Pennsylvania	12,297	1,273	81	10.4	0.66
Rhode Island	1,042	99	12	9.5	1.14
South Carolina	4,380	617	54	14.1	1.24
South Dakota	787	74	8	9.4	0.99
Tennessee	6,137	906	66	14.8	1.08
Texas	23,653	3,903	148	16.5	0.63

(*continued*)

Table B-10   (Continued)

State	Total	Number	Standard Error	Percent	Standard Error
Utah	2,651	255	26	9.6	0.97
Vermont	613	61	7	9.9	1.18
Virginia	7,678	664	59	8.6	0.77
Washington	6,503	661	60	10.2	0.92
West Virginia	1,793	265	22	14.8	1.20
Wisconsin	5,458	601	56	11.0	1.02
Wyoming	518	56	6	10.9	1.22
2006					
Alabama	4,532	650	56	14.3	1.23
Alaska	658	58	7	8.9	1.08
Arizona	6,256	902	71	14.4	1.13
Arkansas	2,748	487	38	17.7	1.38
California	36,160	4,427	160	12.2	0.44
Colorado	4,797	466	52	9.7	1.08
Connecticut	3,457	275	34	8.0	0.99
Delaware	858	80	9	9.3	1.07
D.C.	569	104	9	18.3	1.58
Florida	18,029	2,068	104	11.5	0.58
Georgia	9,334	1,172	76	12.6	0.82
Hawaii	1,254	116	13	9.2	1.01
Idaho	1,472	141	16	9.5	1.06
Illinois	12,633	1,338	85	10.6	0.67
Indiana	6,334	674	59	10.6	0.93
Iowa	2,913	301	33	10.3	1.14
Kansas	2,719	349	34	12.8	1.26
Kentucky	4,106	690	56	16.8	1.37
Louisiana	4,206	713	57	17.0	1.36
Maine	1,313	134	16	10.2	1.20
Maryland	5,607	469	51	8.4	0.90
Massachusetts	6,324	758	61	12.0	0.97
Michigan	9,953	1,323	81	13.3	0.82
Minnesota	5,145	422	47	8.2	0.91

Table B-10   (Continued)

State	Total	Number	Standard Error	Percent	Standard Error
Mississippi	2,887	596	42	20.6	1.46
Missouri	5,797	659	58	11.4	1.01
Montana	930	125	12	13.5	1.26
Nebraska	1,765	180	20	10.2	1.12
Nevada	2,530	241	28	9.5	1.10
New Hampshire	1,308	71	11	5.4	0.84
New Jersey	8,650	762	64	8.8	0.74
New Mexico	1,939	328	29	16.9	1.49
New York	19,021	2,668	119	14.0	0.63
North Carolina	8,847	1,225	79	13.8	0.89
North Dakota	615	70	7	11.4	1.18
Ohio	11,297	1,371	83	12.1	0.74
Oklahoma	3,489	531	47	15.2	1.33
Oregon	3,705	439	45	11.8	1.23
Pennsylvania	12,326	1,397	84	11.3	0.69
Rhode Island	1,054	110	13	10.5	1.19
South Carolina	4,224	474	49	11.2	1.15
South Dakota	770	82	8	10.7	1.06
Tennessee	5,916	879	65	14.9	1.10
Texas	23,208	3,816	147	16.4	0.63
Utah	2,536	235	25	9.3	0.97
Vermont	618	48	6	7.8	1.05
Virginia	7,532	651	58	8.6	0.77
Washington	6,310	502	53	8.0	0.84
West Virginia	1,810	277	22	15.3	1.21
Wisconsin	5,471	555	54	10.1	0.98
Wyoming	516	51	6	10.0	1.17
South Dakota	749	95	8	12.7	1.01
Tennessee	5,901	829	75	14.0	1.18
Texas	21,827	3,705	170	17.0	0.72
Utah	2,346	213	23	9.1	0.92
Vermont	610	52	5	8.5	0.86

(*continued*)

Table B-10   (Continued)

State	Total	Number	Standard Error	Percent	Standard Error
Virginia	7,367	740	71	10.0	0.91
Washington	6,078	766	68	12.6	1.05
West Virginia	1,785	310	23	17.4	1.17
Wisconsin	5,412	528	48	9.8	0.84
Wyoming	487	48	5	9.8	0.98

Note: Numbers in thousands. Standard errors shown in this table are based on standard errors calculated using replicate weights instead of the generalized variance function used in the past. For more information, see "Standard Errors and Their Use" at www.census.gov/hhes/www/p60_243sa.pdf.

Source: U.S. Bureau of the Census, Current Population Survey, Annual Social and Economic Supplements.

For information on confidentiality protection, sampling error, nonsampling error, and definitions, see http://www.census.gov/apsd/techdoc/cps/cpsmar12.pdf.

Footnotes are available at http://www.census.gov/hhes/www/poverty/histpov/footnotes.html.

Author's Note: 1980–2005 data from Table 21 has been omitted. This data can be accessed on the U.S. Census Bureau website at http://www.census.gov/hhes/www/poverty/data/historical/people.html.

Historical Poverty Tables—Footnotes

NA—Not available

1. Implementation of a new March CPS processing system.
2. Implementation of 1970 census population controls.
3. Implementation of a new March CPS processing system. Questionnaire expanded to ask eleven income questions.
4. Implementation of 1980 census population controls. Questionnaire expanded to show 27 possible values from 51 possible sources of income.
5. Implemented three technical changes to the poverty definition. See Characteristics of the Population Below the Poverty Level: 1980; Series P-60, No. 133.
6. Implementation of Hispanic population weighting controls.
7. Implementation of a new March CPS processing system.
8. CPS file for March 1992 (1991 data) was corrected after the release of the 1991 Income and Poverty reports. Weights for nine person records were omitted on the original file. (See P60-184 for further details.)
9. Implementation of 1990 census population controls.
10. Data collection method changed from paper and pencil to computer- assisted interviewing. In addition, the March 1994 income supplement was revised to allow for the coding of different income amounts on selected questionnaire items. Limits either increased or decreased in the following categories: earnings increased to $999,999; Social Security increased to $49,999; Supplemental Security Income

and Public Assistance increased to $24,999; Veterans' Benefits increased to $99,999; Child Support and Alimony decreased to $49,999.

11. Implementation of Census 2000 based population controls.

12. Implementation of Census 2000 based population controls and sample expanded by 28,000 households.

13. Beginning in 2003, CPS ASEC offered respondents the option of choosing more than one race. The 2002 and 2001 CPS ASEC recorded only one race for each respondent. The 3-year averages for 2002 are based on combining the 2003 CPS ASEC race categories shown in the stub with the relevant single race categories of White, Black, American Indian or Alaska Native, or Asian and Pacific Islander recorded in the 2002 and 2001 CPS ASEC.

14. The 2004 data have been revised to reflect a correction to the weights in the 2005 ASEC.

15. The "Outside metropolitan statistical areas" category includes both micropolitan statistical areas and territory outside of metropolitan and micropolitan statistical areas. For more information, see "About Metropolitan and Micropolitan Statistical Areas" at www.census.gov/popest/about/index.html

16. Work experience: Refers to the longest job held in the previous calendar year. The work experience categories are based on the number of weeks worked, and the number of hours worked per week. Full-time year-round: Worked at least 35 hours per week, for at least 50 weeks last year (including paid sick leave and vacations). Not full-time year-round: Worked for at least 1 week last year, but for less than 50 weeks, or less than 35 hours per week, or both.

17. Implementation of Census 2010-based population controls.

A. People of Hispanic origin may be of any race. Data for Hispanic origin not available prior to 1972.

B. Beginning in January 1978, the Bureau of Labor Statistics introduced a new price index for all urban consumers (CPI-U) that forms a continuous series with the earlier index for urban wage earners and for clerical workers as of December 1997.

C. Prior to 1979 unrelated subfamilies were included in all families. Beginning in 1979 unrelated subfamilies are excluded from all families.

Note: The 2003 Current Population Survey asked respondents to choose one or more races. White alone refers to people who reported White and did not report any other race category. The use of this single-race population does not imply that it is the preferred methods of presenting or analyzing data. The Census Bureau use variety of approaches. Information on people who reported more than one race, such as "White and American Indian and Alaska Native" or "Asian and Black or African American," is available from Census 2000 through American FactFinder. About 2.6 percent of people reported more than one race in 2000. Black alone refers to people who reported Black and did not report any other race category. Asian alone refers to people who reported Asian and did not report any other race category. Asian and/or Native Hawaiian and Other Pacific Islander refers to people who reported either or both of these categories, but did not report any other category.

Source: U.S. Census Bureau. "Table 21: Number of Poor and Poverty Rate, by State: 1980 to 2011," 2013. Accessed January 28, 2013. http://www.census.gov/hhes/www/poverty/data/historical/hstpov21.xls

B.II. POVERTY IN THE UNITED STATES, BY AGE, 1966–2011

The following table presents official U.S. government poverty data on the age distribution of the poor (i.e., what percentage and number of the poor were children, adults, or older adults) for each year from 1966 to 2011.

Table B-11   Age Distribution of the Poor: 1966 to 2011

Year	Total Poor		Children under 18		Related children under 18		People 18 to 64 Years		People 65 and Older	
	Number	Percent	Number	Percent	Number	Percent	Number	Percent	Number	Percent
2011	46,247	100.0	16,134	34.9	15,539	33.6	26,492	57.3	3,620	7.8
2010 17/	46,343	100.0	16,286	35.1	15,598	33.7	26,499	57.2	3,558	7.7
2009	43,569	100.0	15,451	35.5	14,774	33.9	24,684	56.7	3,433	7.9
2008	39,829	100.0	14,068	35.3	13,507	33.9	22,105	55.5	3,656	9.2
2007	37,276	100.0	13,324	35.7	12,802	34.3	20,396	54.7	3,556	9.5
2006	36,460	100.0	12,827	35.2	12,299	33.7	20,239	55.5	3,394	9.3
2005	36,950	100.0	12,896	34.9	12,335	33.4	20,450	55.3	3,603	9.8
2004 14/	37,040	100.0	13,041	35.2	12,473	33.7	20,545	55.5	3,453	9.3
2003	35,861	100.0	12,866	35.9	12,340	34.4	19,443	54.2	3,552	9.9
2002	34,570	100.0	12,133	35.1	11,646	33.7	18,861	54.6	3,576	10.3
2001	32,907	100.0	11,733	35.7	11,175	34.0	17,760	54.0	3,414	10.4
2000 12/	31,581	100.0	11,587	36.7	11,005	34.8	16,671	52.8	3,323	10.5
1999 11/	32,791	100.0	12,280	37.4	11,678	35.6	17,289	52.7	3,222	9.8
1998	34,476	100.0	13,467	39.1	12,845	37.3	17,623	51.1	3,386	9.8

Year										
1997	35,574	100.0	14,113	39.7	13,422	37.7	18,085	50.8	3,376	9.5
1996	36,529	100.0	14,463	39.6	13,764	37.7	18,638	51.0	3,428	9.4
1995	36,425	100.0	14,665	40.3	13,999	38.4	18,442	50.6	3,318	9.1
1994	38,059	100.0	15,289	40.2	14,610	38.4	19,107	50.2	3,663	9.6
1993 10/	39,265	100.0	15,727	40.1	14,961	38.1	19,783	50.4	3,755	9.6
1992 9/	38,014	100.0	15,294	40.2	14,521	38.2	18,793	49.4	3,928	10.3
1991 8/	35,708	100.0	14,341	40.2	13,658	38.2	17,586	49.2	3,781	10.6
1990	33,585	100.0	13,431	40.0	12,715	37.9	16,496	49.1	3,658	10.9
1989	31,528	100.0	12,590	39.9	12,001	38.1	15,575	49.4	3,363	10.7
1988	31,745	100.0	12,455	39.2	11,935	37.6	15,809	49.8	3,481	11.0
1987 7/	32,221	100.0	12,843	39.9	12,275	38.1	15,815	49.1	3,563	11.1
1986	32,370	100.0	12,876	39.8	12,257	37.9	16,017	49.5	3,477	10.7
1985	33,064	100.0	13,010	39.3	12,483	37.8	16,598	50.2	3,456	10.5
1984	33,700	100.0	13,420	39.8	12,929	38.4	16,952	50.3	3,330	9.9
1983 6/	35,303	100.0	13,911	39.4	13,427	38.0	17,767	50.3	3,625	10.3
1982	34,398	100.0	13,647	39.7	13,139	38.2	17,000	49.4	3,751	10.9
1981 5/	31,822	100.0	12,505	39.3	12,068	37.9	15,464	48.6	3,853	12.1
1980	29,272	100.0	11,543	39.4	11,114	38.0	13,858	47.3	3,871	13.2
1979 4/	26,072	100.0	10,377	39.8	9,993	38.3	12,014	46.1	3,682	14.1
1978	24,497	100.0	9,931	40.5	9,722	39.7	11,332	46.3	3,233	13.2
1977	24,720	100.0	10,288	41.6	10,028	40.6	11,316	45.8	3,177	12.9
1976	24,975	100.0	10,273	41.1	10,081	40.4	11,389	45.6	3,313	13.3

(continued)

Table B-11 (Continued)

Year	Total Poor		Children under 18		Related children under 18		People 18 to 64 Years		People 65 and Older	
	Number	Percent	Number	Percent	Number	Percent	Number	Percent	Number	Percent
1975	25,877	100.0	11,104	42.9	10,882	42.1	11,456	44.3	3,317	12.8
1974 3/	23,370	100.0	10,156	43.5	9,967	42.6	10,132	43.4	3,085	13.2
1973	22,973	100.0	9,642	42.0	9,453	41.1	9,977	43.4	3,354	14.6
1972	24,460	100.0	10,284	42.0	10,082	41.2	10,438	42.7	3,738	15.3
1971 2/	25,559	100.0	10,551	41.3	10,344	40.5	10,735	42.0	4,273	16.7
1970	25,420	100.0	10,440	41.1	10,235	40.3	10,187	40.1	4,793	18.9
1969	24,147	100.0	9,691	40.1	9,501	39.3	9,669	40.0	4,787	19.8
1968	25,389	100.0	10,954	43.1	10,739	42.3	9,803	38.6	4,632	18.2
1967 1/	27,769	100.0	11,656	42.0	11,427	41.2	10,725	38.6	5,388	19.4
1966	28,510	100.0	12,389	43.5	12,146	42.6	11,007	38.6	5,114	17.9

Note: Numbers in thousands.

Source: U.S. Bureau of the Census, Current Population Survey, Annual Social and Economic Supplements.

For information on confidentiality protection, sampling error, nonsampling error, and definitions, see http://www.census.gov/apsd/techdoc/cps/cpsmar12.pdf.

Footnotes are available at http://www.census.gov/hhes/www/poverty/histpov/footnotes.html.

Historical Poverty Tables—Footnotes

NA—Not available.

1. Implementation of a new March CPS processing system.
2. Implementation of 1970 census population controls.
3. Implementation of a new March CPS processing system. Questionnaire expanded to ask eleven income questions.

4. Implementation of 1980 census population controls. Questionnaire expanded to show 27 possible values from 51 possible sources of income.

5. Implemented three technical changes to the poverty definition. See Characteristics of the Population Below the Poverty Level: 1980; Series P-60, No. 133.

6. Implementation of Hispanic population weighting controls.

7. Implementation of a new March CPS processing system.

8. CPS file for March 1992 (1991 data) was corrected after the release of the 1991 Income and Poverty reports. Weights for nine person records were omitted on the original file. (See P60-184 for further details.)

9. Implementation of 1990 census population controls.

10. Data collection method changed from paper and pencil to computer- assisted interviewing. In addition, the March 1994 income supplement was revised to allow for the coding of different income amounts on selected questionnaire items. Limits either increased or decreased in the following categories: earnings increased to $999,999; Social Security increased to $49,999; Supplemental Security Income and Public Assistance increased to $24,999; Veterans' Benefits increased to $99,999; Child Support and Alimony decreased to $49,999.

11. Implementation of Census 2000 based population controls.

12. Implementation of Census 2000 based population controls and sample expanded by 28,000 households.

13. Beginning in 2003, CPS ASEC offered respondents the option of choosing more than one race. The 2002 and 2001 CPS ASEC recorded only one race for each respondent. The 3-year averages for 2002 are based on combining the 2003 CPS ASEC race categories shown in the stub with the relevant single race categories of White, Black, American Indian or Alaska Native, or Asian and Pacific Islander recorded in the 2002 and 2001 CPS ASEC.

14. The 2004 data have been revised to reflect a correction to the weights in the 2005 ASEC.

15. The "Outside metropolitan statistical areas" category includes both micropolitan statistical areas and territory outside of metropolitan and micropolitan statistical areas. For more information, see "About Metropolitan and Micropolitan Statistical Areas" atwww.census.gov/popest/about/index.html

16. Work experience: Refers to the longest job held in the previous calendar year. The work experience categories are based on the number of weeks worked, and the number of hours worked per week. Full-time year-round: Worked at least 35 hours per week, for at least 50 weeks last year (including paid sick leave and vacations). Not full-time year-round: Worked for at least 1 week last year, but for less than 50 weeks, or less than 35 hours per week, or both.

17. Implementation of Census 2010-based population controls.

A. People of Hispanic origin may be of any race. Data for Hispanic origin not available prior to 1972.

B. Beginning in January 1978, the Bureau of Labor Statistics introduced a new price index for all urban consumers (CPI-UI) that forms a continuous series with the earlier index for urban wage earners and for clerical workers as of December 1997.

C. Prior to 1979 unrelated subfamilies were included in all families. Beginning in 1979 unrelated subfamilies are excluded from all families.

Note: The 2003 Current Population Survey asked respondents to choose one or more races. White alone refers to people who reported White and did not report any other race category. The use of this single-race population does not imply that it is the preferred methods of presenting or analyzing data. The Census Bureau use variety of approaches. Information on people who reported more than one race, such as "White and American Indian and Alaska Native" or "Asian and Black or African American," is available from Census 2000 through American FactFinder. About 2.6 percent of people reported more than one race in 2000. Black alone refers to people who reported Black and did not report any other race category. Asian alone refers to people who reported Asian and did not report any other race category. Asian and/or Native Hawaiian and Other Pacific Islander refers to people who reported either or both of these categories, but did not report any other category.

Source: U.S. Census Bureau. "Table 15: Age Distribution of the Poor: 1966–2011," 2013. Accessed January 28, 2013. http://www.census.gov/hhes/www/poverty/data/historical/hstpov15.xls

B-12. POVERTY BY STATUS AS NATIVE, FOREIGN-BORN, AND CITIZENSHIP STATUS

The following table is official U.S. government poverty data that compare poverty data for individuals born in the United States to individuals in the United States who were not born in this country. As these data show, the poverty rate for people in the United States who were not born in this country is much higher. However, the poverty rate for foreign-born individuals who have become U.S. citizens is actually lower than the poverty rate for individuals born in the United States. As these data reveal, it is individuals who are foreign born but not U.S. citizens who have much higher rates of poverty. One reason for this is because the foreign-born non-U.S. citizen category includes the undocumented, who often have difficulty finding employment because they lack legal status to work in the United States. (See Section 3, "Immigrants," for further discussion on this topic.)

Table B-12 People in Poverty by Nativity: 1993 to 2011

| | All People | | | Native | | | Foreign Born | | | | | | | | |
| | | | | | | | Total | | | Naturalized Citizen | | | Not a Citizen | | |
Year	Total	Number below Poverty	Percentage below Poverty	Total	Number below Poverty	Percentage below Poverty	Total	Number below Poverty	Percentage below Poverty	Total	Number below Poverty	Percentage below Poverty	Total	Number below Poverty	Percentage below Poverty
2011	308,456	46,247	15.0	268,490	38,661	14.4	39,966	7,586	19.0	17,934	2,233	12.5	22,032	5,353	24.3
2010 17/	306,130	46,343	15.1	266,723	38,485	14.4	39,407	7,858	19.9	17,344	1,954	11.3	22,063	5,904	26.8
2009	303,820	43,569	14.3	266,223	36,407	13.7	37,597	7,162	19.0	16,024	1,736	10.8	21,573	5,425	25.1
2008	301,041	39,829	13.2	264,314	33,293	12.6	36,727	6,536	17.8	15,470	1,577	10.2	21,257	4,959	23.3
2007	298,699	37,276	12.5	261,456	31,126	11.9	37,243	6,150	16.5	15,050	1,426	9.5	22,193	4,724	21.3
2006	296,450	36,460	12.3	259,199	30,790	11.9	37,251	5,670	15.2	14,534	1,345	9.3	22,716	4,324	19.0
2005	293,135	36,950	12.6	257,513	31,080	12.1	35,621	5,870	16.5	13,881	1,441	10.4	21,740	4,429	20.4
2004 14/	290,617	37,040	12.7	255,443	31,023	12.1	35,173	6,017	17.1	13,505	1,326	9.8	21,669	4,691	21.6

(continued)

Table B-12 (Continued)

	All People			Native			Foreign Born								
							Total			Naturalized Citizen			Not a Citizen		
Year	Total	Number below Poverty	Percentage below Poverty	Total	Number below Poverty	Percentage below Poverty	Total	Number below Poverty	Percentage below Poverty	Total	Number below Poverty	Percentage below Poverty	Total	Number below Poverty	Percentage below Poverty
2003	287,699	35,861	12.5	253,478	29,965	11.8	34,221	5,897	17.2	13,128	1,309	10.0	21,094	4,588	21.7
2002	285,317	34,570	12.1	251,881	29,012	11.5	33,437	5,558	16.6	12,832	1,285	10.0	20,605	4,273	20.7
2001	281,475	32,907	11.7	249,053	27,698	11.1	32,422	5,209	16.1	11,962	1,186	9.9	20,460	4,023	19.7
2000 12/	278,944	31,581	11.3	247,162	26,680	10.8	31,782	4,901	15.4	11,785	1,060	9.0	19,997	3,841	19.2
1999 11/	276,208	32,791	11.9	246,256	27,757	11.3	29,952	5,034	16.8	11,065	996	9.0	18,886	4,039	21.4
1998	271,059	34,476	12.7	244,636	29,707	12.1	26,424	4,769	18.0	9,864	1,087	11.0	16,560	3,682	22.2
1997	268,480	35,574	13.3	242,219	30,336	12.5	26,261	5,238	19.9	9,732	1,111	11.4	16,529	4,127	25.0
1996	266,218	36,529	13.7	240,459	31,117	12.9	25,759	5,412	21.0	9,043	936	10.3	16,716	4,476	26.8
1995	263,733	36,425	13.8	239,206	30,972	12.9	24,527	5,452	22.2	7,904	833	10.5	16,623	4,619	27.8
1994	261,616	38,059	14.5	238,650	32,865	13.8	22,967	5,194	22.6	7,097	668	9.4	15,869	4,526	28.5
1993 10/	259,278	39,265	15.1	236,745	34,086	14.4	22,533	5,179	23.0	6,973	707	10.1	15,560	4,472	28.7

Note: Numbers in thousands.

Source: U.S. Bureau of the Census, Current Population Survey, Annual Social and Economic Supplements.

For information on confidentiality protection, sampling error, nonsampling error, and definitions, see http://www.census.gov/apsd/techdoc/cps/cpsmar12.pdf.

Footnotes are available at http://www.census.gov/hhes/www/poverty/histpov/footnotes.html.

Historical Poverty Tables—Footnotes

NA—Not available.

1. Implementation of a new March CPS processing system.
2. Implementation of 1970 census population controls.
3. Implementation of a new March CPS processing system. Questionnaire expanded to ask eleven income questions.
4. Implementation of 1980 census population controls. Questionnaire expanded to show 27 possible values from 51 possible sources of income.
5. Implemented three technical changes to the poverty definition. See Characteristics of the Population Below the Poverty Level: 1980; Series P-60, No. 133.
6. Implementation of Hispanic population weighting controls.
7. Implementation of a new March CPS processing system.
8. CPS file for March 1992 (1991 data) was corrected after the release of the 1991 Income and Poverty reports. Weights for nine person records were omitted on the original file. (See P60-184 for further details.)
9. Implementation of 1990 census population controls.
10. Data collection method changed from paper and pencil to computer- assisted interviewing. In addition, the March 1994 income supplement was revised to allow for the coding of different income amounts on selected questionnaire items. Limits either increased or decreased in the following categories: earnings increased to $999,999; Social Security increased to $49,999; Supplemental Security Income and Public Assistance increased to $24,999; Veterans' Benefits increased to $99,999; Child Support and Alimony decreased to $49,999.
11. Implementation of Census 2000 based population controls.
12. Implementation of Census 2000 based population controls and sample expanded by 28,000 households.
13. Beginning in 2003, CPS ASEC offered respondents the option of choosing more than one race. The 2002 and 2001 CPS ASEC recorded only one race for each respondent. The 3-year averages for 2002 are based on combining the 2003 CPS ASEC race categories shown in the stub with the relevant single race categories of White, Black, American Indian or Alaska Native, or Asian and Pacific Islander recorded in the 2002 and 2001 CPS ASEC.
14. The 2004 data have been revised to reflect a correction to the weights in the 2005 ASEC.
15. The "Outside metropolitan statistical areas" category includes both micropolitan statistical areas and territory outside of metropolitan and micropolitan statistical areas. For more information, see "About Metropolitan and Micropolitan Statistical Areas" atwww.census.gov/popest/about/index.html

16. Work experience: Refers to the longest job held in the previous calendar year. The work experience categories are based on the number of weeks worked, and the number of hours worked per week. Full-time year-round: Worked at least 35 hours per week, for at least 50 weeks last year (including paid sick leave and vacations). Not full-time year-round: Worked for at least 1 week last year, but for less than 50 weeks, or less than 35 hours per week, or both.

17. Implementation of Census 2010-based population controls.

A. People of Hispanic origin may be of any race. Data for Hispanic origin not available prior to 1972.

B. Beginning in January 1978, the Bureau of Labor Statistics introduced a new price index for all urban consumers (CPI-U) that forms a continuous series with the earlier index for urban wage earners and for clerical workers as of December 1997.

C. Prior to 1979 unrelated subfamilies were included in all families. Beginning in 1979 unrelated subfamilies are excluded from all families.

Note: The 2003 Current Population Survey asked respondents to choose one or more races. White alone refers to people who reported White and did not report any other race category. The use of this single-race population does not imply that it is the preferred methods of presenting or analyzing data. The Census Bureau use variety of approaches. Information on people who reported more than one race, such as "White and American Indian and Alaska Native" or "Asian and Black or African American," is available from Census 2000 through American FactFinder. About 2.6 percent of people reported more than one race in 2000. Black alone refers to people who reported Black and did not report any other race category. Asian alone refers to people who reported Asian and did not report any other race category. Asian and/or Native Hawaiian and Other Pacific Islander refers to people who reported either or both of these categories, but did not report any other category.

Source: U.S. Census Bureau. "Table 23: People in Poverty by Nativity: 1993 to 2011," 2013. Accessed January 28, 2013. http://www.census.gov/hhes/www/poverty/data/historical/hstpov23.xls

U.S. POVERTY DATA, 2006–2010

The American Community Survey (ACS) is an ongoing survey conducted by the U.S. Census Bureau on an annual basis to provide more current and in-depth information than the census that is conducted only every 10 years. The ACS utilizes the same official government poverty thresholds as the Current Population Survey (see B-1 to B-7).

Documents B-13 to B-20 provide poverty data for the ACS for years 2006 to 2010. The information on poverty in the United States contained in these documents is slightly different from that presented in the historic poverty tables in B-8 to B-12 because they are based on different surveys. The information from the ACS is not the official government data on poverty, but nonetheless it provides additional insight into poverty during the Great Recession.

B-13. POVERTY DATA, 2006

B-13 shows ACS poverty data for the year 2006. The ACS reports a poverty level estimate of 13.3 percent that year, higher than the official 2006 poverty rate of 12.3 percent. The ethnic group with the highest ACS poverty rate was American Indians and Alaska Natives with a poverty rate of 26.6 percent. The poverty rate for non-Hispanic whites at 9.3 percent was the lowest; this was a slightly higher rate than the 8.2 percent reported as the official rate for 2006, although ACS data for all races was slightly higher than the official poverty rates. The ACS also reports on poverty status based on educational attainment for those 25 or older. As B-13 shows, the highest rate of poverty was for those with less than a high school degree.

POVERTY STATUS IN THE PAST 12 MONTHS

2006 American Community Survey.

Table B-13

	United States				
	Total		**Below Poverty Level**		**Percent below Poverty Level**
Subject	**Estimate**	**Margin of Error**	**Estimate**	**Margin of Error**	**Estimate**
150 percent of poverty level	64,644,208	+/–302,381	(X)	(X)	(X)
185 percent of poverty level	82,671,368	+/–320,627	(X)	(X)	(X)

(continued)

Table B-13 (Continued)

	United States				
	Total		**Below Poverty Level**		**Percent below Poverty Level**
Subject	**Estimate**	**Margin of Error**	**Estimate**	**Margin of Error**	**Estimate**
200 percent of poverty level	91,091,199	+/–322,178	(X)	(X)	(X)
Unrelated individuals for whom poverty status is determined	52,994,679	+/–163,505	12,915,675	+/–92,786	24.4%
Male	26,047,553	+/–121,418	5,602,125	+/–57,505	21.5%
Female	26,947,126	+/–74,670	7,313,550	+/–54,013	27.1%
Mean income deficit for unrelated individuals (dollars)	5,523	+/–19	(X)	(X)	(X)
Worked full-time, year-round in the past 12 months	21,695,182	+/–101,638	611,893	+/–15,689	2.8%
Worked less than full-time, year-round in the past 12 months	14,509,870	+/–73,655	5,092,117	+/–52,424	35.1%
Did not work	16,789,627	+/–57,171	7,211,665	+/–54,089	43.0%
PERCENT IMPUTED					
Poverty status for individuals	22.9%	(X)	(X)	(X)	(X)
Population for whom poverty status is determined	291,531,091	+/–25,464	38,757,253	+/–222,238	13.3%
AGE					
Under 18 years	72,482,732	+/–32,656	13,285,569	+/–114,619	18.3%
Related children under 18 years	72,065,732	+/–35,537	12,911,393	+/–114,424	17.9%

Table B-13 (Continued)

Subject	United States				
	Total		Below Poverty Level		Percent below Poverty Level
	Estimate	Margin of Error	Estimate	Margin of Error	Estimate
18 to 64 years	183,477,899	+/–23,413	21,955,093	+/–118,620	12.0%
65 years and over	35,570,460	+/–18,433	3,516,591	+/–25,952	9.9%
SEX					
Male	142,920,792	+/–31,180	16,963,560	+/–118,968	11.9%
Female	148,610,299	+/–28,370	21,793,693	+/–120,471	14.7%
RACE AND HISPANIC OR LATINO ORIGIN					
One race	285,639,455	+/–69,134	37,764,789	+/–223,131	13.2%
White	216,049,704	+/–121,896	22,657,417	+/–166,799	10.5%
Black or African American	35,425,212	+/–41,926	8,968,940	+/–76,397	25.3%
American Indian and Alaska Native	2,280,282	+/–26,072	606,730	+/–19,149	26.6%
Asian	12,880,165	+/–29,281	1,381,226	+/–37,045	10.7%
Native Hawaiian and Other Pacific Islander	415,163	+/–10,310	66,773	+/–7,441	16.1%
Some other race	18,588,929	+/–111,000	4,083,703	+/–64,879	22.0%
Two or more races	5,891,636	+/–63,678	992,464	+/–26,674	16.8%
Hispanic or Latino origin (of any race)	43,306,059	+/–17,762	9,293,416	+/–89,610	21.5%
White alone, not Hispanic or Latino	193,336,042	+/–39,961	17,890,083	+/–138,143	9.3%
EDUCATIONAL ATTAINMENT					
Population 25 years and over	192,247,428	+/–67,154	19,688,040	+/–89,238	10.2%
Less than high school graduate	29,819,730	+/–95,235	7,068,744	+/–53,493	23.7%

(*continued*)

Subject	United States				
	Total		Below Poverty Level		Percent below Poverty Level
	Estimate	Margin of Error	Estimate	Margin of Error	Estimate
High school graduate (includes equivalency)	57,751,630	+/–119,107	6,641,518	+/–53,292	11.5%
Some college, associate's degree	52,060,850	+/–129,959	4,035,084	+/–32,430	7.8%
Bachelor's degree or higher	52,615,218	+/–146,952	1,942,694	+/–22,091	3.7%
EMPLOYMENT STATUS					
Civilian labor force 16 years and over	150,184,796	+/–115,161	11,478,225	+/–74,669	7.6%
Employed	140,627,110	+/–123,365	8,733,238	+/–60,748	6.2%
Male	75,301,768	+/–72,287	3,963,299	+/–38,695	5.3%
Female	65,325,342	+/–92,437	4,769,939	+/–42,726	7.3%
Unemployed	9,557,686	+/–51,495	2,744,987	+/–30,520	28.7%
Male	5,013,286	+/–36,957	1,268,794	+/–21,441	25.3%
Female	4,544,400	+/–36,561	1,476,193	+/–21,176	32.5%
WORK EXPERIENCE					
Population 16 years and over	227,547,350	+/–40,979	26,813,060	+/–133,332	11.8%
Worked full-time, year-round in the past 12 months	93,557,011	+/–104,066	2,317,886	+/–26,418	2.5%
Worked part-time or part-year in the past 12 months	65,679,627	+/–145,799	9,950,481	+/–72,744	15.2%
Did not work	68,310,712	+/–120,160	14,544,693	+/–81,514	21.3%

Table B-13 (Continued)

	United States				
	Total		Below Poverty Level		Percent below Poverty Level
Subject	**Estimate**	**Margin of Error**	**Estimate**	**Margin of Error**	**Estimate**
All Individuals below:					
50 percent of poverty level	16,752,909	+/–139,963	(X)	(X)	(X)
125 percent of poverty level	51,375,624	+/–263,549	(X)	(X)	(X)

	United States
	Percent Below Poverty Level
Subject	**Margin of Error**
Population for whom poverty status is determined	+/–0.1
AGE	
Under 18 years	+/–0.2
Related children under 18 years	+/–0.2
18 to 64 years	+/–0.1
65 years and over	+/–0.1
SEX	
Male	+/–0.1
Female	+/–0.1
RACE AND HISPANIC OR LATINO ORIGIN	
One race	+/–0.1
White	+/–0.1
Black or African American	+/–0.2
American Indian and Alaska Native	+/–0.8
Asian	+/–0.3
Native Hawaiian and Other Pacific Islander	+/–1.7

(continued)

Table B-13 (Continued)

Subject	United States Percent Below Poverty Level Margin of Error
Some other race	+/–0.3
Two or more races	+/–0.4
Hispanic or Latino origin (of any race)	+/–0.2
White alone, not Hispanic or Latino	+/–0.1
EDUCATIONAL ATTAINMENT	
Population 25 years and over	+/–0.1
Less than high school graduate	+/–0.2
High school graduate (includes equivalency)	+/–0.1
Some college, associate's degree	+/–0.1
Bachelor's degree or higher	+/–0.1
EMPLOYMENT STATUS	
Civilian labor force 16 years and over	+/–0.1
Employed	+/–0.1
Male	+/–0.1
Female	+/–0.1
Unemployed	+/–0.3
Male	+/–0.4
Female	+/–0.4
WORK EXPERIENCE	
Population 16 years and over	+/–0.1
Worked full-time, year-round in the past 12 months	+/–0.1
Worked part-time or part-year in the past 12 months	+/–0.1
Did not work	+/–0.1
All Individuals below:	
50 percent of poverty level	(X)
125 percent of poverty level	(X)
150 percent of poverty level	(X)

Table B-13   (Continued)

Subject	United States Percent Below Poverty Level Margin of Error
185 percent of poverty level	(X)
200 percent of poverty level	(X)
Unrelated individuals for whom poverty status is determined	+/–0.1
Male	+/–0.2
Female	+/–0.2
Mean income deficit for unrelated individuals (dollars)	(X)
Worked full-time, year-round in the past 12 months	+/–0.1
Worked less than full-time, year-round in the past 12 months	+/–0.3
Did not work	+/–0.2
PERCENT IMPUTED	
Poverty status for individuals	(X)

Data are based on a sample and are subject to sampling variability. The degree of uncertainty for an estimate arising from sampling variability is represented through the use of a margin of error. The value shown here is the 90 percent margin of error. The margin of error can be interpreted roughly as providing a 90 percent probability that the interval defined by the estimate minus the margin of error and the estimate plus the margin of error (the lower and upper confidence bounds) contains the true value. In addition to sampling variability, the ACS estimates are subject to nonsampling error (for a discussion of nonsampling variability, see Accuracy of the Data). The effect of nonsampling error is not represented in these tables.

Notes:

While the 2006 American Community Survey (ACS) data generally reflect the December 2005 Office of Management and Budget (OMB) definitions of metropolitan and micropolitan statistical areas, in certain instances the names, codes, and boundaries of the principal cities shown in ACS tables may differ from the OMB definitions due to differences in the effective dates of the geographic entities.

Explanation of Symbols:

1. An '**' entry in the margin of error column indicates that either no sample observations or too few sample observations were available to compute a standard error and thus the margin of error. A statistical test is not appropriate.

2. An '-' entry in the estimate column indicates that either no sample observations or too few sample observations were available to compute an estimate, or a ratio of medians cannot be calculated because one or both of the median estimates falls in the lowest interval or upper interval of an open-ended distribution.
3. An '-' following a median estimate means the median falls in the lowest interval of an open-ended distribution.
4. An '+' following a median estimate means the median falls in the upper interval of an open-ended distribution.
5. An '***' entry in the margin of error column indicates that the median falls in the lowest interval or upper interval of an open-ended distribution. A statistical test is not appropriate.
6. An '*****' entry in the margin of error column indicates that the estimate is controlled. A statistical test for sampling variability is not appropriate.
7. An 'N' entry in the estimate and margin of error columns indicates that data for this geographic area cannot be displayed because the number of sample cases is too small.
8. An '(X)' means that the estimate is not applicable or not available.

Source: U.S. Census Bureau. 2012. S1701. "Poverty Status in the Past 12 Months 2006 American Community Survey," Accessed July 3. http://factfinder2.census.gov/faces/tableservices/jsf/pages/productview.xhtml?pid=ACS_06_EST_S1701&prodType=table

B-14. U.S. POVERTY DATA, 2007

The 2007 ACS estimated a poverty rate of 13.0 percent, half a percent higher than the 12.5 percent official poverty rate for that year but lower than the ACS poverty rate of 13.3 percent in 2006. Between 2006 and 2007 the ACS actually reported a decrease in poverty rates across all demographic groups with the exception of year-round full-time workers, for whom the poverty rate held steady at 2.6 percent. This was in contrast to the official data in which increased rates of poverty were reported for whites, blacks, and Hispanics, as well as for children and various other demographic groups.

POVERTY STATUS IN THE PAST 12 MONTHS

2007 American Community Survey 1-Year Estimates. For information on confidentiality protection, sampling error, nonsampling error, and definitions, see Survey Methodology.

Table B-14

Subject	United States Total Estimate	Margin of Error	Below Poverty Level Estimate	Margin of Error	Percent below Poverty Level Estimate
150 percent of poverty level	63,834,717	+/–304,542	(X)	(X)	(X)
185 percent of poverty level	81,815,413	+/–336,493	(X)	(X)	(X)
200 percent of poverty level	90,134,363	+/–352,913	(X)	(X)	(X)
Unrelated individuals for whom poverty status is determined	53,540,968	+/–168,168	12,647,697	+/–84,813	23.6%
Male	26,321,201	+/–120,847	5,454,990	+/–54,978	20.7%
Female	27,219,767	+/–86,561	7,192,707	+/–55,203	26.4%
Mean income deficit for unrelated individuals (dollars)	5,691	+/–18	(X)	(X)	(X)
Worked full-time, year-round in the past 12 months	22,072,747	+/–112,330	575,572	+/–16,735	2.6%
Worked less than full-time, year-round in the past 12 months	14,578,662	+/–75,560	4,933,190	+/–52,971	33.8%
Did not work	16,889,559	+/–60,900	7,138,935	+/–53,857	42.3%
PERCENT IMPUTED					
Poverty status for individuals	23.7%	(X)	(X)	(X)	(X)
Population for whom poverty status is determined	293,744,043	+/–22,700	38,052,247	+/–222,964	13.0%

(*continued*)

Table B-14 (Continued)

Subject	United States				
	Total		Below Poverty Level		Percent below Poverty Level
	Estimate	Margin of Error	Estimate	Margin of Error	Estimate
AGE					
Under 18 years	72,665,911	+/–36,535	13,097,100		+/–115,927
18.0%					
Related children under 18 years	72,252,912	+/–39,200	12,728,964		+/–115,580
17.6%					
18 to 64 years	184,811,647	+/–27,214	21,495,507	+/–114,347	11.6%
65 years and over	36,266,485	+/–18,721	3,459,640	+/–28,269	9.5%
SEX					
Male	144,067,459	+/–31,215	16,576,071	+/–114,864	11.5%
Female	149,676,584	+/–29,327	21,476,176	+/–128,477	14.3%
RACE AND HISPANIC OR LATINO ORIGIN					
One race	287,461,047	+/–69,229	36,998,633	+/–222,763	12.9%
White	217,750,961	+/–106,545	22,283,845	+/–165,925	10.2%
Black or African American	35,680,634	+/–47,848	8,806,842	+/–76,729	24.7%
American Indian and Alaska Native	2,277,716	+/–25,405	576,041	+/–19,468	25.3%
Asian	12,999,694	+/–32,438	1,376,079	+/–34,819	10.6%
Native Hawaiian and Other Pacific Islander	422,191	+/–10,337	66,164	+/–6,585	15.7%
Some other race	18,329,851	+/–116,272	3,889,662	+/–62,889	21.2%
Two or more races	6,282,996	+/–64,252	1,053,614	+/–23,430	16.8%
Hispanic or Latino origin (of any race)	44,470,740	+/–19,426	9,219,100	+/–88,948	20.7%
White alone, not Hispanic or Latino	193,758,737	+/–31,459	17,403,517	+/–141,965	9.0%

| Subject | United States | | | | |
| | Total | | Below Poverty Level | | Percent below Poverty Level |
	Estimate	Margin of Error	Estimate	Margin of Error	Estimate
EDUCATIONAL ATTAINMENT					
Population 25 years and over	194,194,848	+/−68,721	19,285,117	+/−94,152	9.9%
Less than high school graduate	29,301,933	+/−97,953	6,815,218	+/−53,134	23.3%
High school graduate (includes equivalency)	58,253,936	+/−130,931	6,588,614	+/−45,367	11.3%
Some college, associate's degree	52,580,049	+/−125,361	3,990,840	+/−41,226	7.6%
Bachelor's degree or higher	54,058,930	+/−144,490	1,890,445	+/−25,683	3.5%
EMPLOYMENT STATUS					
Civilian labor force 16 years and over	151,275,691	+/−112,739	11,104,708	+/−76,615	7.3%
Employed	141,777,129	+/−109,552	8,468,565	+/−70,663	6.0%
Male	75,806,453	+/−73,960	3,818,556	+/−44,104	5.0%
Female	65,970,676	+/−77,770	4,650,009	+/−40,259	7.0%
Unemployed	9,498,562	+/−48,842	2,636,143	+/−27,220	27.8%
Male	5,100,404	+/−35,300	1,235,682	+/−19,837	24.2%
Female	4,398,158	+/−32,919	1,400,461	+/−22,336	31.8%
WORK EXPERIENCE					
Population 16 years and over	229,670,168	+/−47,495	26,303,799	+/−129,650	11.5%
Worked full-time, year-round in the past 12 months	94,428,260	+/−107,815	2,274,743	+/−28,462	2.4%

(*continued*)

Table B-14 (Continued)

| | United States | | | | |
| Subject | Total | | Below Poverty Level | | Percent below Poverty Level |
	Estimate	Margin of Error	Estimate	Margin of Error	Estimate
Worked part-time or part-year in the past 12 months	66,188,737	+/–150,089	9,645,187	+/–63,901	14.6%
Did not work	69,053,171	+/–117,992	14,383,869	+/–86,378	20.8%
All Individuals below:					
50 percent of poverty level	16,375,097	+/–125,339	(X)	(X)	(X)
125 percent of poverty level	50,863,681	+/–272,095	(X)	(X)	(X)

| | United States |
| | Percent below poverty level |
Subject	Margin of Error
Population for whom poverty status is determined	+/–0.1
AGE	
Under 18 years	+/–0.2
Related children under 18 years	+/–0.2
18 to 64 years	+/–0.1
65 years and over	+/–0.1
SEX	
Male	+/–0.1
Female	+/–0.1
RACE AND HISPANIC OR LATINO ORIGIN	
One race	+/–0.1
White	+/–0.1
Black or African American	+/–0.2
American Indian and Alaska Native	+/–0.8

Table B-14 (Continued)

Subject	United States Percent below poverty level Margin of Error
Asian	+/–0.3
Native Hawaiian and Other Pacific Islander	+/–1.5
Some other race	+/–0.3
Two or more races	+/–0.4
Hispanic or Latino origin (of any race)	+/–0.2
White alone, not Hispanic or Latino	+/–0.1
EDUCATIONAL ATTAINMENT	
Population 25 years and over	+/–0.1
Less than high school graduate	+/–0.2
High school graduate (includes equivalency)	+/–0.1
Some college, associate's degree	+/–0.1
Bachelor's degree or higher	+/–0.1
EMPLOYMENT STATUS	
Civilian labor force 16 years and over	+/–0.1
Employed	+/–0.1
Male	+/–0.1
Female	+/–0.1
Unemployed	+/–0.3
Male	+/–0.4
Female	+/–0.4
WORK EXPERIENCE	
Population 16 years and over	+/–0.1
Worked full-time, year-round in the past 12 months	+/–0.1
Worked part-time or part-year in the past 12 months	+/–0.1
Did not work	+/–0.1
All Individuals below:	
50 percent of poverty level	(X)
125 percent of poverty level	(X)

(*continued*)

Table B-14 (Continued)

Subject	United States Percent below poverty level Margin of Error
150 percent of poverty level	(X)
185 percent of poverty level	(X)
200 percent of poverty level	(X)
Unrelated individuals for whom poverty status is determined	+/–0.1
Male	+/–0.2
Female	+/–0.2
Mean income deficit for unrelated individuals (dollars)	(X)
Worked full-time, year-round in the past 12 months	+/–0.1
Worked less than full-time, year-round in the past 12 months	+/–0.3
Did not work	+/–0.2
PERCENT IMPUTED	
Poverty status for individuals	(X)

Data are based on a sample and are subject to sampling variability. The degree of uncertainty for an estimate arising from sampling variability is represented through the use of a margin of error. The value shown here is the 90 percent margin of error. The margin of error can be interpreted roughly as providing a 90 percent probability that the interval defined by the estimate minus the margin of error and the estimate plus the margin of error (the lower and upper confidence bounds) contains the true value. In addition to sampling variability, the ACS estimates are subject to nonsampling error (for a discussion of nonsampling variability, see Accuracy of the Data). The effect of nonsampling error is not represented in these tables.

Notes:

While the 2008 American Community Survey (ACS) data generally reflect the November 2007 Office of Management and Budget (OMB) definitions of metropolitan and micropolitan statistical areas; in certain instances the names, codes, and boundaries of the principal cities shown in ACS tables may differ from the OMB definitions due to differences in the effective dates of the geographic entities. The 2008 Puerto Rico Community Survey (PRCS) data generally reflect the November 2007 Office of Management and Budget (OMB) definitions of metropolitan and micropolitan statistical areas; in certain instances the names, codes, and boundaries of the principal cities shown in PRCS tables may differ from the OMB definitions due to differences in the effective dates of the geographic entities.

Estimates of urban and rural population, housing units, and characteristics reflect boundaries of urban areas defined based on Census 2000 data. Boundaries for urban areas have not been updated since Census 2000. As a result, data for urban and rural areas from the ACS do not necessarily reflect the results of ongoing urbanization.

Explanation of Symbols:

1. An '**' entry in the margin of error column indicates that either no sample observations or too few sample observations were available to compute a standard error and thus the margin of error. A statistical test is not appropriate.
2. An '-' entry in the estimate column indicates that either no sample observations or too few sample observations were available to compute an estimate, or a ratio of medians cannot be calculated because one or both of the median estimates falls in the lowest interval or upper interval of an open-ended distribution.
3. An '-' following a median estimate means the median falls in the lowest interval of an open-ended distribution.
4. An '+' following a median estimate means the median falls in the upper interval of an open-ended distribution.
5. An '***' entry in the margin of error column indicates that the median falls in the lowest interval or upper interval of an open-ended distribution. A statistical test is not appropriate.
6. An '*****' entry in the margin of error column indicates that the estimate is controlled. A statistical test for sampling variability is not appropriate.
7. An 'N' entry in the estimate and margin of error columns indicates that data for this geographic area cannot be displayed because the number of sample cases is too small.
8. An '(X)' means that the estimate is not applicable or not available. Selected migration, earnings, and income data are not available for certain geographic areas due to problems with group quarters data collection and imputation. See Errata Note #44 for details.

Source: U.S. Census Bureau. "Poverty Status in the Past 12 Months: 2007 American Community Survey 1-Year Estimates," 2012. Accessed July 3, 2012. http://factfinder2.census.gov/faces/tableservices/jsf/pages/productview.xhtml?pid=ACS_07_1YR_S1701&prodType=table

B-15. U.S. POVERTY DATA, 2008

In 2008 the ACS poverty rate estimate was 13.2 percent, an increase over the 13.0 percent ACS estimate for 2007. The 2008 ACS poverty rate of 13.2 percent matched official government estimates of the poverty rate for that year. The ACS reported increased poverty between 2007 and 2008 for all demographic groups reported on except American Indians/Alaska Natives and Asians, for whom the poverty rates decreased slightly, and those of two or more races for which the poverty rate held steady.

POVERTY STATUS IN THE PAST 12 MONTHS

2008 American Community Survey 1-Year Estimates.   For information on confidentiality protection, sampling error, nonsampling error, and definitions, see Survey Methodology

Table B-15

	United States				
	Total		Below Poverty Level		Percent below Poverty Level
Subject	Estimate	Margin of Error	Estimate	Margin of Error	Estimate
150 percent of poverty level	65,339,471	+/–330,682	(X)	(X)	(X)
185 percent of poverty level	83,952,422	+/–353,538	(X)	(X)	(X)
200 percent of poverty level	91,575,702	+/–367,037	(X)	(X)	(X)
Unrelated individuals for whom poverty status is determined	54,574,547	+/–157,680	13,203,946	+/–92,379	24.2%
Male	26,784,725	+/–114,250	5,746,742	+/–61,179	21.5%
Female	27,789,822	+/–85,422	7,457,204	+/–57,050	26.8%
Mean income deficit for unrelated individuals (dollars)	5,944	+/–20	(X)	(X)	(X)
Worked full-time, year-round in the past 12 months	24,344,735	+/–94,353	761,070	+/–16,865	3.1%
Worked less than full-time, year-round in the past 12 months	12,930,496	+/–84,690	4,915,047	+/–55,819	38.0%
Did not work	17,299,316	+/–71,252	7,527,829	+/–61,323	43.5%
PERCENT IMPUTED					
Poverty status for individuals	25.4%	(X)	(X)	(X)	(X)

Table B-15   (Continued)

	United States				
	Total		**Below Poverty Level**		**Percent below Poverty Level**
Subject	**Estimate**	**Margin of Error**	**Estimate**	**Margin of Error**	**Estimate**
Population for whom poverty status is determined	296,184,480	+/–22,192	39,108,422	+/–249,680	13.2%
AGE					
Under 18 years	72,825,003	+/–36,649	13,240,870	+/–125,574	18.2%
Related children under 18 years	72,466,321	+/–39,846	12,919,224	+/–124,903	17.8%
18 to 64 years	186,150,363	+/–30,519	22,174,945	+/–137,161	11.9%
65 years and over	37,209,114	+/–21,307	3,692,607	+/–36,267	9.9%
SEX					
Male	145,300,225	+/–42,387	17,208,986	+/–124,413	11.8%
Female	150,884,255	+/–41,175	21,899,436	+/–141,614	14.5%
RACE AND HISPANIC OR LATINO ORIGIN					
One race	289,400,869	+/–72,949	37,968,515	+/–251,341	13.1%
White	222,850,967	+/–115,641	23,934,719	+/–165,064	10.7%
Black or African American	35,953,688	+/–52,372	8,661,570	+/–84,601	24.1%
American Indian and Alaska Native	2,356,310	+/–30,152	571,104	+/–20,405	24.2%
Asian	13,157,057	+/–29,260	1,384,151	+/–31,920	10.5%
Native Hawaiian and Other Pacific Islander	414,600	+/–10,377	67,605	+/–7,925	16.3%
Some other race	14,668,247	+/–110,441	3,349,366	+/–68,393	22.8%
Two or more races	6,783,611	+/–71,221	1,139,907	+/–28,173	16.8%
Hispanic or Latino origin (of any race)	45,930,650	+/–19,147	9,794,706	+/–103,479	21.3%

(*continued*)

Table B-15 (Continued)

Subject	United States				
	Total		Below Poverty Level		Percent below Poverty Level
	Estimate	Margin of Error	Estimate	Margin of Error	Estimate
White alone, not Hispanic or Latino	194,150,206	+/–35,203	18,027,678	+/–136,340	9.3%
EDUCATIONAL ATTAINMENT					
Population 25 years and over	196,232,110	+/–75,795	19,991,621	+/–104,617	10.2%
Less than high school graduate	28,725,304	+/–116,826	6,863,727	+/–60,146	23.9%
High school graduate (includes equivalency)	55,551,202	+/–109,152	6,421,875	+/–53,265	11.6%
Some college, associate's degree	56,915,004	+/–121,690	4,625,461	+/–38,620	8.1%
Bachelor's degree or higher	55,040,600	+/–165,361	2,080,558	+/–30,946	3.8%
EMPLOYMENT STATUS					
Civilian labor force 16 years and over	155,286,543	+/–128,999	11,823,537	+/–84,351	7.6%
Employed	145,468,862	+/–138,564	9,040,908	+/–67,290	6.2%
Male	77,066,478	+/–91,221	4,105,599	+/–39,063	5.3%
Female	68,402,384	+/–82,108	4,935,309	+/–41,082	7.2%
Unemployed	9,817,681	+/–53,735	2,782,629	+/–32,208	28.3%
Male	5,361,475	+/–39,161	1,339,621	+/–19,053	25.0%
Female	4,456,206	+/–36,107	1,443,008	+/–22,257	32.4%
WORK EXPERIENCE					
Population 16 years and over	231,878,144	+/–38,862	27,186,280	+/–155,870	11.7%

Table B-15 (Continued)

	United States				
	Total		**Below Poverty Level**		**Percent below Poverty Level**
Subject	**Estimate**	**Margin of Error**	**Estimate**	**Margin of Error**	**Estimate**
Worked full-time, year-round in the past 12 months	103,627,775	+/–113,982	2,761,135	+/–34,005	2.7%
Worked part-time or part-year in the past 12 months	58,118,244	+/–128,659	9,388,400	+/–70,876	16.2%
Did not work	70,132,125	+/–128,663	15,036,745	+/–101,085	21.4%
All Individuals below:					
50 percent of poverty level	16,634,799	+/–149,481	(X)	(X)	(X)
125 percent of poverty level	51,988,325	+/–288,015	(X)	(X)	(X)

	United States
	Percent below Poverty Level
Subject	**Margin of Error**
Population for whom poverty status is determined	+/–0.1
AGE	
Under 18 years	+/–0.2
Related children under 18 years	+/–0.2
18 to 64 years	+/–0.1
65 years and over	+/–0.1
SEX	
Male	+/–0.1
Female	+/–0.1
RACE AND HISPANIC OR LATINO ORIGIN	
One race	+/–0.1
White	+/–0.1

(*continued*)

Subject	United States Percent below Poverty Level Margin of Error
Black or African American	+/–0.2
American Indian and Alaska Native	+/–0.8
Asian	+/–0.2
Native Hawaiian and Other Pacific Islander	+/–1.8
Some other race	+/–0.4
Two or more races	+/–0.4
Hispanic or Latino origin (of any race)	+/–0.2
White alone, not Hispanic or Latino	+/–0.1
EDUCATIONAL ATTAINMENT	
Population 25 years and over	+/–0.1
Less than high school graduate	+/–0.2
High school graduate (includes equivalency)	+/–0.1
Some college, associate's degree	+/–0.1
Bachelor's degree or higher	+/–0.1
EMPLOYMENT STATUS	
Civilian labor force 16 years and over	+/–0.1
Employed	+/–0.1
Male	+/–0.1
Female	+/–0.1
Unemployed	+/–0.3
Male	+/–0.3
Female	+/–0.4
WORK EXPERIENCE	
Population 16 years and over	+/–0.1
Worked full-time, year-round in the past 12 months	+/–0.1
Worked part-time or part-year in the past 12 months	+/–0.1
Did not work	+/–0.1
All Individuals below:	
50 percent of poverty level	(X)

Table B-15   (Continued)

Subject	United States Percent below Poverty Level Margin of Error
125 percent of poverty level	(X)
150 percent of poverty level	(X)
185 percent of poverty level	(X)
200 percent of poverty level	(X)
Unrelated individuals for whom poverty status is determined	+/–0.1
Male	+/–0.2
Female	+/–0.2
Mean income deficit for unrelated individuals (dollars)	(X)
Worked full-time, year-round in the past 12 months	+/–0.1
Worked less than full-time, year-round in the past 12 months	+/–0.3
Did not work	+/–0.2
PERCENT IMPUTED	
Poverty status for individuals	(X)

Data are based on a sample and are subject to sampling variability. The degree of uncertainty for an estimate arising from sampling variability is represented through the use of a margin of error. The value shown here is the 90 percent margin of error. The margin of error can be interpreted roughly as providing a 90 percent probability that the interval defined by the estimate minus the margin of error and the estimate plus the margin of error (the lower and upper confidence bounds) contains the true value. In addition to sampling variability, the ACS estimates are subject to nonsampling error (for a discussion of nonsampling variability, see Accuracy of the Data). The effect of nonsampling error is not represented in these tables.

Notes:

While the 2008 American Community Survey (ACS) data generally reflect the November 2007 Office of Management and Budget (OMB) definitions of metropolitan and micropolitan statistical areas; in certain instances the names, codes, and boundaries of the principal cities shown in ACS tables may differ from the OMB definitions due to differences in the effective dates of the geographic entities. The 2008 Puerto Rico Community Survey (PRCS) data generally reflect the November 2007 Office of Management and Budget (OMB) definitions of metropolitan and micropolitan statistical areas; in certain instances the names, codes, and boundaries of the principal cities shown in PRCS tables may differ from the OMB definitions due to differences in the effective dates of the geographic entities.

Estimates of urban and rural population, housing units, and characteristics reflect boundaries of urban areas defined based on Census 2000 data. Boundaries for urban areas have not been updated since Census 2000. As a result, data for urban and rural areas from the ACS do not necessarily reflect the results of ongoing urbanization.

Explanation of Symbols:

1. An '**' entry in the margin of error column indicates that either no sample observations or too few sample observations were available to compute a standard error and thus the margin of error. A statistical test is not appropriate.

2. An '-' entry in the estimate column indicates that either no sample observations or too few sample observations were available to compute an estimate, or a ratio of medians cannot be calculated because one or both of the median estimates falls in the lowest interval or upper interval of an open-ended distribution.

3. An '-' following a median estimate means the median falls in the lowest interval of an open-ended distribution.

4. An '+' following a median estimate means the median falls in the upper interval of an open-ended distribution.

5. An '***' entry in the margin of error column indicates that the median falls in the lowest interval or upper interval of an open-ended distribution. A statistical test is not appropriate.

6. An '*****' entry in the margin of error column indicates that the estimate is controlled. A statistical test for sampling variability is not appropriate.

7. An 'N' entry in the estimate and margin of error columns indicates that data for this geographic area cannot be displayed because the number of sample cases is too small.

8. An '(X)' means that the estimate is not applicable or not available.

Source: U.S. Census Bureau. "Poverty Status in the Past 12 Months: 2008 American Community Survey 1-Year Estimates," 2012. Accessed July 3, 2012. http://factfinder2 .census.gov/faces/tableservices/jsf/pages/productview.xhtml?pid=ACS_08_1YR_S1701&prod Type=table

B-16. U.S. POVERTY DATA, 2009

The ACS estimated poverty rate in 2009 was 14.3 percent, more than a 1 percentage point increase from the 13.2 percent ACS poverty rate in 2008. The 14.3 percent estimate from the ACS matched the official poverty rate for that year, as it did in 2007. The 2009 ACS reported increased poverty for most demographic groups reported. The exceptions were for those 65 years and older, Native Hawaiians/Other Pacific Islanders, and the unemployed (for whom poverty rates decreased) and those who worked full-time year-round (for whom the poverty rate remained steady).

POVERTY STATUS IN THE PAST 12 MONTHS

2009 American Community Survey 1-Year Estimates. For information on confidentiality protection, sampling error, nonsampling error, and definitions, see Survey Methodology

Table B-16

| | United States | | | | |
| | Total | | Below Poverty Level | | Percent below Poverty Level |
Subject	**Estimate**	**Margin of Error**	**Estimate**	**Margin of Error**	**Estimate**
150 percent of poverty level	70,462,042	+/–316,458	(X)	(X)	(X)
185 percent of poverty level	89,952,657	+/–347,411	(X)	(X)	(X)
200 percent of poverty level	97,820,000	+/–359,296	(X)	(X)	(X)
Unrelated individuals for whom poverty status is determined	55,162,150	+/–145,500	14,008,577	+/–91,599	25.4%
Male	27,103,757	+/–111,208	6,327,260	+/–62,104	23.3%
Female	28,058,393	+/–79,349	7,681,317	+/–56,025	27.4%
Mean income deficit for unrelated individuals (dollars)	6,109	+/–20	(X)	(X)	(X)
Worked full-time, year-round in the past 12 months	23,074,552	+/–92,422	722,262	+/–17,979	3.1%
Worked less than full-time, year-round in the past 12 months	13,925,902	+/–84,397	5,277,347	+/–50,516	37.9%
Did not work	18,161,696	+/–74,259	8,008,968	+/–55,156	44.1%

(continued)

Table B-16 (Continued)

Subject	United States				
	Total		**Below Poverty Level**		**Percent below Poverty Level**
	Estimate	Margin of Error	Estimate	Margin of Error	Estimate
PERCENT IMPUTED					
Poverty status for individuals	23.2%	(X)	(X)	(X)	(X)
Population for whom poverty status is determined	299,026,555	+/–24,322	42,868,163	+/–236,589	14.3%
AGE					
Under 18 years	73,347,404	+/–33,624	14,656,962	+/–130,803	20.0%
Related children under 18 years	73,021,591	+/–36,469	14,359,130	+/–129,733	19.7%
18 to 64 years	187,746,677	+/–26,800	24,618,252	+/–125,756	13.1%
65 years and over	37,932,474	+/–23,059	3,592,949	+/–31,855	9.5%
SEX					
Male	146,746,586	+/–40,043	19,183,762	+/–125,667	13.1%
Female	152,279,969	+/–39,542	23,684,401	+/–130,978	15.6%
RACE AND HISPANIC OR LATINO ORIGIN					
One race	291,749,594	+/–78,206	41,551,545	+/–236,440	14.2%
White	224,362,935	+/–140,899	26,270,749	+/–170,746	11.7%
Black or African American	36,423,877	+/–56,122	9,407,955	+/–87,054	25.8%
American Indian and Alaska Native	2,373,209	+/–30,233	647,218	+/–24,055	27.3%
Asian	13,522,332	+/–31,679	1,539,226	+/–32,210	11.4%
Native Hawaiian and Other Pacific Islander	437,793	+/–10,689	66,092	+/–7,994	15.1%
Some other race	14,629,448	+/–130,907	3,620,305	+/–59,008	24.7%
Two or more races	7,276,961	+/–78,662	1,316,618	+/–30,492	18.1%

Table B-16 (Continued)

Subject	United States				
	Total		**Below Poverty Level**		**Percent below Poverty Level**
	Estimate	**Margin of Error**	**Estimate**	**Margin of Error**	**Estimate**
Hispanic or Latino origin (of any race)	47,355,677	+/−21,033	11,130,896	+/−88,341	23.5%
White alone, not Hispanic or Latino	194,504,168	+/−35,767	19,462,966		+/−142,941
10.0%					
EDUCATIONAL ATTAINMENT					
Population 25 years and over	198,178,353	+/−72,860	21,672,041	+/−89,595	10.9%
Less than high school graduate	28,436,354	+/−106,025	7,300,972	+/−56,555	25.7%
High school graduate (includes equivalency)	56,149,122	+/−113,586	7,026,409	+/−45,381	12.5%
Some college, associate's degree	57,536,158	+/−122,065	5,168,482	+/−42,157	9.0%
Bachelor's degree or higher	56,056,719	+/−171,240	2,176,178	+/−28,064	3.9%
EMPLOYMENT STATUS					
Civilian labor force 16 years and over	155,100,289	+/−126,003	13,433,671	+/−75,203	8.7%
Employed	139,813,788	+/−136,230	9,250,760	+/−59,826	6.6%
Male	73,290,558	+/−89,179	4,221,532	+/−36,007	5.8%
Female	66,523,230	+/−84,296	5,029,228	+/−38,768	7.6%
Unemployed	15,286,501	+/−65,258	4,182,911	+/−39,327	27.4%
Male	8,724,114	+/−58,935	2,143,237	+/−30,770	24.6%
Female	6,562,387	+/−44,254	2,039,674	+/−26,290	31.1%

(*continued*)

Table B-16 (Continued)

Subject	United States				
	Total		Below Poverty Level		Percent below Poverty Level
	Estimate	Margin of Error	Estimate	Margin of Error	Estimate
WORK EXPERIENCE					
Population 16 years and over	234,050,989	+/–43,133	29,621,804	+/–139,918	12.7%
Worked full-time, year-round in the past 12 months	98,374,509	+/–122,266	2,666,832	+/–29,640	2.7%
Worked part-time or part-year in the past 12 months	61,065,559	+/–115,429	10,279,853	+/–72,566	16.8%
Did not work	74,610,921	+/–128,458	16,675,119	+/–95,335	22.3%
All Individuals below:					
50 percent of poverty level	18,776,800	+/–151,952	(X)	(X)	(X)
125 percent of poverty level	56,430,295	+/–277,384	(X)	(X)	(X)

Subject	United States Percent below Poverty Level Margin of Error
Population for whom poverty status is determined	+/–0.1
AGE	
Under 18 years	+/–0.2
Related children under 18 years	+/–0.2
18 to 64 years	+/–0.1
65 years and over	+/–0.1
SEX	
Male	+/–0.1
Female	+/–0.1

Table B-16 (Continued)

Subject	United States Percent below Poverty Level Margin of Error
RACE AND HISPANIC OR LATINO ORIGIN	
One race	+/–0.1
White	+/–0.1
Black or African American	+/–0.2
American Indian and Alaska Native	+/–0.9
Asian	+/–0.2
Native Hawaiian and Other Pacific Islander	+/–1.8
Some other race	+/–0.4
Two or more races	+/–0.4
Hispanic or Latino origin (of any race)	+/–0.2
White alone, not Hispanic or Latino	+/–0.1
EDUCATIONAL ATTAINMENT	
Population 25 years and over	+/–0.1
Less than high school graduate	+/–0.2
High school graduate (includes equivalency)	+/–0.1
Some college, associate's degree	+/–0.1
Bachelor's degree or higher	+/–0.1
EMPLOYMENT STATUS	
Civilian labor force 16 years and over	+/–0.1
Employed	+/–0.1
Male	+/–0.1
Female	+/–0.1
Unemployed	+/–0.2
Male	+/–0.3
Female	+/–0.3
WORK EXPERIENCE	
Population 16 years and over	+/–0.1
Worked full-time, year-round in the past 12 months	+/–0.1

(*continued*)

Table B-16 (Continued)

Subject	United States Percent below Poverty Level Margin of Error
Worked part-time or part-year in the past 12 months	+/–0.1
Did not work	+/–0.1
All Individuals below:	
50 percent of poverty level	(X)
125 percent of poverty level	(X)
150 percent of poverty level	(X)
185 percent of poverty level	(X)
200 percent of poverty level	(X)
Unrelated individuals for whom poverty status is determined	+/–0.1
Male	+/–0.2
Female	+/–0.2
Mean income deficit for unrelated individuals (dollars)	(X)
Worked full-time, year-round in the past 12 months	+/–0.1
Worked less than full-time, year-round in the past 12 months	+/–0.2
Did not work	+/–0.2
PERCENT IMPUTED	
Poverty status for individuals	(X)

Source: U.S. Census Bureau, 2009 American Community Survey

Data are based on a sample and are subject to sampling variability. The degree of uncertainty for an estimate arising from sampling variability is represented through the use of a margin of error. The value shown here is the 90 percent margin of error. The margin of error can be interpreted roughly as providing a 90 percent probability that the interval defined by the estimate minus the margin of error and the estimate plus the margin of error (the lower and upper confidence bounds) contains the true value. In addition to sampling variability, the ACS estimates are subject to nonsampling error (for a discussion of nonsampling variability, see Accuracy of the Data). The effect of nonsampling error is not represented in these tables.

Notes: Â·While the 2009 American Community Survey (ACS) data generally reflect the November 2008 Office of Management and Budget (OMB) definitions of metropolitan and micropolitan statistical areas; in certain instances the names, codes, and boundaries of the principal cities shown in ACS tables may differ from the OMB definitions due to differences in the effective dates of the geographic entities. Â·Estimates of urban and rural population, housing units, and characteristics reflect boundaries of urban areas defined based on Census 2000 data. Boundaries for urban areas have not been updated since Census 2000. As a result, data for urban and rural areas from the ACS do not necessarily reflect the results of ongoing urbanization.

Explanation of Symbols:

1. An '**' entry in the margin of error column indicates that either no sample observations or too few sample observations were available to compute a standard error and thus the margin of error. A statistical test is not appropriate.

2. An '-' entry in the estimate column indicates that either no sample observations or too few sample observations were available to compute an estimate, or a ratio of medians cannot be calculated because one or both of the median estimates falls in the lowest interval or upper interval of an open-ended distribution.

3. An '-' following a median estimate means the median falls in the lowest interval of an open-ended distribution.

4. An '+' following a median estimate means the median falls in the upper interval of an open-ended distribution.

5. An '***' entry in the margin of error column indicates that the median falls in the lowest interval or upper interval of an open-ended distribution. A statistical test is not appropriate.

6. An '*****' entry in the margin of error column indicates that the estimate is controlled. A statistical test for sampling variability is not appropriate.

7. An 'N' entry in the estimate and margin of error columns indicates that data for this geographic area cannot be displayed because the number of sample cases is too small.

8. An '(X)' means that the estimate is not applicable or not available.

Source: U.S. Census Bureau. "Poverty Status in the Past 12 Months:2009 American Community Survey 1-Year Estimates," 2012. Accessed July 3, 2012. http://factfinder2 .census.gov/faces/tableservices/jsf/pages/productview.xhtml?pid=ACS_09_1YR_S1701&prod Type=table

B-17. U.S. POVERTY DATA, 2010

The 2010 ACS estimated the poverty rate at 15.3 percent, slightly above the 15.1 percent official poverty rate for that year, and a full 1 percentage point above the ACS 2009 estimated poverty rate. The 2010 ACS reported increased poverty rates for all demographic groups with the exception of those age 65 and over, for whom the poverty rate decreased (this was in contrast to the official poverty measures, which noted a slight increase in poverty for those 65 and over), and those who worked full-time for the entire year (for whom the rate remained steady).

2010 American Community Survey 1-Year Estimates

Supporting documentation on code lists, subject definitions, data accuracy, and statistical testing can be found on the American Community Survey website in the Data and Documentation section.

Sample size and data quality measures (including coverage rates, allocation rates, and response rates) can be found on the American Community Survey website in the Methodology section.

Although the American Community Survey (ACS) produces population, demographic and housing unit estimates, for 2010, the 2010 Census provides the official counts of the population and housing units for the nation, states, counties, cities and towns

Table B-17

| Subject | United States | | | | |
| | Total | | Below Poverty Level | | Percent below Poverty Level |
	Estimate	Margin of Error	Estimate	Margin of Error	Estimate
Unemployed	16,718,430	+/-78,844	4,978,163	+/-44,238	29.8%
Male	9,388,251	+/-58,098	2,549,849	+/-28,330	27.2%
Female	7,330,179	+/-43,095	2,428,314	+/-27,667	33.1%
WORK EXPERIENCE					
Population 16 years and over	237,042,521	+/-46,740	32,039,639	+/-143,762	13.5%
Worked full-time, year-round in the past 12 months	96,019,467	+/-124,168	2,669,443	+/-29,810	2.8%
Worked part-time or part-year in the past 12 months	60,000,021	+/-131,609	10,735,569	+/-72,568	17.9%
Did not work	81,023,033	+/-139,711	18,634,627	+/-104,996	23.0%
All Individuals below:					
50 percent of poverty level	20,413,453	+/-164,628	(X)	(X)	(X)

Table B-17 (Continued)

| | United States | | | | |
| | Total | | Below Poverty Level | | Percent below Poverty Level |
Subject	Estimate	Margin of Error	Estimate	Margin of Error	Estimate
125 percent of poverty level	60,722,408	+/–277,343	(X)	(X)	(X)
150 percent of poverty level	75,366,838	+/–314,872	(X)	(X)	(X)
185 percent of poverty level	95,887,829	+/–346,836	(X)	(X)	(X)
200 percent of poverty level	103,725,710	+/–356,275	(X)	(X)	(X)
Unrelated individuals for whom poverty status is determined	56,018,430	+/–152,233	14,669,595	+/–92,819	26.2%
Male	27,505,388	+/–111,676	6,740,329	+/–55,484	24.5%
Female	28,513,042	+/–81,899	7,929,266	+/–57,684	27.8%
Mean income deficit for unrelated individuals (dollars)	6,293	+/–23	(X)	(X)	(X)
Worked full-time, year-round in the past 12 months	22,560,977	+/–101,710	695,606	+/–15,531	3.1%
Worked less than full-time, year-round in the past 12 months	13,876,401	+/–78,645	5,396,646	+/–56,200	38.9%
Did not work	19,581,052	+/–86,902	8,577,343	+/–66,654	43.8%
PERCENT IMPUTED					
Poverty status for individuals	25.6%	(X)	(X)	(X)	(X)
Female	154,135,860	+/–41,539	25,365,737	+/–128,604	16.5%

(*continued*)

Table B-17 (Continued)

	United States				
	Total		**Below Poverty Level**		**Percent below Poverty Level**
Subject	**Estimate**	**Margin of Error**	**Estimate**	**Margin of Error**	**Estimate**
RACE AND HISPANIC OR LATINO ORIGIN					
One race	293,402,168	+/–78,857	44,577,836	+/–238,231	15.2%
White	224,197,343	+/–136,015	27,951,752	+/–171,930	12.5%
Black or African American	37,200,236	+/–54,789	10,099,631	+/–96,200	27.1%
American Indian and Alaska Native	2,465,461	+/–28,862	701,213	+/–20,355	28.4%
Asian	14,459,936	+/–31,213	1,801,196	+/–35,881	12.5%
Native Hawaiian and Other Pacific Islander	493,951	+/–9,486	92,647	+/–9,700	18.8%
Some other race	14,585,241	+/–120,157	3,931,397	+/–66,523	27.0%
Two or more races	8,132,853	+/–77,114	1,638,120	+/–30,817	20.1%
Hispanic or Latino origin (of any race)	49,703,511	+/–19,654	12,306,535	+/–98,284	24.8%
White alone, not Hispanic or Latino	192,355,136	+/–40,333	20,437,539	+/–135,747	10.6%
EDUCATIONAL ATTAINMENT					
Population 25 years and over	200,754,557	+/–74,823	23,349,887	+/–102,055	11.6%
Less than high school graduate	28,266,989	+/–104,832	7,551,483	+/–56,759	26.7%
High school graduate (includes equivalency)	56,910,186	+/–122,452	7,664,865	+/–58,362	13.5%
Some college, associate's degree	58,267,597	+/–112,817	5,709,144	+/–41,066	9.8%
Bachelor's degree or higher	57,309,785	+/–168,789	2,424,395	+/–27,623	4.2%

Table B-17 (Continued)

Subject	United States				
	Total		**Below Poverty Level**		**Percent below Poverty Level**
	Estimate	**Margin of Error**	**Estimate**	**Margin of Error**	**Estimate**
EMPLOYMENT STATUS					
Civilian labor force 16 years and over	154,986,670	+/–125,651	14,737,735	+/–89,012	9.5%
Employed	138,268,240	+/–144,978	9,759,572	+/–68,769	7.1%
Male	72,060,295	+/–96,756	4,494,037	+/–43,940	6.2%
Female	66,207,945	+/–91,799	5,265,535	+/–48,012	8.0%

Subject	United States Percent below Poverty Level Margin of Error
Population for whom poverty status is determined	+/–0.1
AGE	
Under 18 years	+/–0.2
Related children under 18 years	+/–0.2
18 to 64 years	+/–0.1
65 years and over	+/–0.1
SEX	
Male	+/–0.1
Female	+/–0.1
RACE AND HISPANIC OR LATINO ORIGIN	
One race	+/–0.1
White	+/–0.1
Black or African American	+/–0.3
American Indian and Alaska Native	+/–0.8
Asian	+/–0.2
Native Hawaiian and Other Pacific Islander	+/–1.9
Some other race	+/–0.4

(*continued*)

Table B-17 (Continued)

Subject	United States Percent below Poverty Level Margin of Error
Two or more races	+/–0.4
Hispanic or Latino origin (of any race)	+/–0.2
White alone, not Hispanic or Latino	+/–0.1
EDUCATIONAL ATTAINMENT	
Population 25 years and over	+/–0.1
Less than high school graduate	+/–0.2
High school graduate (includes equivalency)	+/–0.1
Some college, associate's degree	+/–0.1
Bachelor's degree or higher	+/–0.1
EMPLOYMENT STATUS	
Civilian labor force 16 years and over	+/–0.1
Employed	+/–0.1
Male	+/–0.1
Female	+/–0.1
Unemployed	+/–0.2
Male	+/–0.3
Female	+/–0.3
WORK EXPERIENCE	
Population 16 years and over	+/–0.1
Worked full-time, year-round in the past 12 months	+/–0.1
Worked part-time or part-year in the past 12 months	+/–0.1
Did not work	+/–0.1
All Individuals below:	
50 percent of poverty level	(X)
125 percent of poverty level	(X)
150 percent of poverty level	(X)
185 percent of poverty level	(X)
200 percent of poverty level	(X)
Unrelated individuals for whom poverty status is determined	+/–0.1

Subject	United States Percent below Poverty Level Margin of Error
Male	+/–0.2
Female	+/–0.2
Mean income deficit for unrelated individuals (dollars)	(X)
Worked full-time, year-round in the past 12 months	+/–0.1
Worked less than full-time, year-round in the past 12 months	+/–0.3
Did not work	+/–0.2
PERCENT IMPUTED	
Poverty status for individuals	(X)

Data are based on a sample and are subject to sampling variability. The degree of uncertainty for an estimate arising from sampling variability is represented through the use of a margin of error. The value shown here is the 90 percent margin of error. The margin of error can be interpreted roughly as providing a 90 percent probability that the interval defined by the estimate minus the margin of error and the estimate plus the margin of error (the lower and upper confidence bounds) contains the true value. In addition to sampling variability, the ACS estimates are subject to nonsampling error (for a discussion of nonsampling variability, see Accuracy of the Data). The effect of nonsampling error is not represented in these tables.

While the 2010 American Community Survey (ACS) data generally reflect the December 2009 Office of Management and Budget (OMB) definitions of metropolitan and micropolitan statistical areas; in certain instances the names, codes, and boundaries of the principal cities shown in ACS tables may differ from the OMB definitions due to differences in the effective dates of the geographic entities.

Estimates of urban and rural population, housing units, and characteristics reflect boundaries of urban areas defined based on Census 2000 data. Boundaries for urban areas have not been updated since Census 2000. As a result, data for urban and rural areas from the ACS do not necessarily reflect the results of ongoing urbanization.

Source: U.S. Census Bureau, 2010 American Community Survey

Explanation of Symbols:

1. An '**' entry in the margin of error column indicates that either no sample observations or too few sample observations were available to compute a standard error and thus the margin of error. A statistical test is not appropriate.
2. An '-' entry in the estimate column indicates that either no sample observations or too few sample observations were available to compute an estimate, or a ratio of medians cannot be calculated because one or both of the median estimates falls in the lowest interval or upper interval of an open-ended distribution.

3. An '-' following a median estimate means the median falls in the lowest interval of an open-ended distribution.

4. An '+' following a median estimate means the median falls in the upper interval of an open-ended distribution.

5. An '***' entry in the margin of error column indicates that the median falls in the lowest interval or upper interval of an open-ended distribution. A statistical test is not appropriate.

6. An '*****' entry in the margin of error column indicates that the estimate is controlled. A statistical test for sampling variability is not appropriate.

7. An 'N' entry in the estimate and margin of error columns indicates that data for this geographic area cannot be displayed because the number of sample cases is too small.

8. An '(X)' means that the estimate is not applicable or not available.

Source: U.S. Census Bureau. "Poverty Status in the Past 12 Months: 2010 American Community Survey 1-Year Estimates," 2012. Accessed July 3, 2012. http://factfinder2 .census.gov/faces/tableservices/jsf/pages/productview.xhtml?pid=ACS_10_1YR_S1701&prod Type=table

B-18. U.S. POVERTY DATA, 2011

For 2011 the ACS estimated the U.S. poverty rate at 15.9 percent, higher than the official poverty rate for that year of 15.0 percent. Some of the highest poverty rates documented in the 2011 ACS were for children, African Americans, American Indians and Alaska Natives, Latinos, and individuals without a high school diploma.

2011 AMERICAN COMMUNITY SURVEY 1-YEAR ESTIMATES

Supporting documentation on code lists, subject definitions, data accuracy, and statistical testing can be found on the American Community Survey website in the Data and Documentation section.

Sample size and data quality measures (including coverage rates, allocation rates, and response rates) can be found on the American Community Survey website in the Methodology section.

Although the American Community Survey (ACS) produces population, demographic and housing unit estimates, it is the Census Bureau's Population Estimates Program that produces and disseminates the official estimates of the population for the nation, states, counties, cities and towns and estimates of housing units for states and counties.

Table B-18

	United States				
	Total		**Below Poverty Level**		**Percent below Poverty Level**
Subject	**Estimate**	**Margin of Error**	**Estimate**	**Margin of Error**	**Estimate**
Female	66,486,179	+/-90,884	5,564,780	+/-42,903	8.4%
Unemployed	15,897,408	+/-66,142	5,179,420	+/-46,133	32.6%
Male	8,682,907	+/-47,961	2,590,962	+/-29,624	29.8%
Female	7,214,501	+/-45,175	2,588,458	+/-30,840	35.9%
WORK EXPERIENCE					
Population 16 years and over	239,385,366	+/-47,522	33,674,046	+/-139,305	14.1%
Worked full-time, year-round in the past 12 months	97,122,415	+/-128,748	2,862,608	+/-34,505	2.9%
Worked part-time or part-year in the past 12 months	59,243,071	+/-128,164	11,065,556	+/-64,942	18.7%
Did not work	83,019,880	+/-128,994	19,745,882	+/-101,821	23.8%
All Individuals below:					
50 percent of poverty level	21,459,639	+/-151,958	(X)	(X)	(X)
125 percent of poverty level	63,324,455	+/-271,288	(X)	(X)	(X)
150 percent of poverty level	78,288,180	+/-313,983	(X)	(X)	(X)
185 percent of poverty level	98,700,855	+/-349,806	(X)	(X)	(X)
200 percent of poverty level	106,826,236	+/-360,291	(X)	(X)	(X)

(*continued*)

Table B-18   (Continued)

	United States				
	Total		**Below Poverty Level**		**Percent below Poverty Level**
Subject	**Estimate**	**Margin of Error**	**Estimate**	**Margin of Error**	**Estimate**
Unrelated individuals for whom poverty status is determined	56,683,075	+/−175,048	15,290,319	+/−94,968	27.0%
Male	27,796,477	+/−113,161	6,981,559	+/−63,736	25.1%
Female	28,886,598	+/−103,482	8,308,760	+/−56,757	28.8%
Mean income deficit for unrelated individuals (dollars)	6,525	+/−19	(X)	(X)	(X)
Worked full-time, year-round in the past 12 months	22,796,183	+/−111,937	726,896	+/−15,711	3.2%
Worked less than full-time, year-round in the past 12 months	13,737,280	+/−69,994	5,488,930	+/−54,422	40.0%
Did not work	20,149,612	+/−78,992	9,074,493	+/−59,724	45.0%
PERCENT IMPUTED					
Poverty status for individuals	26.0%	(X)	(X)	(X)	(X)
Female	155,186,380	+/−34,397	26,626,754	+/−123,115	17.2%
RACE AND HISPANIC OR LATINO ORIGIN					
One race	295,329,421	+/−96,195	46,644,532	+/−232,566	15.8%
White	225,678,820	+/−110,100	29,260,632	+/−185,461	13.0%
Black or African American	37,510,171	+/−54,242	10,543,367	+/−89,715	28.1%
American Indian and Alaska Native	2,458,045	+/−33,459	724,528	+/−20,286	29.5%

Table B-18 (Continued)

Subject	Total Estimate	Total Margin of Error	Below Poverty Level Estimate	Below Poverty Level Margin of Error	Percent below Poverty Level Estimate
			United States		
Asian	14,728,302	+/–36,874	1,888,398	+/–42,525	12.8%
Native Hawaiian and Other Pacific Islander	491,826	+/–13,604	105,739	+/–9,778	21.5%
Some other race	14,462,257	+/–108,053	4,121,868	+/–75,797	28.5%
Two or more races	8,448,772	+/–94,333	1,807,503	+/–41,599	21.4%
Hispanic or Latino origin (of any race)	50,893,007	+/–19,661	13,126,374	+/–114,607	25.8%
White alone, not Hispanic or Latino	192,557,395	+/–30,976	21,122,952	+/–147,999	11.0%
EDUCATIONAL ATTAINMENT					
Population 25 years and over	202,893,965	+/–68,110	24,702,566	+/–103,402	12.2%
Less than high school graduate	27,933,848	+/–108,733	7,784,811	+/–57,684	27.9%
High school graduate (includes equivalency)	57,305,844	+/–110,771	8,113,171	+/–50,806	14.2%
Some college, associate's degree	59,058,822	+/–112,746	6,211,352	+/–47,338	10.5%
Bachelor's degree or higher	58,595,451	+/–172,265	2,593,232	+/–33,723	4.4%
EMPLOYMENT STATUS					
Civilian labor force 16 years and over	155,489,677	+/–126,178	15,487,311	+/–86,206	10.0%
Employed	139,592,269	+/–128,029	10,307,891	+/–60,928	7.4%
Male	73,106,090	+/–82,998	4,743,111	+/–41,497	6.5%

(*continued*)

Table B-18   (Continued)

	United States				
	Total		Below Poverty Level		Percent below Poverty Level
Subject	Estimate	Margin of Error	Estimate	Margin of Error	Estimate

Subject	United States Percent below Poverty Level Margin of Error
Population for whom poverty status is determined	+/–0.1
AGE	
Under 18 years	+/–0.2
Related children under 18 years	+/–0.2
18 to 64 years	+/–0.1
65 years and over	+/–0.1
SEX	
Male	+/–0.1
Female	+/–0.1
RACE AND HISPANIC OR LATINO ORIGIN	
One race	+/–0.1
White	+/–0.1
Black or African American	+/–0.2
American Indian and Alaska Native	+/–0.8
Asian	+/–0.3
Native Hawaiian and Other Pacific Islander	+/–1.8
Some other race	+/–0.5
Two or more races	+/–0.4
Hispanic or Latino origin (of any race)	+/–0.2
White alone, not Hispanic or Latino	+/–0.1
EDUCATIONAL ATTAINMENT	
Population 25 years and over	+/–0.1

Subject	United States Percent below Poverty Level Margin of Error
Less than high school graduate	+/−0.2
High school graduate (includes equivalency)	+/−0.1
Some college, associate's degree	+/−0.1
Bachelor's degree or higher	+/−0.1
EMPLOYMENT STATUS	
Civilian labor force 16 years and over	+/−0.1
Employed	+/−0.1
Male	+/−0.1
Female	+/−0.1
Unemployed	+/−0.3
Male	+/−0.3
Female	+/−0.4
WORK EXPERIENCE	
Population 16 years and over	+/−0.1
Worked full-time, year-round in the past 12 months	+/−0.1
Worked part-time or part-year in the past 12 months	+/−0.1
Did not work	+/−0.1
All Individuals below:	
50 percent of poverty level	(X)
125 percent of poverty level	(X)
150 percent of poverty level	(X)
185 percent of poverty level	(X)
200 percent of poverty level	(X)
Unrelated individuals for whom poverty status is determined	+/−0.1
Male	+/−0.2
Female	+/−0.2
Mean income deficit for unrelated individuals (dollars)	(X)

(*continued*)

Table B-18 (Continued)

Subject	United States Percent below Poverty Level Margin of Error
Worked full-time, year-round in the past 12 months	+/–0.1
Worked less than full-time, year-round in the past 12 months	+/–0.3
Did not work	+/–0.2
PERCENT IMPUTED	
Poverty status for individuals	(X)

Data are based on a sample and are subject to sampling variability. The degree of uncertainty for an estimate arising from sampling variability is represented through the use of a margin of error. The value shown here is the 90 percent margin of error. The margin of error can be interpreted roughly as providing a 90 percent probability that the interval defined by the estimate minus the margin of error and the estimate plus the margin of error (the lower and upper confidence bounds) contains the true value. In addition to sampling variability, the ACS estimates are subject to nonsampling error (for a discussion of nonsampling variability, see Accuracy of the Data). The effect of nonsampling error is not represented in these tables.

While the 2011 American Community Survey (ACS) data generally reflect the December 2009 Office of Management and Budget (OMB) definitions of metropolitan and micropolitan statistical areas; in certain instances the names, codes, and boundaries of the principal cities shown in ACS tables may differ from the OMB definitions due to differences in the effective dates of the geographic entities.

Estimates of urban and rural population, housing units, and characteristics reflect boundaries of urban areas defined based on Census 2000 data. Boundaries for urban areas have not been updated since Census 2000. As a result, data for urban and rural areas from the ACS do not necessarily reflect the results of ongoing urbanization.

Source: U.S. Census Bureau, 2011 American Community Survey

Explanation of Symbols:

1. An '**' entry in the margin of error column indicates that either no sample observations or too few sample observations were available to compute a standard error and thus the margin of error. A statistical test is not appropriate.

2. An '-' entry in the estimate column indicates that either no sample observations or too few sample observations were available to compute an estimate, or a ratio of medians cannot be calculated because one or both of the median estimates falls in the lowest interval or upper interval of an open-ended distribution.

3. An '-' following a median estimate means the median falls in the lowest interval of an open-ended distribution.

4. An '+' following a median estimate means the median falls in the upper interval of an open-ended distribution.
5. An '***' entry in the margin of error column indicates that the median falls in the lowest interval or upper interval of an open-ended distribution. A statistical test is not appropriate.
6. An '*****' entry in the margin of error column indicates that the estimate is controlled. A statistical test for sampling variability is not appropriate.
7. An 'N' entry in the estimate and margin of error columns indicates that data for this geographic area cannot be displayed because the number of sample cases is too small.
8. An '(X)' means that the estimate is not applicable or not available.

Source: U.S. Census Bureau. "Poverty Status in the Past 12 Months: 2011 American Community Survey 1-Year Estimates," 2013. Accessed January 28, 2013. http://factfinder2 .census.gov/faces/tableservices/jsf/pages/productview.xhtml?pid=ACS_11_1YR_S1701&prod Type=table

B-19. Areas in the United States with Concentrated Poverty 2006–2010

Document B-19 shows the percentage of people living in concentrated areas of poverty based on data from the American Community Survey (ACS) data from 2006 to 2010. The following table looks at census tracts by dividing each into one of four categories based on the poverty rate for that tract. A census tract is a geographic area defined for the purpose of census taking. The column for Category I covers census tracts with a poverty rate that is less than 13.8 percent, and Category IV covers census tracts with a poverty rate of 40.0 percent or more. Census tracts with poverty rates over 20 percent are considered poverty areas.

As B-19 shows, people in poverty are much more likely to live in areas where many other people are also in poverty. Only 3.5 percent of the U.S. population lives in census tracts with poverty rates of at least 40.0 percent, but 12.4 percent of people in poverty live in these very high poverty census tracts. Mississippi was the state with the highest percentage of people (9.1 percent) residing in census tracts with poverty rates of 40.0 percent or more between 2006 and 2010, while Wyoming had the smallest percentage of people residing in these areas (.1 percent). The table below also shows that more people reside in census tracts with poverty rates of 40.0 percent or more in the South and Midwest, than in the Northeast and West.

Table B-19 Distribution of People in Census Tracts by Poverty Levels and by State: 2006–2010

| Area | All Census Tracts | | Category I (less than 13.8%) | | Category II (13.8–19.9%) | | Category III (20.0–39.9%) | | Category IV (40.0% or more) | |
	Number	Margin of Error (+)	Percent	Margin of Error (+)	Percent	Margin of Error (+)	Percent	Margin of Error (+)	Percent	Margin of Error (+)
U.S. Total	296,141,149	14,444	61.4	0.1	16.0	0.1	19.1	0.1	3.5	0.1
In Poverty	40,917,513	273,616	30.6	0.1	19.2	0.1	37.8	0.1	12.4	0.1
Regions										
Northeast	53,322,411	4,205	70.5	0.1	11.1	0.1	14.9	0.1	3.4	0.1
Midwest	64,729,840	4,996	66.2	0.1	14.8	0.1	15.4	0.1	3.7	0.1

South	109,078,089		6,958	53.7	0.1	18.9	0.1	23.4	0.1	4.0	0.1
West	69,010,809		6,114	62.2	0.1	16.2	0.1	19.1	0.1	2.5	0.1
States											
Alabama	4,596,836	0.1	1,125	45.3	0.1	22.7	0.1	27.3	0.1	4.7	0.1
Alaska	674,801		600	76.9	0.4	14.9	0.4	8.2	0.2	–	–
Arizona	6,110,304		1,960	57.4	0.1	14.5	0.1	22.9	0.1	5.2	0.1
Arkansas	2,790,794		1,253	39.4	0.1	24.2	0.2	32.0	0.2	4.4	0.1
California	35,877,036		3,983	61.1	0.1	15.7	0.1	20.5	0.1	2.6	0.1
Colorado	4,773,303		1,113	65.3	0.1	14.5	0.1	18.5	0.1	1.7	0.1
Connecticut	3,434,901		939	78.9	0.1	9.6	0.1	8.8	0.1	2.7	0.1
Delaware	856,004		460	73.2	0.3	17.4	0.3	7.9	0.2	1.6	0.2
District of Columbia	551,331		292	47.8	0.4	17.5	0.4	26.5	0.4	8.2	0.3
Florida	18,107,049		2,209	61.2	0.1	18.4	0.1	17.8	0.1	2.6	0.1
Georgia	9,204,793		1,852	52.3	0.1	18.2	0.1	26.0	0.1	3.5	0.1
Hawaii	1,298,918		675	79.2	0.3	10.2	0.2	9.8	0.2	1.0	0.1
Idaho	1,496,581		701	59.0	0.2	26.9	0.2	12.6	0.2	1.6	0.1
Illinois	12,439,981		1,554	67.4	0.1	13.7	0.1	15.5	0.1	3.4	0.1
Indiana	6,219,801		1,705	63.5	0.1	16.3	0.1	17.3	0.1	2.9	0.1
Iowa	2,916,252		1,019	71.8	0.1	15.0	0.1	11.9	0.1	1.3	0.1
Kansas	2,725,175		949	68.0	0.1	15.3	0.1	14.6	0.1	2.1	0.1
Kentucky	4,157,077		1,299	42.9	0.1	20.4	0.1	32.2	0.2	4.4	0.1
Louisiana	4,302,475		1,008	45.4	0.2	19.0	0.1	28.9	0.1	6.6	0.1

(continued)

Table B-19 (Continued)

Area	All Census Tracts		Category I (less than 13.8%)		Category II (13.8–19.9%)		Category III (20.0–39.9%)		Category IV (40.0% or more)	
	Number	Margin of Error (+)	Percent	Margin of Error (+)	Percent	Margin of Error (+)	Percent	Margin of Error (+)	Percent	Margin of Error (+)
Maine	1,291,988	555	65.0	0.2	20.1	0.1	13.9	0.2	1.0	0.1
Maryland	5,557,115	1,492	82.3	0.1	8.7	0.1	8.0	0.1	1.0	0.1
Massachusetts	6,253,462	1,278	75.1	0.1	9.2	0.1	13.6	0.1	2.1	0.1
Michigan	9,726,785	1,521	61.3	0.1	14.7	0.1	18.3	0.1	5.7	0.1
Minnesota	5,119,104	873	77.2	0.1	11.0	0.1	9.2	0.1	2.7	0.1
Mississippi	2,845,365	962	29.1	0.2	25.2	0.2	36.6	0.2	9.1	0.1
Missouri	5,744,590	1,391	58.6	0.1	19.8	0.1	18.7	0.1	2.9	0.1
Montana	949,414	594	54.7	0.2	24.6	0.3	19.6	0.2	1.1	0.1
Nebraska	1,744,704	764	70.1	0.2	16.0	0.1	12.4	0.1	1.6	0.1
Nevada	2,594,953	923	69.1	0.2	14.1	0.2	15.2	0.2	1.6	0.1
New Hampshire	1,273,957	577	86.4	0.2	8.6	0.1	4.5	0.1	0.5	0.1
New Jersey	8,544,303	1,395	80.0	0.1	7.9	0.1	10.4	0.1	1.7	0.1
New Mexico	1,970,838	842	39.8	0.2	22.3	0.2	33.6	0.2	4.3	0.1
New York	18,710,113	2,408	62.2	0.1	13.1	0.1	19.9	0.1	4.8	0.1
North Carolina	9,013,443	1,647	51.0	0.1	22.3	0.1	23.4	0.1	3.3	0.1

State										
North Dakota	636,048	356	72.1	0.2	13.9	0.2	12.0	0.2	2.0	0.1
Ohio	11,199,642	1,889	63.1	0.1	14.5	0.1	17.4	0.1	5.0	0.1
Oklahoma	3,559,437	1,143	46.2	0.2	23.7	0.1	27.3	0.2	2.7	0.1
Oregon	3,688,75	1,131	56.0	0.2	24.2	0.1	18.4	0.1	1.4	0.1
Pennsylvania	12,199,544	1,948	70.6	0.1	11.3	0.1	14.0	0.1	4.1	0.1
Rhode Island	1,014,029	440	72.5	0.2	5.8	0.2	19.3	0.2	2.4	0.1
South Carolina	4,369,147	1,000	47.4	0.2	21.2	0.2	27.7	0.2	3.6	0.1
South Dakota	771,100	483	64.0	0.2	18.7	0.2	11.9	0.3	5.5	0.1
Tennessee	6,075,066	1,579	47.7	0.1	21.9	0.1	26.1	0.1	4.3	0.1
Texas	23,707,679	2,678	50.2	0.1	17.2	0.1	26.6	0.1	6.0	0.1
Utah	2,613,440	707	76.5	0.1	11.1	0.1	10.1	0.1	2.3	0.1
Vermont	600,114	338	74.6	0.2	15.9	0.2	8.5	0.2	1.1	0.1
Virginia	7,595,386	1,493	74.4	0.1	13.7	0.1	10.3	0.1	1.7	0.1
Washington	6,430,231	1,573	67.6	0.1	16.0	0.1	14.9	0.1	1.6	0.1
West Virginia	1,789,092	785	37.0	0.2	32.0	0.2	28.6	0.2	2.4	0.1
Wisconsin	5,486,658	1,381	73.7	0.1	13.3	0.1	9.7	0.1	3.3	0.1
Wyoming	532,245	09	79.2	0.3	13.5	0.3	7.2	0.2	0.1	0.1

– Represents or rounds to zero.

Note: Details may not sum to totals due to rounding.

Source: Bishaw, Alemayehu. "Areas with Concentrated Poverty: 2006–2010 American Community Survey Briefs." U.S. Census Bureau, December 2011. Accessed July 1, 2012. http:/www.census.gov/prod/2011pubs/acsbr10-17.pdf

B-20. Characteristics of People Living in Concentrated Areas of Poverty in the United States 2006 to 2010

Document B-20 provides additional insight into who is living in concentrated areas of poverty, based on American Community Survey (ACS) data from 2006 to 2010. As this table shows, 46.2 percent of families living in the census tracts with the highest poverty rates (40.0 percent or greater) are single-parent families headed by a female. The majority of families residing in the areas with the highest concentration of poverty have annual incomes between $10,000 and $29,999, and the vast majority have no children, or only one or two children, and rent rather than own a home.

Table B-20 Distribution of People, Families, and Households by Poverty Level of Census Tracts and Other Selected Characteristics:[1] 2006-2010

Characteristics	Category I (Less than 13.8%)		Category II (13.8-19.9%)		Category III (20.0-39.9%)		Category IV (40.0% or more)		Total	
	Estimates	Margin of error (±)	Estimates	Margin of error (±)	Estimates	Margin of error (±)	Estimates	Margin of error (±)	Estimates	Margin of error (±)
People										
United States	**61.4**	**0.1**	**16.0**	**0.1**	**19.1**	**0.1**	**3.5**	**0.1**	**296,141,149**	**14,444**
	181,881,914	56,537	47,305,181	43,430	56,644,210	54,200	10,309,844	24,495	296,141,149	14,444
Region										
Total	181,881,914	56,537	47,305,181	43,430	56,644,210	54,200	10,309,844	24,495	296,141,149	14,444
Northeast	20.7	0.1	12.5	0.1	14.1	0.1	17.7	0.1	18.0	0.1
Midwest	23.6	0.1	20.2	0.1	17.6	0.1	23.1	0.1	21.9	0.1
South	32.2	0.1	43.6	0.1	45.1	0.1	42.5	0.1	36.8	0.1
West	23.6	0.1	23.6	0.1	23.3	0.1	16.7	0.1	23.3	0.1

Age

Total	181,881,914	56,537	47,305,181	43,430	56,644,210	54,200	10,309,844	24,495	296,141,149	14,444
Under 18 years	23.9	0.1	24.1	0.1	26.4	0.1	28.9	0.1	24.6	0.1
18 to 64 years	62.8	0.1	63.0	0.1	62.5	0.1	62.6	0.1	62.8	0.1
65 years and over	13.3	0.1	12.9	0.1	11.1	0.1	8.5	0.1	12.6	0.1
Educational Attainment										
Population 25 years and older	124,298,726	36,788	31,313,635	28,442	35,092,898	36,690	5,472,401	15,141	196,177,660	18,393
Less than high school, no diploma	9.6	0.1	18.2	0.1	25.9	0.1	34.0	0.2	14.6	0.1
High school, diploma	26.8	0.1	32.6	0.1	32.4	0.1	31.1	0.2	28.8	0.1
Some college/no degree	21.1	0.1	21.1	0.1	19.4	0.1	17.3	0.1	20.7	0.1
Associate's degree	8.2	0.1	7.3	0.1	6.2	0.1	4.8	0.1	7.6	0.1
Bachelor's degree or higher	34.2	0.1	20.8	0.1	16.2	0.1	12.8	0.1	28.3	0.1

(continued)

887

Table B-20 (Continued)

Characteristics	Category I (Less than 13.8%)		Category II (13.8–19.9%)		Category III (20.0–39.9%)		Category IV (40.0% or more)		Total	
	Estimates	Margin of error (±)	Estimates	Margin of error (±)	Estimates	Margin of error (±)	Estimates	Margin of error (±)	Estimates	Margin of error (±)
Race and Hispanic Origin										
Total	181,881,914	56,537	47,305,181	43,430	56,644,210	54,200	10,309,844	24,495	296,141,149	14,444
White alone	81.0	0.1	73.2	0.1	58.8	0.1	43.0	0.2	74.2	0.1
White, not Hispanic	74.4	0.1	62.1	0.1	43.3	0.1	26.3	0.1	64.8	0.1
Black alone	7.2	0.1	13.0	0.1	23.3	0.1	38.1	0.1	12.3	0.1
American Indian and Alaska Native alone (AIAN)	0.5	0.1	0.9	0.1	1.5	0.1	2.1	0.1	0.8	0.1
Asian alone	5.5	0.1	3.6	0.1	3.4	0.1	3.2	0.1	4.7	0.1
Native Hawaiian and Other Pacific Islander alone (NHPI)	0.2	0.1	0.2	0.1	0.2	0.1	0.1	0.1	0.2	0.1

Some Other Race alone	3.4	0.1	6.6	0.1	10.2	0.1	11.1	0.1	5.5	0.1
Two or More Races	2.3	0.1	2.5	0.1	2.6	0.1	2.4	0.1	2.4	0.1
Hispanic (any race)	10.7	0.1	18.7	0.1	27.2	0.1	29.5	0.1	15.8	0.1
Poverty										
Poverty universe	**181,881,914**	**56,537**	**47,305,181**	**43,430**	**56,644,210**	**54,200**	**10,309,844**	**24,495**	**296,141,149**	**14,444**
Not in poverty	93.1	0.1	83.4	0.1	72.7	0.1	51.0	0.1	86.2	0.1
In poverty	6.9	0.1	16.7	0.1	27.3	0.1	49.0	0.1	13.8	0.1
Work Experience										
Civilan population in labor force 16 years and older	**98,212,314**	**40,196**	**24,227,261**	**38,201**	**27,090,654**	**53,323**	**4,327,616**	**17,693**	**153,857,845**	**102,651**
Worked full-time, year-round	65.0	0.1	61.8	0.1	58.0	0.1	46.7	0.2	62.8	0.1
Worked less than full-time, year-round	32.7	0.1	34.8	0.1	37.1	0.1	45.9	0.2	34.2	0.1
Did not work	2.3	0.1	3.4	0.1	4.8	0.1	7.4	0.1	3.1	0.1

(continued)

Table B-20 (Continued)

Characteristics	Category I (Less than 13.8%)		Category II (13.8–19.9%)		Category III (20.0–39.9%)		Category IV (40.0% or more)		Total	
	Estimates	Margin of error (±)	Estimates	Margin of error (±)	Estimates	Margin of error (±)	Estimates	Margin of error (±)	Estimates	Margin of error (±)
FAMILIES										
Family Type										
Total	48,931,859	124.722	11,969,590	44.835	13,271,205	58.416	2,081,664	11,447	76,254,318	230,785
Married-couple	80.4	0.2	70.7	0.2	59.9	0.2	43.2	0.3	74.3	0.2
Male householder, no spouse present	5.7	0.1	8.0	0.1	9.6	0.1	10.6	0.2	6.8	0.1
Female householder, no spouse present	13.9	0.1	21.4	0.1	30.5	0.1	46.2	0.2	18.9	0.1
Family Income										
Total	48,931,859	124.722	11,969,590	44.835	13,271,205	58.416	2,081,664	11,447	76,254,318	230,785
No income	0.4	0.1	0.9	0.1	1.6	0.1	3.1	0.1	0.8	0.1
Under $10,000	1.8	0.1	4.6	0.1	8.1	0.1	16.9	0.2	3.7	0.1
$10,000 to $29,999	10.5	0.1	20.8	0.1	28.8	0.2	38.9	0.3	16.1	0.1
$30,000 to $49,999	16.1	0.1	22.5	0.1	23.0	0.1	19.1	0.2	18.4	0.1

$50,000 to $99,999	37.0	0.1	35.1	0.1	28.2	0.1	16.9	0.2	34.6	0.1
$100,000 or higher	34.3	0.1	16.0	0.1	10.3	0.1	5.0	0.1	26.5	0.1
Number of Children in Family										
Total	48,931,859	124,722	11,969,590	44,835	13,271,205	58,416	2,081,664	11,447	76,254,318	230,785
No children	55.2	0.1	54.9	0.1	51.0	0.1	44.7	0.2	54.1	0.1
1 or 2 children	36.6	0.2	36.0	0.2	37.4	0.2	38.7	0.3	36.7	0.2
3 or 4 children	7.7	0.1	8.4	0.1	10.5	0.1	14.2	0.2	8.5	0.1
5 or more children	0.5	0.1	0.7	0.1	1.1	0.1	2.4	0.1	0.7	0.1
HOUSEHOLDS										
Tenure										
Total	70,481,047	120,635	18,591,314	50,080	21,397,812	68,835	3,765,823	15,920	114,235,996	248,114
Owned	74.8	0.2	62.1	0.2	49.7	0.2	31.1	0.2	66.6	0.2
Rented	25.2	0.2	37.9	0.2	50.3	0.2	68.9	0.2	33.4	0.2
Food Stamps										
Total	70,481,047	120,635	18,591,314	50,080	21,397,812	68,835	3,765,823	15,920	114,235,996	248,114
Receiving food stamp/SNAP	4.7	0.1	11.3	0.1	18.7	0.1	30.7	0.2	9.3	0.1
Not receiving food stamp/SNAP	95.3	0.1	88.7	0.1	81.3	0.1	69.3	0.2	90.7	0.1

[1]Poverty status is determined for individuals in housing units and noninstitutional group quarters. The poverty universe excludes children under age 15 who are not related to the householder, people living in institutional group quarters, and people living in college dormitories or military barracks.

Source: Bishaw, Alemayehu. 2011. "Areas with Concentrated Poverty: 2006–2010 American Community Survey Briefs." U.S. Census Bureau, December 2011. Accessed July 1, 2012. http://www.census.gov/prod/2011pubs/acsbr10-17.pdf

B-21. THE SUPPLEMENTAL POVERTY MEASURE IN THE UNITED STATES

The official poverty measure utilized by the U.S. government (see documents B-1 through B-7 earlier in this section) was developed in the 1960s and has been criticized by many experts as inadequate. Some argue that the official poverty measure is inadequate because it does not vary based on the geographic cost of living, and does not account for needs such as child care and medical costs. In response to these and other criticisms, the Census Bureau has begun to develop a Supplemental Poverty Measure (SPM). Table B-21 highlights some of the major differences between the official poverty measure and the SPM. (For further discussion on the measurement of poverty see Section 2, "Measurement of Poverty.")

Table B-21   Poverty Measure Concepts: Official and Supplemental

	Official Poverty Measure	**Supplemental Poverty Measure**
Measurement Units	Families and unrelated individuals	All related individuals who live at the same address, including any coresident unrelated children who are cared for by the family (such as foster children) and any cohabitors and their children
Poverty Threshold	Three times the cost of minimum food diet in 1963	The 33rd percentile of expenditures on food, clothing, shelter, and utilities (FCSU) of consumer units with exactly two children multiplied by 1.2
Threshold Adjustments	Vary by family size, composition, and age of householder	Geographic adjustments for differences in housing costs and a three parameter equivalence scale for family size and composition
Updating Thresholds	Consumer Price Index: all items	Five year moving average of expenditures on FCSU
Resource Measures	Gross before-tax cash income	Sum of cash income, plus in-kind benefits that families can use to meet their FCSU needs, minus taxes (or plus tax credits), minus work expenses, minus out-of-pocket medical expenses

Source: Short, Kathleen. "The Research Supplemental Poverty Measure: 2010." U.S. Census Bureau, November 2011. Accessed July 1, 2012. http://www.census.gov/prod/2011pubs/p60-241.pdf

B-22. THE DIFFERENCE BETWEEN THE OFFICIAL POVERTY MEASURE AND THE SUPPLEMENTAL POVERTY MEASURE, 2009 AND 2010

Document B-22 shows the difference between poverty thresholds based on the official poverty measure and the Supplemental Poverty Measure for the years 2009 and 2010 for a family with two adults and two children.

Table B-22   Two Adult, Two Child Poverty Thresholds: 2009 and 2010

	2009	**2010**
Official	$21,756	$22,113
Research Supplemental Poverty Measure*		
Not accounting for housing status	$23,854	$24,343
Owners with a mortgage	$24,450	$25,018
Owners without a mortgage	$20,298	$20,590
Renters	$23,874	$24,391

*Garner and Gudrais, Bureau of Labor Statistics, October 2011, http://www.bls.gov/pir/spmhome.htm.

Source: Short, Kathleen. "The Research Supplemental Poverty Measure: 2010." U.S. Census Bureau, November 2011. Accessed July 1, 2012. http://www.census.gov/prod/2011pubs/p60-241.pdf

B-23. Different Poverty Measures for People in Poverty in the United States

Document B-23 provides additional detail on the differences between the poverty rate using the SPM measure and the poverty rate using the official poverty measure. As this table shows, the SPM poverty rate was 0.8 percent higher than the official rate in 2010. However, the SPM measure did bring down the poverty rate for children and blacks as compared with the official poverty measure. Applying the SPM measure increased poverty rates more for those age 65 and older than for any other demographical group.

Table B-23 Number and Percent of People in Poverty by Different Poverty Measures: 2010

Characteristic	Number** (in thousands)	Official** Number Est.	Official** Number 90 percent C.I.[1] (+)	Official** Percent Est.	Official** Percent 90 percent C.I.[1] (+)	SPM Number Est.	SPM Number 90 percent C.I.[1] (+)	SPM Percent Est.	SPM Percent 90 percent C.I.[1] (+)	Difference Number	Difference Percent
All People	306,110	46,602	850	15.2	0.3	49,094	908	16.0	0.3	*2,492	*0.8
Age											
Under 18 years	74,916	16,823	378	22.5	0.5	13,622	376	18.2	0.5	*-3,201	*-4.3
18 to 64 years	192,015	26,258	556	13.7	0.3	29,235	602	15.2	0.3	*2,976	*1.6
65 years and older	39,179	3,520	161	9.0	0.4	6,237	216	15.9	0.6	*2,716	*6.9
Type of Unit											
In married couple unit	185,723	14,200	581	7.6	0.3	18,295	622	9.9	0.3	*4,095	*2.2
In female house-holder unit	61,966	17,786	513	28.7	0.7	17,991	552	29.0	0.8	206	0.3

Table B-23 (Continued)

Characteristic	Number** (in thousands)	Official** Number Est.	Official** Number 90percent C.I.¹ (+)	Official** Percent Est.	Official** Percent 90percent C.I.¹ (+)	SPM Number Est.	SPM Number 90percent C.I.¹ (+)	SPM Percent Est.	SPM Percent 90 percent C.I.¹ (+)	Difference Number	Difference Percent
In male house-holder unit	32,224	5,927	289	18.4	0.8	7,317	308	22.7	0.8	*1,391	*4.3
In new SPM unit	26,197	8,690	341	33.2	1.0	5,490	339	21.0	1.2	*-3,200	*-12.2
Race and Hispanic Origin											
White	243,323	31,959	698	13.1	0.3	34,747	728	14.3	0.3	*2,789	*1.1
White, not Hispanic	197,423	19,819	571	10.0	0.3	21,876	605	11.1	0.3	*2,057	*1.0
Black	39,301	10,741	406	27.5	1.0	9,932	388	25.4	1.0	*-810	*-2.1
Asian	14,332	1,737	161	12.1	1.1	2,397	191	16.7	1.3	*660	*4.6
Hispanic (any race)	49,972	13,36	420	26.7	0.8	14,088	459	28.2	0.9	*742	*1.5
Nativity											
Native Born	267,884	38,965	801	14.5	0.3	39,329	85	14.7	0.3	364	0.1
Foreign Born	38,226	7,636	288	20.0	0.7	9,765	327	25.5	0.7	*2,128	*5.6
Naturalized Citizen	16,801	1,910	119	11.4	0.7	2,829	158	16.8	0.9	*919	*5.5
Not a Citizen	21,424	5,727	263	26.7	1.1	6,936	288	32.4	1.2	*1,209	*5.6
Tenure											
Owner	207,290	16,529	565	8.0	0.3	20,205	659	9.7	0.3	*3,676	*1.8

(continued)

Table B-23 (Continued)

Characteristic	Number** (in thousands)	Official** Number		Percent		SPM Number		Percent		Difference	
		Est.	90 percent C.I.¹ (+)	Est.	90 percent C.I.¹ (+)	Est.	90 percent C.I.¹ (+)	Est.	90 percent C.I.¹ (+)	Number	Percent
Owner/mortgage	138,324	8,366	389	6.0	0.3	11,419	471	8.3	0.3	*3,053	*2.2
Owner/no mortgage/ rent-free	72,180	9,036	413	12.5	0.5	9,581	429	13.3	0.6	*544	*0.8
Renter	95,606	29,199	740	30.5	0.6	28,093	76	29.	0.6	*-1,106	*-1.2
Residence											
Inside MSAs	258,350	38,650	932	15.0	0.3	42,929	879	16.6	0.3	*4,329	*1.7
Inside principal cities	98,774	19,584	585	19.8	0.5	20,748	611	21.0	0.6	*1,164	*1.2
Outside principal Cities	159,576	19,066	742	11.9	0.4	22,231	738	13.9	0.4	*3,165	*2.0
Outside MSAs	47,760	7,951	544	16,6	0.7	6,114	449	12.8	0.7	*-1,837	*-3.8
Region											
Northeast	54,782	7,051	327	12.9	0.6	7,969	342	14.5	0.6	*918	*1.7
Midwest	66,104	9,246	410	14.0	0.6	8,678	356	13.1	0.5	*-569	*-0.9
South	113,275	19,210	577	17.0	0.5	18,503	533	16.3	0.5	*-707	*-0.6
West	71,949	11,094	447	15.4	0.6	13,94	512	19.4	0.7	*2,849	*4.0

Table B-23 (Continued)

Characteristic	Number** (in thousands)	Official** Number Est.	Official** Number 90percent C.I.¹ (+)	Official** Percent Est.	Official** Percent 90percent C.I.¹ (+)	SPM Number Est.	SPM Number 90percent C.I.¹ (+)	SPM Percent Est.	SPM Percent 90 percent C.I.¹ (+)	Difference Number	Difference Percent
Health Insurance Coverage											
With private insurance	195,874	9,336	360	4.8	0.2	14,631	464	7.5	0.2	*5,295	*2.7
With public, no private insurance	60,332	22,694	600	37.6	0.8	19,126	559	31.7	0.8	*-3,568	*-5.9
Not insured	49,904	14,571	408	29.2	0.7	15,337	474	30.7	0.8	*766	*1.5

*Statistically different from zero at the 90 percent confidence level.

**Differs from published official rates as unrelated individuals under 15 years of age are included in the universe.

¹Confidence Interval obtained using replicate weights (Fay's Method).

Note: Details may not sum to totals because of rounding.

Table Source: U.S. Census Bureau, Current Population Survey, 2011 Annual Social and Economic Supplement. For information on confidentiality protection, sampling error, nonsampling error, and definitions, see www.census.gov/hhes/www/p60_239sa.pdf.

Document Source: Short, Kathleen. "The Research Supplemental Poverty Measure: 2010." U.S. Census Bureau, November 2011. Accessed July 1, 2012. http://www.census.gov/prod/2011pubs/p60-241.pdf

Recommended Resources

AARP Public Policy Institute. "Boomers and the Great Recession: Struggling to Recover," 2012. Accessed November 30, 2012.http://www.aarp.org/content/dam/aarp/research/public_policy_institute/econ_sec/2012/boomers-and-the-great-recession-struggling-to-recover-v2-AARP-ppi-econ-sec.pdf

Ali, Zaheer. "What About Poor White Kids?" December 20, 2011. Accessed August 5, 2012. http://www.theroot.com/views/what-about-poor-white-kids

Austin, Algernon. "Different Races, Different Recession: American Indian Unemployment in 2010." Economic Policy Institute, November 18, 2010. Accessed July 7, 2012. http://www.epi.org/page/-/pdf/ib289.pdf

Baker, Dean. "The Housing Bubble Pops." *Nation*, September 20, 2007. Accessed July 4, 2012. http://www.cbsnews.com/stories/2007/09/20/opinion/main3281247.shtml

Bane, M. J., and Ellwood, D. "Slipping into and out of Poverty: The Dynamics of Spells." *Journal of Human Resources* 21, no. 1 (1986): 1–23.

Barr, Alistair, and Greg Morcroft. "J.P. Morgan to Buy Bear Stearns for $2 a Share." *Wall Street Journal*, March 17, 2008. Accessed December 10, 2012. http://articles.market watch.com/2008-03-17/news/30763080_1_trading-obligations-bear-stearns-cos-shares

Boushey, Heather. "The 'Man-covery': Women Gaining Jobs in Recovery at a Slower Pace than Men." Center for American Progress, March 9, 2012. Accessed July 27, 2012. http://www.americanprogress.org/issues/2012/03/mancovery.html

Campo-Flores, Arian. "Why Americans Think (Wrongly) That Illegal Immigrants Hurt the Economy." *Newsweek*, May 13, 2010. Accessed July 8, 2012. http://www.thedaily beast.com/newsweek/2010/05/14/why-americans-think-wrongly-that-illegal-immigrants-hurt-the-economy.html

Chance, Matthew, and Christine Theodorou. "As Economic Crisis Bites, Greece's Children Pay the Price," June 16, 2012. Accessed January 1, 2013. http://www.cnn.com/2012/06/15/world/europe/greece-economic-orphans/index.html

Chomsisengphet, Souphala, and Anthony Pennington-Cross. "The Evolution of the Subprime Mortgage Market." Federal Reserve Bank of St. Louis, 2006. Accessed November15, 2012. http://research.stlouisfed.org/publications/review/06/01/Chom PennCross.pdf

Clark, Kim. "The Recession Hits College Campuses." *U.S. News and World Report,* January 27, 2009. Accessed November 26, 2012. http://www.usnews.com/education/articles/2009/01/27/the-recession-hits-college-campuses

Cohn, D'Vera. "Divorce and the Great Recession," May 2, 2012. Accessed November 3, 2012. http://www.pewsocialtrends.org/2012/05/02/divorce-and-the-great-recession/

Constitution Project: National Right to Counsel Committee. "Justice Denied: America's Continuing Neglect of Our Constitutional Right to Counsel," April 2009. Accessed June 16, 2012. http://www.constitutionproject.org/pdf/139.pdf

Crary, David. "Behind the Poverty Numbers: Real Lives, Real Pain." Associated Press, September 19, 2011. Accessed July 4, 2012. http://news.yahoo.com/behind-poverty -numbers-real-lives-real-pain-151738270.html

Dabalis, Andy. "Austerity Pushed 20% of Greeks into Poverty." *Greek Reporter,* November 4, 2012. http://greece.greekreporter.com/2012/11/04/austerity-pushes-20-of-greeks-into-poverty/

Demyanyk, Yuliya, and Otto van Hemert. "Understanding the Subprime Mortgage Crisis." Social Science Research Network, 2008. Accessed October 12, 2012. http://papers .ssrn.com/sol3/papers.cfm?abstract_id=1020396

DeNavas-Walt, Carmen, Bernadette D. Proctor, and Jessica C. Smith. "Income, Poverty, and Health Insurance Coverage in the United States, 2007." U.S. Census Bureau, August 2008. Accessed October 14, 2011. http://www.census.gov/prod/2008pubs/p60-235.pdf

DeNavas-Walt, Carmen, Bernadette Proctor, and Jessica Smith. "Income, Poverty, and Health Insurance Coverage in the United States: 2008." U.S. Census Bureau, September 2009. Accessed October 15, 2011. http://www.census.gov/prod/2009pubs/p60-236.pdf

DeNavas-Walt, Carmen, Bernadette Proctor, and Jessica Smith. "Income, Poverty, and Health Insurance Coverage in the United States: 2009." U.S. Census Bureau, September 2010. Accessed October 14, 2011. http://www.census.gov/prod/2010pubs/p60-238.pdf

DeNavas-Walt, Carmen, Bernadette Proctor, and Jessica Smith. "Income, Poverty, and Health Insurance Coverage in the United States: 2010." U.S. Census Bureau, September 2011. Accessed October 14, 2011. http://www.census.gov/prod/2011pubs/p60-239.pdf

DeNavas-Walt, Carmen, Bernadette Proctor, and Jessica Smith. "Income, Poverty, and Health Insurance Coverage in the United States: 2011." U.S. Census Bureau, September 2011. Accessed October 14, 2011. http://www.census.gov/prod/2011pubs/p60-239.pdf

DeParle, Jason. "Welfare Limits Left Poor Adrift as Recession Hit." New York Times, April 8, 2012. Accessed November 4, 2012. http://www.nytimes.com/2012/04/08/us/welfare-limits-left-poor-adrift-as-recession-hit.html?pagewanted=all&_r=0

Dillon, Sam. "Lines Grow Long for Free School Meals, Thanks to Economy." *New York Times*, November 29, 2011. Accessed June 9, 2012. http://www.nytimes.com/2011/11/30/education/surge-in-free-school-lunches-reflects-economic-crisis.html?pagewanted=all

Duncan, G. J., Kathleen M. Ziol-Guest., and Kalil Ariel. "Early-Childhood Poverty and Adult Attainment, Behavior, and Health."*Child Development* 81 (2010): 306–25.

Federal Reserve Bank of St. Louis. "Natural Rate of Unemployment (Long-Term) (NROU)," 2012. Accessed August 6. http://research.stlouisfed.org/fred2/series/NROU

Food and Nutrition Service, U.S. Department of Agriculture. "The Stimulus Package and SNAP: How the American Recovery and Reinvestment Act Affects SNAP Benefits and Policies," 2012. Accessed November 13. http://www.fns.usda.gov/fns/recovery/ARRA_Powerpoint.pdf

Grow, Brian, and Keith Epstein. 2007. "The Poverty Business: Inside U.S. Companies' Audacious Drive to Extract More Profits from the Nation's Working Poor." *BusinessWeek*, May 21, 2007, 56–67.

Gruenstein Bocian, Debbie, Wei Li, and Keith S. Ernst. "Foreclosures by Race and Ethnicity: The Demographics of a Crisis." Center for Responsible Lending, June 18, 2010. Accessed July 15, 2012. http://www.responsiblelending.org/mortgage-lending/research-analysis/foreclosures-by-race-and-ethnicity.pdf

Haskins, Ron, and Isabel Sawhill. *Creating an Equal Opportunity Society*. Washington, D.C.: Brookings Institution Press, 2009.

Hess, Cynthia, Jeff Hayes, and Heidi Hartmann. 2011. "Retirement on the Edge: Women, Men and Economic Insecurity after the Great Recession." Institute for Women's Policy Research, September 2011. Accessed November 30, 2012. http://www.iwpr.org/publications/pubs/retirement-on-the-edge-women-men-and-economic-insecurity-after-the-great-recession

Huffington Post. "CBO Report Says Deficit Reduction Will Cause New Recession," May 22, 2012. Accessed July 1, 2012. http://www.huffingtonpost.com/2012/05/22/cbo-report-deficit-reduction-recession_n_1537774.html?view=print

Holzer, Harry J., Diane Whitmore Schanzenbach, Greg J. Duncan, and Jens Ludwig. "The Economic Cost of Poverty." Center for Economic Progress, January 24, 2007. Accessed May 20, 2012. http://www.americanprogress.org/issues/2007/01/pdf/poverty_report.pdf

Housing Assistance Council. "Foreclosure in Rural America: An Update," 2011. Accessed November 1, 2012. http://www.ruralhome.org/storage/documents/rcbiforeclosurebrief.pdf

Isaacs, Julia B., Isabel V. Sawhill, and Ron Haskins. "Getting Ahead or Losing Ground: Economic Mobility in America," February 2008. Accessed January 14, 2013. http://www.pewtrusts.org/uploadedFiles/wwwpewtrustsorg/Reports/Economic_Mobility/Economic_Mobility_in_America_Full.pdf

Johnson, Anne, Tobin van Ostern, and Abraham White. "The Student Debt Crisis." Center for America Progress, October 25, 2012. Accessed November 26, 2012. http://www.americanprogress.org/wp-content/uploads/2012/10/WhiteStudentDebt-3.pdf

Johnson, David. "Households Doubling Up." U.S. Census Bureau, September 13, 2011. Accessed November 26, 2012. http://blogs.census.gov/2011/09/13/households-doubling-up/

Johnson, Nicholas, Phil Oliff, and Erica Williams. "An Update on State Budget Cuts." Center on Budget and Policy Priorities, February 9, 2011. Accessed December 18, 2012. http://www.cbpp.org/cms/index.cfm?fa=view&id=1214

Joint Center for Housing Studies. "The State of the Nation's Housing 2011." Harvard University, Graduate School of Design, 2011. Accessed July 18, 2012. http://www.jchs.harvard.edu/research/publications/state-nation%E2%80%99s-housing-2011

Kahn, Lisa B. "The Long-Term Labor Market Consequences of Graduating from College in a Bad Economy," August 13, 2009. Accessed November 26, 2012. http://mba.yale.edu/faculty/pdf/kahn_longtermlabor.pdf

Katz, Michael. *In the Shadow of the Poorhouse: A Social History of Welfare in America.* New York: Basic Books, 1996.

Kim, Marlene. "Unfairly Disadvantaged? Asian Americans and Unemployment during and after the Great Recession (2007–10)," April 5, 2012. Accessed December 6, 2012. http://www.epi.org/files/2012/ib323.pdf

Kochhar, Rakesh, Richard Fry, and Paul Taylor. "Wealth Gap Rises to Record Highs Between Whites, Blacks, Hispanics." Pew Research Center, July 26, 2011. Accessed December 17, 2012. http://www.pewsocialtrends.org/2011/07/26/wealth-gaps-rise-to-record-highs-between-whites-blacks-hispanics/

Lara, David, and Douglas Rice. "Proposals to Cut Domestic Programs Threaten Loss of Housing Assistance for Thousands of Low-Income Families: Current House and Senate Bills Would Fully Fund Vouchers." Center on Budget and Policy Priorities, November 29, 2010. Accessed June 23, 2012. http://www.cbpp.org/files/11-29-10hous.pdf

Lewin, Tamar. "Education Department Report Shows More Borrowers Defaulting on Student Loans." *New York Times,* September 28, 2012. Accessed November 26, 2012. http://www.nytimes.com/2012/09/29/education/report-shows-more-borrows-defaulting-on-student-loans.html

Monea, Emily, and Isabel Sawhill. "Simulating the Effect of the 'Great Recession' on Poverty," Brookings Institution, September 17, 2009. Accessed June 14, 2012. http://www.brookings.edu/~/media/research/files/papers/2009/9/10%20poverty%20monea%20sawhill/0910_poverty_monea_sawhill.pdf

Monea, Emily, and Isabel Sawhill. "An Update to 'Simulating the Effect of the "Great Recession" on Poverty.'" Brookings Institution, September 13, 2011. Accessed June 12, 2012. http://www.brookings.edu/~/media/research/files/reports/2011/9/13 recession povertymonea sawhill/0913_recession_poverty_monea_sawhill.pdf

Morin, Rich. "Rising Share of Americans See Conflict between Rich and Poor." Pew Research Center, January 11, 2011. Accessed July 21, 2012. http://www.pewsocialtrends.org/2012/01/11/rising-share-of-americans-see-conflict-between-rich-and-poor/

Muhammad, Dedrick. "Challenges to Native American Advancement: The Recession and Native America." Institute for Policy Studies, 2009. Accessed October 1, 2012. http://www.ips-dc.org/reports/the_recession_and_native_america

Mutikani, Lucia. "In Recession, Poverty Strikes Middle Class." Reuters UK, January 16, 2009. Accessed July 4, 2012. http://uk.reuters.com/article/2009/01/16/us-usa-economy-poverty-idUKTRE50F0WB20090116

Oliff, Phil, Chris Mai, and Vincent Palacios. "States Continue to Feel Recession's Impact." Center on Budget and Policy Priorities, June 27, 2012. Accessed July 1, 2012. http://www.cbpp.org/cms/index.cfm?fa=view&id=711

Orshansky, Mollie. "Counting the Poor: Another Look at the Poverty Profile," January 1965. http://www.ssa.gov/policy/docs/ssb/v28n1/v28n1p3.pdf

Patterson, James T. *America's Struggle against Poverty, 1900–1994*. Cambridge, MA: Harvard University Press, 1994.

Pavetti, LaDonna, and Liz Schott. "TANF's Inadequate Response to Recession Highlights Weakness of Block-Grant Structure." Center on Budget and Policy Priorities, June 14, 2011. Accessed June 9, 2012. http://www.cbpp.org/cms/?fa=view&id=3534

Peralta, Eyder. "Recession Causes Wider Wealth Gap between White, Minorities." National Public Radio, July 26, 2011. Accessed December 5, 2012. http://www.npr.org/blogs/the-two-way/2011/07/26/138698236/recession-causes-wider-wealth-gap-between-whites-minorities

Pimpare, Stephen. *A People's History of Poverty in America*. New York: New Press, 2008.

Ramakrishnan, Karthick, and Taeku Lee. "National Asian American Survey: The Policy Priorities and Issue Preferences of Asian Americans and Pacific Islanders," October 16, 2012. Accessed November 17, 2012. http://www.naasurvey.com/resources/Home/NAAS12-sep25-issues.pdf

Recovery.gov. "Recovery.gov: Track the Money," 2013. Accessed February 5, 2013. www.recovery.gov

Ross Sorkin, Andrew. "Lehman Files for Bankruptcy; Merrill Is Sold." *New York Times*, September 14, 2008. Accessed July 4, 2012. http://www.nytimes.com/2008/09/15/business/15lehman.html?pagewanted=all

Ruffing, Kathy, Kris Kox, and James Horney. "The Right Target: Stabilize the Federal Debt." Center on Budget and Policy Priorities, January 12, 2010. Accessed July 4, 2012. http://www.cbpp.org/files/01-12-10bud.pdf

Rynell, Amy. "Causes of Poverty: Findings from Recent Research," October 2008. Accessed October 8, 2011. http://www.lruw.org/upload/assets/documents/board/our%20community%20investing/financial%20stability%20initiative/causes%20of%20poverty%20-%20findings%20from%20recent%20research.pdf

Shapiro, Lila. "Missing Workers: 4.9 Million out of Work and Forgotten." *Huffington Post*, February 4, 2011. Accessed June 9, 2012. http://www.huffingtonpost.com/2011/02/04/missing-workers-44-millio_n_818314.html?page=1

Shenn, Jody. "Fannie Mae Tightens Mortgage Standards for Some Home Buyers." Bloomberg, August 22, 2012. Accessed October 10, 2012. http://www.bloomberg.com/news/2012-08-22/fannie-mae-tightens-mortgage-standards-for-some-home-buyers.html

Singer, Audrey, and Jill H. Wilson. "The Impact of the Great Recession on Metropolitan Immigration Trends." Brookings Institution, Metropolitan Policy Program, December 2010. Accessed July 8, 2012. http://www.brookings.edu/~/media/research/files/opinions/2011/1/12 migration frey/1216_immigration_singer_wilson.pdf

Steinhauer, Jennifer. "Debt Bill Is Signed, Ending a Fractious Battle." *New York Times*, August 2, 2011. Accessed July 4, 2012. http://www.nytimes.com/2011/08/03/us/politics/03fiscal.html?pagewanted=2

Streitfeld, Rachel. "Not Even Renters Safe from Foreclosure Storm." CNN, March 8, 2009. Accessed July 1, 2012. http://articles.cnn.com/2009-03-08/us/renters.foreclosure_1_homeless-shelter-renters-foreclosure-rate?_s=PM:US

Sum, Andrew, and Ishwar Khatiwada. "The Nation's Underemployed in the 'Great Recession' of 2007–09." *Monthly Labor Review*, November 2010. Accessed August 5, 2012. http://www.bls.gov/opub/mlr/2010/11/art1full.pdf

Tavernise, Sabrina. "Food Stamps Helped Reduce Poverty Rate, Study Finds," April 9, 2012. Accessed November 13, 2012. http://www.nytimes.com/2012/04/10/us/food-stamp-program-helping-reduce-poverty.html

Tavernise, Sabrina. "Soaring Poverty Casts Spotlight on 'Lost Decade.'" *New York Times*, September 13, 2011. Accessed November 26, 2012. http://www.nytimes.com/2011/09/14/us/14census.html?pagewanted=all

Taylor, Paul, Rakesh Kochhar, Rich Morin, Wendy Wang, Daniel Dockterman, and Jennifer Medina. "America's Changing Workforce: Recession Turns a Graying Office Grayer." Pew Research Center, September 3, 2009. Accessed November 26, 2012. http://www.pewsocialtrends.org/files/2010/10/americas-changing-workforce.pdf

Tiehen, Laura Dean Jolliffe, and Craig Gundersen. "Alleviating Poverty in the United States: The Critical Role of SNAP Benefits." U.S. Department of Agriculture Economic Research Service, 2012. Accessed November 13, 2012. http://www.ers.usda.gov/publications/err-economic-research-report/err132.aspx

U.S. Census Bureau. "Historical Poverty Tables: People," 2012. Accessed December 5, 2012. http://www.census.gov/hhes/www/poverty/data/historical/people.html

U.S. Department of Labor. "African American Labor Force in the Recovery," February 29, 2012. Accessed December 5, 2012. http://www.dol.gov/_sec/media/reports/BlackLaborForce/BlackLaborForce.pdf

U.S. Department of Labor, Bureau of Labor Statistics. "Access to Historical Data for the 'A' tables of the Employment Situation News Release," 2012. Accessed August 5, 2012. http://data.bls.gov/pdq/SurveyOutputServlet

U.S. Department of Housing and Urban Development. "The 2008 Annual Homeless Assessment Report," July 2009. Accessed June 17, 2012. http://www.huduser.org/publications/pdf/4thHomelessAssessmentReport.pdf

U.S. Department of Housing and Urban Development. "The 2009 Annual Homeless Assessment Report to Congress," June 2010. Accessed June 17, 2012. http://www.hudhre.info/documents/5thHomelessAssessmentReport.pdf

U.S. Department of Housing and Urban Development. "The 2010 Annual Homeless Assessment Report to Congress," 2012. Accessed June 17. http://www.hudhre.info/documents/2010HomelessAssessmentReport.pdf

Van de Water, Paul N., and Arloc Sherman. "Social Security Keeps 20 Million Americans Out of Poverty: A State-By-State Analysis," August 11, 2010. Accessed November 4, 2012. http://www.cbpp.org/cms/index.cfm?fa=view&id=3260

Wagmiller, Robert L. Jr., and Robert M. Adelman. "Childhood and Intergenerational Poverty: The Long-Term Consequences of Growing Up Poor." National Center for Children in Poverty, 2009. Accessed October 8, 2011. http://www.nccp.org/publications/pdf/text_909.pdf

Wall Street Journal. "Getting to $787 Billion," February 17, 2009. Accessed July 4, 2012. http://online.wsj.com/public/resources/documents/STIMULUS_FINAL_0217.html

ABOUT THE EDITORS AND CONTRIBUTORS

THE EDITORS

Lindsey K. Hanson, Esq. is a staff attorney at a nonprofit organization in Minnesota, where she represents low-income tenants in housing cases. She formerly represented low-income clients in rural Minnesota in immigration cases and served as court-appointed defense counsel in child protection cases on the White Earth Reservation. She has also planned and implemented literacy and educational programming for low-income children in her work with a variety of nonprofit organizations. In addition, she was a contributing writer for Greenwood's *Battleground: Politics and Government* (2011) and ABC-CLIO's *Encyclopedia of American Indian Issues Today* (2013).

Timothy J. Essenburg, Ph.D. is professor of economics at Bethel University in Saint Paul, Minnesota. He has a keen interest in the revitalization of central city neighborhoods, as is demonstrated in his professional (research and teaching) and personal life. He and his family have lived in the East Phillips Neighborhood of South Minneapolis for 23 years, where in 1998 he co-founded the Banyan Community, a community development corporation. He also has facilitated workshops on antiracism with local churches, Catholic Charities, and Lutheran Social Service. Peace, justice, and the enjoyment of relationships are foundational to his worldview.

THE CONTRIBUTORS

Rojhat B. Avsar, Ph.D. is an assistant professor of economics at Columbia College in Chicago, Illinois.

Behroz Baraghoshi, Ph.D. is an assistant professor of economics at Eastern Connecticut State University in Willimantic, Connecticut.

Mary E. Burton is a research assistant for Carlos Liard-Muriente, Ph.D., associate professor and chair of economics, at Central Connecticut State University in New Britain, Connecticut.

Gerardo Del Guercio has a master's degree in English literature and teaches at École de Langues Shakespeare and Groupe SLC in Montreal, Quebec, Canada.

Bryan Dettrey, Ph.D. is visiting assistant professor of political science at Pennsylvania State University in Harrisburg, Pennsylvania.

Wayne Edwards, Ph.D. is a visiting associate professor of economics at Middlebury College in Middlebury, Vermont.

Charles Hannema, MBA is an associate professor of business and economics at Bethel University in Saint Paul, Minnesota.

Kelsey Hanson, MSW is a recent graduate of the School of Social Work at the University of St. Catherine and St. Thomas in Saint Paul, Minnesota.

Jeff Jacob, Ph.D. is an associate professor of economics at Bethel University in Saint Paul, Minnesota.

Joyce P. Jacobsen, Ph.D. is the Andrews Professor of Economics at Wesleyan University in Middletown, Connecticut.

Eric Larson, Ph.D. is a visiting scholar at the Center for the Study of Race and Ethnicity in America at Brown University in Providence, Rhode Island.

Joyce LeMay, SPHR, MBA is an associate professor of business and economics at Bethel University in Saint Paul, Minnesota.

Carlos Liard-Muriente, Ph.D. is aprofessor and chair of economics at Central Connecticut State University in New Britain, Connecticut.

Steven McMullen, Ph.D. is an assistant professor of economics at Calvin College in Grand Rapids, Michigan.

Stephen Pimpare, Ph.D. is Adjunct Associate Professor of Social Work and Social Policy at Columbia University, NYU, and the City University of New York.

Jack Reardon, Ph.D. is a professor of economics at Hamline University in Saint Paul, Minnesota.

Cara B. Robinson, Ph.D. is an assistant professor of urban studies at the College of Public Service and Urban Affairs at Tennessee State University in Nashville, Tennessee.

Ken Taylor, Ph.D. is a professor of urban missions at New Orleans Baptist Theological Seminary in New Orleans, Louisiana.

Katie Uva is an American History Ph.D. candidate at the Graduate Center of the City University of New York (CUNY) in New York, New York.

Fred Van Geest, Ph.D. is a professor of political science at Bethel University in Saint Paul, Minnesota.

Angela R. Wilder, Ed.D. is an Adjunct Professor of Leadership and Management at Polk State College in Winter Haven, Florida.

Samuel Zalanga, Ph.D. is a professor of sociology at Bethel University in Saint Paul, Minnesota.

INDEX

AARP (American Association of Retired
   Persons), 226
ABS (Asset-backed securities), 47, 49
Absolute measures of poverty, 161, 162
ACA (Affordable Care Act of 2010), 420, 421,
   484, 584, 704
Access to credit
   credit reports, 401
   effect of Great Recession, 397–98
   low-income households, 389, 399–401
   outlook on, 401–2
   overview, 389–90, 397
"Actively seeking work," 494
Adjustable rate mortgage (ARM), 41, 53–54, 87
Adulthood, postponement of, 212
Adults (35–64)
   Great Recession, effects of, 180
   lengths of unemployment, 218
   outlook for, 221–22
   overview of, 218
   poverty, 220–21
   retirement plans, changes in, 219
   unemployment, 218–20
Adverse shock, 14
AEI (American Enterprise Institute), 654–56
AFDC (Aid to Families with Dependent
   Children), 75, 530, 690
Affordability of college, 238
Affordable Care Act of 2010 (ACA), 420, 421,
   484, 584, 704
Africa, 357–58
African Americans
   2008 poverty rate, 171

2009 poverty rate, 172
2010 poverty rate, 173
2011 poverty rate, 174
access to New Deal programs, 76
child poverty and, 202–3
children, 189
chronic intergenerational
   poverty, 144–45, 146
conflict between rich and poor,
   view of, 679
disparity ratio, 93–94
economic mobility, xix, xx–xxi
economy and recession, views on,
   383–84
educational attainment, 192, 196
effects of historical trauma, neighborhoods
   and discrimination on poverty, 146
female-headed households, 190–91
foreclosures, 194–95
Great Depression and, 74–75
Great Recession and, 76–77, 179
homelessness, 195, 446, 448, 449
homeownership, 90, 91, 194
home values, 195
housing crisis and, 194–95
income inequality, 193–94
income losses and increasing disparity,
   193–94
infant mortality rate during the Great
   Depression, 75
injustices against, xx–xxi
life expectancy during the Great
   Depression, 75

long-term unemployment, 193
median wealth, 147
men and unemployment, 337
outlook for, 196
overview of, 188
personal financial situation,
    view of, 381
poverty, 188–91
poverty rates, 693
poverty thresholds, 164
present situation, 188–96
public sector employment, 192, 366
rural families and individuals, 319–20
senior citizens, 190, 225, 311
Social Security and decrease in
    poverty rate, 692
underemployment, 497
unemployment, 191–93
unemployment rate, 380, 511
urban families and individuals, 366
veterans, 374
wealth gap, 195–96
young adults, 210–11, 382
Agricultural sector, 317
Agriculture, Department of (USDA), 161,
    404–5, 407, 409
Aid to Families with Dependent Children
    (AFDC), 75, 530, 690
AIG Insurance, 50, 55, 106
Alabama, 548
Alaska, 288
Alaska Native Claims Settlement
    Act (ANCSA), 288
Alaska Natives, 210–11, 288–92, 374, 561. *See
    also* Native Americans
Alaska Natives Claims Settlement
    Act, 565, 566
Alaskan Native corporations, 542, 565–66
Albania, 8
Allotment process, 287
Alternative banking, 389, 399–401
Alternative Mortgage Transaction
    Parity Act, 40
American Association of Neurological
    Surgeons, 477
American Association of Retired Persons
    (AARP), 226
American Community Survey, 657
American Dream, xviii
American Enterprise Institute (AEI), 654–56
American Humanist Association, xv
American ideals and experience, and
    importance of poverty alleviation, xviii–xxi
American Indian or Native Alaskan (AINA),
    291–92, 561, 562–63. *See also* Native
    Americans

American Jobs and Closing Tax Loopholes Act
    of 2010, 665
American Opportunity Tax Credit (AOTC),
    431–32, 586
American Recovery and Reinvestment Act of
    2009 (ARRA), 5, 108–10, 112
    Earned Income Tax Credit and, 534, 581–82
    food insecurity, 390, 409, 411
    higher education, 431
    homelessness, 392
    homeless program funding, 449
    housing assistance programs, 458
    impact of, 78–79
    impact on local revenue, 546
    Indian Health Service (IHS), 564
    Medicaid and, 419–20
    overview of, 544, 581–83
    Pell grants, 431
    persons with disabilities and, 245
    public sector unemployment and, 192
    state budget shortfalls, 554
    state government spending and, 552
    Supplemental Nutrition Assistance
        Program, 409–11
    Temporary Assistance for
        Needy Families, 533
American Tax Payer Relief Act of 2012,
    585–86, 601
"The American Welfare State" (Tanner), 699
ANCSA (Alaska Native Claims
    Settlement Act), 288
*An Inquiry into the Nature and Causes of the
    Wealth of Nations. See The Wealth of
    Nations* (Smith)
*Annual Homeless Assessment Report to
    Congress* (AHAR), 445
Anti-Catholic sentiment, xxi
Anti-immigrant sentiments, 277–78
Antipoverty programs and budget cutting,
    671–72
Anti-Semitism, xxi
AOTC (American Opportunity Tax Credit),
    431–32, 586
Arab Spring, 601
Arizona, 420, 553, 555, 556, 557
ARM (Adjustable rate mortgage), 41, 53–54, 87
ARRA. *See* American Recovery and
    Reinvestment Act of 2009 (ARRA)
Asian Americans
    child poverty, 234
    educational attainment, 235–36
    female-headed households, 234
    foreclosures, 237–38
    Great Recession, effects of, 181, 238–39
    homeownership, 237, 238
    housing, 237–38

living with parents, 239
long-term unemployment, 236–37
men and unemployment, 337
net worth, 238–39
outlook for, 239
overview of, 232
poverty, 233–34
poverty rates, 163–64, 171, 172, 173, 174, 693
poverty thresholds, 164
senior citizens, 234
underemployment, 497
unemployment, 235–36
unemployment rate, 380, 511
veterans, 374
young adults, 210–11
Asset-Backed Commercial Paper Money Market, 127
Asset-backed securities (ABS), 47, 49
Asset bubbles, 86. *See also* Housing bubble
Asset poverty, 137, 140–41, 143–44
Assets, 121–24, 129
Asylees, 276. *See also* Immigrants
At risk relative poverty rate, 353–54
Attentiveness, xvii
Austerity budgets, 27
Automatic stabilizers, 78, 99
Automobile industry bailout, 106

Baby Boomers, 228, 311–12
"Bailout," economic, 579–81
Bailouts, 19, 24, 87–88
Balance sheet, 120–24, 128–29
Balloon payments, 40
Baltic states, 572
Bank bailouts, 19, 24
Bank crisis, 124–25
Bank failures, 4, 55, 57, 61–62
Banking Act of 1933. *See* Glass-Steagall Act
Banking Act of 1935, 596
Banking crisis, 14
Banking sector, 339
Banking system, 3–4
Banking trends, 15–17
Bank lending to the private sector, 15
Bank of America, 57, 88
Bank of England, 18
Bank of International Settlements, 50
Bank runs, 18, 125
Bankruptcy, 401
Basic needs budget, 138, 151–57, 164–65, 199
Bear Stearns, 19, 54–55, 57, 126, 128
Before-tax money income, 162
Belgium, 19
Belief systems, and importance of poverty alleviation, xiii–xv. *See also* Religious groups

The Bell Curve (Murray and Herrnstein), 677
Bernanke, Ben, 78, 103, 118–19, 131–32
Bernstein, Jared, 108–9
Beveridge Curve, 625
BIA (Bureau of Indian Affairs), 287, 530, 543, 560
BIA Financial Assistance and Social Services program, 567
Bilateral Currency Swaps, 126–27
Bill and Melinda Gates Foundation, 642
Bipartisan Policy Center, 583
Birthrate, 213, 272
Blacks. *See* African Americans
Blanchard, Oliver, 10
BNP Paribas, 18
Boehner, John, 52, 649
Bonds, 44, 47
"Boomeranging," 212, 239
Booth School of Business, 110
Born, Brooksley, 42–43
Brazil, 4, 10, 357, 358, 571, 573
Bridge to Work Program, 209
Broad unemployment rate, 59–60
Brooks, Arthur, 656
Brown v. Board of Education, xx
Budget Control Act of 2011, 566, 585
Budget deficits, in Europe, 24–25
Bureau of Indian Affairs (BIA), 287, 530, 543, 560
Bureau of Labor Statistics (BLS), 161, 209, 226–27, 300–301, 494–95, 502
Bureau of Land Management, 564
Bush, George H. W., 107, 612
Bush, George W.
    Bernanke appointment, 118
    conservatorship of Fannie Mae and Freddie Mac, 106–7
    Economic Stimulus Act of 2008, 104–5, 543, 579–81
    Emergency Economic Stabilization Act (EESA) of 2008, 105–6, 579–81
    federal debt, 612
    fiscal policy, 103–7
    on poverty reduction, 704
    tax cuts, 101
Business cycles, 4, 37, 38, 520, 526, 596
Business cycle synchronization, 17–18
Businesses, tax code changes for in Economic Stimulus Act, 104

Calderón, Felipe, 543, 573
California, 237, 464, 548, 553, 554, 556
Cambodian Americans, 236, 237
Campaign for Human Development, 665
Canada, 9
Cantor, Eric, 657

CAP (Community Action Programs), 692
Capital formation, in Europe, 20–22
Capital gains, 44
Capitalism, Socialism and Democracy
    (Schumpeter), 621
Caribbean, 572
CASE (Christians for a Sustainable Economy),
    637, 671–72
Casinos, tribal, 565
Catholic Charities (CC), 665–66, 667
"A Catholic Framework for Economic
    Life," 664
Catholic Social Teaching (CST), xiv,
    664–65, 668
Cato Institute, 109, 654
CBO (Congressional Budget Office), 174, 414,
    514–15, 601
CC (Catholic Charities), 665–66, 667
CCC (Civilian Conservation Corps), 75
CC-IME (Institute of Mexicans
    in the Exterior), 573, 574
CCT (Christian Churches Together
    in the USA), 669
CDOs (Collateralized debt obligations), 16–17,
    48, 49, 50, 54–55
CDS (Credit default swaps), 16, 19–20, 49–50
Center for American Progress, 213
Center on Budget and Policy
    Priorities, 112, 692
Centers for Disease Control and
    Prevention, 272
Central city neighborhoods, 363–64
Central Falls, Rhode Island, 548
CES (Current Employment Statistics), 502–3
Chained consumer price index, 487–88
Charitable giving, 78
Chavez, Hugo, 574
Check cashing services, 389, 400
Cherokees, 287, 562
Cheyenne River Health Center, 564
Child abuse, 475–77
Child allowances, 204–5
Child Deprivation Index, 199
Child poverty
    1970–2010 poverty rate, 201
    2008 poverty rate, 171
    2009 poverty rate, 172
    2010 poverty rate, 173
    2011 poverty rate, 174
    African Americans, 189
    Asian Americans, 234
    chronic intergenerational poverty, 144–46
    demographic characteristics, 203–4
    educational attainment, 200
    effects of, 145–46
    family mean income, 202

female-headed households, 204
    in geographical areas, 204
    Great Recession and, 77, 180, 200–204
    Hispanic Americans, 202–3, 268–70
    homelessness, 392
    impact of, 147–48, 199–200
    outlook for, 204–5
    overview of, 198–200
    prevalence of, 144
    race and ethnicity, 202–3
    racialization of, 144–45
    social costs of, 200
    social mobility, 199–200
    unemployment, 201–2, 203
    urban families and individuals, 363
    worst-case housing needs, 455–56
Children's Health Insurance Program (CHIP)
    budget shortfalls and, 555
    enrollment, 420–21
    health care assistance, 417
    immigrants, 281
    impact of Great Recession on, 418
    overview of, 390, 418
    as part of Social Security Act, 484
    rural families and individuals, 319
    Ryan budget, 584
Children's Health Insurance Program
    Reauthorization Act (CHIPRA), 421
Child Tax Credit, 112, 531, 583, 586, 669
China, 3, 4, 8, 10, 12–13, 357–58, 571–73, 603
Chinese Americans, 236, 238
CHIP. *See* Children's Health Insurance
    Program (CHIP)
CHIPRA (Children's Health Insurance
    Program Reauthorization Act), 421
Christian Churches Together in the
    USA (CCT), 668
Christianity, on poverty, xiv. *See also* Religious
    groups
Christians for a Sustainable Economy
    (CASE), 637, 671–72
Chronic intergenerational poverty
    African Americans, 144–45, 146
    causes of, 140–41
    children, 144–46
    definition of, 137
    female-headed households, 144
    Hispanic Americans, 144
    impact of neighborhoods on, 146
    overview of, 140
Chrysler, 106
Circle of Protection, 670–72
Citibank, 18
Citicorp, 42
City and social services, 365–66
City governments, 363, 365–66

Civilian Conservation Corps (CCC), 75
Civilian labor force, 502
Civil Rights Act of 1964, xx
Civil Works Administration (CWA), 75
Class conflict, 679–80
Cleveland, 366, 547
Clinton, Bill, 101, 107, 628, 695
COBRA (Consolidated Omnibus Budget
    Reconciliation Act) health insurance
    benefits, 78–79
Collateralized debt obligations (CDOs), 16–17,
    48, 49, 50, 54–55
College endowments, 208, 425–27
College enrollment, increase in, 258–59
College tuition, 391
Commercial Paper Funding Facility, 127
Commercial paper market, 55
Commodity Exchange Act of 1936, 42
Commodity Futures Modernization Act of
    2000, 42, 50
Commodity Futures Trading Commission,
    42–43, 50
Common currency, 22–23
Communities, impact of housing crisis on,
    95–96
Community Action Programs (CAP), 692
Community colleges, 391, 426–29
Community Partnership for Homeless in
    Miami, 446
Community Reinvestment Act (CRA)
    of 1977, 87, 131
Comparative economic size of regions, 8
Compensation, unemployment, 513–15
Competence, xvii
Computers and social media, hiring practices
    and, 440–41
Conference of Labor Statisticians, 494
Confronting Poverty program, 668
Congress, 51–52, 57–58, 94–95. See also
    Legislative response
Congressional Budget Office (CBO), 174, 414,
    514–15, 601
Connecticut, 420, 555
Conservative Revolution, 694–96
Consolidated Omnibus Budget Reconciliation
    Act (COBRA) health insurance
    benefits, 78–79
Construction industry, 334–35, 339, 497,
    509–10, 512
Consumer debt, 398
Consumer Expenditure Survey, 161
Consumer Financial Protection Agency, 81
Consumer Financial Protection Bureau, 627
Consumer Price Index for Food, 408
Consumer sentiment, 156
Consumer Sentiment Index, 158

Consumption, 105
"Contract with America," 695
Corporate bonds, default rate on, 47
Corporate giving, 643–44
Corporate governance, 50–51
Council of Economic Advisors, 162
Council on Veterans Employment, 375
Countrywide Financial, 51, 128
CPS (Current Population Survey),
    406, 411, 502–3
CPS Food Security Control Module, 406
CRA (Community Reinvestment Act)
    of 1977, 87, 131
CRA (Credit rating agencies), 16, 44
Craigslist, 440
Creative destruction, 621
Credit, access to
    credit reports, 401
    effect of Great Recession, 397–98
    low-income households, 389, 399–401
    outlook on, 401–2
    overview, 398–90
Credit boom, as cause of Great
    Recession, 14–15
Credit crunch, 389, 397–98, 626, 642
Credit default swaps (CDS), 16, 19–20, 49–50
Credit derivatives, 49–50
Credit flows, 124
Credit rating agencies (CRA), 16, 44
Credit ratings, 45–46
Credit reports, 401
Credit risk, collateralized debt
    obligations and, 16
Crime, 257, 477
CST (Catholic Social Teaching),
    xiv, 664–65, 668
Culture of poverty thesis, 677
Cummins Emission Solutions, 317
Current Employment Statistics (CES), 502–3
Current Population Survey (CPS),
    406, 411, 502–3
Cut, Cap, and Balance Act, 584–85, 671
CWA (Civil Works Administration), 75
Cyclical poverty, 137, 140, 141–42
Cyclical unemployment, 503–4

Darling, Alistair, 19
Dawes Act, 287
Debt. See Federal deficit and debt
Debt and credit. See Finance, debt and credit
Debt ceiling debates, 583–85
Debt crisis, in Europe, 22–27
Declaration of Independence, xv, 689
Deep poverty rate, 77
Default rates, 47, 56
Deficit, SS and Medicare, 485–89

Deficit and debt, federal, 611–12, 628–30
Deflation, 599, 601
Deflation, problems with, 599–601
Demand-side economics, 101
Denmark, 22
Denver, 364
Depository Institutions Deregulation
    and Monetary Control Act of 1980
    (DIDMCA), 40, 87
Deregulation, 101
Developing nations, 356–58
Dexia, 19
DIDMCA (Depository Institutions
    Deregulation and Monetary Control
    Act of 1980), 40, 87
Differential credit risk, 24
Disability, persons with
    federal government response to, 245
    Great Recession, effects of, 181
    overview of, 241–42
    poverty rates, 242–43
    unemployment, 244–45
    worst-case housing needs, 456
Disability Policy Collaboration, 245
Discouraged workers
    definition of, 504
    as indicator of overall economy, 59
    labor force participation, 218–19
    length of unemployment, 334
    in marginally attached group, 508
    poverty rates and, 436
    recovery and, 338
    underemployment and, 494
Discretionary fiscal policy
    American Recovery and Reinvestment
        Act of 2009 (ARRA), 108–10
    in Bush era, 103–7
    conservatorship of Fannie Mae and
        Freddie Mac, 106–7
    Economic Stimulus Act of 2008,
        104–5
    Emergency Economic Stabilization Act of
        2008, 105–6
    federal debt, 112
    historical background, 100–101
    in Obama era, 107–11
    outlook for, 112–13
    overview of, 99–100
    poverty and, 111–12
    the present, 101–3
    Tax Relief, Unemployment Insurance
        Reauthorization, and Job Creation
        Act, 110–11
Disparate impact discrimination, 440
Disparity ratio for foreclosures, 93
Distribution of income, 151–53, 614–15

Divorce, as secondary effect of Great
    Recession, 477–78
Dodd-Frank Act, 81, 627, 628, 629
Domestic violence, 474–77
Donations from individuals to nonprofits,
    644–45
Double dip recession risk
    outlook for, 601–3
    overview of, 594, 595–97
    present situation, 597–601
"Doubling up," 212, 239, 382, 456, 471
Durability of convergence, 23
Durable goods, U.S. households with, 165
Dust Bowl, 73–74
Dutch Tulip Bulb crisis of 1637, 86

Early Social Security retirement, 219, 221
Earned Income Tax Credit (EITC)
    advocacy for, 669
    ARRA and, 79, 581–82, 583
    assessment of, 695–96
    bipartisan support for, 395–96, 695
    in calculating poverty threshold, 162
    compared to AFDC, 530–31
    expansion of, 586
    fiscal policy, 112
    overview of, 533–34
    Urban Institute on, 659
Earning potential, 200, 208–10
Earnings
    educational attainment and, 257–58
    by educational level, 521–22, 701
    by educational level and sex, 333
EBT (Electronic benefit transfer), 157
ECB (European Central Bank), 18, 543, 572
Economic activity, during recessionary phase
    of business cycle, 38–39
Economic changes, structural
    debt and credit (finance), 626–28
    Dodd-Frank Act, 81, 627, 628, 629
    federal deficit and debt, 629–30
    inevitable changes in market, 620–21
    middle-class income and wealth, 625–26
    outlook for, 630–31
    overview of, 595, 620–21
    potential GDP, 621–23
    unemployment, 623–25
Economic Cycle Research Institute, 598
Economic indicators, 12
Economic insecurity
    basic needs budget, 138, 151–57,
        164–65, 199
    distribution of income and wealth, 151–53
    Economic Security Index (ESI), 77, 138, 153
    macroeconomic performance, 154–56
    measurement of, 138, 150–57

outlook for, 157–58
overview of, 138, 150
societal commitment to public benefits,
    156–57
women, 325–26
Economic mobility, xviii–xxi
Economic performance, 110–11
Economic Policy Institute (EPI),
    164–65, 289, 656–57
Economic Security Index (ESI), 77, 138, 153
Economic stimulus, Bush era, 103–4
Economic Stimulus Act (ESA) of 2008, 5,
    104–5, 543, 579–80
Economy, return to normal. See Normal
    economy, return to
Education
    funding, impact of Great Recession on,
        260–62
    inequality of, 262
    prior economic status and, 253–54
    state budget shortfalls and, 556
    unemployment, 505–8
    young adults, 208–9
Educational attainment
    African Americans, 192, 196
    American Indian or Native
        Alaskan (AINA), 292
    Asian Americans, 235–36
    child poverty and, 200
    concerns over during a recession, 256–58
    earnings by sex and, 333
    Great Recession, impact on, 182, 258–60
    health and, 257
    higher earnings and, 257–58
    Hispanic Americans, 269–70, 272
    outlook for, 262–63
    overview of, 256
    percentage of, 507
    poverty, 261–62
    rates of, 208
    rural families and individuals, 316–17
    suburban families and individuals, 344
    trends in, 213
    unemployment, 29, 257–58, 336, 505–8
    unemployment rates and earnings by, 701
    wage and income, 521–22
    women, 324, 325
Education funding, 260–61
EESA (Emergency Economic Stabilization Act)
    of 2008, 5, 94, 104, 105–6, 543. See also
    Troubled Asset Relief Program (TARP)
EFSP (Federal Emergency Food and Shelter
    Program), 449
Elastic currency, 116
Election of 2012, 585–86
Electronic benefit transfer (EBT), 157

Eligibility, determination of for
    public services, 163
Elwell, Craig, 597
Emergency Economic Stabilization Act (EESA)
    of 2008, 5, 94, 104, 105–6, 543. See also
    Troubled Asset Relief Program (TARP)
Emergency Food Assistance Program, 656
Emergency shelters, 447–48
Emergency Stabilization Act of 2008, 579–81
Emerging economies, 8, 10, 356–58, 543
Employee Retirement Income Security Act of
    1974, 42
Employment, full, 100, 116, 504–5
Employment, importance of, 500–502
Employment Act of 1946, 100, 501
Endowments, 261, 642
Engle, Ernest, 161
Engle's law, 161
Enlightenment philosophy, 500–501,
    687–90, 696–99
Entry-level positions, 209
EPI (Economic Policy Institute),
    164–65, 289, 656–57
Epigenetics, 145–46
Equal opportunity, ideal of, xviii–xix
ESA (Economic Stimulus Act) of 2008, 5,
    104–5, 543, 579–80
ESI (Economic Security Index), 77, 138, 153
Ethics and Religious Liberty Commission, 672
EU (European Union), 20, 353–56,
    543, 572, 601
Europe
    debt crisis, 22–27
    global downturn data, 20–31
    global downturn spreads to, 17–20
    impact of crisis on poverty and
        unemployment, 27–31
    income inequality, 30
    increase in poverty, 27–28
    outlook for, 31–32
    output, capital formation, and
        unemployment, 20–22
    poverty rates, 30
    social protection expenditures, 31
    unemployment by levels of education, 29
European Central Bank (ECB), 18, 543, 572
European Commission, 25, 353
European Recession, 304
European Union (EU), 20, 353–56,
    543, 572, 601
Eurostat, 25
Eurozone, 22–24
Evangelical Protestants, 667–68
Even Start, 412
Exchange rate stability, 23
Expansion, as phase of business cycle, 37

FA (Food for America), 411
FAFSA (Free Application for Federal Student
    Aid), 391, 432
Fair Employment Opportunity Act of 2011,
    392, 442, 526
Fair Housing Act (FHA), 90
Fair Labor Standards Act (FLSA) of 1938, 75,
    690, 691–92
Faith in Public Life, 672
Families, impact of housing crisis on, 95–96
Family finances, by percentile of income, 627
Family formation and size, 470–72, 702–5
Family status, and Native Americans, 292–96
Famine, Affluence, and Morality (Singer), xvii
Fannie Mae, 40
    conservatorship of, 104, 106–7, 128
    Countrywide Financial and, 51
    creation of, 86, 107
    mortgage-backed securities market, 90
Farber, Henry S., 523
FDIC (Federal Deposit Insurance
    Corporation), 125, 581
Federal deficit and debt
    1980–2011, 630
    concerns over, 6
    cutting funding for low-income
        households and, 706
    discretionary fiscal policy and, 101, 103
    Great Recession and, 103, 104, 111
    overview of, 112, 611–12
    as percentage of GDP, 612
    politics of, 583–85
    societal commitment to public
        benefits and, 156–57
    structural economic changes, 629–30
Federal Deposit Insurance Corporation
    (FDIC), 125, 581
Federal Emergency Food and Shelter Program
    (EFSP), 449
Federal Emergency Relief Administration
    (FERA), 75, 404–5
Federal funds rate, 119
Federal Funds Target Rate, 55, 119, 121
Federal Home Loan Mortgage Corporation
    (Freddie Mac). *See* Freddie Mac
Federal Housing Administration, 40
Federal Housing Finance Agency (FHFA), 581
Federal Insurance Office, 627
Federal National Mortgage Corporation
    (Fannie Mae). *See* Fannie Mae
Federal Open Market Committee (FOMC), 43,
    117, 125–26, 596–97
Federal Reserve Act of 1913, 116
Federal Reserve Bank
    balance sheet, 120–24, 128–29
    bank crisis, 124–25

Bear Stearns, 19
combined statements of condition, 122–24
creation of, 116
credit booms, 14
high employment goal, 501
inflation and, 130
map of district banks, 118
monetary policy, nonstandard, 126–30
monetary policy, standard, 119–20
monetary policy and Great Recession, 6, 78
organizational chart, 117
outlook for, 131–32
overview of, 116–18
policy initiatives, 126–27
poverty, 130–31
the present, 118–19
responses to Great Recession, 57–58
Federal Reserve Bank of Chicago, 626
Federal Reserve Bank of Dallas, 25
Federal Reserve Bank of Philadelphia, 515–16
Federal Reserve Economic Data (FRED), 119
Female-headed households. *See also* Women
    African Americans, 190–91
    Asian Americans, 234
    child poverty, 204
    chronic intergenerational poverty, 144
    compared to male-headed households, 332
    Native Americans, 292, 294
    poverty, 326–28
    poverty rates, 163–64, 171, 172, 173
    TANF and, 532
FERA (Federal Emergency Relief
    Administration), 75, 404–5
FHA (Fair Housing Act), 90
FHFA (Federal Housing Finance Agency), 581
Field Emergency Relief Administration, 404–5
Field Foundation, 405
Fighting Poverty with Faith, 667, 669
Filipino Americans, 236, 237–38
Finance, debt and credit, structural changes to,
    626–28
Finance, investment, relationship with
    regulatory agencies and Congress, 51–52
Financial aid, 208, 431–32
Financial assets trade, 17–18
Financial data, during Great Recession, 60–61
Financial literacy, 140–41, 143
Financial Oversight and Consumer
    Protection Act of 2010 (Dodd-Frank), 81,
    627, 628, 629
Financial Services Modernization Act of 1999, 42
Financial Stability and Oversight Council, 627
First marriage, median age at, 212
Fiscal policy, federal
    American Recovery and Reinvestment
        Act of 2009 (ARRA), 108–10

in Bush era, 103–7
conservatorship of Fannie Mae and Freddie
    Mac, 106–7
Economic Stimulus Act of 2008, 104–5
Emergency Economic Stabilization Act of
    2008, 105–6
federal debt, 112
Great Recession, 5–6
high employment goal, 501
historical background, 100–101
in Obama era, 107–11
outlook for, 112–13
overview of, 99–100
poverty and, 111–12
the present, 101–3
Tax Relief, Unemployment Insurance
    Reauthorization, and Job
    Creation Act, 110–11
Fitch, 25, 44
Fixed rate mortgage (FRM), 41, 53–54
Flanagan, Thomas P., 51
Florida, 464, 548
FLSA (Fair Labor Standards Act) of 1938, 75,
    690, 691–92
FOMC (Federal Open Market Committee), 43,
    117, 125–26, 596–97
Food Distribution of Indian Reservations
    program (FDPIR), 412
Food for America (FA), 411
Food insecurity
    food pantries, 410–11, 412
    during the Great Recession, 390, 406–7
    historic background of, 404–5
    internationally, 408
    National School Lunch Program,
        405, 412–13
    outlook for, 413–14
    overview of, 404
    retirees and potential retirees, 310–11
    rising food prices, 407–9
    Special Supplementations for Women,
        Infants and Children (WIC),
        411–12 (see also main entry)
    Supplemental Nutrition Assistance Program
        (SNAP), 409–10 (see also main entry)
Food pantries, 410–11, 412
Food prices, 407–9
Food Security Supplement of the Current
    Population Survey, 406
Food stamp program, 79, 405. See also
    Supplemental Nutrition Assistance
    Program (SNAP)
Ford, John, 73–74
Ford Foundation, 642
Ford Motor Company, 106
Forecast, economic for 2013–2014, 602

Foreclosures
    African Americans, 194–95
    Asian Americans, 237–38
    asset poverty, 143–44
    disparity ratio, 93
    effects of, 5
    during the Great Depression, 77
    impact of, 95–96
    increase in rates of, 53, 92
    rental properties, 454–55
    rural families and individuals, 318
    senior citizens, 226
    urban families and individuals, 364–65
For-profit institutions of higher
    education, 429
Fortis, 19
Foundations, 642–43
Fourteenth Amendment, 276
Fractional reserve banking system, 125
France, 9, 19, 24, 26
FRED (Federal Reserve Economic Data), 119
Freddie Mac, 40, 90, 104, 106–7, 128
Free Application for Federal Student Aid
    (FAFSA), 391, 432
Frictional unemployment, 503–4
Friends of Angelo, 51
"Fringe banking" system, 389, 399–401
FRM (Fixed rate mortgage), 41, 53–54
Full employment, 100, 116, 504–5
Funding liquidity risk, 17

G-20, 543
GA (General Assistance benefits),
    395–96, 529, 534–35
Galbraith, James, 650
GDP. See Gross domestic product (GDP)
General Allotment Act of 1887, 287
General Assistance benefits (GA),
    395–96, 529, 534–35
General Motors (GM), 106
The General Theory of Employment, Interest,
    and Money (Keynes), 100, 691
Georgia, 464, 556
Germany, 9, 20, 22, 24, 27
Gideon v. Wainwright, 462
Gini coefficient, 152–53, 154, 193, 249, 614
Glass-Steagall Act, 42
Global downturn
    banking trends, 15–17
    closer view of, 9–15
    crises spread to Europe, 17–20
    in developing nations and emerging markets,
        356–58
    differing impacts across the world, 12–15
    European data, 20–31
    Great Recession at present, 8–9

outlook, 31–32
overview of, 3–4, 7–8
Gold rush in Alaska, 288
Goldwater, Barry, 694
Goods trade, 17–18
Governance incentive systems, 51
Government debt crisis, 22–27
Government expenditures, during Great
    Recession, 12
Government responses to Great Recession. *See*
    International response; Legislative
    response; Local government response;
    State government response; Tribal
    government response
Government-sponsored enterprise (GSE), 40,
    127, 128, 130
Grameen Bank, 574
Gramm-Leach-Bliley Act. *See* Financial
    Services Modernization Act of 1999
Grand Coulee Dam, 75
Grandparents as primary caregivers to
    grandchildren, 381–82
The Grapes of Wrath (Steinbeck), 73–74
Great Depression, 4–5, 73–76, 474. *See also*
    Great Recession, vs. Great Depression
Great Recession
    compared to other recessions, 119–20
    conditions of, 76
    corporate governance, 50–51
    credit derivatives, 49–50
    data on, 57–62
    definition of, 36–39
    discretionary fiscal policy, 101
    federal fiscal policy, 5–6
    federal monetary policy, 6
    financial data, 60–61
    geographical regions, 9
    vs. Great Depression, 4–5, 73–81
    gross domestic product, 58–59
    housing, 62–63
    housing as part of the American dream,
        39–41
    housing bubble, 39, 52–57
    housing crisis, 5, 88–92
    labor force, 59–60
    neoliberalism, 41–43
    New Deal programs still in place, 78
    outlook, 66
    overview of, 4, 36
    poverty, 63–65, 141–46
    at present, 8–9
    relationships between finance, regulatory
        agencies and Congress, 51–52
    Social Security, 481–82
    structured finance and ratings
        agencies, 44–49

summary of, 65
Treasury securities, 43–44
Greece
    austerity measures, 543, 572
    bailout of, 25
    debt to RGDP ratio, 24
    government debt crisis, 22, 24–25
    Great Recession in, 21, 355–56
    income inequality, 28
    long-term interest rates on
        government debt, 24
    ongoing poverty, 359
    output gap, 22
    poverty in, 28
    total government debt, 26
    unemployment in, 22, 27
Greenspan, Alan, 43
Gross domestic product (GDP)
    adjusted for inflation, 36
    annual growth rate of, 155
    as assessment point for U.S. economy,
        607–11
    in Baltic states, 572
    federal spending as a percentage of, 651–52
    during Great Recession, 58–59, 102
    inflation-adjusted growth rate, 597, 599
    real growth rate 1960–2012, 608
    slow recovery of, 598
    Social Security deficit as percentage of, 486
    unemployment and inflation, 607–9
Gross fixed capital formation, 12–13, 21
Group of 7 (G7), 8, 9
Group of 20 (G20), 570, 575
GSE (Government-sponsored enterprise), 40,
    127, 128, 130
Gupta, Rajat K., 51

Habitat for Humanity, 639
HAMP (Home Affordable Modification
    Program), 94–95, 665
HARP (Home Affordable Refinance Program),
    5, 94–95
Hartford County, Maryland, 548
Harvard University, 381
Haskins, Ron, 686, 700–705
Head Start, 412
Health, as secondary effect, 473–74
Health, educational attainment and, 257
Health and Human Services, Department of
    (HHS), 475–77, 563
Health care, 229, 310, 318–19
Health care assistance
    Children's Health Insurance Program
        (CHIP), 281, 319, 390, 417–18, 420–21,
        484, 555, 584
    health insurance coverage, 421–22, 615–16

Medicaid, 418–20
outlook on, 422–23
overview of, 390, 417–18
Health insurance, 151, 221, 318, 421–22, 615–16
Hellenic Statistical Authority, 356
Hennepin County, Minnesota, 365
Heritage Foundation, 109, 654
Herrnstein, Richard, 677
HHS (Health and Human Services, Department of), 475–77, 563
Higher education
access to for low-income students, 424–25
college enrollment during Great Recession, 425–27
community colleges, 391, 426–29
costs and financial aid, 431–32
funding institutions, 261
impact of Great Recession on institutions, 427–29
outlook on, 432–33
overview of, 390–91, 424–25
private schools, 430–31
for-profit institutions, 429
public 4-year schools, 429–30
Hiring practices
computers and social media, impact on recruitment process, 440–41
mismatched unemployment, 441
outlook on, 441–42
overview of, 391–92, 435
present situation, 435–40
Hispanic Americans
child poverty, 202–3, 268–70
chronic intergenerational poverty, 144
conflict between rich and poor, view of, 679
demographic characteristics, 265
disparity ratio, 93–94
economy and recession, views on, 383–84
educational attainment, 269–70, 272
Great Recession and, 77, 182
homelessness, 446, 449
homeownership, 90, 91, 266
housing needs, 392–93
income, 267–70
median wealth, 147
men and unemployment, 337
outlook for, 271–73
overview of, 265
personal financial situation, view of, 381
poverty rates, 163–64, 171, 172, 173, 174, 693
poverty thresholds, 164
rural families and individuals, 319–20
savings, 270–71
senior citizens, 225, 311

suburban families and individuals, 346
underemployment, 497
unemployment, income, and poverty, 267–70
unemployment rate, 380, 511
veterans, 374
wealth, 265–67
worst-case housing needs, 455–56
young adults, 210–11, 382
Hispanic economic gap, 267
Historical trauma, and poverty, 146, 287–88
Historic injustices, xx–xxi
HMDA (Home Mortgage Disclosure Act) of 1975, 131
Hmong Americans, 236, 237
Home Affordable Modification Program (HAMP), 94–95, 665
Home Affordable Refinance Program (HARP), 5, 94–95
Home equity, 226, 237, 266, 378, 380
Homelessness
African Americans, 195
among whites, 449
definition of, 444
demographics and prevention of, 445–48
families, 445–48
funding for programs, 449–50
during the Great Recession, 77
Hispanic Americans, 446, 449
outlook on, 450–51
overview of, 392, 444
in rural and suburban areas, 448–49
urban families and individuals, 364–65
veterans, 373
Homelessness Prevention and Re-Housing Program (HPRP), 392, 449–50
Home Modification Program, 5
Home Mortgage Disclosure Act (HMDA) of 1975, 131
Homeownership, 5
African Americans, 90, 91, 194
ARRA and, 582
Asian Americans, 237, 238
family income relative to median, 91
Hispanic Americans, 90, 91, 266
increase in, 90
by race and ethnicity, 91
rural families and individuals, 318
senior citizens, 226
urban families and individuals, 364–65
white Americans, 378
Home Owners Loan Corporation, 75
Home values, 96, 195, 237, 378
Homework, time spent on, 260
Hoover, Herbert, 74
Hoover Institution, 654

"Hoovervilles," 74
Hope Tax Credit, 431–32
House Concurrent Resolution 234, 670, 671
Household consumption, during Great
    Recession, 12–13
Household debt, 266, 326, 378–81
*Household Food Security in the United States in
    2011* (USDA), 405
Household income, 248, 249
Housing
    Asian Americans, 237–38
    during Great Recession, 62–63
    prior economic status and, 253–54
    retirees and potential retirees, 310
    rural families and individuals, 318–19
    starts and values, 63
    urban families and individuals, 364
Housing Affordability Index, 62
Housing and Community Development
    Act, 107
Housing and Urban Development,
    Department of (HUD), 90, 318, 445, 449,
    455, 457–58
Housing assistance programs
    demographics of worst-case needs, 455–57
    low-income renters, 392–93, 453–54
    outlook on, 459
    overview of, 392–93, 453
    rental assistance programs, 281, 457–59
    worst-case housing needs, 454–55
Housing bubble
    bursting of, 52–54, 90
    causes of, 39
    Great Recession, 4, 14, 54–57, 88–92
    housing as part of the American
        dream, 39–41
    national housing policy, 5
    origins of, 52
    structured finance and ratings
        agencies, 44–49
    Treasury securities, 43–44
Housing choice voucher program, 457–58
Housing crisis
    African Americans, 194–95
    asset bubbles, 86
    Congressional response, 94–95
    demographics, 93–94
    history of, 266
    history of U.S. housing market, 86–88
    housing bubble and the Great
        Recession, 88–92
    impact on families and communities, 95–96
    local government revenue and, 547
    outlook, 96
    overview of, 5, 85
Housing market, U.S., 80, 86–88, 253–54

Housing overhand, 25–26
Housing starts, 4, 94, 96
HPRP (Homelessness Prevention and
    Re-Housing Program), 392, 449–50
HUD (Housing and Urban Development,
    Department of), 90, 318, 445, 449, 455,
    457–58
Hudson Institute, 654
Human capital, 158
Human Development Index (HDI), 166
Humanism, on poverty, xv
Humanist Manifesto, xv
Humanitarian Repatriation Program, 543, 573
Human rights, xv–xvi
Humphrey-Hawkins Act of 1978, 100, 501
Hungary, 355–56, 359
Hunger. *See* Food insecurity
Hunger USA, 405
Hypo Real Estate, 20

Iceland, 19–21, 22, 572
ICESCR (International Covenant on
    Economic, Social, and Cultural
    Rights), 574
Idaho, 556
IHS (Indian Health Service), 563–64
IMF (International Monetary Fund), 7, 10–12,
    543, 570, 572
Immigrants
    access to public benefits, 281–83
    anti-immigrant sentiment, 277–78
    deportation of, 574
    Great Recession's impact on, 182–83, 277
    outlook for, 283
    overview of, 275–77
    poverty, 278–80
    Social Security deficit and, 489
    unemployment, 237
Immigration system, 280
Incarceration, xxii
Income, 93–94, 249, 267–70. *See also* Wages
    and income
Income, distribution of, 151–53, 614–15
*Income, Poverty, and Health Insurance
    Coverage in the United States* (U.S. Census
    Bureau), 278–79
Income-Based Repayment System, 432
Income distribution, 151–53, 614–15
Income inequality
    African Americans, 193–94
    economic insecurity and, 138
    in Europe, 28, 30
    prior economic status and, 248–49
    statistics on, 152–53
Income share, top 1 percent of, 154
Income to poverty ratio, 65

India, 3, 4, 8, 10, 12–13, 357, 573
Indian Affairs programs, 530–31, 563–64
Indian Americans, 236, 238
Indian Health Service (IHS), 563–64
Indian Removal Act of 1830, 287
Indian Self-Determination and Education
    Assistance Act of 1975, 564
Indian Tribal Governmental Tax Status Act of
    1982, 566
Indicators of economic activity, 12
Individual freedom vs. nobody in need, 697
Individualism, radical, 676, 698
Individuals with Disabilities Education Act
    (IDEA), 245
Infant mortality rate, 75
Inflation, 111, 130, 596, 599, 609, 611
Inflation-adjusted GPD, 597
Inflation rate, 609–11
Initiative on Global Markets, 110
Insider trading, 51–52
Insolvency, 125
Installment lending, 389, 399
Institute of Mexicans in the Exterior
    (CC-IME), 573, 574
Institute on Assets and Social Policy, 225
Institutional constraints for alleviating
    poverty, 686–87
Institutional reform, 690–94
Interest on Excess Reserves, 127
Interest on lawyers' trust accounts
    (IOLTA), 465–66
Interest rates, 6, 14, 53, 119, 399, 400–401
Interfaith initiatives, 637
Interfaith response, 668–70
Intergenerational households, 212, 213,
    381–82
Intergenerational poverty. See Chronic
    intergenerational poverty
Interior, Department of, 563, 564
International Covenant on Economic, Social,
    and Cultural Rights (ICESCR), 574
International Labor Organization, 570–71
International Monetary Fund (IMF), 7, 10–12,
    543, 570, 572
International Organization of Migration
    (IOM), 573, 574
International response
  governmental response, 571–73
  NGO response, 571–74
  outlook for, 575–76
  overview of, 543, 570–71
  at the present, 571
International Social Survey Program, xviii
Internships, unpaid, 209–10
Interreligious Working Group on Domestic
    Human Needs, 669

Investment banks, housing crisis and, 54–55
Investment earnings, 249
Investment properties, 54
Involuntary unemployment, 503–4
IOLTA (Interest on lawyers' trust accounts),
    465–66
IOM (International Organization of Migration),
    573, 574
IQ scores, 677
Ireland, 25, 26, 27, 28, 572
Islam, on poverty, xiv–xv
Italy, 359
  annual output growth rate, 9
  beginning of Great Recession, 20
  debt to RGDP ratio, 24
  government debt crisis, 22, 25, 26–27
  Great Recession in, 21
  long-term interest rates on
      government debt, 24
  poverty in, 28
  total government debt, 26
  unemployment in, 27

Japan, 9
Japanese Americans, 236, 238
JCPA (Jewish Council for Public Affairs), 637,
    667, 668
Jefferson, Thomas, 688, 689
Jesus Christ, on poverty, xiv
Jewish Council for Public Affairs (JCPA), 637,
    667, 668
Jewish response to Great Recession, 668
Jobless recovery, 338
Job market, 391–92
Job tenure, 219–20
John Deere, 573
Johns Hopkins University, 642
Johnson, Lyndon, 161, 612–13, 694
JPMorgan Chase, 19, 57, 126
Jubilee, year of, xiv
Judaism, xiii–xiv, 668
Judicare model, 465
"Justice as Fairness" (Rawls), xvi

Kaiser Family Foundation, 381
Kansas, 557
Kennedy, John, 405
Kentucky, 464
Keynes, John Maynard, 100, 691
Kiva.org, 574
Korean Americans, 236, 238

Labor force, during Great Recession, 59–60
Labor force participation rate, 218, 271–72,
    322–23, 339, 506
Land, Richard, 671

Land ownership on reservation, 287–88
Las Vegas, 39, 364
Latin America, 572
Latin American Community Center, 531
Layoffs, 436
Leech Lake Reservation, 287
Left, political, on the stimulus bill, 79
Legal aid, 393, 464–67
Legal immigrants, 276
Legal permanent residents (LPRs), 276
Legal Services Corporation (LSC), 465–66, 467
Legal system
    legal aid, 464–67
    outlook on, 467
    overview of, 393, 461–62
    public defenders, 462–64
Legislative response
    American Recovery and Reinvestment Act of
        2009 (ARRA), 581–82 (see also main entry)
    American Tax Payer Relief Act of 2012,
        585–86, 601
    economy stimulus and emergency
        stabilization acts, 579–81
    No Budget No Pay Act of 2013, 585–86
    outlook for, 586–87
    overview of, 543–44, 579
    partisan response and debates, 583–85
    Tea Party Movement and mid-term 2010
        elections, 582–83
Lehman Brothers, 54–55, 57, 128
Leverage ratio, 627
Levitt, Arthur, 43
Lewis, Oscar, 677
Liabilities, 121–24
LIBOR (London Inter-Bank Offer Rate), 18
Life expectancy, xxii, 75, 229
Lili'uokalani, Queen, 288
Liquidation, 124
Liquidity backstop, 17
"Listen to Your Pastors" advertisement, 672
Lobbying, tribal, 566–67
Local government response
    budget cuts and tax hikes, 547–48
    General Assistance, 395–96, 529, 534–35
    impact on revenue, 546–47
    outlook for, 549
    overview of, 541–42, 545
Locke, John, 688
London Inter-Bank Offer Rate (LIBOR), 18
Long-term interest rates on government
    debt, 23–24
Long-term unemployment, 76, 193, 218,
    236–37, 250–51, 436
Losing Ground (Murray), 677
Louisiana, 557
Louisville, Kentucky, 365

"Lowering the Debt, Raising the Poor," 668
Low food security, 404, 406–7
Low-income households
    credit, access to, 389, 399–402
    credit reports, 401
    food insecurity, 390, 404–14
    health care assistance, 390, 417–23
    higher education, access to, 390–91, 424–33
    hiring practices, 391–92, 435–42
    homelessness, 392, 444–51
    housing assistance programs, 453–59
    legal system, 393, 461–67
    as renters, 392–93, 453–54
    Social Security, 393–94, 481–91
    underemployment, 493–99
    wages and income, 520–27
    welfare cash assistance programs,
        395–96, 529–36
LPRs (Legal permanent residents), 276
LSC (Legal Services Corporation), 465–66, 467
Luxembourg, 19

Macroeconomic performance, 154–56
Mainline Protestants, 667
Making Work Pay tax credits, 108, 112, 655
Male-headed households, 332, 446
Management sector, 335
Manhattan Institute, 654
Manufactured homes, 317, 318
Manufacturing industry, 298–300, 335, 339
Market economy, 100, 501, 520, 620–21
Marriage, and poverty, 702–5
Marriage rates, 212
Maryland, 464
Massachusetts, 420, 555, 556
Maturity mismatch in bank loans, 15, 16–17
MBS (Mortgage-backed securities), 47–49, 51,
    54–55, 88–90, 127
Mecklenburg County, North Carolina, 548
Median household income, 151, 194
Median wealth, 147
Medicaid, 281, 319. See also Social Security
    ARRA, 554–55, 582
    economic recovery, 615–16
    enrollment growth rates, 419
    explanation of program, 483–84
    funding and programs, 418–20
    increased demand for, 555
    low-income families, 390
    overview of, 390, 417–18
    Ryan budget, 584
    Social Security Act of 1935, 393
Medicare, 223, 229, 417–18, 483–84,
    486, 582, 584
Member Statements for Final Commission
    Report, 112

Men
    Great Recession, effects of, 184–85, 333–37
    lengths of unemployment, 335, 337, 338
    outlook for, 339–40
    overview of, 330–32
    poverty rates, 336, 339
    present situation, 332–33
    recovery and expansion, 337–39
    unemployment, 330
    unemployment by educational
        attainment, 336
    unemployment rate, 509, 512
Mental health, 474
Merrill Lynch, 18, 57
Metropolitan statistical areas
    (MSAs), 320–21, 343
Mexico, 4, 10, 572–73
Michigan, 555
Microlending, 574
Middle class, 625–26
Middle East, 572, 601
Mid-term 2010 elections, 582–83
Midwest region. See Regions of the country
Minerals Management Service, 564
Minimal economic security, xv–xvi
Minimum wage, 151
Mining industry, 334–35
Minnesota, 464, 466, 556
Minority borrowers, 54
Mississippi, 463
Missouri, 557
Mobility, housing market and, 253–54
The Moment of Truth, 112
Monetary policy, federal, 6
    balance sheet, 120–24, 128–29
    bank crisis, 124–25
    credit booms, 14
    high employment goal, 501
    inflation and, 130
    monetary policy, nonstandard, 125–30
    monetary policy, standard, 119–20
    outlook for, 131–32
    overview of, 116–18
    poverty, 130–31
    the present, 118–19
Money Market Investor Funding Facility, 127
Money wiring services, 400
Montana, 466, 553
Moody's, 44
Moore, Stephen, 650
Mortgage-backed securities (MBS), 47–49, 51,
    54–55, 88–90, 127
Mortgage default rates, 64
Mortgage delinquencies, 5
Mortgage pools, in structured finance, 48
Mortgages, 48, 86–87, 92

Mozillo, Angelo, 51
MSAs (Metropolitan statistical areas),
    320–21, 343
Multilateral organizations, 574
Multiplier effect, 108, 534
Murray, Charles, 677
Mutual Fund Liquidity Facility, 127

NAE (National Association of Evangelicals),
    637, 667–68, 671
NAFTA (North American Free Trade
    Agreement) (copy), 299
NAIRU (Nonaccelerating inflation rate of
    unemployment), 504–5, 513, 515, 516
Narrow unemployment rate, 59
National Academy of Science, 165–66
National Asian American Survey, 236
National Association of Evangelicals (NAE),
    637, 667–68, 671
National Bureau of Economic Research
    (NBER), 9, 36, 522–23, 579, 584, 596
National Center for Children in Poverty
    (NCCP), 164–65, 199
National Center for Education Statistics, 192
National Coalition for Asian Pacific-American
    Community Development, 236
National Commission on Fiscal Responsibility
    and Reform, 112
National Council of Churches (NCC), 637, 666
National Financial Condition Index, 626
National Housing Trust Fund, 665, 669
National Labor Relations Act, 75
National Organization of Evangelicals,
    637–68, 671
National Right to Counsel Committee, 467
National School Lunch Program, 405, 412–13
National Student Clearinghouse Research
    Center, 427
Native Americans. See also Tribal government
    response
    family status, 292–96
    female-headed households, 292, 294
    Great Recession, effects of, 183
    historical trauma and poverty, 287–88
    impact of Great Recession on, 563
    injustices against, xxi
    outlook for, 296
    overview of, 286
    poverty among older adults, 296
    poverty rates, 288–92, 293–95, 693
    rural families and individuals, 319–20
    senior citizens, 295–96
    terminology, 286
    unemployment, 289, 291
    veterans, 374
    young adults, 210–11

Native Hawaiian and Other Pacific Islander
    (NHPI), 288–92, 561. *See also* Native
    Americans
Navajo Nation, 562
NBER (National Bureau of Economic
    Research), 9, 36, 522–23, 579, 584, 596
NCC (National Council of Churches), 637, 667
NCCP (National Center for Children in
    Poverty), 164–65, 199
Neighborhoods, impact of on chronic
    intergenerational poverty, 146
Neoliberalism, 41–43
Netherlands, 19
Net worth, 121–24, 225–26, 238–39, 627
Nevada, 466–67, 553
New Deal, 4, 40, 73–76, 78
New entrants to the labor market, 251
New Hampshire, 557
New household formation, 471–72
New Jersey, 466, 553, 555
New Mexico, 556, 557
New Orleans, 348
New York, 463–64, 554
New York City, 363, 366, 548
New York Civil Liberties Union, 463–64
New York Times, 208
New York Times/CBS News Poll, 278
NGOs. *See* Nongovernmental organization
    (NGO) response
NHPI (Native Hawaiian and Other Pacific
    Islander), 288–92, 561. *See also* Native
    Americans
Nixon, Richard, 405, 461
Nobody in need vs. individual freedom, 697
No Budget No Pay Act of 2013, 585–86
Nonaccelerating inflation rate of
    unemployment (NAIRU), 504–5,
    513, 515, 516
Nondiscretionary fiscal policy, 99. *See also*
    Automatic stabilizers
Nonfarm payroll jobs, 502
Nongovernmental organization (NGO)
    response
  international response, 571–73
  outlook for, 575–76
  overview of, 543, 570–71
  at the present, 571
Nonmetro areas. *See* Rural families and
    individuals
Nonprofit organizations response
  budget deficits, 645–46
  corporate giving, 643–44
  demand for services, 645
  endowments, 642
  foundation funding, 642–43
  government funding, 640–62

  individual donations, 644–45
  outlook for, 646–47
  overview of, 635–36, 639–40
Nonprofit Research Collaborative, 644–45
Nonprofit Resources Collaborative, 641, 644
Nonreligious belief systems, and importance of
    poverty alleviation, xiii–xv
Nonstandard monetary policy, 125–30
Nontraditional students, 425–26
Normal economy, return to
  assessment tools, 607
  distribution of income, 614–15
  federal deficits and debt, 611–12
  GDP, unemployment and inflation, 607–11
  health insurance, 615–16
  overview of, 595, 606–7
  poverty, 612–13
  summary and outlook for, 616–17
North Africa, 572, 601
North American Free Trade Agreement
    (NAFTA), 299
North Carolina, 466, 556
North Dakota, 553
Northeast region. *See* Regions of the country
Northern Rock, nationalization of, 18
Not qualified immigrants, 281–82

OASI (Old-Age and Survivors Insurance
    Trust Fund), 483
Obama, Barack
  African Americans, programs to increase
    employment opportunities for, 196
  American Recovery and Reinvestment Act of
    2009 (ARRA), 108–10,
    581–82 (*see also main entry*)
  Bridge to Work Program, 209
  compared to Roosevelt, 73
  Economic Policy Institute and, 657
  federal debt, 612
  fiscal policy, 107–11
  immigration, 277
  No Budget, No Pay Act of 2013, 586
  stimulus legislation, 579
  Tax Relief, Unemployment Insurance
    Reauthorization, and Job Creation
    Act, 110–11
  veterans and, 374–75
Occupy Wall Street movement, 657, 658
ODA (Official development aid), 358
OECD (Organization for Economic
    Cooperation and Development),
    17, 651–52
Office of Economic Opportunity, 162, 692
Office of Financial Research, 627
Office of Management and Budget (OMB), 174
Official development aid (ODA), 358

Ohio, 548, 556
Old-Age and Survivors Insurance Trust Fund
    (OASI), 483
OMB (Office of Management and Budget), 174
Opportunity Society, creation of, 700–705
Optimism gap, 383–84
Oregon, 557
Organization for Economic Cooperation and
    Development (OECD), 17, 651–52
Originate and distribute model, 16
Ornstein, Norman, 656
Orshansky, Mollie, 138, 161–62
Out-of-pocket medical costs, 310
Output, 20–22
Output gap, 21–22
Output ratio, 59, 600, 608, 609
Over-the-counter (OTC) trading
    of derivatives, 42–43

Parents, young adults living with, 212, 239,
    382, 471
Partisan response and debates, 583–86
Path dependency, 687–90, 698–99
Patient Protection and Affordable Care Act. See
    Affordable Care Act of 2010 (ACA)
Paulsen, Hank, 105–6
Pawn lending, 399–400
Payday lending, 389, 400
Payroll tax holiday, 5
Peer ability, 262
Pell grants, 391, 431
Pelosi, Nancy, 52
Penn State University, 199
Pennsylvania, 556
Pension funds, 42, 228
Perceptions of Poverty 2012, 698
Personal Responsibility and Work
    Opportunity Reconciliation Act
    (PRWORA), 530, 532, 695, 704
Pew Charitable Trusts, 643
Pew Hispanic Center, 277, 280
Pew Research Center, 209, 212, 224,
    226, 227, 266, 382, 440,
    649–50, 679–80
Pew Survey, 382
Philosophy, underpinnings for importance of
    poverty alleviation, xv–xviii
Physical security, right of, xvi
Pine Ridge Reservation, 291
Polar political viewpoints, 651–52
Political ideologies
    American views on poverty, 650–53
    conservative views, 654–56
    liberal views, 656–57
    moderate views, 657–60
    outlook for, 660

overview of, 649
think tank perspectives, 653–60
Political participation, 272
Political parties' response to Great Recession.
    See Legislative response
Political viewpoints on poverty, 651, 652–53
Pooling of loans, 16
Poor and rich, conflict between, 679–80
Portugal, 20, 359, 572
    bailout of, 25
    debt to RGDP ratio, 24
    government debt crisis, 22
    Great Recession in, 21
    income inequality, 28
    long-term interest rates on
        government debt, 24
    poverty in, 28
    total government debt, 26
    unemployment in, 22, 27
Positive shock, 14
Potential real domestic gross product (GDP),
    37, 58–59, 621–23
Poverty. See also Low-income households
    adults, 220–21
    African Americans, 188–91
    by age, 171
    by age, location, race, and marital status, 139
    Asian Americans, 233–34
    blame for, 681–82
    characteristics of poor and nonpoor
        families, 703
    developing nations, emerging markets, and
        global downturn, 356–58
    distribution by region, 303, 304
    educational attainment, 257–58, 261–62
    in Europe, 27–28, 30
    Eurozone crisis, impact of, 27–31
    federal fiscal policy, 111–12
    Federal Reserve policy, 130–31
    female-headed households, 326–28
    during the Great Depression, 74
    during Great Recession, 4, 63–65,
        77, 103, 139
    Hispanic Americans, 267–70
    historical trauma, 146, 287–88
    immigrants, 278–80
    marriage, 702–5
    measurement of, 138–39
    monetary policy, 130–31
    perceptions of, 698
    political viewpoints on, 652–53
    rates and economic recovery, 612–13
    recovery, 81
    reduced wages, 523–26
    by region of the country, 302–3
    retirees and potential retirees, 307–8

rural families and individuals, 315–16
senior citizens, 224–25
suburban families and individuals, 345–46
underemployment and, 497–98, 523–26
unemployment and, 523
veterans, 373–74
view of as a large problem, 697
women, 326–27
Poverty, causes and types of
asset poverty in the Great Recession, 143–44
in the Great Recession, 141–46
overview of, 137, 140–41
Poverty, measurement of
alternatives to, 199
overview of, 138–39
poverty thresholds, 138, 151, 162–64,
198–99
present situation, 160–61
senior citizens, 224–25
suggestions for changing, 164–66
in the United States, 161–62
Poverty, reasons to care about
chronic intergenerational poverty in the
Great Recession, 144–46
cyclical and temporary poverty in the Great
Recession, 141–42
outlook for, 147–48
Poverty, societal view of
class conflict and altruism, 679–82
outlook on, 682
overview of, 637–38, 675
philosophical foundation of, 676–78
Poverty alleviation
American ideals and experience, xviii–xxi
conservative revolution, 694–96
Enlightenment philosophy and founding of
the U.S., 688–90
Enlightenment philosophy in modern
society, 696–99
funding for programs, 705–6
institutional constraints, 686–87
institutional reform, 690–94
large-scale cash transfers, 699–700
opportunity society, creation of, 700–705
overview, 685–86
path dependency, 687
philosophical underpinnings, xv–xviii
religious and nonreligious belief systems
and, xiii–xv
self-interest and, xxii–xxiii
worldview, 686
Poverty rates
2008 rate, 171–72
2009 rate, 172–73
2010 rate, 173–74
2011 rate, 174

by age, 170, 172–74, 220–21,
224–25, 490, 692
Alaska Natives, 289
by education and race, 210–11
European Union and Eurozone crisis,
353–56
factors that reduce, 703
families with children under 18, 332
female-headed households, 163–64, 171,
172, 173
in geographical areas, 171–74
during Great Recession, 111, 139, 142
historical rates in the U.S., 169–71
men, 339
men by race and age, 336
by metro and rural locations, 316
Native Americans, 288–92, 293–95
Native Hawaiians, 289
native vs. foreign born population, 279–80
in other recessions, 169
outlook for, 174–75
overview of, 168
for persons with disabilities, 242–43
present situation, 171–74
by race and ethnicity, 170–74, 190,
233, 269, 693
during recessionary phase of business
cycle, 38–39
rural families and individuals, 315–16
senior citizens, 224–25
by sex, 327, 331
suburban families and individuals, 344
unemployment and, 524
United States, vs. international impact, 352
urban families and individuals, 362–63
in U.S., 352
veterans vs. nonveterans, 374
white Americans, 379
by work status, 526
Poverty risk, prior economic status
and, 253–54
Poverty threshold, 138, 151, 162–64, 198–99
Price stability, 23, 116
Primary Credit Rate, 126
Primary Dealer Credit Facility, 126, 127
Prime mortgages, 41, 53
Primerica, 42
Prior economic status
declining wages, 248
education and skill differences, 252
Great Recession, effects of, 182
housing market connections, 253–54
inequality, 248–49
new entrants to the labor market, 251
outlook for, 254
overview of, 248–49

poverty risk and, 252–53
unemployment, 249–51
Private 4-year colleges and universities, 430–31
Private attorneys, pro bono services, 466–67
Privatization of Social Security, 487
Pro bono legal services, 466–67
Program for Economic Recovery, 101
Project-based assisted housing, 457, 458
Property taxes, 365, 541, 546, 547, 552
Property values, decrease in, 260
Protestant Christianity, xiv, 667–68
PRWORA (Personal Responsibility and Work Opportunity Reconciliation Act), 530, 532, 695, 704
Public 4-year colleges and universities, 429–30
Public benefits, 156–57, 281–83
Public defenders, 393, 461–64
Public health care, 319
Public housing, 281, 457–58
Public schools, higher education, 429–30
Public sector employment, 192, 366, 372–73
Public Works Administration (PWA), 75
Purim, xiv
PWA (Public Works Administration), 75

Qualified immigrants, 281–82
QWERTY keyboard, 687

Race. See also specific groups
economic gap, 147
housing crisis, 93–94
poverty rates by, 190, 693
senior citizens and poverty, 225
unemployment by, 191
Racial discrimination, xx, 146, 237
Racine County, Wisconsin, 548
Radical individualism, 676
Rajan, Raghuram, 51
Ratings agencies, and structured finance, 44–49
Rawls, John, xvi, xxii
Reagan, Ronald, 41, 101, 405, 612, 694
Real gross domestic product (RGDP), 7
1973–1980, 37
definition of, 36
in Europe, 21
during global downturn, 8
during Great Recession, 12–13, 58–59
growth forecasts for, 66
growth of, 608
growth rate of in constant prices, 11
growth rate of per capita, 11
vs. potential gross domestic product, 622
Real median household income, 142

Recession, 36–39, 120. See also Great Recession
Recession and Recovery, 657
Recession of 1948, 508
Recession of 1981, 508
Recession of 2001, 14–15, 61, 63
Recovery, as phase of business cycle, 37
Recovery Act. See American Recovery and Reinvestment Act of 2009 (ARRA)
Recruitment process, 440–41
Red-lining, 131
Reducing Poverty Rates, 703
Refugees, 276
Regions, comparative economic size of, 8
Regions of the country
Great Recession, effects of, 183
housing crisis, 93–94
map of, 299
outlook for, 303–4
overview of, 298–300
poverty, 302–3
unemployment, 300–302
worst-case housing needs, 457
Regulatory agencies, 51–52
Relative measures of poverty, 161, 162
Relative poverty median risk gap, 28
Religious belief systems, and importance of poverty alleviation, xiii–xv
Religious groups
antipoverty programs and budget cutting, 671–72
Evangelical Protestants, 667–68
federal budget cutting, 670–72
interfaith, 668–70
Jewish, 668
Mainline Protestants, 666–67
outlook for, 672
overview of, 636–37, 663–64
Roman Catholic Church, 664–65
Rental assistance programs, 281, 457–59
Rental properties, foreclosures, 454–55
Renters, 364
Renters, low-income, 392, 453–55
Rent-to-own, 389, 400
Reservations, poverty on, 289
Reserve credit facilities, 127, 128
Resolution Trust Corporation, 87–88
Responsibility, xvii
Responsiveness, xvii
Restrained credit flows, 124
Retirees and potential retirees
delayed or early retirement, 472–73
disparate impacts, 311
food insecurity, 310–11
Great Recession, effects of, 183–84
health care, 310

housing, 310
outlook for, 311–12
overview of, 306
poverty, 307–8
retirement savings and planning, 308–9
Social Security, role of, 306–7
unemployment, 309
Retirement, 226–28, 472–73
Retirement funds, 151
Retirement plans, changes in, 219, 227–28
Retirement savings, 228, 270–71, 308–9
RGDP. See Real gross domestic
    product (RGDP)
Rhode Island, 553, 556
Rich and poor, conflict between, 679–80
Right, political, criticism of stimulus bill, 79–80
Risk, corporate governance and, 50–51
Robert Wood Johnson Foundation, 642–43
Roman Catholic Church, 664–65
Romer, Christina, 78, 108–9
Roosevelt, Franklin D., 40, 73, 75–76
Rubin, Robert, 43
Running Brave for American Indian Youth, 291
Rural families and individuals
    education and skill differences, 316–17
    foreclosures, 318
    Great Recession, effects of, 184
    Hispanic Americans, 319–20
    homelessness, 448–49
    homeownership, 318
    housing and health care, 318–19
    minorities, 319–20
    outlook for, 320
    overview of, 314–15
    poverty, 315–16
    unemployment, 316–89
Russia, 4, 10, 358
Rust Belt, 364
Ryan, Paul, 583–84, 670

S&P/Case-Shiller Home Price Index, 40, 94
Safety nets, suburban families and
    individuals, 347–48
Sales tax, 552
Sarasota, Florida, 548
Savings, 221, 270–71
Savings and loan (S&L) industry, 86–88
Sawhill, Isabel, 686, 700–705
School Breakfast Program, 405
School funding, local, 260
Schools, quality of, 262
Schumpeter, Joseph A., 621
Schwarzenegger, Arnold, 427, 554
Science, technology, engineering, and
    mathematics (STEM fields), 329
Seasonally adjusted unemployment, 502

SEC (Securities and Exchange
    Commission), 50
Secondary education students, and recession,
    259–60
Secondary effects of Great Recession
    crime and divorce, 257–58, 477–78
    delayed or early retirement, 472–73
    domestic violence, 474–77
    family formation and size, 470–72
    health, 473–74
    outlook on, 478–79
    overview of, 393, 470
    suicide rates, 474, 475
Second global recession, possibility of, 358–59
Section 8 housing choice voucher
    program, 458
Securities and Exchange
    Commission (SEC), 50
Securitization of loans, 15–16
Segregation, xx, 146
Select Committee on Nutrition and Human
    Needs, 405
Self-employment, 339
Self-interest, and importance of poverty allevi-
    ation, xxii–xxiii
Senior citizens
    African Americans, 190, 225, 311
    Asian Americans, 234
    currently in workforce, 473
    foreclosures, 226
    Great Recession, effects of, 180–81
    Hispanic Americans, 225, 311
    homeownership, 226
    Native Americans, 295–96
    net worth, 225–26
    outlook for, 228–29
    overview of, 223–24
    poverty rates, 224–25
    work and retirement, 226–28
    worst-case housing needs, 456
Service industry, 335
Severe material deprivation, 354–55
Sex, female. See Women
Sex, male. See Men
Sheltered populations, 445–47, 449
Shue, Henry, xv–xvi
Singer, Peter, xvii–xviii
Single parent families, economic insecurity
    and, 158. See also Female-headed
    households; Male-headed households
SIVs (Structured investment vehicles), 17
Sixth Amendment, 462
Slavery, xx–xxi
Slicing, 16
Smith, Adam, 100, 688, 690
Smith Barney, 42

SNAP. *See* Supplemental Nutrition Assistance Program (SNAP)
Social contract theory, xv
Social Darwinism, 676
Social media and computers, hiring practices and, 440–41
Social mobility, 199–200, 253
Social protection expenditures, in Europe, 31
Social Security
    Baby Boomers, 229
    beneficiaries, growth of, 485
    benefits overview, 482–83
    delayed or early retirement, 472–73
    Great Recession, 79
    historical emergence of, 481–84
    importance of, 223
    Medicare and Medicaid, 483–84
    outlook on, 491
    overview of, 393–94, 481
    poverty, 489–91
    poverty rates among elderly, 691–94
    role of, 306–7
    solutions to projected deficit, 487–89
    SSDI and SSI, 484
    viability of, 485–86
Social Security Act of 1935, 75, 307, 393, 395, 482, 513, 690, 691–94
Social Security Administration (SSA), 245
Social Security Disability Insurance (SSDI), 245, 246, 281, 484
Social Security Trust Fund, 483
Societal commitment of public benefits, 156–57
Societal response
    nonprofit organizations, 635–36, 639–47
    political ideologies, 635, 649–60
    poverty, societal view, 637–38, 675–82
    religious groups, 636–37
Sojourners, 671, 672
Sound public finances, 23
South Africa, 10, 358
South Carolina, 463, 532
Southeast Asia, 572
Southern Baptist Convention (SBC), 671
Southern region. *See* Regions of the country
South Korea, 573
Spain, 21, 22, 24–28, 359, 572, 573
Special Supplemental Nutrition Program for Women, Infants and Children (WIC), 281, 390, 405, 411–12, 665
Spencer, Herbert, 676
SPM (Supplemental Poverty Measure), 77, 224–25, 267–68, 307–8, 655, 657
Sponsor deeming, 282
Spousal Abuse, 474–75
SSA (Social Security Administration), 245

SSDI (Social Security Disability Insurance), 245, 246, 281, 484
SSI (Supplemental Security Income), 79, 245, 246, 281, 484, 556, 582
Stafford loans, 391, 431
Standard & Poor's, 44, 56
Standard monetary policy, 119–20
State government response
    budget shortfalls, impact of, 555–58
    budget shortfalls, reasons for, 551–52
    budget shortfalls during and after Great Recession, 552–55
    General Assistance, 534–35
    outlook for, 558
    overview of, 542, 550–51
Steinbeck, John, 73
STEM fields (science, technology, engineering, and mathematics), 329
Stewart, Martha, 51
Stimulus package. *See* American Recovery and Reinvestment Act of 2009 (ARRA)
STOCK (Stop Trading on Congressional Knowledge) Act of 2012, 52
Stock market crash of 2008, 308
Structural economic changes
    debt and credit, 626–28
    Dodd-Frank Act, 628
    federal deficit and debt, 629–30
    inevitable changes in market, 620–21
    middle class income and wealth, 625–26
    outlook for, 630–31
    overview of, 595, 619–20
    potential GDP, 621–23
    unemployment, 623–25
Structuralist view, 503–4, 677–78
Structural unemployment, 503
Structured finance, 16, 44–49, 56
Structured investment vehicles (SIVs), 17
Student loans, 208, 210, 226
Subprime mortgages, 5, 41, 53, 89, 90, 92, 107
Sub-Saharan Africa, 357–58, 571
Suburban families and individuals
    educational attainment, 344
    Great Recession, effects of, 185
    Hispanic Americans, 346
    homelessness, 448–49
    outlook for, 348–49
    overview of, 343–44
    poverty, 345–46
    safety nets, 347–48
    unemployment, 345–47
    worst-case housing needs, 457
Suicide rates and Great Recession, 474, 475
Summers, Larry, 43
Sumner, William Graham, 676
Sun Belt region, 363

Supplemental Nutrition Assistance
   Program (SNAP)
   ARRA and, 79, 390
   benefits of, 409
   compared to AFDC, 530–32
   creation of, 405
   funding for, 640
   immigrants, 281
   overview of, 409–10
   Ryan budget and, 584
   suburban families and individuals, 345
Supplemental Poverty Measure (SPM), 77,
   224–25, 267–68, 307–8, 655, 657
Supplemental Security Income (SSI),
   79, 245, 246, 281, 484,
   556, 582
Supply-side economics, 101
Survival of the fittest, 676
Sustainable public finances, 23
Sweden, 27
Switzerland, 20
Systemic risk, 51

Tanner, Michael, 699
Target Federal Fund Rate, 126
TARP (Troubled Asset Relief Program), 105–6,
   543–44, 581. See also Emergency
   Economic Stabilization Act
   (EESA) of 2008
Taxation and transfers, 205
Tax credits, 655
Tax cuts, 100–101, 108, 111
Tax multipliers, 108
Tax policy, 653
Tax Policy Center, 108
Tax rebates, 104–5
Tax Reduction Act of 1975, 695
Tax Reform Act of 1986, 40–41
Tax Relief, Unemployment Insurance
   Reauthorization, and Job Creation
   Act (TRUIRJCA), 108, 110–11, 112,
   431, 483, 544, 583
Tax Relief and Job Creation Act
   of 2112, 583
Teachers, quality of, 262
Tea Party Movement, 582–83, 586–87
Temporary Assistance for Needy
   Families (TANF)
   ARRA and, 79, 582
   budget shortfalls and, 556
   creation of, 695
   female-headed households and, 532
   immigrants, 281
   National School Lunch Program, 412
   overview of, 395–96, 529–33
   passage of, 695

tribal administration of, 562
Temporary poverty, 140, 141–42. See also
   Cyclical poverty
Tennessee Valley Authority (TVA), 75
Term Asset-Backed Securities
   Loan Facility, 127
Term Auction Facility, 126, 127
Term Securities Lending Facility, 126, 127
Texas, 556
Think tanks and political ideologies, 653–60
Timber industry, 564
Time magazine, 50, 73
Traditional students, 426–27
Trail of Tears, 287
Tranching, 16
Traveler's Group, 42
Treasury secretary, 52
Treasury securities, 43–44
Treaties with Native Americans, 287
Tribal Economic Development Bonds, 566
Tribal government response
   Alaskan Native corporations, 565–66
   definition of, 561–62
   demographics of, 562–63
   economic development bonds, 566
   federal budget allocations for Indian Affairs
      programs, 563–64
   lobbying, 566–67
   outlook for, 567–68
   overview of, 542–43, 560–61
   revenue sources, 564–65
   social services, 567
   terminology, 561
Triborough Bridge, 75
Tronto, Joan, xvii
Troubled Asset Relief Program (TARP), 105–6,
   543–44, 581. See also Emergency
   Economic Stabilization Act (EESA) of
   2008
TRUIRJCA (Tax Relief, Unemployment
   Insurance Reauthorization, and Job
   Creation Act), 108, 110–11, 112, 431, 483,
   544, 583
"Tulip mania," 86
Turkey, 571–72
TVA (Tennessee Valley Authority), 75
2010 Hunger in America, 411

UBS, 18
Un-banked individuals, 143
Underemployment
   African Americans, 497
   definition of, 504
   difficulty with definition of, 494–97
   educational attainment, 524
   Hispanic Americans, 497

men, 338–39
number and rate of, 496
outlook for, 498–99
overview of, 394, 493
poverty and, 497–98, 523–26
reduced wages, 523–26
young adults, 209
Underwater mortgages, 5, 53, 77, 96, 310
Underwriting standards, 54
Undocumented immigrants, 276, 277, 278, 280
UN Economic and Social Council, 575
Unemployment
adults, 218–20
African Americans, 76–77, 191–93
American Recovery and Reinvestment
Act of 2009, 108–9
Asian Americans, 235–36
average by region, 302
benefits, 513–15
child poverty, 201–2, 203
cyclical poverty and, 142
economic structural changes, 623–25
educational attainment, 257–58, 505–8
education and, 76, 505–8
in Europe, 20–22
Federal Reserve policy and, 130–31
full employment, 504–5
during Great Recession, 4, 5, 12–13, 59–61,
74, 102, 111, 155, 508–13
health, 474
health insurance coverage, 421–22
Hispanic Americans, 267–70
impact of Eurozone crisis on, 27–31
importance of employment, 500–502
increase during Great Depression, 4
lengths of, 60, 111, 155, 250–51, 335, 337,
338, 437–38, 508–9, 511
lengths of for African Americans, 193
lengths of in other recessions, 156, 510
measurement of, 502–3
men, 330, 334
mismatch of skills and job
openings, 441
Native Americans, 289, 291
in normal economy, 607–9
in other recessions, 156
outlook for, 515–16
over income distribution, 250
overview of, 394–95, 500
for persons with disabilities, 244–45
philosophy of poverty, 680
poverty rates and, 174–75
prior economic status and, 249–51
probability of, 250
ratio of unemployed to job openings, 439
ratio to job openings, 439

during recessionary phase of business
cycle, 38–39
recovery, 80
retirees and potential retirees, 309
rural families and individuals, 316–18
structural economic changes, 623–25
suburban families and individuals, 345–47
tax revenues and, 551
types of, 503–4
urban families and individuals, 366
veterans, 372–73
veterans vs. nonveterans, 372
white Americans, 378–81
women, 325–26
youth, 28
Unemployment compensation, 99, 104, 112,
513–15, 531–32
Unemployment Insurance Modernization Act
of 2008, 658–59
Unemployment rate
1950–2017, 624
1960–2012, 610
1978–1983, 598
1979–1983, 598
2006–2012, 600
African Americans, 380, 511
by age, sex, race, and income quintile,
509–13
as assessment point for U.S. economy,
607–11
data rate, 1960–2012, 610
earnings by education, 701
by educational attainment, 252, 336
by education level, 29
men by race, 335
minority men, 337
by race and ethnicity, 191, 235–36,
268, 380, 513
rate of by educational attainment, 506
rate of in other recessions, 508–9
by region of the country, 300–302
by sex, 323, 331
Unemployment rates and earnings by
education 2011, 701
UN Human Rights Council, 574
UNICEF (United Nations Children's
Fund), 199
United Kingdom, 9, 19, 20
United Nations, 358, 570–71
United Nations Children's Fund
(UNICEF), 199
United Nations Development Programme, 166
United States, annual output growth rate, 9
United States, vs. international impact
developing nations, emerging markets, and
global downturn, 356–58

European Union and Eurozone crisis, 353–56
Great Recession, effects of, 185–86
long-term outlook, 359
outlook for, 358–59
overview of, 351–52
poverty rate, 352
Universal Periodic Review process, 574
University of California–Berkeley, 680–81
Unpaid internships, 209–10
Urban families and individuals
central city neighborhoods, 363–64
city and social services, 365–66
foreclosures, 364–65
Great Recession, effects of, 186
homelessness, 364–65
homeownership, 364–65
housing, 364
outlook for, 366–67
overview of, 362
present situation, 362–66
property taxes, 365
unemployment, 366
worst-case housing needs, 457
Urban Institute, 363, 657–60
USCCB (U.S. Conference of Catholic Bishops), 636, 664–65
U.S. Census Bureau
family formation and size, 470
Income, Poverty, and Health Insurance Coverage in the United States, 278–79
Native American terminology, 286, 561
regional divisions, 298, 299
Supplemental Poverty Measure (SPM), 224–25
U.S. Conference of Catholic Bishops (USCCB), 636, 664–65
U.S. Food Insecurity Rates 1996–2011, 407
U.S. Treasury Securities, 121, 127, 130
Utah, 557
Utilitarian argument for poverty alleviation, xv, xvii–xviii

Variable interest rates, 40
Veil of ignorance, xvi
Venezuela, 574
Vermont, 550
Very low food security, 404, 406–7
Veterans
government responses to Great Recession, 374–75
Great Recession, effects of, 186–87
homelessness, 373
minorities, 374
outlook for, 375–76
overview of, 371–72

poverty, 373–74
public sector unemployment and, 372–73
unemployment, 372–73
Veterans Affairs and Railroad Retirement Board Beneficiaries, 582
Veterans Job Corps, 375
Vietnamese Americans, 236, 238
View of personal financial situation by race/ethnicity, 381
Views on economy and recession, 383–84
Virginia, 466
Virtue ethic of care, xv, xvi–xvii
VISTA (Volunteers in Service to America), 692
Vocational rehabilitation programs, 245
Voluntary unemployment, 503–4
Volunteers in Service to America (VISTA), 692
VOW to Hire Heroes Act, 375

Wachovia, 57, 128
Wages and income, 395
declining, 248
by educational attainment, 521–22
loss of due to unemployment, 523
outlook for, 526–27
overview of, 520
underemployment, 523–26
unemployment and education, interrelationship with, 521–23
Wallis, Jim, 671
Wall Street Journal, 650
"War on hunger," 405
War on Poverty, 78, 138, 161, 162, 594, 613, 691–92, 694
Washington, 463
Washington, D.C., 363, 556, 557
Washington Mutual, 57
Washington Post, 381
Wautoma, Wisconsin, 317
Wealth, Hispanic Americans, 265–67
Wealth distribution, 151–53
Wealth gap
African Americans, 195–96
Hispanic Americans, 267, 271
white Americans, 382–83
The Wealth of Nations (Smith), 100, 688
Welfare cash assistance programs
Earned Income Tax Credit (EITC), 533–34 (*see also main entry*)
General Assistance benefits (GA), 395–96, 529, 534–35
outlook for, 535–36
overview of, 395–96, 529
Temporary Assistance for Needy Families (TANF), 529–33 (*see also main entry*)

Wells Fargo, 57
Western region. *See* Regions of the country
White Americans
    declining home values, increasing debt, and
        unemployment, 378–81
    economy and recession, views
        on, 383–84
    Great Recession, effects of, 187
    homelessness, 449
    homeownership, 380
    household composition, changes
        in, 381–82
    men and unemployment, 337
    overview of, 377–78
    personal financial situation, view of, 381
    poverty rates, 171, 172, 173, 174,
        378, 379, 693
    poverty rates for young adults, 211
    racial wealth gap, 382–83
    senior citizens, 311
    unemployment rate, 380, 511
White House Rural Council, 317
WIC (Special Supplemental Nutrition Program
    for Women, Infants and Children), 281,
    390, 405, 411–12, 665
Wilson, William Julius, 677–78
Wisconsin, 557
Women. *See also* Female-headed households
    earning more than husbands, 324
    economic insecurity, 325–26
    educational attainment, 324, 325
    Great Recession, effects of, 184
    injustices against, xxi
    job tenure, 219
    labor force participation, 506
    outlook for, 327–29
    overview of, 322–25
    poverty, 326–27
    retirement plans, changes in, 219
    rising earning power of, 339–40

senior citizens and poverty, 225, 311
unemployment and economic insecurity,
    325–26
unemployment rate, 509, 512
veterans, 374
young adults, 210–11
Women, Infants and Children (WIC). *See*
    Special Supplemental Nutrition Program
    for Women, Infants and Children (WIC)
Workforce productivity, xxii
Works Progress Administration (WPA), 75
Work status, for persons 16 and older, 525
Work status, poverty rate by, 526
World Bank, 356
World Economic Outlook, 7
World trade, during Great Recession, 12
Worst-case housing needs, 454–56
Wounded Knee Creek massacre, 287
WPA (Works Progress Administration), 75

Young adults (18–34)
    African Americans, 210–11, 382
    Asian Americans, 210–11
    education, 208–9
    Great Recession, effects of, 180
    Hispanic Americans, 210–11, 382
    job prospects and income, 209–10
    life choices during the Great Recession,
        211–12
    living with parents, 212, 382
    outlook for, 212–14
    overview of, 207
    in suburban areas, 346
    underemployment, 497, 498
    women and minorities, 210–11
Youth unemployment, 28
Yup'ik tribal grouping, 562

Zakat, xiv–xv
Zandi, Mark, 108–9